THE EMERGENCE
OF A NATION STATE

The commonwealth of England 1529–1660

Foundations of modern Britain

General editor: *Geoffrey Holmes*

THE TRANSFORMATION OF MEDIEVAL ENGLAND
1370–1529
John A. F. Thomson

THE EMERGENCE OF A NATION STATE
The commonwealth of England 1529–1660
Alan G. R. Smith

THE MAKING OF A GREAT POWER
Pre-industrial Britain 1660–1783
Geoffrey Holmes

THE FORGING OF THE MODERN STATE
Early industrial Britain 1783–1870
Eric J. Evans

THE ECLIPSE OF A GREAT POWER
Modern Britain 1870–1975
Keith Robbins

THE EMERGENCE OF A NATION STATE

The commonwealth of England
1529–1660

Alan G. R. Smith

LONGMAN
LONDON AND NEW YORK

Longman Group Limited
Longman House, Burnt Mill, Harlow
Essex CM20 2JE, England
Associated companies throughout the world

Published in the United States of America
by Longman Inc., New York

First published 1984

British Library Cataloguing in Publication Data
Smith, Alan G. R.
 The emergence of a nation state. —
 (Foundations of modern Britain; 2)
 1. Great Britain — History — Tudors,
 1485–1603   2. Great Britain — History
 — Stuarts, 1603–1714
 I. Title   II. Series
 942.05'3   DA315

 ISBN 0-582-48973-3
 ISBN 0-582-48974-1 Pbk

Library of Congress Cataloging in Publication Data
Smith, Alan Gordon Rae.
 The emergence of a nation state.

 (Foundations of modern Britain)
 Bibliography: p.
 Includes index.
 1. Great Britain — History — Tudors, 1485–1603.
2. Great Britain — History — Stuarts, 1603–1714.   I. Title.
II. Series.
DA315.S64   1984   942.05   83-19629
ISBN 0-582-48973-3
ISBN 0-582-48974-1 (pbk.)

Set in 9½/12 Linotron 202 Times
Printed in Singapore
by Richard Clay Pte Ltd

Contents

Contents

Contents

List of maps

Editor's foreword

So prodigious has been the output of specialized work on British history during the past twenty years, and so rich its diversity, that scholars and students thirst continually after fresh syntheses. Even those who read for the pure pleasure of informing themselves about the past have become quite reconciled to the fact that little can now be taken for granted. An absorbing interest in local situations, as a way to understanding more general ones; a concern with those processes of social change which accompany economic, educational and cultural development, and which often condition political activity too: these and many other strong currents of modern historiography have washed away some of our more comfortable orthodoxies. Even when we know *what* happened, there is endless scope for debate about *why* things happened and with what consequences.

In such circumstances a new series of general textbooks on British history would not seem to call for elaborate justification. However, the five volumes constituting *Foundations of Modern Britain* do have a distinct rationale and they embody some novel features. For one thing, they make a serious attempt to present a history of Britain from the point at which 'Britain' became first a recognizable entity and then a Great Power, and to trace the foundations of this state in the history of pre-eighteenth-century England. The fact that all five authors either have taught or are teaching in Scottish universities, while one has held a chair in the University of Wales, should at least help to remind them that one aim of the series is to avoid excessive Anglo-centricity. The first two volumes, spanning the years 1370–1660, will certainly concentrate primarily on the history of England, emphasizing those developments which first prepared the way for, and later confirmed her emergence as an independent 'Commonwealth', free from Continental trammels whether territorial or ecclesiastical. But the reader should also be aware, as he reads them, of England's ultimate role as the heart of a wider island kingdom in which men of three nations came to be associated. During the period covered by volumes 3 and 4, 1660–1870, this 'United Kingdom of Great Britain' became not only a domestic reality but the centre of an Empire and the possessor of world-wide influence. Space will allow only limited treatment of Ireland and of Anglo-Irish relations until after the Union of 1801. It is appropriate, however, that in the final volume of the series reasserted nationalism should figure almost as strongly as the erosion of imperial status in the story of Britain's slide down the slippery slope from palmy greatness to anxious mediocrity. The terminal date of volume 5, 1975, is deliberately chosen: the year in which Britain, tortured once again by her Irish inheritance and facing demands for Scottish devolution, or even independence, belatedly recognized that the days of complacent self-sufficiency as regards Europe, too, were past.

As well as paying more than mere lip-service to its own title, the present series adopts an irreverent attitude to time-honoured chronological divisions. Those lines of demarcation between volumes which dominated virtually every English history series conceived before 1960 (and, with a few exceptions, have displayed a remarkable capacity for survival subsequently) are seen as a quite unnecessary obstacle to readers' understanding of the way modern historiography has reshaped whole vistas of our island's history in the past forty years. Years such as 1485, 1603, 1689, 1714, 1760 or 1815 established themselves in textbook lore at a time when they accurately reflected the heavily political and constitutional emphasis of traditional history teaching. Even on those terms they have become of limited utility. But equally seriously, the conventions which such divisions perpetuate often make it extremely difficult for authors to accommodate fundamental aspects of social and economic development within their allotted compass. The brutal slicing off of 'Tawney's century' (1540–1640) at 1603 is perhaps the worst of these atrocities; but it is not the only one.

All dates are to some extent arbitrary as lines of division, and all present their own difficulties. It is hoped, none the less, that those selected in this series to enclose periods which are in any case a good deal longer than average, may prove less inhibiting and confusing than some of their predecessors and much more adaptable to the needs of British history courses in universities and colleges.

In one further important respect the authors have kept in mind the practical requirements of students and teachers. Their approach eschews lengthy narrative wherever possible and concentrates, within chapters short enough to be rapidly absorbed, on the development of themes and the discussion of problems. Yet at the same time they attempt to satisfy their readers' need for basic information in two ways: by providing, at appropriate stages, skeletal 'frameworks' of events, chronologically ordered, within which the subsequent analysis and interplay of argument can be set; and by placing at the end of each volume a 'compendium' of factual data, including statistics, on a scale much greater than that of normal textbook appendices.

These compendia are essential companions to the texts and are designed for ready and constant use. The frequent references to them which punctuate so many chapters in this series will be found within square brackets, e.g. [B]. They should be easily distinguishable from the numerous arabic numbers within round brackets inserted in the text, e.g. (117). These refer readers to the Bibliography, in which most items are thematically arranged and serially numbered. Where necessary, specific page numbers (in italic) follow the main reference in the round brackets. In references to articles page numbers are not usually given. References to statutes, also in round brackets, are by regnal year and chapter. Superior numerals are for the references which appear at the end of the relevant chapter. The place of publication of books is London unless otherwise indicated.

Geoffrey Holmes

Acknowledgements

Anyone writing a general book on early modern British history owes a fundamental debt of gratitude to the dozens of scholars whose researches and reflections have enriched our understanding of the period. Some of my debts are implicit in the bibliography and footnotes, but I am very conscious that a large number of more specialized books and articles which could very properly have been included have not found a place. The form of the series demanded a limit on the number of bibliographical items and I have included those which I hoped would be most useful to undergraduates.

I owe a considerable debt to the University of Glasgow which granted me a year's study leave during which most of the book was written. Colleagues at Glasgow have been most helpful. Professor K. G. Robbins and Dr J. A. F. Thomson, authors respectively of the final and first volumes in the series, patiently discussed problems of organization and presentation. I have had many hours of fruitful conversation about the sixteenth and seventeenth centuries with Dr Brian Dietz, Dr Lionel Glassey and Dr Jenny Wormald. Their insights have done much to help my understanding of the period, though they cannot, of course, be held responsible for anything which I have written here. Mr G. B. A. M. Finlayson has been a constant source of encouragement during the preparation of the book and Miss Patricia Ferguson typed the manuscript with her customary skill and care.

My greatest debt, however, is to Professor G. S. Holmes. Ever since I accepted his invitation to write the volume he has been a tower of strength, answering queries and offering advice with unfailing promptitude and good sense. He has read the whole text with meticulous care and has offered numerous suggestions for improvements. I would like to express my most sincere gratitude to him.

My wife has patiently endured the varied moods of an author in the throes of composition. The dedication, to my young daughter and son, is despite the fact that they often did their best to prevent me from finishing the book!

A. G. R. Smith
University of Glasgow
November 1982

List of abbreviations

AgHR	*Agricultural History Review*
APC	*Acts of the Privy Council of England*
CHJ	*Cambridge Historical Journal*
CJ	*Journals of the House of Commons*
EcHR	*Economic History Review*
EHR	*English Historical Review*
HJ	*Historical Journal*
JBS	*Journal of British Studies*
JEH	*Journal of Ecclesiastical History*
JMH	*Journal of Modern History*
LJ	*Journals of the House of Lords*
LP	*Letters and Papers, Foreign and Domestic, of the Reign of Henry VIII*
LQR	*Law Quarterly Review*
P & P	*Past and Present*
PBA	*Proceedings of the British Academy*
TRHS	*Transactions of the Royal Historical Society*

For Stella and Donald

PART ONE

An age of revolution: The era of the Reformation 1529–1558

1529   Legatine court at Blackfriars considers the annulment of Henry VIII's marriage to
       Catherine of Aragon (May–July); court adjourned (July); Henry summoned to
       Rome; writs issued for a meeting of Parliament (Aug); Wolsey indicted under prae-
       munire and ordered to surrender the Great Seal (Oct); More Lord Chancellor –
       persecution of heretics intensified during his period in office (1529–32).
           First session of Reformation Parliament (Nov–Dec); Acts limiting mortuary
       fees and fees for the probate of wills; Act against pluralities and non-residence.
           Victory of Imperialists over the French at Landriano in Italy (June) – Imperial
       control of Italy confirmed.
           Death of the poet John Skelton (June); Simon Fish, *A Supplication for the
       Beggars*.
1530   Oxford and Cambridge universities find in favour of the King's divorce proceed-
       ings, though with dissenting minorities (spring); Henry attempts to convince
       Continental universities of the validity of his divorce claims – mixed verdicts from
       French, Italian, Spanish and German universities (summer). Wolsey in his diocese
       of York (June–Nov) enters into communication with French and Imperial ambassa-
       dors; accused of treason and summoned to London; dies at Leicester Abbey on
       journey south (Nov).
           Mission to the Pope headed by Thomas Boleyn, father of Anne (Jan); petition
       from the English nobility to the Pope on behalf of the King (July) – refused; French
       attempt to mediate with the Pope on Henry's behalf fails (Oct).
           Clergy as a whole accused of praemunire (Dec).
           William Tyndale's Bible burnt (May) – reflects continuing attacks on heresy;
       Tyndale's *Practice of Prelates* attacks Henry VIII's divorce proceedings.
1531   Pardon of the clergy (Feb) for the offence of praemunire in return for payment of
       a large fine; Convocation of Canterbury recognizes Henry VIII as Supreme Head
       of the Church 'so far as the law of Christ allows' (Feb); reports that More will
       resign the Great Seal; Thomas Cromwell joins the inner circle of the King's
       Council; persecution of heresy continues.
           Clement VII issues a brief ordering Henry not to remarry until his case is
       decided (Jan).
           Parliament meets (Jan–Mar): Beggars Act draws distinction between able-
       bodied and impotent poor.
           Sir Thomas Elyot, *The Book named the Governor*.
1532   Parliament meets (Jan–May): Act in Conditional Restraint of Annates; Commons
       'Supplication against the Ordinaries' (Mar) attacks the bishops, complaining about
       the independent legislative powers of the clergy. This leads to the 'Submission of
       the Clergy' (May), which ends the independent legislative power of the church in
       England; resignation of More as Lord Chancellor (May).
           Thomas Cromwell becomes the King's chief minister; death of Archbishop
       Warham (Aug); Anne Boleyn created marchioness of Pembroke (Sept); Anne
       Boleyn pregnant (Dec).
           Discussions with Protestant German states for a possible alliance with England –
       these discussions continue during the 1530s; meeting between Henry VIII and
       Francis I at Boulogne (Oct); earl of Kildare Lord Deputy of Ireland.
           Hans Holbein the Younger settles in England; publication of *A Glass of the
       Truth*, commending Henry's divorce to the English people.

1533   Henry VIII secretly marries Anne Boleyn (Jan); Cranmer archbishop of Canterbury (Feb); Cranmer consecrated (Mar). Parliament meets (Feb–Apr); Act in Restraint of Appeals (Mar). Cranmer pronounces Aragon marriage invalid and marriage between Henry and Anne legal (Apr–May); Ann Boleyn crowned (June). King activates Annates Act of 1532 by letters patent (July). Birth of Princess Elizabeth (Sept).

Truce between England and Scotland.

Statute fixes maximum prices for meat.

1534   Parliament meets (Jan–Mar): First Succession Act; Act in Absolute Restraint of Annates; Act for the Submission of the Clergy. Parliament reconvenes (Nov–Dec): Act of Supremacy; Treason Act; Act for First Fruits and Tenths.

Cromwell appointed Principal Secretary (Apr). Execution of Elizabeth Barton – the Nun of Kent – for treason (Apr). Rowland Lee appointed President of the Council in the Marches of Wales – that Council now begins to exert more effective authority. Irish revolt of 'Silken Thomas', the new earl of Kildare.

Clement VII pronounces the Aragon marriage valid (Mar). Anglo-Scottish peace treaty (May). Treaty between England and Lübeck, leading city of the Hanseatic League; Lübeck recognizes Boleyn marriage (Aug). Death of Clement VII (Sept).

Act limiting ownership of sheep.

1535   Cromwell appointed vicegerent in spirituals (Jan). Visitation of religious houses (1535–36) begins; execution of leading Carthusians (May); Bishop John Fisher made a cardinal by the Pope (May). Executions of Fisher (June) and More (July).

Valor Ecclesiasticus – a valuation of all church property – compiled. Coverdale Bible – first complete English translation.

1536   Death of Catherine of Aragon (Jan). Execution of Ann Boleyn – condemned for incest and multiple adultery (May): Henry's marriage to Anne declared invalid (May); Henry marries Jane Seymour (May).

Last session of Reformation Parliament meets (Feb–Apr): Statute of Uses; Act for the dissolution of the lesser monasteries; Welsh Act of Union; Act abolishing franchises and liberties; Act for Court of Augmentations; Calais Act; Enclosure Act; Beggars Act – significant role for parish.

Parliament meets (June–July): Second Succession Act; Act against papal authority.

Pilgrimage of Grace (Oct–Mar 1537). Creation of new Privy Council. Irish Parliament recognizes royal supremacy; suppression of Kildare revolt in Ireland.

Ten Articles of religion (July) – strong Lutheran influences; royal injunctions to the clergy (Aug); Reginald Pole created cardinal (Dec).

Death of the duke of Richmond, Henry's illegitimate son (June).

1537   Robert Aske, leader of the Pilgrimage of Grace, sentenced to death for treason (May) and executed (July); birth of Prince Edward (Oct); death of Jane Seymour (Oct); reorganization of the Council of the North (Sept); birth of Lady Jane Grey (Oct).

The Institution of a Christian Man (*The Bishops' Book*) – Sept; beginning of surrender of the greater monasteries to the King (Dec); Irish Parliament passes bill for the suppression of the Irish monasteries; execution of 'Silken Thomas', earl of Kildare.

James V of Scotland marries Madeleine, daughter of Francis I of France (Jan); Queen Madeleine dies (July).

'Matthew Bible' – an authorized English translation – published.

1538   Royal injunctions to the clergy (Sept): these include provisions for an English Bible in all parish churches and for the introduction of parish registers of baptisms, marriages and burials. Destruction of the shrine of St Thomas Becket at Canterbury (Sept).

Attack on the Pole family in England.

James V of Scotland marries Mary of Guise (June). Truce of Nice (June) between France and Emperor – leads to fears of an invasion of England by the two great Catholic powers.

1539   Parliament meets (Apr–June): Six Articles Act provides a highly traditional interpretation of church doctrine; Proclamations Act; Act authorizing the dissolution of the greater monasteries; Act authorizing the creation of new bishoprics. New Council of the West established (dissolved the following year).

Fears of invasion of England by French, Imperialists and Scots (spring); great activity to put country in a state of readiness; worst of the danger over by May. Invasion fears revive in the autumn; Cleves marriage treaty signed (Oct) – Henry VIII to marry Anne, sister of the duke of Cleves.

Nicholas Shaxton, bishop of Salisbury and Hugh Latimer, bishop of Worcester, resign their sees in protest against the Six Articles Act.

Coverdale's 'Great Bible'.

1540   Henry VIII marries Anne of Cleves (Jan). Invasion fears subside. Parliament meets (Apr–July): Statute of Wills; Acts passed abolishing the worst abuses of sanctuary and erecting the Courts of Wards and of First Fruits and Tenths. Cromwell created earl of Essex (Apr); Cromwell arrested and attainted (June) and executed (July). Cleves marriage annulled (July). Henry VIII marries Catherine Howard (July).

Henry attempts to woo James V away from French alliance.

Last monastery suppressed (Mar – Waltham Abbey surrenders).

Appointment of clerk of the Privy Council; beginning of the Privy Council register.

Henry VIII founds regius chairs at Oxford and Cambridge.

1541   Catholic conspiracy to raise northern England (Apr) fails; execution of the countess of Salisbury, mother of Cardinal Pole (May). Henry VIII assumes title King of Ireland (June). Progress by the King through northern England (July–Nov).

Death of Queen Margaret of Scotland, widow of James IV and sister of Henry VIII (Oct).

King given evidence of Catherine Howard's immoral conduct, both before and after marriage (Nov); Catherine sent to the Tower (Nov).

Further instructions to parishes to set up vernacular bibles in their churches. Fifth edition of the 'Great Bible' issued.

1542   Parliament meets (Jan–Apr): Act creating the Court of General Surveyors; Cromwell's legislation on price control repealed; Ferrer's case. Execution of Catherine Howard (Feb).

Agreement between Henry VIII and the Emperor Charles V for a joint invasion of France in 1543 (later postponed until 1544). War with Scotland (Aug): Scottish victory at Haddon Rig (Aug); English victory at Solway Moss (Nov).

Birth of Mary Queen of Scots (Dec), death of James V of Scotland (Dec), and accession of infant Mary Queen of Scots.

First Jesuit mission lands in Ireland.

Beginning of the 'great debasement' of the coinage.

Foundation of Magdalene College, Cambridge. E. Hall, *The Union of the*

... *Families of Lancaster and York*.

1543   Parliament meets (Jan–May): attempt to restrict access to the Bible to the upper classes; Act defining the structure of the new Wales. Threat to Cranmer from the conservative faction on the Council. Henry VIII marries Catherine Parr (July).

    Treaty of Greenwich (July) – peace with Scotland and engagement of Prince Edward to Mary Queen of Scots; later annulled by the Scots (Dec). War with France.

    A Necessary Doctrine and Erudition for Any Christian Man (*The King's Book*, May) – endorses the Six Articles.

1544   Parliament meets (Jan–Mar): Third Succession Act – Mary and Elizabeth placed in the line of succession to the throne. Faction threat to Gardiner from reformers on the Council. Sir John Cheke, a notable Protestant scholar, appointed tutor to Prince Edward.

    Edward Seymour raids Scottish lowlands – sack of Edinburgh (May). English invasion of France (June); capture of Boulogne (Sept). Peace of Crespy between France and the Empire (Sept) – England deserted by the Emperor.

    English litany introduced in churches.

    Beginning of the most intensive phase of the 'great debasement'.

1545   Parliament meets (Nov–Dec): Act permits the taking of interest, up to 10 per cent, on loans; the King makes a speech to Parliament (Dec) urging the need for religious unity – this indicates the extent of religious dissent in England.

    French invasion threat: elaborate English preparations on the south coast; French fleet in the Solent, loss of the *Mary Rose*, French landing on the Isle of Wight (July). Engagement between the English and French fleets off Shoreham (Aug); England left in command of the Channel. English invasion of Scotland led by Edward Seymour, earl of Hertford (Sept) – great destruction in the border area.

    R. Ascham, *Toxophilus*, a notable treatise on archery.

1546   Increasing ill health of Henry VIII: illnesses in Mar, July, Oct. Threat to Queen Catherine Parr from conservative faction. Fall of the Howards: the duke of Norfolk and his son the earl of Surrey arrested and sent to the Tower (Dec) – helps the triumph of the reformers by the time of Henry VIII's death. Creation of first regular Navy Board.

    Murder of Cardinal Beaton in Scotland (May). Peace with France by the Treaty of Ardres (June) – England to keep Boulogne for eight years.

    Anne Askew burnt for denying transubstantiation (July).

    Foundation of Trinity College, Cambridge, and refoundation of Cardinal (later King's) College, Oxford, as Christ Church.

1547   Execution of Surrey (Jan). Death of Henry VIII and accession of Edward VI (Jan): govt in the hands of a regency council of 16; Edward Seymour, earl of Hertford becomes Lord Protector (Jan); Hertford becomes duke of Somerset (Feb) and obtains the right to nominate councillors (Mar). Marriage of Lord Seymour of Sudeley, Somerset's younger brother, to Queen Catherine Parr. Courts of Augmentations and General Surveyors combined in Second Court of Augmentations.

    Parliament meets (Nov–Dec): 'Treasons Act' sweeps away a mass of repressive legislation; Act for the dissolution of the chantries; 'Slavery' Act.

    English invasion of Scotland: Scots defeated at Battle of Pinkie (Sept); Somerset begins attempt to consolidate English power in southern Scotland. Death of Francis I; Henry II becomes King of France.

    Publication of the *Book of Homilies*.

1548   Death of Catherine Parr (Sept); Lord Seymour of Sudeley intrigues to marry the Princess Elizabeth; Parliament meets (Nov–Mar 1549).

French Army in Scotland (June); Mary Queen of Scots taken to France (July); Somerset revives English claim to suzerainty over Scotland (Sept).

Much religious dispute and discontent in England in the 'liberal' atmosphere created by the 'Treasons Act' of 1547. Proclamations order the removal of images from churches and the disuse of many 'superstitious' ceremonies – such as the use of ashes and holy water.

Enclosure Commission appointed to enforce existing legislation (June); sporadic riots in southern England.

1549   Parliament of November 1548 continues until March: Act of Uniformity imposes the First Edwardian Prayer Book; tax on sheep and cloth; Act permitting marriage of priests. Execution of Seymour of Sudeley (Mar). New Enclosure Commissions; riots continue in southern England from the spring onwards; major rebellions in the West Country and East Anglia in the summer. Fall of Somerset (Oct): fierce power struggle between Warwick and Wriothesley begins.

War with France (Aug); French besiege Boulogne (Aug).

Edmund Bonner, bishop of London, deprived for opposition to the new Prayer Book (Sept).

First bad harvest of Edward VI's reign.

1550   Warwick, chief power in the State (Feb), exercises his authority through the Lord Presidency of the Council; William Paulet, later marquis of Winchester appointed Lord Treasurer (Feb); Somerset released from the Tower (Feb) and soon rejoins the Council.

Treaty of Boulogne (Mar) – peace with England and Scotland: Boulogne surrendered to France; Scotland abandoned to French dominance.

New ordinal introduced (Feb). Joan Bocher burned for denying the humanity of Christ (May). Hooper objects to the use of episcopal vestments for his consecration to the see of Gloucester: consecration delayed until the following year. Vigorous campaign of Protestantization by Ridley in the diocese of London. Princess Mary refuses to use the new Prayer Book and continues to say mass.

Second bad harvest of Edward VI's reign; local risings continue; boom in English cloth exports reaches its height.

1551   Warwick created duke of Northumberland (Oct); rearrest of Somerset (Oct), tried for treason (Dec).

Gardiner deprived of his bishopric (Feb). George van Parris, a Dutch physician, burned for denying the divinity of Christ (Apr). Hooper's visitation of his diocese of Gloucester reveals the extent of clerical ignorance.

Significant fall in cloth exports – end of the early sixteenth century boom in the cloth trade. Climax of the 'great debasement' of the coinage (June); revaluation of the coinage (July). Third bad harvest of Edward VI's reign; local risings continue; widespread epidemic of 'sweating sickness'; voyage to Morocco.

Sir Thomas More's *Utopia* translated into English.

1552   Execution of Somerset (Jan). Parliament meets (Jan–Apr): Second Edwardian Prayer Book; Act prohibiting the taking of interest on loans; Act directed towards raising funds for the deserving poor. Royal Commission on the revenue courts (Mar), reports (Dec): its recommendations on the amalgamation of courts and on the raising of customs rates not followed up until Mary's reign.

1553   Marriage of Lady Jane Grey and Northumberland's son, Guildford Dudley (May);

death of Edward VI (July); Northumberland tries to alter the succession – the 'reign' of Lady Jane Grey (6–19 July); Northumberland's attempted coup fails; accession of Mary Tudor (July); execution of Northumberland (Aug). Mary asked to marry within the realm (Nov).

Forty-two articles of religion (June). Parliament meets (Oct–Dec): repeal of the Edwardian religious legislation, including the statute permitting the marriage of priests.

Voyage of Willoughby and Chancellor to Muscovy; voyage to the Gold Coast by Captain Thomas Wyndham.

1554   Marriage treaty with Spain concluded (Jan); Wyatt's rebellion (January); Lady Jane Grey executed (Feb). Parliament meets (Apr–May): open conflict in Parliament between Gardiner and Paget (Apr). Mary marries Philip of Spain (July). Pole arrives as papal legate (November). Parliament meets (Nov – continues until Jan 1555). Restoration of the supremacy of the Exchequer over the financial system.

Marian exiles begin to flee abroad.

1555   Parliament of November 1554 continues until January: Act restores papal supremacy (Jan) – former church lands assured to their owners; heresy laws revived. Philip of Spain leaves England (Aug). Death of Gardiner (Nov). Parliament meets (Oct–Dec): First Fruits and Tenths restored to the Church; bill to sequester the lands of Protestant exiles defeated in the Commons.

Beginning of the Marian persecutions: first Protestant martyr John Rogers executed in February; Hooper burned at Gloucester (Feb); Latimer and Ridley tried and burned (Sept–Oct); Cranmer deprived of his archbishopric (Dec); Pole archbishop of Canterbury (Dec). Pole's legatine synod (1555–56) begins its meetings in London.

Very bad harvest. Survey of Crown lands recommended by Privy Council. Foundation of Muscovy Company – first joint-stock company. Naval rebuilding programme.

Foundation of St John's and Trinity Colleges, Oxford.

1556   Philip becomes King of Spain (January). Dudley conspiracy (Mar) – designed to depose Philip and Mary in favour of Elizabeth; Thomas Radcliffe, later 3rd earl of Sussex, becomes Lord Deputy of Ireland.

Burning of Cranmer (March).

Worst harvest of the century; beginning of a series of epidemics. Plans for a full recoinage drawn up and considered, but not implemented.

R. Recorde, *The Castle of Knowledge* – contains the first English mention of the Copernican system.

1557   Philip of Spain returns to England in the spring. Stafford conspiracy, supported by France (Apr). Plantation of Leix and Offaly in Ireland.

War with France (June); combined English–Spanish victory over the French at St Quentin (Aug).

Pole deprived of his legatine powers (Apr); under investigation at Rome for heresy (June).

Epidemics continue.

T. Tusser, *A Hundred Good Points of Husbandry*; R. Recorde's *Whetstone of Wit*, the first English treatise on algebra; George Cavendish completes his *Life of Cardinal Wolsey* (not published until the seventeenth century).

1558   Loss of Calais (Jan). Parliament meets (Jan–Mar): militia system reformed by two statutes; one subsidy voted. Death of Mary and Pole (Nov), Elizabeth ascends the throne. Sir William Cecil becomes Secretary of State and the Queen's principal adviser; Sir Nicholas Bacon, Lord Keeper of the Great Seal; Winchester retained as Lord Treasurer.

New Book of Rates (May): impositions on goods entering and leaving the country made on the sole authority of the Crown. Epidemics continue.

John Knox's *First Blast of the Trumpet Against the Monstrous Regiment of Women*.

England in 1529: Church, State and society

In 1529 the population of England was probably just over 2,500,000. Despite its sparseness by present-day standards that was an increase from a low point which had been reached around 1500, following the series of late medieval epidemics which began with the demographic catastrophe of the fourteenth-century Black Death. The increasing population of the early sixteenth century continued to grow almost continuously until the mid seventeenth century, and this advance in numbers is one of the fundamental facts of the history of the period; the great political and religious events of Tudor and early Stuart England were played out against a background of ever growing numbers of men, women and children [J]. These were overwhelmingly country dwellers. In Henry VIII's reign perhaps 95 per cent of them lived in innumerable villages scattered among the open and enclosed fields and woodlands and waste areas which together made up the English landscape. Towns were small; only London, with 50,000 to 60,000 people in the early sixteenth century, was a major urban unit, containing about 2 per cent of the total population of the country. The larger provincial towns together accounted for perhaps another 2 per cent. Of these probably only Norwich and Bristol reached 10,000 in 1530, and even in such local centres the sights and sounds of rural England were never far away.

The economic and administrative life of the towns was dominated by their merchants, but only the richest citizens of London could vie in wealth, though not in social prestige, with members of the peerage and greater gentry, who stood at the apex of the social as of the political life of the country. The castles and manor-houses of noblemen and gentlemen, scattered throughout England, shared physical domination of the countryside with the great religious edifices – especially the majestic abbeys – which bore witness to the material power as well as to the spiritual authority of the Church. The wealth of the ruling élites in town and countryside was founded on the labours of that great majority of English men and women whose fundamental concern was the events of the agricultural year. If the harvest was good the majority of the population survived without too much difficulty; if it was poor, hardship was the lot of very many and real hunger, perhaps at times even starvation, the fate of some. The productivity of agriculture was low and one of the great challenges of the Tudor age was the problem of feeding the ever-growing population.

The dominance of the agricultural sector is a truism of the economic history of the period, but industry, if of less fundamental significance, was also of considerable importance in the life of the people. Much industrial work was upon the raw materials of agriculture – brewing is an obvious example – and, above all, the manufacture of woollen cloth, founded upon England's large sheep herds, was by far the country's most important industry providing invaluable part-time employment for thousands of men and especially women, who combined the work with their agricultural labours (on the economy and society in the sixteenth and seventeenth centuries see Chs 20 to 22).

The agricultural and industrial workers of sixteenth century England owed allegiance to a hierarchy of State and Church authorities which culminated in 1529 in two striking personalities, King Henry VIII and Cardinal Wolsey. The latter, who had been Chief Minister since the early years of the King's reign, had risen to a position of virtually unprecedented power in the realm (168). As Lord Chancellor since 1515 he held the highest state office under the Crown and dominated the judicial machinery, and although the longevity of William Warham prevented him from achieving the archbishopric of Canterbury he had been archbishop of York since 1514, while his office of papal legate *a latere* [N], conferred on him in 1518, gave him a dominant power in the Church. His love of splendour, so well described by his gentleman usher, George Cavendish,[1] excited both the envy and the denunciation of contemporaries, who sometimes noted sourly that his pomp exceeded that of the King. In the circumstances it is not surprising that to the casual eye the cardinal rather than the King seemed the true ruler of England, the effective head of both Church and State.

Whoever might believe that, both Wolsey himself and Henry knew better. The cardinal, despite the fact that much of his outward prestige came from Rome through his cardinal's hat and his legateship, never doubted that the basis of his power was the King's confidence, and it did not even occur to Henry, with his gigantic ego, that the cardinal was other than his servant. The King was thirty-seven years old at the beginning of 1529, a giant of a man whose growing girth merely emphasized the splendid presence which he had presented to the world since the day he ascended the throne in April 1509 at the age of seventeen. (Much the best biography is (68).) The first two decades of his reign – the years 1509–29 – were, in the words of one recent historian, a 'period of internal tranquility and confidence in the monarchy [unprecedented] since the reign of Edward III in the mid-fourteenth century' (22, *157*). Henry, who presided over this generally happy interlude in England's internal history with supreme self-confidence, was not a diligent administrator – attempts to cast him in that role have been unconvincing (69) – and left the day-to-day business of government to ministers whom he trusted. For nearly two decades Wolsey had been at his right hand, but by 1529 the cardinal's long ministry was drawing to a close.

The administrative system over which King and cardinal presided had a number of basic tasks, common to any sixteenth-century government: to preserve internal order and security; to fight defensive wars; to raise revenue; and to take a general interest in the welfare of the people, especially the poorer sections of the community (98). The institutions of central government – mainly concerned with collecting money and administering the law – were served by a paid bureaucracy (24), but the localities were ruled by unpaid members of the gentry class who dominated the county communities and whose co-operation, especially in their roles as justices of the peace, was essential for the effective administration of the shires (31; 98). These country gentlemen filled most of the seats in the

House of Commons during Henry VIII's reign – as indeed they had done long before (21) – and the Parliaments of which they formed an essential part should be seen essentially as cogs in the government machine rather than as fora for constitutional opposition to the Crown. There was, of course, some opposition to the government in Henry's Parliaments – as for example, in 1523, when there was trouble over finance and foreign policy (25) – but generally Crown and Parliaments co-operated to raise taxes and pass laws. Taxation and legislation were essential for the effective administration of the realm, and the fact that the consent of Lords and Commons was essential in both spheres by 1500 brings home the importance of Parliament's role in the machinery of government (111).

King and cardinal, when they considered the administration of the realm, were concerned not only with England but with Wales and Ireland as well. These two countries were governed on very different bases from England, and the other part of the British Isles, Scotland, with its own kings and its long tradition of hostility to its more powerful southern neighbour, was an important element in England's network of foreign relationships. Wales in 1529 consisted of two parts, the Principality – consisting of the counties of Anglesey, Caernarfon, Merioneth, Flint, Cardigan and Carmarthen – and the Marcher lordships, many of which bounded on English territory to the east. The Principality and the lordships had their own systems of government different both from England and from each other, and although the Principality was a fief of the Crown and many of the lordships had come into royal hands by the early years of the sixteenth century, the whole region was plagued by endemic violence which the ineffective jurisdiction of a Council in the Marches of Wales under Bishop Vesey of Exeter did little to control (102). Ireland, which Henry VIII governed with the title of 'lord' rather than 'king' was divided into the Pale, a comparatively small area around Dublin where the royal writ ran; into Anglo-Irish earldoms, ruled by the descendants of Englishmen who had come to seek their fortunes in Ireland during the Middle Ages; and into Gaelic chieftainships, ruled by native Irishmen (51). Royal authority over the earldoms and chieftainships was limited or non-existent and Ireland as a whole was to prove a formidable thorn in the flesh of English rulers during the sixteenth century.

Ireland was at least nominally part of the King's dominions. To the north, Scotland, a traditional enemy, was ruled by Henry's nephew James V, the son of his elder sister Margaret's marriage to James IV. James, hitherto a minor, began his personal rule in 1528, and Scotland's relationships with England during the 1530s were determined by a combination of factors which included the continuing rivalries of Francis I of France and the Emperor Charles V on the continent of Europe, the Reformation in England, and the 'auld alliance' between France and Scotland. These, taken together, meant that there was ample scope for long-established Anglo-Scottish rivalries to come to the fore during the later part of Henry VIII's reign (see Ch. 5). The strategic importance of Scotland as a back door into England during the latter's conflicts with Continental powers, especially France, had been a familiar element in English foreign policy during the Middle Ages, and the long-established threat to England from north of the border was to continue during the 1530s and for several decades thereafter.

The general background to English foreign policy during the 1530s will be discussed below (Ch. 6). Here it is enough to note that by the later 1520s Wolsey's failure to secure from the Pope an annulment of Henry VIII's marriage to Catherine of Aragon – a failure largely determined by the European diplomatic situation – had fatally weakened his position at home. It led to his fall in the course of 1529 (a fall which illustrated that he was indeed completely dependent on the King's favour) and to a developing crisis for the English Church, already under assault from foreign Protestant ideas. Within a decade that Church, which presented such a formidable institutional face to the world at the end of the 1520s, was to be radically and dramatically changed.

Some notable aspects of the life of the Church in 1529 are worth special attention: its wealth; its unpopularity as an institution in the eyes of many laymen – anticlericalism [N] was very strong in England during the 1520s; the fact that it was being challenged by two heterodox movements, Lollardy and Lutheranism – Protestant beliefs were active in England well *before* Henry's breach with the Papacy; and its dependence on the Crown. The wealth of the Church was founded on its vast landed estates which were the basis of its overall net income of about £270,000 per annum on the eve of the Reformation, about half of that sum going to the monasteries and the rest to the secular clergy. At the same date the Crown enjoyed a total income of about £100,000 a year, not much more than a third of the revenue of the Church. It has been estimated that the Church owned as much as one-fifth of the wealth of England at the time (3; 24; 26). If the foundation of the Church's riches was in its vast landed possessions, the most conspicuous evidence of its power and glory lay in its magnificent buildings, great cathedrals and abbeys and thousands of lesser churches and religious edifices which pious Englishmen had built over the centuries to the greater glory of God and, it must be added, in the hope of aiding their own salvation. These structures often contained great intrinsic wealth in gold and silver plate and even greater treasures in art and books.

The wealth of the Church was one reason for the anticlericalism which was strong in England in the 1520s. Laymen who saw the pomp and splendour of wordly bishops – above all of Wolsey himself – had a reasonable case when they contrasted the life styles of the upper clergy with those of Christ and his Apostles. Moreover, although the overall quality of the clergy was no lower than it had been in the past (169) – it may in fact have been rising – lay standards and demands were now being pitched at much higher levels than ever before. Increasingly well-educated laymen expected more of their clerical mentors and their strictures now had added force through their dissemination in print. Lay criticisms found specific foci in the ecclesiastical courts, in pluralism and in tithes (27), and the extent and ferocity of anticlericalism in London in the early years of Henry VIII's reign was amply illustrated in the notorious Hunne case of 1511 to 1514,[2] which started when Richard Hunne, a substantial London merchant, refused to pay a mortuary fee to the priest who had buried his infant son. The dispute escalated into heresy proceedings against Hunne and reached its climax when he was found hanging from a beam in the bishop of London's prison, to which he had been consigned. Many Londoners believed, whether rightly or not, that Hunne had been murdered, and Bishop Fitzjames wrote in intemperate terms to Wolsey about the hostility of the London populace to the clerical estate. Even more ominously from the point of view of the Church, the affair had repercussions in the Parliament of 1515, where it became involved in disputes about benefit of clergy. The Hunne case is, in fact, the most notable example of that pre-Reformation anticlericalism which found expression in the early years of the Reformation Parliament in such measures as Acts to limit mortuary fees and to restrict the right of clerics to hold a plurality of benefices.

The Hunne episode can be regarded as a manifestation of 'negative' anticlericalism, one of the three different strands in pre-Reformation anticlerical feeling which Professor Scarisbrick has distinguished (68). That negativism concentrated on the denunciation of evils in the institutional Church and found its most virulent expression in the savage and grossly exaggerated strictures of the lawyer Simon Fish, whose *Supplication for the Beggars*, probably published in 1529, was written in the form of a petition from the poor to Henry VIII.

> These are not the [shep] herds but the ravenous wolves going in [shep] herds' clothing, devouring the flock: the bishops, abbots, priors, deacons, archdeacons, suffragans, priests, monks, canons, friars, pardoners and summoners. And who is able to number this idle, ravenous sort which (setting all labour aside) have begged so importunately that they have gotten into their hands more than the third part of all your realm. The goodliest lordships, manors, lands and territories are theirs. Besides this they have the tenth part of all the corn, meadow, pasture, grass, wool, colts, calves, lambs, pigs, geese and chickens. Over and besides, the tenth part of every servant's wages, the tenth part of the wool, milk, honey, wax, cheese, and butter. Yea, and they look so narrowly upon their profits that the poor wives must be countable to them of every tenth egg, or else she . . . shall be taken as an heretic.
> . . .
> And what do all this greedy sort of sturdy, idle, holy thieves with these yearly exactions that they take of the people? Truly nothing, but exempt themselves from the obedience of your Grace! Nothing but translate all rule, power, lordship, authority, obedience and dignity from your Grace unto them! . . .
> Yea, and what do they more? Truly, nothing but apply themselves, by all the sleights they may, to have to do with every man's wife, every man's daughter, and every man's maid, that cuckoldry and bawdry should reign over all among your subjects, that no man should know his own child. . . .
> Tie these holy, idle thieves to the carts, to be whipped naked about every market town till they will fall to labour, that they by their importunate begging take not away the alms that the good Christian people would give us, sore, impotent, miserable people, your beadsmen. . . . (4, *16–19*)

There were, however, two other more positive forms of anticlericalism, one secular, the other religious. The former, of which, indeed, some traces can be found in Fish, argued that much of the Church's wealth should be confiscated and directed to social and educational ends; the clerical estate should have its wings clipped in the general interests of the commonwealth. The latter stressed the need for reform in order to benefit the spiritual life of the Church itself; monasteries should be drastically changed or even swept away altogether and the education of the secular clergy should be improved in order to bring spiritual benefits to all the people of England. The three forms of anticlericalism were not, of course, mutually exclusive, and the second and third types certainly had a notable influence on the plans of Thomas Cromwell (see Chs. 2 and 4).

Although many anticlericals, such as Cromwell himself, had heretical proclivities, anticlericalism did not necessarily imply disagreement with established doctrine. During the 1520s, however, the Church was being challenged by two heterodox movements, Lollardy and Lutheranism (27; 170). Lollardy, which had developed in England in the late fourteenth century under the leadership of the Oxford academic John Wycliffe, anticipated most of the major doctrines of the Reformation except that of justification by faith alone. In the early fifteenth century, however, it was driven underground with the support of the government and continued to survive throughout the fifteenth century only as a clandestine lower-class movement which had its greatest strength among town artisans, though with support among the common people in the countryside as well. Its influence was to be found in almost all parts of the country. Lollardy was always a strongly anticlerical as well as a heretical movement, and its traditions undoubtedly contributed to that anticlericalism among the laity which was, as we have seen, a powerful force in early-sixteenth-century England. Lollard groups, moreover, provided bases in which Lutheran ideas could take root and spread among ordinary people from the 1520s onwards; it is very notable that areas of the country where Lollardy was strong were receptive to the newly developed Protestantism of the Continental Reformation. Lollardy, then, was an important background force to the development of Protestantism in early-sixteenth-century England. On the other hand, it could hardly have brought about a full-scale Reformation on its own. This is because it almost totally lacked support among the ruling classes; during the early fifteenth century it had become associated in their minds with revolt and therefore with a threat to social stability.

Lutheranism did have the dynamic power which early-sixteenth-century Lollardy lacked. The spread of Lutheran ideas among English intellectuals was helped by the humanist ideas associated with the great Dutch scholar Erasmus (1466–1536). Erasmus, of course, never became a Protestant, but humanism stressed the need to return to original sources in all aspects of life and the most important of all original sources was the Bible. Erasmian ideas, therefore, fitted in well with Protestant emphasis on individual interpretation of the Scriptures as the ultimate standard of belief. Erasmus had also launched fierce attacks on the inadequacies and corruptions of the Church, attacks which gave much comfort to Lutherans and other Protestants. Erasmian ideas were certainly influential in England and it is significant that many sixteenth-century English humanists became Protestants. Martin Luther launched his attack on the Old Church in Germany in 1517 and by 1519 his ideas were making themselves felt in England. By 1520 an influential group of English Lutherans was meeting at Cambridge and from there the heresy spread to Oxford. It was soon influential, too, in London and other ports, among native businessmen as well as foreign traders. The first major achievement of the new English Protestantism was William Tyndale's translation of the New Testament, first printed in Germany in 1525. Copies soon streamed into England where they were eagerly snapped up, much to the alarm of the ecclesiastical authorities. This established a native tradition of Bible reading which was clandestine in the 1520s but was, as we shall see (Ch. 2), given official support by Thomas Cromwell during the 1530s.

By 1530, therefore, Protestantism had established a clear base in England. It had won support from intellectuals at Oxford and Cambridge and among businessmen and seamen at London and other ports. It had contacts with Lollard groups and had obtained an English translation of the New Testament. In these circumstances, and given the invention of printing in the mid-fifteenth century, Protestantism was almost bound to develop in England in the years ahead. When Lollardy came to the fore in the later fourteenth century its ideas could only be circulated in manuscripts. Now the vernacular Scriptures themselves were available in print and Lutheran and other Protestant books could also be imported from the Continent in printed editions. This made the circulation of new ideas both much easier and much more rapid. Of course, Henry VIII's breach with the Papacy and the formal rejection of Roman authority during the 1530s had enormous long-term implications for the development of English Protestantism, but it must never be forgotten that the breach with Rome came at a time when England was already subject to strong Protestant influences. Henry's divorce was not, as has too often been implied, the beginning of the Reformation in England, merely an episode, though an immensely important episode, in a longer chain of events.

Just as it is wrong to minimize the extent to which heretical ideas were already influential in England during the 1520s, it is also misleading to exaggerate the troubles of the Church during that decade. A perceptive observer in 1529, unconscious of the dramatic developments of the following decade, would probably have stressed the continuing traditional piety of most Englishmen rather than the influence of heretical ideas or the strength of anticlericalism. The years from about 1480 to 1530 saw a 'great rebuilding' of English urban and rural churches, with parishioners all over the country spending lavish sums on them. That was clearly a sign of pride and general approbation. As Professor Lander says, 'people do not spend vast sums of money upon institutions of which they profoundly disapprove' (21, 2, 148 ff.). We must, therefore, be careful to insist that the religious life of England faced two ways during the 1520s. The rebuilding of churches, which was so obvious to any observer, bore witness to a glow of late medieval piety, while the increasing penetration of Protestant ideas, though less noticeable throughout the country as a whole, pointed to a future which was bound to see ominous challenges to the traditional structure of the Church.

It was in that delicately poised religious situation that Henry VIII introduced his break with Rome in the 1530s, a split which was undoubtedly made easier by the *de facto* dependence of the Church, in many of the most important areas of its life, on the influence of the Crown. In 1529 the bishops, the rulers of the Church in England, were mostly royal nominees whom the Pope appointed to their sees at the request of the monarch. On the financial side the Crown was taking far more money from the Church in the early sixteenth century than was the Papacy (see Ch. 11). As for the canon law of the Church, it was theoretically under the sole control of the Papacy and the clergy. In practice, however, during the later Middle Ages statutes had modified and controlled canon law in important particulars, for example in those relating to benefit of clergy and presentation to benefices (84).

The great conflict between Crown and Papacy during the 1530s was not, of course, the first major confrontation between Church and State in England. Previous medieval struggles, such as the Becket episode in the twelfth century and the disputes over the statutes of Provisors and Praemunire in the fourteenth had always ended in compromise and conciliation. The crisis of the 1530s had a different outcome. It ended in a clear rejection of papal authority and the creation of an English nation state. That outcome was made *possible* by the state of the English Church in 1529, but it was not a conclusion which seemed likely until the early 1530s. The spark which started the chain of events was the King's desire to rid himself of his wife and marry Anne Boleyn.

---

1. George Cavendish, *Thomas Wolsey, late Cardinal, his Life and Death*, ed. R. Lockyer (1962).
2. A. Ogle, *The Tragedy of the Lollards Tower* (Oxford, 1949).

CHAPTER 1

The breach with Rome: origins and accomplishment to 1536

By 1525 Henry VIII had tired of his wife Catherine of Aragon, the widow of his elder brother, Arthur, who had died in 1502. He had married her in 1509, immediately after his accession to the throne, but sixteen years later she had lost her physical attractions and, more important, had failed to secure the succession [B]. It is true that she had borne one healthy daughter, Mary, but the other living children that she had produced had not survived infancy and she had also had numerous miscarriages. By the mid-1520s it must have been clear to Henry that if he was to have a male heir he would first have to find another wife. (For what follows see (25; 27; 68).)

The problem of the succession was no doubt uppermost in Henry's mind when he brooded about his personal problems, but there were other factors which helped to convince him that both his own happiness and the welfare of his kingdom would be best served by repudiating Catherine. After the diplomatic revolution of 1525 in which Henry had broken with his old ally and Catherine's nephew the Emperor Charles V, the Queen was the symbol of a rejected alliance. Moreover, during the later 1520s Henry conceived a growing passion for a court lady, Anne Boleyn, a passion which grew all the fiercer when Anne refused to become his mistress.

In this situation that infinitely flexible instrument, Henry's conscience, began to work overtime. It finally told him that Catherine, who had shared his bed for more than a decade and a half, had never really been his wife at all. In the spring of 1527 he allowed Thomas Wolsey, cardinal-archbishop of York and papal legate, and William Warham, archbishop of Canterbury, to open an investigation, conducted in the strictest secrecy, into the validity of his marriage. Shortly afterwards he informed Catherine that he could no longer regard her as his wife, and that they must separate, news which the Queen received with a combination of incredulity, horror and indignation. She soon made it plain that she was not prepared to accept any verdict pronounced by the English archbishops, but would, as was her undoubted right, appeal to Rome for justice. Thus began Henry VIII's 'Great Cause' [N], which was to have incalculable consequences for subsequent English history.

From 1527 the King's quest for a divorce[1] dominated his affairs. Henry sought to achieve his aim by bringing a variety of pressures to bear upon Pope Clement VII; he presented a legal case which was argued by his representatives at the Curia; he tried to weaken the diplomatic influence which Charles exercised over the Pope through Habsburg military predominance in Italy; he endeavoured to secure the moral backing of the European universities. He could also exert pressure on the Pope through attacks on the rights of the Church in England.

These attacks began in a fairly mild form soon after the Reformation Parliament met in 1529 but only became really significant in subsequent years, with direct and brutal pressure on the English clergy and parliamentary legislation which was designed first of all to curtail and eventually to extinguish papal rights in England.

In order to be able to marry his brother's widow in 1509 Henry had had to obtain a bull from Pope Julius II. This assumed that the marriage between Catherine and Arthur had been consummated and dispensed with the affinity [N] thus created between Catherine and Henry. Henry now argued that the Pope had exceeded his powers in issuing such a bull, maintaining that divine law, from which no Pope could dispense, directly prohibited the marriage. He pointed especially to the biblical passage in Leviticus xx. 21, which stated, 'If a man shall take his brother's wife, it is an impurity: . . . they shall be childless.' It is not clear, however, that this prohibition extended to a *dead* brother's wife; indeed, as Henry's opponents were quick to point out another scriptural passage, Deuteronomy xxv. 5, positively instructed a man to marry the wife of a deceased brother: 'When brethren dwell together, and one of them dieth without children, the wife of the deceased shall not marry to another, but his brother shall take her, and raise up seed for his brother.' There is no doubt, in fact, that Henry's case in law, as he presented it, was a weak one, not only because of the verse in Deuteronomy but because there were precedents for papal dispensations in similar cases. Henry was asking the Pope to declare that some of his predecessors had exceeded their authority. That was a very large demand!

Julius's bull had, as we have seen, assumed that the marriage between Arthur and Catherine had been consummated and Henry maintained throughout the case that Catherine had not come to him as a virgin. The Queen, however, steadfastly maintained that she had, and it seems that she spoke the truth. It has never been clear why Henry told this lie, but, of course, once the lie had been told it became more and more difficult to repudiate it. The situation was especially ironic because Wolsey rapidly saw that acceptance of the Queen's protestations would have given Henry a much stronger case. A non-consummated marriage between Catherine and Arthur would not have created an impediment of affinity between Henry and Catherine, but it *would* have created a different impediment – that of 'public honesty' (resulting from the marriage *ceremony* between Arthur and Catherine) – which also required to be removed by papal dispensation. Julius II's bull had omitted to do this, concentrating instead on the greater impediment of the affinity created by a consummated marriage. If Henry had accepted that the Queen had been a virgin in 1509 he could have made a much stronger legal case, arguing that Julius's bull was inappropriate as it removed an impediment which did not exist while ignoring one that did.

The weak legal case which Henry *did* present clearly hindered his quest for an annulment, but it did not render that quest hopeless. Henry had previously shown himself to be a devoted son of the Church, witness his denunciation of Luther in the *Assertio Septem Sacramentorum* which he wrote in 1521 and for which he obtained from Pope Leo X the title 'Defender of the Faith'. Popes were always anxious to oblige pious monarchs and in different circumstances the legal difficulties might have been overcome by the practised lawyers of the Curia [N]. What really rendered Henry's cause a vain one was the European diplomatic situation. Just at the time he needed the most favourable possible atmosphere at the Curia, the Pope became a virtual prisoner of the Emperor Charles V, following the sack of Rome by the latter's mutinous troops in May 1527. All Henry could then do in the diplomatic field was to encourage Francis I of France in his Italian ambitions in the hope that he might drive the Imperialists out of Italy and thus end or at least substantially reduce Charles's influence at Rome. French successes in 1528 encouraged the Pope to create a commission under Cardinals Campeggio and Wolsey to hear the case in England, but by the end of 1529 Italy and the Pope were once more firmly under Imperial influence and Campeggio's and Wolsey's commission had been revoked. Charles's influence remained predominant in Italy during the following years, the period which saw the continuing failure of Henry's diplomacy at Rome and the decisive moves in England which brought about the breach with the Papacy.

Given the weakness of his legal case and the preponderance of Imperial power in Italy Henry's attempts to influence the Pope by securing the moral backing of European intellectual opinion seem doomed from the start. In 1530 his agents toured the Continental universities seeking verdicts to buttress the favourable opinions which Oxford and Cambridge had been persuaded – though not without difficulty – to pronounce on his case. He secured support from eight foreign universities, including Bologna and Paris, but more were against him, and it rapidly became apparent that the limited academic backing which he had secured would do nothing to sway the Pope. It may be that the idea of collecting opinions from the universities came from a Cambridge don, Thomas Cranmer. In any event, by 1530 Cranmer was in the King's service. When the aged Warham died in the autumn of 1532 Cranmer, already inclined to Protestant views, was Henry's choice to succeed him at Canterbury. Pope Clement, anxious to do the King any reasonable favours, expedited the necessary bulls, and in March 1533 the new archbishop was consecrated after taking the traditional oath of obedience to the Pope. He was careful, however, to make a private protestation beforehand, in which he stated that no oath could bind him to act against his duty to the King. Several months before Cranmer's consecration Henry and Anne Boleyn had begun living together. Anne became pregnant in December 1532 and the following January Henry and she went through a form of marriage. In May Cranmer dutifully pronounced that Henry's marriage to Catherine had been invalid from the start and that his union with Anne was therefore lawful. This was a frontal challenge to papal authority – Clement was still considering the case – as was the Act in Restraint of Appeals to Rome, passed by Parliament in the spring of 1533, the Act which made possible Cranmer's determination of the case in England. Henry, unable to secure a favourable papal verdict, had solved his problem at home. He accomplished this through pressure on the English clergy and parliamentary legislation.

His measures against the English clergy, which began well before the final break with the Papacy, had two purposes. They indicated to the Curia the strength of Henry's determination to achieve his aims and therefore put additional pressure on the Pope to grant an annulment of the Aragon marriage. They also put Henry in a powerful position to obtain his divorce from the English episcopate if the Pope continued to prove recalcitrant. Henry's attacks on the English Church between 1530 and 1532 should not, therefore, be seen in simple terms as *either* a method of putting pressure on the Pope *or else* as an essential prelude to a break with Rome. They allowed the King to keep his options open.

The Reformation Parliament which met for the first time in November 1529 soon launched a series of attacks on abuses in the Church, attacks which revealed the extent of anticlerical feeling. It seems clear that these outbursts, against such grievances as excessive probate and mortuary fees and the holding of benefices in plurality, were spontaneous reactions of the Commons, unprompted by the government. Henry and his advisers must, however, have been delighted by such demonstrations of anticlericalism. They made it plain that any royal attacks on clerical privileges would receive enthusiastic support from influential members of the governing class assembled in Parliament. The royal assault came between 1530 and 1532 in a series of moves which ended in the effective subjugation of the Church in England to royal authority. In 1530 the whole English clergy were charged under praemunire [N] with an offence in the exercise of their jurisdiction. One interpretation has it that they were accused of accepting Wolsey's legatine powers, another that they were indicted for the mere exercise of their normal spiritual jurisdiction which was held to be in derogation of royal authority. In any event in February 1531 they bought a pardon for the large sum of £118,000. The episode was a dramatic warning to the clergy of their insecurity during a period of dispute between their two masters, Pope and King. Henry pressed the point home during the same month by demanding that the clerical estate recognize him as 'Supreme Head' of the English Church. The Convocation [N] of Canterbury, well aware of the direct challenge such a title posed to papal authority, agreed only on condition that the words 'so far as the law of Christ allows' were added. This compromise can hardly have given much satisfaction to either party and the assault on the clergy continued in 1532, now probably under the direction of the King's new minister, Thomas Cromwell. The Commons presented to the King a 'Supplication against the Ordinaries' (i.e. bishops) which complained *inter alia* of the independent legislative powers of the Church. Convocation, browbeaten by the King, was unable to repeat its resistance of the previous year. In May, in a document known as the 'Submission of the Clergy', it gave way completely to the royal demands. All subsequent legislation passed by Convocation was to be subject to royal veto and existing canons were to be surveyed by a Royal Commission of thirty-two, only half of whom were to be clergymen. Any canons found unsatisfactory were to be regarded as null and void. Henry now controlled the legislative machinery of the English Church.

By 1532, then, the King had asserted royal authority over the English clergy. He had not, however, achieved the formal independence from the Papacy which would be necessary both to obtain his annulment at home and to make his control of the English Church secure. That achievement, in its essentials, was the work of the next two years and the instrument used was parliamentary statute. As the ultimate authority in the universal Church the Pope possessed supreme legislative, executive and judicial powers over it; he obtained revenue from it; and, most important of all, perhaps, he was the ultimate arbiter and guardian of its doctrine. His powers and rights in all these fields were swept away in England between 1532 and 1534 in a momentous revolution. (The relevant Statutes can be found in full in (1, vol. III), and in abbreviated form in (3).)

Three Acts deprived him of his English revenues. In 1532 the Act in Conditional Restraint of Annates [G.1(1); N] reduced these payments to the nominal sum of 5 per cent of the first year's income, though a clause in the Act provided that it should not take immediate effect but could be activated by the King by letters patent. This was a clear attempt to blackmail the Pope into compliance with the royal wishes. It failed and in 1533 Henry duly confirmed the Act. In 1534 a further Act abolished the small annates payments which were left [G.1(2)] and in the same year the Dispensations Act deprived the Pope of all his remaining revenues from England. [G.1(3)]

In 1533 the Act in Restraint of Appeals [E.1(1); G.1(4)], perhaps the most famous statute of the Reformation, abolished appeals to Rome in a wide variety of cases, including matrimonial ones. This Act which, as we have seen, enabled Henry to get his divorce in England did not, however, deny appeals to the Pope in matters of heresy. As Professor Scarisbrick has pointed out, even after its passage the Pope was still 'in some minimal way, the head of the Church in England' (68, *317*). If the Act of Appeals drastically reduced the Pope's judicial powers in England, the two annates Acts deprived him of his executive authority. The 1532 Act stated that if the Pope denied or delayed the bulls necessary for the installation of any bishops then they should be consecrated by English authority alone. The 1534 Act went much further providing that bishops were to be appointed by the King alone, though provision was made for the nominal co-operation of cathedral chapters. The 'Submission of the Clergy' of 1532, confirmed by statute two years later (25 Henry VIII, c. 19), by giving the King a veto over both new and existing ecclesiastical laws virtually deprived the Pope of legislative authority in England, and the Dispensations Act completed the 'process by providing that dispensations (licences to depart from canon law) should henceforth be issued in England, not in Rome.

In 1534 the Act of Supremacy [E.1(2); G.1(5)], which assumed in its preamble that the King was head of the English Church, expressly gave him the right to correct heresy. This right, of course, implied the further right to determine which opinions were heretical. The King was, therefore, from 1534 onwards the arbiter of the doctrine of the English Church, assuming in this respect the position previously held by the Pope.

Two further Acts of 1534 endeavoured to provide for the security of the new order which had been established. An Act of Succession (25 Henry VIII, c. 22) vested the inheritance of the Crown in the heirs of Henry and Anne [B], and another Act made it treason to deny the royal supremacy, not merely by deed or in writing but even in spoken words (26 Henry VIII, c. 13). It was a harsh measure, but one which the King and Cromwell clearly deemed necessary to deal with the unrest which they feared might come in the wake of their repudiation of Rome [H]. Finally, an Act against Papal authority in 1536 summarized the revolution of the previous few years with a long attack on the 'pretended power and usurped authority of the bishop of Rome, by some called the Pope' [G.1(6)].

The rejection of the Papacy and the creation of a national English Church in the early 1530s raise a number of issues which have provoked much historical debate. At what stage in the process should a complete breach with Rome be regarded as inevitable? What were the respective roles of the King and Cromwell? And what was the nature of the royal supremacy over the Church which had emerged by 1534? Could it be argued that in some respects the King was exchanging an existing condominium – with an Italian Pope – for a new one – with the English Parliament?

Henry was certainly a man who liked to keep his options open as long as possible. Even as late as 1534 it was provided in the Dispensations Act which had just passed Parliament that it should only come into effect if confirmed by royal letters patent. The King did confirm it soon, but the provision suggests that even at that late date he did not regard his break with the Papacy as final and complete. The delay in activating the statute only makes sense if it was intended to be a means of applying pressure at Rome; there is no point in attempting to blackmail an authority which has already been totally repudiated. On the other hand, Professor Scarisbrick has argued (68, Ch. 9) that from an early stage in the annulment proceedings, perhaps as early as 1530, Henry had resolved on a fairly drastic redefinition of royal and papal authority, although, of course, Scarisbrick would be the first to admit that such a change in the relative positions of Pope and King need not necessarily have produced the complete breach which later occurred.

It seems clear, then, that we cannot regard a total break between England and the Papacy as inevitable as early as 1530. On the other hand, it does seem fanciful to argue that a complete split could have been avoided as late as 1534. Henry's ditherings over the Dispensations Act must be seen in the context of the amount and importance of the anti-papal legislation that had already been passed. Professor Elton has argued (25, Ch. 8) that after the passage of the Act in Restraint of Appeals in the early months of 1533 continuing negotiations with Rome were formalistic only. Indeed he maintains that the final decision to reject the Papacy was taken in the autumn of 1532, when the death of Warham opened up the possibility of appointing a compliant archbishop who could be relied upon to pronounce a favourable sentence on the 'Great Cause' in England. According to this argument Henry's cohabitation with Anne was a result rather than a cause of the final decision to establish an independent national Church. Professor Scarisbrick, on the other hand, believes (68, *309*) that the decisive moment came with the discovery of Anne's pregnancy in January of 1533; it was only then that the final decision was taken to repudiate Rome, and that decision was based on the urgent need to ensure that the expected child would be legitimate. Either of these views seems tenable on the available evidence and it is best to conclude that the decision to break completely with the Papacy was taken some time between the autumn of 1532 and the beginning of 1533. It would certainly be difficult to argue that any other decision was a practical possibility after January 1533.

If it is difficult to decide the exact date at which Henry resolved to cut all ties with Rome it is equally difficult to be sure of the respective roles of the King and Thomas Cromwell in the events of 1530 to 1534. Cromwell, born about 1485 (on

Cromwell see (70; 71)), came from a humble background – his father was a brewer, fuller and blacksmith – and he spent part of his early life abroad, in Italy and the Netherlands, as a soldier and trader. After his return to England he entered Wolsey's service and during the 1520s was one of the most important members of his household. By then he had acquired – we do not know how – a considerable knowledge of English law. On Wolsey's fall he did his best to defend the cardinal's interests while not neglecting his own. He entered the Reformation Parliament and the King's service and by the end of 1530 was a member of the Council, becoming one of its inner circle during the course of the following year. Like Cranmer, with whom he worked closely during the 1530s, Cromwell was a convinced Protestant, though it is impossible to be sure of his exact theological beliefs. He also had strong ideas in the secular field where he embarked on a huge programme of reforms designed both to rationalize and strengthen the administrative structure of the State and also to reform aspects of the English economy and society. From 1532 until his fall in 1540 he was Henry's principal minister and during these years he worked prodigiously hard to achieve his ends.

As a convinced Protestant Cromwell welcomed the rejection of papal authority, though for him this was merely the start of a true reformation of the Church. Henry's divorce proceedings were initiated, as we have noted, three years before Cromwell appeared on the scene. The latter, therefore, began to exert influence in a situation which was already highly conducive to attacks on Rome. The King's actions by 1530 had made a breach with the Papacy conceivable – in that sense Henry himself was undoubtedly 'the man behind the . . . Reformation' (see 52, vol. 2, *173*) – but Elton has argued that it was only after Cromwell became the King's chief adviser in 1532 that a way was found of translating Henry's wishes into practice (25). According to this interpretation Henry knew what he wanted – an annulment of his marriage – but when the Pope refused to grant that demand the King did not know how to proceed. He may have been prepared to *consider* the rejection of papal authority, but he did nothing *in practice* to bring this about. Cromwell showed him the way from 1532 onwards in the series of statutes which accomplished the repudiation of the Papacy. Scarisbrick, on the other hand sees Henry in complete command of the situation throughout (68). Cromwell, for him, was merely 'the executant of the King's designs' (68, *304*) brought to power to carry out plans which Henry had already made. Scarisbrick has argued convincingly that the fundamental ideas behind the break with Rome, ideas which were expounded in the statutes of 1532–34, were all available to Henry by 1530–31, well before Cromwell's admission to the inner ring of royal councillors.[2] There is, however, no doubt that the *specific form* of these statutes, most notably of the great Act of Appeals (52, vol. 2), owed much to Cromwell's careful drafting and revisions. It seems best to conclude that both Henry and Cromwell played vital roles in the rejection of papal authority. Henry initiated the whole train of events when he began his divorce proceedings in 1527 and was fully conversant with the ideas behind the later royal supremacy long before Cromwell became his principal adviser. The latter, on the other hand, gave a new drive and determination to the royal plans and played the dominant role in drawing up the detailed anti-papal legislation of 1532–34 and putting it through

Parliament. The minds of *both* King *and* minister were therefore of the greatest importance in the accomplishment of the schism.

The result of that schism, the royal supremacy over the English Church, was in theory a highly personal authority when it was fully proclaimed in 1534. (For what follows see (25; 68)). The Act of Supremacy of that year was declaratory in form, asserting bluntly that the 'King's Majesty justly and rightfully is and oweth to be the supreme head of the Church of England'. Parliament did not in any sense confer the dignity on the King, it merely recognized a right which had always justly existed, although it had been obscured for centuries by papal usurpations. Armed with this God-given power Henry henceforth issued statements of faith and injunctions to the clergy on his own authority. Subsequent Acts of Parliament which dealt with religious matters recognized this situation. They did not authorize but merely enforced decisions which the King had already made by virtue of his own all-embracing ecclesiastical authority. The theory of the royal supremacy after 1534 was, therefore, plain. The King had replaced the Pope as head of the Church and Parliament's role in religious matters was merely to enforce the royal wishes. This clear-cut theoretical situation was, however, somewhat different in practice. The ecclesiastical statutes which had preceded the Act of Supremacy – measures such as the Annates, Appeals and Dispensations Acts – had been authorized as well as enforced by Parliament. They represented, therefore, a different theory of the royal authority over the Church, a theory which, by joining Parliament's authority with that of the King, gave the latter a much less exalted role in ecclesiastical affairs. Moreover, even after 1534 the King's absolute authority in church matters was limited in practice by his need to secure parliamentary authorization for practical penalties to make that authority effective; only parliamentary statutes could create the punishments necessary to enforce the supremacy throughout the country on a day-to-day basis. As Elton has aptly put it, 'the King's power, however personal to him, was ultimately active by authority of parliament' (25, *197*). In this situation, even after 1534 there was a tension between the 'absolutist' interpretation of the royal supremacy which was certainly favoured by the King himself and a 'constitutional' interpretation, stressing the necessity of parliamentary involvement, which seems to have been favoured by Cromwell and many of the common lawyers. The difficulty was not resolved until the reign of Edward VI, when the latter view prevailed.

We have seen that the 1530s saw a breach with Rome which came about as a matter of state policy. Henry VIII wanted a divorce which the Pope was unable to grant. In that situation he severed England's long-established ties with the Papacy and obtained his wishes from the new national Church of which he made himself the head. This rejection of papal authority was *not* of course, the beginning of the Reformation in England. That, as we have seen, was already active in the 1520s through old Lollard and, above all, new Lutheran influences which were at work upon a lay opinion which was increasingly dissatisfied with the state of the Church. Of course, though Henry's marriage problem did not initiate the Reformation it had the most profound effect upon it. Henry himself would have firmly rebuffed any accusation that in rejecting the Pope he was departing from

Catholic orthodoxy; he would, indeed, have maintained that he was restoring it free from Roman usurpations. It is now clear, however, that in his later years he himself departed far from the traditional teaching of the Church on, for example, the sacraments. Moreover, the withdrawal of obedience from Rome could not but encourage Lutherans and others including Cromwell to see Henry's actions as an opportunity for further changes in the Church at both theological and disciplinary levels. Whatever the King might say about the usurpations of Rome, the papal headship of the Church had been a fact for centuries. Now that the traditional guarantor of orthodoxy had been removed, who could say what the end of the matter would be? The historian can see that the rejection of papal authority made possible the hastening of Reformation in England. If Henry had not sought a divorce in the later 1520s reforming influences in the English Church would still have been there but their progress would surely have been both much slower and much less successful.

---

1. Henry's demand was for an annulment – a declaration that his marriage to Catherine had never legally existed – and strictly speaking it is wrong to use the word 'divorce', which implies the dissolution of a valid marriage. Divorce in the modern sense was, of course, impossible by the law of the Catholic Church, but as it seems pedantic to avoid the word, the terms annulment and divorce have been used interchangeably.
2. Elton, *Reform and Reformation*, Ch. 6, now believes that Cromwell may have influenced Henry's thinking as early as 1530, but his arguments have been challenged and the matter remains open. See Steven W. Haas, 'Henry VIII's Glasse of Truthe', *History*, **64** (1979), 353–62.

CHAPTER 2

The progress of the Reformation, 1536–1547

By 1536 Henry and Cromwell had dismissed the Pope from English life, but they had not reformed the Church. Cromwell certainly wanted such reform, but he had always to tread warily, to ensure that he did not get too far ahead of his master's views. Henry himself had no such reforming fervour, but he did cast covetous eyes on the vast wealth of the ecclesiastical establishment. In the 1530s, with the ordinary royal revenue in decline and heavy expenses to meet, it was obvious that the new national Church would be expected to contribute substantially to the Crown's income. This was made plain by the Act for First Fruits and Tenths, passed by Parliament in 1534 (26 Henry VIII, c. 3). This not only annexed the first year's revenue of bishoprics to the Crown but demanded similar payments from all ecclesiastical benefices, however modest in value. It also provided that from then on all clerics were to pay one-tenth of their net incomes to the Crown each year. This measure brought in an annual income of over £40,000 in the early years of its operation. As a result churchmen were paying much heavier taxation than they had ever done in the days of their obedience to Rome. The royal supremacy was clearly to be an expensive innovation for the Church!

Henry's exactions did not stop there. In 1534 Cromwell and he considered a scheme for the confiscation of all episcopal lands. This came to nothing, but in the following year the compilation of the *Valor Ecclesiasticus* revealed the extent of clerical wealth. This great compendium, an impressive monument to the abilities of Tudor administrators, detailed the income both of secular benefices and of the religious orders. It was made necessary by the Act for First Fruits and Tenths, but its demonstration that the English regular clergy enjoyed a net income of some £136,000 per annum directed attention to the monasteries. In 1536 the first monastic dissolutions took place. (The following account of the dissolution is based on (172) and (173).)

Cromwell clearly played a great part in the whole process of dissolution, but it is important to remember that he acted throughout as the King's servant and that other ministers, especially the duke of Norfolk and Lord Chancellor Audley, played significant roles (173). The financial motives behind the dissolution are obvious. The annexation of the monastic estates to the Crown and the subsequent sale of many of them brought a vast income to Henry. It also helped to tie the landed classes to the new national Church. Noblemen, gentlemen, merchants and yeomen who had bought church lands would, to put it mildly, be apprehensive about the possible consequences of the return of papal authority. Cromwell had promised to make the King rich and the dissolution did just that, at least for a short time, but his motives extended beyond purely financial considerations. As a convinced Protestant who rejected the traditional Catholic stress on the efficacy

27

of works he must have realized that the continuance of a large monastic establishment, committed by its very existence to that theological position, would be a formidable obstacle in the path of the truly reformed Church which he envisaged. Cromwell, moreover, could point to precedents, both in England and abroad, for the successful dissolution of religious establishments. During the 1520s Wolsey had suppressed some twenty-nine English religious houses, an operation in which Cromwell himself had played a prominent role, and during the same decade religious orders had been dissolved in parts of Germany and Switzerland as well as in Scandinavia (172).

It is not clear whether the government intended in 1536 to suppress all the monasteries or merely some of them. The 1536 Act (27 Henry VIII, c. 28), which justified the dissolution of the smaller monasteries on the grounds of the evil life of their inmates as revealed by the royal visitation of 1535, asserted that religion was 'right well kept and observed' in the 'great solemn monasteries of this realm'. This certainly suggests that there was no intention at that time to proceed further, and the fact that Henry himself founded a new abbey, at Bisham, in 1536, lends weight to this interpretation. There is, however, other evidence which suggests that the 1536 dissolutions were unlikely to be the end of the matter (25). The houses which disappeared in that year only enjoyed a small fraction of the total monastic income – not enough to make the King rich; the elaborately organized Court of Augmentations, set up in 1536 to administer the confiscated monastic revenues, seems inappropriate for the comparatively limited business which it gained in that year; the laity's appetite for land was merely whetted, not satisfied, by the opportunities which the 1536 suppressions presented; and finally, the religious objections of Cromwell and his circle to the very existence of monasticism could only be satisfied by a total dissolution. The best explanation of the contradictory evidence is doubtless that Henry and Cromwell proceeded cautiously. They could not know in advance the extent of opposition and resistance to the dissolution and were prepared either to proceed further or call a halt to the process depending on circumstances. When it became clear that there was going to be only limited resistance to their proceedings the arguments for continuing the dissolution became irresistible.

The 1536 Act, which dissolved all houses worth less than £200 a year affected in theory over 300 establishments. Some 80 of these, however, obtained exemptions, largely because of difficulties in accommodating their inmates. The Act allowed the religious affected by it either to take dispensations to leave religion altogether or else to transfer to other houses, and in some parts of the country those who wished to transfer could not be easily accommodated in other establishments. The four following years saw the disappearance of the rest of the religious houses. A few came into the King's hands following the attainder of their abbots for involvement in the Pilgrimage of Grace, but most surrendered to a combination of threats and blandishments from the government, the latter being mainly the offer of pensions to the inmates. An Act of 1539 (31 Henry VIII, c. 13) recognized the surrenders made since 1536, formally vested their possessions in the Crown and provided that the King should enjoy the property of those houses which 'hereafter shall happen to be dissolved'. The last to go was

Waltham Abbey. Its surrender in March 1540 meant that the entire establishment of over 800 religious houses had been dissolved in a period of four years.

The English government did not forget the need to extend its religious ideas to Ireland during the 1530s. It secured the acceptance of the royal supremacy by the Irish Parliament in 1536 though it was much more difficult to put it into practice. By the end of the reign most of the Irish bishops had accepted the new situation, but the general education of the clergy and the laity lagged a long way behind. In 1547 they were far from committed to the Henrician settlement and the events of the rest of the century placed most of them firmly in the Counter-Reformation camp (89). The King and Cromwell also moved against the Irish monasteries. A suppression bill was passed by the Irish Parliament in 1537 and in those parts of the country which were under English control religious houses disappeared. In much of Gaelic Ireland, however, monasteries and friaries continued to exist – the government did not have the physical power to dissolve them. The only systematic study we have of Irish monasticism at this time, however, plays down the significance of the entire process. The dissolution of some monasteries and the survival of others was essentially a minor episode in the history of Ireland.[1]

The results of the dissolution in England were more significant. In the religious sphere it meant the end – apart from the brief Marian revival – of a way of life which over the centuries had produced many remarkable men for the service of the Church. It is true that few sixteenth-century monks and nuns followed their rule with fervour, but most of the 9,000 or so male and female religious who were thrust into the world between 1536 and 1540 probably viewed their fate with distaste. Most of them got pensions – though about 1,800 did not – but these were inadequate for nuns, and though generally sufficient in the case of monks they can have done only so much to console the numerous men – many of them elderly – who must have felt that the whole foundations of their world had collapsed about them. The dissolution in itself did nothing, of course, to make the new national Church Protestant, but it did, as Cromwell and his supporters had hoped, remove an important barrier to acceptance of the Protestant theology of grace. It was also a great blow to the Church as an institution. The loss of all its regular clergy and about half its wealth over a period of four years meant that the new national Church of England was a much less impressive material edifice than its medieval predecessor. Moreover, just as Parliament began to play a significant role in the regulation of ecclesiastical affairs the dissolution robbed the House of Lords of the twenty-nine abbots who had hitherto been an important element in its membership. Afterwards, the Lords was a predominantly secular body.

The cultural effects of the dissolution were also of considerable importance. It is true that, by the 1530s, the monasteries were no longer in the forefront of English educational life as they had been for much of the Middle Ages; but they contained vast treasures in their libraries and works of art, all of which were scattered and many of which were lost. Above all, some of the monastic buildings were among the glories of English architecture, and when they were pulled down or left to decay or converted to secular uses the English towns and countryside lost some of their most imposing features; those who examine the ruins of such abbeys as Rievaulx in Yorkshire begin to understand the extent of the loss. The dissolution also ended the monastic charity which had fed thousands of the poor each year. It has become fashionable to minimize the significance of this loss, especially as the following years saw a great increase in secular donations for poor relief (205), but Professor Knowles pointed out that monastic charity may have amounted to as much as £7,000 to £10,000 per annum (172, *254–6*). This is a large sum and the poor who were no longer fed must certainly have lamented the passing of their monastic benefactors.

The losses of the religious and the poor enabled the Crown vastly to increase its revenues. Henry VIII at least doubled his ordinary income during the 1530s, partly due to his acquisition of first fruits and tenths but mainly as a result of the dissolution (24, *59 ff*) provides a good survey of the financial situation). The monastic lands went initially, of course, to the Crown, but the bulk of them were soon sold, about half during the remainder of Henry VIII's reign and perhaps three-quarters by the accession of Elizabeth. Members of the peerage, merchants and yeomen acquired some, but most went to established gentry families, which thus expanded their holdings, and to the younger sons of such families who acquired land, often in their native counties. The general effect of the land sales was, therefore, to strengthen and expand the upper echelons of landed society – broadly speaking the gentry class – at the expense of both Church and Crown (26).

Whatever their inner feelings few monks actively opposed the dissolution, and the great bulk of the laity accepted the situation with attitudes which ranged from resignation to enthusiasm. It is true that there were demands for the restoration of monasteries during the Pilgrimage of Grace of 1536, but these should be seen in the context of the pilgrims' general resistance to attacks on the northern way of life. Their desire to see monasticism restored was probably fired at least as much by their determination to oppose all measures which could be attributed to the hated Cromwell and his circle as to fervent enthusiasm for the virtues of the religious life. Some monks were, of course, among the most fervent opponents of Henry's rejection of the Papacy, but their fate is best discussed when we consider the general opposition which the religious changes of the 1530s aroused and the government's reaction to it.

If the fall of the monasteries can be seen partly as an attack on the Catholic doctrine of works so, in a rather different way, can the attacks on 'popular superstitions' which Cromwell mounted during the 1530s. The royal injunctions of 1536, drawn up by Cromwell, 'to the intent that all superstition . . . may vanish away', ordered the clergy not to 'set forth or extol any images, relics or miracles for any superstition or lucre, nor allure the people by any enticements to the pilgrimage of any saint . . ., seeing all goodness, health, and grace ought to be both asked and looked for only of God, as of the very author of the same, and of none other'. The 1538 injunctions went much further, ordering the clergy to instruct their flocks, 'not to repose their trust . . . in any other works devised by men's phantasies beside Scripture; as in wandering to pilgrimages, offering of money, candles, or tapers to images or relics, or kissing or licking the same, saying over a number of beads . . . or in such-like superstition' (4, *79, 83*). In September

1538 the shrine of Thomas Becket at Canterbury, one of the great pilgrimage centres of England, was destroyed by order of the government, which duly hastened to seize the huge quantities of treasure which it contained.

These attacks on practices which were part of the everyday life of the people had a much stronger impact on the population at large than the rejection of the authority of a remote Pope, but we cannot know how thoroughly they were carried out at grass-roots level. Many clergymen must have been just as devoted as their parishioners to the old ways, and changes – if they took place at all – were doubtless slow in most parts of the country. The attack on 'superstition', however, just like the dissolution of the monasteries, was an indication from the government that the new national Church was to be different from the old regime.

As we have seen, Protestantism was already at work in England in the 1520s and during the remainder of Henry's reign it made significant advances among limited sections of the population. During the later 1530s the balance of forces at Court did much to encourage the spread of Protestant ideas. Cranmer and Cromwell dominated the scene and bore witness to their Protestantism by securing the appointment of such reforming bishops as Hugh Latimer at Worcester, Nicholas Shaxton at Salisbury and Edward Foxe at Hereford. Some conservatives like Richard Sampson still found places in the episcopate, but the general complexion of the bench of bishops made it much more sympathetic to Cromwellian ideas in 1539 than it had been five years earlier. The reforming line favoured by Cranmer and Cromwell was opposed by a conservative faction headed by Stephen Gardiner, the very able and assertive bishop of Winchester, and Thomas Howard, third duke of Norfolk and head of England's greatest noble family. These men accepted the royal supremacy but did not wish to see other significant changes in the Church. They had the support of some bishops and many conservative nobles and their chance was to come at the end of the decade. Standing behind reformers and conservatives, ready to assert his ultimate authority, was the King. It used to be thought that Henry personally had little truck with novelty in the theological field, but Professor Scarisbrick has demonstrated in fascinating detail that in his later years he moved far from Catholic orthodoxy on important points. It is now clear, for example, that he developed very unorthodox views about four of the traditional seven sacraments – matrimony, confirmation, extreme unction and holy orders (68). The conclusion that he toyed with 'violent novelty' seems a fair one, and it helps to make sense of measures which he permitted or envisaged during his later years. The Ten Articles of 1536, an official statement of doctrine issued by the King's authority as head of the Church, retained only three of the sacraments – baptism, penance and the eucharist. The others were simply ignored. The articles also denied the full doctrine of purgatory and contained many hints of Lutheran ideas. The four 'missing' sacraments were restored in the Bishops' Book of 1537, a document which was not formally licensed by the King, but the restoration was somewhat grudging as it was accompanied by a statement that they were of less dignity than the other three.

The King also allowed his heir Prince Edward to be educated by Protestant tutors, permitted Cranmer to engage in liturgical experiments and may even at the end of his reign have been contemplating the abolition of the mass (on this last point see (68), *475 ff*). The Council which he appointed to run the affairs of England during the minority of his son was certainly dominated by Protestants and it seems unlikely, to say the least, that the King was unaware of the consequences which this would almost certainly have for the theological development of the English Church. All this helps to put into perspective the *official* reaction against Protestant ideas which the King encouraged after 1539. In that year he allowed the conservative Norfolk to pilot through Parliament the Six Articles Act which remained the official doctrinal position of the Church for the rest of the reign. The issues in conflict between conservatives and reformers which it discussed were all settled firmly in favour of the former [G.1(7)]. Cranmer and Cromwell were badly shaken by this measure and Shaxton and Latimer actually resigned their sees. The Act was reinforced by the King's Book of 1543, a formulary, issued with Henry's approval, which confirmed the doctrine of the Six Articles and insisted that all the seven traditional sacraments were necessary for salvation. Only a few people suffered persecution under the Six Articles Act, however, and Protestant ideas continued their advance during the 1540s. Henry's own position was ambivalent. He obviously felt that theological novelty had gone too far for the country at large by 1539 and that it was time to apply the brakes, but we have seen that he continued with his own unorthodox theological investigations behind the scenes and made provisions for his son's minority which helped to produce an overtly Protestant English Church during Edward's reign.

However, Henry's greatest service to the development of English Protestantism was probably his decision to authorize the publication of vernacular bibles in England. There is no doubt that he gave his approval with some reluctance. Cromwell was certainly the driving force behind the decision. In 1535 he was appointed vicegerent in spirituals. Henry's deputy in ecclesiastical affairs. This new office brought home to the hierarchy the realities of the royal supremacy. As vicegerent Cromwell, a layman, took precedence over the archbishop of Canterbury. That symbolized lay control of the Church, but matters of protocol were of limited interest to the vicegerent whose ambition was to use his new powers to reform the Church, always remembering that he could not go faster than Henry would allow. By far his greatest success was his patronage of the vernacular bible (27; 71). In 1535, Miles Coverdale, an English clergyman of Protestant views, published the first complete English translation, probably at Zurich. Cromwell obtained the King's consent to its publication in England and in 1537 persuaded Henry to allow the sale of another translation as well, the so-called 'Matthew Bible'. In 1538 he took a decisive step to ensure that the laity were positively encouraged to read the Bible. He instructed the bishops to urge laymen and women to study the Scriptures. All parish clergymen were to make sure that an English Bible was available in Church for that purpose. Cromwell wanted to make sure that a new and authoritative version was produced for reading by the laity. The task was entrusted to Coverdale and in 1539 he produced his 'Great Bible', which was an outstanding success: it ran through several editions during the next two years. There can be no doubt about the immense significance of this Bible reading for the English laity. Henry attempted in 1543, after Cromwell's fall, to restrict access to the Scriptures to the upper classes, but he failed. Cromwell's work had made sure that laymen and women would think for themselves about the Scriptures – not simply accept what the official voice of the Church said about them. There can be little doubt in fact that study of the Bible was one of the major forces in producing religious disent and discussion in England during the sixteenth and seventeenth centuries. It also contributed enormously to the development of the great English literature of that period which is full of both general debts and specific allusions of the Bible. Cromwell's patronage of the vernacular Bible undoubtedly entitles him to be called one of the outstanding religious reformers of early modern England.

One of the most specific practical achievements of Cromwell as a religious reformer was his introduction of parish registers. In 1538 he ordered all parish priests to keep registers of baptisms, marriages and burials. These have provided later historians with much important statistical material, but their significance at the time was very different; they helped to sort out the marriage problems of many contemporary villagers. Marriages at this time were, by the law of the Church, forbidden within the so-called 'prohibited degrees', which ranged over a very wide spectrum of relationships. These posed especially acute problems in small communities where there was a great deal of intermarriage. Before 1538 such relationships were very difficult to establish because of the lack of adequate records, and this situation gave excessive power without adequate information to the Church courts. The new registers helped, therefore, to provide much-needed details about family relationships. The instruction about parish registers was contained in the royal injunctions of 1538. These, together with the previous injunctions of 1536, were issued by Cromwell in his capacity as vicegerent and were designed both to improve the spiritual behaviour of the clergy and the spiritual education of the laity (92). They constituted, in Professor Elton's words, 'a solid, moderate and . . . necessary reform programme' and even if their intentions were not always realized in practice they are further evidence of Cromwell's determination to improve the condition of the English Church, seen not only as the clergy but also as the whole body of laymen and women.

The cause of reform and the progress of Protestantism were greatly assisted by the products of the printing presses. Between 1525 and 1547 some 800 separate editions of religious works were printed in English, many of them strongly Protestant in content (68). These works must have stimulated the Bible-reading laity of the 1540s to think further about theological problems and formulate their own views on great issues like eucharistic doctrine. This doubtless applied to only a small minority of the population, but it was an articulate self-confident minority which made its voice heard loudly in the reign of Edward VI.

Cromwell's importance as a church reformer was clearly considerable, but there were limits to what he could do in five years. The traditional governmental and judicial machinery of the Church, with its elaborate hierarchy of courts and its ancient canon law, remained basically untouched. The evils of pluralism and the deficiencies of the tithe system continued. An Act of 1539, in which Henry himself had a large hand, did result in the creation of six new bishoprics between 1540 and 1542, though one of them, Westminister, was abolished in 1550 [O.3].

This was, however, a relatively minor adjustment in the pattern of ecclesiastical administration. The basic continuity in the disciplinary life of the Church should help to remind us of another basic continuity – that of the everyday worship of the common people in the parishes. The Pope was condemned and the royal supremacy lauded in sermons, a few images were removed, vernacular Bibles appeared. The long-term effects of the latter in dissolving traditional ideas were, as we have seen, profound, but the immediate impact must be set in the context of the continuity of traditional rituals in the familiar setting of the parish church. Whatever Henry's intentions at the end of his reign, the ancient drama of the mass continued unaltered throughout it, and the priests reinforced their Latin words by continuing to wear the traditional vestments. This well-known scene in church was dramatically altered during the next reign. On Henry's death in 1547 the three leading figures in Church and State, the young King, Protector Somerset and Archbishop Cranmer were all convinced Protestants. Their Protestantism had developed in the later years of Henry's reign, and this suggests that the principal significance of the Protestant ideas which were active from the 1520s onwards was that they made a vitally important impact among the upper and educated classes. That impact never wholly lost its momentum during the official reaction of the 1540s and after 1547 the Protestants came into their own.

That, however, is another story and the basic continuity in parish life throughout Henry VIII's reign must have done much to limit the extent of opposition to the breach with Rome and the theological changes which followed it. Opposition did, however, occur and not merely from the few remarkable men whose actions have always been noted. It also came from common people in the localities, whose attitudes have been revealed by Professor Elton (92). The great bulk of the 'political nation' – the upper ranks of the clergy and the aristocracy and gentry – accepted the royal supremacy without difficulty. The bishops, most of them administrators whose first loyalty was to the King rather than to Rome, fell into line with the single exception of John Fisher of Rochester, the most distinguished theologian on the bench. He was from the start among the most fervent of Catherine's supporters and his attitude led him to the block in 1535. That year also saw the execution of the most famous lay victim of the schism, Sir Thomas More. He defended himself with consummate skill at his trial for treason, but when he was finally condemned he showed that he understood with stark clarity the basic issue at stake. No English authority, whether Crown or Paliament, he proclaimed, could alter the basic constitution of the Church of Christ, which was rightfully headed by the Pope. It was a plea for the unity of Christendom against developing English nationalism, but one that was bound to fail in the circumstances in which it was made. That plea was echoed, in theory, in the demands of the leaders of the Pilgrimage of Grace, the great rebellion which threw the whole of northern England into turmoil in 1536. Many historians, however, play down the significance of religious motives in the Pilgrimage, and even those who do not, lay stress on the rebels' calls for the restoration of monasteries and the dismissal of heretical bishops rather than for the revival of the papal supremacy. If the pilgrims' commitment to Roman authority was doubtful, it was a different matter with those members of the religious orders who opposed Henry's proceedings. The secular clergy generally followed the lead of their bishops in accepting the royal supremacy, but a small but notable minority of religious – Carthusians, Brigettines and Franciscan Observants – took a very different line. They came from the most austere and least corrupt of all the English religious orders of the time and the Carthusians especially received treatment which is quite unjustifiable on any grounds. Professor Knowles has chronicled (172, Ch. 19) the dreadful cruelties to which members of their London House were subjected in attempts to break their spirit; some were chained hand and foot to posts and allowed to starve to death. The fact that the treatment of the monks was legal under the Treason Act of 1534 does nothing to alter the appalling nature of the case.

That Treason Act was the principal weapon in Cromwell's armoury in his investigation of the general opposition to the Reformation which was evident in the localities in the 1530s. Elton has shown that there was extensive grumbling throughout the country about the royal supremacy, about attacks on traditional practices and about the activities of reforming bishops like Latimer. He argues that the malcontents posed a real threat to the State. Other historians are less sure of this[2], but whatever the truth of the matter Cromwell was surely right to take all reasonable precautions. Without a standing army or a paid bureaucracy in the localities he could not afford to take chances. He saw to it that local officials, especially the justices of the peace, as well as private informers kept him up to date with the activities of dissidents in their areas, he considered hundreds of cases which were brought to his attention with great care, dismissed those that seemed frivolous and had the rest tried by the normal processes of the law. Only about sixty-five people were executed as a result of the general grumblings which Cromwell investigated. This is a small number of victims for a momentous revolution like the Reformation of the 1530s. It may be, however, that the extent of the grumbling influenced Henry himself in his decision to call at least an *official* halt to theological innovation at the end of the 1530s. That decision, epitomized as we have seen by the Six Articles Act of 1539, was a setback to Cromwell's own plans. The popular resentment of 'innovations' which the unrest of the 1530s reveals may indicate, however, that the King's decision was a sensible one.

---

1. B. Bradshaw, *The Dissolution of the Religious Orders in Ireland under Henry VIII* (Cambridge, 1974).
2. e.g. P. Williams, *EHR*, **88** (1973), 594–7.

CHAPTER 3

Cromwell and the government of the realm: administrative change in England, Wales and Ireland

The decade of the breach with Rome saw important changes in the administrative structure of the State. The historian of these governmental reforms, Professor Elton, believes that, taken together, they represented a 'revolution' in administration.[1] Other experts disagree. We will examine this issue in Chapter 11. Here we are concerned with the changes themselves. Cromwell, who initiated the reforms, held offices both in the royal household and in the central government machine. He was, for example, appointed to the household offices of Master of the King's jewels and Principal Secretary in 1532 and 1534 respectively and obtained posts in the official bureaucracy as Chancellor of the Exchequer in 1533 and Lord Privy Seal in 1536. It was not, however, any specific job but rather the fact that he was the King's principal adviser for most of the 1530s which gave him the authority to impose his will on the administration. Henry himself was notoriously uninterested in administrative details, and there is no doubt that the restructured government which emerged by 1540 bore overwhelmingly the imprint of Cromwell's personality. The demands of the situations which he faced together with his own genius determined the nature of the reforms.

Cromwell had a number of basic objectives. He wanted to ensure that the royal writ ran fully and uniformly throughout the realm in both secular and religious administration; he wished to strengthen the governmental machinery both at the centre and in the regions in order to make the King's authority more effective; and he was determined to keep the whole process under his personal direction. The first of these aims involved the suppression of privileges in England which hampered or prevented the exercise of full royal authority and also efforts to bring Wales, Calais and at least part of Ireland under firm control within a uniform administrative system. It also involved the translation of the theoretical royal supremacy which has been established over the Church into practical reality through the subordination of episcopal administration to the new office of vicegerent, a post he held himself.

In 1536 an Act of Parliament abolished all significant remaining liberties and franchises [N] throughout the realm. These privileged areas, such as Cheshire and Ely, had come into existence during the Middle Ages and though by the 1530s they were of diminishing significance they still led, as the statute put it, to the 'diminution and detriment of the royal estate' and to 'great delay of justice'. The 1536 Act provided that from then onwards only the Crown could appoint judges and justices of the peace in any part of the realm, that all writs initiating judicial process were to run in the King's name and that only the King could pardon serious crimes. The ancient ecclesiastical liberty of Durham alone retained some independent identity and even there the bishop and his chancellor were now required to exercise authority through a Royal Commission as justices of the peace (27 Henry VIII, c. 24). Four years later another Act (32 Henry VIII, c. 12) ended the most important abuses of the privilege of sanctuary [N] which, over the centuries, had developed into an elaborate system in which hardened criminals were able to shelter, sometimes virtually indefinitely, in sanctuaries which often stood in the middle of important towns, most notably London. The clergy were unable or unwilling to deal with the scandals of the system and in 1540 the most notorious sanctuaries were swept away and the privilege was abolished altogether for individuals found guilty of the most serious crimes, such as murder, arson, rape and burglary. The right of sanctuary was not finally terminated until the reign of James I, but the 1540 Act ended its existence as a serious challenge to the authority of the Crown. There is no doubt, in fact, that through his Acts against liberties and sanctuaries Cromwell rendered royal judicial and administrative authority predominant and virtually uniform throughout the entire realm; a great achievement.

He also turned his attention to the outlying parts of the King's dominions – Wales, Calais and Ireland. In the early 1530s Wales and the Marches were in considerable disorder, largely due to weak guidance from the Council in the Marches. Murder, theft and arson were commonplace throughout the area. In 1534 Cromwell appointed his friend Rowland Lee, bishop of Coventry and Lichfield, as President of the Council. Lee was a man totally devoid of all the human graces which could reasonably be expected in a Christian bishop, but his harsh rule went far to restoring law and order, and in 1536 Cromwell turned to his long-term solution to the problem, the incorporation of Wales into the English administrative system. Parliamentary Acts (27 Henry VIII, cc. 5, 26, See (25; 102)) of that year abolished the distinction between Wales and the Marches, extended parliamentary representation to Wales for the first time, gave Welshmen the benefits of the English common law at the expense of local custom and organized the whole territory into shires with justices of the peace on the English model [E.1(3a)]. It took some time to work the new system out on the ground, but the process was completed three years after Cromwell's death, when an Act of 1543 (34, 35 Henry VIII, c. 26) defined the structure of the new Wales in considerable detail [E.1(3b)]. The union with England seems to have been generally welcomed in Wales and its peaceful assimilation into the mainstream of English administrative and judicial life was one of Cromwell's most notable achievements [O.2]. Two more major landmarks, those of 1603 and 1707, would have to be passed before the 'United Kingdom of Great Britian' finally emerged as a dynastic, administrative and parliamentary unit; but the Act of 1536 represents a big step along that road.

Calais, England's last Continental possession, was also included in Cromwell's 'unitary realm' in 1536, when it was given two parliamentary burgesses. This provision was only part of a massive statute (27 Henry VIII, c. 63) which reorganized the whole administration of the territory, which had been suffering under the incompetent government of the King's deputy, Lord Lisle. Even Cromwell, however, could not make Calais a financial asset and the same applied to England's other overseas possession, Ireland [O.1]. Cromwell's Irish policy (89) was marked by characteristic energy and determination. He spent a great deal of time on the island's problems, he breathed new life into the Irish Parliament and he set the basic terms on which English involvement in Ireland was to be based for centuries ahead; a permanent military garrison in the Pale and the reservation of the office of Lord Deputy for Englishmen. He saw that it would be impossible, at least in the short run, to impose effective royal authority throughout the islands and made no attempt to assert English sovereignty in Gaelic Ireland. On the other hand he tried to enforce English rule effectively in the Pale and the earldoms, though even there.his control was much less effective than he wished. His attitude to those parts of Ireland where he did try to impose English authority was marked by a determination to regard them not as a separate Crown realm but rather as a local unit, like Wales and Calais, under the all-embracing authority of a Crown which directed a unitary realm from a single centre. His Irish policy·in its constitutional aspects should, therefore, as Dr Bradshaw argues, be regarded as one facet of his general aim of asserting the imperial authority of the English Crown on a uniform basis throughout all its territories.

Cromwell wanted to see that royal authority ran effectively throughout the realm in ecclesiastical as well as in secular administration. This involved the translation of the royal supremacy into practical reality in England, an aim which was achieved by 1540 (for what follows see (174). There may, as we have seen, have been differences of opinion between Cromwell and the King about the nature of Parliament's involvement in the royal supremacy, but the two men were almost certainly of one mind when it came to subjecting the episcopate to complete control by the Crown. The supremacy which had been proclaimed in 1534 could have been exercised in either of two ways. It could have been regarded as giving the King merely nominal powers which would be employed in practice by the archbishops of Canterbury and York, or else it could be seen as giving him real powers which placed all episcopal authority in the Church at his mercy. The praemunire proceedings and the pardon of the clergy in 1530–31 suggested to some bishops that the latter interpretation might be the one which the King favoured, and from 1535 onwards Cromwell exercised his powers as vicegerent in a way which made their fears a reality. Between 1535 and 1537 he used the vicegerency to first suspend and then restore the powers of bishops in ways which made plain that all episcopal authority, even the power to ordain, depended ultimately on the King's will. As Dr Bowker has pointed out this demonstration of royal authority rendered the office of vicegerent superfluous. Cromwell had no successor in the post after 1540. He had used it to make the supremacy an administrative reality.

Cromwell's second main objective in administration was closely related to his first; he was determined to improve the government machinery both in the capital and in the outlying parts of England in order to render still more effective the royal authority which he was strengthening by his attacks on liberties and sanctuaries. This second facet of his policy involved the creation of new and the reorganization of old authorities of central and regional government. Part of his work in this sphere was a direct result of the Reformation. The vast new revenues and lands which came to the Crown following the rejection of the Papacy and the dissolution of the monasteries had to be administered and judicial problems arising from that administration had to be dealt with. The most impressive new institution created was the Court of Augmentations set up by Cromwell in 1536 to look after the former monastic estates. It closely followed the organization of a long-established royal honour, the duchy of Lancaster, with a central staff and also receivers in the localities, each of whom collected the revenues of all augmentations lands in a specified geographical area. Many of these newly acquired lands were soon sold on terms which greatly increased the scope of the King's position as feudal overlord of England, a role which brought him a good deal of revenue. The new owners were granted the lands as tenants-in-chief of the King, holding them by the tenure of knight service [N]. In the Middle Ages this had carried the duty of following the King to war, but by the sixteenth century it meant the payment of certain financial dues to the Crown on the death of a tenant. Most important of all, when the heir was a minor his person and lands were taken into royal custody and the resulting wardships [N] brought the Crown substantial profits. In the early years of Henry VIII's reign the feudal revenues were administered on a fairly informal basis, but the increased scale of the business during the 1530s made this situation increasingly unsatisfactory and was one of the principal reasons for the erection, under Cromwell's inspiration, of a formal Court of Wards in 1540 (87; 101). Two other revenue courts were created soon after Cromwell's fall. The Court of First Fruits and Tenths [N], set up in 1540, formalized the administration of the revenues which the Crown had been drawing from the secular clergy since 1535, while a Court of General Surveyors was established in 1542 to administer the older Crown lands, basically those collected by Henry VIII and Wolsey.

Other Cromwellian reforms involved the drastic modification of existing institutions with the objective of producing more effective government. The most important of these concerned the King's Council. During the early years of the reign this was a very large body, reaching at least seventy in number. In 1536 Cromwell reduced it to a 'Privy' Council of about twenty men, nearly all of whom were important administrators. The old Council had been drawn from a very wide spectrum of the notables of the realm — members of the nobility, judges, local worthies and lesser administrators as well as great officers of State. The new Privy Council, on the other hand, resembled both in size and composition the body which was to dominate the administration of Elizabethan England. Its individual members, because they were relatively few in number, rapidly acquired great prestige and authority and despite the vicissitudes – usually exaggerated – which the Council underwent during the reigns of Edward VI and Mary it is difficult to disagree with Professor Elton's conclusion that 'nothing in Cromwell's reforms did more to give drive and reasonable continuity to royal government in Tudor England' (25, *218*).

Cromwell also transformed the office of Principal Secretary, which was a relatively minor post when he acquired it in 1534. As his voluminous papers reveal he turned it into the chief executive instrument of the Crown's domestic and foreign policy, with an authority which ranged over a considerable part of the business of the realm. He was able, of course, to achieve this status for the secretaryship because of his personal pre-eminence in the King's counsels, and none of his immediate successors in the office approached his importance. He had, however, revealed its potential, and the great Elizabethan Secretaries of State, like the two Cecils and Walsingham, conducted business of a range and importance similar to that which Cromwell dealt with in the 1530s.

The creation of a powerful Privy Council and the transformation of the office of Secretary greatly increased the potential power of the central administration, but Cromwell recognized that the more distant parts of the realm required special attention. Regional Councils for the North and the Marches of Wales had existed since Yorkist times but during the 1530s both were strengthened. The Council in the Marches, under the harsh presidency of Rowland Lee began to exert effective authority in Wales from 1534 onwards (102), and the Council of the North was reorganized in 1537, following the upheavals of the Pilgrimage of Grace during the previous year.[2] Its history as a permanent institution really begins with this reform and though it did not at once reduce the North to order it did give the central administration, now centred on the new Privy Council, a more effective voice in these distant regions than it had hitherto exercised. A Council of the West was briefly established in 1539, following the execution for treason in 1538 of Henry Courtenay, marquess of Exeter.[3] It did not survive Cromwell's fall in 1540 and its most important consequence was the establishment of the personal power of its first president, John Russell, later earl of Bedford, who came to replace Courtenay as the dominant influence in the west of England. Here is one instance where Cromwell's attempt at institutional reform failed dramatically.

A third notable characteristic of Cromwell's administrative work was his determination to keep the whole process of change and reform under his personal control. He himself, as we have seen, acquired offices in both the royal household and the official bureaucracy; any post which could be made to serve his purposes was very acceptable. It is notable, for example, that in the early 1530s he used the hitherto insignificant household office of Master of the King's Jewels to create for himself an important role in financial affairs. In the administration of first fruits and tenths he used his servant John Gostwick, who was completely under his domination. As a result the control of this part of the royal revenue remained highly personal as long as Cromwell lived; it was only 'bureaucratized' by the creation of the Court of First Fruits and Tenths in the months following his death. He extended his informal methods to the supervision of the Irish administration and by 1540, as Dr Bradshaw tell us, 'a network of personal servants' provided him with 'an alternative route to the localities in Ireland other than through Dublin' (89, *145*). Thus, Cromwell often worked in highly informal ways through highly 'unbureaucratic' channels.

Whatever Cromwell's methods there can be no doubt about his considerable success in strengthening the administrative machine and extending the effectiveness of royal authority throughout the realm. The suppression of liberties and sanctuaries, the incorporation of Wales, the creation of the Privy Council, the revelation of the potentialities of the office of Secretary, and the firm subordination of the episcopate to royal administrative authority were all outstanding successes. The strengthening of the Councils of the North and in the Marches of

Wales were, it is true, more limited achievements, and although Cromwell's Irish policy has been rightly seen as inaugurating a new if unhappy era in the history of that island, important aspects of it were reversed soon after his death. The overall effectiveness of his regime is perhaps best epitomized by his efficient enforcement of the break with Rome during the 1530s, and this despite his continued dependence on the traditional authorities of local government (92). It can be argued, however, that this reliance points to the major long-term weakness of the Cromwellian administrative reforms. He did not significantly extend the royal bureaucracy into the localities and this meant that unpaid justices of the peace continued to exercise an authority which was essentially a voluntary part-nership with the Crown. Cromwell obtained the co-operation of the vast majority of these local governors, but in the last resort he had no coercive power over them as a body. Under less able men this situation was to reveal serious practical weaknesses in royal authority and ultimately, under Charles I, it was to play a very significant part in bringing the monarchy to its knees. It is fair to note this gap in Cromwell's work, but equally it would be unfair to blame him for it. A man who did so much to strengthen the government of the realm can hardly be faulted for failing to do even more in his eight years of power, especially as the creation of a paid local bureaucracy would have been an enormous task; it was certainly one which none of his successors seriously contemplated.

Some of the administrative machinery created by Cromwell deteriorated in the years after his fall. The secretaryship, for example, declined in authority after 1540 and the report of a notable Royal Commission in 1552 painted an unhappy picture of the state of the financial courts by that year. Having said that, there is little doubt that Cromwell built well. Historians while still accepting the reality now play down the extent of the administrative decline during the 1540s and 1550s. The fact that the State emerged so little scathed from the political, religious, social and economic upheavals of these middle decades of the century is surely due largely to the effectiveness of Cromwell's administrative reforms, above all perhaps to his creation of a strong Privy Council.

---

1. For a detailed account see G. R. Elton, *The Tudor Revolution in Government* (Cambridge, 1953). Elton's most recent discussion is in his *Reform and Reformation: England 1509–1558* (1977), pp. 211 ff.
2. F. W. Brooks, *The Council of the North* (Hist. Assoc., 1953).
3. J. Youings, 'The Council of the West', *TRHS*, 5th ser. **10** (1960), 41 ff.

CHAPTER 4

Social reform in the reign of Henry VIII: Cromwell and the English 'commonwealth'

Cromwell, it is now argued, was not merely a great administrator and policeman, he was also a notable religious and social reformer, a man whose aims extended to a wide vision of a truly reformed Church and State. Governmental efficiency for him was not merely an end in itself, but also a means of realizing this noble aim. We have already discussed his work in the field of religion. Here we are concerned with his social reforms. These have been discussed by Professor Elton in terms of the concept of the 'commonwealth', a word much used in sixteenth century England. It could mean simply the State, but it was also used to denote the well-being of all members of the community. 'Commonwealth' policies basically meant advancing the interests of society by maximizing wealth while at the same time protecting the consumer and the less fortunate sections of the population.

Elton argues that during the 1530s Cromwell produced and put through Parliament a major programme of social and economic reforms which were not only more important than anything which had preceded them, but also of much greater significance than the traditionally better-known commonwealth measures of Edward VI's reign (25; 207). It will not do, however, to exaggerate the originality of Cromwell's work in this field. Professor Scarisbrick has recently given us a convincing picture of Wolsey as a notable reformer, a man who 'transformed the anti-enclosure movement' by efficient investigative methods followed by the prosecution of numerous offenders.[1] Cromwell, then, was following in a tradition which was already active in the Tudor period. He brought to it that emphasis on the use of statutes as well as the detailed planning which was typical of so much of his work (25; 207). He received a flood of advice about reform and his administration included a staff which, in Elton's words, 'worked on the ideas of theorists and reformers to produce legislation for submission to Parliament' (25, *164*). Cromwell himself took an important part in this preparation of Bills and his chief assistants in the task were a team of common lawyers who helped to put the ideas of their master and other intellectuals into suitable form. Cromwell, with his belief in the supremacy of statute, saw Parliament as the instrument which would not merely rid England of the Papacy but would also increases the wealth and ameliorate the social conditions of the new nation state which was created during the 1530s.

His social programme can be discussed in four main areas: he tried to arrest rural depopulation; to promote trade and manufacture; to control the cost of living; and to alleviate social distress. The numerous complaints of the time about rural depopulation turned upon the profitability of sheep-farming; it required a much smaller labour force than arable husbandry and conversions by landlords from arable to pastoral farming, often accompanied by the enclosure [N] of the land involved, led to unemployment for those members of rural society who were driven from the land and often reduced to vagrancy. Such changes in farming practice by reducing the amount of arable land also forced up food prices at a time of rising population. Existing statutes against enclosures and Wolsey's heroic efforts in the earlier years of the century had failed to solve the problem. In 1534 Cromwell introduced drastic legislation (207) to counter, as the bill put it, the greed of men, 'to whom God of his goodness hath disposed great plenty and abundance of substance'. Such men, it was alleged, had been selfishly trying to increase their wealth by acquiring more land and converting it to pasture. The bill provided that no individual should henceforth own more than 2,000 sheep. It also strictly limited the amount of leasehold land a man might possess. This provision was very important for one of the most significant – some historians would say *the* most significant – of the agrarian problems of the early sixteenth century was the engrossing [N] of leaseholds and their conversion to pasture by substantial sheep-owners. The bill passed the Commons but ran into serious trouble in the Lords where even the King's personal intervention could not save the clause about leaseholds. Vested interests in the Upper House had inflicted a severe defeat upon Cromwell and through he counter-attacked with some success in the Commons the final Act (25 Henry VIII, c. 13) was much less severe than he had wished. Individuals were to be allowed to own up to 2,400 sheep and, above all, the previous limits on the acquisition of leaseholds, though they now reappeared, were drastically modified. The Act, despite these changes, did, if it was enforced, go some way to making sheep-farming less profitable and less easy. The extent of enforcement is, of course, the crux of the matter, and this remains unknown as does the effectiveness with which Cromwell's Enclosure Act of 1536 (27 Henry VIII, c. 22) was applied in practice. This was a limited measure which sought to make the extensive existing legislation on enclosures more workable. It maintained that that legislation had failed because it had left the right of enforcement to the lords of the lands involved. They had often neglected their duty and the King was now empowered to intervene and see that justice was done when immediate lords failed to act.

The problems of agriculture were the fundamental ones in the English economy, but Cromwell also sought to promote the manufacture of textiles and the export of cloth, by far the most important branches of the country's industry and overseas trade. Most of the English cloth which was exported at the time was 'undressed' (i.e. unfinished) and the Continental manufacturers who undertook its final preparation made very large profits out of the finishing processes. Men in Cromwell's circle, notably that enthusiastic protagonist of commonwealth reform Clement Armstrong, wanted to stop the export of all unfinished cloth, urging that the finishing process, if undertaken at home, would provide both great additional profits and also substantial extra employment for Englishmen at the expense of foreigners. Their arguments seemed to make good economic sense but ignored the fact that the Netherlands purchasers totally refused to buy finished English cloth at a realistic price. In this situation Cromwell, wiser than James I was to be in 1614, refused to risk a huge upheaval in the English trading system by considering a general prohibition on the export of undressed cloth. He limited himself to promoting various Acts to improve the quality of English cloth and by endeavouring to see that both English and foreign merchants got a fair share of the trade. This policy of limited intervention seems to have worked. His years in office saw a considerable expansion of cloth exports which rose by perhaps 25 per cent in the decade after 1533.

The problems of trade, industry and above all agriculture were intimately bound up with prices, and Cromwell was very concerned about the increase in the cost of living which was evident by the time of his ministry. The previous decade had seen a rapid inflation which especially affected foodstuffs and he hoped to protect the consumer by statutory limitations on the prices which could be charged. During the 1530s a series of Acts imposed restrictions on a wide range of items, including wine, dairy products, poultry and meat. The attempt to fix meat prices has been studied in detail (93). It is an informative story. During the Middle Ages meat and other prices were often regulated by local authorities. In 1529 Wolsey used the Council to fix the price of beef, veal and mutton. Parliament followed the terms of this Council order closely during Cromwell's ministry, when an Act of 1533 set prices for these three meats (24 Henry VIII, c. 3). A Council committee and local officials were given the authority to lower but not to raise the prices fixed in the Act. The London butchers soon maintained that they were in danger of ruin; the prices which they were charged by the graziers were so high, they said, that they could not sell at the statutory price. This complaint led to a proclamation in the summer of 1533 ordering the graziers to sell at a reasonable price and then to another in 1534 denouncing the butchers for still not obeying the statute. Their continued complaints did lead, however, to an Act (25 Henry VIII, c. 1) in the same year which empowered the King to suspend the 1533 statute by proclamation and set more realistic prices if the economic situation made such a change necessary. Renewed representations from the butchers duly led to the envisaged suspension and for the rest of the decade they were allowed to sell at higher prices than the maximum of 1533.

Just as ambitious as Cromwell's efforts at statutory price control was his attempt to alleviate social distress and reduce unemployment and vagabondage through his proposed law of 1536 (25; 207; 208). In the early 1530s poor relief was governed by a statute of 1531 which distinguished between the 'aged and impotent' poor and 'persons being whole and mighty in body and able to labour, having no land, master, nor using any lawful merchandise'. The former might be licensed to beg by justices of the peace, whereas the latter were to be punished by severe whippings (22 Henry VIII, c. 12). The Act had obvious defects; the collection of alms for the deserving poor was totally unorganized and there was no provision for finding work for the able-bodied. These failings were offensive to commonwealth thinkers who rejected the idea of begging and recognized the need to provide work for those fit to undertake it. Deliberations among Cromwell's staff, taking account of commonwealth principles, led to the production of a remarkable draft bill which he accepted and laid before Parliament in 1536. He persuaded the King to recommend it to the Commons, but the extent of opposition rapidly made it clear that it would not pass in its original form. When this became apparent he withdrew the bill and substituted a very much more limited alternative, which he had probably prepared in advance. This duly passed (27 Henry VIII, c. 25). The provisions for the impotent poor were relatively modest in the original bill. They were forbidden to beg and were to be relieved by alms which were to be collected by each parish on a voluntary basis, though it was hoped that constant exhortations from the pulpit would stimulate the generosity of the more prosperous towards their indigent neighbours. The revolutionary proposals were those which affected the able-bodied poor. They were to be employed on a programme of public works such as road-making and bridge-building. They were to receive wages and even medical care and the whole scheme was to be financed by an income tax and administered by a Council to Avoid Vagabonds which was to have the power to make detailed regulations. Any able-bodied man who refused work three times was to be executed. This last provision was doubtless an attempt to separate the genuinely unemployed from those incorrigible 'rogues and vagabonds' whom all Tudor governments feared and punished severely and, as such, it anticipated Elizabethan legislation on the subject.

The Commons rejection of this original bill is hardly surprising in view of its very ambitious contents. The proposed income tax was probably especially unwelcome to them and the final Act scrapped the whole scheme for a public works programme and its attendant administrative and financial provisions. It continued to forbid begging, to give the parish a dominant role in the provision of relief and to provide for the collection of voluntary alms, but these were now to be used to set the able-bodied to work as well as for the relief of the impotent.

How then should we judge Cromwell as a social reformer?[2] His attacks on depopulation were at best a modest success and certainly a pale reflection of what he sought to achieve. His ministry did see a substantial growth of English cloth exports, but this was based on a relatively non-interventionist policy which was a clear rejection of the ideals of commonwealth thinkers like Armstrong with their proposals for the creation of new wealth and employment at home through strict limitations on the export of unfinished cloth. His attempts at price control never really worked and were formally abandoned two years after his death, in 1542, when all the recent legislation on the subject was repealed. The modest Act for poor relief which he obtained in 1536 was a far cry from the grandiose proposals of his original Bill. Cromwell's ambitions in the field of social and economic reform far outstripped, therefore, the practical results which he obtained. His greatest success in economic affairs seems to have been achieved in the field of foreign trade where he rejected commonwealth ideas; his attempts at price control had little chance of success, given both the economic conditions in which he worked and the relatively primitive machinery of enforcement at his disposal; and the ambitious measures to arrest depopulation and help the poor which he laid before Parliament with the King's support were given short shrift by the vested interests of Lords and Commons. Cromwell's work as a social reformer should be seen as part of a long tradition among Tudor statesmen extending back to Wolsey and forward through Somerset to the Cecils. It would therefore be wrong to overemphasize his originality in this field, and although he had some elaborate plans and, as always, worked hard to put his ideas into practice he had limited success. Cromwell the social reformer is far less impressive than Cromwell the administrator or Cromwell the policeman.

---

1. J. J. Scarisbrick, 'Cardinal Wolsey and the common weal', E. W. Ives, R. J. Knecht and J. J. Scarisbrick (eds) *Wealth and Power in Tudor England* (1978), pp. 45 ff.
2. For a line of argument broadly similar to what follows see B. Bradshaw, 'The Tudor commonwealth: reform and revision', *HJ*, **22** (1979), 455 ff.

CHAPTER 5

England, Scotland and the Continent: foreign policy during the Henrician Reformation, 1525–1540

Most of Cromwell's formidable energies during the 1530s were channelled into domestic affairs but he could not escape involvement in foreign policy, a field in which Henry himself took a continuous and often detailed interest. Two basic issues determined English foreign policy between 1525 and 1540. The first of these was the Habsburg–Valois rivalry which was a continuation of the situation which had existed in the years before 1525. That rivalry was personified by Charles V, King of Spain (as Charles I) from 1516 and Holy Roman Emperor from 1519 – ruler of Spain, the Netherlands, much of Italy and parts of Germany – and Francis I, King of France from 1514. The storm centre of their conflict was Italy, but their struggles, which dominated international relations in western Europe for most of the early sixteenth century, had repercussions throughout the Continent [0.4]. English power was a significant, though limited factor in this gigantic struggle. Henry VIII had neither the men nor the money to compete on equal terms with either of his great Continental neighbours – England was a second-class power in terms of resources – but he could play an important role by threatening to put his support behind either Charles or Francis. Each, therefore, wanted English support or at the very least benevolent neutrality in their contest. For England the matter turned on a number of points. There was her traditional enmity with France, her great rival during the Middle Ages (Henry still officially claimed the French throne); there was her accompanying dislike of her northern neighbour and France's ally, Scotland; there was the overwhelming importance of her overseas trading links with the Netherlands, now of course part of the Emperor's dominions. All these facts suggested alliance with the Habsburgs and Henry and Wolsey generally followed this line in the years before 1525. The one obvious objection to a Habsburg alliance was that Charles's power was arguably stronger than that of France, and in such a situation it would be better for England to hold the ring in the balance of power by alliance with the weaker side. This argument was a fair one in itself, but it understandably carried less weight in English eyes than more traditional assumptions about ancient enmities and dynastic and economic advantages.

For much of the period between 1525 and 1540, however, the 'natural' Habsburg–Tudor alliance was rendered difficult or even impossible by the Reformation, the second of the basic issues which affected English foreign policy. The break with Rome had its immediate origins in the divorce of Catherine of Aragon, and the divorcee was Charles's aunt. This fact and Charles's stern disapproval of Henry's schismatical proceedings between 1533 and 1536 meant that the traditional Anglo-Habsburg axis was not a practical possibility: from 1525 to 1536 England's only possible ally between the two great Catholic powers was France,

47

a fact which made relations with Scotland easier. The situation changed somewhat between 1536 and 1538 with the renewal of war between Francis and Charles; an Imperial alliance could again be contemplated, especially as the outbreak of hostilities coincided with the death of Catherine of Aragon. The Franco-Imperial truce of 1538 led, however, to the possibility of a scenario which Henry himself had dreaded but never seriously envisaged and which Cromwell had both dreaded and envisaged; an attack by the two great Catholic powers with help in the North from Scotland upon Henry VIII and his apostate subjects.[1]

Between 1522 and 1525 Henry and Charles were allied in an ambitious attempt to conquer and partition France. By the latter date it was plain that their grandiose dreams were impossible. Both allies lacked the money to continue the war and Charles compounded Henry's misery by repudiating his engagement to the nine-year-old Princess Mary. This had been agreed in 1521 as one of the foundation-stones of the Anglo-Imperial alliance. Henry saw it as the best means of securing a succession about which he was already very worried. The collapse of his French ambitions and the simultaneous rejection of Mary by his ally had a traumatic effect on him. According to Professor Wernham it marked 'the great turning-point' in his reign (30, *111*) and there can be little doubt that this judgement is true in the field of foreign policy. It killed the Imperial alliance stone dead for over a decade and rapidly led to peace and then to an offensive alliance with France. This 'diplomatic revolution' began with a formal end to Anglo-French hostilities in August 1525, and in April 1527 Henry and Wolsey signed a treaty with Francis which committed the allies to war against the Emperor and stipulated that Francis himself or his second son Henry was to marry the Princess Mary. Francis was already trying to break Charles's dominant military power in Italy, and Henry, by then resolved on his divorce, had every practical reason for helping to pry the Pope free from Habsburg control. These hopes were dashed by the sack of Rome by the Emperor's mutinous troops during the following month. Charles had not intended this sacrilegious act but he did not hesitate to exploit to the full the control over Clement VII which it gave him. Wolsey, still in day-to-day control of English policy, was now in a desperate situation. The new French alliance was much disliked in England and he had no money to finance a viable military campaign against the Emperor. On the other hand, as he well knew, failure to gratify the King's wishes for his divorce might lead to measures against the Church in England which he himself could not even contemplate. For the next two years he struggled desperately to secure his master's objectives by diplomatic ends, but his only real hope lay in French military successes in Italy. These came in 1528 and his hopes rose high. They were totally dashed during the following year, however, with the decisive Imperial victory over the French at Landriano. This confirmed Charles's domination of Italy and control of the Papacy and led to Clement's vow to 'live and die' an Imperialist. It was the end of the road for Wolsey. His dismissal in October 1529 marked the end of the phase in which Henry sought to achieve his divorce chiefly by diplomacy.

From 1529 onwards he tried to coerce Clement primarily by allowing or initiating attacks on the rights of the Church in England. Diplomatic moves to advance the divorce proceedings did, of course, continue, but as foreign manoeuvres were no longer the chief means of achieving Henry's 'great matter' and as that continued to be his dominating concern in the years after just as in the years before 1529, foreign policy as a whole came to occupy a less important place in the minds of the King and his advisers. Its chief task was 'to hold the ring and to prevent any interference by foreign powers with the working out of those domestic purposes' (30, *122*). In practice this meant preventing interference from Charles V, a task which was not unduly difficult during these years in view of the number and complexity of the problems which he faced elsewhere. His conflicts with the Turks, the German Protestants and, above all, with France, meant that the situation in England was usually well down his list of priorities. Henry and his advisers worked hard to keep alive French jealousy of the Emperor and, as an additional safeguard, England entered into negotiations for a possible religious and military alliance with some of the German Protestant states. This was the kind of move which Cromwell greatly favoured after his accession to power and between 1532 and 1535 there were discussions with Hamburg, Lübeck and Saxony. Henry himself, however, always disliked the religious implications of alliances with Lutheran states and felt that they were basically unnecessary in view of what he regarded as the irredeemable enmity between Francis and Charles. In this situation none of the negotiations came to fruition and the events of 1535–36 seemed to justify Henry's confidence.

In 1535 the childless duke of Milan, Francesco Sforza, died, and the succession was hotly disputed between Francis and Charles. By the spring of 1536 they were at war in Italy and from then until 1538 England seemed safe from any possible attack. Other events of 1536 made a *rapprochement* between England and the Emperor seem possible. In January of that year Catherine of Aragon died, in May Anne Boleyn was executed, and Henry's subsequent marriage to Jane Seymour not only produced his longed-for male heir with the birth of Prince Edward in October 1537, but also gave him a wife whose legitimacy both Catholics and Protestants could unreservedly accept. In the summer of 1537 Henry welcomed an Imperial ambassador to London and envisaged the golden prospect of being able in future to play Charles off against Francis as well as Francis off against Charles. He had, however, to be careful. In 1537 his nephew, James V of Scotland, was moving closer and closer to France and Henry could not afford to risk too great offence to Francis; that would open up the possibility of an eventual Franco-Scottish assault on England. Such a prospect was remote while the war between Francis and Charles continued, but in June 1538, by papal mediation, they agreed a truce at Nice. This led to persistent rumours of a league between Charles, Francis and James to invade England and reintroduce Catholicism. It is not clear how acute the danger was, but Henry and Cromwell hastened to take precautionary measures both at home and abroad.

Since the beginning of his reign Henry had been building up his navy. He inherited only seven ships from his father, but by the late 1530s he had increased their number to about forty. Improvements in design had been introduced and Henry could always supplement his own ships by requisitioning and arming merchantmen during times of crisis. In 1539, therefore, he was able to assemble a formidable fleet which acted as the country's first line of defence against a possible invasion. The second line was a string of fortresses which were built or rebuilt along the coast of England from Kent to Cornwall from 1538 onwards. Any invader who penetrated these defences would have to face levies of foot soldiers who were mustered in the southern shires in the spring of 1539. These members of the national militia, which was also called out in the North to guard against a possible Scottish assault, may not always have had high military skills, but as a *third* line of defence in the South they were surely a powerful deterrent to invasion. Cromwell and the King also sought allies abroad. Henry continued in his reluctance to commit himself to a league with Lutherans which might imply religious concessions, but in January 1539, when fears of invasion were high, he allowed Cromwell to approach Duke John of Cleves and to continue negotiations with his son William, who succeeded him the following month. The dukes of Cleves had rejected the Papacy but they were not Lutherans. Like Henry himself they had put together an amalgam of doctrine which gave them a religious position of their own. Henry must have had strong fellow feelings with them, but these can at best go only part of the way in explaining his agreement, in October 1539, to marry William's sister Anne. The most acute phase of the invasion scare was over by the spring of 1539, but Cromwell still feared a possible Franco-Imperial alliance and the King was sufficiently convinced by his arguments to marry Anne in January 1540. He disliked his new wife from the start and the Cleves marriage undoubtedly contributed to, though it did not cause, the fall of Cromwell in the summer of 1540, when the marriage was annulled by Cranmer on the ground of its non-consummation. By then it was not only a personal embarrassment to Henry, it had also outlived its political usefulness; Francis and Charles were quarrelling once more about the future of Milan. Henry's continuing scepticism throughout the 1530s about their ability to unite against him was proved right in the end. Despite the fears of 1538–39, he rather than Cromwell had had a more realistic view of the facts of the international situation.

In 1540, free of the dangers of Continental attack, Henry began to make overtures to James V of Scotland with the object of wooing the latter away from his French alliance and drawing him into the orbit of English influence. This move was a recognition of the potential threat which Scotland [O.7] had posed during the invasion crisis of the previous year, a threat which reflected the serious deterioration which had taken place in Anglo-Scottish relations during the 1530s. In the early years of that decade Henry's friendship with France had helped to maintain reasonable relations with Scotland. An Anglo-Scottish truce of 1533 was followed by a formal peace in 1534. These encouraging developments were not, however, maintained. James V, who was now emerging from a long minority and taking the government of Scotland into his own hands was greatly influenced by the powerful Scottish Church which, under its leader David Beaton, naturally opposed close relations with the schismatical Henry. The latter's suggestion that James might make himself rich at the expense of the Church did not help matters and in this situation James turned to France. In 1537 he married Francis's youngest daughter Madeleine and after her early death took another French bride, Mary of Guise, in 1538. The same year saw the beginnings of the threatened invasion of England which has already been discussed and which ultimately led to Henry's approaches to James in 1540.

Discussion of England's role in foreign affairs during the period 1525 to 1540 shows that it was essentially passive and defensive. The rejection of the Papacy during the 1530s was in one sense the result of a a massive failure in English foreign policy: the inability of Henry VIII and his advisers, despite the King's previous services to Rome, to persuade Clement VII to grant an annulment of Henry's marriage to Catherine of Aragon. That failure was almost inevitable given the dominant military position of Charles V in Italy, but the King's obsession with his 'great matter' meant that the foreign policy of the English government from the late 1520s until 1540 was dominated by his domestic needs. Foreign policy during the 1530s was, of course, strongly influenced by the ideas of Cromwell, and his differences with the King, especially about the need for a close alliance with Continental Protestant states, made the conduct of policy less coherent and assured than it might have been. Cromwell's fall in 1540 certainly marked the end of an era in foreign affairs as in so much else. The last years of Henry's rule, the 1540s saw the renewal of the active and aggressive policy, involving war on two fronts, which had characterized the early years of the reign. These wars had important effects on the country's economy.

---

1. The events of 1525–40 are discussed in R. B. Wernham, *Before the Armada* (1966), Chs. 9–11. See also P. S. Crowson, *Tudor Foreign Policy* (1973), Chs. 10–12.

CHAPTER 6

Mid-Tudor Crisis? The economy, war and society, 1540–1560

The middle decades of the sixteenth century have been seen as a period of virtually continuous crisis, affecting most important aspects of English life, social and economic, political and religious. It is certainly true that during the 1540s and 1550s a number of interlinked pressures put enormous strains upon the body politic. Political and religious developments will receive attention in later chapters, but the economic and social background, including the effects of war and disease, may usefully receive attention first. A number of phenomena stand out: a dramatic rise in prices, especially in the price of foodstuffs; a crisis in England's dominant export trade, that in cloth; a series of enormously expensive wars against France and Scotland between 1542 and 1550; runs of very bad harvests between 1549 and 1551 and in 1555 and 1556; and severe influenza epidemics over the years 1556–58, which helped to decimate the population during the later 1550s.

Prices were already rising well before the 1540s, but they sprinted ahead dramatically between 1540 and 1560 in by far the largest proportional increase of the century. During these twenty years the price of foodstuffs doubled while that of industrial goods rose by two-thirds (224). The reasons for these rises will concern us later when we discuss the 'price revolution' of the sixteenth and seventeenth centuries as a whole, but here it is important to note that contemporaries attributed a quite disproportionate blame to the effects of enclosure (the fencing of land) and engrossing (the buying up of farms by an individual, thus leaving previously occupied farmhouses vacant). Their violent denunciations of the iniquities of enclosers during these middle years of the century had significant effects on the policies of Somerset's government, which feared the effects of price rises on social stability. Their fears are understandable when we remember that even in times of relatively static prices a large proportion of the population of early modern England – perhaps as much as a half to two-thirds – lived below or just above the poverty line (the point where they had enough food, drink and clothing to keep them at subsistence level). In these circumstances the huge rise in food prices was especially alarming.

The gravity of the situation was compounded by the troubles of the cloth trade, as cloth was by far England's greatest industry and largest export. The reign of Edward VI saw the end of the boom in the cloth trade which had characterized the early Tudor period. Cloth exports had been depressed during the mid-fifteenth century, but recovery began in Edward IV's reign and during the last two decades of the fifteenth century they stood at around 60,000 cloths a year. A further expansion began about 1500 and by the 1530s exports exceeded 100,000 cloths per annum for the first time. The peak of the boom came in 1549–50[1] when

150,000 cloths went abroad, but during 1550–51 exports fell considerably and by 1551–52 were down to about 100,000 cloths. There was some recovery later in the decade, but it was clear that the boom was over.[2] The slump of the early 1550s obviously had a significant effect on the cloth industry which had expanded during the early years of the century to meet the needs of a growing market both at home and abroad. Now, at a time when domestic as well as foreign demand was almost certainly falling, employers found that they had to cut back on production and this had an effect on many thousands of people throughout England; most of the cloth was produced in their homes by workers who used the wages they received to supplement their often meagre agricultural earnings. In the 1550s, just when the rise in the price of foodstuffs was hitting many of them especially heavily, they found their supplementary income from the cloth industry either cut off or reduced.

Two main explanations have been advanced for the early-sixteenth-century boom in cloth exports and the slump which followed; one turning on 'real', the other on 'monetary' factors. The explanation in the terms of real (i.e. non-monetary) factors lays stress on the increasing demand for English cloth on the Antwerp market in the early sixteenth century. By about 1550, however, there was a glut of cloth at Antwerp. Thus the fall in English exports from 1551; the buyers simply had too much cloth. This is the explanation most widely stressed by experts today. The second explanation, the one in terms of monetary factors, concentrates on the debasements of the English coinage during the 1540s. These made English goods cheaper and therefore more desirable abroad. Before the debasements of the 1540s the value of the £1 sterling had been 26s. 8d. Flemish. In 1551 it was 13s. 4d. Flemish. In other words Flemish money bought twice as many English goods in 1551 as in 1540. In-1551, however, the English currency was revalued and in future Flemish money bought less English goods. This, of course, was bound to be a devastating blow to a market which was already showing signs of serious strain because of the glut of English cloth at Antwerp. This monetary explanation certainly looks attractive to the layman, but it has been challenged on technical grounds by Professor Gould (247). It is probably safest to conclude that real factors in Europe were most important in causing the export boom in English cloth in the early sixteenth century and in later bringing it to an end, but that the debasements and revaluation of the English coinage had some part as well in explaining both the boom and the subsequent slump.

The vast bulk of cloth exports went to Antwerp and the slump of the 1550s illustrated the danger of dependence on a single port. Despite the foundation of the Muscovy Company during Mary's reign, however, it was only under Elizabeth, when the Netherlands market was disrupted by war, that English trade expanded significantly into new areas. Long before then other wars had added to the social and economic problems which England faced during the 1540s and 1550s. Here it is the wars of the 1540s which were crucial; Mary's conflict with France between 1557 and 1558 was a relatively minor episode in this context. Between 1542 and 1550 England was at virtually continuous war with either or both of Scotland and France, and the cost of these wars and of the home defence associated with them was enormous. The figures which Dr Challis provides give a good indication of the scale of the problem. The total cost was perhaps £3.5 m. Taxation provided just under £1 m. of this, and sales of monastic and chantry lands just over £1 m. Borrowing yielded a relatively modest sum, but the greatest amount came from the profits of a massive debasement of the coinage which yielded nearly £1.3 m. between 1544 and 1551 (246). The change in the appearance of coins was dramatic. It has been well described by Sir Charles Oman. Henry VIII 'had taken over from his father the finest, best executed, and the most handsome coinage in Europe. He left to his son the most disreputable-looking money that had been seen since the days of Stephen – the gold heavily alloyed, the so-called silver ill-struck and turning black or brown as the base metal came to the surface.' (quoted in (246, *82*)) Henry's subjects were understandably suspicious of this flood of bizarre-looking coins and the debasements, both by increasing the amount of money in circulation and by undermining public confidence in the coinage, certainly gave a sharp, short-term filip to inflation, a fact appreciated by the author of the *Discourse of the Commonweal*, a notable tract on the ills facing the country, which appeared in 1549 (225). The author was almost certainly Sir Thomas Smith.

Of greater long-term significance than the debasements were the sales of monastic and chantry lands which accompanied them. The dispersal of the bulk of these to the gentry contributed significantly to that growing relative economic strength of the upper reaches of landed society *vis-à-vis* the Crown which was one of the most important developments of the century after 1540. The wars of the 1540s were therefore an economic disaster both for the lower orders in England and, in the longer term, for the Crown itself. By 1551 it was clear that the debasements could no longer be continued and that future land sales on the scale of those of the 1540s were impractical. It was 'the end of an era of affluence' (30, *179*) for the Crown. In future, royal policies, especially in foreign affairs, had to take account of the much more restricted financial resources which were available. The moderation and defensive nature of Elizabethan foreign policy were a reflection of that fundamental fact as well as a commentary on the caution and conservatism of the Queen herself.

If war, by helping to increase inflation, contributed to social distress during the 1540s, bad harvests had similar effects during the following decade. During the years between 1530 and 1548 harvests had generally been good.[3] There were only two really bad harvests during the period (those of 1535 and 1545), six of the remainder were average, and the other eleven were better than that. Especially notable were the six good to abundant harvests which came in a row between 1537 and 1542 [I]; these must at the very least have eased Henry's and Cromwell's task in enforcing the Reformation in vital years soon after the break with Rome. They may not have made malcontents more indulgent to the King's proceedings, but at least they helped to ensure that their discontents were not stimulated too much by the pangs of hunger. After 1548 the situation changed. There were three bad harvests in a row, in 1549, 1550 and 1551 and further very bad ones in 1555 and 1556 [I], the last being the worst of the century, with grain prices shooting up to over twice their normal level (227). The effects of these harvest disasters on the lower orders can be imagined; they led to extreme hardship. Just like the debasements of the previous decade they gave a sharp twist to the already serious inflationary spiral.

The dreadful harvest of 1556 was accompanied and followed by a series of influenza epidemics between 1556 and 1558. These, of course, hit a population many of whom were seriously weakened by lack of food. The story is well summarised by the distinguished seventeenth-century historian John Strype who based his work on a detailed knowledge of sixteenth-century manuscripts.

> What diseases and sicknesses everywhere prevailed! The like whereof had never been known before, both for the lasting and mortality of them: which being hot burning fevers, and other strange diseases began in the great dearth of 1556, and increased more and more the two following years. In the summer [of] 1557 they raged horribly throughout the realm and killed an exceeding great number of all sorts of men. . . . In some places corn stood and shed on the ground for lack of workmen. In the latter end of the year quartan agues were so common among men, women, and young children also, that few houses escaped: and these agues were not only common but to most people very dangerous, especially such as had been sick of the burning fevers before. In 1558, in the summer, about August, the same fevers raged again in such manner as never plague or pestilence, I think . . ., killed a greater number. The winter following also the quartan agues continued in like manner. (quoted (226))

These epidemics and their aftermath produced a great mortality in England between 1556 and 1560 and Professor Fisher estimated that the population of the country may have fallen by as much as 20 per cent during these years. Later research has suggested that the reduction was a good deal more modest – perhaps 6 per cent – but it was still substantial. Following the rapid increase of the early sixteenth century it must have eased inflationary pressures. Food was relatively more plentiful and labour relatively scarcer. The rise in food prices, therefore, levelled off and real wages rose (203; 226). This trend, which continued until at least the late 1560s, must have meant an easing of social tensions during the early years of Elizabeth's reign.

If Elizabeth was relatively lucky in the economic conditions in which her rule opened, her brother and especially her sister were, in contrast, unfortunate in the natural disasters which occurred during their short reigns. Northumberland had to cope with all three harvest failures of Edward's reign during the four years between 1549 and 1553 when he was the effective ruler of England, and the bad harvests, epidemics and soaring prices of the years 1555–58 must have added enormously to the gloom caused in England by Mary's religious persecutions and unsuccessful foreign policy. She was not an able ruler, but it is difficult to discuss the economic context of her reign without concluding that she had much more than her fair share of bad luck. In view of these social and economic difficulties it is perhaps surprising that the governments of the period were not faced with more peasant rebellions than they encountered. The only major revolt of the period which was predominantly social and economic in its motivation was Ket's rebellion of 1549. It is difficult to pinpoint reasons for this comparative lack of lower-class militancy, but it may be suggested that one of the major reasons was the identity of interests between the central government and the local gentry in containing and controlling lower-class discontents. Recent research has revealed moreover (see Chs. 7–9) the extent to which Cromwell's reformed Privy Council worked effectively during most of the troubled middle decades of the century to supervise the everyday business of administration in the localities. This must have gone far in preserving the authority of the central administration in the eyes of local governors who wanted, at practically any cost, to avoid social upheavals.

The history of these years should remind us above all, perhaps, of the dominance of agriculture in the life of the nation (227). This is readily apparent when we remember that the vast bulk of the population worked on the land, that wage-earners might spend 80–90 per cent of their income on food, and that even those, such as textile workers, who engaged in industry, were usually dependent for their raw material on the produce of the land. In these circumstances harvests and the price of food mattered much more to the vast majority of Englishmen than the vicissitudes of foreign trade, important though these might be. They certainly mattered infinitely more than the governmental and administrative changes which we have already examined and which have received so much attention in recent decades. How did the lower orders survive amid the debasements, harvest failures and epidemics of the 1540s and 1550s? Professor Hoskins has painted a notable picture of the grimness of their lives even in 'normal' times (26), and it seems, at first sight, inconceivable that they could have withstood the drastic reduction of their already very low standards of living which these disasters seem to imply. Part of the answer is that many did not survive; we have already noted the demographic catastrophe of the later 1550s. The rest of the answer is more complicated and confident generalizations are difficult, but it does seem clear that many 'landless' labourers in the countryside and even wage-earners in the towns did have access to small plots of land which enabled them to grow at least *some* food. At times of harvest failure and soaring prices this might make the vital difference between starvation and survival. It is also clear that some of these town workers and agricultural labourers were fed by their employers. The *general* significance of this is uncertain because we do not know the percentages of these groups which benefited, but those who did receive such 'payment in kind' were clearly protected from some of the worst effects of the inflation. When all allowances are made, however, the history of the period 1540–60 provides a salutary reminder of the fact that in times of real economic difficulty the majority of sixteenth-century English men, women and children had a bitter struggle just to survive.

1. The yearly figures were calculated from Michaelmas (29 September) to Michaelmas.
2. E. M. Carus-Wilson and O. Coleman, *England's Export Trade 1275–1547* (Oxford, 1963), p. 139; J. D. Gould, *The Great Debasement* (Oxford, 1970), pp. 120, 136.
3. For the methods used by historians in calculating good, average and bad harvests in terms of grain prices see W. G. Hoskins, 'Harvest fluctuations and English economic history, 1480–1619'. *AgHR*, **12** (1964), 28 ff.

CHAPTER 7

Mid-Tudor crisis? Foreign policy and faction in the later years of Henry VIII

The rise in prices was one of the most important developments of Henry VIII's later years as was the continuing advance of the Reformation, made possible partly, as we have seen (Ch. 2), by the ambivalent attitude of the King himself. During these years, too, court factions whose attitudes were coloured by their religious differences, struggled to gain Henry's ear, with 'conservatives' and 'radicals' alternately achieving the upper hand. These domestic conflicts were played out from 1542 onwards against the background of the wars with Scotland and France which occupied so much of the King's attention. These wars direct attention to foreign policy in the post-Cromwellian era.

The major focus and thrust of that foreign policy is an area of controversy among historians. Professor Wernham, following Pollard, believes that Henry's sights were fixed above all on Scotland and that these years marked the culmination of efforts, going back to the mid-1530s, to solve the 'British Problem' by ensuring that all constituent parts of the British Isles were under firm English control (30; 67). Supporters of this interpretation point to the incorporation of Wales into the English administrative and judicial system between 1536 and 1543, the reform of the Council of the North in 1537, the appearance of a Council of the West in 1539, and the assumption by Henry of the title of King of Ireland in 1541. Above all, they argue that the outbreak of war with Scotland in 1542, accompanied by a declaration of English suzerainty over the northern kingdom, reveals that Henry saw his major task in his later years as the final accomplishment of his 'grand design' of a unified Britain. The engagement of Henry's heir, Prince Edward, to the infant Scottish Queen Mary in 1543 gave substance to this dream by opening up the prospect of a unification of the Crowns of England and Scotland on Henry's death. On this analysis the war with France which began in the same year was largely a secondary concern, an interruption to Henry's main business in the North.

This interpretation, which attributes to Henry a grandiose and consistent vision which he retained in the forefront of his mind throughout the later years of his life, is, however, open to serious objections. The administrative reforms of the 1530s, including the union with Wales, the reform of the Council of the North and the creation of a Council of the West were, as we have seen (Ch. 3), essentially a result of Cromwell's genius and drive rather than any determined policy initiated by Henry himself. The assumption of the title King of Ireland represented a rejection of former policies and was long resisted by the King (89). Above all, as Professor Scarisbrick has maintained (68, *424 ff*), it can be cogently argued that Henry's concern with Scotland was secondary to his ambitions against France.

By 1541 Henry had decided to recapture his lost youth by resuming the military career which had marked his early years. Tortuous negotiations with France and the Emperor – once again at loggerheads – led to a tacit agreement with Charles V in the summer of 1542 for a joint invasion of France during the following year. At the same time Henry was trying to persuade James V of Scotland to join the English camp by holding out to him the prospect of a formally recognized place in the English succession. James, under the continuing influence of his clerical advisers, proved deaf to all blandishments and when Henry travelled to York in the autumn of 1541 in the hope of meeting him, James did not come. Henry was furious at the insult and deteriorating relations in 1542 were marked by the growing fierceness of border raids. In the autumn Henry finally lost patience and declared war on Scotland. The timing is significant. It came *after* his agreement to join Charles V in an attack on France. This suggests that his primary preoccupation was with the Continent and that initially he saw the Scottish War merely as a necessary means of securing his northern border. The overwhelming English victory at Solway Moss in November 1542 followed by the totally unexpected death of James during the following month did, however, open up the prospect of more permanent English influence in Scotland. The story of Anglo-Scottish relations between 1543 and 1547 is a saga of missed opportunities on Henry's part. He sought to maximize English influence by playing off against each other the different Scottish factions which were competing for power during the young Queen's minority. He did secure the Treaty of Greenwich in the summer of 1543 which agreed to Mary's eventual marriage to Prince Edward, but his previous and subsequent handling of the touchy Scots was so inept that by the end of the year the Scottish Parliament had annulled the treaty and turned back to the former alliance with France. All that Henry had left was force, but although Edward Seymour, earl of Hertford, mounted a savagely destructive raid on the Lowlands in 1544 the resistance of the Scots was not broken and by the end of Henry's reign the prospect of English control of Scotland seemed remote. The King had squandered his opportunities of 1542–43 by bad diplomacy but, as Professor Scarisbrick reminds us, his subsequent military campaigns in the North were handicapped because 'he would never·expend the necessary troops and money, to conquer and occupy, rather than merely to raid the country. He did this probably because Scotland was a . . . secondary theatre of war.' (68, *426*)

Henry, in fact, concentrated his main efforts on France. It is true that the unexpected turn of events in Scotland in December 1542 caused him to postpone his planned French invasion for a year, but in December 1543 he agreed with Charles V on a joint attack in the summer of 1544 with Emperor and King each supplying 40,000 men. An English army, with Henry himself in attendance, duly crossed the Channel, but the results were, to say the least, disappointing. Initial plans for a joint assault on Paris were never pursued and although Henry captured Boulogne in September, this was a poor substitute for the huge territories in northern and south-western France which he had hoped to win. The Emperor rapidly withdrew from the war and Henry was left to face a projected French invasion in 1545. It did not materialize and in 1546 Francis agreed to a peace by which he yielded Boulogne to England for eight years. Henry's French adventure, with its ambitious and unrealistic aims and limited successes, resembled in many ways his previous wars against France in 1512–14 and 1522–25. For him it was a return to the natural and normal business of kingship – the quest for military glory – and a picture of the reign which stresses the crucial importance for Henry himself of the French Wars of its earlier and later years, gives it a perspective which has often been lacking in recent studies. Diplomatic and military history are now unfashionable subjects among professional historians, but it is arguable that Henry himself saw the divorce and the break with Rome not as the central events of his rule but merely as necessary interruptions in the primary task of a king; winning prestige for himself and his country on the battlefield.[1]

The enormous cost of the wars of the 1540s helped, as we have seen (Ch. 6), to produce the quickening inflation and increasing social distress which marked the middle decades of the century. It was against this darkening domestic background that the faction struggles of the 1540s were played out at Court (for early Tudor faction struggles (88; 85; 25)). During the sixteenth century when the personality and ideas of monarchs were all important it was essential for men who hoped to make their way at Court and in government to gain the ear and confidence of the sovereign. Only those who were successful could hope to share in the wealth and influence which went with royal patronage – that huge range of offices and benefits at the Crown's disposal. The result was factions; men competed fiercely with each other for favours and often drew together in groups to advance their joint interests and block the advancement of their enemies. During recent years historians have been laying more and more stress on the significance of these manoeuvres. Factional struggles both at Court and in the country went on all the time, whereas Parliaments. which in the past have received a perhaps disproportionate amount of attention, were occasional institutions. The study of Tudor factions is only beginning, but when it is well advanced we will probably see how frequently the rivalries of these groupings spilled over into the parliamentary arena and explain many of the tensions and conflicts which occurred there (112).

The primary objective of faction leaders was to advance the wealth and influence of themselves and their followers, but during the mid-Tudor period two complicating factors affected their struggles. The first of these was the Reformation; this gave a religious element to factional politics which had not been present in the years before 1529 but which was to remain one of the major elements in factional struggles for the rest of the early modern period of English history. During the 1530s and 1540s the factions were divided into 'conservatives' and 'radicals'. The conservatives, broadly speaking, were those who accepted the royal supremacy over the Church but opposed further doctrinal changes; their leaders were the duke of Norfolk and Bishop Gardiner. The radicals also accepted the royal supremacy, but wished to use it to introduce Protestant doctrines into the Church. Their leaders were Cromwell and Cranmer in the 1530s, and after Cromwell's execution in 1540, Cranmer and Edward Seymour, earl of Hertford, brother of the King's third wife Jane Seymour and uncle of the heir to the throne, Prince Edward. From 1543 onwards they had the support of the King's sixth and last wife, Catherine Parr. The second complicating factor was the relative weakness of the monarchy during much of the period from 1540 to 1558. It may seem strange to include here the later years of Henry VIII, but there is evidence that, despite the formidable front which he continued to present to the world, the King's physical and mental deterioration contributed to a situation in which he may have been the victim rather than the master of the court factions which contended for power in his shadow. The succession of a minor and a female ruler of limited political abilities meant that the continuing factional struggles of 1547–58 were usually conducted outside the effective control of the Crown, a situation which was only reversed when Elizabeth imposed her will and authority on Court and Council in the early years of her reign.

Factional intrigues were already very apparent during the 1530s, the most notable example being those which attended the fall of Anne Boleyn in 1536.[2] By the beginning of that year Henry was tiring of her and his attention was turning towards another court lady, Jane Seymour, the daughter of a West Country gentleman. Anne's fate was sealed by her failure to produce the longed-for male heir – she miscarried of a boy in January 1536 – and in April and May a series of sensational scandals led to her execution. Her easy manners and the conventions of courtly love which prevailed in her circle were used to press a series of charges against her which included one of incest with her brother Lord Rochford. Several other courtiers were executed for their alleged adultery with the Queen, and the final result of the affair was not only to gratify Henry's desire for Jane Seymour – he married her less than a fortnight after the Queen's execution – but to entrench Cromwell more firmly in power than ever. This last fact is a key to the whole episode. Cranmer's pronouncement that Anne's marriage to the King had been null and void from the start[3] was enough to free Henry, and it is necessary to explain why Cromwell hounded the Queen to death on a series of patently false accusations. The answer is that at the beginning of 1536 he was fighting both for his political influence and for the reforming ideas in which he believed. He had come to power as a supporter of the Protestant Boleyns, but by 1536 had fallen out with Anne. In any event he saw the King's determination to get rid of her and realized the need to do everything he could to fulfil his master's wishes if he was to remain in power. Religious conservatives. such as Henry Courtenay, marquess of Exeter, and Lords Darcy and Hussey also wanted the overthrow of the Queen, though for quite different reasons. Her fall and the subsequent bastardization of Princess Elizabeth would, they believed, bring the Catholic Mary once more to the forefront and they hoped to use Anne's removal to initiate a repudiation of the reforming influences which Cromwell as well as Anne represented. Cromwell's task, therefore, was to secure the overthrow of the Boleyns while at the same time preserving the Protestant cause. It was a very difficult situation but he handled it brilliantly, showing himself a master of factional intrigue. He first of all allied with the conservatives to secure the overthrow and execution of Anne – he could not risk leaving her alive as a possible focus of discontent – and then abandoned them. Their desire to have Mary formally reinstated in the succession was rejected [B] and Mary herself was forced to recognize the royal supremacy and her own illegitimacy, a weakness for which she never forgave herself.

Mary's supporters, defeated in the summer of 1536, raised their heads again in the Pilgrimage of Grace which broke out that autumn. That great uprising, which convulsed much of northern England has produced a large literature in which its causes have been considered at length.[4] It has commonly been seen as a general reaction of northern society against the religious, political and economic policies of Henry and his base-born advisers, most notably Cromwell and Cranmer, and it is difficult to deny the fundamental validity of that judgement. Within this general context some historians have stressed religious, others economic, factors. Most recently it has been argued that the Pilgrimage can be explained primarily in political terms, by the workings of court faction (25). Its real leaders, Professor Elton maintains, were not northerners at all but those elderly courtiers lords Darcy and Hussey who raised the standard of revolt in the North in an effort to overthrow Cromwell and thus reverse the defeat which they had suffered in the earlier part of the year. Their failure further weakened Mary's party and it received yet another blow in 1538 when Exeter and several others who had stood aside from the Pilgrimage were executed following intrigues aimed both at overthrowing Cromwell and reversing the reforming influences at work in the Church.

Faction struggles continued during the 1540s and the first to suffer was Cromwell himself. That great master of intrigue was outmanoeuvred and executed in the summer of 1540. He was condemned unheard by Act of Attainder on charges of high treason that were clearly absurd. The conservatives, headed by Gardiner and Norfolk, managed to poison the King's mind against him for long enough to attain their purpose. They were greatly aided in their task by Norfolk's vivacious niece, Catherine Howard, on whom Henry's roving eye had fallen after the débâcle of the Cleves marriage. Henry undoubtedly blamed Cromwell for the Cleves affair, and the foreign policy which it represented, but the conservatives' decisive triumph seems to have come when they persuaded the King to accept a false charge that his chief minister was a sacramentarian [N] heretic (25; 68). Henry married Catherine Howard soon after Cromwell's execution, but within a year he was regretting the loss of 'the most faithful servant he ever had'.[5] Cromwell had certainly been his greatest minister and it is not difficult to accept Professor Elton's final verdict that he was also 'the most remarkable statesman of the sixteenth century' (25). As we have seen, he was a great administrator and policeman, a notable religious reformer and an ambitious if not very successful social engineer. Above all, in his drafting of the anti-papal legislation of the 1530s he proclaimed the independence of an English nation state which continued to distance itself from European institutions until our own time.

The victory of the conservatives, which was enshrined in the Six Articles Act of 1539, in the fall of Cromwell, and in Henry's marriage to Catherine Howard was less permanent and complete than at first seemed likely. Reforming influences continued to make themselves felt in England, and in 1541 the chief protagonist of such ideas, Archbishop Cranmer, laid before the King evidence about his wife's unchastity before their wedding. It soon became evident that she had almost certainly committed adultery after their marriage as well, and in February 1542 she was executed.[6] The reformers took further comfort from

Henry's final marriage in 1543 to Catherine Parr, a highly educated widow who shared many of their advanced ideas, but the last four years of the reign saw a series of episodes which reveal the continuance of faction struggles based largely on religious rivalries (68; 69). In 1543 the conservatives on the Council, headed by Gardiner, persuaded Henry to authorize the arrest of Cranmer and his incarceration in the Tower on grounds of heresy. Henry, however, warned the archbishop of his impending fate and gave him a ring which he was to produce on his arrest as a sign that he still enjoyed the royal confidence. This Cranmer duly did to the discomfiture of his opponents. In 1544 it was Gardiner's turn. His secretary and nephew, Germain Gardiner, was executed in the spring of that year for denying the royal supremacy, and Cranmer and other reformers on the Council persuaded Henry that he could not have held such dangerous views without his uncle's knowledge and approval. Henry obligingly authorized the bishop's committal to the Tower, but before the Council could act Gardiner, who had been warned by a friend, rushed to the King's side and obtained a full pardon for any offences he might have committed. Two years later it was the Queen herself who was threatened. She was in the habit of airing theological opinions in front of her husband, and when she did this in Gardiner's presence he waxed eloquent on the iniquity of a mere woman, even a Queen, presuming to instruct the Supreme Head of the Church. He secured Henry's approval for an investigation of her alleged heretical activities, but Catherine, learning of the proceedings against her, made her way to the King and convinced him of her innocence. When Lord Chancellor Wriothesley, like Gardiner a conservative in religion, arrived the next day to arrest the Queen, Henry sent him packing with shouts of 'arrant knave! beast! and fool!'.

Cranmer, Gardiner and the Queen, then, all survived the attacks of their opponents, but by 1546 Henry, then fifty-five years old, was clearly a sick man who could not live much longer. This raised the vital question of which of the factions, conservatives or reformers, would hold the levers of power during the coming minority. By the end of the year the answer was obvious; the reformers had won (25). They secured the vital positions in the Privy Chamber, which controlled access to the King, obtained the exclusion of Gardiner from the Council and exploited a charge of treason against Norfolk's son, the earl of Surrey, to secure the arrest of the duke himself. When Henry died in January 1547 the conservatives were in almost total disarray. The men who counted most in the new regime were Edward Seymour, earl of Hertford, the young King's uncle and a convinced Protestant, and Archbishop Cranmer who, at long last, could openly express and exploit his reforming ideas.

The faction struggles of 1536–47 clearly represented attempts by ambitious men to ruin their enemies and keep or gain power for themselves. But they involved much more than personal considerations. The contenders were divided between religious conservatives who wished to avoid further doctrinal changes and reformers who wanted to advance the Reformation. Henry favoured the supporters of each ideological position at different times, but at end of his reign he left the country in the hands of the reformers. This is ironic in view of the fact that at that time the official doctrinal position of the Church was still based on the highly conservative Six Articles of 1539. Two explanations are possible. One is that Henry tacitly accepted many of the Protestant advances of his reign and was prepared to envisage – perhaps even to welcome – the prospect of a truly Protestant England under his son. There is, as we saw, some evidence to support that view, but it must also be pointed out that on his death-bed in 1547 he was the virtual prisoner of the reformers. Whether or not he would have welcomed their triumph at the beginning of his son's reign there was little he could have done by that time to prevent it. This fact raises an important point about Henry's relationship with the factions during his later years. Was he, as Professor Smith tells us (69), their master, exploiting their differences to keep his own hands firmly on the levers of power, or was he rather, as Dr Ives would have it (88), their victim, swayed in random directions by whoever managed to secure his confidence at crucial moments, and often subsequently regretting the conse- quences. Some of the episodes can be interpreted either way. Those of 1543, 1544 and 1546, involving Cranmer, Gardiner and Catherine Parr, can either be regarded as subtle manœuvres by Henry in which he asserted his mastery over both parties or else as the irresponsible and irrational actions of an ageing man of declining mental abilities who was too easily influenced by whoever managed to gain his ear at a particular moment. It seems less possible, however, to see the falls of Anne Boleyn and Cromwell in terms of a King who was in effective control of the situation. It is true that in these episodes Henry got rid of a wife of whom he had tired and of a minister who, he believed, had let him down, but in neither case was the subsequent execution of the victim necessary for the King's purposes, only for those of the opposing faction. In allowing Anne and Cromwell to go to the scaffold Henry's mind was unduly influenced by their enemies, and in the case of the latter, at least, he soon realized his mistake. If Henry was so susceptible to pressure in 1536 and 1540 it is difficult to imagine that he was not similarly impressionable during his declining years in the 1540s. It seems fair to conclude, therefore, that he was probably more often the victim than the master of faction.

The later years of Henry VIII's reign were difficult ones for England. The King was at best in only partial control of the court intrigues which surrounded him, he did not always give a firm lead in religious affairs and, above all, he pursued a disastrous and expensive foreign policy which contributed to the growing price inflation which was to dominate the domestic economic scene during the reigns of his son and elder daughter. On the other hand the routine government of the country during these years was conducted by Cromwell's reformed Privy Council, which began to keep a regular record of its proceedings in 1540. Its generally effective oversight of the localities ensured that, despite wars, economic difficul- ties and religious and factional strife, England was essentially a well-administered country. It is doubtful if that fact brought much comfort to Henry as he lay on his death-bed. Administrative details had always bored him, and he left them to 'lesser' men while he concentrated on more congenial activities, such as war, pleasure and theological debate. It is probable that success in war, with the glory that would bring for himself and his country, was his highest ambition, but he is remembered today. and rightly so, primarily as the man who broke England's ties with the Papacy. The details of his foreign policy and of his ruinously expensive wars soon faded into the background of history, but the breach with Rome and the Protestant Reformation which preceded, accompanied and followed it had momentous consequences for the whole subsequent history of the British Isles.

---

1. See P. R. Roberts, *EHR*, **86** (1971), 358 ff.
2. E. W. Ives, 'Faction at the Court of Henry VIII: the fall of Anne Boleyn'. *History*, **57** (1972), 169 ff; G. R. Elton, *Reform and Reformation*, 250 ff.
3. The grounds were that Henry's previous sexual relations with her sister Mary had created a canonical impediment to the marriage.
4. For good general discussions with different emphases see A. G. Dickens. 'Secular and religious motivation in the Pilgrimage of Grace', *Studies in Church History*, IV (ed. G. J. Cuming, 1967), pp. 39 ff; C. S. L. Davies, 'The Pilgrimage of Grace reconsidered', *P & P*, **41** (1968), 338 ff.
5. *LP*, XVI, 285.
6. For the full story L. B. Smith, *A Tudor Tragedy, the Life and Times of Catherine Howard* (1961).

CHAPTER 8

Mid-Tudor crisis? Edward VI: the rule of Somerset

The nine-year-old boy who ascended the throne at the beginning of 1547 was already at that early age firmly committed not merely to his father's break with the Papacy but also to the advancement of Protestant doctrines of which Henry, despite the ambivalent attitude of his later years, had never formally approved. Edward's fervent Protestantism must have given great comfort to his principal ministers in Church and State, Archbishop Cranmer and Edward Seymour, earl of Hertford, the King's uncle, created duke of Somerset at the beginning of the new reign. Cranmer's doctrinal views continued to develop throughout his career. He abandoned belief in transubstantiation during the 1530s and by the end of Henry's reign may no longer have believed in a real presence in the sacrament. (For a brief discussion of Cranmer's doctrinal evolution, see (27, *186 ff*).) Somerset's precise theological position is debatable, but there is no doubt that he consorted with radicals like John Hooper and Thomas Becon during Edward's reign, associations which suggest that he was inclined more towards extreme than moderate Protestantism (96).

Somerset rapidly emerged as the chief power in the State, with quasi-regal authority. By the terms of Henry VIII's will the government of the realm during Edward's minority was vested in a Council of sixteen named men. There were, however, no restrictions imposed on the way they exercised their authority and within three days of Henry's death they had accepted Somerset's elevation to the office of Lord Protector. This coup was engineered by Somerset with the help of Sir William Paget, an experienced administrator who was probably Henry's ablest lay councillor at the end of his reign. Two months later, in March, Somerset obtained the right to appoint members of the council. By the spring of 1547, therefore, he had achieved a dominant position, and his fellow councillors were rewarded for their acquiescence in the flood of new and higher titles and grants of land which came their way during the course of 1547.

It has traditionally been argued that the tone of Somerset's rule was set by a great 'liberalizing' statute passed by the first Parliament of the reign, which met in November 1547. This 'Treasons Act' (1 Edward VI, c. 12; statutes from the beginning of Edward VI's reign are in (1, Vol. IV)) swept away a mass of repressive legislation, including the medieval heresy laws, Henry's harsh additions to medieval treason legislation, the Six Articles Act, and all restrictions on the printing or study of the Scriptures [H]. It also repealed the controversial Proclamations Act of 1539 (31 Henry VIII, c. 8), which had ordered that royal proclamations should be obeyed 'as though they were made by act of Parliament'. Somerset, partly on the basis of this statute, partly on the basis of his social policy, has been seen as a man ahead of his times, an idealist who believed in toleration and had a genuine concern for the poor. His rule, it has been argued, finally collapsed in 1549 because of the opposition of traditionally minded councillors who feared social revolution (28, vol. 1; 97). Somerset certainly believed in a much wider toleration than either Henry VIII or Mary – there were no executions for heresy during the Protectorate – but it must be remembered that in 1547 he and his fellow Protestants believed that open discussion of religious matters would help their cause and that there were limits to what was allowed; the 1547 Act, after repealing all Henry's treason legislation, immediately reintroduced one aspect of it: denial of the royal supremacy was still to be treason. The repeal of the Proclamations Act was probably designed to give Somerset more personal power; he had thereafter the right to issue proclamations without the signed approval of fellow councillors. Moreover, the 1547 Act as a whole should be seen in the perspective of a new reign. Monarchs often rejected the unpopular measures or men of their predecessors – witness Henry VIII's execution of Empson and Dudley – and the 1547 statute was certainly in this tradition; Protector and Parliament saw it partly as a means of gaining support for the new regime.

The 1547 Act should therefore be seen in the context in which it was passed as well as a reflection of Somerset's own views. The Protector's character was a complex one, but it is no longer possible to depict him simply as the frustrated idealist of the traditional interpretation. Recent work (96) has shown him to be much more conventionally minded. In a greedy age he was an exceptionally acquisitive man, building up, both before and after his accession to power, a great landed estate. Much of this was at the expense of the bishopric of Bath and Wells – a commentary on the limits of his idealism. The focal point of his entire policy during the Protectorate was not a series of schemes to relieve the poor but rather the enormously expensive Scottish War which, by contributing to inflation, fed social distress. He was also an impossible colleague. His arrogance and aloofness soon made him many enemies among the nobility and gentry on whom he ultimately depended and the concern which he did show for the poor – a concern which should be seen in the context of traditional Tudor social policy – was vitiated by the way in which he aroused hopes among the 'lower orders' which he did not have the ability to fulfil.

The Scottish War which Somerset had inherited from Henry VIII was his central preoccupation (96). He had been the principal English military commander in the war during the old King's later years, when he had shown himself an able soldier. During the Protectorate he tried to subdue Scotland by establishing a series of garrisons in the southern and eastern parts of the country, a policy which merely stiffened Scottish resistance and drew the Scots more and more under French influence, the very situation which Somerset wished to avoid. In the summer of 1548 a large French army landed in Scotland and Mary Queen of Scots was transported to France where she was duly to become the wife of the dauphin. These developments revealed the essential bankruptcy of Somerset's policy and marked the effective end of the ambition, which he had taken over from Henry VIII, of securing a marriage between Edward and Mary which would eventually have led to a united Britain. He persisted, however, in continuing the war and the following year Henry II of France formally entered the struggle and attacked Boulogne. Somerset's Protectorate ended with a large French army entrenched in a Scotland which was fiercely hostile to England and a new French War in which the loss of Boulogne, which Henry VIII had won at such a high cost, seemed inevitable.

The disasters of Somerset's foreign policy were compounded by its high cost – he spent over £350,000 on garrisons and military operations in Scotland – and by the fact that it occupied time and attention which might more usefully have been devoted to the domestic scene, where he faced religious and social problems. In the religious field the vital question was how far and how fast Protestantism could be introduced. The Treasons Act of 1547, by repealing the Six Articles of 1539, proclaimed that Catholic doctrines were out of favour and another 1547 statute, which dissolved the chantries [N], also attacked traditional ideas. There were over 2,000 chantries throughout the country (27; 53). They had originally been condemned by a Henrician Act of 1545 (37 Henry VIII, c. 4) which had not denounced them on doctrinal grounds but had asserted that the money which would be produced by their seizure was necessary to pay for the French and Scottish Wars. Henry died before the Act could be put into effect and the new statute, made necessary by his death, took a different line [G.2(8)]. The ostensible reason for the dissolution was now the superstitious errors which chantries had encouraged, notably 'vain opinions of purgatory and masses satisfactory, to be done for them which be departed'. The new Protestant government was doubtless sincere in its dislike of the theological implications of the existence of chantries, but it was desperate for money and most of the lands, worth perhaps as much as a quarter of the former monastic property, were soon sold. The end of the chantries meant the disappearance of institutions which had for centuries been part of the everyday social scene, intimately bound up with the hopes and fears of the population at large, and Professor Dickens has rightly emphasized the profound psychological effect which the dissolution had on 'the cohesion and morale of the nation'. The government was seen to be seizing and using religious endowments for its immediate secular needs, and the fact that a limited proportion of this total chantry income was devoted to educational purposes hardly altered the basic point.

Other notable pieces of religious legislation during the Protectorate included an Act of 1549 allowing priests to marry [G.2(9)] – as many as a third did in some dioceses – and the Act of Uniformity [E.2(6); G.2(10)] which accompanied the 1549 Prayer Book. That latter Act had considerable constitutional significance. We have seen (Ch. 1) that after 1534, despite the theoretically 'absolutist' nature of the royal supremacy in the Church, there was another view which stressed the role of Parliament in its exercise. That view was strengthened by the accession of a minor who was unable to exercise the supremacy personally and its triumph was enshrined in 1549, when Parliament authorized as well as enforced the Act of Uniformity which imposed the new Prayer Book. Here for the first time an English Parliament clearly and unequivocally assumed control of the doctrine and ceremonies of the Church. It was a momentous moment in both constitutional and ecclesiastical history and all subsequent sixteenth and seventeenth-century rulers had to live with its consequences. The Prayer Book itself introduced a form of worship which retained many conservative features; the structure of the mass was largely unchanged and the familiar 'scenic apparatus' of worship with the accustomed medieval vestments was retained. For ordinary men and women the great novelty of the new services must have been the fact that they were now conducted in English rather than Latin. The book was essentially the work of Cranmer, though it took account of the differing views of other bishops, which centred on eucharistic doctrine. Here there were important changes in Catholic tradition, which insisted that each mass was a sacrifice which supplemented the one which Christ had made on the Cross. Now the latter was held to be complete and sufficient in itself; masses were henceforth to be regarded as commemorative services. The sacred host was to be administered with the words, 'The Body of our Lord Jesus Christ which was given for thee preserve thy body and soul unto everlasting life.' This phraseology clearly recognized a real presence in the sacrament, but Cranmer certainly did not intend it to imply a recognition of the doctrine of transubstantiation. The extent of its ambiguity became apparent when Gardiner, then in disgrace in the Tower, announced that he was ready to accept it in the latter sense. This was certainly straining the wording but it does reveal the extent to which conservatives could take comfort from the contents of the book ((27, *217 ff*) gives an excellent brief account of the First Prayer Book). Cranmer's and almost certainly Somerset's own views were more radical than those which they now sanctioned, but their freedom of action was restricted by the obvious dangers of attempting radical changes at the time: some conservative bishops disliked the comparatively limited alterations which *were* made; ordinary men and women were attached to their familiar services; and the foreign situation demanded restraint: England could not afford to provoke the enmity of the Emperor at a time of hostility with Scotland and France (96). In this domestic and international context the 1549 Prayer Book appears, in fact, as a shrewd, statesmanlike measure. Somerset, whose general reputation is now so much under a cloud, should be given full credit for his role in its introduction.

Somerset, who was aware of the need for caution in religious affairs, was less sensible in his social policies (96). The most remarkable aspects of these were the expectations which they aroused among the peasantry and the fact that Somerset persisted with them after their initial failures in 1548; a reflection perhaps of his stubbornness as well as of his genuine desire to help the poor. The policies themselves were entirely conventional and should not be attributed to the influence of an organized group of 'commonwealth men' [N] working to secure amelioration of the condition of the peasantry. No such group existed (55), and Somerset's attempts to restrict enclosures should be seen as part of a long tradition of paternalism going back through Cromwell and Wolsey to the Middle Ages. We now know, of course, that enclosure was not the main cause of the social distress of the period; the inflation of the time was caused much more by the coinage debasements made necessary by the wars of the 1540s. This recognized by Sir Thomas Smith, the Protector's Secretary of State, who wanted a restoration of the currency. That reform would, however, have cut off the supply of money for the Scottish War which Somerset regarded as all important and he rejected Smith's advice in favour of the views of John Hales, a Chancery official who became the champion of the anti-enclosure movement. The result was Enclosure Commissions in 1548 and 1549. These raised both the hopes of the poor and the fears of the rich when they toured the country, and their failure to produce effective reforms must have been largely responsible for the widespread riots and disturbances which convulsed much of southern England in 1548 and 1549. Hales's attempt to secure the passage of agrarian reforms in the parliamentary session of 1548–49 also failed when his bills to promote dairy-farming and prevent engrossing were rejected. The government did, however, secure a tax on sheep and cloth. This was designed essentially to raise revenue, but as it would obviously make sheep-farming less profitable it could be represented as a useful piece of social engineering which might promote the growing of grain.

If Somerset's social policies were both conventional and a failure, his conduct of government, also a failure, was highly unconventional. He had attained supreme power through the acquiescence of his fellow councillors, and common sense as well as custom suggested the need to maintain their support by consulting them regularly. In fact Somerset did almost precisely the opposite. During his period of power he sought their advice only occasionally and even failed to exploit the administrative expertise of men like Paget in the government of the realm. The Privy Council faded into the background during his regime and the result was that when he needed the councillors' support during the revolts of 1549 he found himself politically isolated; men like John Dudley, earl of Warwick resented his arrogance and also recognized that he was an incompetent administrator (54; 95). His preference for a highly 'personal' style of government is confirmed by his use of proclamations, documents issued by Tudor monarchs to announce decisions and administer the realm. Following the repeal of Henry VIII's Proclamations Act in 1547 he was able to issue these without the signatures of twelve fellow councillors and he made full use of his opportunities; during the years 1547–49 he employed proclamations far more frequently and with more severe penalties than any other early Tudor ruler. In these circumstances it is not surprising that Professor Heinze concludes that it was during the Protectorate that proclamations posed their greatest threat to the supremacy of parliamentary statutes (93).

Somerset's high-handed use of prerogative powers in his proclamations fits in well with the picture of an aloof man who found it difficult to take advice. It now seems clear that it was essentially these personal qualities which brought him down in 1549. Members of the Privy Council did not object to his Scottish and social policies as such – subjugation of Scotland and justice for the poor were highly conventional objectives with roots deep in English history – but rather to his incompetence in their execution. Above all, they resented their exclusion from an effective role in government and when major rebellions broke out in the West Country and East Anglia in the summer of 1549 they seized the opportunity to bring the Protectorate to an end. The West Country revolt was caused principally by the new English Prayer Book, which the rebels denounced as a 'Christmas game', that in East Anglia by agrarian discontents.[1] The idea that Somerset was personally sympathetic towards the rebels will not bear examination – they were 'lewd, seditious and evil disposed persons' – but his fellow councillors could argue that his enthusiastic promotion of the Enclosure Commissions had given him an understandable, if undeserved, reputation among the lower orders as a social revolutionary (96). This was an excuse to get rid of him; the real reason, as we have seen, was the arrogance and incompetence which had led him first of all to engross and then to mismanage the business of the realm. By October 1549 he found himself virtually isolated, and on the 11th of that month he was arrested. He was released from the Tower in February of the following year and soon rejoined the Council, but he could not resign himself to the lesser position which he now occupied and his plotting against the new regime led to his rearrest in October 1551 and execution at the beginning of 1552. The years of his power had been disastrous ones for England. It would be wrong to deny his genuine if conventional concern for the poor, but he alienated his Council colleagues by his arrogance and high-handed methods while pursuing a foreign policy which was both unsuccessful and enormously expensive. His religious settlement, with its compromises and evasions which pleased neither conservatives nor radicals, was arguably a sagacious measure the best possible for the country in circumstances when it was dangerous to go either too slowly or too fast, but it was unlikely to be permanent. All in all he left his *de facto* successor John Dudley, created duke of Northumberland in 1551, a most unenviable inheritance.

1. A good recent study is J. Cornwall, *The Revolt of the Peasantry 1549* (1977).

CHAPTER 9

Mid-Tudor crisis? Edward VI: the Northumberland regime

As the historical reputation of Somerset has plummeted in recent years that of Northumberland[1] has risen. In many ways his early career resembled that of the Protector. He rose to prominence in the later years of Henry VIII when he won a deserved reputation as a soldier and also acquired substantial property. During the Protectorate he enhanced both his dignity – he became earl of Warwick in February 1547 – and his wealth. After he became the chief power in the State he showed that he shared Somerset's appetite for ecclesiastical property, though without the latter's strong personal commitment to Protestantism. The combination of greed and religious opportunism which he displayed, together with his attempt to alter the established line of succession on Edward VI's death, gave him an unenviable historical reputation which has only recently been seriously challenged. (The best brief description of the Northumberland regime is (54, *29 ff*).) No one should doubt that he was a selfish and ambitious man – so were almost all the courtiers and crown servants who surrounded him – but it can be argued that his policies, in view of the daunting difficulties which he faced, were generally sensible and effective.

Northumberland did not have a dominant position in October 1549; he only gained a controlling role in the State by February 1550 as a result of a ferocious power struggle, the full details of which have only recently been revealed. (95) It was generally believed that Somerset's fall would lead to a religious reaction and there is no doubt that many members of the Council wanted at least a halt to the Reformation. Their leader, Thomas Wriothesley, earl of Southampton, tried to brand Northumberland as an accomplice in Somerset's follies. In this situation Northumberland found an invaluable ally in Archbishop Cranmer who naturally feared the religious consequences if the conservatives won. By exploiting Cranmer's influence with the fanatically Protestant Edward, Northumberland was able to secure the addition of a number of his own adherents to the Privy Council and to vote Southampton and his supporters out of office. There could be no question of a new Protectorate but Northumberland took the office of Lord President, a post which gave him control of the Council's procedure. He used that office to restore the effective conciliar government which Somerset had abandoned.

Northumberland realized that it was pointless to continue the Scottish and French Wars which had been such a drain on England's resources during the later years of Henry VIII and throughout the Protectorate. The Treaty of Boulogne in March 1550 has been described as 'the most ignominious . . . signed by England during the century'.[2] Boulogne was surrendered to France, the English troops were to leave Scotland and the marriage between Edward and Mary

71

Queen of Scots was tacitly abandoned. It was certainly an inglorious settlement, but Northumberland should not be blamed for his realism in cutting England's losses. The wars could only have been continued at a cost which might have imposed an intolerable strain on England's social fabric.

The ending of war allowed Northumberland to concentrate on the principal domestic task of any government, the preservation of law and order. Here he faced immense difficulties. There was continuous unrest and disaffection among the 'lower orders' throughout his rule; hardly surprising in the aftermath of the 1549 rebellions and especially ominous in view of the economic situation which he had to face. This was far worse than in Somerset's time, when harvests had been good. Northumberland had, however, to cope with the effects of the three bad harvests of Edward's reign as well as of the 1551 crisis in the cloth trade. In these circumstances, faced with soaring grain prices and a slump in the country's main industry, he demonstrated a concern for social justice which was probably more effective than Somerset's better-known measures. It is true that the sheep tax was abolished and the Enclosure Commissions abandoned, but there were more prosecutions for depopulation than in Somerset's time and some important social legislation was passed, including Acts of 1552 to protect arable-farming and to prohibit usury (the lending of money at interest, which had been permitted, subject to certain restrictions, in 1545 (5 & 6 Edward VI, cc. 5, 20)). In 1552 also a new Poor Law was introduced (5 & 6 Edward VI, c. 2). It was concerned mainly with the collection of funds for the relief of the deserving poor and provided a hint of the compulsion which was to be applied under Elizabeth. Any person who had the means to contribute to poor relief but refused to do so was to be exhorted by his local parson. If this proved ineffective, he could be sent to the bishop who would try to 'induce and persuade him . . . by charitable ways and means'.

If Northumberland's social policies can be seen largely as a more effective continuation of those of his predecessor, the religious settlement which he permitted in 1552–53 represented a real break with the compromise of 1549; it committed England clearly and unequivocally to the Protestant camp. Cranmer, who presided over the settlement, had given Northumberland vital support during the power struggle of 1549–50 and now he achieved his reward in a Prayer Book and Articles of Religion which reflected many of the theological ideas to which he had been committed since the beginning of the reign (27). The 1552 Prayer Book changed the structure of the old mass and abolished its very name; it now became a communion service. The scenes within churches were transformed to take account of the new approach, with the replacement of altars by communion tables and the rejection of medieval vestments in favour of a simple surplice. The words accompanying the administration of the host were altered to the form, 'Take and eat this in remembrance that Christ died for thee, and feed on him in thy heart by faith with thanksgiving', phraseology which suggests a commemorative rite rather than a real presence in the sacrament. This interpretation is reinforced by the Council's ruling that kneeling to receive communion, which was still required, did not imply 'any real and essential presence . . . of Christ's natural flesh and blood'. In June of the following year, less than a month before the King's death, he gave the royal assent to forty-two doctrinal articles which were strongly influenced by Calvinism (27), especially on the key doctrine of predestination. These, together with the Prayer Book itself, formed the foundation of the Elizabethan settlement of 1559–63.

It is impossible to be certain of the reaction of clergy and people to the new Prayer Book during the few months of Edward's reign in which it was in operation, though we may suspect that the illiterate masses did not take kindly to the changed scene in their parish churches. Whatever their private views, however, there was no repetition of the Prayer Book rebellion of 1549, a fact which may tell us something of the effectiveness of Northumberland's government of the realm compared with that of Somerset. The centrepiece of that government was his restoration of the authority of the Privy Council under his own guidance and control (54; 95). He appreciated that Somerset's neglect of the Council was the key factor in his downfall and after using the office of Lord President to establish his own control over its work and composition he set about the task of restoring its efficiency. He accepted a plan put forward by Paget which ensured that business was conducted according to a fixed routine, and by the end of 1550 the Council was once more in effective charge of the administration of the realm. He added twelve new councillors to the board after February 1550, and in 1551 it reached a maximum size of thirty-three. The working membership was a good deal smaller, however, and this helped to preserve administrative efficiency, just as the enhanced membership strengthened Northumberland's political control. Northumberland accompanied his restoration of Council authority with a much more cautious use of proclamations than that practised by Somerset. He not only issued them less frequently and with much less severe penalties but also showed a greater concern for founding them on parliamentary statutes (93). In this field, just as in his emphasis on the Council as an administrative institution, he was returning to the practices of Cromwell's day. Like Cromwell, too, he had plans for the reform of the governmental machine. Here he was concerned with promoting not only efficiency but also economy; very necessary in view of the Crown's desperate financial position. The proliferation of revenue courts during and after Cromwell's ministry had produced a situation in which, by 1549, the royal revenue was collected and administered by no less than five institutions, with the Exchequer, traditionally the principal body for dealing with the royal finances, occupying a relatively unimportant role. The unsatisfactory nature of this situation was compounded by corruption in some of the courts – for example in the Court of Wards – and in March 1552 a Royal Commission was set up to investigate the revenue courts and make recommendations for reform.[3] It reported in December, astonishingly quickly in view of the amount of detailed work which it undertook. Its thoroughness was a tribute to the efficiency of its members and especially to the work of the experienced bureaucrat Sir Walter Mildmay, who played a leading role in its proceedings. After making a detailed analysis of the Crown's revenues and of the inadequacies of the five courts the commissioners put forward two possible solutions; either the courts should be reduced to two, with an office for Crown lands and the Exchequer in charge of all other revenues or else they should all be merged into the Exchequer. The recommendations do not seem to have been included in the final report as it was

presented to the Council[4] and they were not acted upon – and then only in part –
until Mary's reign, but the work of the Commission is one striking demonstration both of the commitment of Northumberland's regime to reform and of
the practical efficiency with which it could go about the task.

By the end of 1552, then, despite all the problems which he faced, Northumberland had a firm grip on the realm. His whole position, however, depended on
the continued survival of the King, and by early 1553 it was clear that Edward's
always precarious health was deteriorating rapidly. The signs of tuberculosis made
it plain that he would not live long and Northumberland realized that he would
either have to acquiesce in the accession of the Catholic Mary and his own inevitable downfall or else make a desperate attempt to alter the succession as
enshrined in a statute of 1543. That 'third Succession Act' of Henry VIII's reign
had left the throne, assuming that Edward himself died childless, first of all to
Mary and then to Elizabeth [B]. Now Northumberland with the agreement – some
historians would say on the initiative (28, vol. 2) – of Edward himself endeavoured to bypass not only Mary but also Elizabeth and secure the throne for Lady
Jane Grey, a descendant of Henry VIII's younger sister Mary, who was married
in May 1553 to Northumberland's eldest son, Guildford Dudley. The plot failed,
mainly because on Edward's death the political nation as a whole refused to
accept such a blatant interference with the succession as established by law. But
its collapse, which now looks so inevitable, seemed much less certain at the time,
and Northumberland's gamble, given the stakes involved, should perhaps be seen
as worth the attempt. Its failure led to his execution, but he could have expected
little power in the new reign if he had tamely accepted Mary's accession. Success,
on the other hand, would have brought the glittering prize of the Crown within
the grasp of his family.

Northumberland went to the scaffold abjuring his Protestant faith, a great
propaganda victory for the new Catholic government, but it has been argued (54)
that this seeming apostasy was in fact consistent with his religious attitude
throughout his life. That, so the argument goes, was based on the conviction
that a man was bound to accept the religious views of the government in power,
whatever these might be. It is impossible now to say whether or not Northumberland really held such extreme Erastian [N] opinions, but neither this rejection
at the very end of his life of the Protestantism which he had supported during his
days of power nor his futile attempt to alter the succession should be allowed to
conceal the successes of 'a genuine reform administration, the first since Cromwell's fall' (25, *358*). It must surely be concluded that Northumberland, despite
his unhappy end, was a much more realistic and effective ruler than the traditionally overpraised Somerset.

One of the most important developments of Northumberland's rule was the
religious settlement of 1552–53 and it has been argued that the 'one positive
achievement' of Edward's reign as a whole was in religion (22). The importance
of the Edwardian period in that field is not in doubt in view of its contribution
to the Elizabethan settlement, but the extent to which Protestantism had taken
root in the country at large by 1553 is a controversial subject. (For differing views

see e.g. (24, *253 ff*; 25, *367 ff*).) It is certainly clear that by that date it had won influential converts among members of the ruling and educated classes. The six years of the reign saw a barrage of Protestant propaganda which ranged from the crude invective of men like John Bale, who wrote scurrilous diatribes against the mass, to the reasoned pronouncements of distinguished Continental theologians who came to England and spread a wide variety of the ideas of the European Reformation, including those of Calvin and Zwingli. The Italian Peter Martyr was appointed to a chair at Oxford in 1548, and the following year Martin Bucer, the most distinguished of the immigrants, was made Regius Professor at Cambridge. He had originally been won over from Catholicism by Luther, but his theological opinions developed independently and during the rest of his life he moved gradually to a Zwinglian position, a slow doctrinal development, so like that of his patron Cranmer, which reflected a sincere and continuing search for the truth. His death in 1551 removed from the scene the man who was perhaps best suited to develop still stronger ties between English and Continental Protestantism, though the links which had already been established made England in Edward's reign an important European centre of theological discussion (27). The influence of men as varied as Bale and Bucer, whose only common ground was a sincere anti-Catholicism, is difficult to assess. The crude invective of the former and the academic expositions of the latter must have done something, in their very different ways, to win converts to Protestantism, but it is impossible to do more than guess at the number and long-term influence of such conversions.

The Protestant propaganda and preaching which was permitted or encouraged during the reign bore witness to the official policies of both Somerset and Northumberland, directed at securing a break with traditional Catholic opinions. One indication of their success can be gained by examining the preambles of wills. Only a minority of the population, mainly gentry, clergy, the wealthier members of urban communities and the most prosperous members of the peasantry, made wills, so it must be emphasized that the trends which they reveal tell us nothing about the opinions of the bulk of the population. Traditional Catholic usage in a will was to mention the Blessed Virgin and the Saints and the omission of such a reference can be taken as an indication of at least some sympathy with reforming ideas. Analysis of wills in Nottinghamshire and Yorkshire in 1547 shows that about 60 per cent included traditional formulae while the remainder did not. By 1553 the proportions were approximately reversed (27). These figures reveal both the extent to which reforming influences were being felt among the more prosperous members of society in parts of the Midlands and of the even more conservative North by the end of Henry VIII's reign and their continuing influence under Edward VI. Evidence which comes from southern England is more striking. Already by 1547 some 60 per cent of wills proved in Kent suggest reformist influences and by 1553 the figure was 90 per cent; the Reformation had clearly made a considerable impact in the upper reaches of society in Cranmer's own diocese by the end of Edward's reign (251).

Evidence which comes from Mary's reign can also tell us a good deal. Her first Parliament, which met in 1553, repealed all the Edwardian religious legislation, thus restoring the position at the end of Henry VIII's reign. A substantial minority in the Commons, perhaps 80 out of 350, voted against the measure (54). Such opposition to the policies of a strongly Catholic government must surely indicate a sincere devotion to Protestantism, and such commitment to the Reformed faith was certainly true of the group of nearly 800 men, women and children who, fearing persecution, fled abroad from 1554 onwards. These 'Marian exiles' almost all came from the upper and educated strata of society; gentry, clergy, theological students, merchants. This is not surprising – working-class Protestants would not normally have the money to find their way abroad – but some members of the 'lower orders' did show during Mary's reign not only that they had been converted to Protestant beliefs but also that they were prepared to die for their faith; of nearly 300 men and women who were burnt for heresy by Mary's government between 1555 and 1558 the vast majority belonged to the poorer sections of the community.

The sacrifices of the Marian martyrs and exiles reveal commitments to Protestantism which must, in the vast majority of cases, have been made by the end of Edward's reign, and the evidence which we have considered so far suggests that reforming ideas had strongly influenced a substantial number of the upper and educated classes in some parts of the country. Certainly, the appeal of Protestantism, with its emphasis on vernacular Bible reading and on the priesthood of all believers was bound to be initially strongest among the literate minority of English men and women. It is much more difficult, however, to decide how representative the Marian martyrs were of lower-class opinion. The vast majority of victims came from the south and east of the country, with only a handful in the west and north, and it is clear that the grass-roots influence of the Reformation on much of northern England was extremely limited by 1553, especially in Lancashire where it had made virtually no impact at all by that date, except to provoke resentment (175). Moreover, 300 or so lower-class victims in southern and eastern England, while impressive as a testimony to the heroism and devotion of individuals, must be set in the context of a total English population of some 3,000,000 in the mid-sixteenth century. All the evidence we have, indeed, is compatible with the view that reformed ideas had strongly influenced only a tiny minority of the lower classes by 1553 (53). Poorer men and women, mostly illiterate, had to be educated in Protestant doctrines before they could be sincerely converted to them. Such education had to come essentially from the clergy, and it was only during Elizabeth's reign that substantial numbers of preachers, familiar with the new doctrines, emerged from the universities. Protestantism, then, may have influenced only a minority of the nation by the end of Edward's reign, but it is vital to remember that that minority included those men who were to form the governing circle during the early Elizabethan period. The Protestant 'party' of Edward's reign, represented by clerical exiles like Grindal and lay compromisers like Cecil, who stayed at home during the Marian reaction, were to get their chance again from 1558 onwards.

The House of Commons seems to have acquiesced with little dissent in the religious settlements of Edward's reign, but it was a different story in the Lords, where a substantial minority opposed all the Protestant innovations of the period. Dr Loach, while making this point, emphasizes that the general relationship between government and Parliament during the Edwardian period was one of co-operation; in important fields like social and economic policy Crown, Lords and Commons were in broad agreement (54). The governing class also showed basic unity at the very end of the reign when it rejected Lady Jane Grey in favour of the lawful heiress to the throne, the Princess Mary. The latter thought that this revealed a basic enthusiasm for her religion; it showed primarily, in fact, the attachment of the political nation both to the Tudor dynasty and the rule of law. Mary, despite her deficiencies as a ruler, was at least an adult, and her brother's reign revealed that under a child selfish men could easily use the Crown's resources for private ends. Both Somerset and Northumberland ruthlessly exploited ecclesiastical property and royal lands and patronage to reward their followers and enrich themselves. Their selfish exploitation of the State's assets came at a time when the Crown's growing financial plight made it plain that ambitious foreign policies like those of the 1540s were now beyond the Crown's resources. By 1553 the two principal financial foundations of the war of 1542–50 were no longer available; debasements of the coinage had been brought to an end in 1551 and could not be renewed without intolerable social strains, while most of the new lands which the Crown had acquired at the Reformation had been sold. The reign of Edward VI, therefore, marked a watershed between a brief period during the later years of Henry VIII when large amounts of cash were found relatively quickly and (if the inflationary costs are ignored) easily, and the remainder of the Tudor and early Stuart era, when equivalent sums could only be secured, if at all, with the greatest difficulty.

---

1. Although John Dudley, earl of Warwick, did not become duke of Northumberland until 1551 I have referred to him throughout this chapter by that title.
2. A. F. Pollard, *Cambridge Modern History*, II (Cambridge, 1903), p. 499.
3. W. C. Richardson, ed., *The Report of the Royal Commission of 1552* (Morgantown, West Va., 1974).
4. G. R. Elton, 'Mid-Tudor finance', *HJ*, **20** (1977), 737 ff.

CHAPTER 10

Mid-Tudor crisis? The reign of Mary

With the accession of Mary England had once more an adult sovereign, able to exercise personal authority. The obvious advantages of this were, however, restricted by two considerations; she was a woman and she had limited aptitude for government. There had been no female ruler in England since Matilda in the twelfth century – not a happy precedent – and in 1558, shortly before Mary's death, John Knox published his *First Blast of the Trumpet Against the Monstrous Regiment of Women*. In this tract he wrote that 'to promote a woman to bear rule, superiority, dominion or empire above any realm, nation or city is repugnant to nature; contumely to God, a thing most contrary to his revealed will and approved ordinance; and finally, it is the subversion of good order, of all equity and justice'.[1] Most men of the day would have agreed with these sentiments, if not necessarily with the violence with which Knox expressed them, and Mary's government, simply because it was government by a woman, had grave disadvantages. These were compounded by the Queen's personal characteristics. (For discussion of Mary's character see (29). Loades's detailed work is now the standard history of the reign.) Her entire life until her accession had been bound up with preserving her royal dignity, revering the memory of her mother and clinging to the Catholic faith which was the centre-piece of her existence. Her very difficult position during the reigns of her father and brother had made her wary and mistrustful of all their advisers and she never fully trusted the experienced councillors, such as Gardiner and Paget, whom she inherited from them. This may be understandable, but it did not help the effective government of the realm, especially in view of her reliance on the advice of the Imperial ambassador, Simon Renard. Her dominant aim, when she attained the Crown, was to end the schism with the Papacy and make England once more part of Catholic Christendom. That for her was a matter of principle and on principles she was inflexible, a fact which could give rise to grave political problems. She also longed for marriage and a child, partly to give her personal happiness but mainly to ensure that Catholicism would be preserved after her death.

Mary's marriage to Philip of Spain, with its implications for English foreign policy, and the restoration of Catholicism were the dominant issues of her reign in the eyes of contemporaries and have rightly remained the foremost concerns of later historians, despite recent stress on the creative financial and administrative developments of the period. With the benefit of hindsight it is easy to assume that her policies were doomed to failure from the start, but that is much too simple an assumption. By January 1555 it looked, in fact, as if she had succeeded: she had achieved the marriage she wanted and believed that a child was on the way; the links with Rome had been restored; a serious rebellion had been crushed; and the country was at peace. After that, it is true, things went badly wrong, but in the early months of 1555 the disastrous ending of the reign nearly four years later could not reasonably have been anticipated.

Mary was resolved from the start to marry her cousin, Philip of Spain, although her councillors were not aware of her determination until two or three months after the start of the reign. She formally notified them of her intentions at the beginning of November and although all of them accepted the *fait accompli* a majority were almost certainly against the marriage. There was also opposition in the first Parliament of the reign; in November the House of Commons presented a petition asking the Queen to marry within the realm, a request which Mary rejected with angry words. In January 1554 the marriage treaty was concluded. It safeguarded Elizabeth's rights to the succession if Philip and Mary had no children, provided that foreigners were not to be appointed to English offices, and declared that England was not to be drawn into Philip's wars against her will. Philip was, however, to join Mary in the exercise of sovereign powers, and public reaction to the treaty seems to have been generally hostile; Englishmen feared that, whatever might appear on paper, they were about to become a subordinate part of the Habsburg Empire ((29, Ch. 4) for a discussion of the Spanish marriage). At the end of January rebellion broke out in Kent, led by Sir Thomas Wyatt, a prominent member of the local gentry. Other revolts, planned in the West Country, in Leicestershire and in the Welsh borders, did not get off the ground and Wyatt, who marched on London, was defeated, partly because of the courage which the Queen herself showed in the crisis. Professor Loades had argued that the rebellion was mainly an anti-Spanish demonstration (29; 141) and it was certainly designed to prevent the marriage, but there also seem to have been strong Protestant motives behind the episode (251) and it may be best to regard it as a general commentary on the depth of discontent which some of Mary's subjects felt with her policies after the first few months of her reign.

Philip arrived in England in the summer of 1554, but his immediate marriage to the Queen did not bring Mary the personal happiness she craved. She idolized her husband, but it is clear that he did not return her feelings. Moreover, early in 1555 it became apparent that the child which she believed she was carrying was an illusion. Philip, never popular in England, left in August of the same year and did not return until the spring of 1557, when he successfully drew the country into his war with France. That war has traditionally been seen as a disastrous folly which demonstrates Mary's subservience to her husband's will. There is something in this arguement – the majority of the Privy Council certainly opposed involvement in a conflict which England could not afford – but the conduct of the war was a good deal less incompetent than has usually been supposed and it enabled many of those who had previously been involved in sedition against Mary's government to play military roles which, in Mr Davies's words 'provided an opportunity . . . to reunite a deeply divided ruling class (54, *163*). The final outcome of the war, the fall of Calais in January 1558, was due largely to a successful gamble against heavy odds by Henry II of France, but of course it was this loss of England's last outpost on the Continent which made the deepest impact at home; a fitting start to the last unhappy year of the reign. Philip's involvement of England in an unsuccessful war and the failure of the Spanish marriage to produce an heir should not, however, be allowed to obscure the positive advantages which it offered the Queen at the start of her reign; a husband who stood above domestic factional politics as no Englishman could easily have done and alliance with the ruler of England's most important trading partner, the Netherlands. There were sound reasons for the marriage; its failure lay not in the idea but in the results: the Queen's inability to produce a child, the association of the match with an unsuccessful foreign policy, and the links which came to be made in the minds of Englishmen between the Spanish alliance and persecuting Catholicism.

It is unlikely that Philip, as has sometimes been assumed, tried to exercise a moderating influence over the religious persecutions which began in 1555 (29), but there is no doubt that the responsibility for the policy lay not with him but with the Queen and Cardinal Pole, who believed it their bounden duty to root out heresy. Before the persecutions began Mary had succeeded in formally restoring England to the Roman allegiance. She firmly believed that all legislation against the Papacy was *ipso facto* null and void but found to her dismay that she had to proceed through Parliament; only that body could remove penalties which its predecessors had imposed. In 1553 a statue of her first Parliament [G.3(11)] abrogated all the Edwardian religious legislation, thus restoring the position at the end of Henry VIII's reign and in January 1555, in her third Parliament, a second 'Statute of Repeal' [G.3(12)] abolished all Acts passed against the Papacy since the beginning of 1529. There was, as we have seen (Ch. 9), a substantial minority opinion in the Commons which opposed the repeal of the Edwardian legislation, but the restoration of the ties with Rome seem to have been accepted without trouble by both Houses of Parliament once the landed classes were guaranteed quiet possession of the former monastic lands which they held. The government also experienced no difficulty in reviving the medieval heresy laws during the same Parliament [G.3(13)] and it was under these laws that nearly 300 individuals were burned at the stake between February 1555 and the end of the reign (27; 29; 177). A few of the victims, notably Cranmer, Ridley, Latimer and Hooper, were among the great of the realm, but the vast majority were humble men and women whose cruel sufferings brought increasing signs of resentment from the crowds which invariably flocked to the executions. The persecution involved an enormous administrative effort by both the ecclesiastical and civil authorities in southern and eastern England where the vast bulk of the burnings took place, with thousands of investigations and interrogations of suspects. By 1558 it had failed to extirpate heresy, but this is not to say that the task was hopeless. Mary and Pole had only three and a half years to do their work and Counter-Reformation attacks on Protestantism in other parts of Europe (for example in areas of southern Germany) show that persecution *could* work effectively in the sixteenth century.

The sacrifices of the martyrs, soon enshrined in that Elizabethan best seller John Foxe's *Acts and Monuments* (better known as Foxe's 'Book of Martyrs') gave dignity to the Protestant cause which had all too often seemed lacking in Edward VI's day when it could be associated with the squalid struggles of members of the nobility and gentry for ecclesiastical property. None of the lay leaders of Protestantism were among the martyrs, but they were well represented among the 800 or so exiles who, fearful of their fate in a Catholic England, fled to the Continent from 1554 onwards (27; 178). These men like Sir Anthony Cooke, the father of four brilliant daughters all of whom were to make distinguished matches in the Elizabethan period, and Sir Francis Knollys, later a distinguished Elizabethan councillor, waited the end of the Marian regime, as did clerics like Edwin Sandys, Edmund Grindal, Richard Cox and John Jewel, all of them eventually to become Elizabethan bishops. The exiles often quarrelled among themselves – as in the celebrated 'Troubles' at Frankfurt – but their disputes over points of liturgy and doctrine were less important than the fact that they were a 'party' in exile, a group of men whose common cause was to see the restoration of a Protestant England. While they awaited that happy day they endeavoured to bring it closer by helping to inspire and finance a flood of Protestant books and writings which all the efforts of Mary's government were unable to keep out of England (29).

While the exiles dreamed of the collapse of Catholicism at home, Cardinal Pole, papal legate and, after Cranmer's deposition at the end of 1555, archbishop of Canterbury as well, was endeavouring to lay foundations on which the restored Church would endure. Pole, who had Yorkist royal blood in his veins (he was a great-nephew of Edward IV) had refused to accept the Henrician schism and lived abroad until Mary's reign. He was created a cardinal in 1536, but went through his own theological agonies when he had an intense personal struggle about acceptance of official Church teaching on the doctrine of justification. He finally conquered his doubts on the grounds that obedience to the official voice of the Church and especially to the Papacy must take precedence over all other considerations. His main task on his return to England, was to re-establish Catholicism in the hearts and minds of people who had been weaned away from the Old Faith by twenty years of anti-Roman propaganda. He failed. A few religious houses were restored (172), actions were brought against clergymen who had married between 1549 and 1553, and heretics, as we have seen, were vigorously pursued. Such concentration on legalism, however, could hardly inspire ordinary people with a genuine enthusiasm for the Catholic faith. What was needed was a sustained missionary effort to educate the masses, and this was almost entirely lacking. Even in the conservative North there was little sign of a grass-roots Catholic revival (except perhaps in Lancashire) and it is easy to understand Professor Dickens's verdict that Mary and Pole – who rejected the offer of Jesuit help – 'failed to discover the Counter-Reformation' (27, *280*). That is not, however, the end of the matter. It is important to recognize the brevity of the time during which Pole exercised effective authority over the English Church; his legatine powers lasted for only two and a half years, as he was deprived of his commission by Paul IV in April 1557. By June of that year he was under investigation at Rome as a suspected Lutheran, and it is understandable in these circumstances that both his opportunities and energies for ecclesiastical reform flagged during the last eighteen months of the reign.

In the short time he did have at his disposal Pole's work should be judged, partly at least, in terms of his own priorities (176). He believed that schism had been brought about by the actions of a small group of evil men. The people as a whole had been misled and would return to the old faith if traditional practices and doctrines were restored in a quiet and orderly manner. These ideas explain Pole's concentration on legalism (essential for re-establishing the old ways), his distrust of too much preaching (which might stir up theological controversies which he wished to avoid) and his long-term plans for an episcopate and clergy who would be effective and worthy pastors for their flocks. His legatine synod, held in London in 1555–56, provided for the establishment of diocesan seminaries for the education of the clergy. This was a pioneering step, later taken up at the Council of Trent with important consequences for the quality of the clergy in the Catholic Church as a whole, but it required many years for highly trained pastors to have an impact on the country at large, and Pole's imaginative scheme died with him as far as England was concerned. He also saw to it that competent men like White of Winchester, Christopherson of Chichester, Pate of Worcester and Goldwell of St Asaph were appointed to the episcopal bench. A number of the new bishops, like Pole himself, has considerable pastoral gifts, and the fact that they had little time or opportunity to use them must not conceal the fact that the Marian episcopate was a potentially formidable spearhead for a genuine Catholic revival. Its behaviour on Elizabeth's accession can be contrasted dramatically with that of the Henrician episcopate at the time of the schism. Then only Fisher defended the Roman Supremacy. In 1559 only one bishop – Kitchen of Llandaff – accepted the new Protestant settlement. If Mary and Pole had lived for another ten or twenty years they might have achieved a genuine reconversion of the masses to Catholicism, though it must be said that in the short term their persecutions won them little support and a good deal of hostility among the people. As it was the English religious situation in 1558 was confused. There were vocal Catholic and Protestant minorities, but the population as a whole, buffeted and confused by the religious upheavals of two decades, probably waited with resignation on the decisions of their betters. It can be guessed that most of them were attached to traditional rituals and practices, which added colour to their daily lives, but indifferent to and often ignorant about the doctrinal subtleties and controversies which filled the learned works of the day.

While Englishmen debated the dramatic events of religion and foreign policy, less spectacular developments in government and administration helped to lay some of the foundations of the Elizabethan State. The Privy Council, despite the fact that it attained a membership of over forty and was divided by factions which the Queen could not always properly control, exercised a reasonably effective oversight of routine administration, a task made doubly necessary by the background of virtually continuous disaffection and conspiracies against which councillors worked (29; 54). Mary's government, therefore, accepted the tradition of administration through the Council, which had been broken by Somerset and revived under Northumberland, and was to be further developed by Elizabeth. It also carried out a reform of the revenue courts which stemmed from the report of the 1552 Commission, though the final measure, under the aegis of Lord Treasurer Winchester, did not exactly follow either of the commissioners' recommendations. In 1554 Winchester annexed the Courts of First Fruits and Tenths and of Augmentations to the Exchequer, thus making the latter, for the first time since the fifteenth century, once more responsible for the vast bulk of the royal revenues.[2] The Court of Wards and the duchy of Lancaster continued to manage their own resources, and the former especially remained a most important source of royal patronage. The 1554 reform established the basic pattern of financial administration for the rest of the Tudor and early Stuart periods. It was, therefore, a very important measure, though it is doubtful if it achieved the economy in administrative expenses which had been hoped for. Its most important results were probably to introduce the more efficient Augmentations methods into parts of the Exchequer machinery and to make the head of the Exchequer, the Lord Treasurer, who had previously been responsible for only a small portion of the royal revenues, into a kind of minister of finance. Indeed the status of the Lord Treasurer was greatly increased from 1554 onwards and thereafter the occupants of the office, notably the Cecils under Elizabeth and James I, were often the principal ministers of the Crown.

Two other reforms (29; 244; 248) brought substantial long-term benefits to the royal finances. In 1555 a Privy Council committee recommended that a survey should be made of all the Crown lands, with a view to increasing their value. This was done, further valuations were made in 1557, and soon afterwards a Commission was ordered to raise rents and entry fines [N] accordingly. The net revenue of the Crown lands rose, on the basis of one calculation, by over £40,000 per annum between the end of Edward's and the beginning of Elizabeth's reign, and although Professor Loades has cast doubts on the reality of the figure (29), it seems reasonable to conclude that improved methods of estate management did result in a substantial rise in the Crown's land revenues under Mary. There is certainly no doubt about the importance of the second reform, increased customs rates. The 1552 Commission on the revenue courts suggested a revision of these rates, which were still fixed on the basis of valuations of 1507 which took no account of the inflation of the intervening decades. Implementation of the proposal was delayed, however, until May 1558, when a new Book of Rates substantially increased existing valuations. As a result, the customs, which brought in only £29,000 in the fourth year of Mary's reign, raised £83,000 in the first year of Elizabeth's. The new book, inspired by Winchester, was issued on the Crown's authority alone, without the consent of Parliament, and the constitutional principle involved was to give rise to major disputes in the reign of James I. More immediately, the improved customs and land revenues which Mary's government obtained were of crucial importance for Elizabeth's finances. It was she, not Mary, who reaped the benefit, perhaps to the tune of £90,000 a year altogether. When it is remembered that the total royal revenue in Elizabeth's early years amounted to about £265,000 per annum (98) – just enough for her to manage if she practised strict economy – the crucial significance of the Marian reforms can be appreciated. They were fundamental for Elizabeth's solvency and thus for the Elizabethan achievement as a whole.

Mary's reign also laid the foundations for the Elizabethan militia and navy and prepared the way for the recoinage of 1560–61. The navy, built up so impressively under Henry VIII, had suffered severely during the economies of the Northumberland regime when no new ships were built, old vessels were sold and repairs were generally neglected. A rebuilding programme began in 1555 and reached a very high level in 1558–59 when as much tonnage was built in a single year as in the entire five years before the Armada. Moreover, the financial administration of the navy was greatly improved in 1557 when a regular peacetime allocation was made for its upkeep. That was intended to cover the repair of ships which needed attention and the man in charge of the operation was the ubiquitous Winchester, the genius behind so many mid-Tudor administrative and financial reforms. These naval improvements enabled the English fleet to play an honourable part in the French War of 1557–59 and Elizabeth was able to use the much improved fleet created by her sister in her naval intervention in Scotland in 1560 which played an important role in ousting the French-dominated government of Scotland and thus in creating a Protestant regime on England's vital northern border.[3] Reform of the navy had begun before the outbreak of war in 1557. The war itself, by revealing the inadequacies of home defence, led to reform of the militia system. That was based on the obligation of all able-bodied men to defend the country in time of need, but few tended to turn up when summoned, and the weapons of those who did appear were often quite inadequate, being based in theory on the provisions of a thirteenth century statute. In 1558 two Acts (4 & 5 Philip and Mary, cc. 2, 3) of Mary's last Parliament reformed the system; one, the 'Arms Act', modernized the whole system for the provision of weapons, while the other, the 'Militia Act', attempted to make the mustering system itself more effective by penalizing absences and administrative corruption. These Acts were the foundation of the military system which prevailed throughout Elizabeth's reign and, despite their undoubted inadequacies, they were an improvement on the previous situation (55).

The ability to maintain effective naval and military systems was based in the long run on financial solvency and stability and here Mary's government played a significant role, not merely by its reforms in the customs and in the administration of the royal lands but by the plans for a recoinage which it drew up (246). Northumberland had stopped debasing the coinage in 1551 but the base money which existed at the time was not withdrawn from circulation, creating a situation in which good-quality and base coins were in use together. In the summer of 1556 a group of privy councillors considered 'which ways may best be devised for the reformation of the coins'. As a result a plan for a full recoinage was being actively discussed at the end of the year and by the summer of 1557 a decision was in the balance. In the end the government did nothing, and Dr Challis concludes that it was 'sheer failure of nerve that caused the scheme to fall through'. That may be true, but the decision is very understandable in view of the appalling economic situation of the time with the worst harvest of the century in 1556–57 and a devastating influenza epidemic at the same time. It would surely have been irresponsible for a government to risk the further upheavals of a major currency reform in such conditions. In any event the Marian plans of 1556–57 undoubtedly form a basis for the recoinage of 1560–61 and it is clear that 'Elizabeth could never have tackled the problem of the coinage either as quickly or as effectively as she did had it not been so thoroughly aired amongst government officials in the immediately preceding years' (246, *118*).

The creative role of Mary's government in the field of coinage reform has only recently been recognized. So too has its role in the making of what Professor Tittler has called 'a national urban policy' (54, *74 ff*). He argues that during the years 1540–58, and especially in Mary's reign, Crown, Council and Parliament gave urban communities 'conscious support' which became 'more precise in detail, more comprehensive in scope and more regular in execution than ever before' (54, *75*). In previous years merchants and craftsmen had been given rights to regulate conditions in their own trades and industries, but such rights had been seen in terms of particular trades and specific industries. Three Acts (1 & 2 Philip and Mary, c. 7; 2 & 3 Philip and Mary, c. 11; 4 & 5 Philip and Mary, c. 5) of Mary's reign, however, dealt with the problems of retail trade and of cloth-making on a national basis in an attempt to prevent rural incursions on urban rights in these fields.

These Acts represented co-operation in the economic field between Crown and Parliament, both of which had to agree to the statutes, and it has been argued that co-operation rather than conflict was the general theme of Marian parliamentary history (54). Dr Loach sees little active opposition during the reign, either in the Lords or in the Commons, to the Crown's religious policies and thinks that the 'critical spirit' which Neale detected in the 1555 Parliament has been much exaggerated. It is certainly true that the older school of parliamentary historians has been unduly obsessed by the idea of conflict and that much of the parliamentary history of Mary's reign and indeed of the entire Tudor period can and should be written in terms of co-operation between Crown, Lords and Commons, the three elements in the parliamentary trinity.[4] That truth must not, however, be allowed to obscure the reality of the conflicts which *can* be detected between the Crown and some members of the Marian House of Commons. The eighty or so members – a substantial minority – who voted against the repeal of the Edwardian religious legislation certainly opposed government policy as a matter of principle and the concern of a majority of Commons members for the sanctity of property rights was very evident in 1555 when a bill to sequester the lands of Protestant exiles abroad was actually defeated in the Commons. The House may have opposed the measure on secular rather than on religious grounds, but that did not affect the reality of their opposition. Moreover, the government had troubles of another kind in the parliamentary arena. In April 1554, in the second Parliament of the reign, there was an unseemly struggle between Gardiner and Paget, the Queen's two most prominent councillors, when the former vainly tried to push through a religious programme which had not been approved by the Privy Council as a whole. Faction struggles within the Council were a normal aspect of government, but it was unheard of for them to spill over into Parliament and the Queen's failure to prevent this incident is a reflection of her lack of effective political control over her leading advisers (for this incident see (29, *168 ff*)). There was, therefore, a good deal of routine co-operation as well as some conflict between Crown and Parliament during Mary's reign. Both elements were normal throughout the Tudor period and it is wrong to stress one to the exclusion of the other. Faction fights among councillors in open Parliament are another matter and were not repeated until the Jacobean period; Elizabeth saw to that.

Mary's failure to exercise clear and continuous authority over her councillors can be taken as a good indication of her limitations as a ruler, but her ineffectiveness should not be exaggerated. She did succeed in enforcing her will over the return to Rome, over her marriage with Philip and over the declaration of war against France·in 1557 – probably the three major decisions of the reign – and that despite the fact that in the two latter cases substantial majorities in her Council were against her. Mary did not lack resolution when her vital personal concerns were involved, but it was a different matter when it came to routine application to business, where her attention was patchy and uncertain. This is explained to some extent by the poor health which plagued her throughout the reign, but it did not make the task of her ministers any easier. She had able advisers, such as Paget and Gardiner, even if they could not always agree, and she also had William Paulet, marquis of Winchester, one of the key figures of the Tudor age. The full details of his contribution to the reforms of the 1550s have yet to be revealed, but there is no doubt that he was a creative administrator, the vital link between the ages of Cromwell and Burghley. The positive administrative reforms which he inspired, so vital as we have seen to Elizabeth's early successes, make nonsense of Pollard's cruel and too celebrated epigram that 'sterility was the conclusive note of Mary's reign'.[5] Moreover, the failures of the Marian regime, especially in the religious field, were by no means inevitable. Here, as we saw, the short time-span of the reign was crucial. Mary died after only five years realizing that the Protestant Elizabeth would reverse her policies. It was a bitter knowledge for her to bear as death approached and brought home the importance of her failure to bear the Catholic heir who might ultimately have carried on her work; her own 'sterility' was the great tragedy of her political as well as of her personal life. Ill luck certainly dogged the later years of her reign. She had no control over the dreadful economic conditions of 1555–58, perhaps the worst of the entire century with.their bad harvests and terrible epidemics, and it is too easy to forget that the gloom which surrounded these years was due at least as much to natural disasters with their heavy tolls in malnutrition and deaths as to religious persecution and foreign policy failures. Mr Davies has recently coined a much better epigram than that of Pollard. He himself applies it to the French War, but it can equally well be used as a verdict on the reign as a whole; 'luck ran against the Queen' (54, *185*).

The death of Mary can be seen as marking the end – or the beginning of the end – of the 'mid-century crisis' of Tudor England. But should we talk in such apocalyptic terms? It may be that the application of the word 'crisis' to a period of at least eleven and in the case of some historians (W. R. D. Jones in (209) covers the period 1539–63) of over twenty years obscures as much as it illuminates. It seems essential at least to distinguish in discussion between the English people and the English State. There is obviously much to be said for the view that the middle decades of the century were a period of crisis (or perhaps better of crises) for the *people* of England. The years 1540–60 saw unprecedently rapid changes in the economy and in religion, arguably the two areas which affected most intimately the lives of ordinary Englishmen; historians are now emphasizing the profound psychological as well as material shocks which these upheavals must have meant for hundreds of thousands of men and women who had been accustomed to much less volatile conditions.[6] It is doubtful, on the other hand, if the Tudor *State* was ever in quite as serious difficulties as the word 'crisis' implies. Between 1540 and 1558 the throne was occupied successively by a sick and rapidly ageing bully, a boy who was too young to rule and a woman of limited political abilities. In these circumstances what is significant and remarkable is not the weakness of government, but its relative strength. At no time during the period, except perhaps at the end of Somerset's Protectorate, was there a serious threat of the breakdown of administration, surely the fundamental test of a 'crisis' in the life of a state. The middle decades of the century certainly produced severe difficulties for the governments of the time, but the English State which Elizabeth inherited in 1558 was a fully functioning polity.

---

1. D. Laing, ed., *The Works of John Knox*, IV (Edinburgh, 1855), p. 373.
2. For the 1554 reform see G. R. Elton, *The Tudor Revolution in Government*, pp. 223 ff; W. C. Richardson; *The History of the Court of Augmentations* (Baton Rouge, 1961), pp. 246 ff.
3. M. Oppenheim, *History of the Administration of the Royal Navy* (1896), pp. 109 ff; T. Glasgow, 'The Navy in Philip and Mary's War, 1557–8', *Mariner's Mirror*, **53** (1967), 321 ff; 'The maturing of naval administration, 1556–64', *Mariner's Mirror*, **56** (1970), 3 ff.
4. For results of this cooperation, the legislation passed by Mary's Parliaments see, D. M. Loades, *The Reign of Mary Tudor* (1979), pp. 274 ff.
5. A. F. Pollard, *The Political History of England 1547–1603* (1910), p. 172.
6. See e.g. J. D. Gould, 'The price revolution reconsidered', *EcHR*, 2nd ser. **17** (1964–65), 265; A. G. Dickens, *The English Reformation*, p. 215.

CHAPTER 11

The early Tudor revolution: the significance of the Reformation era, 1529–1558

If the idea of a mid-Tudor crisis is familiar to students of the period, so is the theory of an early Tudor 'revolution'. That concept, so prominent in the works of Professor Elton, is based on the belief that the changes which took place in the three decades between the beginning of the Reformation Parliament and the accession of Elizabeth were so numerous and important that they transformed the English polity.

It is true that the practical powers of the Papacy and the Church had been strictly limited by the Crown during the later Middle Ages, but Dr Harriss's argument (84) that the changes of the 1530s were therefore of relatively limited significance will not bear examination. No medieval monarch had claimed the title of Head of the Church or the right to decide its doctrine, but these were the claims made by Henry VIII and his successors. In the short term the headship brought the Crown vast new prestige and powers. Monarchs were now respon- sible not only for the welfare of their subjects' bodies, as they had always been, but also for the theoretically even more important welfare of their souls. This added dramatically from Henry VIII's reign onwards to the already very great charisma of the monarchy, which also assumed direct control over all aspects of the life and work of the clergy. In the longer term, however, the headship was much less beneficial for royal authority. As a result of the Reformation political and religious dissent became inextricably linked. Catholics and Puritans under Elizabeth and the early Stuarts were usually regarded as a political threat to the State as well as a religious threat to the State Church, both of which were now headed by the monarch. The religious difficulties of the later sixteenth and early seventeenth centuries, with all their consequences for the monarchy, were there- fore largely a result of the royal headship of the Church introduced during the 1530s, a headship which was regarded by many religious dissidents as particularly shocking during the reign of Elizabeth when, under the modified title of Supreme Governor [N], it was held by a woman.

The changes of the 1530s also led to the formal establishment of an English 'nation state', a realm subject to no outside authority. Long before then, of course, foreigners had noted that Englishmen had a good conceit of themselves – an Italian observer wrote about 1500 'they think that there are no other men than themselves and no other world than England' (quoted (177, 26)) – but the break with Rome led to a much increased sense of national self-consciousness, an enhanced feeling that England was both very different from and much superior to other European states. Formal proclamation of English autonomy was made in the Cromwellian preamble to the 1533 Act of Appeals which asserted that England was 'an empire . . . governed by one supreme head and king' with powers over the clergy as well as the laity, and in the Act of Supremacy of 1534 which explicity gave to the King those doctrinal powers over the Church which had not formally been withdrawn from Rome in the previous year (24 Henry VIII, c. 12; 26 Henry VIII, c. 1). The duality of medieval life, with Church and State each supreme in its own field and the former under the control of a distant Pope was thus ended and, despite the brief re-establishment of Roman authority under Mary, the feeling of national identity and uniqueness continued to grow, reaching an apogee in the reign of Elizabeth when it was given classic expression in one of the most influential works in the whole of English literature. John Foxe's *Acts and Monuments*, published in 1563 and universally known as the 'Book of Martyrs' was a resounding statement of the theory that Protestant England was God's 'elect nation', superior to the enslaved Papists of the Continent and entirely independent of all authority apart from that of the Crown (278). That was the theory of English and later of British nationhood which was to prevail from then onwards until the 1970s, when membership of the European Community once more subjected the country to the decisions of an external authority.

The Reformation, which enhanced the position of the Crown within the newly proclaimed English nation state, also helped to increase the role and status of Parliament within the polity. During the 1530s Parliament played an essential role in the enforcement of the Reformation, and from 1549 onwards it authorized as well as enforced doctrinal changes in the Church, a situation which led to important conflicts between Crown and Parliament in the late sixteenth and early seventeenth centuries. At the same time its composition and the relative relationships of its constituent parts underwent important modifications. In the early years of the sixteenth century, during the reign of Henry VII, bishops and abbots had outnumbered secular peers in the Lords. By the Reformation Parliament the situation had changed; there were then fifty ecclesiastical and fifty-seven secular lords – a rough balance (114). The dissolution of the monasteries, however, removed the twenty-nine abbots from the Upper House, leaving the lords spiritual in a very definite minority. This has been the position in the House of Lords ever since and it is particularly ironic that the decisive change occurred just before Parliament as a whole began to assume control in matters of doctrine. The dominance of the Crown and laity over the English national church from the sixteenth century onwards owes much, therefore, to the changes in the composition of the Upper House which took place during the 1530s, Just at the time that the membership of the Lords was fundamentally modified, its status *vis-à-vis* the Commons was also changed. By 1500 the assent of the Lower House was necessary for the making of new laws, but at the beginning of the sixteenth century bills originating in Lords and Commons were still treated in different ways in order to emphasize the continuing superior status of the Upper House. It was only during the 1530s that this situation was changed with the Commons being treated for the first time as completely equal partners with the Lords in the legislative process. During that decade, too, the Crown, which had previously stood outside Parliament, became an integral part of the body, thus creating the situation which has prevailed since then, with supreme legislative authority over the English or British nation state being wielded by a 'mixed' sovereign body of

King in Parliament. During the 1530s the legislation which Parliament passed also underwent a transformation. Acts became much longer and more numerous and began to deal with new matters of profound importance; the ecclesiastical changes of the Reformation. One aspect of the differences is revealed by noting that in the printed *Statutes of the Realm* all extant legislation from Magna Carta until 1509, a period of 294 years, fills 1,092 pages, while the laws of Henry VIII's reign, which occupied 37 years, fill almost as much space, 1,032 pages (52, vol. 2).

If the Reformation significantly enhanced the status of both Crown and Parliament, it drastically weakened the Church as an institution. Before the 1530s the Church in England had been part of the vast entity of Catholic Christendom with its own legislative authority independent of that of Crown and Parliament and subject in theory to a foreign monarch, the Pope. After 1540 it was firmly subordinated to the lay authority of Crown and Parliament and severed from the international Catholic institutions to which it had owed allegiance for hundreds of years. At the same time the 'plunder of the Church' by the laity proceeded apace. The seizure of its monastic and chantry and much of its episcopal property from the 1530s onwards meant that by the accession of Elizabeth the Church's wealth must have been reduced to about one-third of its pre-1529 levels. This enormous change in its material position was paralleled by the destruction of its entire monastic establishment and the disappearance of thousands of regular clergy. Moreover, the much poorer post-Reformation Church paid substantially larger sums in taxation to the Crown than its pre-Reformation predecessor had ever paid to Pope and King together. Professor Scarisbrick has calculated that between 1485 and 1534 the Church paid in all an average of about £17,300 per annum in taxation, with £4,800 going to the Pope and £12,500 to the King. Between 1535 and 1547, on the other hand, the average yielded by clerical taxation was about £47,000 a year, all of it, of course, going to the Crown (171). In view of these figures and of the property losses already noticed it is not surprising that Scarisbrick concludes that the Reformation was a 'fiscal catastrophe' for the English Church (171, 53).

As a result of the Reformation, too, England's position in Europe was greatly changed. Pre-Reformation England, despite the notorious xenophobia of many of its inhabitants, saw itself essentially as a constituent part of Catholic Europe. The Henrician schism, as we have seen, significantly affected the country's relations with Catholic rulers like Charles V and by the later sixteenth century the Elizabethan nation state, under the considerable influence of Foxeian propaganda, saw itself as basically different from and superior to a still largely Catholic Continent. Stark words of comparison may exaggerate the contrast between pre-1529 and post-1558 attitudes, and Elizabeth herself was certainly no Protestant crusader, but there can be no doubt that the change in England's international outlook between the 1530s and 1560s was profound and lasting. After 1558 England was the principal Protestant power in Europe and this gave her a role which she could never entirely ignore or neglect.

The important long-term effects of the Reformation on England's international relations were, it can be argued, matched by its long-term consequences for England's socio-political development. It is true that the sales of church property

between the 1530s and 1550s did not lead to a revolution in the structure of society-
the bulk of the lands went to already established families – but this huge transfer
of wealth led to a relative weakening of the economic position of both Church
and Crown relative to that of the upper reaches of landed society, especially the
gentry. Further land sales during the Elizabethan and early Stuart periods
continued and enhanced the trend and it has been argued by both contemporary
and later commentators that there were significant links between this fundamental
shift in economic power and the political upheavals of the mid-seventeenth
century (214; 215). Whatever the truth of that idea, the Reformation gave the
nobility, gentry and yeomen who had purchased former monastic and chantry
lands a vested interest in the changes of these years which no doctrinal reaction
could hope to undo. Mary secured a formal return to Rome with relative ease in
1554–55, but she did so only because she struck a bargain with the landed classes.
Their material gains in land were safeguarded by Act of Parliament (1 & 2 Philip
and Mary, c. 8), and even the Queen, who bitterly disliked the bargain, was
forced to accept that without it there was no chance of Parliament, that citadel
of noble and gentry power, accepting once more the authority of the Papacy.

The Crown's acquisition of ecclesiastical revenues and property during the
1530s and the subsequent sale of much of the former monastic land on the basis
of feudal tenures necessitated the creation of new administrative and judicial institutions like the Courts of Augmentations, First Fruits, and Wards. These changes,
together with reforms in the Privy Council and the secretaryship, have been seen
by Professor Elton as the centre pieces of an 'administrative revolution' (91).
(Professor Elton restates his views most recently and most moderately in (25,
211 ff).) Medieval administration, he argues, was essentially 'household' administration, a governmental system where the mainsprings of administrative action
were to be found in the royal household. Modern administration, on the other
hand, which was introduced by the changes of the 1530s, was fundamentally
'bureaucratic', dominated by great institutions of State capable of carrying on the
government of the country to a large extent independently of the monarch. This
theory has provoked considerable discussion,[1] but there is still no general agreement about its validity. Recent research has, as we have seen, shown that the
Privy Council, following the Cromwellian reforms of the 1530s, did continue to
supervise the general administration of the country with a good deal of efficiency
during the troubled middle decades of the century (Chs. 9 and 10), but it is also
clear that by 1550 the financial institutions which had been created or inspired by
Cromwell were not doing their work satisfactorily, a situation recognized by the
Royal Commission of 1552 and the restoration of Exchequer supremacy two years
later. That latter reform, despite the fact that it introduced improved administrative methods into the Exchequer machinery, can be regarded as in one sense
a return to a traditional medieval system where the Exchequer controlled the
bulk of the royal revenue. Medievalists, in fact, have been unhappy with descriptions of medieval administration as essentially 'household' government, and there
is no doubt that Elizabethan government was a good deal less formal and
contained *more* 'household' elements than Elton's interpretation would seem to
allow (see Ch. 13). It does, therefore, seem dangerous to argue that there was

a revolution in administrative methods during the 1530s, especially in view of recent discoveries about the considerable governmental importance of an indubitably 'household' institution, the King's Privy Chamber, during that decade[2] and the absence of any fundamental reforms in local government where the dominant role of unpaid JPs continued.

It can indeed be argued that the union with Wales and the virtual abolition of sanctuaries and franchises during the 1530s were much more drastic breaks with the past than the administrative changes at the centre. They formed a part of Cromwell's grandiose scheme to subject all outlying parts of the realm to royal authority in a uniform way. This concept of direct governmental control of the whole of the State's territory through uniform law and practice was not fully realized under Cromwell, but he did make great strides towards its accomplishment. It is surely for *that* concept and for his practical role in the creation of a powerful Privy Council and secretaryship rather than for any imagined 'bureaucratization' of the central government machinery that Cromwell the administrator deserves to be remembered. If the 1530s did not witness a decisive shift from 'household' to 'bureaucratic' methods of government, the decade did, however, see an important stage in the 'secularization' of administration. That process had been going on for some time, made possible by the spread of education among the laity during the later Middle Ages, but it received a notable impetus at the time of the Reformation. Before 1530 many of the most notable governmental offices were still dominated by clerics; from the 1530s onwards, as examination of the lists of Lord Chancellors, Keepers of the Privy Seal, and King's Secretaries shows, they were almost entirely occupied by laymen.

One of the most important tasks of the lay councillors who increasingly controlled the administration from the later years of Henry VIII's reign onwards was the raising of taxation, and it has been suggested that here too the 1530s saw a fundamental break with the past, with the establishment by Thomas Cromwell in the Subsidy Acts of 1534 and 1540 of a 'new principle' of taxation by which Parliament granted supply to the Crown not, as had been traditional, for war or the defence of the realm, but for the ordinary peacetime expenses of government. This according to Professor Elton was Cromwell's 'most revolutionary achievement of all' and he argues that the principle was maintained throughout the rest of the Tudor period.[3] It must be said at once that if any such new principle *was* established it did not make the Crown rich – witness the notorious and necessary parsimony and economy of Elizabethan government – but it seems unlikely in fact that any such idea was introduced. Careful analysis of the Subsidy Acts of Edward's, Mary's and Elizabeth's reigns suggests rather that, although grants certainly were made in peacetime, these were always for extraordinary purposes, usually defence, and never for ordinary expenses.[4] Indeed, it seems likely that the traditional medieval idea that the King should 'live of his own', only turning to Parliament for help in time of emergency, was maintained throughout most of the early modern period, only coming to an end, as Professor Chandaman has argued, after the revolution of 1688.[5]

If some historians are doubtful of ideas about revolutions in taxation and administrative methods during the early Tudor period, it seems likely that an increasing number of them will lay emphasis in the years ahead on the important legal developments of the period. These, according to their historian, Dr J. H. Baker, constituted a 'legal revolution', and although much work remains to be done upon their causes it is already clear that they were of fundamental import-ance for the whole later course of the common law (131; 132; 134). Much of the story can only be told in terms of highly technical procedural changes and a full account would require a survey of the whole field of the common law, in both its civil and criminal aspects. It is the tale of 'a quiet reformation from within. What in the Church had called for fire and steel was achieved in the law by wit and stealth; for the new law of the renaissance period was made not by flouting the old learning, but by sneaking round it.' (134, *163*) Here we can touch, and then superficially, on only two of the most important aspects of the changes, those in the land law, which altered it 'almost beyond recognition' (132, *3*), and those in the work and relative importance of the central courts.

Land in medieval and early modern England was the fundamental source of wealth, prestige and power, and the land law, governing all aspects of its pos-session and control, was therefore of fundamental political, and social as well as legal importance.[6] By 1500 English feudalism as an effective military system was long since dead, but the traditional tenures were maintained, with all land being held by its possessor of a superior lord and ultimately therefore of the King himself. On the death of a tenant his heir was theoretically supposed to pay a series of dues to his overlord, and the greatest burdens of all fell on the King's own tenants-in-chief, who held land immediately of the Crown. By 1500, however, lawyers had elaborated a system which enabled tenants, through employment of the 'use' [N] to hand over property to their successors without the need to pay these burdensome death duties. The essence of the use was that the tenant conveyed his land to trustees who held it on his behalf and adminis-tered it according to his instructions. As common law land could not be disposed of by will, no such provisions had to be made during the tenant's lifetime. Once they had been made, however, he could in practice order the trustees to dispose of the land as he thought best. He could thus provide for younger sons and distant relatives who would not have inherited anything under normal feudal rules and he *could* do so in his will; the point was that the land in theory remained with the trustees, it was only the *use* which passed to others on the tenant's death. This system obviously made for social flexibility and by 1500 most of the land of England was held in use. The disadvantage of this from the Crown's point of view was that it deprived the King of his feudal revenues; as long as the number of trustees was maintained the legal 'tenant' of the lands never died and therefore the Crown never benefited. In 1532 Henry VIII laid before Parliament a scheme by which he would obtain feudal revenues once more, but only from part of the land in question. This compromise was rejected by the Commons, but in 1535 the King obtained a verdict from the common law judges that uses were illegal. Armed with this judgement he forced the Statute Uses (27 Henry VIII, c. 10) through Parliament in 1536. He agreed that uses made before 1536 should remain valid, but in return the statute vested the legal title to the land in the beneficiary of the use. The statute gave the Crown effective feudal rights over *all* the lands of tenants-in-chief and was a great financial success, but by abolishing the practical power of tenants to devise land by will it enforced complusory primogeniture in future, thus making for a more rigid society. The obvious dissatisfaction of the landed classes, expressed strongly by some of them in the Pilgrimage of Grace, led to the Statute of Wills of 1540. (32 Henry VIII, c. 1) This gave the Crown feudal rights over only one-third of a tenant's lands and provided that tenants might leave the other two-thirds by will. The statute, therefore, gave tenants for the first time the clear right to dispose of freehold land by will, and thus marked the end of an epoch in the history of the land law. Despite its relative moderation it left the Crown with a considerable revenue and patronage from 'fiscal feudalism' (101). It also, together with the Statute of Uses, introduced new complications into the land law which were 'perhaps the worst legacy of the sixteenth-century legal revolution' (131, *241*) and led to bitter complaints from landowners up to at least the time of Oliver Cromwell.

The Statutes of Uses and Wills were relatively striking landmarks in the legal changes of the period. Just as important, if less dramatic, were the changes which took place in the work of the central courts. There was a great increase in their business at the expense of ecclesiastical and local courts, new courts such as Star Chamber and Requests rose to prominence, and the relationship of the two main common law courts, King's Bench and Common Pleas, underwent important modifications. During the fifteenth century the business of King's Bench and Common Pleas suffered at the expense of Chancery which offered litigants the advantages of speedier and more effective procedures. The greatest threat was to King's Bench which heard a much smaller proportion of cases than Common Pleas, and it became clear that if it was to justify its continued existence it would have to offer litigants and the lawyers who advised them improved remedies and procedures. It did this between about 1490 and 1550. The chief procedural advantage of Chancery was its use of bills, which enabled plaintiffs to begin cases without the delays and inconveniences involved in the employment of writs. King's Bench began to use procedure by bill before 1500, but it only became firmly established during the early sixteenth century when the court also made many important innovations in substantive law. As a result the decline in its business was halted during the 1530s and there was an impressive expansion in its work from the 1540s onwards. Common Pleas, with perhaps ten times as many cases as King's Bench at the beginning of the century, took a much more conservative stance than the latter court with regard to new remedies and procedures. As a result, although it did not lose business in absolute terms, it gained little of the vast increase in litigation which took place during the Tudor period. Much of that flooded into King's Bench from the mid-sixteenth century onwards, despite the fact that the bulk of it concerned matters, such as actions for debt, which had traditionally been reserved for Common Pleas. The long-term result of this encroachment of King's Bench on Common Pleas business, an encroachment in which the third central common law court, the Exchequer, joined in a major way during the seventeenth century, was to make most of the traditional business of Common Pleas triable in each of the major courts. King's Bench continued to have most success in attracting cases, and by the beginning of the eighteenth century, having by then engrossed most of its rivals' litigation, it dominated the judicial scene.

The changing legal framework upon which we have touched is one of the less familiar aspects of the new English polity, the 'nation state' which emerged during the early sixteenth century. That was an entity which was a good deal stronger than historians have sometimes supposed. The years 1529–58 were a period of unprecedented economic, religious and political change but, as we have seen, attempts to describe the 1540s and 1550s as a time of continuous crisis for the State are unhelpful. This conclusion, broadly confirmed at local level by Mr Clark in his important study of Kent (251), is given added weight by the relative ease with which, in the years immediately after 1558, Elizabeth established the regime which was to guide England through 'a long period of relative stability. It is evident, in fact, that beneath the more dramatic upheavals in society and govern-ment which marked the period 1540–58 the administration of the country went on in a much more effective way than has traditionally been supposed. The Privy Council, in particular, despite the political rivalries among its members, was an efficient administrative machine, the vital link between the centre of government and the localities. This tradition of relatively effective administration – with a brief but important hiatus under Somerset – clearly owed much to Cromwell's work. He may not have introduced a revolution in administrative methods, but this is not to deny that his reforms contributed fundamentally to the underlying stability which is one of the notable features of the English State during this period of dramatic change.

The relatively strong English State of the period might, however, have been stronger still if Henry VIII and Somerset had not pursued foreign policies which were so expensive that they necessitated the transfer of the bulk of the church lands acquired by the Crown at the Reformation to the aristocracy, the yeomanry and above all the gentry. The result was greatly to strengthen the upper reaches of secular landed society as a whole within the State. Members of the gentry class especially, who acquired most of the lands, also obtained the revenue and the potential political influence which went with them. The alienation by the Crown of so much land during the wars of the 1540s surely makes that decade of decisive importance in the evolution of the English monarchy and indeed of the English constitution and English society as a whole. If Henry VIII had been able to retain and pass on to his successors the bulk of the landed resources which he had won in the 1530s the whole future development of England might have been very different; it could have resulted in a seventeenth-century English monarchy much closer to the absolutist systems of the Continent than the Jacobean and Caroline regimes which actually emerged. This, of course, is speculation, but it is one of the great 'might have beens' of English history. Henry's squandering of his newly acquired resources during the disastrous wars of his later years, a process continued by the needs of Somerset's Scottish policy, ensured that such a devel-opment was unlikely if not completely impossible. By Mary's reign it was clear that the English State, even with good financial management, could not afford war (29).

The Reformation, then, brought only short-term financial benefits to the

Crown and it is likely that there was no dramatic change during the early sixteenth century either in administrative methods or in the principles on which Parliament granted direct taxation but, despite these caveats, it is surely right to see the period 1529 to 1558 as a 'revolutionary era': the number and importance of the changes which did take place during these thirty or so years makes it difficult to deny the validity of such a verdict. The Church lost its independent institutional existence and well over half its wealth; the Crown acquired greatly enhanced dignity and considerable long-term problems by its assumption of ecclesiastical supremacy; Parliament, substantially altered in composition by the exclusion of the abbots from the Upper House, increased its prestige and authority by first enforcing and then authorizing new doctrine for the Church; an English 'nation state', independent of all external authority, was proclaimed; the upper ranks of landed society substantially enhanced their wealth and potential political power; England's relations with and attitude towards the Continent were considerably modified; there was significant progress in ensuring that royal authority was dispensed uniformly throughout the realm in accordance with a common code of law; and developments in legal procedures and substantive law took place which were to transform the common law in the years ahead.

It has been suggested that there was yet another revolutionary change – or at least an attempt at one – besides those which we have already considered; that the reign of Henry VIII saw the effort to create a 'Tudor despotism'. Henry and Cromwell, buttressed by the new royal authority over the Church, tried, it is argued, to reject traditional restrictions on the monarchy's secular authority and create an absolutism untrammelled by law.[7] This seems on the face of it to be a strange argument when it is remembered that leading contemporary authorities were unanimous that the King was subject to the law; that the law could only be changed with the consent of the Lords and Commons, expressed in Parliament; and that that consent could never be taken for granted: the Henrician period contains many examples of determined and sometimes successful opposition to the Crown in Parliament (see, e.g. (114)). This might seem to indicate that the idea of Tudor despotism should immediately be dismissed. The issue, however, is less simple than that: laws could only be effective safeguards against despotism if they were generally obeyed by the Crown. But here, too, there is scant comfort for supporters of the concept of despotism; in his detailed study of the operation of government policy during the 1530s Professor Elton has demonstrated in great detail the almost painful adherence of the Cromwellian regime to the letter of the law (92). A much more difficult point remains. Were some of the laws, even though passed with the consent of Parliament, so blatantly dangerous and unjust that they raised the possibility or even the reality of despotic rule? Relevant here are the Proclamations Act of 1539 [E.1(4)] and the treason legislation and Acts of Attainder [N] of the reign.

In a recent full discussion of the Proclamations Act, Professor Heinze has shown beyond much doubt that it cannot legitimately be regarded as an instrument of despotism (93), but the treason legislation (135) and Acts of Attainder[8] were harsh – even savage – measures with tyrannical implications. The cruel destruction of the London Carthusians, members of the most saintly of all the religious orders, under the 1534 Treason Act (26 Henry VIII, c. 13) was 'the biggest blot on the record of Henry and Cromwell' (*25, 193*). Acts of Attainder, though clearly *legal* in the sense that they reflected the supremacy of statute, were equally clearly *unjust* – many of the victims were innocent of the charges, were denied due process at common law and were condemned unheard. Such facts cannot be denied. It must be remembered as well, however, that Henry and Cromwell were trying to enforce a revolution – the Reformation – and in a revolutionary situation harsh measures are often necessary. Also, the policy was enforced through the normal institutions of government, controlled by members of the political nation, the aristocracy and gentry, who themselves provided many of the victims of the attainders of the reign. Henry depended for the success of his rule on the general co-operation and obedience of the gentry class as a whole: with no standing army, no effective police force and no large, paid bureaucracy in the localities he had no machinery for enforcing a despotic rule upon the political nation. Without the voluntary assistance of the local governors administration in the localities would simply have collapsed. Henry retained the loyalty of the vast majority of the gentlemen of England even while he unjustly condemned a small minority of their fellows to the cruel death reserved for traitors.

There is no doubt, then, that the regime of Henry and Cromwell, men engaged in carrying through a revolution, was harsh. In the case of a number of individuals, such as the Carthusians and the political victims of Acts of Attainder, it was cruel, arbitrary and tyrannical. On the other hand, it never approached a general despotism. There was always a very high regard for the letter of the law and Cromwell and the King, even if they had wished to establish arbitrary rule throughout the country (and there is little evidence that they did), had no machinery to enforce such a tyranny.

---

1. See most notably the debate between Drs G. L. Harriss and P. Williams on the one hand and Professor Elton on the other in *P & P*, **25** (July 1963), **29** (Dec. 1964), 31 (July 1965), and **32** (Dec. 1965).
2. D. R. Starkey, 'The King's Privy Chamber, 1485–1547' (Cambridge University Ph.D. thesis, 1973).
3. G. R. Elton 'Taxation for war and peace in early Tudor England', *War and Economic Development*, ed. J. M. Winter (1975), pp. 33 ff.
4. G. L. Harriss, 'Thomas Cromwell's "new principle" of taxation', *EHR*, **93** (1978), 721 ff.
5. C. D. Chandaman, *The English Public Revenue 1660–1688* (Oxford, 1975), p. 2.
6. See A. W. B. Simpson, *An Introduction to the History of the Land Law* (1961).
7. The latest statement of this view is J. Hurstfield's 'Was there a Tudor Despotism after all?', *TRHS*, 5th ser., 17 (1967). It is convincingly rejected in G. R. Elton, *Studies in Tudor and Stuart Government and Politics*, vol. I, pp. 260 ff.
8. S. E. Lehmberg, 'Parliamentary attainder in the reign of Henry VIII', *HJ*, **18** (1975), 675 ff.

An age of conservatism: The Elizabethan achievement, 1558–1585

PART TWO

1558 Loss of Calais (Jan.). Parliament meets (Jan–Mar): militia system reformed by two statutes; one subsidy voted. Deaths of Mary and Pole (Nov), Elizabeth ascends the throne. Sir William Cecil becomes Secretary of State and the Queen's principal adviser; Sir Nicholas Bacon, Lord Keeper of the Great Seal; Winchester retained as Lord Treasurer.

 New Book of Rates (May): impositions on goods entering or leaving the country made on the sole authority of the Crown. Epidemics continue.

 John Knox's *First Blast of the Trumpet Against the Monstrous Regiment of Women*.

1559 Parliament meets (Jan–May): Acts of Supremacy and Uniformity – Queen 'Supreme Governor' of the Church; liturgical settlement founded on 1552 Prayer Book.

 Philip II offers to marry Elizabeth and is refused (Feb). Peace with France in the spring by the Treaty of Câteau-Cambrésis: effective surrender of Calais to the French. Protestant revolt in Scotland against the Queen Regent, Mary of Guise (May). Death of Henry II of France (July), accession of Francis II, husband of Mary Queen of Scots.

 Deprivation of the Catholic bishops in England; also of a limited number of lower clergy (*c*. 300). Matthew Parker archbishop of Canterbury (July). Royal injunctions to the clergy: a Bible to be available in every church; priests once more permitted to marry (but on royal, not on statutory authority).

1560 Robert Dudley in dominant position at English Court as Queen Elizabeth's favourite (Aug.); death of Amy Robsart, Dudley's wife, in mysterious circumstances (Sept). Irish Parliament imposes the Royal Supremacy and the Book of Common Prayer in Ireland.

 England sends naval and military help to the Scots rebels (Treaty of Berwick, Feb); French troops withdraw from Scotland (Treaty of Edinburgh, July); papal jurisdiction and the mass abolished in Scotland (Aug).

 Death of Francis II of France, husband of Mary Queen of Scots (Dec), accession to French throne of Charles IX.

 Recoinage of 1560–61 begins (Dec).

 Geneva Bible published in English translation – note its Calvinist tone and its cheapness. Westminster School founded.

1561 Lady Catherine Grey, a possible claimant to the succession, sent to the Tower for marrying without the Queen's consent (Aug). Ambrose Dudley, the favourite's elder brother, created earl of Warwick.

 Negotiations for a possible marriage between Elizabeth and King Eric of Sweden. Return of the widowed Mary Queen of Scots from France to Scotland (Aug); Elizabeth refuses her passage over English soil.

 Steeple of Old St Paul's in London burnt down.

 Recoinage completed (Oct).

 Gorboduc, the first English tragedy in blank verse, performed; Sir Thomas Hoby translates *The Courtier* by Castiglione.

1562 Elizabeth plans and then cancels a journey to York to meet Mary, Queen of Scots (summer). Elizabeth catches smallpox and almost dies (Oct) – no agreement on the succession among privy councillors. Robert Dudley admitted to the Privy Council (Oct).

England intervenes (Oct) in the first of the French religious wars on the Protestant side.

John Hawkins' first voyage to the West Indies carrying slaves from West Africa to the Spanish colonies.

Jewel's *Apology*.

1563   Parliament meets (Jan–Apr): differences over the succession issue between Queen and Parliament; Statute of Artificers regulates conditions of employment of the mass of the population in great detail; Beggars Act introduces element of compulsion in the collection of funds for poor relief; 'Cecil's fast' introduced by an Act which made Wednesdays as well as Fridays 'fish days' – Act repealed in 1585; Act ordering the translation of the Bible and Book of Common Prayer into Welsh.

The Thirty-nine Articles (a revision of the Forty-two Articles of 1553) approved by Convocation as the doctrinal foundation of the English Church; a set of Puritan measures – including provisions for a considerable simplification of church ritual – narrowly defeated in Convocation.

Severe outbreaks of plague in London and other parts of England.

John Foxe's *Acts and Monuments* published. Byrd appointed organist at Lincoln cathedral.

1564   Robert Dudley created earl of Leicester; discussions about a possible marriage between Leicester and Mary Queen of Scots; reports of a possible marriage between Mary Queen of Scots and Henry, Lord Darnley.

Treaty of Troyes with France (Apr) – English claims to Calais formally renounced; peace restored between the two countries.

Hawkins's second voyage to the West Indies.

Birth of William Shakespeare (Apr).

1565   Darnley travels to Scotland (Feb); marriage of Darnley and Mary, Queen of Scots (July); growing resentment by Darnley of the influence of Mary's favourite, David Riccio. Beginning of the deputyship of Sir Henry Sidney in Ireland.

Elizabeth orders an inquiry into vestiarian practice in the Church (Jan): this reveals wide differences.

1566   Parliament meets (Sept, and continues until Jan 1567): differences over the succession issue between the Queen and Parliament; Parliment asks the Queen to marry; notable series of Puritan bills in the House of Commons; Elizabeth refuses to allow Parliament to give statutory confirmation to the Thirty-nine Articles.

Murder of David Riccio (Mar); birth of Prince James of Scotland (June).

Parker's *Advertisements* (March) prescribe the wearing of the surplice at church services; this leads to the intensification of the 'vestiarian controversy'.

1567   Murder of Darnley (Feb); subsequent marriage of Mary Queen of Scots to James, earl of Bothwell (May); Mary defeated by Scottish opposition lords at Carberry Hill (June) and imprisoned; abdication of Mary Queen of Scots (July) and accession of James VI to the Scottish throne at the age of one year – James Stuart, earl of Moray, becomes regent.

Arrival of the duke of Alba with a Spanish army in the Netherlands (Aug).

Hawkins, accompanied by Francis Drake, sails on his third voyage to the West Indies (Oct).

Foundation of Rugby School.

1568   Death of Lady Catherine Grey (Jan). Mary Queen of Scots escapes from captivity, repudiates her abdication and is defeated by the Regent Moray at Langside (May). Mary flees to England (May). Investigations into Mary's conduct in Scotland undertaken in England (Oct–Dec).

Incident at San Juan de Ullua during the course of Hawkins's third voyage to the West Indies (Sept). Elizabeth seizes Genoese bullion designed to pay Alba's troops in the Netherlands (Dec) – worsening relations between Spain and England.

Seminary to train English Catholic priests founded at Douai in the Netherlands by Father William Allen.

First Welsh Eisteddfod held.

1569   Plot to marry Mary Queen of Scots to the duke of Norfolk (spring); Norfolk–Leicester conspiracy against Cecil; Norfolk arrested and sent to the Tower (Oct); earls of Northumberland and Westmorland ordered to London, refuse and rise in revolt – the 'rebellion of the Northern Earls' (Oct): rebellion collapses (Dec). Fitzmaurice revolt in Ireland (1569–73) begins.

Return of Hawkins and Drake to England (Jan).

1570   Revolt and defeat of Leonard Dacre in northern England (Feb). Norfolk released from the Tower (Aug).

Assassination of the Regent Moray in Scotland (Jan). Negotiations between France and England for a possible marriage between Elizabeth and Henry, duke of Anjou, later Henry III.

Pius V issues the bull *Regnans in Excelsis* excommunicating and deposing Elizabeth (Feb); John Felton publishes the bull in England and is later (Aug) executed for high treason. Thomas Cartwright extolls Presbyterianism in his lectures on the Acts of the Apostles at Cambridge.

R. Ascham's *Schoolmaster*.

1571   William Cecil created Lord Burghley (Feb). The Ridolfi Plot, involving the deposition of Elizabeth with Spanish aid: Norfolk involved. Norfolk arrested once more following his involvement in the Ridolfi Plot (Sept).

Parliament meets (Apr–May): difficulties between Elizabeth and Parliament over the issue of the succession (Mary, Queen of Scots' position involved); 'Strickland's Bill' in Parliament seeks to amend the Prayer Book in a radical direction; an Act makes it high treason to bring papal bulls into England; statutory confirmation given to the Thirty-nine Articles; Treasons Act makes it high treason to deny the Royal Supremacy or call the Queen a heretic; statute allowing interest of up to 10 per cent on loans.

Ecclesiastical canons provide a disciplinary basis for the Church of England.

Foundation of Jesus College, Oxford, and of Harrow School.

1572   Norfolk condemned to death (Jan) and executed (June) for his part in the Ridolfi Plot. Death of Lord Treasurer Winchester (Mar), Burghley appointed to the treasurership (July). Parliament meets (May–June): further difficulties between Queen and Parliament over the succession, once again involving the issue of Mary Queen of Scots; Poor Relief Act provides important definition of vagrancy and introduces national poor rate system to support deserving poor.

Treaty of Blois with France (Apr) – defensive alliance between France and England (the 'diplomatic revolution' of 1572). Massacre of St Bartholomew in France: murder of thousands of Huguenots (Aug). The eighteen-year-old duke of Alençon, Anjou's younger brother, succeeds him as suitor to the thirty-nine-year-old Elizabeth.

Expedition by Francis Drake to seize Spanish treasure in the New World (May).

Presbyterian *Admonition to the Parliament*; M. Parker, *De Antiquitate Britannicae Ecclesiae*. Foundation of the Society of Antiquaries.

1573   Sir Francis Walsingham appointed Secretary of State (Dec). Creation of the 'trained bands': specially armed and trained elements of the militia.

Fall of Edinburgh Castle, in the hands of Mary Queen of Scots' partisans, to a combined Anglo-Scottish force (May); Protestant party under the Regent Morton dominant in Scotland.

Renewal of trade between England and Spain following the interruption after 1568.

John Whitgift's *Answer to the Admonition*. Birth of William Laud (Oct).

1574   Convention of Bristol between England and Spain (Aug) – settlement of Anglo-Spanish claims and counter-claims following the English seizure of the Genoese treasure in December 1568. Death of Charles IX of France, accession of Henry III (previously duke of Anjou). Bernardino de Mendoza arrives in England as Spanish ambassador (July).

First Catholic seminary priests from abroad come to England.

Walter Travers' *Full and Plain Declaration of Ecclesiastical Discipline*, the Presbyterians favoured replacement for the Prayer Book, published.

1575   Death of Matthew Parker (May); Edmund Grindal archbishop of Canterbury (Dec). Two Dutch Anabaptists burnt at Smithfield (July).

William Byrd and Thomas Tallis, *Cantiones Sacrae*; Christopher Saxton's *County Atlas of England and Wales*; Archbishop Parker leaves his great collection of manuscripts to Corpus Christi College, Cambridge. Birth of Lionel Cranfield (Mar).

1576   Parliament meets (Feb–Mar): notable parliamentary speech by Peter Wentworth on the issue of freedom of speech, Wentworth imprisoned in the Tower by order of the House for his remarks about the Queen (Feb); Elizabeth remits the sentence (Mar); Poor Relief Act – stocks of raw materials to be provided throughout the country to give work to the unemployed.

Grindal, ordered by the Queen to suppress the prophesyings, refuses in a famous letter (Dec). Ecclesiastical canons issued.

First of three voyages of Martin Frobisher in search of a north-west passage to China.

William Lambarde's *Perambulation of Kent*; Humphrey Gilbert's *Discourse to Prove a North-West Passage*. Shoreditch Theatre built.

1577   Grindal suspended (June); John Aylmer, an opponent of Puritanism, appointed bishop of London; John Whitgift becomes bishop of Worcester.

Drake begins his circumnavigation of the world (Nov); second voyage of Frobisher in search of a north-west passage.

R. Holinshed, *Chronicles*; W. Harrison, *Description of England*. The Curtain Theatre in London opened.

1578   Secret marriage of Leicester to Lettice Knollys (Sept). John Hawkins appointed Treasurer of the Navy.

James VI of Scotland nominally assumes the reins of government (Mar). Alexander Farnese, duke of Parma, appointed Governor of the Netherlands by Philip II (Oct). Revival of marriage negotiations between Elizabeth and Alençon (now duke of Anjou).

English College removed from Douai to Rheims.

Third voyage of Frobisher in search of a north-west passage.

John Lyly, *Euphues*; *Leicester's Commonwealth*, a savage attack on Elizabeth's favourite, published.

1579   A major Irish rebellion (the Desmond rebellion of 1579–83) begins. Alençon visits England to undertake a personal courtship of Elizabeth (Aug); the Privy Council advises the Queen against the proposed marriage (Oct).

An English College founded at Rome under the supervision of the Jesuits. Eastland Company formed for trade with the Baltic.

Plowden's *Law Reports*; Spenser's *Shepherds Calendar*; John Stubbe's *Gaping Gulf* – a fierce attack on the Alençon marriage proposal. Stubbe sentenced to have his right hand amputated.

1580   Philip II of Spain inherits Portugal and its empire. Negotiations for Alencon marriage continue.

Arrival in England of Fathers Campion and Parsons, the first Jesuits to reach the country (June).

Drake returns to England after completing his circumnavigation (Sept). Voyage of Arthur Pett and Charles Jackman in search of a north-east passage to China. First treaty between England and the Ottoman Empire.

J. Stow, *The Chronicles of England* (*Annals* in later editions).

1581   Parliament meets (Jan–Mar): recusancy fines raised to £20 a month.

Alençon pays a second visit to England (Nov).

Arrest of Campion (July); Campion executed (Nov).

Francis Drake knighted by the Queen (Apr). Foundation of the Levant Company.

Publication of William Lambarde's *Eirenarcha*; Richard Mulcaster's *Positions*, a notable treatise on education, urges the education of girls.

1582   Alençon leaves England (Feb) – effective end of the marriage negotiations between him and Elizabeth.

Philip II's general, Parma, begins the conquest of Flanders and Brabant. Graduated pay, according to rank, introduced into the Royal Navy.

London's first waterworks established. Edinburgh University founded.

1583   The Throckmorton Plot: Catholic plot for the deposition of Elizabeth with foreign aid; Throckmorton arrested (Oct).

Death of Grindal (July); John Whitgift archbishop of Canterbury (Aug). Whitgift demands subscription to his 'three articles'.

Sir Humphrey Gilbert's voyage to the New World: he annexes Newfoundland, but leaves no colonists; Gilbert drowned on return voyage.

Burghley's *Execution of Justice in England*, justifies the death penalty for Catholic priests; T. Smith, *De Republica Anglorum*, the classic contemporary account of the Elizabethan Constitution. The Queen's Players formed by Sir Edmund Tilney, Master of the Revels.

1584   The Spanish ambassador, Mendoza, expelled for complicity in the Throckmorton plot (Jan); execution of Throckmorton (July). Parliament meets (Nov, and continues until Mar 1585): differences between the Queen and Parliament over the succession, involving the issue of Mary Queen of Scots.

Death of the duke of Alençon-Anjou (June); the Protestant Henry of Navarre becomes heir to the French throne. Assassination of William of Orange (July). Treaty of Joinville between Spain and the French Catholic League (Dec): an alliance to prevent the succession of Henry of Navarre to the French throne.

Whitgift accepts qualified subscription to his 'three articles': Whitgift's actions in 1583–84 lead to the 'grand design' of Field and others to create a secret Presbyterian Church within the Church of England.

Ralegh sends a fleet to the New World; it lands in what later became Virginia.

William Allen's *True, Sincere and Modest Defence of English Catholics*, a reply to Burghley's *Execution of Justice*.

Reginald Scot's *Discovery of Witchcraft*. Emmanuel College, Cambridge, founded by Sir Walter Mildmay.

1585   Catholic League dominant in France; the duke of Parma makes substantial military advances against the Dutch rebels; Treaty of Nonsuch (Aug): Elizabeth promises military aid to the Dutch rebels; English expedition to the Netherlands under Leicester (Dec) – beginning of war between England and Spain.

Parliament of November 1584 continues until March: Act against Jesuits and seminary priests.

First English colony founded in Virginia; foundation of Barbary Company to trade with North Africa; first of three voyages (1585–87) of John Davis in search of a north-west passage; Drake sets out on a plundering voyage against the Spanish West Indies (Sept).

CHAPTER 12

The establishment of the Elizabethan Regime: the settlements in England and Scotland, 1558–1563

It is both fashionable and just to stress the difficulties which had made Mary an embittered woman when she came to the throne in 1553. It is less fashionable but equally just to point out that Elizabeth had had a scarcely less difficult early life before her accession in 1558. She was bastardized before she was three, following the annulment of her mother's marriage to Henry VIII in 1536, and the stigma was not removed when she was put into the line of succession in 1543 failing direct heirs to both Edward and Mary (35 Henry VIII, c. 1). During Edward's reign she had to deal with the attentions of the Protector's brother, Thomas Seymour, a handsome, ambitious and reckless man who wished to marry her as a step towards achieving power in the State, and under Mary she had to cope with the government's suspicions about her possible involvement in plots like Wyatt's rebellion, as well as Mary's justified doubts about her religious soundness. She emerged as Queen at the age of twenty-five, having grasped the need for both caution and dissimulation. Her hot Tudor blood had drawn her towards Seymour, but her rational mind learnt from that episode the need to put her personal inclinations behind the needs of her royal state – a lesson she was to remember in her later relations with her favourite, Robert Dudley, earl of Leicester. She carefully avoided being drawn into any of the plots of Mary's reign, and if her Protestantism was never seriously in doubt – the whole story of her birth was tied up with the breach with Rome – she was no religious fanatic and conformed, if with a marked lack of enthusiasm, between 1553 and 1558. The political abilities which she developed and demonstrated during her early life marked her out as the possessor of an able mind. That had been trained from childhood in the humanist tradition by capable tutors like Roger Ascham and she was a learned young woman, even something of a 'bluestocking', when she took over the government of the country.

Mary, as we have seen (Ch. 10), had been desperately unlucky in the economic background against which she had to work. Elizabeth was much more fortunate [I; K; L]. The harvest situation up to the outbreak of war with Spain was generally favourable with only five bad harvests compared with thirteen good and ten average ones in the years from 1558 to 1585 (227). This better-than-normal succession of harvests must have made a significant contribution to the reduced inflation rates which marked the period from about 1560 to the early 1590s; food prices, which had doubled between 1540 and 1560, rose by less than 25 per cent between 1560 and 1590. During the first decade of the reign prices may even have fallen from the average level of the 1550s (224), and in this relatively short-term context the restoration of a sound currency in 1560–61 and the sharp fall in population during the epidemics of the later 1550s were probably of decisive importance. The fall in population especially, by reducing the demand for food, led to a considerable easing of inflationary pressures and a rise in real wages during the 1560s.

These fundamental economic trends must have gone a long way in helping to stabilize the Elizabethan regime by the 1570s and 1580s, but in the very first years of the reign they could not be anticipated, especially as the harvest history of the period 1558–63 was poor, with two bad, two good and two average harvests. In the short term the success – perhaps even the survival – of the new government depended on the way in which the Queen tackled the serious political and religious problems which confronted her. In 1558 she faced three fundamental tasks: she had to establish an effective administration centred on the Privy Council; she had to create a new religious settlement; and she had to bring the war with France to an end while keeping a careful eye on Scotland where French influence was dominant.

The first task was the creation of an administration. This was basically done in the three months between November 1558 and January 1559 (29; 99). At Court Elizabeth made sweeping changes which symbolized her personal rejection of the Marian past. Among the leading officials of the royal household only Sir John Mason, the Treasurer of the Chamber, retained his post, while there was a clean sweep of Mary's Catholic ladies-in-waiting who were replaced by Protestant relatives of the Queen and the wives and daughters of Elizabeth's new courtiers and officials. More fundamentally important were the changes in the Privy Council. Mary had left a Council of thirty-nine. Elizabeth soon reduced this to nineteen. She had soothing words for those whom she did not appoint; 'let them not think the same for any disability in them', she stated, 'but that for I do consider a multitude doth make rather discord and confusion than good counsel' (quoted (99, *29*)). It is plain, however, that many of the Marian councillors who were dropped did have 'disabilities' in the Queen's eyes, either as strong Catholics who had been personal favourites of her sister or else as largely nominal members who had swelled the theoretical size of the Council without making effective contributions to its work. She did retain ten of Mary's councillors, seven peers and three commoners. These were either great magnates like the earls of Arundel, Pembroke, Derby and Shrewsbury, men who wielded enormous power in their localities, or else experienced administrators like Lord Treasurer Winchester, Sir John Mason and Sir William Petre. Of the nine new members only two were peers. One was Francis Russell, second earl of Bedford, an outspoken Protestant with wide lands in the west of England; the other, William Parr, marquis of Northampton, was the brother of Queen Catherine Parr, newly restored to the title which he had lost in 1553 for his support of Lady Jane Grey. The seven new commoner members were almost all men of experience, generally gained at Court or in government under Edward VI. They included two cousins of the Queen on her mother's side, Sir Richard Sackville and Sir Francis Knollys, as well as her faithful steward, Sir Thomas Parry. An important new member was Sir Nicholas Bacon, who became Lord Keeper of the Great Seal, but by far the most significant appointment was that of Sir William Cecil who was made Secretary of State, thus returning to an office which he had occupied under Northumberland. It was an able team which even in 1559 was dominated by the 'official' element of government and household men who were to increase their supremacy still further during the reign at the expense of the 'magnates'. All the members were laymen – with the theoretical exception of Nicholas Wotton – and the average age was about fifty, just twice that of the Queen herself. Although it contained strong Protestants like Russell, Knollys and, to a lesser extent, Cecil himself, their influence was balanced by that of conservatives like Arundel, Shrewsbury and Derby, men who were not supporters of the Papacy but who had welcomed the return of the mass under Mary. The membership of the Council, designed to preside effectively over the administration of the country, bore witness to the Queen's determination to extend her patronage to the representatives of as wide a spectrum of religious opinion as possible, from strongly committed Protestants to religious conservatives who stopped short of upholding the Roman Supremacy.

The sweeping changes at Court and the significant alterations in the membership of the Privy Council were not paralleled by purges in either central or local administration. Most of the personnel of the central administrative departments retained their posts – that was only to be expected at a time when such offices were regarded as a form of property – and there were relatively few dismissals from the all-important Commissions of the Peace in the localities during the first half-dozen years of the reign. Administrative was reinforced by judicial continuity; none of the Marian judges – all strongly conservative in religion – were removed from the bench.

It can be said, then, that by the beginning of 1559 the Queen had created an administration which made her general intentions clear. It was obvious that she was determined to reject once more the papal authority which her sister had restored, but she had also made it plain that she wanted to exclude as limited a number of her subjects as possible from her favour; only open supporters of Rome, whether clerical or lay, were totally rejected in the highest reaches of government. By January 1559, when Parliament met to provide a new religious settlement, it was clear that the Queen would lay a bill restoring the Royal Supremacy before it. This was certainly done, but little else about the making of the religious settlement of 1559 is clear. Two main views can be distinguished. One, put forward by Sir John Neale in 1950 (179), has long held the field; the other, current before Neale's work, has recently been revived and extended by Dr N. L. Jones.[1] Neale argued that in 1559 the Queen did not intend to enact a Protestant Prayer Book for the Church. She wished, he maintained, merely to restore the Royal Supremacy, postponing a decision about the form of worship to be adopted until a later date, after the matter had been discussed in Convocation. The final settlement which emerged after Easter did, however, contain an Act of Uniformity enforcing a new Prayer Book as well as an Act of Supremacy, and Neale explained this defeat for the Queen by pressure from radical Protestants in the House of Commons, by her dependence on returned Marian exiles for staffing the upper reaches of her new Church following the refusal of all but one of the Marian bishops to accept the restored Royal Supremacy, and by the greater freedom of manœuvre which the government possessed after the

Peace of Câteau-Cambrésis with France in March 1559. That treaty, the argument goes on, made it less necessary for her to pursue a religious policy which was moderate enough to retain the friendship of Philip II of Spain, a friendship which was quite imperative while England was at war with the other great Catholic power, France. Elizabeth, when she was finally brought to accept a Prayer Book, would, Neale maintained, have favoured the more conservative Edwardian Book of 1549 whereas the radicals both inside and outside the Commons would have preferred something more extreme than the 1552 Book. In this situation compromise was finally reached on a version of the 1552 Book. This analysis of events sees the 1559 settlement essentially as a defeat for the Queen and as a qualified triumph for the Marian exiles, both clerical and lay, who spearheaded the campaign for a radical settlement.

Dr Jones has argued, on the other hand, that the settlement which emerged in 1559 was basically what Elizabeth wanted. She introduced at the start a new Prayer Book based on the Edwardian Book of 1552 and her programme was accepted without difficulty by the House of Commons which amalgamated the government's Supremacy and Uniformity Bills into a single measure which was, however, successfully opposed in the Lords. It was the resistance of the Marian bishops and of a group of conservative peers in the Upper House which caused the decisive trouble for the government. They removed the provisions for Protestant uniformity and reduced the effectiveness of the supremacy proposals. Faced with the possible wreckage of her plans, Elizabeth arrested two bishops and kept a number of conservative peers away from the Lords when the session resumed after Easter. New Supremacy and Uniformity Bills were introduced which once again rapidly passed the Commons. The bishops in the Upper House remained adamant in their resistance, but the Lords as a whole, perhaps mollified by the title of Supreme Governor rather than Supreme Head, which was now proposed for the Queen, accepted the Supremacy Bill fairly easily. The Uniformity Bill had a much rougher passage. It was passed by only three votes, and it is likely that if the government had not taken the steps already described to keep away some of its most notable opponents it would have failed altogether. This version of events obviously sees the 1559 settlement as a triumph for both the Queen and a House of Commons which supported her throughout. The difficulties came from a conservative House of Lords which almost torpedoed the royal plans.

It is impossible to be sure which, if either, of these two interpretations is correct; the limited documentary evidence available does not permit of certainties. The issue is, however, an important one. Much of the religious and parliamentary history of Elizabeth's reign has traditionally been constructed around the 1559 settlement, and if Dr Jones is right and there was no radical Protestant opposition to the Crown in 1559 then Neale's picture of such an opposition during the 1560s, an opposition which he sees are deriving from the events of 1559, must be called in question. This is an issue which can be pursued further in a different context (see Ch. 15); what is important here is to note that in 1559 Queen, Lords and Commons *did* finally agree, however enthusiastically or reluctantly, to Acts of Supremacy [E.3(7); G.4(14)] and Uniformity [G.4(15)] which formed the basis of the government and worship of the Church of England until our own day.

The Act of Supremacy's provision that the Queen was to be 'Supreme Governor' [N] rather than 'Supreme Head' of the Church may have made little practical difference as far as ecclesiastical government was concerned, but it did have important theoretical implications. As Head of the Church Henry VIII had regarded himself as a semi-ecclesiastical personage, a kind of 'lay bishop' governing the Church from inside. As Supreme Governor Elizabeth was very clearly a lay person governing the Church from outside. This change of title can be regarded, perhaps, as a concession to both Catholics and the more radical Protestants, each of whom denied or doubted, though for very different reasons, that *any* lay person, let alone a woman, could be Head of the Church. The Act of Uniformity imposed the second Edwardian Prayer Book of 1552, with a number of modifications. Two of these were of especial importance. The wording of the 1549 Prayer Book, which indicated a real presence in the sacrament, was prefixed to that of the 1552 Book, which suggested that the communion service was a commemorative rite (see Chs. 8 and 9). The 1559 version, therefore, allowed communicants to stress or minimize the idea of a real presence, depending on which section of the wording they emphasized. This was an effort at comprehension, at persuading as wide a section of the community as possible to accept the Prayer Book. The second crucial modification dealt with vestments. It ordered that those used by the clergy should be the ones authorized in the second year of Edward VI, a proviso which theoretically enforced the use of the medieval mass vestments. It was this provision, bitterly resented by the more radical Protestants even in the much modified form in which the government tried to enforce it, which led to the vestiarian controversy of the 1560s (see Ch. 18).

None of the Marian bishops except Kitchen of Llandaff would accept the settlement and they were duly deprived, together with many of the other dignitaries of the Marian Church. The lower clergy were much more amenable. It is impossible to be certain how many went so far in their opposition as to warrant expulsion from their parishes but it was probably only about 300 (24). Many of the thousands who remained, however, were no doubt either hostile or indifferent to the new services and it remained to be seen whether or not the settlement would take root in the country at large. Four years after the governmental and liturgical basis of the Elizabethan Church had been settled by the Acts of Supremacy and Uniformity it received its doctrinal foundation in the Thirty-nine Articles of 1563 [G.4(16)], a revision by Archbishop Parker of the Forty-two Edwardian Articles which had been given effect for a brief period in 1553. They provided, in Professor Dickens's words, 'a decisively Protestant interpretation of the faith' (27, *251*), and though they embodied a number of different religious traditions and contained ambiguities which allowed theologians of different points of view to accept them either enthusiastically or reluctantly, there can be no doubt about the strong Calvinist elements which they contained and which were to give the Elizabethan Church its dominant theological flavour.

The religious settlement and the creation of a new administration were two of the most urgent problems which faced the Queen in 1558. A third was the foreign situation. England and France were still at war and it was clear that Elizabeth had little practical chance of regaining Calais. The Treaty of Câteau-Cambrésis in the spring of 1559, which brought the war to an end, ceded the town to France for eight years, after which the French were to return it or pay 500,000 crowns (30). It was a face-saving formula for England, but it could hardly be doubted that Calais had gone for good. The long-term effects of the loss were in fact beneficial – Calais had been a constant drain on English resources – but the settlement was unquestionably an inglorious one. It was more than redeemed the following year by events in Scotland where Mary of Guise was Regent for her daughter, Mary Queen of Scots. French influence in Scotland was one of the main reasons why peace had been essential in 1559 – the Treaty of Câteau-Cambrésis had removed at least temporarily the possibility of a Franco-Scottish invasion from the North – but the prospect of long-term French control of Scotland, a prospect reinforced when Mary Queen of Scots became Queen Consort of France in 1559, was clearly a most serious threat to English security. A Protestant-inspired revolt in Scotland against the Queen Regent broke out in May 1559 and, urged on by Cecil, Elizabeth sent first of all money and then naval and military help to the rebels. The result was the Treaty of Edinburgh of 1560, by which French troops were withdrawn from Scotland and the Protestants left in control of the country, a victory which they symbolized a few months later by abolishing papal jurisdiction and outlawing the mass in Scotland (30; 99). It was a famous victory for Elizabeth no less than for the Scottish Protestants; her northern border was much more secure with the emergence of a Scottish regime free from French dependence and strongly hostile to the religion of the staunchly Catholic French Crown.

Although Elizabeth and her advisers were primarily preoccupied with political and religious problems during the early years of the reign they did not forget the needs of the economy. Their objective here was to restore stability after the upheavals of the previous decades and the two principal measures which they adopted or secured with this aim in view were the restoration of the coinage in 1560–61 and the Statute of Artificers of 1563. The ending of debasements in 1551 had not, as we have seen, meant the withdrawal of the existing base coins from circulation and Mary's plans for a full restoration of the currency were not put into effect (see Ch. 10). They did, however, enable Elizabeth's government to act relatively quickly at the beginning of her reign. Between December 1560 and October 1561 the remaining base coins were withdrawn from circulation and converted to fine silver money in an operation which was a great technical success; the Crown made a profit of about £50,000 (246). By far the most significant result of the recoinage was, however, the restoration of domestic and foreign confidence in the currency during the 1560s. The Queen and her advisers appreciated the importance of this and resolutely adhered to a 'sound money' policy for the English coinage during the rest of the reign. No less important than the restoration of the coinage in the government's policy of promoting social stability was the Statute of Artificers of 1563 (56; 98). The original bill was substantially amended as it went through Parliament and it is impossible to analyse here the whole of the long and complicated Act which emerged, but the government's main intentions can be illustrated from the clauses dealing with compulsory labour in agriculture. These provided that all males between the ages of twelve and sixty who were not exempt on a number of specifically defined grounds were to work in agriculture. This reflected the government's concern both with securing an adequate supply of agricultural labour and with combating the growing evil of vagrancy. If successful it would have boosted agricultural production, contributed to the strength of national defence – agricultural workers were potential militia recruits – and have reduced the menace of the tramp; significant contributions to economic, political and social stability. The government's success clearly fell very far short of its intentions – vagrancy, for example, seems to have increased during the reign – but the provisions do show the way in which the minds of the Queen and her ministers were working.

The Statute of Artificers was passed five years after the start of the reign and it can be argued that by 1563 Elizabeth had laid the political, religious and economic bases of her government. A new administration had been created under the supervision of a small, effective Privy Council; England's international position had been greatly improved by the conclusion of peace with France and above all the removal in 1560 of the threat of her northern border; the government, liturgy and doctrine of the Elizabethan Church had been formulated; and economic and social stability had been encouraged by the recoinage and the Statute of Artificers. The general tone of the new regime was cautious, moderate and – granted its fundamental opposition to papal authority – conservative. It had made promising beginnings, but it remained to be seen how well the Queen and her advisers could build on these in the years ahead.

1. *Faith by Statute: Parliament and the Settlement of Religion 1559* (1982).

113

The Queen and her ministers: the Elizabethan Privy Council and central administration

Elizabeth's first task after she ascended the throne was, as we have seen, the creation of an administration centred on the Privy Council, and throughout her reign her most constant preoccupation was with the government of the country in the broadest sense; in other words with the day-to-day conduct of foreign and domestic business. In this she obviously relied to a great extent on her ministers and she rapidly established relationships with them founded on their duty to give advice when she asked for it and their obligation to carry out whatever decisions she herself made irrespective of their own opinions on the matter. These were classic principles of Tudor government and the Queen was determined to stick to them. Even in the greatest affairs of State she did not always ask her ministers' advice. In 1586 the earl of Leicester, then in command of the English forces fighting against Spain in the Netherlands, complained that he was not receiving advice from the Privy Council. Sir Francis Walsingham, the Secretary of State, replied that the councillors well understood his complaints but, 'her Majesty retaining the whole direction of the causes of that country to herself and such advice as she receiveth underhand, they know not what to write or to advise'. Of course, she usually *did* consult her Council, but she was quite prepared to ignore its advice on occasion. In the summer of 1562 she was preparing to travel to York to meet Mary Queen of Scots. All the councillors, when consulted, advised against the journey, but Elizabeth made it plain that she was determined to go and later cancelled her plans only because of a change in the international situation (98). Sir William Cecil, created Lord Burghley in 1571, exerted far greater political influence over the Queen than any other statesman of the age, but he knew the limits of his authority as he made plain to his son and political heir Sir Robert Cecil in 1596. 'In such matters as I differ in opinion from her Majesty', he declared, 'I will not change my opinion by affirming the contrary, for that were to offend God . . ., but as a servant I will obey her Majesty's commandment and no wise contrary the same . . . after that I have performed my duty as a councillor.' Other ministers were sometimes less sensible or else less subtle than Burghley, but the Queen soon made it plain where power lay. One famous story, which may have gained in the telling but makes the point well, relates how she humbled Leicester when he presumed too far. 'If you think to rule here I will take a course to see you forthcoming', she told the proud earl, 'I will have here but one mistress and no master.' (5, *141–2*)

Elizabeth, so clearly determined to rule her own house, kept her servants on their toes by taking a direct interest in all aspects of administration. Her interference in small matters often profoundly irritated her ministers, but she was always careful not to become involved in *too many* trivial details. One vital aspect of her genius was her ability to pick and trust good advisers like the Cecils, Walsingham, Sir Nicholas Bacon, Sir Thomas Egerton and Sir Walter Mildmay – men whom she trusted with a wide initiative in routine matters. William Cecil had a very special place among them. In 1558, when she appointed him to the Council, she indicated that he was to be her chief adviser and told him, 'I give you this charge, that you shall be . . . content to take pains for me and my realm. This judgement I have of you that you will not be corrupted by any manner of gift and that you will be faithful to the state.' (75, *29–30*) It was a judgement and trust that he confirmed and fulfilled in forty years of diligent service, the longest partnership between sovereign and minister in the whole of English history.

As Secretary of State and later as Lord Treasurer the elder Cecil was the most notable of the group of ministers and officials who formed by far the most important element in the Elizabethan Privy Council. The 'magnates', who owed their position as councillors to their great estates as well as to the Queen's confidence, may have numbered as many as six in 1563, but thereafter their role was reduced and at the end of the reign only one man, Gilbert Talbot, earl of Shrewsbury fell into that category. Indeed, the reduction in the size of the Privy Council during the course of the reign, from nineteen in 1559 to fourteen in 1603 was achieved largely by squeezing out the great provincial notables who were prominent in the 1560s. This emphasized that in the Queen's eyes the Council was designed essentially to exercise effective administrative authority in the country rather than to satisfy the political ambitions of members of the nobility who had traditionally seen a place on the Council as a mark of their status within the State (86). Under Elizabeth they had to look elsewhere for such recognition.

We have seen that one of the Council's principal duties was to give advice when the Queen asked for it. Its other two major roles were its administrative and judicial (or quasi-judicial) work.[1] The advice which the Queen obtained from her councillors was seldom unanimous – the Council's united front in the Mary Queen of Scots episode in 1562 was a rare occurrence – and throughout the reign Elizabeth was usually able to consider differing arguments from her principal advisers before making major policy decisions. The most important of all the issues which divided the Council was probably the question of whether or not to send military aid to the Dutch rebels in their struggle against Spain. From the 1570s two groups of councillors emerged, a 'war party' headed by Leicester and Walsingham, both strong Puritans, who were anxious to help the Protestant Dutch, and a 'peace party', headed by the more cautious Burghley. During the early 1580s Leicester and his supporters seem to have outnumbered Burghley and his adherents on this issue. Elizabeth, however, did not make her decisions by counting the heads of her councillors. She was determined to preserve peace as long as humanly possible and refused to be pushed into war until 1585, when national security was clearly at stake (103).

The Council's duty to advise the Queen on matters of high policy may have been the most dramatic aspect of its work, but its most constant preoccupation was with its routine administrative tasks. It concerned itself with everything that went on in England and the pages of the Privy Council Register bear eloquent witness both to the multiplicity and the diversity of its business. It exercised, for example, detailed supervision over the work of those ubiquitous local agents the justices of the peace, and when war came after 1585 it played the major role in organizing defensive and offensive operations against Spain. Its burdens were increased by the demands of private petitioners who bombarded it with pleas for assistance in injustices which they claimed to have suffered. Specific courts did exists to hear such complaints, but petitioners clearly felt it worth while to pester the most influential body in the land with their troubles. Consideration of such private pleas hindered the Council's more pressing preoccupations with public affairs and in 1582 it ordered that from then on, 'no private causes arising between parties for any action whatsoever which may receive order and redress in any of her Majesty's ordinary courts shall be received and preferred to the Board, unless they shall concern the preservation of her Majesty's peace or shall be of some public consequence to touch the government of the realm'.[2] This decision seems, however, to have made little difference to the flood of petitions and in 1589 and 1591 the Council had to repeat and re-emphasize its former prohibition in orders[3] which seem to have had as little effect as the 1582 decree itself.

The increasing number of private suitors is one indication of the growth in the Council's work which undoubtedly took place during the Elizabethan period. Another is the increasing frequency of Council meetings. In the earlier years of the reign the Council seems, as a rule, to have met only three times a week, either in the morning or in the afternoon. By the 1590s, however it was meeting almost every day, sometimes in both mornings and afternoons (98). By that time it had to cope not only with the ever growing importunities of private petitioners but much more importantly in its own eyes with the increased duties involved in supervising the war with Spain and superintending the greatly expanded scope of the work of local government officials which took place during the later sixteenth century.

The Privy Council's concern with private suitors reflected its inheritance of the duty of the medieval King's Council to see that justice was done to all the monarch's subjects and although it was not, in the strict technical sense, a court, debate among historians as to whether it exercised judicial or merely 'quasi-judicial' functions may seem a largely sterile exercise (cf.(3, *101*) and (98, *24–5*)). It enforced its decisions in disputes between individuals by arresting and imprisoning those who refused to accept its decrees. Roger Windham, a Norfolk gentleman who was twice gaoled until he agreed to comply with a Council order compelling him to pay compensation to other parties, and many others like him, were only too well aware of the effective judicial authority which councillors exercised.

Under the supervision of the Privy Council and the Queen the country was administered by a number of central agencies which existed to help fulfil the basic but limited objectives which Elizabeth's government set itself (98). These were principally to keep law and order; to defend the country: to raise enough money to provide for administration and defence; and, some way behind the other three, to take a paternalistic interest in the welfare of the Queen's subjects. Many of these tasks were undertaken by local officials, but great central institutions like the courts of King's Bench, Common Pleas, Star Chamber, Chancery and

Exchequer and the Navy Board played vital roles. A key part in the maintenance of both domestic and foreign security was played by the Secretary of State. The secretaryship under Elizabeth enjoyed once more the kind of position which Thomas Cromwell had given it during the 1530s, when he had had a hold on almost all the affairs of the realm. Under Elizabeth three men, each of great ability, held the secretaryship for most of the reign; Sir William Cecil from 1558 to 1572, Sir Francis Walsingham from 1573 to 1590, and Sir Robert Cecil from 1596 onwards. They raised it to the heights which it had achieved by the end of the century when Robert Cecil wrote of it, 'All officers and counsellors of princes have a prescribed authority by patent, by custom or by oath, the secretary only excepted.' He, in contrast, had 'a liberty to negotiate at discretion at home and abroad . . . all matters of speech and intelligence' (quoted (98, *47–8*)). It was this broadly defined responsibility for the security of the realm which inspired Walsingham to build up his famous – or notorious – spy system, which played a major role in the capture of Catholic priests at home and in securing useful foreign intelligence (74).

Central institutions like Chancery and the Exchequer were staffed by official 'civil servants', men who received a salary and fees for their prescribed administrative duties, but there were probably less than 1,000 central government officials all told at this time, some hundreds in London and the rest in the provinces (56, *106–8*), and to consider only established civil servants would give a false impression of the machinery of government. Ministers and leading officials could not have done their work without the help of their personal assistants, who occupied no official position in the State. These men were merely members of their masters' households, subject to immediate dismissal at the will of their employers and often dependent for their livelihood on the gratuities which they received from hopeful suitors who sought to gain a minister's or an official's favour through a good word from his secretary. Burghley's personal assistants, given their master's key role in government, were important figures in the administration of the realm and we have a good deal of information about their activities, especially those of Michael Hickes, who was his patronage secretary from 1580 to 1598 (75; 104). The work of Hickes and his colleagues in Burghley's service can be paralleled by the duties performed by the private secretaries of other Elizabethan ministers like Sir Francis Walsingham, who had a large number of confidential clerks between 1573 and 1590, and Sir Robert Cecil, who had four personal assistants in 1603. The existence of these private secretaries and the importance of their work reminds us of the danger of applying labels like 'bureaucratic' to Elizabethan government. The very essence of Elizabethan ministers' households, where so much of the administrative work of the country was done, was that they were *not* bureaucratic machines. Each minister or official organized the duties of his assistants precisely as he thought best at any given time. Elizabethan government was clearly a mixture of 'bureaucratic' and 'household' elements, combining the official machinery of institutions like Chancery and the Exchequer with the informal processes of administration which took place within the personal offices of the leading ministers and officials.

The Queen's attitude towards administration was extremely conservative and

Burghley, also a cautious man, shared her attitudes. There is no evidence that they ever thought of making substantial alterations or innovations in the government machinery in an effort to achieve greater efficiency. Their conservatism is very evident in the key area of finance, which was Burghley's special responsibility after he became Lord Treasurer in 1572. Elizabeth has been praised by historians for her government's solvency which was in striking contrast to the bankruptcies of her Continental competitors. Her ordinary revenue – consisting principally of customs dues, rents from the royal lands, feudal revenues, the first fruits of benefices and the profits of justice – rose from about £200,000 per annum in the early years of the reign to about £300,000 a year at the end (98, 8).[4] This was at a time when food prices rose by about two-thirds and industrial prices by rather less than one-third (224), so the Queen's regular revenue seems to have at least kept pace with inflation. Elizabeth kept her ordinary expenditure to a necessary minimum, and by the later part of her reign she was saving about £100,000 a year from her ordinary revenue. She used this surplus, together with parliamentary subsidies and the money from land sales and naval prizes, to finance her war effort against Spain. It was a remarkable achievement that after eighteen years of very expensive warfare at the end of the reign she died only about £350,000 in debt (98).

There is, however, another side to this financial success story. Elizabeth was never notably generous in rewarding her servants, and the financial stringencies of her later years led to a notable growth of corruption in the public service as courtiers and officials, deprived of adequate rewards from their mistress, accepted larger and larger gratuities, sometimes indistinguishable from outright bribes, from the suitors who sought their favour. James I's notorious generosity was in part a reaction to Elizabeth's miserliness in her last years and it can be forcibly argued that the Queen and Burghley, by neglecting opportunities to increase their ordinary revenue, left the Stuarts, faced by ever rising government costs, in a much less happy financial position than was necessary. This can be illustrated by examining the history of customs duties, of the royal land revenues and of feudal dues during the Elizabethan period. As we have seen above (Ch. 10), as a result of the Marian reform of 1558 customs revenues rose to £83,000 a year at the beginning of Elizabeth's reign. During the period 1599–1603, the last five years of the reign, they averaged about £96,000 a year (245). This was a poor performance at a time of rapid inflation and it can be explained by the methods by which duties were levied. Some dues, most notably those on exported cloth and imported wines, were imposed on the quantity rather than the value of the goods traded. Thus, as prices rose the customs realized a smaller and smaller proportion of the true value of the wares. Other duties were theoretically levied upon the value of the goods, but the valuations in Mary's book, which had been fairly realistic when it was issued in 1558, were not increased during Elizabeth's reign and rapidly fell out of line with the true worth of the commodities (248). In allowing this situation to develop and continue Burghley clearly permitted a fall in the real value of the customs which a more active and realistic policy could have avoided.

The royal land revenues received similarly conservative treatment. During the reign they increased from about £78,000 to about £100,000 a year (245), an increase of between a third and a quarter at a time when food prices were rising much more quickly. Part of this poor performance can be explained by land sales, but there is no doubt that the rents on royal lands were far below realistic valuations. A great series of surveys instituted in the early years of James I's reign revealed the extent of the problem. The manor of Barking in Essex, for example yielded rents of £103 a year in 1609 but the true annual value was £682! (75) Not all manors, of course, were undervalued by 600 per cent, but there was clearly scope for very substantial increases during the Elizabethan period and Burghley's and the Queen's failure to take action, at a time when private landlords were sharply increasing their rentals, cost the government a great deal of much needed revenue. The history of the feudal dues, which were collected by the Court of Wards, tells an equally striking story. Wardship [N] and its associated burdens brought the Crown an average revenue of just under £15,000 per annum during the Elizabethan period. Burghley was Master of the Court for most of the reign, controlling its policies from his appointment in 1561 until his death, still in office, thirty-seven years later. Income from wardship was actually higher at the beginning of his mastership, when it stood at over £18,000 a year, than at the end, when it had fallen to less than £15,000 per annum, and if allowance is made for inflation the fall in real terms was a very substantial one. Changes in policy after his death showed what could be done. Before the end of Elizabeth's reign Burghley's successor, Robert Cecil, had raised the annual revenue from the Court to over £22,000 and during the 1630s it reached a peak of over £80,000 a year.[5]

This lack of basic reforms in the financial system throughout Elizabeth's reign is perhaps the most striking illustration of the Queen's and Burghley's fundamental conservatism. The latter's failure to take even modest steps to achieve increases which were both possible and very necessary in the Crown's regular revenue contrasts sharply with the innovations of his predecessor, Winchester, which made Elizabeth's own solvency possible. Burghley served Queen and country faithfully, but it is difficult to avoid the conclusion that his financial policies, which must have received the approval of his equally conservative mistress, were not in the Crown's long-term interests. Founded basically, no doubt, on a desire to preserve the stability of the regime they left his successors in the office of Lord Treasurer in charge of an old-fashioned financial machine which brought the government a much smaller proportion of national resources than it might reasonably have enjoyed. Even more important, perhaps, it accustomed the landed and trading classes to a situation in which they paid a very small part of their income in taxation. When they were called upon to give more under the early Stuarts their reluctance and resentments caused major difficulties for the Crown. It is only fair to add, however, that if royal and ministerial conservatism stored up trouble for the future, it did, indeed, in the shorter term, buttress the stability which was one of the notable features of the Elizabethan regime during the 1570s and 1580s, the 'high Elizabethan period' to which men looked back so nostalgically during more troubled times in the seventeenth century. That stability was partly founded, too, on the effective administrative control of a powerful Privy Council and on the Queen's recognition of the fundamental need to secure the co-operation of the politically conscious classes – the nobility, gentry and wealthier citizens of the towns. She obtained that co-operation largely by allowing them access to patronage through Court and Parliament and by ensuring that their very various voices were heard there.

---

1. For the Elizabethan Privy Council see A. G. R. Smith, *The Government of Elizabethan England*, pp. 13 ff; M. B. Pulman, *The Elizabethan Privy Council in the Fifteen-Seventies* (Berkeley, 1971).
2. *APC 1581–2*, pp. 394–5.
3. *APC 1589–90*, pp. 181–2; *APC 1591*, p. 240.
4. There is a useful summary of the financial situation under Elizabeth in P. Williams, *The Tudor Regime* (Oxford 1979), pp. 70 ff.
5. J. Hurstfield, 'The profits of fiscal feudalism, 1541–1602', *EcHR*, 2nd Ser., **8** (1955–6), 55; H. E. Bell, *An Introduction to the History and Records of the Court of Wards and Liveries*, Table A.

CHAPTER 14

Patronage and faction

Elizabeth's government had a number of methods of securing compliance with its wishes (for a good general discussion (see 24, *351 ff*)). As last resorts the terror of the treason laws and the use of armed force might be employed, but the Queen and her ministers were only too well aware of the relatively limited coercive powers they had at their disposal. Without a standing army, an effective police force or a substantial paid bureaucracy in the localities they relied heavily on political persuasion to enforce their will. The homily of obedience, designed to be read in churches for the edification and education of the Queen's subjects, emphasized her God-given right to issue orders which it was her subjects' bounden duty to obey or, at the very least, not to resist. Failure to carry out the Queen's lawful commands would lead to anarchy. Then, 'no man shall ride or go by the highway unrobbed; no man shall sleep in his own house or bed unkilled; no man shall keep his wife, children and possessions in quietness: all things shall be common: and there must needs follow all mischief and utter destruction both of souls, bodies, goods and commonwealths' (5, *139*). It would be wrong to underestimate the effect which such moral teachings had on the minds of Elizabethans of all classes who were instinctively predisposed towards acceptance of the philosophical and theological ideas behind them, founded on belief in a 'great chain of being' (277) on which all living creatures had their appointed place, with God at the very top and lesser authorities, especially princes, exercising 'divine right' in their duly constituted roles lower down the hierarchy.

If propaganda from the pulpit was one way of encouraging the Queen's subjects to obey her authority, another was the ritual aspects of the Elizabethan Court which was one of the most splendid and ceremonious in Europe. Awed visitors commented on the pomp and pageantry which took place within the royal palaces (see Ch. 26), but the Queen was aware of the need to impress as wide a circle of her subjects as possible and those in the southern parts of the realm were able to witness the imposing progresses which she undertook during the reign to outlying royal castles or manors, to the seats of local nobility and gentry, and to provincial towns. The common people, who lined the roads to watch the spectacle were treated not only to sights of royal magnificence which were designed to impress them with both the might and the majesty of the sovereign, but also, on occasion, to calculated displays of royal graciousness. The Spanish ambassador, writing in 1568, described how she sometimes 'ordered her carriage . . . to be taken where the crowd seemed thickest, and stood up and thanked the people' (quoted 72, *207*). Elizabeth was clearly well aware of the impact which a few gracious words might have on her ordinary subjects, who were anyway very ready to be impressed by the visual aspects of monarchy, but she realized that in securing the obedience of the 'political nation', that comparatively limited group of men whose co-operation was essential for the effective government of the country, charm and an appeal to moral and spiritual obligations were not enough. She had to follow policies which were at least generally acceptable to them – here her instinctive conservatism struck answering notes in the minds of the majority of the governing classes – and to satisfy their material interests. She endeavoured to fulfil this latter need by the use of patronage.

Elizabeth had numerous benefits and rewards at her disposal (24; 56; 75; 98): grants of honours, such as peerages and knighthoods; a vast array of offices at Court, and in Church and government; leases, on highly favourable terms, of royal lands; the grant of export licences, monopolies and customs farms, all of which conferred valuable economic privileges on the recipients; and pensions and annuities, which were conferred both on favoured courtiers and on retired servants of the Crown. The great majority of those who benefited from this stock of patronage came from the 2,500 or so men who, at any one time, took a direct interest in Elizabethan politics. The vast majority of these were country gentlemen and Professor MacCaffrey has estimated that about 40 per cent of them usually held court or governmental places 'worth a gentleman's having'. If that figure is correct – and it is, of course, a well-informed guess – then the Queen was able to bind the material interests of a very substantial proportion of the Elizabethan political nation to the fate of her government through the use of merely part of her patronage. The high proportion who benefited is an indication that she wanted to spread the favours at her disposal as widely a possible, to secure, in Professor MacCaffrey's words, 'not . . . the adherence of a party or faction but . . . the goodwill and confidence of a whole class' (56, *98, 99, 108*).

Most members of the political nation and the vast majority of other suitors for royal favour had no direct contact with or access to the sovereign and had to pursue their claims through intermediaries. Many of them did this by letter while others thronged the Court, trying to persuade influential ministers, officials and royal favourites to take up their cause. The privy councillors and high officials who stood between the sovereign and the mass of clients were both the recipients and distributors of patronage. They held their own positions and influence from the Queen's grants and favour and they used their authority to advance the suits of others, either through recommendations to Elizabeth or else by disposing directly of that large portion of the royal patronage which was committed to them by virtue of their offices. In this situation the leading courtiers and ministers were themselves besieged by clients and they had their own personal assistants who protected them from excessive importunities and recommended or delayed the suits of humble and sometimes even of exalted clients. Burghley was overwhelmed with suitors. His household biographer recorded that he 'drew upon him such multitude of suits as was incredible but to us that saw it, for besides all business in Council or other weighty causes, and such as were answered by word of mouth, there was not a day . . . wherein he received not threescore, fourscore and an hundred petitions' (75, *38–9*). Michael Hickes, his patronage secretary, who dealt with the great bulk of these suits, became both an influential and a wealthy man, and the way he carried out his duties illustrates the workings of the patronage machine (75). Clients usually asked him either to approach Burghley when the latter was in a receptive mood and then press their causes, or else to deliver letters to his master on their behalf. Hickes expected payment for his services and he received a flood of gratuities from grateful or hopeful clients. These might be considerable: one suitor, for example, paid £20 for services rendered and another promised £100 if he obtained his wishes.

The activities of a man like Hickes, who numbered among his correspondents some of the greatest men in the realm, reveal the complexities which often faced Elizabethan suitors for patronage. George Hastings, earl of Huntingdon, was one of the leading noblemen of the realm, a man who had independent relationships with both the Queen and Burghley, but in 1597 he thought it worth while obtaining Hickes's help in settling a wardship negotiation in which he was involved and for which Burghley, as Master of the Wards, held ultimate responsibility. Hickes's position in Burghley's private office, which clearly gave him opportunities to help men like Huntingdon, enabled him to dash completely the hopes of humbler suitors, as William Nevill made clear in 1595 when he reflected on the failure of his previous suits to Burghley. The crux of the matter, he was convinced, was his failure to secure Hickes's co-operation and he promised that the latter could name his own 'composition' (i.e. gratuity) in return for help in his present petition (75).

The difficulties which both exalted and humble suitors could encounter in their quest for benefits suggest that the pursuit of patronage was often a time-consuming business. It could also be a humiliating one. Francis Bacon and Edmund Spenser knew what they were talking about when they reflected upon the search for favour. 'The rising unto place', wrote Bacon, 'is laborious, and by pains men come to greater pains; and it is sometimes base, and by indignities men come to dignities.'[1] Spenser told a similar story in his poem, *Mother Hubbard's Tale*, where he lamented:

> Full little knowest thou that hast not tried,
> What hell it is in suing long to bide:
> To lose good days, that might be better spent;
> To waste long nights in pensive discontent;
> To speed today, to be put back tomorrow;
> To feed on hope, to pine with fear and sorrow,
> To have thy Prince's grace, yet want her Peer's;
> To have thy asking, yet wait many years.[2]

Many clients clearly felt that such delays and possible humiliations in the quest for patronage were more than outweighed by the prospect of ultimate success. Appointment to a minor office such as a stewardship of royal manors could do much to further both the fortunes and prestige of a local gentleman, and at the level of high national politics great offices of State which were disposed of by the Queen alone were glittering prizes which marked royal confidence in the fortunate recipient and usually also gave him a prominent role in the distribution of patronage at a lower level. In this situation, where ministers and officials dispensed as well as received patronage, the number of the clients who thronged around a councillor or courtier was a mark of his standing in the State. If he was unable to confer benefits on enough of them, his following would melt away and seek patronage elsewhere. The result was factions, each of which competed for as large a share as possible of royal favours (88; 100).

The Queen, determined throughout her reign to ensure a wide distribution of patronage, made it plain that no one faction leader would be allowed to monopolize her confidence and thus control the patronage machine. She saw that such a situation would deprive her of much of the sovereign power which she always jealously guarded and both contemporary and later commentators have rightly seen her manipulation of the factions as one of the secrets of her success in government. Sir Robert Naunton, an Elizabethan who wrote an account of the Queen and her ministers during the seventeenth century, summarized her policy as well as anyone has ever done when he wrote, 'The principal note of . . . [Queen Elizabeth's] reign will be that she ruled much by faction and parties which herself both made, upheld, and weakened, as her own great judgment advised.' (5, *141*) Historians in their discussion of the factions of the reign have generally concentrated in the period up to the 1580s on the followers of Burghley and Leicester and in the 1590s on the adherents of Essex and Robert Cecil, but the picture which emerges may distort a situation in which other leading noblemen and ministers, men like the duke of Norfolk and the earl of Arundel in the early years of the reign and the earl of Nottingham and Lord Cobham in the later years of the century, probably controlled substantial and significant amounts of patronage (85). Detailed knowledge of the structure of the Elizabethan factions awaits further research, but it is already apparent that while there may up until now have been excessive concentration on the Cecils, Leicester and Essex, it will not do to go to the other extreme and suppose that all prominent councillors were important cogs in the patronage machine. Thomas Radcliffe, earl of Sussex, for example, an influential councillor during the 1570s, seems to have been of very limited importance in the distribution of patronage.[3]

The existence of a significant number of factions headed by leaders of different attitudes – notably towards religion – meant that a wide spectrum of opinion was represented in the distribution of patronage. Elizabeth refused throughout her reign, to accept Puritan programmes for the reform of the Church but her favourite, Leicester, was strongly committed to the Puritan cause and his influence helped to ensure that Puritan voices were heard, if seldom heeded, in the highest counsels of the land, and that men of Puritan sympathies were not excluded from prominent ecclesiastical positions, still less from powerful secular offices. Leicester himself gave some idea of the importance of his role in church patronage in a letter which he sent in 1576 to the Puritan preacher, Thomas Wood. He stated:

> There is no man I know in this realm that hath showed a better mind to the furthering of true religion than I have done, even from the first day of her Majesty's reign to this. . . . Look of all the bishops that can be supposed that I have commended to that dignity since my credit any way served, and look whether they were not men as well thought of as any among the clergy before. Look of all the deans that in that time also have been commended by me. . . . Beside this, who in England hath had or hath more learned chaplains belonging to him that I, or hath preferred more to the furtherance of the church of learned preachers? (5, *130–1*)

Leicester's patronage of bishops like Edwin Sandys of Worcester, who eventually became archbishop of York and who was sympathetic to many Puritan ideas, can be contrasted with the attitude of Sir Christopher Hatton, a prominent courtier who held important office in the royal household before becoming Lord Chancellor in 1587. Hatton was very unsympathetic to the Puritan cause and his growing influence during the 1570s can be seen in appointments like that of John Aylmer, who began his episcopate in London in 1577 with strong attacks on the Puritans (182).

The quest for patronage inevitably centred on the Court where the leading men of the realm gathered about the Queen, but the influence of the factions penetrated into the shires where they ensured both that the voices of the country were heard at Court and that the voices of the Court were heard in the country. These voices differed at least as much in the localities as they did at the centre of power, and men of the most varied opinions in Norfolk or Kent could make their views known at Court through their patrons there (153; 251). This gave these local notables a feeling of close involvement in the political process, and during the Elizabethan period there was no suggestion of that alienation of country attitudes from Court values which was to become a conspicuous feature of English life during the reign of Charles I. The Elizabethan Court included within its bounds men of varied political and religious views whose intimate links with county society gave a fundamental and vitally important stability to the Elizabethan system. The Queen was able to carry most of the 'local governors' throughout the country with her in most of her policies for most of her reign. This was because, though they might not always agree with all that she was doing, they knew that their own different views would at least get an airing at Court.

The workings of the Elizabethan patronage machine thus helped to bring stability to the country for the greater part of the reign. Until the 1590s, despite Leicester's occasional extravagant gestures, no one really challenged its fundamental premise; that no one man or faction could hope to monopolize the Queen's confidence and with it the distribution of her favours. Burghley, whom she trusted more than any of her other servants, was too wise to attempt to push his very great influence further than the Queen would have allowed and contemporaries who thought that he engrossed her entire patronage were wide of the mark (75). The situation changed, as we shall see, with Essex's vaulting ambitions during the 1590s, but until then the patronage machine served the Queen's purposes effectively. It enabled her to distribute her favours among a wide cross-section of her most prominent subjects while at the same time ensuring that Court and country were linked by ties of mutual self-interest which gave their leading members either the reality or the hope of substantial material benefits in the service of their sovereign.

---

1. F. Bacon, *Essay 'Of Great Place'*.
2. E. Spenser, *Mother Hubbard's Tale*, ll. 895–902.
3. Susan Doran, 'The political Career of Thomas Radcliffe, 3rd earl of Sussex' (London University Ph. D. thesis, 1977).

CHAPTER 15

Conflict and co-operation: Elizabeth and her Parliaments

During the early Tudor period there were disagreements and even at times conflicts between Crown and Parliament. These marked the rule of Henry VIII as well as the reigns of his son and elder daughter, but they should be seen as a normal part of political life and were less important than the co-operation between Crown, Lords and Commons which was the normal and expected state of affairs and which produced the vast mass of early-sixteenth-century legislation which is set out in the pages of the *Statutes of the Realm* (see (54; 114; 115) also Chs. 9 and 10 above). There is no doubt that there was a considerable increase in the prestige and authority of Parliament during these years. The Reformation Parliament of 1529–36 was not only of unprecedented length, with eight sessions over a period of seven years, it also discussed matters of unprecedented importance, the ecclesiastical legislation of the Henrician Reformation. As a result Parliament acquired enhanced dignity not only in the eyes of its own members but also almost certainly in those of the nation as a whole. Henry VIII, who did nothing to discourage this growth in parliamentary prestige, made the point well when he stated in 1542, 'we at no time stand so highly in our estate royal as in the time of Parliament' (3, *270*). During Henry VIII's reign, it is true, Parliament's precise role in ecclesiastical affairs was uncertain, but under Edward VI it assumed, in the Statute of Uniformity of 1549, authority in doctrinal matters which later sovereigns – notably Elizabeth – might dislike but could never wholly reject. The early sixteenth century also saw significant changes in the composition of Parliament, both of the House of Lords and of the House of Commons. As we have seen above (Ch. 11), as a result of the dissolution of the monasteries the Lords became primarily secular in composition. As far as the Commons is concerned, the important point to notice is the growth in the number of members [D.2]. There were 296 MPs at the beginning of the sixteenth century and exactly 400 at Elizabeth's accession in 1558 (118). This great expansion was basically the result of the desire of local gentlemen for parliamentary seats – by the sixteenth century it was a significant mark of prestige to secure election to the Commons – and the workings of the patronage system ensured that successive sovereigns were persuaded by court and government notables to create the new borough seats necessary to fulfil at least some of the growing demands from the shires. There was little rationality in the choice of the boroughs enfranchised. Many were, from the start, small and intrinsically unimportant – among the 'rotten boroughs' of the eighteenth century – but the courtiers and country gentlemen who secured their creation were well satisfied. The latter got the seats in the Commons which they desired and the former the gratitude of the gentlemen they had patronized and thus the strengthening of their own influence in the country.

During the reign of Henry VIII the Commons also notably advanced its rights and privileges. In 1515 it gained control over the attendance of its members; these in future had to obtain a licence from the Speaker if they wished to leave before the end of a session (6 Henry VIII, c. 16). In 1523 the vague right to free speech which the Commons traditionally enjoyed was formalized at the request of Sir Thomas More, who was then Speaker (3). The whole question of free speech was to lead to trouble during Elizabeth's reign, and it is important to note that what More asked for and got was the right to oppose freely matters which were *legitimately* before the House. It was not intended to allow members to discuss high affairs of State without the Crown's consent. In 1542, as a result of Ferrers's case (3, *267–70* where it is misdated 1543), the Commons obtained the right to enforce, on its own authority, the traditional freedom of members from arrest on private suits [E.1(5)]. That had hitherto been enforced by the Crown on members' behalf, but it is significant that the new authority of the Commons did not extend against the Crown, and during Elizabeth's reign members such as Peter Wentworth and Anthony Cope were arrested on the Queen's orders while Parliament was in session, usually on the grounds of unconstitutional actions outside the House (117, vol. 2).

During Elizabeth's reign some MPs attempted, not very successfully, to advance their early Tudor privileges. In 1586, in the celebrated Norfolk election case, the Commons asserted a right to decide disputed elections to the House themselves, to the exclusion of the authority of the Lord Chancellor, who had traditionally had the final voice in such matters [E.3(9)]. The claim, however, was not recognized by the Crown and the Commons did not attempt a consistent defence of their position. In 1589 they went a long way towards recognizing once more Chancery's rights in this field. The issue came up again, as we shall see (Ch. 30), in the Buckinghamshire election case in James I's reign (117, vol. 2). As far as the fundamental privilege of free speech was concerned, the Queen refused to make any concessions to those who wished to extend its limits. In 1593 she restated [E.3(10)], through the Lord Keeper, the traditional position of 1523, and throughout her reign she tried to maintain a careful distinction between 'matters of State' which might only be discussed by MPs with royal consent, and 'commonwealth' affairs which could properly be initiated by private members. The result was a royal interpretation of the Commons rights which probably reduced their practical freedom of speech to a level below that of the reign of Henry VIII.

Though MPs did not make significant additions to their privileges during Elizabeth's reign the size of the Commons continued to grow [D.(2)]. Another 62 seats were added, giving a total membership of 462 by the end of the reign. Moreover, the 'quality' of the membership continued to improve. During the early Tudor period the gentlemen who flocked in ever increasing numbers into the Commons as representatives of the newly enfranchised boroughs were increasingly wealthy and well educated. The 'invasion' of the boroughs by country gentlemen continued under Elizabeth – her later Parliaments contained four gentlemen to every townsman – and more and more of them had a higher education at either a university or an inn of court or both. In the 1563 Parliament

139 MPs were in that position, in 1584, 219, and by the 1593 Parliament 252 MPs, well over half the total, had had either a university or a legal education (118).

Sir John Neale has argued that this growth in the 'quality' of the House and the self-confidence which went with it was one of the major reasons for the formidable front which MPs were able to present in opposition to the Crown during the Elizabethan period, and his two large narrative volumes (117) are essentially a story of conflict between the Crown on the one hand and members of the House of Commons on the other. Neale does, of course, emphasize that the conflicts were always within carefully defined limits – he continually stresses the *fundamental* loyalty of virtually all MPs to the Crown – but any reader of his work is inevitably left with the impression that the central focus of Elizabethan parliamentary history should be study of the differences between the Queen on the one hand and very many MPs on the other. It is a story which fits in well with the traditional Whig view of early modern English history, a view which sees English freedoms developing in the sixteenth and seventeenth centuries as a result of growing conflicts between Crown and Commons. Neale's vivid picture also indicates a continuing growth in the prestige of Parliament and especially of the House of Commons, which, he argues, 'reached maturity in Elizabeth's reign' (118, *307*). This is a debatable point. We have already seen that the Commons failed to extend its privileges significantly beyond the limits of the early sixteenth century during the Elizabethan period, and this aspect of Neale's thesis may depend upon an optical illusion fostered by the increased evidence which enabled him to present such a detailed picture of discussions within the Lower House. Elizabeth herself did not think that Parliaments were unduly popular with her subjects and openly declared her pride in summoning them as seldom as possible. 'Her Majesty', Lord Keeper Puckering told the assembled Lords and Commons in 1593, 'hath evermore been most loth to call for the assembly of her people in Parliament and hath done the same but rarely and only upon most just, weighty and great occasions.'[1] She certainly summoned them less often than her predecessors. Between 1529 and 1558 never more than two years and often only a single year lapsed without a summons of Parliament, whereas under Elizabeth there were only thirteen sessions in forty-five years and three consecutive years often passed without a meeting (119).

During Elizabeth's reign, in fact, the co-operation between Crown and Parliament which had been the most important feature of early Tudor parliamentary history continued. There were, of course, conflicts and disagreements as well, but Neale's picture both exaggerates their extent and the importance of the role which Puritan members of the Commons played in those which did occur. Neale concentrated heavily in his account on the great dramatic incidents in the parliamentary history of the reign: religion, the succession, free speech, and the monopolies debate in 1601, and within this context he stressed both the capacity of the Puritans for organized opposition to the Crown and the skill with which the Queen managed the House of Commons for most of the reign. The foundations of his views about Puritan influence were the role which he assigned them in securing a religious settlement in 1559 which was a good deal more radical than the Queen would have liked, and his discovery of a Puritan 'Choir' in the Parliament of 1563–66, a core of over forty radicals who continued the pressures of 1559 upon the Crown, this time mainly on the issue of the succession, and continued to direct or inspire Puritan moves in later Parliaments. We have seen however, that it is doubtful if there was any conflict at all between the Queen and radical Protestants in the 1559 Parliament (above, Ch. 12), and it has been argued that the Choir, far from being an 'opposition' clique contained men of the most varied political views and cannot legitimately be seen as a Puritan pressure group (112). In this context it may be noted that Thomas Norton, seen by Neale as a leader of the Choir and one of the greatest parliamentary agitators of the reign, now appears in the work of Dr Michael Graves as a man who, despite his moderate Puritanism, was essentially a professional layer and legislator who often co-operated with privy councillors and who played an extremely important role in the detailed business of the House, sitting on innumerable committees and furthering much routine legislation. It is a convincing picture and emphasizes the dangers of Neale's concentration on the more dramatic aspects of a man's parliamentary career to the exclusion of his more mundane concerns in the Commons.[2]

The religious differences which arose throughout the reign between the Crown and Puritan members of the Commons turned, as Neale has emphasized, upon the desire of Puritans to modify the Church settlement established in 1559 and the Queen's determination to resist such attempted changes [G.4(19)]. Such Puritan pressure, which can be seen in major incidents in 1566 and 1571 and in an attempt to establish a full-blown Presbyterian system in 1587 can be interpreted, if one follows Neale's views, as a continuation of agitation by radicals who had been partly successful in imposing a religious settlement on the Queen or, if one follows Dr Jones's interpretation, as the desire of men who had been broadly satisfied with the government's plans in 1559 to press ahead with reform. Whichever view is favoured, the most notable thing about the agitation is surely its failure. The Queen was quite unmoved and the 1559 settlement remained at the end of the reign, as at the beginning, the foundation of the Elizabethan Church. The question of the succession [B] produced major differences between Queen and Commons in 1563 and 1566 and came to the fore again several times later on in the reign, notably in 1571, 1572 and 1584, always on these latter occasions in connection with attempts by MPs to secure the formal exclusion of Mary Queen of Scots. Elizabeth resolutely refused to debar Mary, just as in 1563 and 1566 she had resisted sustained pressure to name a successor from the Lords and the Privy Council as well as the Commons. The especially difficult situation which she faced in 1566 when she was virtually isolated in the face of the determination of her councillors and Parliament to obtain a formal declaration about the succession illustrates the fact that Commons conflicts with the Queen usually caused her major anxieties only when they had the support of the Lords and often of the Council as well. It was the combined agitation of Council, Lords and Commons against Norfolk and Mary Queen of Scots in 1572 which secured the former's execution in the face of royal reluctance and the even greater pressure which they employed in 1586–87 which finally brought Mary herself to the block. In striking contrast, agitation in the Commons over free speech in 1566, 1576 and 1587 produced no extension of the House's rights in that field, although Peter

Wentworth's disrespectful words about the Queen in 1576 led to his imprisonment in the Tower by order of the House itself [E.3(8)]. The attitude of the Commons towards Wentworth in 1576 suggests indeed that he was essentially a maverick, a man whose views on free speech, which were of great significance for the future, were too far ahead of their time in the Elizabethan period. His advocacy of the House's right and duty to discuss all high matters of State would, if accepted, have overturned the entire basis of Tudor personal monarchy. It makes the Queen's fierce determination to resist very understandable.

The monopolies debate in 1601, the last conflict of the reign, was a much greater potential threat to the Crown's authority than the essentially unrepresentative agitations of Peter Wentworth. It involved a challenge to the royal prerogative of making regulations for the control of trade and industry. Elizabeth had issued numerous grants of monopolies which gave individuals the sole right to make or distribute particular products. This was one method of rewarding royal servants, for the grants brought considerable profits to the recipients. Monopolies were, of course, always unpopular with consumers as they tended to raise prices, and during the 1590s the bulk of the population had to pay for them against a background of serious economic depression. A dutiful and restrained attack on the system in the Parliament of 1597 gave way to fierce agitation in 1601 following the government's failure to take adequate action to improve the situation. Monopolies affected members of all religious persuasions, and the Commons pressure which forced the Queen to withdraw the most objectionable grants and to expose the rest to challenge in the common law courts was a triumph for the House as a whole. It was arguably the only notable purely Commons victory of the reign.

Agitation in the Commons alone, if one excepts the events of 1601, seems to have done little to change or modify Elizabeth's policies. It usually required sustained pressure from the Lords and at least some of her Council as well to move the Queen and even then, as on the succession issue in 1566, she sometimes resisted all persuasion. It is hard to avoid the judgement that the political influence of the Commons in Elizabeth's reign was very limited and this conclusion, reinforced to some extent by the skill with which Elizabeth managed her Parliaments, reminds us that the Commons was not and did not regard itself as essentially a body of agitators. Its basic role was to co-operate with the Crown and the Lords in passing legislation. The passage of laws demanded, of course, parliamentary management, and the methods by which Elizabeth influenced the Commons and helped to control the flow of business there have received a good deal of detailed attention (for a summary see (98, *33 ff*). Through the magic of her personality and judicious use of privy councillors, the Speaker and the committee system she generally managed to get her way. She could also sometimes use the Lords to kill Commons bills of which she disapproved and there was always the royal veto to quash bills which had passed both Houses but which she either disliked or wished to consider further. Neale did show that the Queen called Parliament to secure the passage of necessary legislation – subsidy bills and other important government measures. In no less than twelve out of their thirteen sessions Elizabethan Parliaments granted supply – one or more subsidy [N] on each occasion – and they often produced other important government legislation as well. Moreover, numerous bills introduced by private members of both Houses and dealing with matters of national, local or personal concern were either passed or considered. Neale only touched on a fraction of that legislation and he neglected almost entirely the private bills and Acts which were of crucial concern to individual members of both Houses or the localities where they lived or which they represented. It is arguable, however, despite his neglect, that Parliament should be regarded more as a legislative than as a political institution. The mass of Elizabethan Acts which it passed and the even greater number of bills which it considered are only now beginning to receive from historians the attention which they deserve. When we know more about this legislation we will be able to present a rounded picture of the parliamentary history of the reign.

In the most important contemporary treatise which dealt with the nature and function of Parliament, Sir Thomas Smith stressed its legislative at the expense of its political role (5), and Elizabeth demonstrated that she heartily endorsed his emphasis. Although virtually all her Parliaments were asked to pass or consider important government legislation – especially subsidy bills – only one was called specifically to debate an important political question which did not require legislation. That was the 1586 Parliament, summoned to advise the Queen on the fate of Mary Queen of Scots. Some members of the Commons insisted throughout the reign, as we have seen, in discussing political and religious matters without the Queen's approval, but this did not prevent the passage of 438 public and private Acts during the Elizabethan period, an average of about 34 per session of Parliament. That is not a bad record of legislative activity for sessions which averaged less than ten weeks in length, and the point is reinforced when it is noted that the first seven sessions of Parliament, between 1559 and 1581, which passed 144 public and 107 private Acts also considered at least 514 other bills which failed to pass (112; 119). If the government wanted money and laws from Parliament rather than political advice many private members shared its priorities. The Peter Wentworths of the House of Commons were highly untypical and most members of both the Upper and the Lower Houses probably saw meetings of Parliament as essentially occasions for legislation to further the interests of the nation as a whole and their own local and private concerns. Many important public bills were introduced or substantially modified on the initiative of 'backbench' members. Good examples are the Statute of Artificers, in its origins a government measure, which received additions about apprenticeship in the Commons, and the very important legislation on the poor in 1597, which was actually initiated by private MPs (56; 117, vol. 2). It was, of course, perfectly proper for private members to take the lead in such public 'commonwealth' business, but the bulk of them probably laid at least as much emphasis on the private legislation which could further their individual or local interests. The nineteen private Acts of the 1563 session included statutes confirming the liberties of Exeter and the privileges of Southampton, but the great majority, no less than fifteen, dealt with the strictly private affairs of the nobility and gentry. It must have been highly important to the landed classes to know that in Parliament they could have attainders reversed and difficulties about their landed estates resolved, and this aspect of the parliamentary scene, with its emphasis on Lords and Commons as fora for the vital if usually unspectacular business of the 'political nation' lends emphasis to the argument that one of the most important roles of Elizabethan Parliaments was to act as stabilizing institutions. As Professor Elton has pointed out, in addition to legislative activity which satisfied the needs of many private members, the Commons in the Elizabethan period was a place where ambitious men could further their careers by attracting the attention of the Queen and her principal advisers. By her reign all those who were appointed to the Privy Council and who were not peers had first of all served an apprenticeship in the Commons (113). It is not suggested, of course, that this was the only reason for their appointment, but it looks as if men who wished to scale the political heights realized that a seat in the Commons was likely to be a vital step in their careers.

Elizabethan Parliaments, which did much to realize the legitimate needs and ambitions of their members and contributed in these ways to achieving the political stability which was one of Elizabeth's fundamental aims, consisted of three elements, Queen, Lords and Commons, but the attention which has until recently been focused on the first and third elements of this trinity has unduly obscured the role of the Lords. Elizabethan peers, unlike some of their contemporaries in the Commons, do not seem to have kept parliamentary diaries and it is impossible to reproduce for Elizabethan Upper Houses the cut and thrust of debate in the Commons which is familiar as a result of Neale's work. During the later sixteenth century, however, the Upper House remained very important. Over Elizabeth's reign as a whole the majority of bills which came before Parliament were, it is true, introduced in the Commons, but the Lords still had a very significant share in the legislative initiative. In some sessions it was notably important in this respect, as in 1563 when 32 out of the 51 Acts finally passed started in the Lords and even in 1576 it had first view of 17 out of the total of 37 Acts passed (112). The idea that the Lords was very subservient to the Crown is almost certainly an exaggerated one. In 1559 it may have been the Upper House rather than the Commons which nearly wrecked the religious settlement, and in 1563 and 1566 the Lords were almost as determined as the Commons in pressing the Queen to name a successor. Their advice was unsuccessful on these occasions, but in 1587 similar pressure from them played an important role in bringing Mary Queen of Scots to the block. Moreover, the influence of individual peers on members of the House of Commons has not yet received the attention it deserves, and when more work has been done on this important topic the importance of the Elizabethan House of Lords may be further enhanced. From 1571 onwards, when Burghley sat in the Upper House, he managed government business in the Commons from there. This made the Lords the Crown's 'operations centre' in Parliament, and near the end of the reign the peers showed that they were still capable of winning a battle of wills with the Lower House, even in a matter which was traditionally a Commons preserve. In 1593 they bullied the Commons into granting three rather than two subsidies (117, vol. 2).

The parliamentary history of Elizabeth's reign, as it is now emerging, suggests a less dramatic and contentious picture than that presented by Neale. There was certainly opposition to the Crown in both Lords and Commons – that was part of the normal give and take of the political process – but it is wrong to exaggerate its importance or to overestimate the extent of Puritan influence in the Commons or the trouble which it caused the Queen. In the view of the government and almost certainly of most members as well Parliament's principal task throughout the reign was to pass laws, and the bulk of its time was spent in discussing essentially non-contentious matters. In providing the public legislation which both the Queen and her subjects wanted and in satisfying the private needs and ambitions of a cross-section of the political nation, it acted as an important stabilizing force in Elizabeth's essentially conservative regime.

---

1. J. E. Neale, 'The Lord Keeper's speech to the Parliament of 1592/3', *EHR*, **31** (1916), 130.
2. M. A. R. Graves, 'Thomas Norton the Parliament man', *HJ*, **23** (1980), 17 ff.

CHAPTER 16

The Crown and the localities: Elizabethan local government and justice

Members of the Elizabethan House of Commons who frequently talked about their 'country' were usually referring to their native shire rather than to England as a whole, and such particularism was even more common among those lower down the social hierarchy who frequently lived out their entire lives without leaving the county in which they had been born. Such attachment to individual localities reminds us that Elizabethan society and government were founded firmly on the bedrock of county institutions. For the vast majority of Elizabethans of all classes government was essentially local government. The gentry of the shires dominated it in their roles as justices of the peace and as members of such influential bodies as local subsidy and sewers commissions, and the lower orders, who might rarely come in contact with the central government at all, were only too well aware of the ever present eyes of local JPs and village officials.

During the sixteenth century the authority of the sheriff, traditionally the most important local official, continued a long decline which had begun in the later Middle Ages.[1] The powers of justices of the peace, in contrast, grew significantly, and new posts of lord and deputy lieutenant were created. Sheriffs, despite their reduced influence, still carried a heavy workload and the numerous administrative and judicial responsibilities together with the limited powers of the office go far in explaining why so many Elizabethan gentlemen were reluctant to accept appointment to a sheriffdom, even though the office lasted for only one year. Sheriffs did, however, come into their own at times of parliamentary elections, when they presided at the county courts where knights of the shire were chosen. On these occasions they often resorted to ingenious trickery to get their favoured candidates elected (118), and it is clear that they were then determined to exercise to the full the real power which they no longer possessed in most other fields. The office of lord lieutenant, which by 1600 had replaced that of sheriff at the head of the county hierarchy, was a Tudor creation which came into being as a result of the dangers of the early Reformation years (90). Henry VIII's reign saw only its tentative beginnings, but during the Northumberland regime lieutenants were sent into many counties and it looks as if the duke contemplated making the office a permanent part of the administrative system. Mary, however, returned to the earlier practice of appointing lieutenants only for specific reasons and at irregular intervals and it was only during Elizabeth's reign that the office came into its own. The 1580s, the years of invasion threats around the time of the Armada, saw important developments which were a significant stage on the way to making the lieutenancy a permanent feature of the administration. Between 1585 and 1587 lieutenancy commissions were issued for nearly all the English shires, and after the defeat of the Armada in 1588 continuing threats from

Spain meant that the new lieutenants were allowed to retain their posts. The office was essentially military in character and during the last fifteen or so years of Elizabeth's reign, when lieutenancies were held by great officers of State like Burghley himself and Lord Admiral Nottingham, who could not possibly attend to all the detailed work in person, deputies undertook an increasingly significant role in the work of the office; indeed the office of deputy lieutenant was essentially an Elizabethan creation.[2] The lieutenants and their deputies were primarily responsible for the training and equipment of the militia and the unpopularity of military service among the common people, especially during the years from 1585 onwards, when levies were raised for service abroad, in France and the Low Countries, made their task extremely difficult. Lieutenants also exercised some oversight of government economic regulations in the areas under their control, supervised the recusants in their districts and were responsible for the collection of the loans which the Queen raised on occasion to cover extraordinary expenses. These were often unpopular tasks, but by the end of the reign the lieutenants had come to form a vital link between central and local government. They kept the Queen and her ministers informed of the views of the shires, conveyed the Privy Council's orders to their localities and exercised influence in the appointment of new justices of the peace (153). The Queen seems to have chosen well: it was never found necessary to remove a lieutenant from office during the reign.

Beneath the lieutenants and their deputies were the justices of the peace, the key figures in local administration. The office, unlike that of lieutenant, was a medieval creation, but the numbers and powers of the justices increased significantly during the sixteenth century. At its beginning there were on average less than 10 JPs per shire, but by the middle of Elizabeth's reign the average was 40 or 50 and there was a further expansion in the last years of the century. In Wiltshire numbers increased from 30 in 1562 to 52 in 1600, in Norfolk from 34 in 1577 to 61 in 1602 and in Kent from 56 in 1562 to 96 during the 1590s (98; 153; 251). The growth in numbers was only partly the result of the greatly increased amount of work devolved upon JPs during the sixteenth century. Only a minority of justices seem to have been active at any one time and the pressure for increasing the size of the commissions seems to have come from the local gentry who regarded appointment to the office more and more as a mark of social prestige. To be left out of the ranks of the justices came to be seen as an affront to the status of a prominent gentleman's family and it was the government which tried, without success, to limit the number of justices throughout Elizabeth's reign.

There is no doubt, of course, that the active justices had to cope with a rapidly increasing volume of work, both administrative and judicial. William Lambarde, the notable Kentish lawyer and antiquary, whose *Eirenarcha* is the classic account of the work of Elizabethan JPs, listed 306 statutes which by the 1590s required the justices' assistance for their enforcement. Of these 133 predated 1485, 60 were made between 1485 and 1547, 38 were passed in the reigns of Edward VI and Mary, and 75 belonged to the Elizabethan period between 1559 and 1597.[3] Some of the Elizabethan statutes, in particular, contained very important and complicated provisions and the great statutes dealing with apprenticeship, vagrants and the poor, the centrepieces of Elizabethan social legislation, in themselves imposed very heavy workloads on justices. Statutes were one source of the justices' authority and they convey some idea of the burden of their administrative tasks. The other foundation of their power was the Commission of the Peace which was issued each year and emphasized the judicial aspects of their work. The Commission had achieved a fixed form by 1485 and retained it for most of the Tudor period. In 1590, however, largely because of the increased work of the justices, it was substantially revised in a form which lasted for over 300 years. It gave the justices the right to hear and determine a wide variety of criminal and civil cases. The more important of these judicial duties as well as some of the justices' administrative tasks could only be performed at quarter sessions, but much routine work could be done by justices either singly or in small groups. Lambarde devoted 288 pages of his book to the work of the justices out of quarter sessions[4] as opposed to 243 pages on the sessions themselves.[5] A single justice wielded extensive criminal jurisdiction, including the right to commit culprits to gaol in cases of breach of the peace and powers under statutes relating to thefts of horses and to unlawful games and hunting. Lambarde's remark that in such cases a justice having 'the whole matter committed to himself alone, ought to be wary and circumspect, lest . . . he rashly condemn the guiltless' is sufficient comment on the possible abuses inherent in wide authority devolved on individual justices, but it is clear that the amount of work which they undertook either alone or in twos and threes was essential to prevent quarter sessions being completely swamped with business.

Quarter sessions, as the name implies, were supposed to be held four times a year, though additional meetings might be called if the pressure of business made this essential. All the justices of the shire were supposed to be present, but attendance was very irregular and the work was performed by the core of hard-working gentlemen who bore the brunt of the judicial and administrative work in each of the counties. Meetings usually lasted for only one day but were conducted with all the formality which befitted important judicial gatherings. The civil jurisdiction of justices in sessions was limited, but they had very extensive powers on the criminal side where their authority was hardly less than that of the central courts at Westminster or the justices of assize. They tried cases of murder, assault, witchcraft, burglary, vagrancy, failure to attend church and a host of other crimes and misdemeanours and meted out harsh punishments which included frequent floggings. Torture, which was unknown to the common law although sometimes employed by the Privy Council in affairs of State, was never used, and after 1590 the most serious cases were in practice reserved for the justices of assize (136). Even so, the fact that eighteen offenders out of the sixty-five tried were hanged at the Derbyshire winter sessions of 1598 reveals both the continuing power of the justices and the severity with which it was sometimes exercised. The justices also used quarter sessions for the performance of some of their most important administrative tasks, such as the fixing of wage rates and the oversight of some aspects of the Poor Law, and the whole proceedings, on the administrative as well as on the judicial side, must have been a firm reminder to the lower orders of the extent of the powers which the local gentry wielded over the details of their daily lives and conduct.

The county was the fundamental unit of local government, but beneath it other smaller units, notably hundreds and parishes, played significant roles. Hundreds were important units for taxation purposes, justices often organized themselves by hundreds when carrying out some of their lesser administrative and judicial duties, and the militia was mustered hundred by hundred. The chief officers of a hundred were its two high constables who had a variety of financial, military and police duties. Much more important by Elizabeth's reign than the hundred was, however, the parish, which rose to prominence in the machinery of secular government in the period after the Reformation. From the reign of Henry VIII onwards it was given important duties in the field of poor relief, Mary's government made it responsible for the upkeep of highways, and during the Elizabethan period it established itself as a major unit of local administration, with a new executive staff of overseers of the poor and surveyors of roads who joined its traditional officials the constables and churchwardens. Elizabethan towns had their own ruling bodies, but although the details of borough administration differed substantially throughout the realm, the tendency during the Tudor period was towards closed corporations controlled by small groups of wealthy merchants. Even Norwich, which had a very liberal constitution by Elizabethan standards, had a government which was a compromise between oligarchy and democracy.

This brief survey of local government institutions demonstrates that important creative changes took place in the administration of the shires during the later sixteenth century: the great expansion in the work of the justices of the peace which had begun in the early Tudor period and which was to continue in the early seventeenth century proceeded apace; the developments in the office of lord lieutenant created an important new link between the centre and the localities and was a vital stage in the evolution of an office which has retained prominence until our own day; and the establishment of the parish as a major unit of secular government is one example of the way in which an essentially ecclesiastical institution could be changed and developed after the Reformation. Moreover, as Mr Clark has pointed out in his important study of Kent, the extension and intensification of local government which these and other changes of the period illustrate and imply, played an important role in bringing about the increasing stability which marked most county societies in the later sixteenth century (251, *111 ff*). That stability was illustrated in Kent by the relative unimportance of popular disturbances in the county in the years after 1558, when the riots which did occur never got out of hand or posed a serious threat to the established order. In Elizabethan Kent, as in most of the rest of England, the local governors were firmly in charge of the situation.

Control over local government was exercised by the Queen and Privy Council. That control could not be too strict. Justices – despite a nominal fee – were effectively unpaid and, in the last resort, the Crown relied on their voluntary co-operation to keep the wheels of administration moving. If the class as a whole refused to enforce a particular royal demand there was little the Queen could do.

Throughout the reign the value of subsidies fell sharply; a subsidy brought in almost £140,000 in 1559, only about £80,000 in 1601. Allowing for inflation that was a fall of well over a half in real terms. The major culprits were the subsidy commissioners and assessors, local gentlemen, many of them justices of the peace, who refused to make realistic assessments of gentry wealth and remained unmoved by the growing stridency of government complaints during the reign. In 1594 the government ordered that any commissioners who were JPs and assessed themselves at less than £20, 'must look to receive the disgrace to be put out of the commission'. This ultimate threat was of no avail: subsidies continued to decline in value under James I and the landed classes continued to be taxed on a small and falling proportion of their true wealth (245). This illustration of central government impotence in the face of determined resistance by the entire governing class in the localities should not be allowed to conceal the fact that *individual* justices could not afford to oppose the Crown too often on *specific* matters in which they did not have the backing of virtually all their fellows. The Queen had no hesitation in ordering the removal of JPs who had displeased her. In 1595, for example, she looked through the entire list of justices and indicated that some names were to be removed from the next commission. The reaction of most justices to the stream of instructions which they constantly received from the Privy Council was, however, probably one of moderately diligent obedience when the orders did not conflict with their direct personal interests. They considered that they knew what was best for their own localities, but were prepared to obey higher authority when it seemed reasonable to do so. As the Elizabethan Council was a body of able and efficient men – and always included prominent representatives of the gentry class – its commands usually seemed sensible enough to local notables. The Norfolk justices who reported to the Council in 1586 the efforts which they had made to maintain food supplies and keep down prices (5) were typical of those thousands of Elizabethan JPs who ran sixteenth-century local administration with an eye to the economic needs of their inferiors and in general co-operation with a central government whose paternalistic aims they fully shared.

The constant exhortations of the Privy Council are evidence that it worked hard to try and ensure the effectiveness of local government. The varied responses to its orders – seen in very different fields like taxation and the control of food supplies – is a reminder that the extent of its success was determined by the willingness and ability of the local governors to obey its commands. Their attitudes are best recorded in studies of individual counties, and recent books on Norfolk, Kent, Lancashire, Essex and Sussex reveal both the variety of local conditions and the very different attitudes of important groups of JPs in different parts of the realm (137; 153; 175; 191; 251). These contrasting details cannot be pursued here but they show that, amidst the relatively uniform institutions of local administration, each county had its own problems and its own ways of dealing with them. Early modern England has been seen as a federation of counties (see e.g. 254), each with its individual ethos, and while this argument can sometimes be carried too far there is no doubt that local patriotism and particularism greatly helped to emphasize the distinctive features of life in the varying regions of

England. The extent of government control, the workings of the patronage system and the religious complexions of the governing benches of justices varied so widely in Lancashire, Kent and Norfolk, to take just three examples, that the common institutions of these counties – sheriffs, lieutenants, quarter sessions, parishes and the like – conceal as much as they reveal. An understanding of the institutions of local government and their development in the Elizabethan period is vital in any general picture of local society. So too, however, is an appreciation of the need to put flesh on the bare bones of institutional developments by studying individual county societies in all their multifarious activities. A start has been made on such studies for the Elizabethan period, but the excellence of the work of scholars like Hassell Smith, Clark and Haigh should remind us that much still requires to be done. We need detailed studies of more Elizabethan counties.

1. For a discussion of the institutions of Elizabethan local government see A. G. R. Smith, *The Government of Elizabethan England* (1967), pp. 85 ff.
2. G. Scott Thomson, 'The origin and growth of the office of deputy-lieutenant', *TRHS*, 4th ser. **5** (1922), 150 ff.
3. W. Lambarde, *Eirenarcha* (1599 edn), pp. 608 ff.
4. Lambarde, *Eirenarcha*, pp. 74–362.
5. Lambarde, *Eirenarcha*, pp. 363–606.

CHAPTER 17

The development of the Church of England

In no respect were differences in local circumstances more marked than in matters of religion. County studies reveal much about the impact of the Elizabethan religious settlement in the localities. It was there, at grass-roots level, that the Church created by the Acts of Supremacy and Uniformity had to win support. In 1559 that Church lacked adequate doctrinal, disciplinary or philosophical bases. During Elizabeth's reign efforts were made to provide such foundations and to remedy other glaring weaknesses in the ecclesiastical establishment. A doctrinal basis, which permitted a spectrum of theological belief within a clearly Protestant framework, was, as we have seen above (Ch. 12), created by the Thirty-nine Articles of 1563, and the 1560s and 1570s also saw advances on the disciplinary and philosophical fronts. From the reign of Henry VIII onwards plans had been made for a complete revision of the medieval code of canon law, but these never reached fruition and in Elizabeth's reign the discipline of the Church was founded on a variety of royal injunctions, canons approved in convocation and episcopal articles and instructions. Many of these orders were of doubtful legal standing and there was no effort to create a coherent code from them before the reign of James I. Despite these limitations, canons like those of 1571 and 1576 did go some way in establishing a framework of conduct for the clergy.[1] They dealt in detail with the duties of all ranks of ministers from bishops downwards, and if they had been fully obeyed would have produced both admirably disciplined clergymen and a well-instructed laity. In reality, they remained an ideal no less for bishops than for their subordinates, but the fact that they had been promulgated at least gave diligent clergymen something to aim at and educated laymen a yardstick by which to measure the performance of their spiritual mentors.

On the philosophical side the great name in the early years of the reign is that of John Jewel, a Marian exile who was appointed bishop of Salisbury in 1559 and published his *Apology of the Church of England* in 1562.[2] Catholics maintained that the new English Church was a mere political creation, an act of expediency to meet the government's needs in 1559. Jewel firmly rejected such criticisms, affirming with powerful arguments that it was, in fact, a return to early Christian practices which had been destroyed by the excesses of medieval Catholicism. 'We have come as near as we possibly could', he stated, 'to the Church of the apostles and of the old . . . bishops and fathers, which Church we know hath . . . been sound and perfect . . . a pure virgin, spotted as yet with no idolatry nor with any foul or shameful fault; and have directed according to their customs and ordinances not only our doctrine but also the sacraments and the form of common prayer.' (5, *119*) He laid great emphasis on the importance of the Bible, but

Puritans, who later took comfort from that fact, had also to recognize that Jewel held very strongly to the view that they should not destroy the unity of the Church for non-essentials, such as the obligation to wear vestments. Jewel, however, died in 1571, before the development of the main Puritan challenge to the Church. His defence of the new establishment was directed essentially against the Catholics, and the Puritans were not fully answered at a high intellectual level until the publication of Hooker's work during the 1590s.

The health of the Church depended in the first resort upon the condition of the clergy. All Mary's bishops, with the exception of Anthony Kitchen of Llandaff, refused to accept the new order and were deprived. The result was a bench of bishops totally inexperienced in episcopal administration. Many of those appointed in the early years of the reign made up for this in a pastoral zeal which reflected their own ideals as well as the enormous problems which they had to face when confronted by a clergy and laity many of whom were at best indifferent and at worst openly hostile to the new Church. The new archbishop of Canterbury, Matthew Parker, had not been an exile, but almost all the other major sees, such as York, London, Durham, Winchester, Salisbury, Norwich, Ely, and Coventry and Lichfield went to men who had fled abroad in Mary's reign. Most of them, like Grindal at London, laid a stress on preaching and on the education of both clergy and laity which was different from the emphasis which the Queen herself put on conformity to legally established practices. It was this difference of views which led to the greatest ecclesiastical crisis of the reign, the suspension of Grindal from office in 1577, two years after his promotion to Canterbury following the death of Parker in 1575. That suspension has rightly been seen as a watershed in the history of the Elizabethan episcopate and from the 1570s onwards, as the first generation of bishops died, they were replaced by successors who shared the emphasis which the Queen laid on the disciplinary rather than the pastoral aspects of their office. Men like John Aylmer, bishop of London from 1577, John Piers, bishop of Rochester from 1576 and of Salisbury from 1577 and, above all, John Whitgift who was appointed to the see of Worcester in 1577 and succeeded Grindal at Canterbury in 1583, showed little of the leniency towards Puritanism which had marked the episcopates of many of their predecessors. Such differences among the bishops should not, however, as Dr Houlbrooke has pointed out, be allowed to obscure the fact that, in Elizabeth's reign 'for the first time in many centuries there was established in England a body of bishops who were nearly all normally resident in their dioceses [and] regular in visitation' (53, *98*).

In contrast with the wholesale episcopal deprivations of 1559, few of the lower clergy were ejected from their parishes in the early years of Elizabeth's reign. Only about 300 (24) carried their opposition to the new Church far enough to warrant that ultimate sanction – a small proportion in a country which had about 9,000 parishes – but this is not to say that those who remained were either enthusiastic about or even moderately pleased with the new services which they were required to conduct. Many of them had continued in their ministries through all the changes of Henry's, Edward's and Mary's reigns, and apathy and bewilderment as well as a strong desire to maintain their livelihood doubtless explains the nominal conformity of very many of them in the early years of the reign. Three conspicuous weaknesses which affected the lower clergy at the beginning of the reign were their insufficient numbers, their inadequate training and their poverty. As a result of the upheavals of the Henrician and Edwardian Reformations the number of ordinations had fallen sharply and in 1558 many parishes had no resident minister. Between 10 and 15 per cent of livings seem to have been vacant at Elizabeth's accession and in some localities the situation was much worse; some areas of the sees of London and Canterbury, in the most populous parts of the realm, had vacancies in a third of their parishes (165). These vacancies were filled up during the course of the reign, but it was more difficult to ensure that parish priests were adequately trained. Here too, however, progress was made. The proportion of graduates among the clergy rose almost everywhere, especially during the last two decades of the century, although there were still very wide variations in different parts of the country. In the diocese of Worcester 19 per cent were graduates in 1560, 23 per cent in 1580 and 52 per cent by 1620. In Coventry and Lichfield only 14 per cent had a degree in 1584 and 24 per cent in 1603. The situation was very different in the favoured see of Oxford where 38 per cent were graduates at the beginning of the reign, a proportion which rose strikingly during the second half of the century (27; 165). These figures show that much remained to be done before the ideal of a fully graduate clergy was achieved, but also that the Elizabethan period was a vital stage on the way towards that goal, which was virtually attained by the reign of Charles I, when the overwhelming majority of recruits to the Church were graduates. A degree suggested that its possessor had the inherent intellectual abilities necessary to make a suitable minister of God's word, but a higher education alone did not guarantee pastoral success. Potential ordinands had to undergo an examination, usually conducted by an archdeacon, which tested their religious zeal and the reality of their vocation, as well as their more formal educational qualifications. Most of those rejected seem to have been refused on account of insufficient knowledge of the Scriptures and Nicholas Wallys, who sought admission in the diocese of Ely in 1568, found that his BA was not enough to compensate for his ignorance of the Bible. In some dioceses – such as Ely – fairly rigorous standards seem to have prevailed in these examinations from the early years of the reign, and it is clear that in the later sixteenth century bishops were able to demand generally higher standards in terms of learning and pastoral ability from those who sought entry to the ministry; here probably are the beginnings of the emergence of that clerical 'profession' with increasingly stringent educational, pastoral and preaching standards which Dr O'Day has distinguished as a recognizable entity by the early seventeenth century (165).

If standards among the lower clergy did show signs of growing professionalism during the reign it is clear that much remained to be done before the Puritan ideal of a preaching minister in every parish was achieved. It was the desire of both the Puritan clergy and laity throughout the country to bring the word of God, adequately expounded from the pulpit, to as wide a cross-section of the population as possible, which led to the development of the office of lecturer. This became a permanent feature in many parishes in the later sixteenth century.

Local gentlemen, town corporations or groups of parishioners provided funds for the establishment of lectureships which were conferred on learned men – usually but not always with Puritan sympathies – who then preached regularly in parishes which had been accustomed to only occasional sermons (184). These lectureships, of course, bypassed the normal channels of ecclesiastical discipline and the later Elizabethan episcopate was generally hostile to them as a challenge to hierarchical authority. Lecturers were often much better paid than parish clergymen and there can be no doubt that one of the greatest obstacles which the bishops faced in their quest for a well-educated ministry was the financial inadequacy of many church livings (53; 192). The bishops generally found that their own incomes were reduced as Elizabeth continued the assault on episcopal lands which had begun under Henry VIII and Edward VI, and at a lower level as well the laity exploited ecclesiastical income which should properly have been devoted to the support of the clergy. Laymen enjoyed the income of nearly 4,000 of the 9,000 or so parish benefices, usually allowing the clergymen who served the spiritual needs of the parishioners only a meagre stipend out of the 'impropriated' [N] revenue. Even in the other parishes, where the full income came to the incumbents, it was often insufficient to support a wife and family in suitable style and in 1585 Whitgift complained that only about 600 livings in the country were adequate for a learned minister (27, *309–10*; 165, *127*). Parish ministers depended on the tithes [N] collected from the laity for the bulk of their income and an Act of 1549 (2 & 3 Edward VI, c. 13) which effectively reduced the number of tithe payers and made tithes more difficult to collect exacerbated the economic problems of many already inadequate livings. The low incomes of the majority of parish clergymen throughout and after the Elizabethan period must have restricted the number of able men who were potential recruits for the ministry. In these circumstances the achievement of Elizabeth's bishops in raising clerical standards, partial and incomplete though it was, was a considerable one. They had legitimate cause to complain about those Elizabethan gentlemen, often the holders of impropriated tithes, who were loud in demanding improved standards in the parishes and yet showed little inclination to help in providing the economic resources which would help to attract the best men into the regular ministry of the Church. Such generosity as they did show towards the clergy was usually expended on the support of lecturers who were often, as we have seen, effective rivals to the established parish system.

Despite all the difficulties which the Church faced there were more and better educated clergymen at the end of Elizabeth's reign than at the beginning. The success of their ministry depended ultimately on their ability to influence the minds of the laity. Fundamental in this respect was the extent to which the authorities were able to secure the regular attendance of the population at church. The Act of Uniformity of 1559, which provided that all men and women should attend church on Sundays and holy days, imposed a fine of 12d for each absence, 'to be levied by the churchwardens of the parish where such offence shall be done' (1 Eliz., c. 2). In 1581, at a time of especially strong anti-Catholic feeling, the penalty was raised to £20 a month for all those over sixteen who absented them-selves from Sunday services (23 Eliz., c. 1). That very heavy penalty could have been paid, when it was actually imposed, only by the more prosperous gentry families, and even the much more modest fine of 1559 was beyond the resources of poorer parishioners. These fines were designed primarily to drive Catholic sympathizers into their parish churches, but they were never systematically levied and it seems clear that large numbers of men and women absented themselves from Sunday worship throughout the reign. The 'lower orders' were notorious for their reluctance to come to church. Sir Nicholas Bacon, Lord Keeper of the Great Seal, commented in 1563 that 'the common people in the country universally come . . . seldom to common prayer and divine service'[3] and it seems that the authorities concentrated their efforts in enforcing attendance on those above a certain social level. Archbishop Grindal's injunctions for the province of York in 1571 stated that all lay people should come to church, 'especially householders' (276, *160*); the absence of the poorer members of the community was clearly regarded with a certain equanimity. Mr Clark has estimated that 'something like a fifth of the population of Kent stayed away from church on a regular basis in the late sixteenth century', the great majority of them poor and ignorant people (251, *156*). Even when men did come to church they often made their contempt for or indifference towards the proceedings plain. Bacon complained that those who *did* attend services were too often 'vainly occupied' during worship. The kind of behaviour he had in mind was doubtless typified by that of members of the congregation whose attitudes were vividly described by their parish priest in 1603. 'My parishioners', said Nicholas Breton, '. . . are a kind of people that love a pot of ale better than a pulpit . . ., who, coming to divine service more for fashion than devotion, are contented after a little capping and kneeling, coughing and spitting, to help me to sing out a psalm, and sleep at the second lesson.' Those who lived far off, he continued, did not even bother to stay until the end of the proceedings but left early, 'glad to be gotten home to dinner'. That was doubtless unseemly behaviour, but it was better than the conduct of a Somerset parishioner who, on one occasion during the 1590s, shouted at a long-winded preacher that it was time he stopped so that the maids might go milking, or than the indecency of a Cambridgeshire man whose 'most loathsome farting, striking, and scoffing speeches' in church in 1598 occasioned 'the great offence of the good and the great rejoicing of the bad'.[4] In view of the number of poor parishioners who stayed away altogether from church and of the attitude of some of those who did attend, it is not surprising that many Elizabethans were deeply ignorant of the Christian religion. An Essex minister reported in 1598 that the lower orders did not even understand the Lord's Prayer, and a few years later another reported that in a parish of 400 he had found only 10 per cent who had any real knowledge of basic Christian tenets. The situation was at its worst in the 'dark corners' of the land, parts of the North and Wales. The Puritan divine John Penry reported that in Elizabethan Wales thousands of people knew nothing of Christ – 'yea almost . . . never heard of him' (276, *164–5*).

The indifference or hostility of many men and women towards the Established Church was doubtless encouraged at the beginning of the reign by the attachment of a large proportion of the population to traditional forms of Catholic worship and throughout it by the inadequacy of the machinery for enforcing ecclesiastical discipline on the laity. By the 1570s the authorities seem to have succeeded in suppressing most 'superstitious' images and ceremonies in parish churches and thus in gradually weaning people away from the visual appeal of the old religion, but the frequently lax attitude of churchwardens, local notables and church courts helped to ensure that the ideal of a wholly church-going population remained, as we have seen, a dream (24). Ignorance, indifference or hostility on the part of a large percentage of the population towards the Church should not, of course, be regarded as anything essentially new – the same attitudes were common during the Middle Ages – and in the Elizabethan period, as in former times, the bulk of the population doubtless did attend their local churches, even if they were not always inspired by or even interested in what they heard there.

By the late 1580s, despite all its difficulties, the Church had begun to put down roots in the country. It was still faced with hostility or indifference on the part of substantial numbers of the people and there continued to be considerable poverty among the lower ranks of the clergy. On the other hand, the numbers and training of those entering the priesthood had gradually improved since the beginning of the reign and the Church had begun to establish doctrinal and phil-osophical bases for its claim to be a true Christian body descended from the Church of the Early Fathers. Its successes, such as they were, can be attributed largely to the lack of any really serious doctrinal divisions among the clergy, to the identification of the Church with the authority of the Crown and, above all, perhaps, to the passage of time. By 1588 thirty years had gone by since the settlement and most men and women in the country had got used to the new services and ideas which they saw and heard in their churches. The importance of habit can hardly be overestimated. By the 1590s it was working in favour of the Church rather than, as in the 1560s, against it, and that is perhaps the key to understanding why the Elizabethan Church, for all its faults, had won a firm place in national life before the end of the reign. It faced, of course, the hostility of Catholics, who totally rejected it, and the attacks of Puritans, who wished to reform or transform it. In its relationship with the Puritans the 1570s and early 1580s were probably a turning-point for the Church. After Grindal's suspension in 1577 and still more after Whitgift's appointment as archbishop in 1583 it was clear that Puritan discontents with the Establishment were likely to increase rather than to diminish, as had seemed likely during the archiepiscopate of the compassionate and pastorally minded Grindal. In the 1580s and 1590s the Church of England waged a war on two fronts, against both Puritans and Catholics rather than the single struggle against the Catholic enemy which a continuation and development of Grindalian policies might have made possible.

---

1. E. Cardwell, *Synodalia* (Oxford, 1842), I, pp. 111 ff, 132 ff. For comments see V. J. K. Brook, *A Life of Archbishop Parker* (Oxford, 1962), pp. 267 ff; P. Collinson, *Archbishop Grindal* (1979), p. 227.

2. Published in Latin as *Apologia Ecclesiae Anglicanae*, but soon translated into English and later into several foreign languages as well. A good modern edition is J. E. Booty, *An Apology of the Church of England* (Ithaca, 1963).
3. P. Collinson, 'Sir Nicholas Bacon and the Elizabethan *Via Media*', *HJ*, **23** (1980), 268.
4. Collinson, *HJ*, **23** (1980), 268; J. Hurstfield and A. G. R. Smith, *Elizabethan People*, p. 136; K. Thomas, *Religion and the Decline of Magic*, pp. 161–2.

CHAPTER 18

The challenge to the Church: Puritan opposition and Catholic threat

The name 'Puritan' [N] began to be applied during the 1560s to describe strong Protestants who criticized the newly established Elizabethan Church on the grounds that it needed reform (182). It was a word of abuse, rejected by those to whom it was applied – 'the adversary', said a petition addressed to the Privy Council about 1580, 'very cunningly hath new-christened us with an odious name . . . of Puritanism; we detest . . . the name' (196, *14*) – and scholars have differed as to precisely who should be comprehended within the term. The major difficulty is whether Separatists [N], who wished to leave the Church altogether, should be included.[1] It is arguably best to use the widest description possible and we may follow Professor Kearney in defining Puritanism as the 'circle of discontent both within and without the Established Church from the 1560s onwards. . . . What was common to all [the critics] . . . was a vision of what the Church of Christ ought to be if it were stripped of externals and inessentials. Where they differed . . . was in their view of what was external and inessential'.[2] Although some scholars have argued differently,[3] it seems difficult to maintain that there were significant theological divisions between the Puritans and their opponents, all of them strongly influenced by Calvinism, especially on key issues like grace and predestination. As far as church government was concerned, many moderate Puritans accepted the episcopal office, though they laid stress on its pastoral rather than on its disciplinary aspects. Here their attitude was very similar to that of many of the early Elizabethan bishops, and in the early days of Grindal's achiepiscopate it seemed that a real alliance between hierarchy and Puritans might be possible on the basis of a commonly shared belief in the need for moderate church reform and strong opposition to the Catholic menace (on Grindal, see (181)). More extreme Puritans, who believed in a Presbyterian form of government for the Church, were probably never as influential in the 1570s and 1580s as the propaganda of their opponents has led some historians to believe, and the Separatists, who wished each congregation to be master of its own affairs and rejected the whole idea of a national Church, were never more than a tiny minority throughout the reign. These divisions among the Puritans on matters of ecclesiastical government undoubtedly weakened the ability of the Presbyterians to resist Archbishop Whitgift's onslaughts upon them in the later years of the reign but, as Professor Dickens has reminded us, it will not do to make too firm distinctions between 'Anglicans' and 'Puritans' for the greater part of the Elizabethan period (27; *313 ff*). Such distinctions imply theological divisions which, as we have seen, probably did not exist, and the Puritans can best be seen in a general sense as those strongly committed Protestants who laid the greatest possible stress on Bible reading and on hostility to the Catholic enemy. The latter implied the rejection of all 'superstitious' practices remaining from the medieval past in the English Church and explains the heat aroused by the 'vestiarian controversy' of the 1560s, when Puritans resisted the attempts of the hierarchy, driven on by the Queen, to impose the use of the surplice at ecclesiastical services (182).

Puritans were to be found in significant numbers in all sections of Elizabethan society except the lowest. Puritan emphasis on individual reading and understanding of the Gospels – a religion of the mind rather than of the eye – meant that the illiterate masses, who laid stress on the visual aspects of worship, were largely unaffected by the movement. Indeed, as we have seen, many of the 'lower orders' were ignorant of the basic tenets of Christianity. If it did not seem a contradiction in terms it would be tempting to include Marian exiles among the bishops, men like Grindal and Sandys, who enforced the Queen's instructions on vestments very reluctantly, if at all, among the ranks of the Puritans, and it is certain that some of the greatest noblemen of the realm, like Ambrose Dudley, earl of Warwick, Henry Hastings, earl of Huntingdon, a relative of the Queen and a possible heir to the throne, and Francis Russell, earl of Bedford, were strongly committed to the 'godly' cause. Most important of all was the Queen's favourite, Robert Dudley, earl of Leicester, who rapidly became the great champion and defender of Puritanism at Court and in the country, and the influence of these men and their many like-minded allies among the gentry was vital both in protecting Puritanism in the localities and in ensuring that Puritan ministers were presented to livings under their patronage. Among the stoutest champions of the movement were upper-class ladies like the Yorkshire heiress Margaret Hoby whose extreme piety is revealed in the diary which she kept at the end of the reign. Her account of a day in her life reveals the extent to which religious devotions dominated the minds and occupied the time of some at least of the most committed supporters of Puritanism.

> In the morning after private prayers and order taken for dinner I wrote some notes in my testament till ten o'clock; then I went to walk and, after I returned home, I prayed privately, read a chapter of the Bible and wrought [i.e. embroidered] till dinner time. After, I walked awhile with Mr Rhodes and then I wrought and did some things about the house till 4. Then I wrote out the sermon into my book preached the day before and, when I had again gone about the house and given order for supper and other things, I returned to examination and prayer. Then I walked till supper time and, after catechising, meditated awhile of that I had heard, with mourning to God for pardon both of my omission and commission, wherein I found myself guilty, I went to bed (5, *129*).

A man like Secretary of State Sir Francis Walsingham had less time than Lady Margaret to devote to his prayers, but he carried his Puritan piety into his view of the international scene with which he was so largely concerned in his office. 'What juster cause can a prince that maketh profession of the Gospel have to enter into wars than when he seeth confederacies made for the rooting out of the Gospel and religion he professeth?' (98, *18*) asked Walsingham rhetorically when advocating active English intervention against Spain in the Netherlands. His vision of the world, in which the fight against the Catholic Antichrist was all important, irrespective of immediate national interests, was not, of course, shared by the Queen, but it must have been similar to that of other Puritans in high official places – men like Sir Walter Mildmay, Chancellor of the Exchequer, and Robert Beale, clerk of the Privy Council, who helped to keep Puritan views in the forefront of the political arena where they were heard, if seldom heeded, by the Queen. Puritans were also prominent, of course, among merchants and other leading townsmen (53), but the idea that the Puritan ethic was essentially one of hard-headed capitalism, dominated by the profit motive, will not bear examination. Dr Knappen has proved beyond reasonable doubt that Puritanism was essentially an 'other worldly' religion, extremely suspicious of capitalist tendencies and emphasizing traditional aspects of economic morality like the 'just price' (183, *339 ff*). In their economic views, in fact, Puritans generally shared the ideas of other members of the Church of England and of the government itself, though with their usual sense of fierce commitment they were quick to take a lead, as in the parliamentary legislation on the poor in 1597, when there was an obvious social need.

Puritanism, then, in its mainstream and more moderate aspects, should be regarded as a movement for reform in the Church which had much in common with the views of the more evangelically inclined members of the hierarchy. The Puritan ideal of a literate, Bible-reading laity who led godly lives under the direction of a learned preaching ministry in a Church purged of Popish remnants was also the ideal of Archbishop Grindal. The trouble came when the Queen, dissatisfied with the lack of order in the Church, tried to enforce the use of the surplice in the 1560s. Bishops like Grindal, who disliked the Queen's orders, nevertheless agreed that the use of the vestment was a 'thing indifferent' which the prince might lawfully require. Puritans, not burdened with the responsibility of high office under the watchful eye of Elizabeth, agreed that the matter was not in itself a vital one but maintained that, as there was no command in the Bible to wear such a vestment, its use could not properly be demanded. Such attitudes hardened over the years and the more extreme Puritans, resentful of the hierarchy's attitude, followed Thomas Cartwright into Presbyterian ideas during the 1570s and 1580s. This aroused the deepest suspicion in Elizabeth, who believed that Presbyterianism was subversive of royal authority. She began to take a hard line towards the Puritan movement as a whole and when she tried to suppress the prophesyings [N], those exercises for clerical education which were supported by Grindal and many of his fellow bishops, the stage was set for a confrontation between the Crown and the Puritan leadership which culminated in Whitgift's assult on Puritanism in the 1580s [G.4(18)] and his destruction of the organized Presbyterian wing of the movement in the early 1590s. The details of that conflict have been vividly described by Professor Collinson ((182), see also Ch. 28), and it is important to note with him that the growing extremism of some sections of the Puritan movement during the 1570s and 1580s was largely a reaction to the Queen's and eventually Whitgift's hostility to the moderate Puritanism of the early years of the reign.

This important conclusion reinforces the thesis that a moderate 'Grindalian' approach to Puritanism throughout the reign might have produced a largely united Church of England by the late 1580s instead of the divided body, containing a number of Presbyterian sympathizers, which Whitgift faced during his archiepiscopate. It can be argued that a large part of the explanation for this situation lies in the fundamentally different attitudes of the Queen and the Puritans towards the Church. The latter saw its deficiencies as scandals which needed immediate and sustained efforts at reform supported by government, clergy and all sections of lay society. Elizabeth was equally aware of the defects, but she regarded them much more philosophically. 'Thus much I must say', she said of the Church to the assembled Lords and Commons in Parliament in 1585, 'that some faults and negligences may grow and be, as in all other great charges it happeneth, and what vocation without'. Her major concern was with conformity to the Prince's lawful commands in the ecclesiastical no less than in the secular sphere. She dreaded the 'new fangleness' of the Puritans – a probable reference to the Presbyterian threat – and pronounced it 'dangerous to a kingly rule' (5, *115*). She exaggerated both the strength of the Presbyterians and their hostility to her government, but such as they were she had been largely responsible for bringing them about by her lack of sympathy for the moderate Puritanism which at the start of her reign had sought effective church reform. In 1603 that moderate Puritanism was still a formidable force among the literate laity after its comparatively small Presbyterian wing had been destroyed as an organized force by Archbishop Whitgift (see Ch. 28).

By 1588, the year of the Armada, it was clear that Puritanism, whatever its ultimate fate, had already made a significant contribution to English religious life. The early Elizabethan bishops, the generation whose members began to die off during the 1570s, had been sympathetic to many proposals for moderate reform and Archbishop Grindal himself had been suspended in 1577 for refusing to suppress the prophesyings which Puritan ministers and laity so strongly supported. The tacit goodwill of members of the hierarchy during the early years of the reign, together with the help of Puritan noblemen and gentlemen, meant that Puritan ideas and attitudes took root among large numbers of the educated laity during the 1560s and 1570s. The preaching tradition of the Church of England, one of its notable features, was established largely by Puritans like 'silver-tongued' Henry Smith, whose sermons still convey a strong sense of the physical realities of hell (5), and such men were able to use the pulpit to spread their message because the workings of the patronage system gave Puritan gentlemen the right to present their favoured candidates to many parish benefices. Other radical clergymen found an outlet in the urban lectureships which became such a feature of the Elizabethan ecclesiastical scene and Puritan merchants and gentlemen did much to begin the civilization of the 'dark corners of the land', those regions in Wales and the north of England where their charity brought schools and other benefits which began to draw these parts of the realm into the main stream of English life (193). The Puritans also had their failures. The greatest was their inability to secure changes in the 1559 religious settlement, which the Queen continued throughout the reign to regard as sacrosanct, and the more extreme forms of Puritanism had a limited impact in the country at large. The Separatists, though active from the 1560s right through the reign, were always a tiny, unrepresentative minority, and the Presbyterians, though more numerous, were still always a limited group and never fully united under a common programme. The comparative ease with which Whitgift was able to destroy their organization during the 1590s suggests that the threat which they posed to the Establishment should not be exaggerated.

Members of the Established Church, whether or not they were Puritans, shared that common hatred of Catholicism which was one of the distinguishing features of Elizabethan society and which can be seen consistently in Elizabethan parliamentary debates. The Puritan threat to the Church came from within. It represented the views of a body of men who wished to reform the Establishment, not to destroy it. The Catholic threat, in contrast, came from outside the Church and, indeed, part of it came from outside the country as well. It was, therefore, at the beginning of the reign, a threat to the independence of the 'nation state' which had been established when Henry VIII had rejected the Papacy during the 1530s and been renewed when Elizabeth had once more cast off papal authority in 1559. It can be argued that the Catholic threat was *potentially* at its greatest in the years up to the 1570s – before the Church of England began to strike roots in the country at large. During these early years of the reign, however, there was no effective Catholic challenge to the government. This can be explained partly by the lack of any clear lead from abroad – Rome made no pronouncement against the Queen – and the consequent drift of many Catholic laymen into the Established Church, and partly by the fact that the government did not begin energetic persecution of Catholic dissenters until the 1570s; which meant that Catholics did not until then have the martyrs around which a cause can so often rally (24; 185; 187). When the Catholic challenge did come, as a result of important developments from 1568 onwards, it had, therefore, a comparatively small body of committed domestic supporters behind it – a fact which decisively weakened it as a threat to the Protestant Establishment. The flight of Mary Queen of Scots to England in 1568 and her imprisonment there made her a focus for Catholic loyalties in England and the rebellion of the northern earls, though it had important political and economic motives as well, was designed to restore Catholicism. These events (186) which greatly alarmed Elizabeth's Protestant ministers, were preludes to the papal bull [N] *Regnans in Excelsis*, issued by Pius V in 1570, in which he excommunicated and deposed the Queen [G.4(17)]. The issue of the bull forced the hard core of English Catholics into open opposition to the Crown. This took two forms, political and religious. The political threat centred at first around various plots to depose Elizabeth and replace her by Mary, conspiracies like the Ridolfi Plot of 1571. the Throckmorton Plot of 1583 and the Babington Plot of 1586, all of which included provision for Catholic foreign aid. In 1587, as a result of her involvement in the Babington Plot, Mary Queen of Scots was executed. In the later years of the reign, from 1585 onwards, there was war with Spain and the threat of a Spanish invasion of England. Philip II certainly regarded his war against the heretical Elizabeth as a crusade, and his ultimate aim was her removal from the throne and a Catholic restoration. These political challenges, which involved only a tiny minority of fanatics at home or assaults on England from abroad, were regarded with horror or distaste by most of the

English Catholic laity whose religious differences with the Queen did not readily convert them either into supporters of assassination or of a foreign conquest of England. They made their position plain enough at the time of the Armada in 1588, when the Catholic nobility and gentry demonstrated their fundamental political loyalty to the regime.

More serious was the religious resistance, which centred on the missionary priests who came to England from 1574 onwards from the seminary at Douai in the Spanish Netherlands which had been founded in 1568 by Father William Allen, an English Catholic exile who was later made a cardinal. These missionaries were fired with the zeal of the Counter-Reformation and were happy to face the prospect of martyrdom if they could bring spiritual guidance and comfort to their fellow Englishmen. About 100 secular priests had arrived by 1580 when they were joined by Fathers Campion and Parsons, the first Jesuits to reach England. By the end of the reign there may have been about 400 secular priests and a dozen Jesuits in the country (57; 186). These men stiffened the resolve of the hard core of Catholics who had remained loyal to the Papacy throughout the early years of the reign and, even more alarming for the government, began to make new converts. As a result it intensified penal legislation against the Catholics (for a brief summary see (24, 275 *ff*)). Already in 1571, it had been made treason to bring papal bulls into the country and by 1585 (13 Eliz., c. 2; 27 Elix., c. 2) priests could be condemned to death merely for being priests [H]. Between 1581 and 1603, 180 Catholics were executed for treason, over 120 of them priests (186). Government propagandists insisted that these men suffered not for their religion but because they opposed the Crown on temporal matters, while Catholic apologists maintained that they suffered for their faith. Burghley himself took part in the debate with his *Execution of Justice in England*, published in 1583, and Allen replied the following year in his *True, Sincere and Modest Defense of English Catholics*. Both sides, of course, were right. At a time when politics and religion were inextricably intertwined and Popes claimed the right to depose heretical rulers, Catholics who suffered death were both martyrs for their religion and traitors to the realm.

The transparent sincerity and faith of the missionary priests made them the spearheads of the Catholic revival of the later years of Elizabeth's reign. Their lay flock, however, was often at odds with their zeal. By 1590 there was a strong tendency to quietism among the Catholic laity; a desire to be allowed to live their lives and practise their faith free from government persecution but with the implicit recognition that they were a small minority in an essentially Protestant England which would remain committed to the Reformed faith. This very important difference of outlook turned, as Professor Bossy has shown (188), on the essentially different backgrounds of the two main elements among those who secured the survival of Catholicism during the Elizabethan period, the Catholic gentry and the missionary priests. In the years after 1559, when so many Catholics were drifting away from the old faith, its survival depended largely on sympathetic members of the aristocracy and gentry who were able to use their social authority to preserve Catholic practices in their own houses for their families, servants and tenants. This 'seigneurial Catholicism' varied greatly in strength in different parts of the country, but everywhere the Catholic gentry were concerned essentially with the preservation of their households and the practice of the old religion under their own authority in these households, an attitude which was both essentially passive – there was no missionary spirit about it – and based on the idea of lay leadership of the Catholic cause. The views of the missionary priests were obviously very different. They envisaged themselves rather than the gentry as the leaders of English Catholicism and their burning faith and zeal for conversions was very different from the essentially cautious devotion to the forms of the old religion which was the mark of so much of the gentry Catholicism of the period. This split among the Catholics was to come to a head in the 1590s, but it was already obvious before the last decade of the reign and gave some comfort to a government whose hope of seeing Catholicism die out gradually with the passage of years had been shattered by the successes of the missionary priests.

By 1590, in fact, Catholicism in England had been saved partly by the support and protection of the Catholic gentry, especially in the early years of the reign, and partly by the work of the missionary priests from the later 1570s onwards. The missionaries' enthusiasm did, however, as we have seen, divide as well as inspire a Catholic cause which in 1590 still depended very heavily on members of the gentry and the nobility. Indeed the missionaries, those traditional heroes of Elizabethan Catholicism, appear in a less favourable light than is usual in Dr Haigh's recent general survey of Elizabethan Catholicism (190), where he argues that they concentrated too much of their effort on the south and east of England, where Catholicism was comparatively weak, and above all that they had paid too much attention to the gentry, too little to Catholic sympathizers among the 'lower orders'. As a result they helped to produce the late Elizabethan Catholic community which Bossy has so brilliantly described; a small distinctive minority concentrated around gentry sympathizers. What Haigh is saying, in fact, is that the seminary priests might have retained the allegiance of a much larger proportion of the English population for Catholicism if they had gone about their task in a different way. It is an interesting speculation, but we should surely remember that the missionaries *had* to turn to the Catholic gentry for protection: if they had involved themselves to a greater extent with the common people many more of them would probably have been caught, with the possible consequence of a collapse of the whole Catholic mission. As it was, it was obvious by 1590 that the government had little chance of completely extinguishing Catholicism. Equally clearly the Catholics had still less chance of re-establishing an officially Catholic England even if, as a body, they were prepared to make such an attempt. Most of them were not. Some of the missionary priests were willing to accept the foreign aid which would be necessary in any realistic attempt to overthrow the government, but the Catholic laity were almost all loyal to the Queen and wanted only to be left to practise their religion quietly. In effect, if not yet in theory, they had recognized the existence of the English nation state and its idiosyncratic national Church. That was a momentous development.

1. See e.g. H. F. Kearney, 'Puritanism and science: problems of definition', *P & P*, **31** (July 1965), 104 ff; B. Hall, 'Puritanism: the problem of definition', *Studies in Church History*, II, ed. G. J. Cuming (1965), pp. 283 ff.
2. Kearney, P & P (July 1965) 105.
3. J. F. H. New, *Anglican and Puritan: the Basis of their Opposition 1558–1640* (1964).

CHAPTER 19

Exploration and foreign policy

The strong hostility of the vast majority of Elizabethans towards Catholicism coloured their attitude towards the continent of Europe. This ideological commitment, so obvious in the thinking of a man like Walsingham, was not shared by the Queen, who regarded England's great Catholic neighbours France and Spain with the cool eye of the secular politician. Her attitude towards foreign policy was founded on a pragmatic desire to preserve the country's security. The well-known explorations undertaken by Englishmen during her reign, which have seemed so exciting to later historians, were of relatively minor concern to the Queen and her ministers, whose attention was overwhelmingly fixed on the European mainland, the central focus of English foreign policy.

In exploration England followed the lead which was set by the Portuguese and Spaniards in the fifteenth and early sixteenth centuries (for an excellent brief account see (47)). There was an initial burst of activity in the reign of Henry VII when John Cabot, a Genoese who entered the service of the English Crown, undertook two voyages to North America. He was followed by his son Sebastian who tried to find a north-west passage round America to Asia in 1509, but exploration was at a low ebb in the reign of Henry VIII and it was only under Northumberland that there was significant new activity. The voyage of Willoughby and Chancellor along the northern coast of Russia in 1553 was designed to find a north-east passage to Asia. Although it failed in that task it opened up the trade with Russia which led to the Muscovy Company's charter of 1555. Other voyages of Edward VI's reign, in 1551 and 1553, led to trade with Morocco and the Gold Coast of Africa and Elizabeth encouraged such African ventures after her accession in 1558. During the Elizabethan period Englishmen built on the foundations laid in the reigns of Henry VII and Edward VI with a continuing search for north-west and north-east passages to Asia which were designed to secure a share of the lucrative trade of the Far East. Elizabethan explorers also made new initiatives, notably attempts to found colonies in North America as well as efforts to discover and exploit the vast continent which was then generally believed to occupy the whole southern part of the globe.

Between 1576 and 1578 Martin Frobisher made three voyages in search of a north-west passage and his failures did not deter John Davis who made another three between 1585 and 1587. Davis penetrated further into northern waters than any previous explorer, but lack of money compelled him to give up his quest when he mistakenly believed that he was on the point of success. The Edwardian efforts to find a north-east passage had, as we have seen, led to the creation of the Muscovy Company and explorers continued to dream of finding a north-east passage. These hopes did not die until the voyage of Pett and Jackman in 1580 showed that they were impracticable. The quest for a north-west passage did not produce the immediate gains in trade which had resulted from Willoughby's and Chancellor's expedition to Muscovy in 1553, but it did lead to the first efforts to found English colonies in the New World. Sir Humphrey Gilbert undertook a voyage in 1583 with the objective of founding such a colony as an advance base for further exploration in search of the passage, but although he formally annexed Newfoundland he did not actually leave colonists there. The first colonies were created in Virginia in 1585 and 1587 under the auspices of Sir Walter Ralegh whose objectives probably included their use as a base for further exploration. The 1585 colony soon ran into difficulties with food shortages and troubles with the Indians and the colonists returned home the following year. The second colony, that of 1587, ended in disaster. When a further expedition arrived three years later with supplies it found that the 150 colonists had disappeared. It seems that they had voluntarily left the fort which they had erected but their final fate has never been discovered. These were inauspicious beginnings to the great British North American Empire of the seventeenth and eighteenth centuries, but they were preludes to the creation of the first successful English colony in the reign of James I. The quest for the fabled southern continent whose northern coast was believed to stretch right along the fringes of the Indian, Atlantic and Pacific oceans was designed to lead ultimately to the creation there of a wealthy English empire which might rival those of Spain and Portugal. Francis Drake was chosen to make the initial voyage and his instructions included the discovery of suitable places for English trading posts. He made no attempt to carry out these orders, however, and in his great voyage of 1577–80 turned away to plunder the Spanish colonies on the western coast of South America before completing the first English circumnavigation of the world with his return home in 1580.

The motives behind these voyages of exploration combined religious, social and economic elements. After the Reformation, Englishmen were even less inclined than they had been previously to accept the papal division of the non-European world between Spain and Portugal which had been decreed in the late fifteenth century. Explorations and still more the settlement of colonies, which violated the papal bull, fed both the nationalistic and Protestant pride of Elizabethans, who were also looking for possible new homes for a surplus population which made growing demands on often inadequate food supplies as the sixteenth century advanced. Above all, perhaps, they sought new trading outlets to compensate for the increasing difficulties which they encountered in their traditional markets in the Netherlands. (on overseas trade, see (238; 241).) That quest, which, by the end of the reign, extended into distant continents, was accompanied by a substantial growth in the size of the country's merchant fleet and was of the utmost significance for England's later history. With hindsight we can see that it pointed the way to the creation of the great British trading and colonial empires of the seventeenth to nineteenth centuries. But that was in the future. In the Elizabethan period itself trade remained overwhelmingly European and English foreign policy was dominated not by colonial issues but by developments on the European mainland.

The general direction of foreign policy, as of all other high matters of State, was controlled by the Queen, and Professor Wernham has shown from internal evidence in the state papers that Elizabeth was personally acquainted with much of the detail as well as the broad outlines of foreign policy (30). The Principal Secretaries, the ministers chiefly concerned with foreign affairs, could do little without her knowledge. Elizabethan foreign policy was very clearly the Queen's policy although, of course, she usually formulated it after consultation with her privy councillors. The practical responsibility for enforcing and defending that policy fell upon the army and the navy. Historians have traditionally given the Elizabethan Army a poor press,[1] but recent authorities have taken a more favourable view (145; 146), stressing both the difficulties which faced the Crown and the improvements which were made. The country was reluctant to pay the large sums necessary for an efficient military establishment, and given this fact and the deep-seated corruption in army administration the creation of the 'trained bands' [N] in 1573 was an achievement of some note. These consisted of men chosen at the annual musters because they seemed especially fit for military service. They were given special equipment and training and as a result the militia, which was mustered in strength in 1558 to defend the country against threatened invasion from the Armada, was not as worthless an organization as has sometimes been suggested. On the other hand, it would be optimistic to conclude that it could have offered effective resistance for long to the famed Spanish infantry if they had managed to establish a substantial bridgehead on English soil. Fortunately, although the army fought campaigns abroad and in Ireland, it never had to face that ultimate test. Some of the men sent on overseas service were from the trained bands but the great majority were untrained volunteers and conscripts, many of the latter rogues and vagabonds. It was unpromising military material and it is surprising that the men, so many of them the dregs of society, consistently cheated and exploited by their officers, poorly fed and subjected to a stern disciplinary code, fought as well as they sometimes did in France and the Low Countries.

The crucial role in England's war against Spain was played not, however, by the army, but by the navy, whose moment of greatest glory came in 1588 with its defeat of the Armada (the fundamental work on the navy remains (144)). In 1559 the Queen possessed 22 effective ships of more than 100 tons in weight and by 1603 the number had grown to 29. These royal vessels were, of course, supplemented by armed merchantmen during times of crisis and the increase in both the number and size of merchant ships which began during the 1570s enabled the Queen to assemble the formidable fleet which faced the great Spanish challenge of 1588. Moreover, the reign saw very important developments in the design and striking power of new ships built for the navy. Under the auspices of Sir John Hawkins, who held the vital office of Treasurer of the Navy from 1578 until his death in 1595 and who made his influence felt behind the scenes in earlier years, ships were made longer and narrower and thus faster and more seaworthy. They were also given heavier guns than before. Many older ships were modified or rebuilt along the new lines and it is clear that Hawkins was the organizer of victories in the struggle against Spain. As a result of his work the fleet became a highly efficient fighting force by the standards of the time, and it demonstrated its technical superiority against the Armada in 1588.[2] It achieved its feats despite frequently appalling conditions for the seamen who manned the Queen's ships. Overcrowded quarters, bad food and virtually non-existent sanitation caused frequent disease. Hawkins did his best to improve pay and conditions, but he could make little real impression on the problems given the limitations both of the Crown's finances and of the medical knowledge of the time.

For Elizabeth her navy was essentially a defensive instrument, a means of protecting England against possible invasion. As such it reflected the essentially defensive nature of her entire policy. She had no desire whatsoever for any extension of English territorial power on the Continent; she merely wished the country to be secure. This involved excluding as far as possible from the British Isles the influence of the two great European military powers, France and Spain, who were England's potential enemies. It also meant a careful watch on the coast-line of northern Europe from Britanny to the Netherlands. It was important to ensure that neither France nor Spain dominated the entire stretch of coast and thus gained a very wide launching pad for a possible invasion of England. The twists and turns of Elizabeth's policy and the vacillations which contemporaries and later historians have found both so irritating and bewildering were designed with these essential aims in mind; they reflected her efforts to hold the ring between France and Spain, to ensure that neither became too great a threat to English security. It is important to remember too that, although Spain came to be the greater threat to England, this was not apparent at the beginning of the reign when France was the main danger, and deep-seated distrust of France continued to be a major consideration of Elizabeth's policies throughout her life, especially in the years up to the 1580s. The Queen hoped to realize her aims without wars. She had a genuine hatred of war with all its waste of human and material resources and, above all, her instincts told her that a decisive war would produce a new international situation which might be more unwelcome to England than the one which had preceded it. Her foreign policy in fact reflected her deep political conservatism, her preference for living with problems rather than attempting fundamental solutions.

Between 1558 and 1585 she had considerable success. Despite her interventions in Scotland in 1560 (see above, Ch. 12) and in the first of the French religious wars in 1562–63 (30) she avoided major military commitments. The situation in Scotland did give her considerable anxiety. The return of Mary Queen of Scots in 1561 was the prelude to years of turmoil which centred on Mary's marriage in 1565 to Henry, Lord Darnley, a match which gave her son James, born in 1566, an added claim to the English throne; Darnley, like his wife, had Tudor royal blood in his veins. In every other way, however, the marriage was a disaster. Darnley's contemptible character, apparent soon after the wedding, contributed to his murder in 1567, an act in which Mary's complicity has been strongly suspected but never proved. Her subsequent marriage to James, earl of Bothwell, her imprisonment and her eventual flight to England in 1568 to escape the wrath of her subjects are among the best-known episodes in Scottish history. Already in 1567, she had been replaced on the Scottish throne by her infant son James VI, and from the later 1560s until 1586 Anglo-Scottish relation fluctuated, with Elizabeth exploiting the goodwill of the Protestants to create a party favourable to the English alliance and doing her best to thwart the pro-French and Catholic influences which were still strong in Scotland. Between 1570 and 1573 there seemed a chance that Mary's remaining supporters in Scotland might gain the upper hand, but Elizabeth's material support for a succession of Anglophile regents helped to ensure that by the latter date the King's party was firmly in control. In the early 1580s when James himself, still in his early teens, had assumed nominal control of the kingdom, it seemed that there might be a renewed threat from the north, led by the plausible Esmé Stuart, created duke of Lennox by his cousin, the young King. Lennox's aims centred on his personal advancement, but Spanish agents hoped to use him to further the Catholic cause and his influence clearly posed a potential threat to English security at a time when growing Spanish power looked increasingly menacing throughout western Europe. Lennox's fall in the autumn of 1582 was, therefore, a relief for Elizabeth. England's 'postern gate' in the North was once again closed to foreign enemies.

James himself, as he grew to manhood during the 1580s, remained fundamentally loyal to the Protestant faith in which he had been brought up, and this and his growing hope of succeeding to the English throne on Elizabeth's death helped to produce the Treaty of Berwick of 1586 which committed England and Scotland to an offensive and defensive alliance and provided James with a much-needed English pension of £4,000 a year. By the mid-1580s, in fact, it was clear that the pro-English Protestant ascendancy which had been established in Scotland in 1560 with the Queen's help, had come to stay. That was one of the greatest of Elizabeth's achievements abroad, as it was the essential foundation upon which James VI's peaceful succession to the English throne in 1603 was built; the united Great Britain which seemed so far away in 1558 was within a step of realization by the later years of the Elizabethan era.

A year before the Treaty of Berwick Elizabeth had sent troops to the Netherlands to assist the Dutch rebels there against their Spanish overlords. This outbreak of open if undeclared war between England and Spain in 1585 was a major defeat for Elizabeth; she had persistently tried to avoid it. Eighteen years before, in 1567, the duke of Alba had arrived in Brussels with a substantial army to crush the revolt of the Netherlands against Spain. It was 'one of the turning-points of western European history' (30, *290*) and posed an obvious threat to English security. If Alba obtained firm control of the Netherlands, with all its wealth of shipping, he would be in an ideal position to launch an attack, with his seasoned troops, on the heretical Elizabeth. The latter detested rebels and was no Protestant crusader, but strongly Protestant members of her Privy Council, such as Leicester and Walsingham, urged her, during the 1570s, to intervene on the Dutch side (see above, Ch. 13). The Queen concluded a defensive treaty with France in 1572, but she refused to commit herself to open war in the Netherlands until she had little choice in the matter. By 1585, however, England had either to fight or face the prospect of Spanish domination of the whole of western Europe. That international scenario, so gloomy from the English point of view, was the result of a series of events in the late 1570s and early 1580s which produced a dramatic change in the European balance of power in favour of Spain (30). The death in 1578 of King Sebastian of Portugal in an African war meant the accession of his aged and celibate uncle, Cardinal Henry. Philip II was the next heir by blood to the Portuguese throne and on the Cardinal-King's death in 1580 he duly entered into his inheritance, adding the Portuguese Empire, the second greatest in the world, to the largest of all, his own vast Spanish dominions. Especially alarming from England's point of view was Spain's acquisition of the powerful Portuguese fleet. In July 1584 the assassination of William of Orange, the linchpin of the Dutch rebels in their struggle against Spain, opened up the prospect of both the political and military collapse of Dutch resistance in the face of Philip's great general, the duke of Parma, who was already making substantial military progress against the rebels. Finally, in 1584 and 1585 the French monarchy, in the person of Henry III, surrendered to the influence of a French Catholic League, in the pay of Philip II, which was determined to exclude Henry III's heir, the Protestant Henry of Navarre, from the French throne in favour of a Catholic claimant. By 1585, therefore, England alone seemed to stand in the way of a complete Spanish domination of the Netherlands and France which would have brought the whole of western Europe under Philip II's effective control and given him the entire north-western coastline of the Continent as a base from which to assault England.

Elizabeth's intervention in 1585 clearly could not have been delayed if the country's security was to be preserved. Indeed, Professor Wilson has argued forcibly that Elizabeth did too little too late (150). By 1585, he points out, there was no chance of bringing the Southern Netherlands back into a united front with the North in the struggle against Spain; the southern provinces had been decisively reconciled with Philip II in 1579. What Elizabeth should have done, he argues, was to intervene decisively in the Low Countries during the 1570s in a much more favourable diplomatic situation and before there had been the crucial split between North and South. If she had done this, as a majority of her privy councillors wanted, she might, Wilson believes, have helped to secure the creation of an independent Netherlands, with both northern and southern provinces united in freedom from Spain. These arguments have a superficial attraction, but there is surely more to be said on the other side. Elizabeth did not *want* an entirely independent Netherlands; she wished them to remain under a Spanish overlordship which she believed was necessary to keep French influence out. It might have been in England's best interests if she had taken a different view – though this is not as clear as Professor Wilson seems to think – but the fact is that she did not. Moreover, during the mid-1570s there seemed a real chance that the Queen might get what she *was* aiming at – a return of the whole Netherlands to something like the position which they had occupied under Philip II's father, the Emperor Charles V; nominal subjection to Habsburg sovereignty but with a wide degree of political freedom, and it looked as if this might come about without large-scale English military intervention (30). Above all, perhaps, there is the financial issue. The cost to the Queen of military intervention in the 1570s would have been enormous (as it was to be in the 1580s). One of the reasons for her success in both foreign and domestic affairs was her solvency, and this depended on keeping out of expensive foreign adventures as long as she possibly could. Of course, it was plain by 1585 that the money would have to be found, England's fundamental security, perhaps her very survival, was then at stake, but this seems a poor reason for arguing that it should have been found in the much more balanced international situation of the 1570s when the vast growth of Spanish power in the early 1580s could hardly have been foreseen.

In the years between 1558 and 1585, in fact, Elizabeth's foreign policy served the country well. She had made modest improvements in England's defensive strength on land and developed the power of the Royal Navy as an effective instrument of war while at the same time avoiding major foreign adventures. This latter aspect of her policy was eminently sensible – indeed, it was essential – at a time of considerable financial stringency and it did allow her to accumulate some reserves which could be well employed when she was reluctantly drawn into war in the late 1580s (see above, Ch. 13). The fact that the Queen had to go to war at all in 1585 was a major defeat for her policy, but her desire to avoid armed conflict, however strong, had by then to be subordinated to the first of all her responsibilities; the need to preserve the security and integrity of the realm.

---

1. e.g. Sir Charles Oman, *A History of the Art of War in the 16th Century* (1937), pp. 372–3.
2. M. Lewis, *The Spanish Armada* (1960).

PART THREE

Renaissance Society: Life, mind and culture under the Tudors and Stuarts

CHAPTER 20

Population, prices and agriculture

One of the many factors which determines a country's ability to wage war effectively is the size of its population. In this respect England was at a disadvantage compared with both its Continental rivals France and Spain, with perhaps a third of the population of the former and a half of that of the latter at the end of the sixteenth century. England's population had, however, increased very substantially between the Henrician Reformation and the death of Elizabeth. Indeed, the population rise of the sixteenth and early seventeenth centuries and the price rise which accompanied it were among the most significant social and economic phenomena of the period and they had important effects on the country's most important source of wealth and employment, its agriculture.

Between 1500 and 1650 the population of England rose by between 200 and 250 per cent while the price of agricultural products went up by about 700 per cent and of industrial goods by about 300 per cent. If we take the period from the 1540s – by which time the rise in agricultural prices was already well advanced – until the 1650s the figures are less dramatic, with agricultural prices rising by over 300 per cent and industrial prices by about 250 per cent while population almost doubled ((44; 203; 224), see also [J] and [K]). Even on this set of figures, however, it is clear that agricultural prices rose at a considerably higher rate than the population increase. One conclusion seems plain. In sixteenth- and early-seventeenth-century England it was both necessary to increase agricultural production to feed a growing population and profitable to do so; the potential stimulus which the population rise gave to more extensive and intensive agriculture suggests that there were large profits to be made by improving landlords who were prepared to produce for the market.

The difficulties of making accurate estimates of population in a pre-census age are notorious, but the massive recent study (203) by Messrs Wrigley and Schofield, based on a detailed examination of over 500 parish registers, provides as reliable a guide as we are likely to have in the foreseeable future. The application of refined mathematical techniques to these registers has enabled the authors to reconstruct the population history of England from the sixteenth century onwards in a detail and with a sophistication never before achieved. They themselves would be the first to admit that their results remain imperfect, but they are certainly a major advance on anything that has gone before [J].

Wrigley and Schofield only start in the 1540s, but the population rise which they chart had already begun – scholars are divided as to whether it began in the later years of the fifteenth century or the early years of the sixteenth (203). By 1541 the population of England reached almost 2,800,000. It touched 3,000,000 by the early 1550s, fell back during the terrible influenza epidemic of the later

1550s, then forged ahead again to reach 3,500,000 by the later 1570s and 4,000,000 by the mid-1590s. The 4,500,000 mark was achieved in the second decade of James I's reign and 5,000,000 by the middle 1630s. By that time the rate of increase was slowing down, but the population continued to rise until 1657 when it stood at about 5,300,000. After that it fell back, recovered, and then fell again, so that in 1733 it was still about 5,300,000 (203). The population of Wales, which is not included in these figures, probably did not exceed about 200,000 in 1500 (203).

This growing English population was much more mobile than used to be thought (206). A good deal of the movement can be accounted for by young men and women who left their native villages for agricultural labour or indoor service in nearby communities or else sought apprenticeships or other employment in towns. The most venturesome might go to London, which grew throughout the sixteenth and seventeenth centuries to an extent which made it both the wonder and the scandal of the age. Its population, around 50,000 or 60,000 in the 1520s, reached about 200,000 at the end of Elizabeth's reign and about 400,000 in the middle of the seventeenth century. These figures represented about 2 per cent of the total population of the country in the 1520s, 5 per cent in 1600 and 8 per cent in the 1650s, and the growth of London's population, both absolutely and relatively, is an accurate illustration of its central and increasingly significant role during the period in the social, economic and administrative life of the nation. The vast growth of London was fuelled entirely by migration from smaller towns and from rural areas – death-rates in the city were so high that London could not even keep its population steady by natural increase. Provincial towns also grew more rapidly than the population of the country as a whole; the leading provincial centres, which accounted for about 2 per cent of the population of England in the 1520s, had perhaps 3 per cent of the country's inhabitants in 1650. Their relative growth was, therefore, much more modest than that of London and the pattern varied substantially among individual towns. Most, like London, relied on immigration from the countryside for their population increase, but they were much less powerful magnets than the metropolis and the rural influxes into their streets were neither as substantial nor as continuous in relative terms as the great flood of men and women who entered London throughout the period. Some towns, such as Coventry and Southampton, which were expanding in the early years of the sixteenth century, failed to maintain their growth, and the population of the former was probably slightly less in 1603 than it had been in the 1520s. Others, such as York and Exeter, grew substantially between the early sixteenth and mid-seventeenth centuries. The important textile city of Norwich expanded rapidly between the 1570s and the 1620s, when it reached a population of over 20,000. Then, however, it stagnated for several decades. This lack of any *general* pattern of urban growth in England in the period 1500–1650 and the relatively modest increase in the percentage of the population living in the leading provincial towns during the period helps to remind us of the overwhelmingly rural nature of English society in 1650 as in 1500. London, of course, was *sui generis*. If the urban population of England rose from about 4 per cent of the total in 1500 to about

11 per cent in 1650, it must be remembered that London accounted for 8 per cent of the latter figure (256, 257).

The virtual doubling of England's population between the 1540s and 1650s obviously represented an excess of births over deaths during the period as a whole and scholars have speculated as to whether this should be explained primarily by changes in fertility or mortality, that is to say in the birth- or death-rates. Wrigley and Schofield have now argued convincingly that changes in fertility and mortality were *both* of very great importance between 1540 and 1650, although changes in fertility were relatively more important between 1551 and 1571 and changes in mortality between 1571 and 1611. The late Elizabethan era was a 'golden period of low mortality' in which expectation of life at birth exceeded forty years, a figure not reached again until the nineteenth century (203, *230, 242 ff*).

During the early seventeenth century, as we saw, the rate of population growth began to slow down and by the 1650s the population was falling. It is now clear that one of the major reasons for this was a declining birth-rate which can be linked to a long-term fall in real wages. The grim economic conditions which prevailed for the lower orders of society during much of the sixteenth century and which led to a steady decline in their standard of living meant that many men and women either married later in life or never married at all. Those women who did marry had, therefore, a smaller number of years in which to bear children. The great population boom of the sixteenth and early seventeenth centuries ended largely because men and women became convinced that economic conditions were not favourable to early marriage or indeed to marriage at all (203).

The sixteenth- and early-seventeenth-century population rise was accompanied, as we shall see, by more extensive and intensive agriculture, but the fact that agricultural prices between the 1540s and 1650s rose more quickly than either the rate of population growth or than wage rates suggests that agricultural productivity did not keep up with the demands of the expanding population. In these circumstances the numbers of poor and vagrants grew. By the end of the sixteenth century, in fact, England was over-populated in relation to available resources. This led to famines, to some redistribution of the population within England and to suggestions that surplus people might colonize empty territories abroad. England escaped the worst of the terrible *crises de subsistence* which affected great areas of continental Europe in the sixteenth and seventeenth centuries and led to mass starvation in, to take just one example, parts of France. The country did, however, suffer famines in 1597–98 and 1623 in which men and women starved to death. The crises were at their worst in northern England, especially in Cumbria, but in 1597–98 there were famine deaths in the south-west as well as in the north of England (204; 206). Inhabitants of villages with a growing population but limited economic opportunities might, as we have seen, drift into provincial towns or seek their fortunes in London. They might also, however, move into other rural areas which seemed to offer better prospects for a livelihood. There was, during the period 1500–1650, a movement away from arable-farming areas to regions of pastoral agriculture and to forest and fen areas where extensive common lands were still often available. The Isle of Axholme in the Lincolnshire fens was an area where poor cottagers enjoyed not merely extensive common rights but also had employment opportunities in local industries. It saw a substantial population increase in the last years of the sixteenth century and during James I's reign. The late sixteenth and early seventeenth centuries also saw a flood of writings advocating English colonies abroad. One reason frequently suggested for their establishment was to provide homes and opportunities for the country's surplus population, some of the 'many millions which yearly do increase amongst us', as one writer put it, with not a little exaggeration, in 1612 (44,57–8; 206, *126 ff*).

Many of the colonists who did leave England in the early seventeenth century were doubtless delighted to escape from rising prices at home. Just like the population increase of the period, the general outlines of the price rise of 1500–1650 have long been well known to historians, though, just like their colleagues among the demographers, experts in the field rightly stress the difficulties and limitations of the evidence from which price series must be constructed (225). It is important, in discussing the price rise, to distinguish between foodstuffs and industrial products. One well-known series [K], which uses a measure of 106 for the price of a composite unit of foodstuffs in the first decade of the sixteenth century and an index number of 217 for the same food in the 1540s suggests that food prices rose to a level of 723 in the 1640s, an increase of nearly 700 per cent in 140 years. At the same time a sample of industrial goods increased in value from 98 units in the decade 1500–10 to 127 in the 1540s and 306 in the 1640s, an increase of just over 300 per cent during the period as a whole.

In accounting for the rise in agricultural prices, the harvest failures of the 1550s and 1590s and the general inflationary pressures of war during the 1540s and 1590s were certainly significant – the 1540s, 1550s and 1590s all saw much greater than average price rises – but these are usually and rightly regarded as relatively minor factors compared with the three explanations which traditionally dominate discussions of the price rise. Two of these are 'monetary' factors, the debasements of the 1540s and bullion imports from abroad; one a 'real' factor, the population increase of the period (44; 225; 246). We have already examined the 'great debasement' of 1544–51 in another context (Ch. 6). It may have doubled the amount of money circulating in the economy and it certainly had a significant effect on the very sharp upward thrust of prices between 1540 and 1560. It is also fairly clear now, thanks to the work of Dr Challis, that substantial quantities of Spanish silver from the New World entered England during Elizabeth's reign and contributed to inflationary pressures. Above all, perhaps, population pressure on relatively inelastic food supplies explains both the extent and the sustained nature of the price rise over the whole period up to 1650. It is especially important to notice in this context that the rise in the price of industrial goods was much less steep than the increase in agricultural prices. The principal though not the only reason for this was probably the differential demand for agricultural and industrial products. Men and women had to eat, and in the difficult times of the sixteenth and early seventeenth centuries spent a high proportion of their available income on food. Relatively little was left over to purchase industrial goods and the law of supply and demand then ensured that the price of the latter rose to a comparatively modest extent.

The great upward surge of agricultural prices ended about the middle of the seventeenth century, though industrial prices continued to forge ahead for the next three decades. Some reduction of bullion inflow may have contributed to this slackening of the overall price rise, but that was almost certainly a minor factor. More important was the easing of population pressure upon the means of subsistence – the population of England, as we have seen, entered a long period of decline and stagnation from the 1650s onwards. In these circumstances a fall in food prices could be expected and the continuing rise in the price of industrial goods can doubtless be explained by the fact that real wages were higher in the period 1650–80 than they had been in the early decades of the seventeenth century. Men and women, therefore, had more money to spend on comparative 'luxuries' and industrial workers, now in a buoyant market, were able to charge comparatively more for their goods (44).

The combined population and price rises of the sixteenth and early seventeenth centuries led to an increasing economic polarization between those at the bottom of the rural pyramid – agricultural labourers whose wages were approximately halved in real terms during the period 1500–1650 ((63), see also [L]) – and those who were able to produce for the market, notably the many prosperous gentlemen and yeomen to whom Tawney and Campbell have drawn attention (215; 211). We have already noted (Ch. 6) the fundamental importance of agriculture in the life of the country during the early modern period, when the vast majority of people either worked on the land or in occupations, like the cloth and leather industries, which were dependent on agriculture.[1] Interrelationships between town and country were close, with large numbers of townsmen growing food on plots of land within urban areas and a great many agricultural workers and their families heavily engaged in and dependent upon industrial work, most notably in textiles, to maintain their livelihood.

It is important to stress the variety of the farming scene. Both the leading modern authorities (63; 229) on English agriculture during this period emphasize the diversity of the agricultural regions of England. There were, however, two major farming areas, which can be divided by a line drawn between Teesmouth in the North-east and Weymouth in the South-west. North and west of this line was an area of mainly pastoral farming in the high lands of the region, and south and east of it was the mainly mixed farming carried out in lower lands where the emphasis was on arable produce but where livestock were also an important element in the agricultural economy. Already by 1500 much land had been enclosed (230), but the continuing enclosures of the sixteenth century gave rise to great emotion among contemporaries and have stirred some later historians to similar cries of moral outrage. The most common charge against enclosers was that they turned their lands into sheep pastures, because wool was a more profitable commodity than other forms of farm produce. Sheep-farming certainly involved much lower labour costs than arable-farming but the corollary, of course, was that agricultural labourers might be driven from their land by greedy sheep-farmers. The picture is a familiar one from the sermons and general anti-enclosure propaganda of the period, but it is exaggerated and misleading. In highland England enclosure was seldom a problem. Land was generally plentiful and, in the words of Dr Thirsk, 'the highland zone consisted for the most part of land which was either completely enclosed by the beginning of the sixteenth century, or, if the land was worth enclosing at this time, could and often did undergo painless enclosure' (63, 6). Trouble did come in the predominantly grain-growing areas of the Midlands where land was relatively scarce and where the traditional open-field system of farming, which depended for its successful operation on the enforcement of common rights, had a strong hold. Even in the South and East, however, many open fields had either disappeared by the beginning of the sixteenth century or indeed had never been known at all in the farming practices of some areas. In 1500, for example, substantial parts of Kent and Essex were already enclosed.

There is no doubt that in the worst-affected areas of the Midlands enclosure could involve serious social problems – in Leicestershire, for example, where about 10 per cent of the land was enclosed during the sixteenth century (45; 46) – but it should also be remembered that many sixteenth- and early-seventeenth-century enclosures were economically progressive. Farmers who fenced their own land in order to raise its productivity were helping to feed the growing population of sixteenth-century England as well as securing their own economic advantage, and much of the enclosure of the period, as is now generally recognized, was designed to improve arable methods rather than to introduce sheep runs. Clearly, enclosure was a complex phenomenon with widely differing results in different areas of the country. Its progressive elements – the links between enclosure and more scientific agriculture – direct attention to the theory that the introduction of new agricultural techniques in the late sixteenth and seventeenth centuries produced changes in English agriculture which were more important than those of the later eighteenth century. This is Dr Kerridge's well-known thesis that the 'agricultural revolution' took place in the sixteenth and seventeenth rather than in the eighteenth and nineteenth centuries (229). Kerridge bases his ideas essentially on the introduction of new techniques and crops into English agricultural life. These, he believes, gave a great filip to agricultural productivity. One of these techniques was alternate or, as Kerridge prefers to call it, 'up and down' husbandry, a system in which comparatively short periods of arable-farming were followed by much longer periods of pastoral farming. This, it is argued, produced both much better stock and much higher grain yields, on occasion, Kerridge believes, four times as high as the best medieval yields. This practice of alternate husbandry, he maintains, expanded very rapidly during the century 1560–1660; by the latter date it was prevalent in 'half the farmland' (229, *194, 331*).

Another innovation which spread in the early seventeenth century was the floating of water meadows, in which pasture-land was flooded to protect it against winter frost and stimulate earlier than usual growth of spring grass. This made possible the maintenance of larger sheep flocks. New crops such as coleseed were also introduced. These were invaluable as fodder and enabled farmers to keep larger numbers of livestock alive each winter. Larger herds of livestock meant more dung for fertilizing the soil, and this in turn helped to increase its yield.

These were clearly significant improvements, but did they amount to an 'agricultural revolution'? It is crucial to discover how many farmers adopted the new techniques. Far fewer seem to have done so than Kerridge believes. One of his critics argues that he 'strains the evidence to prove the widespread adoption of up-and-down husbandry' and another suggests that 'the new techniques that were widely disseminated geographically were not widely dispersed socially, and vice-versa'.[2] If we had reliable evidence about the output of English farms during this period we might be able to settle the matter conclusively. Unfortunately, no reliable figures exist. It has been estimated that the average yield of wheat per acre rose from 8½ bushels in 1450 to 11 bushels in 1650 – figures which probably give little comfort to Dr Kerridge – but these estimates are little better than sophisticated guesswork (63).

Dr Kerridge's technical innovations may not have constituted an 'agricultural revolution' but they must have gone some way towards increasing the food supply during the sixteenth and early seventeenth centuries. More important, however, in this respect was probably the extension which took place in the area of land under cultivation. That had expanded greatly during the population boom of the thirteenth century, but had contracted in the later fourteenth and fifteenth centuries following the population losses after the Black Death. In the sixteenth and early seventeenth centuries much marginal land was reoccupied or opened up for the first time in many parts of the country from Cumberland and Westmorland in the North to Sussex and Kent in the South. Perhaps the most notable examples are to be found in the drainage of marshlands which gathered pace from the 1560s onwards, culminating in the celebrated schemes of the earl of Bedford in the fenlands of Cambridgeshire and adjacent counties during the 1630s.

We do not need, therefore, to accept the concept of an agricultural revolution in early modern England to agree that during the sixteenth and early seventeenth centuries English agriculture responded in notable ways to the challenges imposed on it by a rising population. The extension of the area under cultivation, the adoption of new agricultural techniques, the introduction of economically beneficial enclosures and the energy of improving landlords all helped to produce sufficient food to enable England to avoid the major subsistence crises which plagued her European neighbours. It is true, of course, that men and women died in the comparatively small-scale famines of the 1590s and 1620s and that the achievements of English agriculture must have seemed very limited to the hundreds of thousands of men and women whose standard of living fell relentlessly in the bleak economic conditions of the period and who were constantly afraid that they would not have enough to eat. The achievements were, however, real, and, given the scale of the problem, impressive.

---

1. A. J. and R. H. Tawney, 'An occupational census of the seventeenth century', *EcHR*, 5 (1934–35), I, 25 ff.
2. G. E. Mingay in *AgHR*, **17** (1969), 152; J. Thirsk in *History*, **55** (1970), 261.

CHAPTER 21

Industry and trade

We have seen above (Ch. 20) that at least one historian has favoured – probably wrongly – the idea of an 'agricultural revolution' in early modern England. Long before that case was advanced the distinguished American historian Professor John Nef argued that there was an 'industrial revolution' in the same period, and although experts on English overseas trade have not used the word 'revolutionary' to describe the commercial changes of the years before 1660 they have seen the sixteenth and early seventeenth centuries as a time of vital preparation for the 'commercial revolution' of the later seventeenth century.

The intimate links between sixteenth-century agriculture and industry, already noted in Chapter 20, were of decisive importance in determining the nature of industry during this period. These links can be illustrated by discussing industrial materials, the men who processed these materials and the seasonal nature of a good deal of industrial work. Much of the industry of the time, as Professor Coleman points out, 'consisted of the direct processing of agricultural products in order to meet the three basic needs of life – food and drink, shelter, clothing' (232, *12*). This could be seen in the work of such men as millers, brewers, builders and the producers of textiles, all of whom worked upon the raw materials of the agricultural economy. Many of these industrial workers, most notably those in the textile industry, worked in agriculture as well as in the manufacturing process, and the seasonality and casual nature of much industrial work was determined both by the exigencies of the weather and the demands of the harvest season. All this makes it plain that there was no clearly defined 'industrial sector' in the economy. Agriculture and industry, just like country and town, were too intimately linked for this to be possible.

If one of the most notable features of the industry of the period was its intimate links with and fundamental dependence upon agriculture, another was its labour-intensive rather than its capital-intensive nature. The existence of a substantial body of unemployed or underemployed labour – a situation inherent in the agricultural conditions of the time – helps to explain the enormous importance of the 'domestic system' of production which dominated the woollen industry and was also common in other major manufactures such as leather,[1] linen and hosiery production. The domestic system can best be illustrated from its most important component, the cloth industry. Clothworkers made the cloth in their own homes with raw materials supplied to them by clothiers who then bought the cloth back. The system expanded with great rapidity during the sixteenth and early seventeenth centuries, giving much needed by-employment to many rural families. Its growth was reflected in the greatly increased production of cloth per head of population. That probably grew two- or threefold between the late fifteenth and

172

mid-seventeenth centuries, an increase which was founded upon the expansion of overseas and probably also of home demand for the product (44; 232). The governments of the day favoured this expansion of the woollen industry, but they did so as much for its social as for its narrowly economic benefits. The fact that it absorbed so much underemployed labour made it a potential stabilizing force in the life of the country, and this greatly appealed to governments which were constantly worried about the potential threat which a large body of needy poor might pose to the social fabric.

Just as the domestic system of production dominated the woollen industry, the woollen industry itself dominated the whole industrial scene, with its huge if unquantifiable production for the domestic market and its crucial role in England's export trade, where, as we shall see, woollen textiles were as predominant at the end of our period as at its beginning. There were no major technical innovations in the manufacture of woollen cloth in the sixteenth and seventeenth centuries, but there were two main types of product, the old broadcloths, which traditionally dominated the industry, and the 'new draperies', lighter cloths which came into increasing prominence in the late sixteenth and early seventeenth centuries. The manufacture of the old heavy woollen broadcloths, though found in many parts of the country from Lancashire in the North to Kent in the South, was concentrated in three main areas, the West Country, East Anglia and the West Riding of Yorkshire. The reasons for these concentrations are still not altogether clear, but one major explanation probably lies in the existence in the three areas of large pools of underemployed labour, men and women who were eager to supplement their income through the domestic system (232). Demand for these broadcloths slumped in the early seventeenth century [M.3], with short-term crises in the industry like those of 1614–16, 1620–24 and 1640–42, all of which should be seen against a long-term trend in fashion away from heavy woollens and towards the lighter new draperies, which made an increasing impact on the export market from the later sixteenth century onwards.

The new draperies were worsteds, made from combed, long-staple wool rather than the carded, short-staple wool of the old broadcloths. They were usually lighter, more varied and often cheaper than the old heavy woollens, and their introduction into England was principally due to the migration of Protestants from the Low Countries during the 1560s and 1570s (235). These refugees, fleeing from Spanish Catholic persecution, settled mainly in southern and eastern England, especially in East Anglia. The immigrants already had strong trading links with southern Europe where their comparatively lightweight woollens were much more attractive than the traditional heavy English cloths, and the growth of the new draperies as an important element in the English export trade in the early seventeenth century partly reflected the growing prominence of southern as opposed to northern Europe in the English trading system.

The overwhelming preponderance of cloth-making in the English industrial history of the sixteenth and early seventeenth centuries, a process based on the extensive exploitation of labour, on low fixed capital and on limited technical innovation is in itself sufficient to raise a priori doubts about the thesis of an industrial revolution in early modern England, an idea propounded by Professor

J. U. Nef during the 1930s.[2] Nef's thesis was founded on three main arguments: the expansion of the coal industry which took place in England during the sixteenth and seventeenth centuries; the development, over the same span of years, of the iron industry; and the large amounts of fixed capital and new technical methods which, he believed, were employed in industry during the period. The figures which he produced for the coal industry certainly look spectacular. Between the 1550s and the 1680s, according to his statistics, coal production in England and Wales increased from about 170,000 tons per annum to about 2,500,000 tons a year, a fourteenfold increase (233). This coal was used for both domestic and industrial purposes and Nef argued that it greatly facilitated the growth of towns, especially London, whose ample domestic fuel was imported from the great northern coalfield in Northumberland and Durham. Moreover, urban expansion encouraged the development of industries like brewing, paper-making, and soap-boiling, which used coal in their manufacturing processes. Another important industry which benefited was shipbuilding; new ships had to be built to handle the growing coastal traffic in coal between Newcastle and London.

The development of the iron industry is the second major plank of Nef's thesis and we know that the output of iron increased from about 5,000 tons per annum in the 1550s to about 24,000 tons a year in the middle of the seventeenth century (236). The iron industry did not use coal as a fuel – it was totally dependent on charcoal for the smelting process – and Nef believed that during the seventeenth century a nationwide shortage of timber developed as a result of the insatiable demands of the iron industry. Finally, Nef drew attention to the new technical methods and large amounts of fixed capital employed by some of the developing industries of the period.

Other historians have united to reject or modify Nef's conclusions.[3] Professor Coleman has pointed to the very dubious nature of Nef's figures for coal production (44, *84–5*; 232, *46–7*) – the expansion of the coal industry was plainly a good deal less spectacular than those suggest – and it is clear that although coal was employed in industry in the mid-seventeenth century, its main use then was still as a domestic fuel. It is also clear that the national timber shortage which Nef described is a myth. The development of the iron industry was not held back by any overall scarcity of wood, but its output did rise relatively slowly in the early seventeenth century, when it was unable to meet domestic demand. England in these years was still heavily dependent on Swedish iron imports (236). As for large-scale industries and new technical methods, the former were very untypical – though the building of giant houses like the Cecil mansions of Theobalds and Hatfield and the work of the big naval dockyards of the day did employ very large numbers of men – and the latter were confined to industries like mining and metallurgy which were of limited importance compared with the manufacture of textiles, which, as we have seen, was not affected by significant technical changes. Moreover, as Dr Thirsk has recently suggested, a major aspect of industrial expansion from the later sixteenth century onwards almost certainly lay in the growth of a great variety of 'consumer' industries which have hitherto been largely neglected by historians but which were labour intensive and demanded only modest capital outlays. One of these was stocking-knitting, which may have given by-employment to as many as 100,000 people at any one time during the early seventeenth century. Another was the pin industry which started from nothing in the early sixteenth century but was strongly entrenched by the 1620s, providing considerable employment in London and parts of Gloucestershire (234).

Nef's 'industrial revolution', in fact, emerges as an unconvincing amalgamation of dubious statistics about the coal industry, of mistaken assumptions about the production of iron and of concentration upon a few untypical examples of large-scale enterprises in untypical industries. During the sixteenth century England was in fact a backward country industrially when compared with her Continental neighbours. From the mid-sixteenth century she started to catch up, and the period 1550–1650 is better seen as an important stage in this catching-up process and an essential preparation for what was to follow in the century after the Restoration than as the era of a mythical early industrial revolution. As Professor Coleman puts it, 'the import of continental skills and techniques, via immigrant labour and, in some cases, capital, is one of the major themes of Tudor and Stuart industrial history' (44, *69–70*). Another theme is the absolute expansion of industry during the period 1500–1650, best seen perhaps in the dramatic development of cloth production and in the growth of Dr Thirsk's 'consumer' industries. Behind this industrial advance, sustaining and encouraging it, were the twin forces of population increase and price inflation. These increased the labour supply and led to steep falls in the standard of living of many members of the community who were unable to grow food for the market and thus take advantage of the soaring prices of agricultural products. Many of these men and women were able to survive only by exploiting the by-employments which were increasingly to be found in the growing textile and consumer industries of the period. The wages they earned there gave them the resources to keep body and soul together and the goods which they produced either went for export or else were bought by those prosperous members of the community – from gentlemen downwards – who had benefited from the rise in agricultural prices and were therefore in a position to spend a growing proportion of their income on a range of industrial goods. It should not be forgotten, however, that for a substantial part of the English population most industrial products were far down their list of priorities. They had more than enough to do to secure the most basic necessities of life in the form of food, clothing, and shelter, and until the standard of living of the great mass of the English population could be raised well above subsistence level there was little prospect of a 'mass market' at home for the products of industry.

The significant if less than 'revolutionary' advances in English industry which have just been described were matched by important developments in the country's internal and overseas trade. The overseas trade, which can be at least partially quantified, has dominated textbooks at the expense of the unquantifiable but arguably even more important internal trade ((237) now provides an excellent survey). England lacked the extensive internal tolls and customs which were common on the Continent at this time. Their absence undoubtedly helped the development of internal trade, but in our own day the lack of toll records has hindered the efforts of historians to learn more about the trade. There can be no doubt, however, that the great bulk of domestic products were consumed within the country and in this situation and with a doubling of the population during the sixteenth and early seventeenth centuries there is a very strong *prima facie* case for seeing internal trade as a significant vehicle for economic growth and development.

It is clear, in fact, that there was a very considerable network of internal trade, both in terms of goods carried and of methods of transport employed (237). The most important goods were grain, wool and woollens, and minerals, such as coal, iron and tin, and there was an extensive trade in livestock which, by the early seventeenth century, included important droving trades in cattle and sheep from Wales, Scotland and Ireland. There were three main methods of transport – rivers,[4] coastal routes[5] and roads – and relative transport costs were of funda-mental importance in internal trade during the period. Rivers and coastal shipping were most suitable for bulky goods of relatively low value, like cereals and coal, and from the late Elizabethan period onwards considerable efforts were made to improve river navigation. At the same time, the considerable growth in English shipping tonnage which took place in the late sixteenth and seventeenth centuries reflected in part a significant growth in the coasting trade: by 1660 about half of England's total shipping tonnage may have been engaged in fishing and coasting (239). Road transport, despite its cost disadvantages compared with river and sea carriage, was the basis of most trades and most notably of the wool trade, which remained of such fundamental importance to the economy throughout our period. Early modern English roads have traditionally had a bad press from historians, but it has recently been argued that they may have been a good deal better than used to be thought, and certainly the sixteenth and early seventeenth centuries saw improvements in the vehicles which used the roads, with the introduction of much larger wagons, capable of carrying substantial quantities of goods about the countryside.

London stood at the centre of England's internal trade. We have already noted its huge growth in the period 1500–1650 (Ch. 20). As it expanded it stretched its tentacles further and further afield over the countryside and virtually the whole of England, from the North to the West, became involved in supplying the varied needs of the metropolitan market (63; 231). By the mid-seventeenth century it was drawing food supplies from as far afield as Berwick, Cornwall and Wales (231). Another piece of evidence which illustrates the importance of internal trade is the extent of specialization among the 800 or so market towns of England in the early seventeenth century. As Professor Everitt has shown, over 300 of these specialized in marketing one commodity, which was often distributed far and wide throughout the country (63).

The stress which is now being laid on the significance of England's internal trades in the early modern period helps to put the country's overseas trade into perspective. That remains of great importance, but it should be realized that it was not only less significant than the agriculture upon which the basic livelihood of the community depended but also less important in terms of total value – though not of long-term national potential – than the much more poorly docu-mented internal trade which has just been examined. Comparison of England's overseas trade in the 1530s and 1540s with the situation a century later reveals some crucial similarities as well as a number of significant differences.[6] One fundamental similarity was the dominance of the export trade by woollen textiles. In the mid-sixteenth century cloth accounted for about 80 per cent of the value of all exports, and in the mid-seventeenth century, when it included the new draperies, it accounted for over 80 per cent (44; 45). Imports, in contrast, both in the sixteenth and seventeenth centuries, were not dominated by a single item but consisted of a wide range of raw materials and manufactured goods. Non-woollen textiles, like linen, canvas and fustians, were of considerable significance, as were wine, oil and dyestuffs, and a variety of metalwares. Luxury goods like spices and Mediterranean foodstuffs also featured in the list (44). In the mid-seventeenth century, just as in the mid-sixteenth, England's export trade was dominated by London. In the later years of Henry VIII's reign about 90 per cent of the country's cloth exports were shipped from the capital and although by the early seventeenth century the outports had regained some ground about 75 per cent of textile exports were still going through London in 1640 (44; 247). The overwhelming bulk of England's trade remained throughout the seventeenth century, as it was in the sixteenth, intra-European. In the 1560s most of the trade 'was still conducted in European waters, from Holland to southern Spain, with various northern French ports, such as Rouen and La Rochelle, following Antwerp as the main sources and destinations' (44, *62*). In 1621 only 6 per cent of London's imports came from Asia and America and even in 1700 85 per cent of English exports still went to European destinations (44; 45).

The dominance of European markets in both the import and export trades, the supremacy of London in overseas trade, the variety of imports and the over-whelming preponderance of textile exports – these familiar trading patterns, common to the period 1530–1640 as a whole – would be generally accepted by historians. It is much more difficult to assess the changing volume and value of English overseas trade during the whole period between 1500 and 1640. There is no doubt that the early sixteenth century saw a considerable expansion in cloth exports [M.1], but the great trade boom of these years was followed by the much more difficult period between 1550 and 1650, difficult not only for English exporters but also for historians. The period from the 1550s to the end of the seventeenth century was 'the most barren of continuous commercial statistics for any time in English history since before 1275' (44, *61*). Historians, thrown back on fragmentary figures, come to very different conclusions. Dr Clarkson writes that 'the combined value of trade in old and new draperies from London rose by about 75 per cent in the first forty years of the seventeenth century', while Professor Coleman's figures show a slight drop in the value of total textile exports between the early years of James I's reign and 1640 (44; *64*; 45, *126*; see [M.3]). In this situation cautious judgements are in order, but it is certainly clear that the volume and value of English trade were rising much less rapidly in the years between 1550 and 1640 than they had been in the first half of the sixteenth century.

The difficulties which are encountered in assessing changes in the value and volume of English overseas trade in the period 1550–1640 do not prevent historians from agreeing on a number of important differences in the overseas trading picture of 1640 compared with that of 1550. These differences are just as important in assessing the trade history of early modern England as the similarities which we have already examined. One major change was in the nature of the woollen goods exported. The old broadcloths which dominated the cloth exports of the mid-sixteenth century were increasingly challenged by the new draperies which, as we have seen, were produced in increasing quantities in England from the 1560s onwards. By the early years of James I's reign these lighter woollens were taking over 20 per cent of the textile export market and by 1640 they were taking over 40 per cent [M.3]. The future lay with them and with their late-seventeenth century offshoots. Another substantial change in the pattern of trade was the very considerable expansion of the geographical area, both inside and outside Europe, within which it operated. In the later years of Henry VIII the great bulk of English overseas trade was channelled between London and the port of Antwerp, then the commercial metropolis of Europe. Between the 1550s and the 1580s, however, war between France and Spain and then the revolt of the Netherlands against Spain shattered Antwerp's pre-eminence. This led to a much wider diffusion of English trade to other Netherlands towns, to Germany and into the Baltic. English merchants also turned to the Mediterranean from the later years of Queen Elizabeth's reign onwards. At the beginning of the seventeenth century as much as 90 per cent of English cloth exports were still going to the markets of northern and central Europe, but by 1640 the figure was less than 70 per cent, statistics which illustrate the extent of penetration of Mediterranean markets by English exporters whose new draperies were making increasing inroads in Spain and Italy by the time of the Civil War (64; 238). The early years of the seventeenth century also saw the beginnings of the Far Eastern and American trades which were to be of such crucial importance in England's economy in the years after 1660, but were of strictly limited significance before that date (238).

The period between the 1550s and the mid-seventeenth century also saw significant changes in the organization of English trade with the creation of many new chartered companies and the rise and decline of the joint-stock principle. The Merchant Adventurers, the established company which controlled English cloth exports to Antwerp in the early sixteenth century, lost their position of supremacy with the expansion of English trade outside their monopoly area in northern Europe. New companies, created with government approval to regulate trade in different regions included the Muscovy Company of 1555, the Eastland Company of 1579, the Levant Company of 1581, the Barbary Company of 1585, the East India Company of 1600 and the Virginia Company of 1606. Some of these companies, like the Merchant Adventurers and the Eastland Company, were regulated companies, controlling the conduct of trade without operating a common fund of capital, but others, such as the Muscovy and East India Companies, were joint-stock organizations, with investors sharing in the profits of voyages in proportion to the capital which they contributed to the common fund. The joint-stock principle was important in the establishment of distant trades like those to Russia and the Far East, but companies sometimes abandoned it after they were firmly established in their ventures and among the joint-stock companies founded before 1660 only the East India Company ever made a large contribution – though admittedly it was a very substantial one – to the total of English overseas trade (238). Indeed all trading companies came under increasing attack from those who resented both their monopolies and their dominance by small cliques of London merchants, and in 1604 there was a major 'free trade' debate in the House of Commons in which these resentments found full expression (258). By the mid-seventeenth century several trades – including those to France, Spain and America – were virtually free from company control. The 'free traders' success should not, however, be exaggerated. Company control of English overseas trade was never as great as either the companies' contemporary critics or some later historians have suggested. As Professor Davis reminds us, 'most trade was carried on by individuals and small partnerships' (238, *41*).

The expansion of English trading horizons in the late sixteenth and early seventeenth centuries was accompanied by a growing English shipping industry. More and larger ships were needed for distant trades to Asia and America and the country's mercantile fleet, which totalled about 50,000 tons in the 1570s, expanded to about 115,000 tons in 1629 and 150,000 tons in 1640. At the same time the number of larger ships – over 200 tons – grew from 14 in the 1570s to about 150 in 1629 (44; 239). Moreover, during the sixteenth and early seventeenth centuries English merchants showed an increasing determination to secure the benefits of English trade for themselves, a resolution which was strengthened by the rise and challenge of the Dutch. During the 1540s only about 50 per cent of English cloth exports were in native hands, with Hanse merchants taking the lion's share of the remainder. By the 1550s Englishmen's share of the export market had risen to over 70 per cent and in 1597 the Hansards were expelled from London (44; 238). The early seventeenth century saw the growing challenge of the Dutch carrying trade, but the Navigation Act of 1651 was a sign of the joint resolution of the English government and merchant community to keep as much trade as they possibly could in native hands.

The growing control by English merchants of the trade of their own country, the expansion of the English shipping industry largely to meet the needs of new and more distant trades, the establishment of many chartered companies, the considerable expansion of the geographical area of English trade, and the major change in the nature of English woollen exports with the rise of the new draperies and the decline of the old broadcloths are areas of change to consider alongside the continuities in England's overseas trade which have also been discussed. The general impression to emerge from this picture of continuity and change is perhaps that progress was more limited than is often supposed. We are told that in 1660 England was on the eve of a 'commercial revolution'[7] and the reality of the advances which took place in the later seventeenth century cannot be denied. We can see, too, that the bases for many of these later seventeenth-century advances can be found in the expansion of shipping and the foundation of colonies in, and companies trading to, America and Asia, developments which took place in the late sixteenth and early seventeenth centuries. It must be remembered, however, that we have the benefit of hindsight, and an impartial observer in the mid-seventeenth century would have been at least as likely to stress the problems as to eulogize the possibilities of English trade. At that time there was little sign of the great expansion of the American and Far Eastern trades which took place after the Restoration. Much more obvious were the continuing and overwhelming dependence of English trade on the export of woollen textiles, the challenge from the Dutch, reflected in the passage of the Navigation Act of 1651, and the recurring trade crises of the period, not least the slump at the end of the 1650s which ushered in the Restoration.

---

1. For the leather industry, L. A. Clarkson, 'The leather crafts in Tudor and Stuart England', *AgHR*, **14** (1966), 25 ff; 'The organisation of the English leather industry in the late sixteenth and seventeenth centuries', *EcHR*, 2nd ser., **13** (1960–61), 245 ff.

2. J. U. Nef, 'The progress of technology and the growth of large scale industry in Great Britain, 1540–1640', *EcHR*, **5** (1934–35), 3 ff; 'Prices and industrial capitalism in France and England, 1540–1640', *EcHR*, **7** (1936–37), 155 ff; *The Rise of the British Coal Industry*, 2 vols (1932); *War and Human Progress* (Cambridge, Mass., 1950).

3. D. C. Coleman, 'Industrial growth and industrial revolutions', *Economica*, New Series, **23** (1956), 1 ff; *Industry in Tudor and Stuart England*; *The Economy of England*, pp. 82 ff; L. A. Clarkson, *The Pre-Industrial Economy in England*, pp. 99, 106–7, 115–6; F. J. Fisher, 'Tawney's century', *Essays in the Economic and Social History of Tudor and Stuart England*, ed. F. J. Fisher (Cambridge, 1961), p. 6; P. J. Bowden, 'Agricultural prices, farm profits and rents', *The Agrarian History of England and Wales*, IV, pp. 607–9; S. M. Jack, *Trade and Industry in Tudor and Stuart England* (1977).

4. T. S. Willan, *River Navigation in England 1600–1760* (Oxford, 1936).

5. T. S. Willan, *The English Coasting Trade 1600–1750* (Manchester, 1938).

6. On overseas trade see R. Davies, *English Overseas Trade 1500–1700* (1973); B. Supple, *Commercial Crisis and Change in England, 1600–1642* (Cambridge, 1959); W. E. Minchinton, ed., *The Growth of English Overseas Trade in the 17th and 18th Centuries* (1969); G. D. Ramsay, *English Overseas Trade in the Centuries of Emergence* (1957); F. J. Fisher, 'Commercial trends and policy in sixteenth century England', *EcHR*, **10** (1939–40), 95 ff; L. Stone, 'State control in sixteenth century England', *EcHR*, **17** (1947), 103 ff; A. Friis, *Alderman Cockayne's Project and the Cloth Trade* (Copenhagen, 1927); B. Dietz, 'England's overseas trade in the reign of James I', A. G. R. Smith, ed., *The Reign of James VI and I* (1937), pp. 106 ff.

7. See R. Davis, *A Commercial Revolution: English Overseas Trade in the Seventeenth and Eighteenth Centuries* (Hist. Assoc., 1967).

CHAPTER 22

The social structure and social change

The economic changes of the sixteenth and early seventeenth centuries took place within a social framework which was described by notable contemporaries like the scholar and statesman Sir Thomas Smith, who wrote his *De Republica Anglorum* in the 1560s, the clergyman William Harrison, whose *Description of England* was published in the 1570s and the foreign intelligencer and minor government official Thomas Wilson, who wrote his *State of England anno. dom. 1600* at the end of Elizabeth's reign. Harrison, in his description of the social structure, stated:

> We in England divide our people commonly into four sorts, as gentlemen, citizens or burgesses, yeomen, and artificers or labourers. Of gentlemen the first and chief (next the king) be . . . dukes, marquises, earls, viscounts, and barons, and these are called gentlemen of the greater sort, or (as our common usage of speech is) lords and noblemen; and next unto them be knights, esquires, and last of all, they that are simply called gentlemen. . . .
>
> . . . Citizens and burgesses have next place to gentlemen, who be those that are free within the cities, and are of some likely substance to bear office in the same. . . .
>
> . . . Yeomen are those which by our law are called *legales homines*, freemen born English, and may dispend of their own free land in revenue to the sum of 40s. sterling. . . .
>
> . . . The fourth and last sort of people in England are day labourers, poor husbandmen, and some retailers (which have no free land), copyholders [N], and all artificers, as tailors, shoemakers, carpenters, brickmakers, masons, etc. . . .'
> (6, vol. i. *105–34*)

That is a bird's-eye view of English society as it appeared to an educated Elizabethan, and Harrison would have agreed with later historians that the major dividing line was between the gentlemen and the rest. Sir Thomas Smith provided us with the classic contemporary description of a gentleman. 'Whosoever studieth the laws of the realm, who studieth in the universities, who professeth liberal sciences, and to be short, who can live idly and without manual labour and will bear the port, charge and countenance of a gentleman, he shall be called master, for that is the title which men give to esquires and other gentlemen, and shall be taken for a gentleman. . . .' (7, *39–40*)

Gentlemen, of course, included a very wide range of wealth and status. At the top were the titled nobility, Harrison's 'gentlemen of the greater sort', an exclusive body of 54 men in 1529. By the end of Elizabeth's reign there were still only 55 of them – the Queen was always reluctant to create new peerages – but numbers did expand considerably under James I and Charles I, reaching 126 English peerages in 1628. In 1641 there were 121 peers (217). The sale of peerages during the period of Buckingham's supremacy did something to devalue the status of noblemen, but this point should not be pushed too far. In 1641 the peerage included, as it had always done, some relatively poor men (217), but the over-whelming majority of the nobility throughout the period remained very large landowners, among the richest men in the country. Below the peers were knights, esquires and ordinary gentlemen, and in 1611 the hereditary rank of baronet was introduced between the titular nobility and the knights (217) – baronetcies being sold by the needy James for a flat payment of £1,095 each. Included among the gentlemen were many of the clergy, not only bishops and dignitaries like arch-deacons and cathedral canons but also, in accordance with Smith's definition, university graduates who included a growing percentage of the parish ministers in the early seventeenth century. Also included were the increasingly numerous and wealthy lawyers, other highly educated professional men such as physicians, and many of the wealthier citizens of the towns who theoretically came into Harrison's second group. Many of these citizens, however, possessed substantial landed estates in the country and were far wealthier than the great majority of 'mere' gentlemen. Just as their income came from both landed and mercantile wealth, so they straddled two social groups, those of the gentlemen and the burgesses.

The social divide between gentlemen and the rest of the population was also a political one. The gentlemen of England, with the addition of a number of the wealthiest citizens of the towns (men who, as we have seen, often ranked as members of the gentry class) comprised the 'political nation', that small minority of the population who took a significant day-to-day interest in the running of the country and might hope to influence the way in which England was governed (see above, Ch. 14).

The second group in society, the citizens and burgesses, were, according to Smith, 'such as not only be free and received as officers within the cities, but also be of some substance to bear the charges' (7, *41–2*). His emphasis on the wealth of the leading townsmen was echoed by Thomas Wilson who wrote that 'it is well known that at this time there are in London some merchants worth £100,000 and he is not accounted rich that cannot reach to £50,000 or near it . . .' (8, *21*). Wilson certainly exaggerated – London merchants who were worth a good deal less than £50,000 were certainly considered rich men by their contemporaries – but there is no doubt that the handful of magnates at the top of the London mercantile community were enormously rich; the wealthiest of all Sir John Spencer was probably worth more than £300,000 when he died in 1610, almost certainly the richest man in the country (5, *2*). Merchants in provincial towns were, of course, much less rich, and quite unable, in contrast to their London brethren, to vie with members of the peerage. Leading citizens of towns like Norwich and Bristol did, on the other hand, rank with substantial members of the gentry in their respective counties, and the relatively liquid nature of their wealth, much less tied up in land than that of rural gentlemen, enabled them to take a leading role in the charitable benefactions which were such a notable feature of the period (205).

The yeomen, the third of Harrison's groups, were defined by him as 40s. freeholders, a description repeated by Smith (7, *42*). These definitions do, however, distort historical reality. Many early modern Englishmen described by their contemporaries as yeomen held no freehold land at all, or very little, and, in any event, by the late sixteenth and early seventeenth centuries, due to the ravages of inflation, a 40s. freeholder who had no other source of income, would have been a virtual pauper. It is best, in fact, to describe the yeomen in economic terms, as prosperous farmers. They probably comprised at least 100,000 families during the Elizabethan period. The fourth category of the population, which included the vast majority of the Queen's subjects, obviously comprised men and women in a wide range of economic circumstances, from relatively prosperous husbandmen and artificers to the poor and destitute. In good times the better-off members of this group might live reasonably well, but they had few reserves to fall back on in difficult economic circumstances, and the paupers, of course, had no possessions at all. Politically the 'fourth sort', as Smith affirmed, had 'no voice nor authority . . . and no account is made of them but only to be ruled' (7, *46*). That is the authentic voice of a Tudor gentleman commenting on the place of the 'lower orders' in society.

The people who comprised these social groups, so varied in status, wealth and political influence, were highly mobile geographically. The geographical mobility of the lower orders (see above, Ch. 20) has only been comparatively recently demonstrated by historians and it is now clear that many of the vagrants who so alarmed the authorities of the early modern English State were not criminals but migrants in search of subsistence (65). The mobility of the upper ranks of society has, in contrast, long been an accepted fact. Local gentlemen moved frequently about their 'countries' – those country societies which played such a large role in the political and social life of the England of the day – visiting neighbours and attending assemblies of local notables, especially quarter sessions. They also travelled outside their native shires, especially to London, which became more and more of a magnet as the sixteenth century went on. The idea of a London season, demanding the attendance of all who had claims to fashion and elegance developed with great speed between 1590 and 1620 and the flood of gentlemen taking up residence in the metropolis so alarmed King James that in the years after 1614 he issued numerous proclamations ordering the country gentry to return to their native shires where they could be well occupied maintaining law and order and providing hospitality and employment. These proclamations were, it is hardly surprising to report, almost totally ignored (217).

There was, then, extensive geographical mobility at all levels of society. Early modern English men and women moved about the countryside, sometimes in search of pleasure, often, in the case of the lower orders, in search of work. Many vagrants left a trail of petty and sometimes of more serious crimes behind them in the districts through which they moved. What, however, about social mobility? There were certainly plenty of individual cases of that downward and upward social movement which in all places and all ages penalizes the incompetent and unfortunate and rewards the able and lucky. Among the latter we can mention Sir Michael Hickes, the son of a London mercer who, after an education at university and Inn of Court, entered the service of Lord Burghley, married a wealthy widow and ended life as a prominent Essex gentleman. His brother, Baptist, had even greater worldly success rising through his moneylending activities to the dizzy heights of the peerage; he was created Viscount Campden in the early years of Charles I (75).

Individual social mobility is one thing, a change in the basic structure of society quite another, and most historians assume that there was no such basic change in sixteenth- and early-seventeenth-century England. There certainly *were* some significant alterations in the relative importance of different social groups. Professor Stone's thesis that the period saw a decline in the authority and status of the peerage remains controversial, but other sections of the upper reaches of society grew significantly in size and wealth, notably the gentry (see Ch. 35), the merchants and the professional classes, such as doctors and lawyers. Thomas Wilson, commenting at the end of Elizabeth's reign on the fortunes of the common lawyers remarked that 'within these 40 or 50 years, since the practice of civil law hath been as it were wholly banished and abrogated, and since the clergy hath been trodden down . . ., and since the long continuance of peace hath bred an inward canker and rest in men's minds, the people doing nothing but jar and wrangle one with another, these lawyers by the ruins of neighbours' contentions are grown so great, so rich and so proud that no other sort dare meddle with them. Their number is so great now that, to say the truth, they can scarcely live one by another'. (8, *24*) Wilson certainly exaggerated – the great majority of lawyers were less rich than he suggests – but his picture, if applied to the relatively small but very influential legal élite, is a valid one. The upper reaches of Elizabethan and early Stuart society were clearly expanding significantly in numbers and wealth and their growing prosperity was shared by large numbers of yeomen who took advantage of the agricultural opportunities offered by the expanding market for food (211).

On the other hand, at the bottom of the social heap the poor and vagrants were also growing in numbers both relatively and absolutely. William Lambardes, notable scholar and expert on local administration, considered some of the reasons in a speech of 1594 when he drew particular attention to the effects of the war with Spain, but he made no reference to what historians would now see as the main cause, the growing pressure of an expanding population on limited resources (5, *28 ff*).

The increasing prosperity of the richer groups in society and the pauperization of large numbers among the lower orders represented a striking economic polarization between the upper and bottom ranks of Englishmen. But there was more to it than that. The increasing division between the richer and poorer elements was paralleled by a growing split between the 'respectable' members of society and the rest. Dr Wrightson has argued with conviction that in the period between 1580 and 1660 the 'middling sort' – those members of rural and urban society who stood below but not too far below the traditional governing classes of countryside and town – allied with their betters, whose cultural values they increasingly came to share and adopted an increasingly hostile and distant attitude towards the rural masses (206).

All these social changes, taken together, were the result of a variety of economic and cultural influences among which the population and price rises and the educational and religious changes of the period were of crucial significance. The price and population rises were of decisive importance in producing the increasing economic polarization of society, while the educational and religious developments helped to create and highlight cultural divisions between the 'respectable' and the rest. The growth in educational facilities increased the literacy of many of the 'middling sort' (see Ch. 24) and the religious changes associated with the Reformation inculcated in them high standards of personal conduct which often found expression in a Puritan piety which was scandalized by the frequent immorality and religious indifference of the 'lower orders'.

The increasing polarization of English society during the sixteenth and early seventeenth centuries between 'respectable' elements and the rest of the population was of profound importance both then and for the future. Whether or not it represented a fundamental change in the structure of society is, perhaps, a debating point. Certainly, it is arguable that by 1660 English society can be legitimately analysed within either of two broad conceptual frameworks; the gentlemen and the rest, or the 'respectable' and the rest. That is a choice which historians looking at society in the early years of our period do not really have – they are thrown back on the traditional distinction between the gentry on the one hand and those beneath them on the social scale on the other – but the concept of the 'respectable' and the rest, which originated in our period, had a long history before it; it was still a very powerful idea at the end of the Victorian era and, indeed, beyond. Here, perhaps, is one of the foundations of modern British society which has not received sufficient recognition from historians of the early modern period.

Sixteenth- and seventeenth-century governments no doubt welcomed, in general terms, the growth of an avowedly respectable element among the 'middling' ranks of the population. Their general policy towards social change was, however, to prevent it, an attitude which was held by the authorities of the 1640s and 1650s almost as much as by those of the pre-revolutionary era. Governments' motives were both theoretical and practical. The theoretical motive behind the desire to maintain the established social hierarchy was the belief that it was part of God's divine plan for the universe. This idea, part of the mental furniture of educated Elizabethans, was founded on the concept of a great 'chain of being', with God at its apex and angels, men, animals and inanimate objects ranged in their due order below. The hierarchy of men and women in their appointed stations in life was thus a reflection of the divine order of the universe (275; 277). The theory of the chain of being was expounded with great clarity by Tudor and Stuart preachers in the homily of obedience, which was frequently read in churches and provided a vigorous defence of existing social relationships.

Almighty God [stated the homily] hath created and appointed all things in heaven, earth, and waters, in a most excellent and perfect order. In heaven He hath appointed distinct and several orders and states of archangels and angels. In earth He hath assigned and appointed kings, princes, with other governors under them,

in all good and necessary order. . . . Every degree of people in their vocation, calling
and office hath appointed to them their duty and order: some are in high degree,
some in low, some kings and princes, some inferiors and subjects, priests and
laymen, masters and servants, fathers and children, husbands and wives, rich and
poor: and everyone hath need of other: so that in all things is to be lauded and
praised the goodly order of God. . . . (5, *138–9*)

One way in which Tudor governments sought to make their theoretical defence
of the social hierarchy visible was sumptuary legislation, regulating in great detail
the clothes which were considered appropriate for the different orders of society.
The existence of numerous statutes and proclamations on this subject is as
revealing as the fact that they were honoured much more in the breach than in
the observance – both native and foreign commentators were agreed that the
men and women of the day tended to dress above their station.[1]

The desire of early modern governments to prevent social change was, of
course, founded on practical as well as theoretical considerations. A prime task
of any government is to prevent disorder, and early modern administrations feared
that social changes might lead to a breakdown of law and order with serious
consequences for the stability of the country. They therefore sought to control
the greed of the upper classes as well as the discontents of the lower orders.
Sixteenth-century governments believed – wrongly as we now know – that enclosure and engrossing were responsible for many of the worst economic ills of the
country and they tried to limit the rapacity of landlords and prevent the depopulation of the countryside by legislation and by Commissions of Enquiry which
tried to maintain tillage and reverse conversions from arable to pastoral farming
((46, *36 ff*), see above, Ch. 20). They also sought to help the deserving poor and
punish sturdy rogues and vagabonds – enormous tasks in view of the greatly
increased number of paupers and vagrants, due mainly to the population rise and
price inflation of the period. Between 1531 and 1597 a series of Acts created an
increasingly sophisticated system of relief for the deserving poor – defined as the
aged and infirm poor and pauper children – and over the same period legislation
also provided for the severe punishment of rogues and vagrants, with penalties
ranging from the relative 'mercy' of savage whippings to the horrors of the 1547
Act, 'the most savage . . . in the grim history of English vagrancy', which
provided that vagabonds were to be branded and then condemned to lives of
temporary or, in some cases, even permanent slavery. That draconian measure
was too harsh even for sixteenth-century standards – it was repealed in 1549 – but
the general severity of sixteenth-century legislation against vagrancy reveals the
extent to which the Tudor governing classes lived in terror of the tramp (98; 210).

The determination of gentry-dominated governments after 1640 to maintain
the social hierarchy and prevent substantial social change was motivated by the
continuing desire of the gentlemen who retained power during the 1640s and
1650s to preserve the social order in face of attacks on it by radical revolutionaries: this was a major theme of the Interregnum and the prevalent social conservatism of the gentry can be seen in all the Parliaments of the 1650s – the Rump,
Barebone's and the Parliaments of the Protectorate (see Part V). In 1660 when
the gentlemen of England united to welcome back the King it was clear that they

had succeeded in their objective of preserving the existing social framework. In succeeding they did, of course, preserve their own dominance. The most significant dividing line in English society may be seen by that time as being either between its 'respectable' members and the rest or between the gentry and the rest, but if the first of these conceptual frameworks is adopted it must obviously be recognized that the gentry were the politically and socially dominant element within the 'respectable' group in society. Even the growing urbanization and the commercial and financial 'revolutions' of the late seventeenth and early eighteenth centuries failed to change that situation substantially, though they did modify it.

1. F. E. Baldwin, *Sumptuary Legislation and Personal Regulation in England* (Baltimore, 1926); W. Hooper, 'The Tudor Sumptuary Laws', *EHR*, **30** (1915), 433 ff; J. Hurstfield and A. G. R Smith, *Elizabethan People*, pp. 30 ff.

CHAPTER 23

Law and Order

As we saw when considering the attitude of Tudor administrations towards social change, a primary task of any early modern government was to preserve law and order within the country. Governments had to try to prevent crime, riots and rebellions and, if prevention proved impossible, to catch and punish the criminals and suppress the riots and rebellions. Coercion, therefore, was the last resort of the government. It hoped to achieve its aims by persuading people to obey the law voluntarily, by taking measures to remove, as far as possible, the reasons for riots and by reducing the means of violence available to citizens.

The most important vehicle for exhorting people to obey the law was the pulpit. Theoretically the entire population was expected to attend church on Sundays, and even if the reality fell considerably short of the theory ministers still had a captive audience each week which comprised the majority of adults. Admonitions to obey the instructions of duly constituted authority rained down on parishioners. We have already noted the words of the homily of obedience (Ch. 22), so popular with parish ministers, and its sentiments were strongly echoed in innumerable sermons throughout our period. That powerful preacher Thomas Lever, well known as a critic of upper-class greed during Edward VI's reign, thundered in 1550 against oppressed members of the lower orders who took the law into their own hands just as much as against the avaricious landlords who treated them unjustly. It was wrong, he affirmed, for rich men to 'make strait laws to save their own goods', but even worse for the poor to rebel and thus produce greater chaos than even the most evil of laws. The duty of subjects to duly constituted state authorities, he went on, was very great. They must pay all taxation demanded 'and not . . . be curious to know for what cause it is asked' (55, *30–1*). Governments, which greatly valued the words of ministers who preached obedience to the law, also exhorted the population to obey its commands in innumerable statutes and proclamations of the period, and government propagandists, including no less a man than William Cecil himself, took time to explain the Crown's case on some of the burning issues of the day. In 1583 Cecil published his *Execution of Justice in England*, a justification of the government's harsh laws against Catholic missionaries on the grounds that they were a political threat to the English nation state (56).

Tudor monarchs and ministers also tried to remove some of the reasons for riots and to reduce their subjects' opportunities for violence. They endeavoured throughout the sixteenth century to take measures against enclosers and engrossers (see above, Ch. 22) and recognized in 1563, in the Statute of Artificers, that the wages paid in many places to working men were 'too small and not answerable to this time, respecting the advancement of prices of all things belonging to the said servants and labourers', although they then somewhat spoiled the effect by laying down maximum rather than minimum wage-rates (24, *177–8*). An obvious way of reducing the opportunities for violence was to regulate the possession of guns and swords. The growing use of firearms in the sixteenth century was of considerable concern to governments, and from 1514 onwards a series of statutes attempted to regulate their possession and use. An Act of 1542 spoke of the 'divers, detestable, and shameful murders, robberies, felonies, riots, and routs with crossbows, little short handguns and little hagbuts'. In 1579 a proclamation castigated local officials for failing to enforce the laws against the carrying of guns, and in 1600 the government stated that 'licentiousness hath grown so far as it is usual not only with common and ordinary persons travelling by the highways to carry pistols and other kinds of pieces, but that ruffians and other lewd and dissolute men . . . wheresoever they go or ride in the highways and streets . . . do in secret manner go provided of such means to do mischief'. The government also worried about swords. In 1562 the Queen prohibited the wearing of 'long swords and rapiers, sharpened in such sort as may appear the usage of them can not tend to defense, which ought to be the very meaning of wearing of weapons in times of peace, but to murder and evident death' (24, *223–4, 236–7*).

Such statutes and proclamations suggest that sixteenth-century governments had, at best, limited success in controlling the use of offensive weapons, and there is no doubt that crime and violence continued to be endemic both among the lower orders and upper strata of sixteenth-century English society. By the end of the century, however, there are signs that the land-owning classes were acquiring more peaceful habits; by 1600 more and more propertied men were turning to the lawcourts rather than to weapons to solve their disputes (24; 217).

The criminal activities of the upper classes, probably on the wane by 1600, were obviously more spectacular than those of the lower orders, but the great majority of criminals came from the poorer strata of society. When the persuasions of ecclesiastical and government propaganda failed to deter these men from illegal activities they had to be caught and brought before the courts as a preliminary to punishment. In early modern England, however, where there was no professional police force or prosecuting service, it was often very difficult to produce suspected criminals in court. The great majority – perhaps as many as 80 per cent – escaped trial (133). Throughout the period minor courts – like manorial courts leet, presided over by the steward of the manor – continued to exercise criminal jurisdiction, but the more serious crimes were tried by justices of the peace in quarter sessions and by judges from the central courts who toured England twice a year in order to hold courts of assizes in the localities; from at least as early as the 1570s most serious felonies were tried before the assize judges. At the top of the hierarchy of criminal courts was King's Bench at Westminster, but it was of limited importance in terms of the *number* of serious criminal cases which came before it; it heard far less than assizes (133; 136).

Contemporaries lamented the extent of crime and disorder in the country and most later historians have accepted their picture of an increasing crime rate, We must remember, however, that it is common in all societies and ages for men to bewail the amount of criminal activity and that the incomplete state of the English criminal records of the period and the difficulties of interpreting those which we do have, render the task of quantification difficult if not impossible. We can, however, draw some tentative conclusions from the material available. We have seen that there is reason to believe that the amount of upper-class violence was declining by 1600 and Professor Cockburn's analysis of serious crimes in the counties of Essex, Hertfordshire and Sussex between 1559 and 1625, most of them committed by members of the lower orders, suggests that that pattern may be more generally applicable throughout the population as a whole. He shows that criminal activity, as measured by trials at assizes in these three counties, increased substantially during the Elizabethan period and then fell back during James I's reign (133, *50 ff*). There were two broad categories of criminal cases; those against the person and those against property (133, *54 ff*). Crimes against the person, most notably homicide, assault and witchcraft, were much less common than those against property: of over 7,500 people indicted [N] at assizes in the three counties under review nearly 5,500, about 73 per cent, were accused of theft. Most thieves were either vagrants or members of the lower strata of the settled population, and it is probable that their crimes were primarily the result of economic hardship. Cockburn has found three sudden increases in the number of property offences coming before the courts in Elizabeth's reign, each of which can be identified with a period of sharply rising food prices. The most dramatic increase of all came during the economic blizzard of 1596–98, when the number of crimes against property rocketed in each of our three counties (133). The conclusion seems clear. Most serious crime in sixteenth- and early-seventeenth-century England was theft, most thieves came from the lower orders and most stole so that they could buy food. On the other hand, although crime does seem to have increased during the Elizabethan age, it is much less clear that it grew during the period 1500–1640 as a whole. Upper-class violence may have have been declining by James I's reign, and, if we are to believe Professor Cockburn's figures, serious crime among the lower orders may also have been past its peak by that time. It would certainly be fitting if a great sixteenth-century 'crimewave' really did ebb during the days of the ultra-pacific James I with his horror of both foreign and domestic violence, the latter well epitomized in his condemnation of the practice of duelling (217, *242 ff*).

If the machinery for catching thieves and other criminals was very imperfect, with perhaps as few as 20 per cent of those who committed crimes brought before the courts, those who did stand trial had a very good chance of escaping the full rigour of the often ferocious penalties which their crimes theoretically entailed. Any criminal convicted of the theft of goods worth more than 12d. could be hanged, and during the sixteenth century the number of felonies – crimes which carried a death sentence – was substantially enlarged. Trial juries, however, were often sympathetic to the accused who were brought before them. Perhaps a quarter of those indicted were found not guilty and jurors saved from the gallows a substantial if unknown number of those whom they did convict by undervaluing stolen goods so as to reduce their value below 12d. and thus make the criminal liable to a public whipping rather than hanging (136). Even of those convicted of felony only about 10 per cent were actually executed. Many who were first-time offenders escaped through their ability to read, an accomplishment which made them eligible for benefit of clergy for some felonious offences, while others were saved from the ultimate penalty by judges who substituted other sentences, such as service in the navy (136).

Assize judges were sometimes criticized by local magistrates for what the latter regarded as their undue leniency to criminals. In practice, however, in the absence of an effective prison system in the England of the day and with comparatively few criminals able to pay a substantial fine, the judges had at their disposal few meaningful punishments short of death. That is a clear indictment of early modern criminal law, and if only 20 per cent of criminals were tried at all and a mere 10 per cent of those convicted of felony were executed, the law cannot realistically have acted as a great deterrent to men who often stole to provide the neccessities of life for themselves and their families. In such circumstances it seems safe to agree with Dr Williams that 'it is unlikely that Tudor lawcourts had much impact on the ordinary crime-rate' (24, *232–3, 252*; 136, *132*).

The great bulk of the felonious offences tried at assizes were against property and the great majority of those tried belonged to the lower orders. The law's severity might be mitigated – often against the wishes of the average country gentleman – by assize judges, but the severity was there largely to keep the poor in their place, to prevent them from plundering the possessions of their betters. That interpretation of the role of the sixteenth-century criminal law, so natural for propertied contemporaries, has been echoed by modern scholars who have stressed the 'class bias' of the law. The gentlemen of early modern England certainly thought that the rigours of the legal system were necessary to preserve their own position in society and this helps to explain, as we shall see (Ch. 43), the determined resistance of the great majority of lawyers and gentlemen to any radical reform of the law during the revolutionary decades of the mid-seventeenth century.

The everyday criminal activities of the lower orders were an irritant to the government and the governing classes. More serious in their eyes were, of course, the riots and rebellions which marked the period. A riot was technically and assembly of three or more people to commit an illegal act, but we are concerned here with rather larger disturbances. Dr Wrightson has argued (206, *173–4*) that riots were of two main kinds, food riots, involving the seizure or detention of food by a crowd, and enclosure riots, which involved the destruction of the fences which had been built around hitherto open fields or commons. This distinction may be useful for purposes of analysis, but it should be remembered that it is in some ways artificial; complaints about the high price of food might lead to attacks on enclosures. Sixteenth- and early-seventeenth-century rioters had limited objectives. They certainly did not wish to overthrow the social order – although government propaganda sometimes suggested that they did – merely to assert certain basic rights to which they believed all men were entitled, above all the right to subsistence – enough to eat and drink at reasonable prices. Mr Clark has shown that popular protest was endemic in Kent in the period 1558–1640.[1] The Kentish rioters were – predictably – the poor, and – more surprisingly perhaps – they included many women, perhaps driven to despair because of difficulties in feeding their families. The numbers involved in individual riots in Kent were not large, probably never exceeding 100, and the worst riots were in years of acute economic difficulty, especially the 1590s. It is an unsurprising picture and it can be fleshed out by consideration of two riots in 1596, those at Canterbury and Hernhill, which 'had a common theme: the shortage of grain at reasonable prices'.

Much Kentish wheat went to feed the insatiable demand of London and this led to periodic crises in corn supplies within the county itself. The most serious of these came during the bad harvests of 1594–97. By the second of the four harvest failures of these years, that of 1595, the grain stored in Kent from previous good harvests had all been used up, and London buyers began to offer prices well above the market rate. The Kentish magistrates wanted strict control of corn exports from the county, but in February 1596 they were overruled by the Privy Council. It was about this time that the Canterbury and Hernhill riots occurred. The Canterbury disturbances took place in the poor suburb of St Dunstan's. populated by low-income families and including many paupers and criminals. The bad harvest of 1595 caused crisis conditions in the parish with a huge increase in burials, many of which must have been at least indirectly due to the food shortage. In these circumstances the sight of carts departing for London laden with precious supplies of grain was too much for some of the inhabitants and perhaps fifteen to twenty people were involved in the detention of two grain wagons. They only agreed to disperse when the dean of Canterbury ordered that the carts should not continue on their journey. It is notable that the 'rioters' behaved in the most restrained way. They detained the wheat but did not steal any of it and they harmed nobody. Hernhill, a village to the north-west of Canterbury, had a great many poor inhabitants, some of them squatters, others the victims of the village's deteriorating local economy; the tanning industry which provided its principal by-employment was in decline. The Hernhill agitators, who were probably never more than twenty-five in number, wanted action from a local justice of the peace to reduce the price of corn, but the conspiracy ended with a raid on the barn of a Catholic landowner and the theft of some of his grain.

Better known than the Kentish riots of the 1590s are the Oxfordshire 'revolt' of 1596 and the Midlands 'rising' of 1607. The former involved only between ten and twenty men and was caused by a combination of high corn prices and anger at enclosures which had been carried out in the western part of Oxfordshire. Its leaders talked about seizing weapons from the houses of gentlemen and throwing down enclosures, and one of them is said to have talked about murdering members of the gentry. The plot was betrayed, however, and the ringleaders arrested. The local notables and the government took the affair very seriously, a reflection of the fact that even a minor conspiracy could set alarm bells ringing in the highest quarters. It is notable, too, that the Privy Council did not ignore the plotters' complaints. In January 1597 it questioned some Oxfordshire gentlemen about their enclosing activities (24). The Midlands rising in the early years of James's reign was the result of complaints against enclosures in a part of England which was, as we have seen (Ch. 20), the area of the country worst affected by the enclosure movement. As a result, risings broke out in Leicestershire, Northamptonshire and Warwickshire under the leadership of John Reynolds, nicknamed Captain Pouch. Some hedges were broken down, but the revolt was easily suppressed by local landowners.[2]

All the riots and risings which we have been considering were limited protests by small numbers of men and women against what they regarded as intolerable injustices. As such they were part of a long tradition of riots and revolts which went back to the Middle Ages and was to continue into the eighteenth century. There were also, of course, a number of much more serious rebellions between 1529 and 1660, and Dr Williams has argued plausibly that these were, broadly speaking, of two types, those in which the leaders attempted to seize political power, and those which were rather protests in force which did not seek to over-turn established authority, merely to remedy grievances ((24, *313 ff*), see also (140)). As such, the latter group can, not unfairly, be regarded as demonstrations on a very much larger scale than but still similar to the minor riots and revolts which we have just been examining. These large-scale protests were the Pilgrimage of Grace of 1536, Ket's rebellion of 1549, and the south-western rebellion of the same year. The Pilgrimage was the result of a combination of economic, political and religious discontents, and historians are still debating which of these different sets of motives was the most important (see above, Ch. 7). On the other hand, whichever of the motives we emphasize, we can surely agree that 'fundamentally the Pilgrims were protesting against an unprecedented intrusion by the Crown into their local communities and traditional ways'. The Pilgrimage was, in fact, 'the archetypal protest movement of the century' (24, *321, 316–17*), combining noblemen, gentlemen and commoners in a gigantic effort to secure redress of their grievances from a Crown to which they loudly and probably genuinely professed loyalty. Ket's rebellion of 1549 and the south-western rising of the same year had none of the upper-class support which had marked the Pilgrimage. These were movements of the common people, the former essentially economic – a protest against a variety of agrarian grievances in East Anglia, including enclosures, high rents and the overstocking of the common lands by the large sheep-flocks of the gentry – the latter primarily religious – a rejection of the new English Prayer Book imposed on the country in 1549.

All these protest movements, both the large-scale rebellions of 1536 and 1549 and the comparatively minor riots and revolts which were endemic throughout the sixteenth and seventeenth centuries, were notable for their essential moder-ation. The rioters and rebels showed very little physical violence to their oppo-nents and, despite the fact that there was almost no support for such movements from landowners after the Pilgrimage of Grace, there were few signs of serious class conflict in the uprisings; the protesters, in so far as their grievances were economic, made highly conservative demands, asking for a return to traditional moral values in economic relationships. There is no convincing evidence that they ever sought to challenge the established social hierarchy.

In the other major rebellions of the period the leaders attempted, either overtly or covertly, to seize political power. This can be seen in the overthrow of Somerset in 1549 (if that can properly be termed a 'rebellion' at all), in the

Jane Grey episode in 1553, in Wyatt's rebellion in 1554, in the rebellion of the northern earls in 1569 and in the Essex revolt of 1601. With the exception of the first, a revolt against a 'regent', all of them failed. No legitimate monarch was toppled until the 1640s. Indeed, the failure of the rebellions in which the leaders sought to overthrow the government illustrates, *inter alia*, the strong grip which the Tudor monarchy had on both the imagination and the perceived self-interest of the political nation.

The major rebellions of the Tudor period had no successors in the early Stuart period before the dramatic events of the 1640s. The 'Great Rebellion' of 1640 onwards was, of course, *sui generis* (see Chs. 34–44). It began as a protest, escalated into an attempt to seize political power, continued with civil war and the overthrow of the monarchy, produced an outburst of radical religious, political and social ideas unprecedented in English history, either before or since, and only ended with the restoration of the monarchy in 1660. The Great Rebellion, indeed, illustrates the way in which the continuing pressure of events could radicalize a movement which began as a protest and ended as a full-scale religious and political revolution with social revolutionaries waiting in the wings in the vain hope that they might make the revolution their own. The outbreak of civil war in 1642 reflected the ultimate breakdown of that ordered society which the propertied classes strove so hard to maintain during the sixteenth and seventeenth centuries, a society founded on intellectual assumptions which were completely hostile to the idea of revolts against duly constituted authority and on a criminal law which sought to keep the lower orders in their place through harsh – if not always effectively applied – penalties.

---

1. P. Clark, 'Popular protest and disturbance in Kent, 1558–1640', *EcHR*, 2nd ser., **29** (1976), 365 ff.
2. E. F. Gay, 'The Midlands revolt of 1607', *TRHS*, 2nd ser., **18** (1904), 195 ff.

CHAPTER 24

Education and science

All the major rebellions of the sixteenth and early seventeenth centuries failed, with the minor exception of the palace *coup d'état* which ousted Somerset and the major exception of the 'Great Rebellion' which overthrew the monarchy, the House of Lords and episcopacy during the 1640s. That rebellion has often been described by historians as the 'English Revolution' (see Ch. 35, and see (38; 281)) – one of the most notable 'revolutions' in the ever growing list which historians of Britain are compiling for the sixteenth and seventeenth centuries – and the terms 'educational revolution' and 'scientific revolution' are also familiar to students of early modern English history. Indeed, some historians have detected important links between the educational changes of the period on the one hand and the political upheavals of the mid-seventeenth century on the other.

There is no doubt that the sixteenth and early seventeenth centuries saw a considerable expansion of educational facilities, at both school and higher educational levels. Two preliminary points should be made about this growth; it was an accelerated continuation of an expansion which was already in progress in the fifteenth century (21), and it was not a linear trend taking place continuously throughout the early modern period but rather a progression by fits and starts in which the years 1580–1610 were a time of 'educational recession' (262, *169*).

There were, in the words of Professor Stone, 'three different, if often overlapping forms' of school education during the period. First of all there was the teaching of basic literacy – the elementary ability to read and write – in so-called 'petty' schools; secondly, a type of schooling which helped to prepare children for apprenticeships, and which included instruction in practical aspects of mathematics and the keeping of accounts; and finally there was the grammar school, dominated by its classical curriculum with a heavy concentration on Latin grammar (263). Figures which have been produced to illustrate the growth in the number of schools include those of Professor Jordan, who counted 410 new schools started between 1480 and 1660 in the 10 English counties which he surveyed, and those of the nineteenth-century Schools Inquiry Commission which listed 435 endowed schools established throughout the country between 1500 and 1660 (205, *291*; 262, *165*). Neither of these lists is complete – both, for example, omit a good many private fee-paying schools – but the general trend is clear, a great expansion of school education at all levels.

Higher education too was growing at a considerable rate at the universities of Oxford and Cambridge. It also grew at the Inns of Court, which provided both for aspiring barristers and for those who merely wished to obtain a smattering of legal education. New colleges were founded at the universities – Jesus and

Wadham at Oxford in 1571 and 1612 and Emmanuel and Sidney Sussex at Cambridge in 1584 and 1596 to take four examples – and the number of university entrants rose from about 650 a year during the 1560s, to about 770 per annum during the decade of the 1580s. Numbers then fell back slightly until the second decade of the seventeenth century when they resumed their upward march, reaching about 1,050 during the 1630s. Those who entered the Inns of Court rose in numbers from about 160 a year during the 1560s to perhaps 275 per annum in the 1630s. Adding to these figures young men who were educated at home or abroad to university standard and deducting from them the 50 per cent or so of entrants to the Inns of Court who had already studied at university, we get an approximate figure of 780 entering higher education each year during the 1560s and about 1,240 entrants per annum during the 1630s. In the 1640s numbers fell sharply, and although they recovered a little in the 1650s they never matched their pre-Civil War peak throughout the rest of the seventeenth century. In fact, 'in quantitative terms English higher education did not get back to the level of the 1630s until after the First World War'; in 1931 male university entrants formed about 2.3 per cent of their relevant age group compared with the 2.5 per cent going on to higher education in 1640 (263).

There were a number of reasons for this expansion of the educational system in early modern England (251; 263; 205). It may have been associated at all levels with a growing desire among parents that children should be allowed to develop as far as possible their individual personalities and potentialities, and it was certainly linked, at both the theoretical and practical levels, with the religious changes of the time. English Puritans, so influential in society during the Elizabethan and early Stuart periods, believed in the value of education as a weapon against sin and idleness – above all it enabled people to read the Bible – and they demonstrated their commitment both by the education which they provided for their children and the substantial financial contributions which they made during the period for the founding of schools and the improvement of the universities. Moreover, the Reformation which had, as we have seen (Ch. 11), broken the grip of the clergy on many of the highest offices of State, led to an increasing demand for lay administrators in *all* ranks of state service, and as the sixteenth century advanced it became more and more advantageous in seeking such posts to have some knowledge of the law. Then there was the influence of sixteenth-century humanists and educators, men like Colet and Mulcaster, who taught that a bookish education centred on the classics would not merely help its recipients to serve the State effectively but would also make them more 'rounded' individuals, able to converse intelligently not merely with their equals but perhaps also with their social superiors. Education, in other words, helped men to acquire status, and at a time when land was changing hands at great speed many purchasers hoped to secure social as well as material advantages for their children by giving them a higher education. In addition, the growing number of gentlemen who flocked to the Inns of Court went there not merely to prepare themselves for coping with the administrative and legal burdens of the office of JP, which many of them would be called upon to exercise, but more generally to gain a minimum of legal knowledge which might help them in the conduct of their personal affairs in an increasingly litigious age.

The great growth in educational facilities which took place had to be paid for. Broadly speaking, there were three sources from which the money could come: the State; the individual parents whose children obtained educational benefits; and private benefactors who left money for educational expansion. The old view of the disastrous role of the State in education in the sixteenth century was put forward long ago by A. F. Leach,[1] who believed that many of the schools which existed at the time of the Reformation were dissolved or impoverished after the dissolution of the chantries in 1547. His ideas are no longer tenable. It is clear that during and after Edward VI's reign, when the Chantry Act was passed, steps were taken by either the State or town corporations to reform and improve the educational establishments which existed in 1547. Even if we take the narrow context of Edward VI's reign itself, it is clear that there were more grammar schools in England in 1553 than in 1547 (22). The State plainly did not sweep away an existing system of education by depriving it of funds, but it is also clear that the impetus for the great expansion of the educational system did not come from the government. Part of it came from the money provided by individual parents whose children obtained educational benefits. At school level they supported the growing number of fee-paying schools which were established during the period, and even in the large number of 'free' schools, where the boys were not charged for instruction, there were many incidental expenses which parents had to meet, such as payments for writing materials and books and 'voluntary' gifts to the masters of the schools, often necessary because of the low level of teachers' salaries. At the universities and Inns of Court, where life could be expensive, students were also usually dependent on money from their parents, and more and more parents were not merely willing but able to pay for the education of their children. We have seen (Ch. 20) that there was a redistribution of national wealth in early modern England with a growing gap between the upper and middling ranks of society on the one hand and the impoverished masses on the other, and this meant that not merely the gentry but many of the 'middling' groups – yeomen and moderately prosperous townsmen – had the means as well as the desire to invest in their children's education. The third major source of money for educational expansion was private benefactors and Professor Jordan has demonstrated that their role was crucial. They founded hundreds of new schools and poured money into the universities both to improve facilities there and to establish numerous scholarships to support deserving students. Although these benefactors came from all parts of the country and from almost all social backgrounds there are two notable facts about them; one is the dominance of London benefactors, the other the decisive contribution made by the merchant classes in general and the merchants of London in particular (205).

So far we have considered the number of children and adolescents entering the educational system. The great expansion in the number of schools and in university places might suggest that Professor Stone's term 'educational revolution' is justified; but before we come to that conclusion we should look further at the social groups in the community which were affected and at the content of education. Professor Jordan argued that the great expansion of school facilities made education available to all sections of the community, however poor. By 1660, he stated, schools in Norfolk were so distributed and available that there was one 'within the reach of any poor and able boy who thirsted for knowledge and who aspired to escape the grip of poverty'.[2] This statement is almost certainly untrue; the opportunity for schooling remained, in practice, beyond the reach of very many boys. The great majority of the poorest people in the community – labourers, husbandmen and the urban poor – required their children's help from an early age to support the family. It did not matter to these people – the bulk of the community – whether education could be obtained free for their children or not. The latter had to be put to work to earn their own bread from as early an age as possible (263; 264). The groups above the level of the rural and urban poor all benefited to a greater or lesser extent, the gentry probably most of all (263; 264). This is the picture which one would expect in an era when education was prized and educational facilities were expanding. Those at the top of the social scale benefited most. The lower down one went the more opportunities diminished. Girls' chances were limited in the extreme. The grammar schools and universities were closed to them, and though the wealthiest might receive an excellent education at home from distinguished teachers – a system which produced notable bluestockings, like Queen Elizabeth and the learned Cooke sisters – only the tiniest minority could expect any education beyond the bare-literacy which could be acquired in the petty schools (206).

The study of literacy, like that of demography, is one of the growth points of early modern historical studies, and, like the latter, it lacks a satisfactory statistical basis. It is now possible, however, to make some fairly sophisticated guesses about the extent of literacy in sixteenth- and early-seventeenth-century England, guesses founded on men's and women's ability to sign their names.[3] The sequence of educational instruction at the time was such that children would almost always learn to read before they could write, and Dr Cressy has argued that a signature indicates that the writer's literary skills were probably somewhere in the range between a crude reading ability and genuine fluency in writing. This is probably acceptable as a generalization, although there must have been all sorts of individual exceptions to the rule. On the basis of that criterion, and working on the signatures and marks made during the 1640s by over 40,000 men in over 400 parishes in 25 counties, the overall male literacy rate in England on the eve of the Civil War was probably about 30 per cent [O.5]. At the same time it was probably about 10 per cent among women. Figures for earlier periods are even less certain, but 'reasonable guesses' by Dr Cressy are 10 per cent male and 1 per cent female literacy in 1500 rising to 20 per cent male and 5 per cent female literacy at the time of Elizabeth's accession (262, *72, 176*). The literacy of the different social groups paralleled, as one would expect, their educational opportunities. Gentry and clergy, almost wholly literate by the early seventeenth century, were well ahead of yeomen and tradesmen, who, in turn, were well ahead of husbandmen and labourers. The literacy of tradesmen and yeomen – members of the 'middling' groups in society – did in general improve substantially over the period 1500–1650 as a whole, but this was not true of husbandmen and labourers. The overall illiteracy of husbandmen in pre-industrial England was about 80 per cent; as Cressy says, 'they rested near that plateau relatively unmoved by the educational and political developments of the sixteenth and seventeenth centuries' (262, *156*). More surprisingly, regional variations in literacy seem to have been relatively slight, with no very great differences among counties. The greatest variations were from parish to parish *within* individual counties (262), a fact which reveals the need for the most detailed local investigations if we are to explain the educational patterns of each shire.

The 'educational revolution', which looks an impressive concept when we compile statistics of new schools established and of greatly increased numbers in higher education, seems a good deal less impressive after this examination of the different groups in the community who benefited – or failed to benefit – from the changes: the extent of illiteracy among husbandmen, labourers and women, the great bulk of the population, in the mid-seventeenth century makes it very clear that the educational changes of the period were highly selective in their impact. Further doubts about the validity of the word 'revolution' arise when we turn to the content of education.

In schools the study of Latin grammar and Latin literature remained, as in the fifteenth century, the principal concern, though it is true that these studies, under humanist influences, were often based on texts which were much nearer to the originals than their medieval predecessors. The principal function of the universities in the years before the Reformation was the training of a clerical élite with a notable emphasis on the study of scholastic theology and canon law. The Reformation era saw the abolition of canon law studies and increasing humanistic influences, but the content and effectiveness of teaching in the universities over the whole period from the late sixteenth to the mid-seventeenth centuries has given rise to considerable debate among historians (259; 260; 261; 266). Professor Curtis, for example, stresses the advances and innovations made during the period, emphasizing the role of college tutors like Richard Holdsworth, Fellow of St John's, Cambridge, from 1613 to 1620, in introducing modern methods and studies which lay outside the formal curriculum. Professor Charlton, on the other hand, who emphasizes the conservatism of the universities, points to the continuing importance of scholastic methods and to the role of Aristotle at the centre of university studies for most of the seventeenth century. Teaching in 'new' subjects like mathematics and science was, he admits, available, but he stresses that only a small minority of dons had any substantial interest in these subjects. When the experts are divided in this way it is best to be cautious, but three points seem clear. First of all, the universities remained in the sixteenth and seventeenth centuries, as they had been in the fifteenth, primarily seminaries for the clergy, producing that ever growing number of graduates who, by the early seventeenth century, had gone far to making the Church of England a graduate body at parish level. That is a fact which people like Curtis and Stone, with their emphasis on the new role of the laity in the student body, tend to underestimate. Contemporaries, however, did not generally make that mistake and radical critics of the conservatism of the universities laid much stress during the 1640s and 1650s on their dominance by clerical interests (272). Secondly, the best teaching in mathematics and science during the period took place not at Oxford or Cambridge but at Gresham College in London, founded during the 1590s with money and property left by the great Elizabethan financial expert Sir Thomas Gresham (281). Thirdly, the gentry who emerged from the universities were, on the whole, profoundly conservative in their political ideas. This was not the view of Thomas Hobbes who, writing in the 1660s, saw the pre-Civil War universities as centres of secular radicalism – 'the core of [the] rebellion' (5, *82–3*). His words were, however, written after the dramatic events of the 1640s and 1650s, and it can be argued that the radicalization of the views of some gentlemen during these decades was due largely to the pressure of events and tells us little of pre-1640s ideas (see Ch. 35). Indeed, the overwhelming majority of the country gentlemen in the House of Commons were profoundly conservative in their attitudes, both during the 1620s and in the early months of the Long Parliament. They demonstrated this in their relentless search for precedents, in their devotion to the idea of a 'balanced' constitution and in their stress on Charles I as innovator. In these circumstances Charlton's words about the conservatism of the views which were propagated by the universities seem generally convincing; they 'showed every sign of reluctance to accept new ideas and to assimilate them into their courses of study' (259, *152*).

But that is not the end of the matter. If the universities were not hotbeds of seditious gentry in the pre-1640 period they were unquestionably the nurseries of those highly educated Puritan ministers who in the late Elizabethan and early Stuart periods poured out of such colleges as Emmanuel in Cambridge to bring their ideas to many of the parishes of England. The continuing role of the universities as training centres for the clergy of the Established Church was, as has just been noted, an example of conservatism, of continuity with the past, but the Puritanism of many of the clergy who emerged was, in contrast, a *radical* factor of the very greatest importance in the overall history of the period up to 1660. Historians who today are once again stressing the crucial significance of religion in the events of 1640–42 (see Ch. 35) should surely stress the significance of the production by Oxford and especially by Cambridge colleges of this godly clerical élite. These puritan clergymen founded their faith firmly on their biblical studies, but, of course, reading the vernacular Bible was, by the early seventeenth century, a very widespread activity of the educated laity, many of whom adopted Puritan ideas of varying hues as a result of their personal meditations on the Scriptures. Such Bible reading was conducted mainly outside the formal educational system (196), but if there was an 'educational revolution' in early modern England it may be that it should be seen, in the widest sense, largely as a product of such biblical studies. The expansion of the formal educational system and such changes as did take place in the curriculum at both school and university level may have been of lesser significance in their impact upon society at large than the influence of Bible reading on the substantial literate minority of the nation. Bible readers, who might be prepared to challenge the formal authority of the Church in the light of what they read in the Gospels, were also often prepared, in the last resort, to take the most resolute action to defend the faith on which they believed their salvation depended; they showed that clearly during the 1640s.

Study of the vernacular Bible in sixteenth- and seventeenth-century England was a central aspect of the life of many of the literate men and women of the time. It was a much smaller minority who took an active interest in the important scientific changes of the period, changes which were to culminate in the later seventeenth century in the epoch-making Newtonian synthesis of 1687. Developments in English science in this period must, of course, be seen against the background of the European 'scientific revolution' as a whole. During the sixteenth and seventeenth centuries the work of a galaxy of notable scientists such as Copernicus, Tycho Brahe, Kepler, Galileo, Newton, Vesalius and Harvey transformed educated men's views of the universe and of their own bodies (267; 268; 269). By the time of the Restoration the earth-centred Ptolemaic cosmos with its finite boundaries and its heaven above the sphere of the fixed stars – a picture which dominated the minds of men in the 1530s – had been replaced for many by the sun-centred Copernican universe, boundless, perhaps infinite, with no obvious place in it for heaven and the souls of the elect. At the same time, through the work of anatomists like Vesalius and physiologists like Harvey, men learnt important new information about the structure and functioning of their bodies.

There were important English and Scottish contributions to this developing body of knowledge. The greatest of all the physiological advances of the period, the discovery of the circulation of the blood, was announced in 1628 in the (*De Motu*) *Cordis* of William Harvey, who served as physician to both James I and Charles I. The *De Motu* is a model of inductive reasoning, based on careful observations and experiments. Previously men had believed that blood ebbed and flowed upwards and downwards in their veins and arteries, but Harvey calculated that the amount of blood pumped into the arteries by the heart in half an hour was greater than the total amount of blood in the body and insisted that it was impossible to account for this except on the basis of his circulation theory. Harvey's was a work of genius, but even more notable British contributions came in the physical sciences. Newton's *Principia* came after the end of the period under consideration, but in the years before the Restoration much important work in mathematics and astronomy came from British pens (270; 271). In mathematics Robert Recorde, John Dee, Thomas Harriot and the Scotsman John Napier all made important contributions. Recorde, who died in 1558, invented the = sign for 'equal'; Dee, a remarkable polymath, had wide-ranging mathematical interests; Harriot did fundamentally significant work in algebra; and John Napier, well known to schoolboys as the inventor of logarithms, published that very useful discovery in his *Descriptio* of 1614. William Gilbert, one of the great Elizabethans, brought out his *De Magnete* in 1600. It has been described as 'the first physical treatise to be based on experiment'. It took twenty years to write and in it Gibert demonstrated that the earth was a great magnet, a fact which could be used to explain all terrestrial magnetic phenomena (271, *156*). In astronomy the great theme is the reception of Copernicanism in England. Copernicus's *De Revolutionibus* was published in 1543 and the earliest known mention of it in an English book is in Recorde's *Castle of Knowledge* of 1556. Dee had two copies of the *De Revolutionibus* in his great library, but it was Thomas Digges, the son of a distinguished scientific father, who became the leading English propagandist of Copernicanism and in 1576, in his *Perfect Description of the Celestial Orbs*, he described and defended the Copernican system and added his own assertion that the universe was infinite; an issue on which Copernicus had never committed himself. Digges in fact, was 'the first modern astronomer of note to portray an infinite heliocentric universe, with the stars scattered at varying distances throughout infinite space' (270, *164–5*). It must not be suggested, of course, that Copernican ideas immediately carried all before them in England. The truth is far more complex. It is clear that by the early seventeenth century belief in the old Ptolemaic picture of the universe was in rapid decline among educated men, but by then Copernicanism had to compete with another rival, the system invented by Tycho Brahe in the later years of the sixteenth century. That was a compromise between the Ptolemaic and Copernican versions. It had all the planets revolving around the sun, but the entire group of sun and planets then revolved around the earth. The earth was thus left stationary at the centre of the universe and the Tychonic theory was very popular among those who felt that the Ptolemaic picture was out of date but still found it difficult to accept Copernicus's idea of a moving earth. It was only about 1650 that the popularity of the Tychonic began to fall well behind that of the Corpernican system in astronomical writings (270).

No discussion of the English science of the period should omit the name of Francis Bacon who did no notable scientific work himself but had important things to say about both the methodology and usefulness of science. Bacon stressed the importance of experiments and emphasized the need for their systematic use to build up a body of knowledge from which general theories could be established and then tested. He described his inductive method in his *Novum Organum* of 1620. Induction, he stated, 'derives axioms from . . . particulars, rising by a gradual and unbroken ascent, so that it arrives at the most general axioms last of all. This is the true way but as yet untried' (268, *72*). Bacon believed that scientific discoveries would give men new power over nature and that this in turn would lead to improvements in material prosperity which would make men happier. If Digges was a prophet of the infinite universe which dominates the minds of men today, then Bacon was a forerunner of those present-day propagandists – now perhaps declining in number – who see scientific advances as a cure for the ills of mankind.

Bacon was not, of course, a professional scientist, and his interest in the subject was a reflection of the growing popular concern with science during the sixteenth and seventeenth centuries. This can be seen in the large and growing number of scientific books which were published. Over 10 per cent of the books published in England in our period dealt with the natural sciences, and the great majority of them, about 90 per cent, were in English. These vernacular scientific books were aimed at a wide range of readers, and their growing number, together with the distinguished original work done by English scientists in the Elizabethan and early Stuart periods, helps to justify Professor Hill's argument that 'in the eighty years before 1640 England, from being a backward country in science, became one of the most advanced (281, *15 ff*). Further major advances were, of course, made in England in the later years of the seventeenth century and, as we shall see, historians are now arguing about the relative importance of the 1640s and 1650s on the one hand and of the post-Restoration era on the other in this story of continuing scientific developments (see Ch. 43). Whatever conclusions are reached about the relative importance of the periods 1558–1640, 1640–1660, and 1660–1700, there can be no doubt that the scientific changes of the sixteenth and seventeenth centuries as a whole – whether we call them a 'revolution' or not – transformed men's understanding of the universe and of their own bodies. Great breakthroughs in ideas were made. Harvey's views about the functioning of the body and Digges's about the nature of the universe are, in broad terms, readily comprehensible and convincing to the modern 'man in the street', whereas the physiological and astronomical ideas of early-sixteenth-century Englishmen are not.

The astronomical, mathematical and physiological advances of the sixteenth and seventeenth centuries have tended to dominate modern textbooks on 'the history of science', but subjects such as alchemy and astrology, which would now be regarded as 'unscientific' were probably of equal interest and concern to early modern scientists. Today, alchemy – which was founded on a mistaken 'four elements' theory of matter[4] – seems a bizarre activity of the past. Astrology, however, is still a notable feature of the popular press and the casting of horoscopes a common pastime, though clearly few people take these activities seriously. The foundation of astrology – the idea that the heavenly bodies have an influence on the earth – has, however, a basis in fact, and astrology, as we shall now see, was an important feature of English social life at all levels during the sixteenth and early seventeenth centuries when it grew in popularity partly as a result of the Reformation.

---

1. A. F. Leach, *English Schools at the Reformation* (1896).
2. W. K. Jordan, *The Charities of Rural England 1480–1660* (1961), p. 165.
3. See D. Cressy, *Literacy and the Social Order*; 'Levels of illiteracy in England, 1530–1730', *HJ*, **20** (1977), 1 ff.
4. E. J. Holmyard, *Alchemy* (1957).

CHAPTER 25

Aspects of English life and mind: I – 'Magic': beliefs in astrology and witchcraft

The Reformed churches of the sixteenth century, including the Church of England, endeavoured to deny the efficacy of the 'magic' of the medieval Church and to prohibit its practice. The magical elements in pre-Reformation Catholicism, many of them, of course, perversions of the official teachings of the Church, originated in the early days of Christianity, when the Apostles frequently attracted converts by working miracles. By the beginning of the sixteenth century the life of the Church was full of popular beliefs which had miraculous implications (276). The adoration of saints and pilgrimages to their shrines were founded on the belief that holy men and women of the past had supernatural powers of intercession with the Almighty; the ecclesiastical authorities had a wide range of rituals and formulae which were designed to convey God's blessing on everyday objects such as houses and crops; the chantries, with their prayers and masses for the dead, gave the impression that salvation was possible through mechanical formulae; above all, the sacraments of the Church, and especially the mass, were associated with magical power: in popular belief much stress was laid on the ability of the priest, by the mere ritual pronunciation of the words of consecration, to change the character of material objects – the miracle of transubstantiation was debased as the power of the clergy to 'make God'. The medieval Church, therefore, appeared as 'a vast reservoir of magical power, capable of being deployed for a variety of secular purposes' (276, 45).

The Protestant reformers, in rejecting the magical elements in pre-Reformation church practice, made a particular point of attacking transubstantiation, the heart of Catholic 'miracle' religion (276). They regarded it as a spurious and dangerous assertion of supernatural power by the priesthood, and by 1552 the English Church had reduced the ancient mass to a commemorative rite. Men and women, however, continued to hunger for the comfort which so many of the ancient rituals had brought to their daily lives, which were so exposed to the vagaries of chance as manifested in such phenomena as disease and the weather. Not surprisingly, they sought solace in substitute 'magics'. Among the most popular of these were the science of astrology and witchcraft beliefs, both of which provided early modern English men and women with explanations for the misfortunes and seemingly random events of their lives, and held out hopes that appropriate action – consultation with an astrologer or denunciation of a witch – would, *inter alia*, explain their situations, give them hope for the future and secure the punishment of those who could be held responsible for their misfortunes.

The principles of sixteenth-century English astrology were founded on a body of learning which had originated in ancient Babylonia (276). Astrological ideas were further developed by the Greeks, Romans and Arabs, and the English interest in the subject, at a relatively low ebb at the beginning of the sixteenth century, expanded enormously during the years after the Reformation and continued at a high level until the end of the seventeenth century. Although the subject, in all its ramifications, was by 1500 a very complicated one, the main ideas are simple enough. Astrologers and the very large number of their contemporaries who shared their ideas believed that the heavenly bodies exerted an influence on events on earth and that the nature of that influence at any particular time depended on the precise position of the heavenly bodies at that moment. By drawing a map of the heavens at a specified point in time – a horoscope as it was called – an astrologer could analyse the situation and assess its implications for his client. Also, given the necessary astronomical information, he could contruct horoscopes for future moments in time and thus hope to predict the influences which the heavens would exert on later occasions. There were four main branches of the astrologer's art. First of all, general predictions, which applied to society as a whole rather than to individuals and involved such matters as forecasting future harvests and the likely course of politics and wars. Then there were nativities, which involved making a map of the sky at the time of a person's birth and forecasting that individual's future prospects from it. Thirdly, there were elections, which involved selecting the best time for a particular action. Finally, there were horary questions, problems which the astrologer tried to resolve by considering the exact state of the heavens at the moment when the question was put to him.

Astrology in sixteenth- and seventeenth-century England was, therefore, an elaborate 'science' with detailed rules of procedure. Its influence penetrated to virtually all strata of the population. At the very top, Queen Elizabeth had her own astrologer John Dee, whom we have already met[1] as an important mathematician; it was Dee who chose the most auspicious day for her coronation. William Lilly, one of the most notable English astrologers of the seventeenth century, kept a record of the occupations or status of some of his numerous clients. That shows that they ranged from aristocrats and gentlemen to female servants and even paupers, and included professional men, tradesmen and a large proportion of seafarers and military men (276). Another important indication of the popularity of astrology can be seen in the number of almanacs which were sold during the sixteenth and seventeenth centuries. These little pocket-books, which contained a great deal of astrological information, were published in their thousands. They were the only books apart from the Bible to be widely distributed at almost all levels of society. By 1659 Lilly's almanac, *Merlinus Anglicus*, was said to be selling nearly 30,000 copies a year and by the 1660s perhaps one family in three bought an almanac each year (274; 276).

Almanacs even more than the Bible were the 'popular press' of the day and the practices of leading astrologers reflected the extent of interest in the subject. Elizabethan and Stuart England was full of astrologers, many of whom worked part-time, combining their casting of horoscopes with other occupations. There were, however, whole-time professionals as well and at the top of the tree were the well-known practitioners with extensive London clienteles, men like Simon Forman, William Lilly and John Booker (276). Forman, who can be taken as an example of that London élite, was a Wiltshireman, born in 1552, who was an unlicensed medical practitioner in London from the 1580s onwards, but gained his greatest fame as an astrologer. The extensive papers which he kept about his cases have survived and from them it has been possible to reconstruct in detail the workings of a sixteenth-century astrological practice (273). He handled a huge volume of business, casting over 1,000 horoscopes a year between 1597 and 1601, and his clients, like those of Lilly, were drawn from every social group from the nobility down to servant-girls. They included clergymen, like the dean of Rochester, Dr Thomas Blague, whose wife Alice was also on his books. The Church officially disapproved of astrology, which it regarded almost as a rival religion, but this did not prevent individual clergymen from being among its most fervent devotees. Blague used Forman's services to assess his chances of obtaining a bishopric, for which he was almost pathetically ambitious. His failure to get the hoped-for preferment was probably largely due to his awful wife who spent her husband's wealth, as Forman tells us, on 'her own lust and pleasure' (273, *129 ff*). Forman himself was no mean performer when it came to sexual activity. His practice seems to have given him numerous opportunities to indulge himself and he became a remarkable sexual athlete. His work also brought him substantial material returns; he left £1,200 when he died in 1611, a large sum for a man who had started with nothing. Astrology could clearly be a highly profitable business for its leading exponents.

The clients who flocked to consult Forman and his colleagues had a wide variety of problems to set before them, but these were of two main kinds; sometimes they sought information which they were unable to obtain elsewhere, often they wanted advice. In the first category came queries about lost property, missing persons and ships and unidentified illnesses; in the second, requests for help with personal decisions. Some clients whose inquiries were in the latter category wanted to know about career prospects and Forman had a set of rules showing 'in what trade or science a man shall best . . . live by' (276, *314*), but the most numerous requests for advice seem to have been about romantic and family problems. Women, in particular, wanted information about their future husbands, and there were consultations with men worried about the legitimacy of their children and parents anxious about the conduct of a problem son (276).

The astrological beliefs which remained so strong throughout our period only began to decline during the last years of the seventeenth century when the impact of the astronomical discoveries of the sixteenth and seventeenth centuries was fully felt in the astrological field. Astrological theory had depended above all else on the maintenance of the Aristotelian distinction between the perfect unchanging heavenly bodies and the changeable earth; this was essential in explaining the one-way astrological influence which the stars were supposed to exercise. When the discoveries of the sixteenth and seventeenth centuries revealed the earth as itself a planet among other heavenly bodies and the latter as being made of the same material as the corrupt and constantly changing earth, this essential distinction vanished. With it went belief in astrology as a viable intellectual system. At about the same time new explanations began to be given for misfortunes which astrologers had been called upon to predict or explain. To take just one example, at the end of the seventeenth century mathematicians began to explore the extent to which even chance happenings and misfortunes could be predicted on an overall statistical basis. This made possible the growth of scientific insurance which safeguarded men and women in a number of fields where they had hitherto been exposed to disasters which they had attempted to predict or forestall through astrological inquiries (276). Into the astrologer's shoes came the actuary.

Sixteenth- and seventeenth-century attitudes towards astrology were clearly paralleled by the pattern of witchcraft beliefs. These too were at their height in the sixteenth and early seventeenth centuries only declining significantly during the years which saw the turning away from astrology as a valid intellectual system (57; 276; 279; 280). Technically, any kind of magical activity, whether designed for good or evil, might be called witchcraft, but for practical purpose witches can be defined as men or women (much more frequently the latter) who were believed to be able mysteriously to injure others. Their activities might take many forms, such as impeding domestic work like the making of butter or beer, and the killing or injuring of farm animals. The most serious and most common accusation in England, however, was of injuring or killing other people. It is necessary to distinguish between witchcraft beliefs in England on the one hand and Scotland and the Continent on the other. Belief in witchcraft goes back to the dawn of human history, but a new element was added to European witchcraft in the later Middle Ages, the idea that the witch owed her powers to a pact which she had made with the Devil. This belief, propagated by the Church, turned witchcraft into a Christian heresy, but the idea of the diabolical pact was slow to penetrate to England. It can be found in the writings of English experts from the late Eliza-bethan period onwards, but it was only from the early years of the seventeenth century that the idea of the pact with the Devil featured at all prominently in English witchcraft trials, and even then it was by no means an essential feature. That was a very different situation from the one prevailing in Continental coun-tries like Germany where there were massive persecutions on the basis of the demonic pact from the later Middle Ages onwards, or in Scotland, where the full Continental theory, though it arrived late, was applied in the great witchcraft trials which took place in the winter of 1590–91 (57; 276; 280).

In England, where witchcraft continued to be presented as an anti-social crime rather than as a heresy throughout our period, it is impossible to calculate accu-rately the number of witchcraft accusations or even of prosecutions; many of the former were not followed up and the incomplete nature of the judicial records at our disposal does not allow a precise total for the latter. It is clear, however, that in the 'Home Circuit' – the five counties of Essex, Kent, Hertfordshire, Surrey and Sussex – 513 people were indicted for witchcraft between 1560 and 1700. The peak period for prosecutions was Elizabeth's reign with the climax coming during the 1580s and 1590s; of the 307 prosecuted at the Essex assizes between 1560 and 1680 (Essex had far more prosecutions than any of the other Home Counties) 163 were tried between 1560 and 1600, with 111 of the pros-ecutions coming in the period 1580–1600. It seems likely in fact that there were more trials throughout the country as a whole under Elizabeth than there were during the entire seventeenth century (276; 279). Only a minority of those tried were executed – 112 out of the 513 people tried at Home Circuit assizes between 1560 and 1700 – but it has been estimated that executions over the Kingdom as a whole may have numbered as many as 1,000 between 1542, when the first statute against witchcraft was passed, and 1736, when the last witchcraft law was repealed. The figure of 1,000 may be a substantial overestimate, but there were certainly at least as many and probably more witchcraft executions than Catholic martyrdoms in sixteenth- and seventeenth-century England (276; 279).

These statistics and the prosecutions which they represent can be understood only in terms of a combination of psychological, sociological and intellectual explanations of the phenomenon of early modern English witchcraft (276; 279). It is clear from the judicial records that most witches were poor women, given to cursing and making images of people who had offended them, the idea being to injure or cause the death of the victim. Witches, being almost all from the lower strata of society, could not realistically hope to take their enemies to law (an expensive business) or use ordinary physical force against them. They attempted, therefore, to achieve their ends by supernatural means. Most of the alleged victims of witchcraft were more prosperous than those whom they accused of the crime, and their accusations often followed unneighbourly behaviour by them towards the witch, whom they blamed for subsequent misfortunes. In 1659, for example, Frances Rustat of Hertfordshire was 'strangely handled, with great pain, racking and torment'. She accused old 'Goody Free' of causing her troubles and added that she had never been well since she had taken eggs from the old woman without paying for them. This was typical of the pattern in witchcraft accusations when, as Mr Thomas emphasizes, 'it tended to be the witch who was morally in the right and the victim who was in the wrong' (276, *553*). The supposed victims of witchcraft clearly often had guilt complexes about those whom they accused, and the whole phenomenon of sixteenth- and seventeenth-century witchcraft was largely a reflection of the breakdown of the traditional cohesion of village life under the pressures of social and economic change. The price and population rises of the period led, as we have seen (Ch. 20), to a growing number of poor, many of them widows or unmarried women (groups from which witches were traditionally drawn), and more prosperous members of the community were both increasingly resentful of the burdens which these paupers imposed upon them and at the same time uneasily aware of their Christian duty to give them charity.

If the witches came from the poorest classes in the community and their victims from groups often just above them in the social scale those who were responsible for witchcraft prosecutions came on the whole from the educated classes. There had always been upper-class men who were sceptical about witchcraft, notably James I himself in his later years (57), but it was only towards the end of the seventeenth century that this attitude became prevalent in the top ranges of society (276; 279). Why is still not altogether clear, though it was almost certainly caused in part by the collapse of Renaissance Neoplatonism – with its belief that the universe was full of occult influences – before the mechanical philosophy which came into increasing prominence in the last decades of the seventeenth century.

What is clear is that the growing scepticism of the educated classes led to the end of witchcraft prosecutions in England. The last witch trial in an English civil court took place at Leicester in 1717 and in 1736 Parliament repealed the 1604 Act which had theoretically governed witchcraft prosecutions for over a century. It is significant that it replaced it by a measure which prohibited accusations of witchcraft but imposed penalties on men and women who claimed to be able to use magical powers. Witchcraft, which had been a 'terrifying reality' for millions of English men and women of all classes in the sixteenth and early seventeenth centuries, was regarded by educated opinion in the early eighteenth century as a 'vulgar fraud'. It was a different matter, however, with the lower orders and informal witchcraft accusations continued to be a familiar part of rural life for much longer; indeed, alleged witches were lynched in nineteenth-century England (276).

Witchcraft and astrology, which helped to provide sixteenth-century men and women with explanations for everyday events were, in part, substitutes for the 'magic' of medieval Catholicism, which had given solace to so many bewildered pre-Reformation Englishmen. The Reformation, with its attacks on the rituals of the old Church, turned more and more men and women towards these new magics. Belief in astrology and witchcraft, prevalent throughout the sixteenth and early seventeenth centuries, only came to an end among the educated sections of the community in the years around 1700. Among the reasons for that 'decline of magic' one at least stands out for its long-term significance as well as for its immediate importance; the impact of the scientific revolution, which received its supreme statement in England in the work of Isaac Newton.

----

1. See above, Chapter 24. On Dee see P. J. French, *John Dee: the World of an Elizabethan Magus* (1972).

CHAPTER 26

Aspects of English life and mind: II – A golden age of English culture

The astrological and witchcraft beliefs of sixteenth- and seventeenth-century Englishmen, though clearly of the greatest social significance, are not normally emphasized in studies of the cultural life of the period. These, which traditionally and rightly stress the glories of late-sixteenth and early-seventeenth-century cultural developments in England, concentrate on aspects of the social scene like court life, on the building and rebuilding which took place throughout much of England, on music and, above all, on literature and the theatre.

The term 'Court' has been used by some early modern English historians to include all those who held profitable offices or benefits from the Crown as opposed to those, described as the 'Country', who did not (see Ch. 33). In the much more restricted sense in which it is employed here it means the monarchs and their immediate entourage, together with the settings in which they moved and the interests which they pursued. The splendours of the post-Reformation English Court, so well known from numerous contemporary descriptions, had their origins in the fifteenth century, when Edward IV maintained a lavish display, while Henry VII, notorious for his parsimony in other matters, spent relatively heavily on the glorification of the new dynasty. Among other things, he founded the Yeomen of the Guard, still today a national institution. The real flowering of Tudor court life came, however, in the reign of Henry VIII, when the events of the Reformation placed the King on a pinnacle of prestige, power and dignity well above that occupied by previous monarchs. Henry was a man who, in any event, enjoyed gorgeous displays, and the majesty of the Court during his reign reflected both his personal predilections and his new role as Head of the Church as well as of the State. During the later 1530s another bodyguard, the gentlemen pensioners or 'spears', was added to the court establishment (85; 91). These men, with their splendid uniforms, complemented the Yeomen of the Guard, and like the latter they still make a fine show today on ceremonial occasions; in their modern form, as the gentlemen-at-arms, they are the sovereign's closest body-guard.

Queen Elizabeth, like her father, gloried in the splendours of a Court which reflected her own dignity and the majesty of the realm. Paul Hentzner, a German traveller who visited England in 1598, left a fine description of a ceremonial procession to chapel which he saw while the Queen was at Greenwich. An excerpt from his account gives the flavour of the occasion.

> First went gentlemen, barons, earls, knights of the garter, all richly-dressed and bare-headed; next came the Chancellor, bearing the seals in a red silk purse, between two [attendants] one of which carried the royal sceptre, the other the sword of state in a red scabbard studded with golden *fleurs de lys*, the point upwards; next came

the Queen . . . very majestic. . . . She had in her ears two pearls with very rich drops . . ., upon her head she had a small crown . . ., and she had on a necklace of exceeding fine jewels. . . . That day she was dressed in white silk, bordered with pearls the size of beans . . .; her train was very long, the end of it borne by a marchioness. Instead of a chain she had an oblong collar of gold and jewels. As she went along in all this state and magnificence she spoke very graciously, first to one, then to another, whether foreign ministers or those who attended for different reasons. . . . Whoever speaks to her it is kneeling [though] now and then she raises some with her hand. . . .

The ladies of the Court followed next to her, very handsome and well-shaped, and for the most part dressed in white. She was guarded on each side by the gentlemen pensioners, fifty in number, with gilt battle-axes. In the ante chapel . . . petitions were presented to her, and she received them most graciously, which occasioned the acclamation of, 'Long live Queen Elizabeth!' She answered it with, 'I thank you, my good people.' In the chapel was excellent music. As soon as it and the service was over . . . the Queen returned in the same state and order and prepared to go to dinner. . . . (98, 2)

Elizabeth on that occasion, as on so many others in her life, showed that she had the 'common touch'; she knew how to play to the gallery of the general public, those ordinary men and women who flocked to see her whenever she appeared in public. That was a reflection of the fact that the Elizabethan Court always remained a 'popular' institution, in touch with the feelings and aspirations of the great majority of the Queen's subjects. That was seen, for example, in its patronage of drama; Shakespeare's plays, with their appeal both to courtiers and to the common people, symbolized a fundamental unity between the Court and ordinary men and women. By the reign of Charles I the situation had changed beyond recognition. Charles, like Elizabeth, maintained a splendid and cere- monious Court, but increasingly, as the years passed, that Court was more and more out of touch with and unsympathetic to the cultural aspirations of the masses, unashamedly esoteric where the Elizabethan Court had been avowedly popular. In the 1630s the interests of Charles and his courtiers in painting, in architecture and in music were far removed from those of the vast majority of his subjects, and the growing cultural isolation of the Court is well symbolized by its patronage of masques, those prodigiously expensive entertainments which combined the arts of poet, painter, architect and musician for the benefit of a narrow circle of courtiers (5; 37; 60; 73)

This change in the general ambience of court life represented a much wider change; a change from Queen Elizabeth, who saw herself as the personification of the ideas, attitudes and ambitions of her people as a whole, to King Charles, who sat at the centre of an élitist culture which propagated religious and artistic ideas which found little response among the generality of Englishmen. (On religious ideas see Chs 32, 33.) The very different Courts of Elizabeth and Charles I were, therefore, in themselves, symbols of the general success of the Queen's reign and the very obvious failure of that of Charles; the one a sign of the essential unity of the nation, the other of its division.

The late Elizabethan and early Stuart periods, the years which saw the apogee of the 'popular' court culture of the Queen's reign and the turning away to élitism under Charles I, were also the time of a great building and rebuilding throughout much of England of the houses of yeomen and those above them on the social scale (217; 218). There were two aspects of the phenomenon; first of all the physical building, rebuilding or substantial modernization of houses which ranged from the great mansions of the aristocracy to the modest farmhouses of yeomen, and secondly a notable increase in household furnishings and equipment, including books. These improvements were made possible by the growing prosperity of the men concerned, all of whom might hope to benefit from selling food for the market at a time of rising agricultural prices. Many yeomen radically altered their medieval houses, inserting ceilings in halls which had previously been open to the rafters. This produced a living space in the lower part of the house and a sleeping area above, and these in turn were frequently divided into smaller rooms by the use of partitions. Such changes in turn necessitated more windows and fireplaces. This type of reconstruction, which gave the middling ranks of rural society much greater privacy in their homes, was usually accompanied by the introduction of more, and more elaborate, furniture and domestic fittings and equipment, including such luxuries as cushions and wall-hangings. Moreover, the incidence of book ownership among the more prosperous members of society grew substantially during our period. This is demonstrated, for example, by the researches of Mr Clark on the richest 30 per cent or so of the citizens of the three Kentish towns of Canterbury, Maidstone and Faversham between the 1560s and 1630s. Only about 8 per cent of the Canterbury sample owned books during the 1560s, about 46 per cent in the 1630s. The Maidstone figures show 21 per cent of the sample owning books in the 1560s, rising to 44 per cent in the 1630s, but the trend is the same as in Canterbury and is confirmed by the Faversham figures which reveal 15 per cent of the sample as bookowners in the 1560s and 49 per cent in the 1630s. These figures apply to men – women were much less likely to own books – and must, of course, be used with caution; the odd book or two in a house did not constitute a library (251). Nevertheless, the general improvement in the housing conditions of the middling ranks of Elizabethan and early Stuart men and women, which gave them sufficient household goods to live a tolerably comfortable existence and the occasional book to stimulate their minds, did mean that 'culture' in the broadest sense was becoming much more widespread in the Elizabethan period than it had ever been before. Even at that elementary level it was, of course, beyond the grasp of the majority; most husbandmen and labourers and their families continued to live an illiterate existence in primitive one-roomed cottages (63).

Most yeomen during the period seem to have rebuilt or improved existing houses rather than constructing entirely new ones. It was a different story, however, at the very top of society where peers and members of the upper gentry built vast mansions, a large number of them entirely from scratch. Most of these 'prodigy' houses were constructed between 1580 and 1620 and, in the words of Professor Stone, 'many . . . still lie heavily about the English countryside like the fossilized bones of the giant reptiles of the Carboniferous Age' (217, *551*). They were partly a reflection of the new 'civil culture' of the upper ranks of society – the last private castle in England, Thornbury in Gloucestershire, had been built as long ago as the early years of Henry VIII – but were, above all, symbols of the conspicuous consumption of the highly status-conscious members of the peerage and upper gentry, each of whom tried to outdo his rivals while at the same time providing a fitting place to entertain Queen Elizabeth or King James, who might reasonably be expected to honour a member of the aristocracy with a visit. The great Lord Burghley, who constantly complained of his poverty – he was actually one of the richest men in England – did not hesitate to proclaim his status in his houses. He rebuilt the family seat at Stamford Baron in Northamptonshire, completing it in 1589. The result, Burghley House, a huge edifice, is one of the most impressive of all surviving Elizabethan houses. Another of his great mansions, Theobalds, is no longer standing, but it was one of the wonders of the age. He built it in Hertfordshire between the 1560s and 1580s, when it was one of the largest buildings in England, standing in a magnificent park 8 miles in circumference (75).

The later Elizabethan period and the reign of James I, the years in which the house-building of the gentry and aristocracy reached its height, were also a great age of English music (287). It has indeed been argued that 'in the reign of Elizabeth England reached the highest concentration of musical genuis in all her history and led Europe in this field' (23 , *439*). Other scholars might qualify that statement but still point to the glories of English music in the later sixteenth century. During our period there were notable achievements in both sacred and secular music. In the former field three great mid-century composers Christopher Tye, Thomas Tallis and Robert White produced works of very high quality. Their younger successors in the Elizabethan and Jacobean periods, Orlando Gibbons and William Byrd, produced the first distinguished music specifically for Anglican services; they were among the greatest European composers of the day. There was also much notable secular music; many fine collections of songs appeared in the years between the Armada and 1630. Among the best of the song writers were John Dowland and Thomas Morley. The madrigal, a musical form introduced from Italy, had achieved very great popularity in England by the later Elizabethan period and in 1594 Morley produced the first completely English collection of these songs. Perhaps the greatest English writer of madrigals, however, was John Wilbye, who died in 1614.

Two of the sovereigns of the period, Henry VIII and Elizabeth, took a very considerable interest in music. Henry was not only a notable patron of musicians, he was no mean performer in his own right: he played the lute, the organ and the virginals (a keyed musical instrument very popular at the time), sang well in a powerful voice and composed songs (68). Elizabeth, who patronized Tallis and Byrd, was another royal musician in her own right. She was an elegant singer and played on the lyre, lute and virginals. When Sir James Melville visited her Court in the early years of the reign as the representative of Mary Queen of Scots he admired her abilities. 'My lord of Hunsdon drew me up to a quiet gallery', he wrote in his *Memoirs*, many years after the event, '. . . where I might hear the Queen play upon the virginals. . . . After I had hearkened awhile, I took by the tapestry that hung before the door of the chamber and, seeing her back was toward the door, I entered within the chamber . . ., and heard her play excellently well. . . .' (5, *15*; 73, *205–6*) The personal involvement of Queen Elizabeth in the music of her day appropriately symbolized what was surely – with the possible exception of the mid to late nineteenth century – the greatest age of private and spontaneous music-making in English history. James I did not have the musical accomplishments of his predecessor, but the great age of English music person-ified by Gibbons and Byrd and the secular song writers extended into his reign. In the same way, the great literary efflorescence of the age was a Jacobean as much as a late Elizabethan phenomenon.

The Elizabethan and Jacobean periods, the age of Shakespeare, hold a unique place in English literature (there is an excellent brief survey in (*283*)). The Britain in which we live would be an infinitely poorer place without Shakespeare's plays and the other great literary works of the early modern period; they are indeed among the foundation-stones of our cultural heritage. That great literature was written in language which grew increasingly flexible and rich as the sixteenth century advanced, owing much to the importation of foreign words as well as to the influence of contemporary writers like Jewel, Foxe, Spenser, Bacon and, of course, Shakespeare himself. Among the greatest of the literature was the Bible, as translated by William Tyndale and Miles Coverdale in the early sixteenth century and rendered into even finer English prose in the Authorized Version of 1611. We have already noted its fundamental importance in the history of English thought (Ch. 2), and the flowing phrases of the translations were one of the major influences on writers of both prose and poetry throughout the sixteenth and seventeenth centuries. Cranmer's Prayer Book, too, touched great heights of literary inspiration.

The early Tudor period, which produced the first great English translations of the Bible, was also the age of John Skelton, with his direct, sometimes uncouth, but always striking verse, and of the courtier poets Sir Thomas Wyatt and Henry Howard, earl of Surrey, who introduced the sonnet into England. Surrey, whose literary brilliance was matched by his political ineptitude – he went to the block at the end of Henry VIII's reign – was also responsible for important experiments in blank verse, a dramatic form which reached its ultimate grandeur in the work of Shakespeare. The early Tudor period was only, of course, a prologue to the glories of the Elizabethan and Jacobean ages. In poetry and drama the names of Sidney, Spenser, Marlowe, Johnson, Donne, Herbert, Kyd and Lyly spring to mind as among the most notable of a galaxy of talent, while in prose the works of Foxe, Hooker, Bacon, Burton and indeed, of James I himself, command attention. It is only possible here to mention a few examples from these men's pens, but it would be wrong not to notice Spenser's *Faerie Queene*, written towards the end of the long Elizabethan age, a masterly allegory full of marvellous imagery, in which he celebrated the success of Elizabeth's rule in an orderly society. It is both a great work of art and a political commentary. Then there was that tempestuous young genius Christopher Marlowe, whose colourful character matched the sweeping grandeur of his four tragedies written, like the *Faerie Queen*, in the concluding years of the Queen's reign. Of these, *Tamburlaine*, the story of the fourteenth-century Tartar hero, and *Dr Faustus*, the tale of a magician who sold his soul to the Devil in return for universal knowledge, are especially notable and contain some truly magnificent lines in blank verse. If Marlowe was the greatest tragedian before Shakespeare himself, John Lyly was perhaps the finest practitioner of comedy before the advent of the Bard. His plays, which almost all use mythological subjects, were very popular at Court, not least perhaps because Lyly catered for courtiers' interests by including references to contemporary topics. Among the prose writers Hooker is notable for his judicious and measured style (see Ch. 28), while Francis Bacon's *Essays*, originally published in 1597 and extended and revised in later editions, are written with an economy of style and a distinction of mind which make them a delight to read. Bacon, of course, could be cruel. The essay 'Of deformity', was probably a reflection of his hatred for his tiny, hunchbacked cousin, Robert Cecil, who, he believed, had obscured his own great talent.

> Deformed persons are commonly even with nature: for as nature hath done ill by them, so do they by nature; being for the most part (as the Scripture saith) void of natural affection; and so they have their revenge of nature. . . . Whosoever hath any thing fixed in his person that doth induce contempt, hath also a perpetual spur in himself to rescue and deliver himself from scorn. Therefore, all deformed persons are extreme bold: first, as in their own defence, as being exposed to scorn; but in process of time by a general habit. Also, it stirreth in them industry, and especially of this kind, to watch and observe the weakness of others. . . . Again, in their superiors it quencheth jealousy towards them, as persons that they think they may at pleasure despise; and it layeth their competitors and emulators asleep, as never believing they should be in possibility of advancement till they see them in possession. So that . . . deformity is an advantage to rising. (12, *131*)

Bacon, who never achieved high office under Queen Elizabeth, eventually came into his own under James I, and his new master, like Bacon himself, wielded a facile pen. James's literary abilities can be seen to good advantage in his colourful *Counterblast to Tobacco* of 1604, an anti-smoking manifesto which would win high praise from the modern medical profession.

> And for the vanities committed in this filthy custom, is it not both great vanity and uncleanness that at the table, a place of respect, of cleanliness, of modesty, men should not be ashamed to sit tossing of tobacco pipes and puffing of the smoke of tobacco one to another, making the filthy smoke and stink thereof to exhale athwart the dishes and infect the air when very often men that abhor it are at their repast? . . . Have you not reason . . . to be ashamed and to forbear this filthy novelty, so basely grounded, so foolishly received, and so grossly mistaken in the right use thereof? In your abuse thereof sinning against God, harming your selves both in persons and goods, and taking also thereby the marks and notes of vanity upon you. . . . A custom loathsome to the eye, hateful to the nose, harmful to the brain, dangerous to the lungs, and in the black stinking fume thereof nearest resembling the horrible stygian smoke of the pit that is bottomless. (9, *89–91*)

When James was writing his *Counterblast*, William Shakespeare, the universal genius of our literature, was at the height of his powers. Shakespeare's world-wide fame today is a reflection of his unparalleled ability to move the minds and hearts of readers and playgoers who can only marvel at his ability to both portray and comment upon the whole gamut of human emotions and ambitions. His sonnets and other poems have, of course, received enormous attention, but in the last resort it is his plays – the comedies, the histories and the tragedies – that are the basis of his immortality. In the cycle of historical plays written in the 1590s he provided a magnificent literary view of fifteenth-century English history which had such influence that it is only comparatively recently that historians have broken free from its mould. His *Richard III*, for example, is a caricature, but one which has fixed itself irrevocably in the minds of thousands of men and women over the centuries.

> I, that am rudely stamp'd and want love's majesty
> To strut before a wanton ambling nymph;
> I, that am curtail'd of this fair proportion,
> Cheated of feature by dissembling nature,
> Deform'd, unfinish'd, sent before my time
> Into this breathing world, scarce half made up,
> And that so lamely and unfashionable
> That dogs bark at me, as I halt by them;
> Why, I, in this weak piping time of peace,
> Have no delight to pass away the time,
> Unless to see my shadow in the sun
> And descant on mine own deformity:
> And therefore, since I cannot prove a lover,
> To entertain these fair well-spoken days,
> I am determined to prove a villain,
> And hate the idle pleasures of these days.
> Plots have I laid, inductions dangerous,
> By drunken prophecies, libels, and dreams,
> To set my brother Clarence and the king
> In deadly hate the one against the other.[1]

In the early years of the seventeenth century, following the histories, came the great tragedies, *Macbeth, Hamlet, King Lear* and *Othello*, plays which have delighted theatregoers from that day to this. Audiences have been enthralled by set-piece speeches like Hamlet's magnificent soliloquy on life and death.

> . . . To die, to sleep;
> To sleep: perchance to dream: ay, there's the rub;
> For in that sleep of death what dreams may come
> When we have shuffled off this mortal coil,
> Must give us pause. There's the respect
> That makes calamity of so long life;
> For who would bear the whips and scorns of time,
> The oppressor's wrong, the proud man's contumely,
> The pangs of dispriz'd love, the law's delay,
> The insolence of office, and the spurns
> That patient merit of the unworthy takes,
> When he himself might a quietus make
> With a bare bodkin? who would fardels bear,
> To grunt and sweat under a weary life,
> But that the dread of something after death,

The undiscover'd country from whose bourn
No traveller returns, puzzles the will,
And makes us rather bear those ills we have
Than fly to others that we know not of?
Thus conscience does make cowards of us all.[2]

Shakespeare's words are magnificent but his plays were meant to be seen, not read, and they have always been best appreciated by the spectator in the theatre rather than by the reader at home.

The greatest literary figures of the post-Shakespearian age were John Bunyan and John Milton, men whose work was profoundly influenced by the the the revolutionary decades of the mid-seventeenth century (see Ch. 43). Indeed, historians must never forget the links between history and literature. Imaginative writing can, if used with caution, illuminate social attitudes. Ulysses' famous speech on degree in Shakespeare's *Troilus and Cressida* is a case in point.

. . . O! when degree is shak'd,
Which is the ladder to all high designs,
The enterprise is sick. How could communities,
Degrees in schools, and brotherhoods in cities,
Peaceful commerce from dividable shores,
The primogenitive and due of birth,
Prerogative of age, crowns, sceptres, laurels,
But by degree, stand in authentic place?
Take but degree away, untune that string,
And hark! what discord follows; each thing meets
In mere oppugnancy : the bounded waters
Should lift their bosoms higher than the shores,
And make a sop of all this solid globe:
Strength should be lord of imbecility,
And the rude son should strike his father dead:
Force should be right; or rather right and wrong –
Between whose endless jar justice resides –
Should lose their names, and so should justice too.[3]

That stress on the need for order would have been echoed by virtually all Elizabethans. Many of them would also have shared the sentiments of Sir Walter Ralegh who wrote about the corruptions of court life in his early-seventeenth-century poem, *The Lie*.

Say to the Court it glows,
And shines like rotten wood,
Say to the Church it shows
What's good, and doth no good.
If Church and Court reply,
Then give them both the lie. (5, *164*)

These words of Shakespeare and Ralegh are the reflections of two men of genius upon different aspects of the contemporary scene. As such they are social documents as well as literary gems. Elizabethan poetry and prose, when judiciously used, can be among the most revealing sources for the history of the age. Indeed, Ralegh's strictures on corruption at Court are a suitable intro-duction to our next major theme: the breakdown of the Elizabethan system in the later years of the reign.

---

1. *Richard III*, Act I, Scene i, lines 16–35.
2. *Hamlet*, Act III, Scene i, lines 64–83.
3. *Troilus and Cressida*, Act I, Scene iii, lines 101–18.

PART FOUR

An age of transition: The breakdown of the Elizabethan system, 1585–1642

1585   Catholic League dominant in France; the duke of Parma makes substantial military advances against the Dutch rebels; Treaty of Nonsuch (Aug): Elizabeth promises military aid to the Dutch rebels; English expedition to the Netherlands under Leicester (Dec) – beginning of war between England and Spain.

      Parliament of November 1584 continues until March: Act against Jesuits and seminary priests.

      First English colony founded in Virginia; foundation of Barbary Company to trade with North Africa; first of three voyages (1585–87) of John Davis in search of a north-west passage; Drake sets out on a plundering voyage against the Spanish West Indies (Sept).

1586   Whitgift appointed to the Privy Council (Feb) – a symbol of the fact that he was the first and only Elizabethan ecclesiastic to exercise significant political influence. Babington Plot – Mary Queen of Scots agrees to the murder of Elizabeth; Babington arrested (Aug) and executed (Sept). Parliament meets (Oct, and continues until Mar 1587): Norfolk election case (the Commons claim the right to decide disputed elections); both Houses of Parliament petition the Queen for the execution of Mary Queen of Scots (Nov).

      Treaty of Berwick (July): defensive alliance between England and Scotland. Death of Sir Philip Sidney in the Netherlands (Oct).

      Drake returns to England with substantial booty (July). English colonists in Virginia return home. Thomas Cavendish begins his circumnavigation voyage of 1586–88 (July).

      Star Chamber decree (Jan) tightens censorship of the Press. W. Camden, *Britannia*.

1587   Execution of Mary Queen of Scots (Feb). Parliament of October 1586 continues until March: Cope's Bill and Book (Feb) – parliamentary attempt to introduce a Presbyterian form of church government; remarkable parliamentary speech by Peter Wentworth on the issue of free speech (Mar). Sir Christopher Hatton becomes Lord Chancellor (Apr).

      Drake's raid on Cadiz (Apr) does much damage to Spanish Armada preparations. Leicester relinquishes his command in the Netherlands (Oct).

      William Allen made a cardinal (Aug). Henry Barrow and John Greenwood, leaders of the London Separatists, imprisoned.

      Second English colony in Virginia founded.

      C. Marlowe writes *Tamburlaine*.

1588   Spanish Armada (July): defeated by an English fleet under Howard of Effingham. Death of Leicester (Sept).

      Death of John Field (Mar). First (Oct) of the *Marprelate tracts* of 1588–89.

      First Welsh Bible published. Thomas Hariot, *Brief and True Report of the New Found Land of Virginia* – recommends the use of tobacco as a medicine.

1589   Parliament meets (Feb–Mar): the House of Commons partially withdraws from its stand on the Norfolk election case.

      Elizabeth dispatches the Portugal expedition (Apr–June): this fails to achieve any of its objectives against Spain. Assassination of Henry III of France (July): accession of Henry of Navarre to the French throne; civil war in France; Elizabeth sends English troops to assist Henry of Navarre in the French Civil war (Sept). James VI of Scotland begins his voyage (1589–90) to Denmark; he marries Princess Anne of Denmark (Aug).

Bancroft's sermon at Paul's Cross (Feb) in which he implies that bishops hold their office *iure divino*. Beginning of Whitgift's onslaught of 1589–92 on organized Presbyterianism. Further *Marprelate tracts* issued before the secret press is found and confiscated: these brilliant but scurrilous attacks on the bishops discredit Presbyterianism in the eyes of moderates.

Henry Barrow's *True Description of the Visible Congregation of the Saints*; Richard Hakluyt, *Principal Navigations*.

1590   Death of Walsingham (Apr): secretaryship of state left unfilled. Notable reform of the Commission of the Peace.

Thomas Cartwright and other Puritan leaders arrested and brought before the High Commission.

Virginia colony of 1587 found abandoned by a relief expedition.

Edmund Spenser, *The Faerie Queene* (books 1–3), published; Peter Bales, *Writing Schoolmaster*, includes a shorthand system.

1591   Death of Hatton (Nov). Growing prominence of Sir Robert Cecil in state affairs, doing much of the work of the Secretary's office.

Expedition against the Azores by Lord Thomas Howard and Sir Richard Grenville (Mar) – leads to Grenville's famous fight in the *Revenge* and his subsequent death (Sept). England sends forces (May) to defend Britanny against the arms of Spain and the French Catholic League.

Cartwright and other Puritan leaders brought before Star Chamber.

Publication of Sir Philip Sidney's *Astrophel and Stella*, gives impetus to the popularity of the sonnet.

1592   Birth of George Villiers, later duke of Buckingham (Aug). Death in the Netherlands of the duke of Parma (Dec).

Sir John Burrows captures the great Portugese galleon *Madre de Dios* with a huge treasure.

Thomas Kyd, *The Spanish Tragedy*. Trinity College, Dublin, founded.

1593   Parliament meets (Feb–Apr): Lord Keeper Puckering, on behalf of the Queen restates the traditional 1523 interpretation of free speech; three subsidies voted after strong pressure by the Lords on the House of Commons; Peter Wentworth raises the issue of the succession, is arrested, and dies later (1597) in the Tower; severe Acts against recusants and sectaries symbolize the growing assurance of the Church of England, under Whitgift's strong leadership, against its enemies. Beginning of a great rebellion (1593–1603) in Ulster which imposed a severe and mounting financial burden on the Crown during the next decade. The earl of Essex admitted to the Privy Council.

Henry IV of France announces his conversion to Catholicism (July).

Execution of the Separatists John Greenwood and Henry Barrow (Apr).

Plague.

Richard Hooker publishes the first four books of his *Laws of Ecclesiastical Polity*; Richard Bancroft; *Survey of the Pretended Holy Discipline*, openly asserts the divine right of bishops. C. Marlowe killed in a brawl at the age of 29.

1594   Alleged plot to murder the Queen by her Portugese physician Dr Lopez: Lopez arrested (Feb) and executed (June).

Death of Cardinal Allen (Oct).

First of four bad harvest years. JPs who assessed themselves at less than £20 a year for taxation purposes told that they would be put out of the Commission of the Peace.

Parsons' *Conference About the Next Succession* advocates the claims of the Spanish Infanta.

1595   Hugh O'Neill, earl of Tyrone, openly joins the Irish rebellion.

Henry IV of France formally declares war on Spain (Jan). Expedition by Drake and Hawkins to the West Indies (sails Aug): death of Hawkins during the expedition (Nov).

Whitgift's nine Lambeth articles, a strongly orthodox statement of Calvinist theology. 'Wisbech stirs' among the Catholic priesthood in England begin.

Second of four bad harvest years. Ralegh's first voyage to Guiana.

1596   Sir Robert Cecil appointed Secretary of State (July). Oxfordshire revolt (Nov).

Death of Drake on West Indies expedition (Jan). The Spaniards capture Calais from France (Apr). Cadiz expedition (June–Aug) led by Howard of Effingham and Essex: Cadiz and much Spanish shipping burnt; large quantities of Spanish treasure seized. Second Spanish invasion armada dispersed by gales off Finisterre (Oct).

Third of four bad harvest years.

Blackfriars Theatre, London, opened. Foundation of Sidney Sussex College, Cambridge.

1597   Parliament meets (Oct, and continues until Feb 1598): issue of monopolies raised in the Commons.

'Islands Voyage' by Essex (August), fails to capture the Spanish treasure fleet. Third Spanish invasion armada dispersed by storms off the coast of France (Oct).

Fourth bad harvest year.

First edition of Bacon's *Essays*; James VI, *Demonologie*; W. Shakespeare, *Romeo and Juliet, Richard II* and *Richard III* published.

1598   Parliament of October 1597 continues until Feb: three subsidies granted; legislation on the poor and vagabonds, on charitable trusts and on discharged soldiers and sailors. Tyrone inflicts a serious defeat on English forces at the Battle of the Yellow Ford in Ulster (Aug). Death of Burghley (Aug) – beginning of the climax of the power struggle between Essex and Robert Cecil.

Peace of Vervins between France and Spain (May). Earl of Cumberland sacks Puerto Rico. Death of Philip II (Sept), accession of Philip III to the Spanish throne.

George Blackwell appointed archpriest in England by the Pope: beginning of the 'archpriest controversy'.

James VI's *Trew Law of Free Monarchies* published; J. Stow, *Survey of London*.

1599   Essex Lord-Lieutenant of Ireland: lands in Ireland (Apr), concludes treaty with Tyrone and returns to London (Sept). Birth of Oliver Cromwell (Apr). Thomas Sackville, Lord Buckhurst, appointed Lord Treasurer (May). Robert Cecil Master of the Court of Wards (May).

Philip III plans a further armada against England: the 'Invisible armada'.

Globe Theatre built. James VI, *Basilikon Doron*. Shakespeare's *Julius Caesar* first acted.

1600   Mountjoy, Lord Deputy of Ireland (1600–3), arrives in Ireland (Feb). Essex condemned to lose all his offices and to imprisonment at the Queen's pleasure (June); released in August but not restored to favour; he plans to recover his influence by force.

Gowrie conspiracy in Scotland (Aug): James VI seized but later released. Will Adams lands in Japan (Apr) – the first Englishman in Japan; he makes his home there until his death. East India Company founded (Dec).

Fortune Theatre, London, opened. Shakespeare's *Henry V* and *Merchant of*

Venice published; Ben Jonson, *Every Man out of his Humour*; W. Gilbert, *De Magnete*, a pioneer study of magnetism.

1601   Essex revolt (Jan) – fails; trial of Essex, condemned to death and executed (Feb). Parliament meets (Oct–Dec): great debate on monopolies; four subsidies granted; Poor Laws of 1597–98 reissued in only slightly modified form; Queen Elizabeth makes her 'Golden speech' (Nov).

Spanish forces land at Kinsale in southern Ireland (Sept); Mountjoy besieges Kinsale (Oct) and defeats Tyrone before Kinsale (Dec).

First East India Company voyage from London.

1602   Robert Cecil conducts a secret correspondence with James VI to prepare his way to the English throne.

The Spaniards at Kinsale surrender (Jan).

A gvt proclamation of Nov 1602 offers concessions to secular priests who will swear an oath of allegiance to the Crown.

Shakespeare's *Merry Wives of Windsor* published; Sir David Lindsay, *Satire of the Three Estates*; Richard Carew, *Survey of Cornwall*. Bodleian Library at Oxford opened.

1603   Death of Queen Elizabeth (Mar) and accession of James VI of Scotland who receives an ecstatic welcome on his journey south as James I of England; he reaches London in May. Tyrone surrenders: end of the Irish War (Mar). Ralegh dismissed as Captain of the Guard (Apr) and later (July) committed to the Tower, suspected of complicity in a plot (the 'Main Plot') to dethrone the King in favour of his cousin Arabella Stuart; Ralegh tried for treason and condemned to death (Nov) but reprieved (Dec). Cecil raised to the peerage as Lord Cecil of Essendon (May). The 'Bye Plot' against the King, inspired by the Catholic priest William Watson, enraged at the continued levying of the recusancy fines (June).

13 'Appellant' priests sign a 'Protestation' of allegiance to the Queen (Jan). Puritan 'Millenary Petition' presented to James on his journey south (Apr). James orders that the collection of the recusancy fines should continue (May).

Plague.

First publication – in imperfect form – of *Hamlet*.

1604   James's first Parliament meets (first session, Mar–July): Buckinghamshire election case; Apology of the Commons; 'free trade' debate; debates on 'union' with Scotland; marriage of priests given statutory authority; Act against recusants confirms the anti-Catholic statutes of the last reign (July), but James promises not to enforce it meantime; statute forbids bishops to alienate their lands, even to the Crown. James proclaimed King of 'Great Britain' (Oct).

Treaty of London (Aug) – peace with Spain; proposal for the marriage of James's heir, Prince Henry, to the Infanta Anne, daughter of Philip III. Sir Arthur Chichester becomes Lord Deputy of Ireland (Oct).

Hampton Court Conference (Jan); death of Whitgift (Feb); Richard Bancroft archbishop of Canterbury (Oct); 1559 Prayer Book reissued with minor modifications; important church canons (Sept): Bancroft institutes a campaign for clerical subscription to these canons. James issues a proclamation ordering the banishment of priests.

Great Farm of the customs; beginnings of a trade boom which lasted until 1614.

Othello by W. Shakespeare (first production); James I, *Counterblast to Tobacco*.

1605   Robert Cecil created earl of Salisbury (May). Second session of James's first Parliament meets (Nov, and continues until May 1606): Gunpowder Plot (5 Nov) – the end of an era in English Catholic history.

Bancroft's campaign against Nonconformist ministers continues; some driven from their livings.

Francis Bacon, *Advancement of Learning*; Michael Drayton, *Poems*.

1606　Parliament of Nov 1605 continues until May: severity of the recusancy laws increased; new oath of allegiance imposed on Catholics; 3 subsidies granted. Trial of the Gunpowder conspirators (Jan); 8 executed (Jan–Feb), including Guy Fawkes. Proclamation by James I for a new national flag combining emblems of Scotland and England (Apr). Third session of James's first Parliament meets (Nov, and continues until July 1607): session dominated by the question of 'union' with Scotland, with the Commons showing a marked lack of enthusiasm for the project. Marriage of the earl of Essex and Lady Frances Howard, daughter of the earl of Suffolk. Visit to England of James I's brother-in-law, Christian IV of Denmark – marked by much drunken disorder at Court.

Bate's case: the judges confirm the King's right to levy impositions without the consent of Parliament.

Expedition departs to colonize Virginia.

Macbeth probably written (first published 1623); first performance of B. Jonson's *Volpone*.

1607　Midlands 'rising' against enclosures (May). Flight abroad of Tyrone and other Ulster lords (Sept) – leads to the confiscation of much Ulster land and its plantation by English and Scottish settlers. Robert Carr, the King's Scottish favourite, knighted. Bacon appointed Solicitor-General.

Dispute over 'prohibitions' between Bancroft and Chief Justice Coke reaches a head, with Coke reasserting the right of the common law courts to decide which cases properly belonged to ecclesiastical jurisdiction.

Establishment of an English colony at Jamestown in Virginia.

Publication of Dr John Cowell's *Interpreter*, a law book containing controversial constitutional opinions; J. Norden, *The Surveyor's Dialogue*.

1608　Death of Buckhurst (Apr); Cecil Lord Treasurer (May). Calvin's case (the *post nati*): judges decide that Scots born after James's succession to the English throne are his natural-born subjects within England as well as Scotland.

Treaty of mutual defence between England and the United Provinces (June).

A New Book of Rates and new impositions exploit the decision in Bate's case and lead to a considerable rise in Crown revenue, soon amounting to £70,000 per annum.

Shakespeare's *King Lear* published; Thomas Middleton, *A Mad World My Masters*; Captain John Smith, *A True Relation of Virginia*.

1609　Confrontation between Coke and James I over the boundaries between the common law and ecclesiastical jurisdiction (Feb). Birth of Edward Hyde, later earl of Clarendon (Feb). James I signs a document entailing most of the Crown lands then in his possession. Ralegh's Sherborne estate granted to James's favourite, Robert Carr.

Twelve-year truce between Spain and the United Provinces begins.

Shakespeare's *Sonnets* published; also *Troilus and Cressida* and *Pericles*.

1610　Fourth and fifth sessions of James's first Parliament meet (Feb–July; Oct–Dec): important debates on impositions, the Great Contract and Cowell's *Interpreter*. *The Interpreter* burnt by the common hangman. Prince Henry created prince of Wales (June). Imprisonment of Arabella Stuart, pretender to the throne, for marrying William Seymour, earl of Hertford, a claimant of the Suffolk line.

Assassination of Henry IV of France (May).

Death of Bancroft (Nov).

Henry Hudson discovers Hudson's Bay (Aug).

J. Speed, *Theatrum* – a notable collection of maps; first performance of *The Alchemist* by Ben Jonson.

1611 James's Scottish favourite Robert Carr created Viscount Rochester. (Mar). Escape from captivity (June), flight from England, recapture and reimprisonment of Arabella Stuart. Creation of the title of baronet: the title is openly sold.

Negotiations for a marriage between the Elector Palatine, a leading German Protestant prince, and James's daughter Elizabeth; also for a marriage between Prince Henry and the Infanta Anne.

George Abbot archbishop of Canterbury. Theological controversy between King James and the Dutch Arminian Conrad Vorstius, with James defending traditional Calvinist doctrine. William Laud elected president of St John's College, Oxford. Authorized Version of the Bible published.

Shakespeare's *Tempest* written (published 1623). John Donne, *An Anatomy of the World*.

1612 Death of Robert Cecil, earl of Salisbury (May): Treasury put in commission; James resolves to be his own Secretary of State; Sir George Carew Master of the Wards. Death of Prince Henry (November).

Formal signing of the marriage contract between the Elector Palatine and Princess Elizabeth (May).

Two English heretics burnt for their Arian and Anabaptist doctrines – the last burning of heretics in England.

Colonization of the Bermudas (the 'Somers Islands') from Virginia.

Second (revised and enlarged) edition of Bacon's *Essays*; John Smith, *A Map of Virginia*. Foundation of Wadham College, Oxford.

1613 Essex divorce case: the countess wants to marry the royal favourite, Carr; divorce granted (Sept), after strong pressure from the King; Sir Thomas Overbury ('the favourite's favourite') opposes the divorce and is sent to the Tower where he dies (Sept). Carr created earl of Somerset (Nov) before his marriage to Lady Essex (Dec). Coke appointed Chief Justice of King's Bench; Bacon Attorney-General.

Marriage of James's daughter Elizabeth to Frederick, Elector Palatine (Feb). Fears of a Spanish invasion of England. Sarmiento, later count of Gondomar, appointed Spanish ambassador in London.

First performance of Shakespeare's *Henry VIII*.

1614 James issues a proclamation against duelling (Jan). The 'Addled Parliament' meets (Apr–July): further disputes over impositions; no legislation passed. Ralph Winwood – a strong opponent of Spanish influence – appointed Secretary of State (Mar). Death of the earl of Northampton, a possible Lord Treasurer (June). Thomas Howard, earl of Suffolk, appointed Lord Treasurer (July); Somerset succeeds to Suffolk's previous office of Lord Chamberlain. First meeting between George Villiers and the King (Aug).

Discussions for a Spanish marriage for Prince Charles between James and Sarmiento; discussions continue later in the year at the Spanish Court.

Alderman Cockayne's scheme for the prohibition of the export of undyed cloth: Merchant Adventurers Charter suspended (Dec); Cockayne in control of the cloth trade to northern Europe; leads to a crisis in the cloth industry during the next 3 years.

John Napier of Merchistoun publishes his *Descriptio* – the discovery of logarithms; Sir W. Ralegh, *History of the World*; J. Selden, *Titles of Honour*.

1615   Villiers made a gentleman of the bedchamber (Apr); Somerset's unreasonable behaviour becomes increasingly unacceptable to the King. Rumours about the possible murder of Overbury in the Tower become public; Somerset and his wife arrested on suspicion of the murder (Oct). Death of Lady Arabella Stuart in the Tower (Sept). Lionel Cranfield knighted and appointed Surveyor-General of the Customs – a significant stage in his rise to power.

       James receives Spanish terms for a marriage between Prince Charles and the Infanta; these provide for a possible Catholic succession to the throne; James decides to proceed with the negotiations. Embassy of Sir Thomas Roe to the Court of the Mogul Emperor at Agra.

       Inigo Jones appointed Surveyor of the King's Works; W. Camden, *Annals* (deals with the Elizabethan period up to 1588).

1616   George Villiers Master of the Horse (Jan) and knight of the Garter (Apr), created Baron Whaddon and Viscount Villiers (Aug). Earl and countess of Somerset tried for Overbury murder (May) and found guilty: James remits the death sentence. Bacon becomes a privy councillor (June). Prince Charles created prince of Wales (November). Dismissal of Coke as Chief Justice of the King's Bench as a result of the 'case of commendams' (Nov).

       Negotiations proceed for Prince Charles's marriage to the Infanta Maria of Spain despite difficulties over the religious provisions of the marriage treaty.

       Ralegh released from the Tower (Mar) to prepare for his voyage to Guiana; Spanish ambassador Sarmiento protests against the proposed voyage.

       Death of Shakespeare (Apr). Collected *Works* of Ben Jonson published.

1617   George Villiers created earl of Buckingham (Jan). Resignation and death of Lord Chancellor Ellesmere; Bacon Lord Keeper of the Great Seal (Mar). James I visits Scotland (May–Aug). Death of Sir Ralph Winwood, the anti-Spanish Secretary of State (Oct).

       Spanish theologians insist on effective toleration for English Catholics before a marriage between the Infanta and Prince Charles is agreed; negotiations proceed.

       Merchant Adventurers Charter restored: end of the Cockayne scheme.

       Ralegh leaves on his voyage to Guiana (June).

1618   Bacon Lord Chancellor (Jan); Sir Robert Naunton Secretary of State (Jan); Buckingham made a marquis (Jan). Lord Treasurer Suffolk dismissed (July): Howard influence in eclipse; Buckingham now dominant. Execution of Ralegh (Oct) following his return to England after clashes with the Spaniards in South America. Cranfield's major financial reforms begin.

       Bohemian revolt against Habsburg authority: beginning of the Thirty Years War. Spanish marriage negotiations suspended – James unable to satisfy Spanish demands.

       Opening of the Synod of Dort in the United Provinces (Nov): this discusses the theological differences between Calvinists and Arminians.

       James I issues his *Book of Sports*, permitting traditional Sunday entertainments such as dancing: the *Book* much disliked by Puritans. John Selden's *History of Tithes*: raises doubts about the rights of the clergy in this field.

1619   Buckingham becomes Lord High Admiral (Jan). Death of Queen Anne (Mar). Secretary of State Sir Thomas Lake, a dependent of the Howards, dismissed.

       Elector Palatine chosen King of Bohemia (Aug); accepts the Crown (Sept) – James dismayed by this affront to the Habsburgs by his son-in-law.

       The Synod of Dort's Calvinist pronouncements against Arminianism (May) are strongly supported by James I.

First colonial Parliament meets at Jamestown in Virginia (June); Sir Edwin Sandys becomes Treasurer of the Virginia Company.

Inigo Jones begins the banqueting house at Whitehall. Harvey outlines his discovery of the circulation of the blood in lectures at St Bartholomew's Hospital in London.

1620 Secret treaty between England and Spain for the marriage of Prince Charles and the Infanta Maria.

Battle of the White Mountain (Oct): Frederick loses Bohemia; the Palatinate is invade by the Imperialists.

Growing economic depression; considerable unemployment in the cloth industry. The Pilgrim Fathers settle at Plymouth in New England (Dec).

Bacon's *Novum Organum*, his grand scheme for improvement of the sciences.

1621 James's third Parliament meets (Jan–June): revival of impeachment and attack on monopolists; fall of Bacon (May); two subsidies granted. Lionel Cranfield becomes Lord Treasurer. Parliament resumes (Nov–Dec): Commons Protestation (Dec).

Resumption of war between Spain and the Dutch; Elector Palatine arrives in exile at the Hague (Apr); death of Philip III of Spain (May), accession of Philip IV.

William Laud appointed bishop of St David's.

First visit of van Dyck to England; R. Burton's *Anatomy of Melancholy*; T. Mun, *A Discourse of Trade*.

1622 Reconciliation between Buckingham and the Howards. John Digby, earl of Bristol, sent to Madrid to complete negotiations for the Spanish match; Prince Charles promises to visit Spain to advance the marriage negotiations. War in the Palatinate continues.

F. Bacon, *History of the Reign of Henry VII*.

1623 Charles and Buckingham undertake a trip to Madrid (Feb–Oct): they return offended and resolved on war with Spain. Buckingham made a duke: the first non-royal duke in England since Norfolk's execution in 1572.

Massacre of Amboyna (Feb): murder of East India Company servants by the Dutch; James fails to take effective action in support of the Company.

First collected edition of Shakespeare's *Plays* – the First Folio.

1624 James's fourth Parliament meets (Feb–May): resolution for war with Spain; three subsidies granted (appropriation of supplies); Statute of Monopolies passed; legal maximum rate of interest on loans reduced from 10 to 8 per cent; Cranfield impeached and dismissed (May).

Mansfield expedition to recover the Palatinate fails. Accession to power of Richelieu in France (Aug). French marriage treaty (Nov): marriage agreed between Prince Charles and the French Princess Henrietta Maria.

Trade improves after the depression of 1620–24. Virginia taken over by the Crown as England's first royal colony (June).

Richard Montagu's *New Gag* – a statement of Arminian doctrine – published.

1625 Death of James I (Mar), accession of Charles I. Marriage of Charles I and Henrietta Maria (May). Charles's first Parliament meets (June–Aug): two subsidies granted; tonnage and poundage granted for only 1 year by the Commons, the Lords refuse to accept this and Charles continues to collect the customs revenue without parliamentary authorization throughout his reign; first significant parliamentary attacks (led by John Pym) on Arminianism. Scottish Act of Revocation directed against the holders of former ecclesiastical property by Charles (Oct).

Beginnings of war with Spain; Cadiz expedition in the autumn a disaster for England.

Feoffees for impropriations set up to buy impropriated tithes: they act essentially in the Puritan interest.

Plague.

Daniel Mytens appointed painter to Charles I. Third, further enlarged edition of Bacon's *Essays*. William Camden's *Annals* published, completing the story of Elizabeth's reign up to 1603.

1626   Charles's second Parliament (Feb–June): attempt to impeach Buckingham; no supply granted; Commons complain about the collection of tonnage and poundage without parliamentary consent. Digges and Eliot sent to the Tower for managing the impeachment of Buckingham (May).

A forced loan raised to support the war with Spain (Sept).

York House debate on religious doctrine: Buckingham supports the Arminian position. Laud appointed bishop of Bath and Wells.

John Donne, *Five Sermons*.

1627   Darnel's case (the 'Five Knights' case', November): the judges rule that the King's 'special command' is a sufficient cause for imprisonment. Laud appointed to the Privy Council.

Beginnings of war with France: expedition to La Rochelle and the isle of Rhé, under Buckingham's command, to help the French Huguenots – a disaster, just like the Cadiz expedition of 1625.

Archbishop Abbot suspended from office.

1628   First session of Charles's third Parliament (Mar–June): Petition of Right; 5 subsidies granted; attacks on Arminianism; Oliver Cromwell returned to Parliament for the borough of Huntingdon. Weston Lord Treasurer (July). Assassination of Buckingham (Aug). Thomas Wentworth raised to the peerage and appointed President of the Council in the North.

Fall of La Rochelle to the forces of Louis XIII of France (Oct).

Laud appointed bishop of London.

Alexander Leighton's *Appeal to Parliament*, a ferocious attack on the bishops; William Harvey's *De Motu Cordis* published; Edward Coke, *First Institute*.

1629   Second session of Charles's third Parliament (Jan–Mar): Commons pass three resolutions against Arminianism and against tonnage and poundage not voted by Parliament; Charles dissolves Parliament: beginning of the 'personal rule'. Wentworth appointed to the Privy Council (Nov).

Treaty of Susa (Apr): peace with France.

Beginning of the trade slump of 1629–31.

Rubens, in England on a political mission for Philip IV of Spain, undertakes artistic work for Charles I during his stay and is knighted by the King.

1630   Arrest of Alexander Leighton (Feb): sentenced in Star Chamber to a savage punishment, including mutilation, for his attack on the bishops. Birth of Prince Charles (later Charles II, May). Extensive fines levied on freeholders worth £40 per annum who had failed to take up knighthood.

Treaty of Madrid (Nov): peace with Spain.

Laud becomes Chancellor of Oxford University (April).

Bad harvest. Beginning of large-scale emigration to New England. Foundation of Guinea Company.

1631   The King and Laud try to raise money for the repair of the fabric of St Paul's in London.

A *Book of Orders* instructs local officials to see that poor relief is effectively administered.

Sir John Eliot's *Monarchy of Man* stresses the powers of the Crown.

1632 Wentworth appointed Lord Deputy of Ireland (Jan). Death of Sir John Eliot in the Tower (Nov).

Foundation of Maryland.

Van Dyck, court painter to Charles I, settles in England. William Harvey appointed physician to Charles I.

1633 Charles I's Scottish coronation (June). Wentworth takes up his office in Ireland (July). Birth of Prince James (later James II, Oct).

Death of Archbishop Abbot (Aug); Laud archbishop of Canterbury (Aug). Feoffees for impropriations dissolved on Laud's initiative because of their Puritan sympathies.

Large fine imposed by the Crown on the city of London (Mar).

Book of Sports of 1618 reissued; John Donne and George Herbert publish books of *Poems*. W. Prynne, *Histriomastix* – an attack on the theatre as a source of immorality.

1634 Obsolete forest laws enforced over a wide area in order to secure large fines for the Crown. Savage Star Chamber sentence on Prynne for his attack on the theatre with its implied rebuke to the royal family: his ears are cut off (May). Death of Sir Edward Coke (Sept). Sir Robert Heath, Chief Justice of Common Pleas, dismissed (Sept); succeeded by Sir John Finch (Oct). Ship money imposed on the maritime counties (first writ of ship money, Oct).

Charles negotiates with Spain for a treaty against the Dutch.

Laud begins a 3-year visitation of the province of Canterbury.

First settlement in Maryland.

Milton's *Comus*.

1635 Death of Lord Treasurer Weston (Mar): Treasury put in Commission with Laud as one of the commissioners. Ship money extended to inland counties (second writ of ship money, Aug). Fines for violation of forest laws continue.

War between France and Spain formally declared (May).

Commission of Depopulation (May): commissioners directed to compound with guilty landowners on payment of a fine. Increased customs duties levied in a New Book of Rates.

John Selden, *Mare Clausum* – sets out England's claims to sovereignty of the seas.

1636 William Juxon, bishop of London, appointed Lord Treasurer (Mar). Third writ of ship money (Oct).

Wentworth makes a statement before the English Privy Council about the successes of his Irish administration *vis-à-vis* the Church, finance and the army.

Van Dyck, *Charles I on Horseback*.

1637 The common law judges are asked by the Crown to give an opinion on the legality of ship money (February). Burton, Bastwick and Prynne, Puritan pamphleteers, are mutilated for their attacks on the Arminian bishops (June). John Lilburne receives a harsh sentence in Star Chamber for refusing to answer questions put to him. Hampden's case on the legality of ship money heard in Exchequer Chamber: arguments of counsel (Nov–Dec). Forest fines continue.

Bishop Williams, the most prominent remaining Calvinist on the bench of bishops, sent to the Tower for his opposition to Laudian ideas. Papal agent received at Court. New Prayer Book imposed on Scotland.

Star Chamber decree imposes severe restrictions on the Press. Milton's *Lycidas* written.

1638   Verdict in Hampden's case: 7 to 5 for the King (final judgement in June). Scottish national covenant (Feb); the marquis of Hamilton sent as royal commissioner to negotiate with the Scots (June); he returns to England (July). Hamilton back in Edinburgh in Aug with royal permission for the holding of a General Assembly and a Scottish Parliament; third visit to Scotland by Hamilton in Sept: the King makes large concessions: Assembly and Parliament summoned, Prayer Book revoked. The concessions fail in the face of Scottish suspicions. Wentworth, in Ireland, stresses the need for strong measures to reduce the Scots to obedience.

1639   First Bishops' War: Charles raises troops to bring the Scots to obedience, but there is no actual fighting; pacification of Berwick (June). King allows Spanish troops to march across southern England (summer). Wentworth returns from Ireland: he reaches London in Sept and becomes one of the King's chief advisers. Decision taken at the end of the year to summon Parliament. Beginning of 'taxpayers' strike' of 1639–40: breakdown of effective royal control of local government in England.

Battle of the Downs (Oct): Spanish fleet defeated in English waters by the Dutch.

1640   Wentworth created earl of Strafford and Lord Lieutenant of Ireland (Jan). Death of Lord Keeper Coventry, Finch appointed Lord Keeper (Jan). Short Parliament meets (Apr–May): dissolved without voting supply. Second Bishops' War (Aug–Oct): English forces defeated by the Scots: Treaty of Ripon (Oct) – Charles agrees to pay the Scots £850 a day until a settlement is made. Long Parliament meets (Nov): attack on the judges; monopolists expelled from the Commons; impeachment of Laud and Strafford; Commons condemn the new Arminian canons of 1640 and declare that Convocation has no power to bind either the clergy or the laity without the consent of Parliament (this declaration is approved by the Lords the following year); 'Root and Branch' Petition against episcopacy submitted to the Commons by London citizens (Dec).

Press censorship breaks down.

1641   Long Parliament continues its first session until Sept: Triennial Act (Feb); Act against dissolving the Long Parliament without its own consent (May); execution of Strafford by Act of Attainder (May); Tonnage and Poundage Act (June); Star Chamber and High Commission abolished (July); Ship Money Act (Aug).

Discussions in the Commons on the 'root and branch' issue (from Feb onwards) bring disagreements among members. From June onwards opposition leaders in the Commons demand that appointments of royal ministers should be subject to parliamentary approval.

Second session of Long Parliament begins (Oct): Grand Remonstrance, passed by 159 votes to 148 (Nov); parliamentary leaders demand control of the militia (Dec). Supporters of the parliamentary opposition gain control of the gvt of the city of London (Dec).

Trip to Scotland by Charles I (Aug) does little to further the royalist cause there. Catholic rebellion in Ireland (Oct).

1642   Attempt by the King to arrest the 'five members' (Jan); the King leaves London (Jan). The Long Parliament continues: Bishops' Exclusion Bill passed (February), Militia Ordinance passed by the Lords and Commons (Mar).

Gradual beginning of hostilities between supporters of the Crown and supporters of the parliamentary opposition. The King denied entry to Hull by Sir

231

John Hotham (Apr); the King issues Commissions of Array (June); the navy declares for Parliament (July); the King raises his banner at Nottingham (Aug); Battle of Edgehill (d[1], Oct); royalist forces advance to Turnham Green (pv, Nov); Eastern Association established (Dec).

Long Parliament orders the closing of all theatres.

---

1. d = drawn or indecisive battle; pv = parliamentarian victory; rv = royalist victory.

CHAPTER 27

The war with Spain and its consequences, 1585–1603

The outbreak of open if undeclared war with Spain was, as we have seen, a defeat for the peace-loving Elizabeth. She could, however, take some comfort from the fact that she had been able to delay it until 1585. That date can, indeed, be seen as the culmination of the 'high Elizabethan period', those middle years of the Queen's reign in which her successes were very obvious and in which the domestic difficulties of the war years lay in the unforeseen future. There is no doubt that Elizabeth had considerable achievements behind her by 1585. The Protestant Church which had been established in 1559 was beginning to put down roots in the country; sound money had been re-established in 1560–61 and the disastrous debasements of the 1540s were in increasingly dim if still potent memory; the Crown was solvent and, indeed, the Queen was saving money from her meagre ordinary revenue; the patronage system, under Elizabeth's ever vigilant eyes, was working successfully to bring stability to the country; relations between the Queen and her Parliaments, despite periodic difficulties over such matters as religion and the succession, had been, on the whole, a story of co-operation; English traders were expanding their horizons and thus lessening the country's traditional and dangerous dependence on a Netherlands market which was increasingly disrupted by civil strife; and the Queen and her small, powerful Privy Council kept a firm control on administration and generally carried most of the political nation in the localities with them in most of their policies. Above all, perhaps, major wars had been avoided.

There was, of course, another side to the story. Catholicism had been contained but not extinguished; the Puritans, under increasing attack from Archbishop Whitgift, were very unhappy both with the state of the Church and with the attitudes of a hierarchy increasingly dominated by a bench of bishops who laid stress on their administrative rather than on their pastoral functions; the ordinary revenue was much lower than it need have been and the Queen and Burghley achieved solvency only through economies which were unpopular with many members of the political nation in peacetime and which gave rise to anguished cries from the nobility and gentry in the much more difficult financial and economic conditions of the 1590s; overseas trade was not expanding significantly in either volume or value; and the Queen and Council, without a substantial paid bureaucracy, a professional police force, or a standing army, lacked effective coercive power in the localities. These difficulties for or limitations on royal authority seemed in 1585 much less significant than the catalogue of Elizabeth's achievements, but in the war years of the 1590s the limited financial resources available and the difficulties which the war helped to produce and intensify in the localities suggested that English society was not effectively organized to fight even an essentially defensive war: it was not good at raising the two fundamental resources needed for war – money and troops – and when the next great round of military demands was made on the country in a less favourable political atmosphere in the 1620s, the result was a major crisis for the monarchy in 1628–29.

In 1585, then, Elizabeth embarked on a war which was to reveal the weaknesses of the country in an era when no state could realistically hope to avoid war indefinitely. No ruler of the time hoped to avoid a major conflict with more fervour than the Queen. By the 1580s even she realized that her hopes had failed. The consequences of that failure were obvious by the time of her death in 1603. The Queen's aims remained basically the same throughout the war (56). She was determined to ensure that neither France nor the Netherlands fell under total Spanish domination, but was equally convinced that the revivified France which began to emerge under Henry IV during the 1590s must not be in a position to dominate the northern European coastline where it would be at least as great a threat to English security as a triumphant Spain. It was basically for this reason that she was so determined to secure a Netherlands which was still under nominal Spanish overlordship – necessary to keep France out – but with a wide degree of local independence – essential to limit effective Spanish power. Her war aims, in fact, reflected almost exactly the aims of her foreign policy in time of peace, and they did so because she was resolutely convinced that they provided the best means of maintaining that English security which it was her overriding desire to preserve. The war continued for the rest of her life and was fought on the Continent (in the Netherlands and France), at sea and in Ireland, where Spain tried to exploit the major rebellion which broke out there during the mid-1590s. We cannot discuss the details of the war and the merits or defects of Elizabeth's strategy – this has been done by Professor Wernham (56, *340 ff*) in an article which is generally sympathetic to the 'cautious common sense' which was the hallmark of the Queen's military and naval decisions – but it is vital to remember that it was fought in a period of serious economic difficulties for the country.

War, famine and plague were the three great scourges of early modern European society and England had to endure all three together during the 1590s. The decade opened with a run of good harvests, but from 1594 to 1597 there were four terrible years in a row with two of the four worst harvests of the century in 1596 and 1597 [I]. It was during this time of harvest catastrophe that Shakespeare's Midsummer Night's Dream was written, and a well-known speech by Titania almost certainly refers to these natural disasters in words which brilliantly evoke the blighted fields of the time.

> The ox hath therefore stretch'd his yoke in vain,
> The ploughman lost his sweat, and the green corn
> Hath rotted are his youth attain'd a beard;
> The fold stands empty in the drowned field,
> And crows are fatted with the murrion flock.[1]

There was a serious outbreak of plague in 1592–93. Thousands died in London alone and other parts of the country were seriously affected. In Kent, for example, it spread rapidly throughout the country and remained a serious problem until 1595. Another outbreak in 1603, while the war was still dragging on, was even more violent (251; *243*). The terrible harvests of the mid-1590s were probably the most important factor in the spiralling inflation of the decade, the worst since the middle years of the century: food prices rose by over 35 per cent during the 1590s [K] and in the worst harvest years there were food riots in many parts of the country.

The war certainly contributed to the social distress which was bound to follow these natural disasters. The greatly increased government expenditure made necessary by the military and naval ventures of the period contributed – though probably to a lesser degree than the harvest failures – to the high inflation of the last years of the reign (224), and the needs and misdeeds of discharged soldiers and sailors returning from the wars were important elements in the problems which the poor and vagrants posed for the government during the 1590s. The sixteenth century as a whole was an unhappy time for the poorer members of society and one set of figures suggests that during the last decade of Elizabeth's reign the standard of living of working men in town and country reached its lowest level in the whole of recorded English history [L]. The Elizabethan period was, therefore, undoubtedly an 'iron' rather than a 'golden' age for the less fortunate members of the community, and the genuine concern of members of the political nation for the impotent poor together with their fears of sturdy rogues and vagabonds led to a great elaboration of the Poor Law which culminated in the statutes of 1598 (98). As we have seen (Ch. 10), an Edwardian Act of 1552 had provided a hint of compulsion in the collection of poor relief and in the early Elizabethan period Acts of 1563, 1572 and 1576 (5 Eliz., c. 3; 14 Eliz., c. 5; 18 Eliz., c. 3) provided that compulsion, ordered justices of the peace to impose specific rates of taxation in the localities for poor relief and commanded that stocks of raw materials should be provided in towns so that the unemployed could be given work. These provisions were codified and improved in the statute of 1598 (39 Eliz., c. 3), which remained the basis of the English poor relief system until the early nineteenth century. The timing of that statute, which was being discussed in Parliament at the height of the economic crisis of the 1590s, reflected the government's and the political nation's preoccupation with the needs of the deserving poor just as another major statute (39 Eliz., c. 4) of the same year bore witness to their fears of vagrancy and their determination to punish rogues and vagabonds severely; they were to be whipped and returned to their native parishes. Discharged soldiers were seen as a special category among both the deserving and vagrant poor and separate Acts of 1598 dealt with the problems which they posed (39 Eliz., cc. 21, 17). A special rate was to be levied in every parish for the relief of sick and maimed soldiers and mariners, but discharged soldiers and sailors who had taken to vagrancy were subjected to the most severe penalties. They were ordered to settle down to some lawful work and those who did not were to be executed. The ferocity of this provision, so much harsher than that against ordinary rogues, clearly indicated the extent of the problem which former soldiers and sailors were posing to law and order; the effects of the war with Spain could be seen in the activities of discharged soldiers in the streets of

London and in the counties of southern England as well as in the presence of English armies in the Netherlands and France.

If the war undoubtedly contributed to the social strains and difficulties of the 1590s it had a more mixed effect on the country's economy as a whole. It led to the development of a privateering 'industry' in which English gentlemen and, above all, merchants financed voyages for the capture of Spanish prizes (212). These brought in between £100,000 and £200,000 per annum and as English imports from Spain, which stopped on the outbreak of war, had amounted to between £100,000 and £120,000 a year, it seems fair to conclude that 'the returns of privateering were worth at least as much as those of the Iberian trade' (212, *128*). That was perhaps a small consolation to those merchants who were heavily committed to the trade in English cloth to Spain, and 'outports' like Bristol and Chester which depended largely on Spanish markets suffered severely during the war. On the other hand, their difficulties led to an increasing concentration of trade and wealth in London, where great merchants like Sir Paul Bayning and Sir Thomas Myddleton accumulated large liquid capital reserves from their privateering ventures. It has been argued that this accumulation of wealth in London was essential for the successful launching of such great ventures as the East India trade and the Virginia Company in the early years of the seventeenth century (212), and there can be no doubt that the war played a vital part in the expansion of England's mercantile marine which was a feature of the 1580s and 1590s (212; 239). The new ships which were built, many of them specifically for privateering, required captains and crews, and the experience which these men gained of ocean-going seamanship during the war stood them in good stead in the days of peace after 1604 when many of them took part in the eastern trade and in American colonization. In Dr Andrews' words, 'the contribution of these two decades . . . to England's maritime strength made possible her rise to commercial pre-eminence in the following century' (212, *232*).

If the Spanish War had mixed short-term effects on the English economy but brought substantial long-term benefits to trade and shipping, its effects on the country's international position were almost entirely beneficial. This seems obvious if we compare England's situation in 1585, when Elizabeth dispatched Leicester to the Netherlands, with the position at the Queen's death in 1603. At the former date there seemed a real possibility that both France and the whole of the Netherlands might fall under the control of a Spanish monarchy which had vastly increased its strength during the early 1580s. That would have left an isolated England to bear the full brunt of a Spanish attack, and if England had fallen it is difficult to see how Protestantism could have survived against the triumphant forces of the Counter-Reformation. Elizabeth was no protestant crusader and it is a fallacy to see the Dutch struggle against Spain in simplistic religious terms – many of the northern Netherlanders were Catholics – but there is no doubt that the Anglo-Spanish War of 1585–1604 was a decisive event in the struggle of Counter-Reformation Catholicism to suppress the Reformation. Elizabeth's intervention in the Netherlands and later in France made sure that neither Catholicism nor Spain would win a complete victory. When she died in 1603 the independence of the French monarchy was assured and the Northern Netherlands was divided from Spain. It was not the ideal solution from the Queen's point of view – she wanted as we have seen a united Netherlands under nominal Spanish sovereignty – but the fact that the Southern Netherlands remained under Spain's control was some guarantee that France's influence would not be allowed to extend too far along the coasts facing England's sensitive south-eastern shore. Above all, the threat of Spanish hegemony over western Europe had been re-moved. It was a turning-point in the history of the Continent. The future, though this was not yet obvious, lay with the north-western states of France, the United Provinces and England. England, in short, was far more secure in 1603 than she had been in 1585.

If the international effects of the war were favourable for England, its domestic political consequences were ominously bad. The Queen was growing old during the 1590s. She had always been a woman of peace, never at home in a war situ-ation. She became more and more out of sympathy with the times, anxious to bring the war to an end but unable to devise feasible ways of doing so. The general slackening of her grip on government, which was a feature of these years, was partly due to increasing age but probably as well to a general weariness with the war and its associated problems. She missed the great ministers and courtiers who had served her in the earlier years of the reign; Leicester died in 1588, Sir Walter Mildmay in 1589, Sir Francis Walsingham in 1590, Sir Christopher Hatton in 1591. The most important of all, Burghley, did live on until 1598, but he like his mistress was old, a political dinosaur bankrupt of new ideas. The Queen in these last years of her reign often appears as an irascible and embittered old woman.[2]

The Spanish War, which cost Elizabeth so much in terms of worry and nervous energy during her declining years, imposed very heavy burdens on the country at large. We have already discussed its social costs; the financial consequences were even more striking. Vast sums were spent on the navy, on the military expeditions to the Netherlands and France and on the Irish rebellion, which became entangled with the war and was by far the biggest single item in the Queen's expences from the mid-1590s onwards. Her ordinary revenue, now running at perhaps £300,000 a year, was quite inadequate for such demands upon her purse and she met part of the cost by selling Crown lands and borrowing. She also imposed heavy burdens on the localities and turned to Parliament for assist-ance. Individual counties were expected to provide funds for equipping their local militia for home defence and also to raise troops for service abroad. Such demands were especially heavy in southern England, and it has been estimated that Kent spent over £10,000 during the war years on local defence preparations as well as raising at least 6,000 men for service overseas. The war thus had 'a deleterious, disruptive impact on county society' (251, *225–6*). It was a broadly similar story in Norfolk where attempts, at a substantial cost, to make the militia more effective led to local protests which overflowed into Parliament, especially in 1597 and 1601 (153). Parliament itself voted ten subsidies between 1593 and 1601 and during the years 1590–1603 Elizabeth received an average of £135,000 a year from parliamentary taxation compared with about £50,000 per annum during the period 1558–70 (98). The Parliaments of these years were well aware of and sympathetic to the Queen's needs, but they used the extra leverage which their growing financial contributions gave them in the monopolies crisis of 1601 when they forced the Queen to concede the substance of their demands. The monopolies issue was itself largely a by-product of the war. Monopolies – the sole right to make or distribute particular products – stemmed from the Crown's prerogative right to regulate the economic life of the country. Originally they were allowed to reward inventors or encourage new manufactures. They became increasingly numerous and highly objectionable only in the last fifteen or so years of the reign – the period of the war with Spain. Then numerous monopolies were granted which affected already established industries, making large profits for the grantees but raising prices for consumers at a time of considerable economic hardship. During these years the Queen was saving every penny she could for the war and had even less money than usual to bestow on her courtiers and officials. One way she could reward them without direct cost to the Crown was by granting them patents of monopoly. The fury of the Commons in 1601, when Sir Robert Cecil commented on their disorderly behaviour, 'more fit for a grammar school than a court of parliament', forced the Queen to cancel the most objectionable patents and to subject the rest to scrutiny in the common law courts (117, vol. 2 pp *376 ff*).

The granting of a large number of monopolies was one indication of the domestic financial stringency which the Crown faced as a result of the Spanish War. Another was the growth of corruption in the public service, a phenomenon to which Sir John Neale first drew our attention in a famous lecture (100). As the enormous cost of the war compelled the Queen to reduce her favours and gifts to suitors – she herself apologized in 1600 because the war had forced her to 'restrain her bountiful hand from rewarding her servants' – there was an increasingly ferocious struggle for those that remained, with clients offering larger and larger gratuities, which soon became indistinguishable from outright bribes, to courtiers and middlemen who might further their suits. This situation was given added significance by the breakdown of the classic Elizabethan patronage system in these years. That had depended for its successful working on no courtier or minister trying to achieve a monopoly of power. Burghley and even Leicester had honoured this convention, but the rising star of the Court in the 1590s, Leicester's stepson and potential political heir, Robert Devereux, earl of Essex, refused all moderation. He wanted everything for himself and his supporters, and the Queen's refusal to grant him high political office or to reward his clients as he thought they deserved led him to wild and irresponsible actions. Elizabeth may have hoped for a repetition during the last years of her reign of the situation which had prevailed during the 1570s and 1580s when Burghley and Leicester, the trusted minister and the favoured courtier, had been the two main channels through which her patronage flowed. Sir Robert Cecil, Burghley's younger son and political successor, was prepared to play his father's role but Essex's vaulting ambitions made such a scheme unworkable, and when it became obvious that his manœuvres had lost him the Queen's trust and he saw that he was faced with bankruptcy and the probable ruin of his position as a faction leader he gambled on rebellion. He lost and was executed, but his failure no less than if he had succeeded meant that one man now dominated the patronage scene. Essex's dictum 'he who is not with me is against me', had virtually reduced the factions to two by 1601; his own and Cecil's. His fall left only the latter's.

> Little Cecil trips up and down,
> He rules both Court and Crown,

wrote a lampoonist after Essex's execution. His words were essentially true. Between 1601 and 1603 Cecil exercised greater power than even his father had ever wielded and certainly more than the Queen would have wished (98). The patronage system which had served her so well for most of her reign became a destabilizing influence in the State during the last years of her life, and it is difficult to avoid the conclusion that she herself was largely to blame. She was usually a sound judge of men, but she perserved with Essex long after it was obvious that he was a danger to, rather than a useful servant of, the State. It was another sign that she was growing old.

The domestic events of the 1590s illustrated, therefore, the inadequacy of the Crown's revenue to fight an effective war without making demands on the localities which roused strong resentments there, resentments which might spill over into the parliamentary arena. Even with substantial local taxation and unprecedented parliamentary grants Elizabeth only managed to wage an essentially defensive war and that at the cost of limiting rewards to servants and courtiers at home and making the country pay an increasing share of the cost of her 'civil service' through the growth of such indirect taxation as monopolies. The unpopularity of these, as revealed in no uncertain terms in the Parliament of 1601, illustrated the dangers of adding to the cost of living in such ways, especially at a time of severe economic hardship when the principal problem of the lower orders was one of sheer physical survival. The breakdown of the patronage system with the ambitions and death of Essex was a symbol of domestic failure, an indication that the Queen's judgement was growing less sure in her old age. All these developments, taken together, produced a feeling of *fin de siècle*; Englishmen were awaiting a new reign. In this unhappy domestic atmosphere religious developments also gave cause for concern.

---

1. W. Shakespeare, *A Midsummer Night's Dream*, Act II, Scene i, lines 93–7.
2. See e.g. the letters of her godson Sir John Harington, *Nugae Antiquae* (1804), pp. 235, 314–5, 318, 320–3.

CHAPTER 28

Catholics, Puritans and the Church of England, 1588–1603

By 1588, as we have seen (Ch. 17), the Church of England, despite the many difficulties which it faced, had begun to strike roots in the country. The Puritans within it were under continuing assault from Archbishop Whitgift who started his rule at Canterbury in 1583 determined to reduce them to conformity (see above, Ch. 18). As for the Catholics, it was clear by the end of the 1580s that their religion was not going to 'wither away' as the government had hoped. The influence of Catholic landowners had enabled them to protect the practices of the old religion on their estates for themselves, their families and their tenants, and the influx of missionary priests from the 1570s onwards gave the Catholic cause a new idealism and enthusiasm which was a priceless asset to it (see above, Ch. 18). The attitude of Catholics to the dramatic events of 1587–8 – the execution of Mary Queen of Scots and the coming of the Armada – also showed, however, that, as a body, they were not prepared to take a lead in efforts to overthrow the government. As Professor Hurstfield put it, with only slight exaggeration, by 1590 'it had . . . become certain that . . . in terms of religion the Catholic movement was invincible to the Queen; in terms of politics it was invincible to her enemies' (56, *382*). The years between the defeat of the Armada and the end of the reign saw important trends and events for Catholicism and Puritanism as well as significant developments in the Church of England.

The Church continued to establish itself as the national ecclesiastical institution. By the end of the reign it had represented the official face of English religion for over forty years, and the weekly attendance of the majority of the population in most parts of the country at their parish churches gave it and its ministers a unique position as a disseminator of news and propaganda as well as theological and moral teachings. It had become an integral part of the lives of men and women, most of whom could by 1603 remember no other official religion. Moreover, during the 1590s the quality of the clergy, which had been improving continuously if slowly throughout the reign, gave cause for increasing satisfaction as the number of well-trained graduates entering the parish ministry rose still further. During these years, too, the Church received its greatest philosophical justification when Richard Hooker published the first four books of his *Laws of Ecclesiastical Polity* in 1593 (for a good brief summary see (186, *315 ff*)). Jewel's *Apology* of 1562 had been directed essentially against Catholic criticisms, but Hooker's great work, though a formidable justification of the Church's position vis̀ -vis both Catholics and Puritans, concentrated on the attacks of the latter, with their denunciations of the popish rites and ceremonies which, they claimed, still disfigured the Church. His work as a whole – the fifth book was not published until 1597 and the last three until the middle years of the seventeenth century – was a remarkable intellectual achievement, 'a manifesto to which the Church [still] returns at every crisis to seek justification and vindication' (quoted (186, *315*)), and it was given added force by the magnificent if measured prose in which it was written. Its flavour can be tasted in a passage in which Hooker deals with the attacks of the Puritans on the continuing 'popish superstitions' in the Church.

> Concerning rites and ceremonies there may be fault either in the kind or in the number and multitude of them. The first thing blamed about the kind of ours is that in many things we have departed from the ancient simplicity of Christ and his Apostles, we have embraced more outward stateliness, we have those orders in the exercise of religion which they who best pleased God and served him most devoutly never had. For it is out of doubt that the first state of things was best, that in the prime of the Christian religion faith was soundest, the Scriptures of God were then best understood by all men. . . . The glory of God and the good of his Church was the thing which the Apostles aimed at and therefore ought to be the mark whereat we also level. But seeing those rites and orders may be at one time more which at another time are less available unto that purpose, what reason is there in these things to urge the state of one only age as a pattern for all to follow? It is not, I am right sure, their meaning that we should now assemble our people to serve God in close and secret meetings; or that common brooks or rivers should be used for places of baptism . . .; or that all kinds of standing provision for the ministry should be utterly taken away and their estate made again dependent upon the voluntary devotion of men. In these things they easily perceive how unfit that were for the present, which was for the first age convenient enough. (quoted 5, *121–2*)

This brief excerpt shows how adeptly Hooker put his finger on one of the weaknesses of the Puritan position; the fact that, despite their repeated stress on the need to follow the letter as well as the spirit of the Bible, they did *not* in fact suggest that the Church of England should continue all the practices of the primitive Church as these were revealed in the New Testament.

Hooker defended the government of the Church of England by bishops, but he did not claim that episcopacy was necessary for a true church. It was during the post-Armada years, however, that two new theological tendencies, which presaged the Arminian [N] developments of the 1620s and 1630s, came to the fore in England. These were attacks on the Calvinist doctrine of predestination [N] and defence of the concept of *de iure* episcopacy [N]. In the pre-Armada years no prominent English churchman had asserted that bishops were necessary for a true church. Whitgift himself stated that God had not ordained any specific form of church government and that the matter was therefore a 'thing indifferent' which might lawfully be established by the Prince. Elizabeth was determined on episcopacy and therefore all her subjects, both clerical and lay, should follow her lawful orders. It therefore produced something of a sensation when in February 1589 Richard Bancroft, a prominent clergyman who was then a member of the High Commission and who became bishop of London in 1597 preached a sermon at Paul's Cross in London in which he implied if he did not explicitly state that bishops held their office *iure divino*. During the early 1590s other English clergymen *openly* asserted episcopal divine right and Bancroft himself did so in 1593 in his *Survey of the Pretended Holy Discipline*, a scathing attack on the Puritans.

These ideas were certainly confined to a small minority of clerics, but they alarmed influential laymen like the Queen's cousin Sir Francis Knollys who appreciated the potential threat which they posed to religious peace. He was proved right during the Laudian supremacy of the 1630s, as were the defenders of that other Elizabethan theological orthodoxy, the Calvinist doctrine of predestination, the idea that God in his inscrutable purpose had preordained some men and women to eternal bliss and others to eternal damnation irrespective of their actions on earth.· Calvinism was the predominant theology in Elizabethan England but it did not go unchallenged, and long before the 1590s some clerics expressed anti-Calvinist views in which they laid stress on man's free will to work out his own destiny in this world. These disputes came to the fore in 1595 when the heads of a number of Cambridge colleges took action against William Barrett, a young don who stressed free will rather than predestination. A long controversy followed, the upshot of which was Whitgift's nine Lambeth articles of 1595. These were strongly Calvinist in tone and supported predestinarian orthodoxy, but the whole dispute had alarmed the Queen and in December 1595 she ordered Whitgift to stop further discussion of predestination, 'a matter tender and dangerous to weak, ignorant minds'. The conflicts over predestination, just like those over the status of bishops, clearly affected only a limited group among the clergy and an even smaller number of laymen during the 1590s, but they had ominous implications for the future. The balanced 'Anglicanism' which Hooker propounded and defended during the 1590s represented a formidable intellectual challenge to the Puritan position, but its strength lay in the fact that it did so without denying any of the theological orthodoxies which were shared by virtually all members of the Church of England, whether they were Puritans or not, during the Elizabethan period. The new ideas about episcopal divine right and free will which came to the fore during the 1590s were quite another matter. They raised the possibility of a serious theological split at some future date in a Church of England which had, since Elizabeth's accession, been dominated by Calvinist theology. The fact that the new King, James I, was very unsympathetic to these new ideas for almost his entire reign, concealed the danger until the middle 1620s, but after that date the attempts of a sympathetic monarch and archbishop, Charles I and Laud, to force them on the Church as a whole made for the most serious unrest and division within it.

Whitgift's lack of sympathy with the new theological trends of the 1590s did not prevent him from making direct assaults on the Puritans which resulted in the suppression of the organized Presbyterian movement in the Church. Professor Collinson has demonstrated (56, *127 ff*; 182, *222 ff*) that the Presbyterian movement, in so far as it existed at all, was largely a response to rather than a cause of Whitgift's measures. In 1583, soon after his appointment to Canterbury, he required all clergymen to subscribe to three articles acknowledging the royal supremacy, affirming that the Prayer Book contained 'nothing in it contrary to the word of God' and asserting that the Thirty-nine Articles were 'agreeable to the word of God' [G.4(18)]. Some Puritans had misgivings about the first and third of these articles and none could conscientiously accept the second. The penalty for failure to subscribe was ultimately deprivation and the result was a crisis for the Church which was only resolved in 1584. Whitgift came under strong pressure both at Court and in the Council from noblemen like Leicester and ministers like Burghley and Walsingham who were both sympathetic to Puritanism and particularly critical of Whitgift's policies at a time when the government needed all the support it could get in face of the danger of Catholic subversion, and in the later months of 1584 he was forced to allow the majority of doubtful ministers to subscribe with qualifications. As a result only a very few were deprived of their livings. Professor Collinson believes that this was the 'great crisis' of the Church of England during Elizabeth's reign. 'If three or four hundred ministers had been . . . under . . . threat of deprivation when parliament assembled in November 1584', he wrote, 'episcopacy might be unknown in the British Isles today.' Whitgift's reluctant and tardy moderation had 'ensured the ultimate confusion of his enemies' (182, 272). Whatever the truth of such speculations it seems clear that it was largely as a result of Whitgift's actions in 1583–84 that John Field, the great organizer of Elizabethan Puritanism, and others among the more extreme leaders of the movement set about their 'grand design'of creating a secret Presbyterian Church within the Church of England. They had mixed success, but embryo Presbyterian organizations were set up in many parts of the country and there were provincial and national meetings which anticipated the creation of a full-scale Presbyterian alternative to the Established Church.

The Presbyterian movement, however, fell apart in the early 1590s. Field died in 1588. He was irreplaceable as an organizer and the defeat of the Armada in the same year, by removing the immediate threat of Catholic invasion, helped to create a favourable atmosphere for the attack which Whitgift, supported by the Queen and Lord Chancellor Hatton, launched against Presbyterianism in the years from 1589 onwards. In 1589 and 1590 the papers of the leading Presbyterians were seized and searched for incriminating evidence. The material collected in this way was used in the prosecution of nine ministers, including Thomas Cartwright, the intellectual father of Elizabethan Presbyterianism, before the Courts of High Commission and Star Chamber. The government hoped to prove that Presbyterianism had been a seditious threat to the State, and although it failed to do so it had succeeded by 1592 in driving the Presbyterian movement underground for the rest of the reign.

The destruction of Presbyterianism as an organized force in the early 1590s must not, however, be allowed to conceal the reality of the influence of Puritan religion in England during the last decade of Elizabeth's reign. Presbyterianism had found its strongest supporters among the clergy, and the fact that most of the Puritan laity were moderate men who were prepared to accept episcopal government of the Church helps to explain the ease with which Whitgift was able to defeat the Presbyterians. It is probable, indeed, that moderate Puritanism, despite of the deaths between 1588 and 1590 of some of its most important supporters in the Privy Council – men like Leicester, Mildmay and Walsingham – grew stronger than ever among the laity during the 1590s, a period which saw ever more vocal demands for a preaching ministry, a growing emphasis on the sanctity of the sabbath and the increased prominence of 'household religion', in which pious heads of families took the lead in spiritual exercises for the benefit of themselves, their families and their servants (196). The distinguished preacher and scholar William Perkins was, in Professor Hill's words, the 'high priest' (196, *502*) of this moderate Puritanism which was the dominant strand of opinion in criticism of the Established Church from the 1590s until the re-emergence in strength of Presbyterianism and the development of much more extreme forms of religious opposition during the 1640s.

By 1603, then, it was clear that the more extreme Puritans – the Presbyterians – had failed to make a lasting impact on the Elizabethan Church. The Separatists, always a tiny minority, did show considerable energy during the 1580s and 1590s under the leadership of Robert Browne, Henry Barrow and John Greenwood, but the last two were executed for sedition in 1593 and these men – whether or not one thinks they should be included among the Puritans (see above, Ch. 18) – held congregationalist views which placed them well outside the mainstream Puritanism of the rest of the Church's Protestant critics who, whether they favoured an episcopalian or a Presbyterian form of government, were united in their belief in a Church which was organized and disciplined on a national basis. We have seen (Ch. 18) the extent of the contribution which Puritan influences had made to the life of the Church of England by 1588 and, although the 1590s saw the destruction of organized Presbyterianism, these years also confirmed and indeed increased the influence of moderate Puritan values among many members of the laity who were more than ever devoted to the ideals of a preaching ministry and who laid increasing stress on the development within their own households of Puritan spiritual values which emphasized Bible reading and the sanctity of the sabbath.

The 1590s, which saw these important trends in the history of Puritanism, probably witnessed a growth in the number of Catholics in some areas of the country and a decline in their strength in other regions. It certainly saw the development of an open split in the Catholic camp between those who refused to consider any compromise with the government and those who wanted a *modus vivendi* with it. The records of recusancy suggest a dramatic rise in the number of Catholics in parts of the North during the later years of the reign (24). In the West Riding of Yorkshire, for example, there were 271 presentments for recusancy in 1575–80 and 1,136 in 1603–4. In Lancashire the number of recorded recusants grew from about 300 in 1578 to over 3,500 in 1604. Such figures represent the energy of the local officials who prosecuted suspected Catholics as well as the actual size of the recusant community, but after making all allowances for a substantial improvement in the machinery of prosecution during the later years of the reign, the reality of the increase in Catholic numbers can hardly be in doubt. Moreover, there were many men and women in the North who had Catholic sympathies but conformed reluctantly to the Anglican settlement, attending its services only occasionally and with marked lack of enthusiasm. The story in the south and east of the country is rather different. There the number of committed Catholics almost certainly fell during the later years of the reign. In Kent, for example, the Catholic community suffered a 'severe battering' during the last two decades of the century and by 1603 it had been reduced to a few 'small pockets of active Catholics' (251, *179*). Such mixed fortunes for Catholicism in different areas of the country doubtless reflected both the relative fertility of the conservative North as a field for the missionary priests to plough as well as the greater effectiveness of the government's penal measures against Catholics in those parts of the country which lay nearer to the centre of its power in London. Elizabeth in 1603 no less than in 1588 could take comfort from the fact that, taking England as a whole, the Catholic threat was being contained. Indeed, by 1603 the government could hope to benefit from divisions within the Catholic leadership which came into the open during the 1590s.

As we have seen (in Chapter 18), the Catholic laity demonstrated its essential loyalty to the Crown during Armada year, but there were always some priests – especially Jesuits – who took the view that it was their duty and that of their co-religionists to give aid to a Catholic foreign power which was prepared to invade England to overthrow the heretical Elizabeth. Other priests inclined much more to the patriotic views of the overwhelming mass of the Catholic laity, and between 1595 and 1603 these two factions within the priesthood fought bitter battles over the possibility of coming to terms with the Protestant Establishment (56; 186; 189). We cannot go into the details of the 'Wisbech stirs' of 1595 onwards or into the 'archpriest controversy' of the years after 1598. These were largely concerned with disputes within the priesthood about the government of the Catholic Church in England, but the 'Appellants' of 1598, a group of secular priests who appealed to Rome against the activities of the archpriest, George Blackwell, and his Jesuit and secular supporters were anxious to reach an agreement with the English government which would allow them to exercise their priestly office in return for a denial of the Pope's power to depose secular rulers. The upshot was a government proclamation of November 1602 which distinguished between the Jesuits and their allies and those secular priests who were prepared to come to terms with the government. The former were ordered to leave the country, but the latter, provided they would swear allegiance to the Queen, were to receive more favourable treatment. Thirteen Appellants then signed a 'Protestation' of allegiance to the Queen in January 1603 in which they explicitly denied the deposing power of the Pope. This seemed a promising scenario for a compromise between the Appellants and the government, but that proved impossible. It soon became apparent that the two sides had been talking at cross purposes. The government was only prepared to grant immunity from the penal laws to priests who both took an oath of allegiance to the Crown and at the same time agreed to cease performance of their priestly functions in England. The Appellants, on the other hand, were only prepared to take such an oath if the government allowed them freedom to exercise their spiritual ministry. The failure of the negotiations should not, however, be allowed to conceal their significance. The events of the 1590s showed the beginnings of a shift of attitudes both among some members of the priesthood towards the government and of the government towards a Catholic community, the great bulk of whose members were increasingly quietist in their attitudes (188). These were the first tentative indications that a formal agreement between an English government and at least a section of the Catholic priesthood might some day be possible.

CHAPTER 29

Revolt in Ireland and the crisis of Elizabeth's last years

Thomas Cromwell had not tried to create an Irish national state. His policy, as we have seen, had been to impose effective rule in the Pale and the earldoms, which he regarded as part of the unitary state centred on London which he was trying to create (see above Ch. 3). That policy did not survive his execution and from 1540 until the end of Henry VIII's reign the most important figure in Irish history was the new Lord Deputy, Sir Anthony St Leger, a Kentish gentleman who had gained first-hand experience of Ireland when he paid a six-month visit to the country in 1537 as head of a Royal Commission. His chief adviser was Thomas Cusack, an Anglo-Irish lawyer who had estates in County Meath (89). Together they aimed at creating by friendship and conciliation a united national state for Ireland. The essential aspect of their policy was the idea of 'surrender and regrant'. The Gaelic chieftains were asked to become feudal vassals of the Crown and to introduce English law and customs into their territories. In return the King would formally recognize their previously insecure titles to their lands. Moreover, Henry was persuaded in 1541 to assume the title of King of Ireland, thus giving a national superstructure for the whole island. It was an ambitious plan which, if it had succeeded, might have brought about the reconciliation of English, Anglo-Irish and Gaelic interests. It did, however, need time if it was to have a chance, and the expenses which it involved – St Leger made large financial concessions to the Irish lords who accepted conciliation – became too great for Henry to bear during the last years of his life when he was desperate for money for his French and Scottish Wars. Between 1547 and 1558 the whole policy collapsed in ruins with first of all forcible attempts to export the Edwardian Reformation wholesale to Ireland and then, under Mary, the occupation of Irish lands by English settlers. St Leger did have two further periods of office as Lord Deputy after his recall in 1548, but neither Edward's nor Mary's governments trusted him fully, and the decision, in 1557 during the lord deputyship of the earl of Sussex to seize and confiscate the territories of Leix and Offaly to the west of the Pale and 'plant' them with English settlers was a very clear sign that conciliation had been replaced by aggression. The stage was set for the Irish troubles of Elizabeth's reign which culminated in the Great Revolt of the 1590s.

The history of Ireland under Elizabeth is essentially the story of the forcible imposition of English authority over the whole island, and Dr Canny has argued that the late 1560s and early 1570s were a vital period in the story (162). During these years the English government accepted plans put forward by Sir Henry Sidney, who was Lord Deputy for much of the period between 1565 and 1578, for the assertion of English authority throughout the island. The intention was to reduce the financial drain which Ireland was making on the Crown's revenues –

it was hoped that in due course it would become self-financing – but by 1576 it was clear that this hope was a mirage. Meanwhile, Sidney's assaults on the Gaelic lordships had provoked fierce resistance, and despite his establishment of presidencies in Munster and Connaught which were designed to control these provinces in the English interest, it was obvious by the end of his second deputy-ship in 1578 that his work had merely led to a further alienation between English and Irish. The Irish, always regarded as inferior by their English masters, were now seen as little better than barbarians, while the English were more and more disliked by the Irish – now increasingly influenced by the Counter-Reformation – both as Protestants and as conquerors. This growing hostility was especially important as Sidney's attitudes survived his departure from the Irish scene. Many of the soldiers and adventurers who had served in Ireland during his deputyship remained behind to press for a continuing policy of conquest which would serve both their thirst for military adventure and their hopes of enrichment, and his four successors as Lord Deputy were all strongly influenced by his ideas. In these circumstances it is not surprising that there was a major rebellion in 1579–83 which involved papal and Spanish help for the rebels and demonstrated the dangers which Counter-Reformation Catholicism might pose for English authority in the island. These dangers became much greater with the outbreak of war with Spain in 1585, and the Great Irish Revolt of the 1590s was an obvious opportunity for the Spaniards to assail England through her back door in Ireland.

Rebellion broke out in Ulster in 1593, but it was not until Hugh O'Neill, earl of Tyrone, came out into the open against the government in 1595 that its full significance became apparent (51). O'Neill was a man of considerable military and political abilities and he succeeded in creating a reasonably disciplined army out of the motley Irish forces which he gathered together. In 1598, in Ulster, he inflicted a crushing defeat on the English Army at the Battle of the Yellow Ford. This led to a virtual collapse of English authority in most of the island and when the earl of Essex arrived in 1599 as Lord Lieutenant he had the unenviable task of facing what amounted to a national revolt against English rule. His period in office, as is well known, was a further disaster for England's position. He marched south instead of attacking the greater threat which came from the North, and when he did move towards Ulster on the direct orders of the Queen it was only to arrange a truce with Tyrone before rushing back to London to defend himself against Elizabeth's fury. At the beginning of 1600, therefore, Tyrone was by far the most powerful man in Ireland and any idea of a speedy English conquest of the whole island seemed ludicrously optimistic. This, however, is what was accomplished between 1600 and 1603 by the new Lord Deputy, Charles Blount, Lord Mountjoy, a remarkable general whose outstanding energy during his deputyship included the waging of winter campaigns, virtually unknown at the time.[1] In September 1601, when he had already made very considerable progress in subduing the revolt, Spanish aid for the rebels arrived in the form of a force of 4,000 experienced infantry which landed at Kinsale on the south coast. Mountjoy invested the town and in December, in a crucial battle, he heavily defeated the forces which Tyrone had marched south from Ulster to aid his Spanish allies. The latter surrendered at the beginning of 1602 and the war was virtually over, though Tyrone himself did not give up the struggle until six days after Elizabeth's death.

By 1603, then, England had imposed her political and military authority throughout Ireland. It was a considerable achievement, especially as only a few years earlier it looked as if the whole island might rapidly slip out of English control and become a base for foreign attacks in the Catholic interest on the English mainland at a time when Elizabeth was growing old and the issue of the succession was increasingly dominating English politics. The genius of Mountjoy ensured that Ireland was no threat at the time of the Queen's death, but the English conquest of the island had been a very heavy drain on the Exchequer – it had cost about £2m. to crush the rebellion (56), by far the greatest expense the Queen faced during the later 1590s, despite the continuance of the Spanish War at sea and on the Continent. It must also be emphasized that the English success was narrowly political; attempts to impose the Reformation on the Irish people had clearly failed by 1603. Indeed, the reigns of Edward VI and Elizabeth, with their efforts to Protestantize Ireland, ensured that the island would become a pawn in papal and Spanish attempts for the overthrow of Elizabeth. The failure of these should not be allowed to conceal the success of the Catholic Church in keeping the allegiance of the great mass of Irishmen. Throughout Elizabeth's reign both the Gaelic Irish and the old Anglo-Irish colonial stock remained true to the Catholic religion. It was only the 'new English' conquerors who were Protestants and that merely increased the dislike which most Irishmen already felt for them on other grounds (51).

Despite the growing religious and cultural alienation of most Irishmen from England during the Elizabethan period, they could take some satisfaction from the fact that in 1603 Irish Catholics still retained the vast bulk of the land in their hands. The various 'plantations' of Mary's and Elizabeth's reigns did, of course, see land forfeitures, but it was not until the seventeenth century, from the reign of James I onwards, that really massive quantities of Irish land were expropriated for the benefit of immigrant Protestants. The Irish problem is still, of course, in the 1980s, one of the great issues troubling Britain. Many of the roots of that problem up to and beyond the nineteenth century were laid in the Tudor period: the establishment of political and military control by a minority English establishment; the attempt to impose Protestantism and its rejection by the vast mass of Irishmen; the growing English belief in Irish inferiority and the resentments which this produced in Ireland. When, in the seventeenth century, Englishmen and Scotsmen began to expropriate huge quantities of Irish land the situation reached the fully explosive state which was to continue for so many years. The Irish problem, which has undoubtedly been one of the most important aspects of the modern British experience was, therefore, firmly founded in the Tudor period, though it was to be still further intensified during the following century.

Elizabeth's death, as we have seen, virtually coincided with Tyrone's surrender and one of her principal legacies to James I was an Ireland which, if sullen and resentful, was fully under English control. It is always emphasized that James's accession, by uniting the crowns of Scotland and England, allowed the exercise of a single royal authority from Land's End to John O'Groats; it should more often be added that he was the first English sovereign who exercised something approaching effective political authority over the whole of Ireland. His accession to the English throne was peaceful [B]. The way had been paved by Cecil in a famous correspondence with James conducted in great secrecy during the last two years of Elizabeth's life (56, *389 ff*). The Queen herself was much less popular in the last years of her reign than is sometimes supposed. The very difficult economic conditions, the indecisive and expensive war with Spain and the execution of Essex – more popular with the mass of the population than he deserved to be – all cast their shadow over the last years of a woman who seemed more and more to have outlived both her time and her usefulness. Sir Francis Bacon made the point when he wrote that Elizabeth could not 'answer the votes either of servants or subjects to a full contentment, especially in her latter days, when the continuance of her reign (which extended to five and forty years) might discover in people their natural desire and inclination towards change so that a new court and a new reign were not to many unwelcome'. Sir Walter Ralegh said the same thing both much more succinctly and much more cruelly when he coined the pointed epigram that the Queen was 'a lady whom time had surprised'.[2]

Such remarks provide a salutary corrective to tendencies to treat 'the Elizabethan period' as a single era of virtually uninterrupted triumphs and remind us that the early, middle and later periods of the reign each had its own atmosphere and problems. We have already assessed the extent of the Elizabethan achievement by 1585 (Ch. 27), and we have now noted both the failures and the successes of the Queen's later years. Any temptation to exaggerate her successes during the last decade of the reign should be resisted, but it must also be emphasized that although the years 1585–1603 *did* see the beginnings of 'the breakdown of the Elizabethan system', its achievements at the time of the Queen's death were still considerable. The Spanish War had ensured the preservation of the country's basic independence and security – the most important task which any government had to fulfil; the country's domestic peace was maintained – the Essex rebellion was hardly a serious threat; and in ecclesiastical affairs organized Presbyterianism had been crushed and Catholic divisions had been exploited. On the other hand, the conquest of Ireland, though it provided a short-term political success for Elizabeth's government at the very end of the reign, contained the seeds of future tragedy; Catholicism had not been rooted out in England; moderate Puritanism was arguably stronger in the 1590s than it had ever been before; and the beginning of new theological trends in the English Church, associated with assertions of the divine right of bishops and attacks on the doctrine of predestination, raised the dangerous if still remote possibility of a major ideological split in an establishment which had hitherto been dominated by Calvinist theology. The grimness of life for the bulk of the English people during the 1590s was due primarily to natural disasters over which the government had no control, but the inflationary pressures of war undoubtedly added to their sufferings. The financial consequences of the war contributed to the growth of corruption in the public service and the collapse of the classic Elizabethan patronage system which were among the most important domestic political developments of the last years of the reign. Above all, perhaps, the government's need for war finance in these years imposed strains on its relationships both with Parliament and with the localities which emphasized the important truth that the English governmental system was not well equipped to raise the money for war. The end, during Edward VI's reign, of the very brief 'era of affluence' for the Crown which had characterized the later years of Henry VIII meant that the English State could not afford expensive wars. Elizabeth had the very good sense to realize this, and the Spanish War which she entered so reluctantly was an essential, defensive struggle for English survival. Even so, the tensions which it provoked in a county like Norfolk and which soon made themselves felt in Parliament were a warning that future governments should try very hard to keep out of armed conflicts. It was hardly a lesson which James I needed to be taught – like Elizabeth he knew the virtues of peace – but Charles I's government forgot the lesson both in the later 1620s and then again in the years after 1637. It was that more than anything else which led to a major crisis for the monarchy in 1628–29 and the complete collapse of its effective authority in England in 1639–40.

---

1. For Mountjoy, C. Falls, *Mountjoy, Elizabethan General* (1955).
2. Quoted by J. Hurstfield, *Man as a Prisoner of his Past: the Elizabethan Experience* (A. H. Dodd Memorial Lecture, Cardiff, 1980), p. 16.

CHAPTER 30

The reign of James I to 1618: I

James I's reception in England on his journey southwards to take up his inheritance reflected both Elizabeth's relative lack of popularity during her declining years and the natural inclination of most men to welcome a new face and hope for personal benefits from a new regime. The King himself long remembered the warmth of that initial reception. 'Shall it ever be blotted out of my mind', he stated in 1604 in his first speech to an English Parliament, 'how at my first entry into this kingdom, the people of all sorts rid and ran, nay rather flew to meet me; their eyes flaming nothing but sparkles of affection, their mouths and tongues uttering nothing but sounds of joy, their hands, feet and all the rest of their members in their gestures discovering a passionate longing and earnestness to meet and embrace their new Sovereign.'[1] He was already a very experienced ruler when he took over the government of England. He had inherited the Scottish throne on his mother's abdication in 1567 when he was only a year old and during the whole of his adult life he had wrestled, with considerable success, with the problem of Scotland (48; 49; 57). The dominant secular issue of his Scottish reign was relations with the nobility, and James saw the need to cooperate with and conciliate them, a policy he continued after 1603. He had considerable success in controlling the Estates, the Scottish Parliament, in the interests of the Crown and showed similar skill in the ecclesiastical field, where he disliked the power and pretensions of the Presbyterian ministers with their insistence on the Church's divine right to control its own affairs free from the authority of either Crown or Estates. In 1596 their leader, Andrew Melville, lectured him on his subordination to the Church and called him 'God's silly vassal', but already by 1603 James had managed to begin the revival of episcopacy within the Scottish Church and to assert his control over the General Assembly. He continued both his ecclesiastical and his secular policies with much success after he became King of England, and although it is arguable that the sureness of his touch in Scottish affairs declined during the last years of his life there can be no doubt about the general success of his Scottish reign. He was one of the most successful of all the kings of Scotland.

The Scottish economy seems to have expanded during James's reign with significant developments in trade and industry (57), but the country remained a poor one, dominated by a primitive agriculture 'static in technology and inefficient in organisation' (57, 60), and the King, in the years before 1603, had unrealistic dreams about the wealth of England or at least about the extent to which he would be able to exploit English resources for his own purposes. He was a man of generous instincts, reluctant to say no to courtiers and ministers who plagued him with demands for rewards after 1603 and he had other admirable personal qualities, like his love of learning and above all, perhaps, of peace. He had also, of course, much less praiseworthy traits in his character, notably an overweening vanity and a total inability to draw the line between legitimate generosity and gross extravagance. His greatest weakness as an administrator in England was his laziness. He believed that the details of government could be left to subordinates while he went out hunting, and although in the early years of the reign the labours of Robert Cecil, who was his chief minister until 1612, concealed some of the worst results of this royal neglect it inevitably meant that James did not have a firm grip on the English governmental machine. This became a serious matter under Cecil's much less able successors, and it may be that James, who had been used to a less elaborate administrative set-up in Scotland, was misled by his successful conduct of government there into thinking that he could deal equally well with English affairs on an informal and *ad hoc* basis.

James certainly had one piece of good fortune during the early years of his English reign; the economic situation in the country was generally favourable [I; K]. In the years between 1603 and 1618 there were only three bad harvests – those of 1608, 1613 and 1617 – and the reign opened with a succession of four good ones during the years 1603–06 (227). In this favourable situation agricultural prices actually fell back between 1600 and 1610 from their very high level of the 1590s, and in 1620 food prices were only 10 per cent above the level of 1600, a figure which can be compared with the 36 per cent rise which took place during the single decade of the 1590s. When food prices were relatively stable men and women had enough money to buy other goods, and the 15 per cent rise in industrial prices between 1600 and 1620 suggests that there was an increasing demand for non-essentials which most people could not afford during times of rocketing food prices (224). This general impression of relative prosperity is reinforced by the trade boom which followed the ending of the Spanish War in 1604 and lasted until 1614 (57; 242). English trade during James's reign remained overwhelmingly intra-European, centred on London, and dominated by the export of woollen cloth, but there was a significant shift of trade from northern to southern Europe which was associated with the growing prominence of the 'new draperies', lighter and cheaper cloths which took a larger share of exports at the expense of the heavy woollens which had traditionally been dominant. There was also a notable growth of trade with the Far East through the East India Company which established itself as a major force in trade during the reign. The post-war boom ended abruptly in 1614 when a period of long-term decline began. The Cockayne Project of 1614, an ill-advised attempt to insist on the export of fully finished English cloth rather than on unfinished articles, met with such hostility from the Dutch finishing industry that the export of English cloth fell catastrophically. The outbreak of the Thirty Years War followed in 1618 and this led to currency manipulations and debasements in Germany and eastern Europe which were disastrous for English cloth exports there. The worst of the crisis was over by the end of the reign, but there was no recovery of the optimistic spirit among the merchant community which had marked the boom decade of 1604–14.

If the economic situation during the early years of the reign was a favourable one, the financial prospects for the Crown were a good deal less rosy. Here James inherited a difficult position. Elizabeth's last years had been marked by an extreme miserliness which had displeased her courtiers and ministers, and the advent of a new sovereign in 1603 and the end of war in 1604 raised both their hopes and their expectations. At the same time James's limited ordinary revenue had to pay for rising government costs – he, unlike Elizabeth, had a wife and family to support – and he was not helped by continuing if moderating inflation during his reign. James was eager to respond to the demands for money and favours which engulfed him, but he simply could not afford to be too generous without either substantial parliamentary assistance or a large increase in his ordinary revenue. The former could be expected only in time of war or national emergency and Parliament – though it did vote subsidies in 1606 and 1610 – did not expect to make large extraordinary grants after the conclusion of peace in 1604. The reluctance of the Commons to open their purses was reinforced by James's quite unjustified extravagances. It was one thing to argue that greater liberality to royal servants was needed in the new reign, quite another to justify what actually happened. Royal expenditure soared during the first decade of James's rule. During the last years of Elizabeth ordinary expenditure had been not more and perhaps substantially less than £300,000 per annum. By 1614 it was running at well over £500,000 a year. The vast bulk of that increase went not on such items as defence and the diplomatic service, which saw only modest rises in their costs, but in the household, the wardrobe, the chamber, the privy purse and in fees and annuities. That represented expenditure by James on his own pleas-ures and also his lavish rewards to favourites and courtiers, many of them Scotsmen like Sir John Ramsay and Lord Hume (60; 244). John Hoskyns, a prominent parliamentary critic of royal extravagance, voiced a general feeling when he stated in the House of Commons in 1610 that 'the royal cistern had a leak, which, till it were stopped, all our consultation to bring money unto it was of little use'.[2]

If Parliament would not rescue the King from his financial troubles by a series of extraordinary grants the obvious solution, given James's clear determination to spend large sums of money both on himself and on his servants, was to increase the ordinary revenue at his disposal. We have stressed that Elizabeth and Burghley, by refusing to attempt such increases, had passed on to James a much less favourable financial inheritance than was necessary (see above, Ch. 13). Robert Cecil, created earl of Salisbury in 1605 and made Lord Treasurer in 1608, had none of his father's inhibitions about increasing ordinary revenue. Obvious sources were the Crown lands, feudal dues and customs duties. Salisbury turned his attention to each of them and in 1610 he attempted a fundamental reorgan-ization of the whole financial system with his Great Contract of that year.

At the end of Elizabeth's reign the royal land revenues, including those of the duchy of Lancaster, were about £100,000 a year. Between 1604 and 1610 Salisbury and Buckhurst, his predecessor as Lord Treasurer, inspired perhaps by rapidly rising rents on private estates, instituted a series of surveys designed to reveal the extent to which the royal lands were undervalued and thus provide the basis for a substantial raising of rents and entry fines. The surveys were not, however, completed for the whole country and their abandonment, due perhaps to the other pressures on Salisbury's time during the last three years of his life, meant that there was no hope of raising Crown rents to anything approaching an economic level. By 1619, as a result of land sales since the beginning of the reign and of lax Exchequer administration, the total revenue from land had fallen to about £85,000 a year (75; 244). Salisbury had already succeeded in substantially increasing the revenue from feudal dues in the last years of Elizabeth and the continuance of this policy of maximizing the Crown's gains from this source meant that wardship revenue stood at between £23,000 and £25,000 per annum during the period 1613–15 and reached over £36,000 a year by the end of the reign (87). This was a modest success for the government, but Salisbury's great achievement was in increasing customs duties. This was done partly by farming the customs, partly by the introduction of impositions [N] and a new Book of Rates in 1608 (245; 249). The collection of customs by poorly paid officials directly appointed by the government led to much inefficiency and corruption and during Elizabeth's reign experiments were tried with farming parts of the customs out to businessmen who paid an annual rent to the Crown and then kept for themselves any gains which they made above that sum. In 1604 this system was extended to the main body of the customs which were leased at a rent of £112,000 per annum. This was successively raised in subsequent years and in 1614 it stood at £140,000 a year. That was an increase of nearly a half on the late Elizabethan receipts and the Jacobean customs were further boosted by the new impositions of 1608. The path for these was prepared by the important legal judgment in 1606 in Bate's case [E. 4(16)] in which the judges ruled in favour of the Crown and against John Bate, a Levant Company merchant who had refused to pay an import duty on his currants on the grounds that it had not been approved by Parliament, merely imposed by royal authority. He was on weak legal ground – impositions had been introduced both under Mary and Elizabeth – and the judges' formal recognition of the Crown's right to impose duties for the regulation of trade meant that Salisbury could safely go ahead with the additional customs which he introduced two years later. These, combined with a new Book of Rates, brought in about £70,000 a year and had profound constitutional implications. If the government could raise customs revenue at will in this way, then it would have at its disposal a flexible and expanding source of income which might render parliamentary supply less and less important. This possibility was not lost on members of the House of Commons as the conflicts between MPs and government over impositions in the parliamentary sessions of 1610 and 1614 showed very clearly.

Salisbury's success in increasing customs duties has to be set against the failure of his Great Contract of 1610 (55). That was introduced at the end of the only really sustained effort which was made during the reign to reduce the royal debt. That had risen to over £700,000 in 1606 but by 1610, by using the parliamentary subsidies granted in 1606 and by selling Crown lands, Salisbury had reduced it to under £300,000. The Great Contract which he then laid before Parliament looked at first as if it might succeed in changing the whole basis of the royal finances. In the form in which it was provisionally agreed in the summer of 1610 it abolished the Crown's rights of warship [N] and purveyance [N] in return for an annual sum of £200,000. During the summer recess, however, both King and

Commons had second thoughts, and after Parliament resumed the agreement foundered amidst mutual recriminations. Its failure marked both the last attempt at a radical reorganization of the financial system before the Civil War and the loss of James's confidence in Salisbury, the scheme's principal protagonist. The latter's success in increasing customs revenue by over £100,000 a year during his ministry was not enough to close the gap between revenue and expenditure. This could only have been done if there had been substantial economies as well, and James was not prepared to make these at this stage in his reign. As a result, deficits on the ordinary account continued and the royal debt rose once more, reaching £900,000 in 1618.[3] By that time James had had to face the parliamentary storms over impositions which were features of both the 1610 and 1614 sessions.

It is, indeed, traditional to stress the difficulties which arose between James and his Parliaments, both in the years before and after 1618. In the earlier period there were two Parliaments, that of 1604–10, which had five sessions, and the 'Addled Parliament' of 1614 (57; 58; 121; 123; 124). In both of these there were serious differences between Crown and Commons. In 1604 the Buckinghamshire election case [E. 4(11)], which turned upon the claim of the Commons to decide disputed elections to the House themselves rather than to leave the decision to Chancery led to an assertion by the King that 'they derived all matters of privilege from him and by his grant', and to a counter-assertion by MPs in the Apology, a document justifying their proceedings in 1604, that their privileges and liberties were their 'right and due inheritance, no less than . . . lands and goods [E. 4 (12)]'. It was a point of principle about which members of the House clearly felt very strongly and the issue was to rumble on during the reign and give rise to a serious clash in the Parliament of 1621. James's desire for a real as opposed to a merely personal union between England and Scotland also brought him into conflict with the Commons. In his opening speech to Parliament in 1604 he made an eloquent and picturesque plea for such a union [E. 4(13)]. 'What God hath conjoined', he said, 'let no man separate. I am the husband and all the whole isle is my lawful wife. I am the head and it is the body. I am the shepherd and it is the flock. I hope, therefore, no man will be so unreasonable as to think that I, that am a Christian king under the Gospel, should be a polygamist and husband to two wives.'[4] James was too sensible to expect rapid progress towards complete legal and institutional unity, but he hoped that both his English and Scottish Parliaments would take modest steps in that direction in the early years of his reign. The issue of the union was the principal business in his English Parliament both in the first session of 1604 [E. 4(14)] and in the third, in 1606–7, but to James's dismay English MPs showed a contempt for and hostility towards the Scots which led them to reject many of his initial proposals, including a suggestion for mutual naturalization [E. 4(15)]. Hostile English laws against the Scots were, it is true, repealed, but the King, angry and disillusioned by the narrow attitudes of his English subjects, never forgave the Commons for their virtual rejection of what was for him undoubtedly the most important parliamentary project of his entire reign. The two sessions of 1610 saw the failure of the Great Contract and the clash over impositions [E. 4(17)]. The latter gave rise to those fears among MPs which were voiced by James Whitelocke, when he argued that 'if this power of imposing were quietly settled in our kings, considering what is the greatest use they make of assembling of parliaments, which is the supply of money, I do not see any likelihood to hope for other meetings in that kind because they would provide themselves by that other means' (11, *262*). In 1614 a court faction headed by Henry Howard, earl of Northampton, opposed the summoning of another Parliament and when the advice was ignored spread rumours in the Commons about government attempts to pack Parliament which, together with further disputes about impositions, were largely responsible for wrecking the session and securing the dissolution of the Parliament before any legislation could be passed.

The clashes over impositions have been described by Professor Russell as 'the only profound constitutional conflict of the reign of James I' (121, *9*). It can be argued that the disputes over the status of Commons privileges were of equal significance, but, whatever the final verdict on this matter, there is no doubt that Russell is right when he argues that the result of the impositions debates was a virtually total victory for the Crown. The 1614 Parliament was the only occasion in James's reign when the Commons threatened to withhold supply to enforce their wishes, and the King rejected their attempt to blackmail him into giving up impositions in return for a sum unlikely to have exceeded two subsidies. It is easy to see why he did so. Subsidies, which had been falling in value throughout the Tudor period and continued to do so in the early seventeenth century were now worth only about £70,000 each. In purely financial terms there was no inducement to James to give up his annual revenue of £70,000 from impositions unless he got a grant of at least one subsidy *every year*. There were no conceivable circumstances in which Parliaments would have made such grants in peacetime, and the inability or unwillingness of early Stuart Houses of Commons to satisfy the Crown's financial needs has led modern scholars to lay increasing stress on their impotence in clashes with the government.

If recent scholarship has increasingly questioned traditional ideas about the growing power of Parliament in James's reign and indeed in the whole period before the 1640s, it has also shed grave doubts on the idea that Jacobean parliamentary conflicts were due primarily to the stupidity and inflexibility of James himself. In his important study of the 1604 session (58, *43 ff*) Mr Munden has demonstrated the King's moderate and conciliatory attitude for much of the time and has suggested that most of the trouble may have come from a group of great lords at Court and in the Council who misled the King about the intentions of the Commons. Members of Parliament certainly laid great stress in the Apology on the activities of 'misinformers', and it may be that the clashes of court factions which certainly helped to wreck the 1614 Parliament and which provoked further trouble in the 1621 and 1624 sessions were already at work behind the scenes in 1604. Members of the Upper House may have played a significant role in that session in encouraging the Commons opposition to James's plans for closer union between England and Scotland which, as we have seen, came to a head in 1607, and the role of the House of Lords, which certainly remained of the greatest importance throughout James's reign, requires further study both in terms of its own institutional importance and in its relationships with and influence on the Lower House.

So far we have stressed the difficulties between Crown and Parliament during the early years of James's reign and there is no doubt that the conflicts which did occur were real and in some cases of considerable importance. It is essential to remember, however, that the first Parliament of the reign showed that it could still fulfil in full its primary task; the passage of legislation which represented that co-operation between King, Lords and Commons which was considered necessary both for the successful government of the realm and as a general demonstration both at home and abroad of the health of the body politic. During its five sessions the 1604–10 Parliament passed 97 public and 130 private Acts, a total of 227 pieces of legislation (1, vol. IV). It was, however, the end of an era. The legislative output of the six following Parliaments, those of 1614–28, was meagre (see Ch. 32). The passage of legislation involved the successful organization of business in both Houses of Parliament, but during James's reign there was little sign of those government legislative programmes which had been characteristic of the Tudor period. This fact helps to lend credence to the idea, popularized by Professor Notestein (120), that private MPs 'won the initiative' in James's reign by wresting control of Commons procedure from the government. We cannot examine the details of this argument, which turns largely on the significance of developments in the committee system, but it has recently been challenged in an article[5] which seems sure to lead to further debate about the relative roles of privy councillors and private members in the Jacobean House of Commons.

The role of court factions in the parliamentary history of James's reign, now increasingly appreciated by historians, is a reminder that in the early seventeenth century, no less than under Elizabeth, the ambitions of the factions and the workings of the patronage machine were the central feature of political life (the best study is (78) see also (57, 140 *ff*)). Until his death in 1612 Salisbury remained James's principal minister but he had to share power both with the Howard clan, headed by the earls of Northampton, Suffolk and Nottingham, and with Scottish favourites like Ramsay, Hume, Dunbar and Hay. These men were all greedy for wealth as well as influence. Salisbury amassed an enormous fortune during James's reign and Northampton, who had had little money in 1603 was worth perhaps £80,000 at his death in 1614. Salisbury combined personal greed with a genuine desire for reforming the royal finances and it has recently been argued that the generally maligned Northampton was also a major protagonist of reform.[6] The Scottish favourites were more blatant in their extravagance and corruption and their attitude can be epitomized by that of Lord Hay whose motto was 'spend and God will send'. As Master of the Wardrobe he certainly spent money like water and God, in the person of James I, saw that he was never in need. Clarendon estimated that 'in a very jovial life', he spent 'above four hundred thousand pounds which . . . he received from the Crown', but 'left not a house or acre of land to be remembered by' (quoted (78, *16*)). These years also saw the rise to influence of the first major favourite of James's English reign. Robert Carr, created Viscount Rochester in 1611 and earl of Somerset in 1613, was a Scot who had come to England on James's accession and after Salisbury's death he shared influence with the Howards. Their supremacy was challenged by a group of peers which included the earl of Pembroke and Archbishop Abbot who disliked both the Howards' Catholic sympathies and their friendship towards Spain. These men put forward George Villiers, a remarkably handsome young gentleman from Leicestershire, as a candidate for James's favour, and after Somerset had lost power, as a result of involvement in a squalid murder case, Villiers came to dominate the Court. The dismissal of Lord Treasurer Howard in 1618 on charges of gross corruption meant the effective end of Howard influence and inaugurated an era in which Villiers, now earl of Buckingham, was the greatest power in the land. James's undoubted homosexual tendencies found their full expression in his love for his new favourite. 'Christ had his John, and I have my George', he told his Privy Council in 1617 with pathetic and near-blasphemous satisfaction and the flood of royal bounty which had been spread widely in the early years of the reign was heavily concentrated in its latter part on the new prime favourite who, with his large and rapacious family, was an army in himself. Villiers had, however, come to power as a protagonist of reform against the corruptions of Howard rule before 1618, and his initial patronage of Cranfield suggests that he was sincere enough in his desire for administrative improvements provided these did not touch his own pleasures and profits too closely. By 1618, therefore, Buckingham had achieved, with James's full consent, the position which Essex had craved and Elizabeth had refused in 1601: a dominant role in the distribution of patronage and with it effective control of the government. It was the climax of years of political intrigue at Court in which James had shown himself unable or unwilling to stem a flood of corruption which was epitomized by the open sale of honours and offices.

The early years of the reign also saw the well-known clashes between the King and the greatest lawyer of the day, Sir Edward Coke, over legal issues which have often been discussed in the wider context of a conflict between the royal prerogative and the common law. The significance of such disputes should not, however, be exaggerated. Professor Jones has shown (*57, 177 ff*) that the idea of conflict between prerogative and common law courts misrepresents a more complex reality in which the difficulties between them should be seen as part of a wider problem of defining the boundaries of the respective jurisdictions of *all* courts. The differences between James and Coke were real enough on specific issues – like whether or not judges had the right to resist discussions with the King in cases in which the royal prerogative was involved (the 'case of commendams' which led to Coke's dismissal in 1616). Such differences should however, be seen in the context of general agreement on fundamental constitutional principles; the dominant constitutional theory in Jacobean England, shared by King, parliamentarians and lawyers alike, was of a balanced constitution founded on certain inalienable rights possessed by both Crown and subjects. The parliamentary debates in 1610, which revealed that King and Commons differed profoundly over the point of balance in the matter of impositions, showed equally clearly that they were committed to the fundamentals of a rule of law which would safeguard both

King and people (57; 105). There was no struggle for sovereignty in Jacobean England, and James's difficulties with Coke arose to a considerable extent from his genuine if sometimes misguided desire to set himself up as a peacemaker when different parts of the legal system came into conflict. He was very eager to play a similar peacemaking role in the English Church and in the wider world of European diplomacy.

---

1. *CJ*, I, p. 142.
2. E. R. Foster, ed., *Proceedings in Parliament 1610*, II (New Haven, 1966), p. 344.
3. R. Ashton, 'Deficit finance in the reign of James I', *EcHR*, 2nd ser., **10** (1957–58), 15 ff.
4. *CJ*, I, p. 143.
5. S. Lambert, 'Procedure in the House of Commons in the early Stuart period', *EHR*, **95** (1980), 753 ff.
6. L. L. Peck, 'Problems in Jacobean administration: was Henry Howard, earl of Northampton a reformer?', *HJ*, **19** (1976), 831 ff.

CHAPTER 31

The reign of James I to 1618: II

James's accession aroused hopes among both Catholics and Puritans and appre-hensions in the minds of the hierarchy. During the 1590s, when his main ambition had been to secure his peaceful succession to the English throne and he had needed as much support south of the border as he could get, he had given the impression that both the Protestant critics of the Establishment and Catholic dissenters might hope for better things under his rule. Archbishop Whitgift and the hierarchy on the other hand, who knew that James was a learned man, deeply interested in theology, were not sure of his personal preferences. It soon became apparent that both the hopes of the Catholics and the Puritans and the fears of the hierarchy had been exaggerated, but that is not to say that James was totally unsympathetic to the critics of the Church. The fundamentals of church govern-ment in England, where respectful bishops were a welcome change from outspoken Scottish Presbyterian ministers like Andrew Melville, suited him very well, but he was prepared to look at the Church for himself and try to improve any details which he thought required reformation. It was an attitude which fitted in well with his general conception of his role as a British Solomon, whose wisdom would, he expected, be accepted by all.

James's theological position augured well for his rule over the Church. He had been brought up in the stern Calvinism which was prevalent in Scotland, and although he disliked the Presbyterian ethos of the Scottish Kirk he had no quarrel with its theology, This meant that when he came to England he found himself in the mainstream Elizabethan theological tradition with its emphasis on predestin-ation. He had no time for either the free-will views or ideas about episcopal divine right which had begun to stir up controversy in the Church during the 1590s, and he combined these theological attitudes with a determination to do something about the 'plunder of the Church' which had begun in Henry VIII's time with the dissolution of the monasteries and had continued during the reigns of Edward VI and Elizabeth with attacks on the chantries and on episcopal lands. In 1604 an Act of Parliament (1 Jac. 1, c. 3) forbade bishops to alienate their lands, even to the Crown. James also proposed to hand back to the Church impropriated tithes in royal hands – these, he suggested, should be used to augment the stipends of impoverished ministers – and he wanted the universities to follow his example. The latter proposals, however, came to nothing in face of the hostility of Whitgift and Bancroft who persuaded the King to drop them on the grounds that they would reduce the resources available for the support of the élite of learned men in the ministry and thus have a serious long-term effect on the quality of the clergy (192).

Whitgift and Bancroft were similarly dismayed by James's decision to hold a conference to discuss Puritan criticisms of the Church, but on this issue they were not able to persuade him to change his mind. On his journey south from Scotland Puritan ministers had presented him with the Millenary Petition [G.5(20)], in which they set out their grievances against the Established Church and asked for redress. The result was the Hampton Court Conference held in January 1604. The petition was essentially a moderate document (182), reflecting in its demands the Puritan attitudes which had come to the fore during the 1590s following the suppression of Presbyterianism. It is clear that the petitioners were looking for changes in detail in the government and worship of the Church rather than fundamental limitations on the powers of the bishops or drastic changes in the Prayer Book. As they themselves put it in the preamble to the petition they were not 'factious men affecting a popular parity in the Church, nor . . . schismatics aiming at the dissolution of the state ecclesiastical' (i.e. neither Presbyterians nor Separatists); instead they were looking for the redress of 'divers abuses . . ., particular griefs'. At the conference itself James showed his independence of both hierarchy and Puritans, deciding some matters in favour of one side, some in favour of the other (194). The upshot was a long list of reforms affecting both the government and the worship of the Church and Professor Curtis has argued that this shows that the Conference 'cannot be called a total failure' (194, *12*). It is difficult to deny the validity of that conclusion, but many of the intended reforms were never carried out. The committees which were set up to put the decisions into practice were dominated by hostile bishops and James did not superintend their work closely. Here is a striking illustration of one of his great weaknesses. He was too lazy to follow up decisions at the level at which they mattered most – their execution. There was, however, a notable exception. The conference is best remembered today for its authorization of a new translation of the Bible. Its appearance owed much to James's continuing interest and support between 1604 and 1611 (76) and with its sonorous prose, which has echoed from so many pulpits from his day into the twentieth century and which has influenced both the content and the style of so much great literature, it is perhaps the King's most important and lasting memorial. Only a few Puritan ministers – probably not more than ninety (195) – were so dissatisfied with the results of Hampton Court that they were prepared to refuse conformity to the Prayer Book as it was reissued with minor modifications in 1604. They were deprived of their livings as a result of Bancroft's campaign against them in 1605. These men represented the small minority of ministers who had regarded the ceremonies and polity of the Elizabethan Church as actually unlawful. They had remained within the Church in Elizabeth's reign hoping for better days under her successor, but when it was plain that James was, at best, prepared to make only minor concessions to accomodate them they felt that they had to leave. Professor Collinson has argued with conviction (182, *463 ff*) that these 'radical' Puritans were the ancestors of the independents who were to make such an impact on English religious and political life during the middle years of the seventeenth century, but in James's reign their influence was small. This is understandable in the general context of the King's ecclesiastical policy in the years after Hampton Court.

It is true that there was a good deal of grumbling about religion in the Parliament of 1604–10, with the introduction by the Commons of bills against pluralities, to provide for a learned ministry, to remove scandalous ministers, and to prevent clergymen being appointed JPs. These summed up typical seventeenth-century lay views about the clergy, 'that they should be poor, pure, learned and unworldly' (10, *127*). They infuriated James, who regarded them as an unwarranted interference with his right to legislate for the Church. There was also Commons support for the deprived ministers and complaints about the fact that the canons of 1604 – the most important official statement yet about the doctrines and practice of the Church – had been issued on the authority of Crown and Convocation alone and not submitted for parliamentary approval. Such differences between King and Commons recall similar Elizabethan conflicts. They never got out of hand and the second decade of James's reign in particular was a period of general peace for the Church which reminded some moderate Puritans of the hopeful days of Grindal in the 1570s. Here James's appointments to the episcopal bench were very relevant. Most bishoprics went, as Dr Cross has put it, 'to men whose theology and ideas on church government closely resembled those of the early Elizabethan bishops' (53, *33*). Bancroft, who was archbishop of Canterbury from 1604 to 1610 was an obvious exception and it was his attitude which caused a good deal of the religious trouble in Parliament during the first decade of the reign. In 1611, however, James appointed as his successor George Abbot, a Calvinist of the old school, and he nominated one Calvinist to succeed another in the see of York in 1606 when Toby Mathew was appointed on the death of Mathew Hutton. Both Matthew and Abbot continued in office into Charles I's reign. Other key sees, most notably London, were filled with similarly committed Calvinists and there was a general impression of 'harmony' between the hierarchy and the Puritans during these years (60). James gave his whole-hearted support to the Calvinist pronouncements of the Synod of Dort in the United Provinces in 1618–19, and in these circumstances it is not surprising that he was very unsympathetic to supporters of 'Arminian' views in England, men like William Laud, who rejected orthodox ideas about predestination. Laud became a client of Buckingham, but when the favourite pressed for his advancement the King replied with much insight, 'He hath a restless spirit and cannot see when matters are well, but loves to toss and change and bring things to a pitch of reformation in his own brain.' It was not until 1621, and then with a very bad grace, that he agreed to Laud's appointment to the minor Welsh see of St David's (197). The best evidence for the religious peace of the later years of James is indeed to be found in the Parliaments of 1621 and 1624, which were 'remarkable for a dearth of religious grievances' (60, *128*), founded on the satisfaction of godly gentlemen in the House of Commons that they had a King who was both theologically sound and prepared to allow a wide practical degree of toleration to moderate Puritans.

In general, then, the Puritans could take a good deal of satisfaction from James's reign, as, indeed, could all moderate members of the Church of England. It was a time of basic religious peace for the Crown's Protestant subjects, a peace which seems all the more impressive in the light of the religious turmoils within the Church during the late 1620s and 1630s. As far as the Catholics are concerned, James's actions were founded on a combination of his personal outlook and the need to take account of the views of his Protestant subjects, considerations which sometimes pulled him in different directions. He himself had a much more moderate attitude towards the Catholic faith then the vast majority of his people. In 1604, in a speech to Parliament, he acknowledged Rome 'to be our Mother Church, although defiled with some infirmities and corruptions'. He did not want it destroyed, but reformed, and indicated that he was prepared to consider a measure of practical toleration for peaceable members of the Catholic laity. On the other hand, he fulminated against those clergy who supported the deposing power of the Pope (186, *365–6*). James's attitude to Catholics should be seen, in fact, in the context of his general desire for peace in all areas of life, both domestic and international. It was bound up with his foreign policy, in which he saw himself as the peacemaker of Europe, marrying his children into both Protestant and Catholic princely families on the European continent.

The attitude of his Protestant subjects, forcibly expressed in Parliament, was very different. They demanded the rigorous application of the penal laws and, on occasion, still harsher measures against recusants. The King obviously had to take their views into account, and, as a result, during his reign his practical attitude to Catholics varied. After the Gunpowder Plot of 1605 he supported harsh measures against them, but as the reign went on and his desire for a Catholic marriage for his son Charles came to the forefront there was a considerable degree of toleration. Over twenty Catholic priests were executed during the reign, but it is notable that there were no executions after 1618 (186). Indeed, as Professor Bossy has stressed (57, *91 ff*), the Gunpowder Plot marks the end of an era in English Catholic history. In the Elizabethan period Catholics had been heavily engaged in political intrigues and plots; after 1605 they relapsed into political quietism. The number of Catholics grew from about 35,000 in 1603 to perhaps 60,000 in 1640 and the number of priests in the same period from about 250 to 750. Much of the increase certainly took place in James's reign. During the Jacobean period, too, the priesthood seems to have concentrated more and more on the household education of the gentry families who continued to provide the backbone of the Catholic cause. There are interesting similarities here with the development of Puritan 'household' religion from the 1590s onwards and the upshot, as far as the Catholics were concerned, was the formation of a distinctive community which, during James's reign, became increasingly well instructed in its religion and in the moral and social duties which went with it. It can be argued that James's attitude towards this increasingly numerous but increasingly docile Catholic population was on the whole sensible and reasonably successful. He permitted enough practical toleration to prevent further outbreaks of violence like the quite untypical Gunpowder Plot, but maintained sufficient restrictions to prevent an unacceptably large number of conversions. As a result, the Catholic community in 1625 was not a serious threat either to the authority of the Established Church or to the integrity of the English nation state.

The more vocal Puritans, who were critical of James's relative leniency towards Catholics at home, were equally resentful of what they saw as his pro-Catholic attitudes abroad, especially during the second decade of his reign. In Scotland, before his accession to the English throne, James had tried to stay on good terms with all foreign powers. He put his success down to his own skill, but it was very largely due to the fact that Scotland was of minor importance in European politics; Continental rulers were pleased enough to have James's friendship but their general goodwill was largely a mark of indifference to Scottish attitudes. James assumed that the same policy of general friendship would work equally well when he ruled the much more important kingdom of England, but his genuine desire to act as the peacemaker and arbiter of Europe, always a very difficult task, proved impossible in the international situation which prevailed after 1618.[1] He started sensibly by concluding an honourable peace with Spain in 1604, in which he refused to give up English claims to trading or settlement rights in the New World and asserted the entitlement of the Dutch, who continued the struggle, to raise volunteers and money in England. From then on he tried hard to bring about and preserve peace in Europe. He played an important role as mediator in securing the Dutch truce with Spain in 1609 and a significant part in settling the succession to the duchies of Julich, Cleves and Berg, territories on the lower Rhine which threatened to embroil much of Europe in war between 1609 and 1614. His policy of keeping on good terms with both Catholic and Protestant powers is best reflected, however, in his marriage plans for his children. Negotiations for such marriages began soon after his accession to the English throne and in 1613 there was much rejoicing in England when he married his daughter Elizabeth to Frederick, the young Elector Palatine, one of the principal Protestant princes in Germany. English Protestants, so delighted at this seeming commitment by James to the Protestant camp, were much less pleased with the plans for a Catholic match for the two royal princes, Henry and Charles. Repeated negotiations to marry Henry to a Spanish infanta had come to nothing by the time of his death in 1612, but from 1614 onwards discussions were resumed between England and Spain with the prospective bridegroom now the new heir to the throne, Prince Charles. James continued these negotiations for most of the rest of his life, and the hostility which they aroused among his Protestant subects was well expressed near the end of his reign in the Parliaments of 1621 and 1624 (125; 126; 127).

James's desire to act as a European conciliator was a tribute to his genuine humanity and love of peace as well as a reflection of his vanity, but it could hardly survive the outbreak of the Thirty Years War in 1618. The most serious criticism of his foreign policy is, indeed, his failure to appreciate the significance of the changed international situation after that date. The Spanish invasion of the Palatinate, the hereditary territory of his son-in-law, in 1620, should have indicated to him that he now had to choose between a Spanish match for Charles and support of the Protestant cause. England was the principal Protestant power in Europe, and the choice should have been as clear to him as it was to most of his subjects, but James could not easily abandon the policies of a lifetime. The last years of his reign saw the ageing King struggling to reconcile his Protestant duties with his continuing desire for friendship with Spain. That was by then a hopeless task, but the tragic collapse of James's dreams at the end of his reign should not blind us to the basic realism which lay behind his passion for peace. He knew that England was not equipped either militarily or financially to fight a war, and in these circumstances his determination to avoid armed conflict was eminently sensible. The effectiveness of his methods of preserving peace are open to debate – it has been argued, for example, that he should have tried to reach an effective understanding with France in the early years of the reign[2] – but it will no longer do to see him as the dupe of Gondomar, the influential Spanish ambassador to England between 1613 and 1622[3] or to repeat Professor Willson's conclusion that his foreign policy 'proved the most shameful failure of his reign' (76, *273*). There was much to be said for it in practical terms during the period up to 1618, and even after that date, although James showed a fundamental lack of realism in trying both to aid his daughter and her husband and at the same time to preserve good relations with Spain, his belief that a major war could only bring trouble for England was amply confirmed by the events of 1625–29.

Whatever the judgement on James's foreign policy, there can be no doubt that his reign marked a crucial stage in the history of British overseas expansion, with the establishment of the first permanent English colonies (47, 57). James, as we have seen, had refused in 1604 to recognize Spanish claims to a monopoly of trade and territory in most of the New World and in practice the Spanish authorities made little difficulty about most of the English colonial ventures of the reign. Settlements were founded at Jamestown in Virginia in 1607 and at Plymouth in New England in 1620, each originally with about 100 inhabitants. In 1624, when Virginia had a population of about 1,200, it was taken over by the Crown as England's first royal colony, although the settlers received confirmation of privileges which had originally been granted to them by the Virginia Company in 1619 and which included the right to make laws for their own benefit. By the end of the reign, too, tobacco had been established in the colony as a valuable export crop and, despite the King's dislike of smoking, expressed in his well-known *Counterblast to Tobacco* (see Ch. 26), its popularity in England secured the colony's economic future for many years. The Plymouth settlement remained small during James's reign, with 200 inhabitants in 1624. Unlike the Virginia colonists they were Separatists who had fled from England to America via the United Provinces to obtain freedom of worship. The great migration of moderate Puritans, who had remained within the Church of England, only took place during the Laudian regime of Charles I's reign, when they founded further colonies in New England. The colonies, which had such great long-term significance for England's economic expansion, did not begin to make a sizeable contribution to English trade until the middle of the seventeenth century, and in James's reign colonial propagandists stressed the value of tropical colonies as opposed to those in temperate climates. Tropical settlements, it was argued, might provide not only gold and silver but also goods like silk, pepper, dyestuffs and sugar, which would help the balance of trade by ending England's dependence on foreigners for the supply of such exotic wares. Such hopes led to several vain attempts to establish an English settlement in Guiana on the borders of Brazil. Interest in that area culminated in Ralegh's voyage of 1617, but his embroilment with Spaniards against the King's express orders led to his execution the following year by an enraged James who was quickly accused of sacrificing one of the greatest Englishmen of the day to unrealistic dreams of Spanish friendship. James's greed for the fabled wealth of Guiana had persuaded him to permit Ralegh's expedition, but despite its obvious desire to subserve England's economic interests the government's attitude towards colonial enterprise was essentially a passive one; limited to encouraging and supporting the efforts of private enterprise.

The English colonists in America had numerous encounters with native Indians, whom they regarded as barbarians, and a similar attitude towards the Gaelic inhabitants of Ireland was common among their fellow countrymen who stayed at home. James expressed this feeling well in 1612 when he wrote of the virtues of bringing 'civility, order and government amongst . . . [the] barbarous and unsubjected' Irish (76, 322). The great Irish event of his reign was the plantation of a colony of English and Scots in Ulster (51). The excuse for this was the flight abroad in 1607 of Tyrone and other Ulster lords who were afraid that the growth of English authority was depriving them of their traditional status. What followed was a catastrophe for the native Irish in the north of the country. The greater part of the territory of six counties was confiscated by the government and assigned primarily to English and Scottish immigrants and to army officers who had served the Crown in Ulster. The Irish were left with between a quarter and a fifth of the land. Ulster had previously been a Gaelic stronghold, but the great plantation of James's reign made it a British colony and established the foundations of the modern Northern Ireland problem by the permanent introduction of a large Protestant Scottish and English population which dominated the political and social scene. The dismal prospects for future social peace which the Ulster plantation implied were reinforced by the continuing and futile efforts of the government to force Protestantism on the native population throughout Ireland. By 1618 all the main ingredients of the 'Irish Problem' as it has continued until the present day, were already present. That is a sad epitaph on James's Irish rule.

A survey of the British scene in 1618 suggests, however, that James's failures were matched by his successes. He was the first sovereign to rule the three kingdoms of England, Scotland and Ireland and his failures in Ireland should be set against his successes in Scotland. He had made peace with Spain and had successfully kept England out of war. The first permanent English colonies in America had been established. The Church of England was essentially at peace and the English Catholics, while increasing in number, were no longer a serious political threat to the State. He had had his troubles with Parliament, but had emerged as the *de facto* victor in the important struggles over impositions in 1610 and 1614. Moreover, parliamentary legislation, the concrete sign of co-operation between Crown, Lords and Commons, had continued to be passed in considerable quantities in the sessions of 1604–10. His clashes with Sir Edward Coke should be seen essentially as a difference of personalities rather than as a conflict of principle between the prerogative and the common law. On the other side of the coin, the years between 1612 and 1618, which were marked by the ascendancy of the Howards at Court, were arguably the most blatant period of corruption in England during the whole century and a half from the reign of Henry VIII to the

266

Restoration, and the exactions of courtiers during these years contributed to the financial difficulties which were James's most intractable problem and which had inflated his debt to some £900,000 by 1618. The fact that the debt was caused largely by the King's chronic inability to economize was no consolation, and the failure of the Great Contract in 1610 was an indication that radical plans to change the whole basis of the financial system were unlikely to succeed. Most distressing of all in James's eyes, was the failure of his pet project for institutional union between England and Scotland to make significant progress. This and the dislike which his new English subjects openly showed for his Scottish countrymen clearly enraged him. Historians have talked a great deal about the growing disillusion-ment of many Englishmen with James as his reign progressed. There is clearly much truth in this, though a great deal of their discontent probably stemmed from their anti-Catholic and anti-Spanish prejudices as much as from intrinsic demerits in the King's policies. Perhaps we should hear more of *the King's* growing disil-lusionment with England. This was very evident by the middle years of the reign[4] and was founded largely on the feeling that he was not appreciated by his subjects at his true worth. In this situation he found more and more consolation in his love for his favourite Buckingham, whose shadow loomed so large during the last years of the reign.

---

1. There has been no satisfactory general discussion of James's foreign policy since the first five volumes of S. R. Gardiner's *History of England* (1883). J. R. Jones, *Britain and Europe in the Seventeenth Century* (1966), Ch. 2, is an illuminating sketch. G. M. D. Howat, *Stuart and Cromwellian Foreign Policy* (1974), Chs 2 and 3, is superficial.
2. M. Lee, Jnr, *James I and Henry IV, An Essay in English Foreign Policy, 1603–10* (Urbana, Ill., 1970).
3. A realistic view of the relationship between James I and Gondomar is now provided by C. H. Carter, 'Gondomar: ambassador to James I', *HJ*, **7** (1964), 189 ff.
4. The point is stressed by Dr J. Wormald in *History*, **68**, 187 ff.

CHAPTER 32

The ascendancy of Buckingham, 1618–1628

During the ten years between 1618 and 1628 Buckingham, who was made a duke in 1623 – the first non-royal duke in England since Norfolk's execution in 1572 – dominated the Court as the prime favourite first of all of James I and then of Charles I. The fact that he was able to retain power on James's death and indeed to exercise an even more complete dominance for the rest of his life over the very different Charles suggests that it is wrong to dismiss him as a man of no abilities. He had the skill to monopolize the counsels of two successive kings of England – no mean feat – and he showed some abilities as an administrator after 1619 when, as Lord High Admiral, he helped to repair the damage done to the fleet during the preceding period of Howard control (77; 78; 144). James was in the last years of his reign while Buckingham's star was in the ascendant, but the traditional picture of a King sinking into dotage between 1618 and 1625, 'a broken, debauched and repulsive old man' (76, *425*), is a caricature which will not bear examination. James had suffered for much of his life from a painful illness which has been – rather unconvincingly – identified as porphyria, a rare metabolic disease, and the extensive medical notes left by his physician record that his health deteriorated considerably after 1618 with severe attacks of pain sometimes accompanied by delirium.[1] Recent work on the last years of his rule, especially on its religious and parliamentary history, has, however, rightly laid stress on the considerable skill and shrewdness which the sick and ageing James could still show (125–7). Charles, from the start of his reign, had a much less sure touch. He talked a lot less about his powers and rights than James but was much more energetic than his fundamentally lazy father and his desire to get things done, granted the limited and inadequate administrative machinery for enforcing the royal will in the localities, was a recipe for trouble, as the events of the 1630s showed very clearly. Moreover, as a committed Arminian he embarked on religious policies which were anathema not merely to Puritans but to the vast mass of moderate members of the Church of England. His attempt to enforce his religious views on reluctant subjects has rightly been described by Professor Russell as a 'catastrophic' (125, *423*) error, but its disastrous impact was not felt in the country at large until the 1630s, and during the early years of his reign, the period 1625–30, the difficulties which England faced were primarily due to the wars with Spain and France to which Buckingham and Charles committed a largely reluctant nation.

The events of Buckingham's ascendancy were played out against a background of better-than-average agricultural conditions, marred principally by a bad harvest in 1622 which led to famine in the spring of 1623 [I]. Food prices were virtually static during the 1620s as a whole and the price of industrial goods actually fell [K], but this cessation of inflationary pressures at home was not matched by a similarly happy situation for England's foreign trade which had hardly begun to recover from the problems of the early 1620s before it was again depressed by plague and war at the beginning of Charles I's reign (57; 224; 227–8; 242). The war with Spain to which England was virtually committed before the death of James lasted from 1625 until 1630, and between 1627 and 1629 the country was also at war with France. The story of the events leading up to the Spanish War is well known (36, Vol. 5) and cannot be retold here, but it is important to remember that from the outbreak of the Thirty Years War in 1618 until Charles's and Buckingham's trip to Madrid in 1623 James, despite all the international difficulties and domestic opposition which his plans encountered, continued to press for a Spanish match for his son. When his two 'sweet boys' returned from their Spanish trip determined on war he was horrified. They ruthlessly wore down his opposition though he did die before effective war began in 1625. Having abandoned the Spanish match Buckingham turned to France, but Charles's marriage to the French princess, Henrietta Maria, soon after his accession was unpopular in England because of the Queen's nationality as well as her Catholicism and it did not prevent the outbreak of war with France in 1627. England was therefore committed to war with the two great Catholic powers at the same time – a situation she had always traditionally sought to avoid – and Buckingham and Charles must be severely criticized for allowing this to happen, even though the French must take their share of the blame for the events which led up to war (125). (For a much more favourable view of Buckingham's foreign policy than the one given here see (77).)

The importance of the wars of 1625–30 for the domestic history of England was very great. The threat or reality of war was the principal reason for the summoning of the five Parliaments which met between 1621 and 1629 (125). The initial enthusiasm of MPs for war with Spain, probably never as great as historians once believed, soon evaporated when its cost and its failures became clear. The Parliaments of the 1620s voted twelve subsidies altogether, but these were not nearly sufficient to meet the government's needs, and it had to resort to borrowing, to the sale of Crown lands and to such dubious unparliamentary taxation as the forced loan of 1626. Moreover, war preparations in the localities put enormous pressures on county societies, with such inevitably unpopular measures as the levying of local rates to support the large number of troops impressed and the billeting of such troops on civilian households where their conduct gave rise to cries of anguish from many of the afflicted householders (for the effects in Kent see (251, *328 ff*)). The stresses which resulted between local society and central government were inevitably reflected in the Parliaments of 1626 and 1628–29, when MPs were vociferous both in their condemnation of the burdens which the conflicts had imposed on their constituents and in their denunciations of the failures which marked the conduct of the war, most notably such fiascos as the Cadiz expedition of 1625 and Buckingham's 1627 voyage to the island of Rhé to help the French Huguenots. The events of those years in fact hammered home the lesson which had been increasingly obvious to intelligent observers since Mary's reign; that England could not afford major wars. The defensive war against Spain in the 1590s, a conflict generally accepted in England as necessary, had put severe strains on society in the last years of Elizabeth. The offensive wars against Spain and France during the later 1620s, much less obviously in England's interests, much less successful, and conducted by a royal favourite who was already very unpopular on other grounds, led to a major crisis between the Crown and the governing classes at the end of the 1620s, a crisis symbolized by the widespread resistance to the forced loan of 1626 and by the Petition of Right, which MPs compelled the King to accept in the Parliament of 1628.

The forced loan of 1626 reflected the crisis in the Crown's finances caused by war, but the military conflicts of the years from 1625 onwards merely exacerbated and intensified royal financial difficulties which were the most persistent problem of the later as they had been of the earlier years of James I's reign. Buckingham was certainly no more and perhaps indeed less corrupt than the Howard clan whom he ousted from power in 1618 and 1619, but he made very large demands upon the royal purse, which were highly unpopular among those members of the political nation who did not have his favour and who were therefore virtually excluded from the Crown's patronage. Buckingham had not forgotten in 1618, however, that he had been helped to power by reformers who were anxious to attack the gross administrative malpractices of the Howard era and he was not averse to reforms which did not affect his own profits and comforts too closely. His most important protégé was Lionel Cranfield, a merchant who rose to the highest financial office in the State and who was, apart from Robert Cecil, the most important reformer of James's reign (on Cranfield see (78; 220)). Cranfield obtained his first government post in 1615, but it was only from 1618 onwards that he achieved high office, becoming Master of the Wardrobe, Master of the Wards, a Treasury commissioner and finally, in 1621, Lord Treasurer. From 1618 until 1624 he was, apart from Buckingham, the most important royal minister. He tried to increase revenue by such methods as raising the rent of the customs farmers and the rates of customs duty paid by aliens, but his most notable efforts were directed towards reducing expenditure. He made onslaughts on the royal household, the Navy Office, the Ordnance Office, and the wardrobe, applying strict business methods to their notoriously lax administration. He saved £18,000 a year in the household alone, where his vigilant eye extended as far as 'cast off fish, bottles and jugs'. These were now to be sold. In the wardrobe, where he succeeded the profligate Hay, there was enormous scope for savings. Cranfield cut its costs to the Crown from £42,000 to £20,000 a year and still made a considerable profit for himself. Such economies, applied over a long period, might in due course have wiped out the £900,000 debt of 1618, but time was not on Cranfield's side. The darkening international situation of the early 1620s led to increased spending on defence and foreign embassies and Cranfield found, in any event, that his retrenchments were not allowed to eat into Buckingham's own enormous profits. He himself was vulnerable to attack from his own large private gains, and when he opposed Buckingham's determined efforts to drag the country into war with Spain in 1624, the favourite joined with parliamentary supporters of the war to overcome James's reluctance to dispense with his treasurer. At the time of his fall the debt stood at about £1 m. (245). Like James, Cranfield saw clearly that England could not afford war, and he was the most important single casualty of the determination of the prince and Buckingham to get their way on that issue.

The Parliament of 1624, which impeached [N] Cranfield, was the second of the five Parliaments of the 1620s, and historians have rightly stressed the importance of these assemblies (the definitive treatment is now (125)). The principal reason for their summons, as we have seen, was the financial needs of the Crown, faced with the prospect or reality of war, and only the Parliament of 1626, in which the Commons demanded the impeachment of Buckingham in return for supply refused to vote subsidies. Those of 1621 and 1625 each granted two, that of 1624 three [E.4(24)], and that of 1628 five. It was not nearly enough, but it is only fair to remember that the Commons, despite their hostility to the ineffective conduct of the war and their other grievances against Buckingham, were not prepared to starve the Crown totally of funds at a time of national danger. The most notable financial innovation of these years, the Commons decision in 1625 to grant the Crown tonnage and poundage – the ancient customs duties which they traditionally voted for life at the beginning of each reign – for one year only, was a result of the impositions disputes of James I's reign. In 1624 Solicitor-General Heath had cited the Jacobean Tonnage and Poundage Act of 1604 as a justification for the levying of impositions, and the Commons in 1625 were determined to produce an Act which would not allow such an interpretation. There was no time to do this in 1625, hence the grant for one year only. They fully intended to give Charles these traditional revenues for life in due course, but the Lords' refusal to pass the grant for one year only left him with no legal authority at all for the main body of the customs. He continued to collect them none the less and the ill feeling which this unfortunate situation created continued until the time of the Long Parliament.

The money which the Crown demanded in each of the Parliaments of the 1620s to subserve its foreign policy and the resulting wars obviously helped to keep the European situation in the forefront of members' minds, but the Commons plea to James in 1621 that Charles should not marry a Spanish princess, a petition which enraged him as an invasion of the royal prerogative, seems to have arisen from a misunderstanding by members, who believed that James would welcome their intervention. They could not, however, ignore his subsequent insistence, harking back to the disputes of 1604, that their privileges were at his mercy [E.4(21)], and the result was the Protestation of 1621 in which they insisted that these privileges were 'the ancient and undoubted birthright and inheritance of the subjects of England' [E.4(22)]. That important statement of principle was issued four years before the outbreak of war with Spain. The Petition of Right [E.5(26)], the most important document produced by the Parliament of 1628, was, in contrast, the result of three years of unsuccessful war, and it stated the Commons four main grievances arising from that war; the martial law and billeting of troops on civilians which accompanied it, the arbitrary taxation, represented by the forced loan of 1626, which followed it, and the arbitrary imprisonment of the 'five knights' [E.5(25)] and others who refused to pay the loan. The King finally assented to the Petition and the Commons thought that they had won his acceptance of their interpretation of the law on these points. Charles, however, took the view that the Petition was only a statement of existing law, which he interpreted in a rather different way from the Commons. He showed that very clearly by such actions as the imprisonment of Sir John Eliot following the dissolution of Parliament in 1629.

The subsidy debates and the conflicts over the rights of the Commons and of the subject which were such important issues in the Parliaments of the 1620s had their origins, in the last resort, in the needs of the Crown's foreign policy during that decade. The attempt to impeach Buckingham, which dominated proceedings in the 1626 session, also turned to a considerable extent on the nation's fortunes abroad. It reflected the failure of the war effort which he was directing as well as his general unpopularity as the engrosser of royal patronage. It probably had little to do with his open conversion to Arminianism, which was still too recent to have penetrated deeply into the minds of most members. There is no doubt, however, that the issue of Arminianism was of growing importance in the Parliaments of the later 1620s, when members expressed increasing alarm at the dangers it posed to the peace of the Church. The climax came in 1629 when the Speaker was forcibly held down in his chair while three resolutions condemning Ariminianism and tonnage and poundage not voted by Parliament were passed. That was an act of violence which gave Charles justification for dispensing with Parliament. It was the beginning of eleven years of 'personal rule'.

The disagreements between the Crown and the Parliaments of the 1620s were universally regarded as shameful, a sign of failure. King, Lords and Commons all stressed the need to work together to secure the stability of the State at home and to preserve England's international reputation, which suffered severely when the king and the representatives of his people were seen to be at loggerheads, especially when the country was at war. The struggles of court factions, which spilled into the parliamentary arena during the 1620s just as they had done in 1614, were symbols of the determination of individuals to increase their power in the State at the expense of their rivals while at the same time giving support to policies which they favoured. Elizabeth had managed to prevent faction rivalries from playing too great a part in parliamentary proceedings, but the events of the Parliaments of 1621 and 1624, in which the careers of Bacon and Cranfield were ruined, and those of 1626, in which a formidable coalition in Lords and Commons made a determined effort to remove Buckingham, show that James and Charles could not match her skills in this field (78; 125). Moreover. the Parliaments of the 1620s were very unsuccessful as legislative institutions ((1, vols IV, V); vol. V contains the statutes from the beginning of Charles I's reign). As we saw, the Parliament of 1604–10 passed a large number of public and private Acts. The story between 1610 and 1640 was very different. Three of the six Parliaments of these years – those of 1614, 1621 and 1626 passed no legislation at all (apart from the 1621 Subsidy Acts) and the Parliaments of 1625 and 1628 passed only eight statutes each, all of them public Acts. The record of the 1624 session, with thirty-five public and thirty-eight private Acts, was certainly very respectable, but it must be seen in the context of the general lack of legislation in the thirty years after 1610. Most strikingly, perhaps, it was the only Parliament in that entire generation to pass *any* private legislation at all, and as individuals and the localities which they represented saw such private legislation as one of the most important reasons for parliamentary assemblies, that fact alone would suggest that the Parliaments of the period were failing in one at least of their primary tasks. The failure to pass laws was the result of a variety of factors: the inability of the Parliaments to manage their business effectively; the lack of government legislative programmes; the time consumed by high political matters, such as impeachment proceedings; and the early dissolution of some of the Parliaments as a result of their conflicts with the Crown.

The Parliaments of the 1620s, failures as legislative institutions, also failed to impose their will upon the Crown (121). During that decade they attacked the collection of impositions and tonnage and poundage without parliamentary consent, tried to remove Buckingham from Charles I's side and denounced such measures as the forced loan of 1626 and the arbitrary imprisonment of those who refused to pay it. Despite threats to withhold supply unless they got their way they won none of these battles, though they thought in 1628, at the time of the passage of the Petition of Right, that they had gained some of their objectives. The King's actions in 1629 and afterwards showed them their mistake. It can be argued, however, that the Parliaments of the period did have three conspicuous successes. One of these was the revival in 1621 of the medieval procedure of impeachment [E.4(20)] by which the Commons could lay charges of crimes or oppressions by individuals before the Lords.[2] Such proceedings could not force a monarch to get rid of a minister whom he was determined to keep – witness the Buckingham case in 1626 – but it did put a powerful propaganda weapon into the hands of peers and MPs. More significant, perhaps, was the growing recognition both among MPs and in the country at large that the House of Commons was 'the representative of the people'. The researches of Professor Derek Hirst (122) have taught us that a much higher proportion of the population than used to be supposed had the right to vote at elections and that MPs generally paid a great deal of attention to the wishes and grievances of their constituents. The significance of this in the war years of the 1620s, when the localities were groaning under the burdens of the government's financial and military demands, hardly needs emphasizing. By the time of the Parliament of 1628–29, and indeed before it, it was clear that the complaints which members of the Commons were expressing were not merely their own but represented the disgruntled voices of ordinary men and women in the shires. It was an ominous warning to the Crown. The third parliamentary success was the development of a 'true opposition' by 1628, a body of Commons opinion united in principle against what it saw as the government's arbitrary actions during the two previous years and determined to erect a bulwark against such actions in the future. It was this attitude which produced the Petition of Right, and although the irresponsible actions of some leaders of the Commons, like Eliot and Holles, wrecked the session of 1629 and enabled Charles to inaugurate his period of personal rule with an attack on the excesses of his parliamentary opponents, the wide spectrum of opposition which existed by then in both the Commons and the country at large to the King's conduct of government since his accession was a warning that, if he continued in highly unpopular causes, then any future demands upon the country for money for military purposes might provoke a reaction of incalculable consequences.

The parliamentary attacks on Buckingham in 1626 reflected dislike among the political nation at his engrossment of patronage as well as dismay at his unsuccessful conduct of the war. Buckingham's control of patronage was never complete even when his authority was at its height under Charles I – William Herbert, earl of Pembroke, for example, still had independent influence (125) – but he did achieve as nearly monopolistic a position as any man could reasonably hope to attain. He worked hard at placing and rewarding his clients and accumulated for himself an enormous income, which he spent lavishly, and a string of titles and offices which can be read in full in the Commons articles of impeachment against him,[3] which reveal that he had accumulated every rank in the peerage, from duke to baron, a fitting symbol of his dominant position in the State. The open sale of titles and offices had begun before his rise to power, but during the years of his supremacy it became more blatant. Between 1615 and 1628 about thirty English and forty Irish and Scottish peerages were sold for about £350,000 altogether. The Crown got less than half the money, with most of the remainder going to Buckingham. It was a policy which brought the peerage as a whole into some disrepute and created tensions between old and new members of the House of Lords (35; 217). Buckingham's control of almost the entire stock of royal patronage made him bitter enemies among those who were excluded from his favour, but it also enabled him to reward men of a wide variety of opinions. In 1625 both the Arminian Laud and the Puritan John Preston were among his most enthusiastic clients, and although his attitude towards ecclesiastical patronage became much less eclectic after his open commitment to Arminianism in 1626, it is important to stress that, especially in James's reign, the dominance of the patronage machine by a single favourite did not mean the monopoly of office by men of a single viewpoint.

Buckingham's open support of Arminianism soon after Charles's accession reminds us that the great theme of religious history between 1625 and 1629 is the entrenchment of the Arminian party in power at Court (60; 125). During these years the religious peace which had marked James's last years came to an end. James himself seems to have begun to waver in his hitherto firm support for Calvinism during the very last year of his life, but it was on Charles's accession that the Arminians came into their own. In the summer of 1625 he took under his personal protection Richard Montagu, whose attack on predestinarian Calvinism in his book the *New Gag*, published in 1624, had shocked Archbishop Abbot, outraged orthodox clergy and led to a parliamentary assault on Arminian doctrines by John Pym. Buckingham made his position clear in February 1626 when, at a debate at York House on the subject of Montagu's writings, he supported the Arminian against the Calvinist position. Between 1626 and 1628 publication of predestinarian views was effectively prohibited and Charles and Buckingham made their religious position equally clear by their appointments to bishoprics. In 1626 Laud was translated from the poor and remote see of St David's to Bath and Wells and in 1628 he moved to London. The great prize of Canterbury still eluded him, as Abbot lived on until 1633, but by 1629 other key sees including York, Winchester, Norwich and Chichester were filled by leading Arminians, the last named going to Montagu. By the beginning of the personal rule, therefore, the Arminians had begun to grasp the levers of power within the Church. Their ascendancy was by no means complete and was challenged by surviving Calvinists like Abbot himself and John Williams, bishop of Lincoln, but it was clear that, given the staunch support of the King, the future lay with them. It was an ominous prospect for the Church, and real trouble came during the 1630s when the Laudian bishops tried to impose their will at the grass-roots level of parish life.

The entrenchment of Arminianism at the Court by 1629, at a time when the vast majority of Protestant Englishmen disliked its doctrines, was one sign of that growing split between the Crown and influential local opinion which was a most significant development of the 1620s. That split, which created profound diffi- culties and agonies for members of the political nation, who needed influence both at Court and in the shires if they were to play out satisfactorily their vital role in the administration of the country, has been described by some recent historians as a split between 'Court' and 'country', and there can be little doubt that the alienation of Charles from the great majority of his influential subjects, which was to reach its height during the 1630s, was already well advanced by 1629. Gentlemen were coming to believe that the King could not be trusted to respect either the fundamental constitutional privileges which they believed were their birthright or the Church doctrine in which they had been brought up.

The assassination of Buckingham in 1628 and the dissolution of Parliament in 1629 marked the end of an era. Charles resolved to rule without Parliaments for the foreseeable future and he brought the French and Spanish Wars to an end in 1629 and 1630. They had been disastrous failures for England, both in the humiliating military and naval reverses which the country had suffered and in their effects on the domestic scene. Their lesson was clear. Charles had to keep out of war. The effective start of the Spanish War had come only after Charles's accession in 1625 and it is important to distinguish in any general assessment of Buckingham's ascendancy between the last years of James's reign and the early years of Charles. The period 1618–24, despite its difficulties, appears in retrospect as a relatively happy time for both England and Scotland. These were years of peace abroad and basic religious calm at home compared with the foreign disas- ters and Arminian experiments of 1625–29. The parliamentary history of the 1620s, so generally treated as a unity by historians, can now be depicted more realistically as a mirror of the different political and religious moods which prevailed before and after 1625, and Professor Russell, who makes that convincing point as one of his major conclusions, goes on to ask how far the change in mood which made the Parliaments of 1621 and 1624 so much happier assemblies than those of 1626 and 1628 represents a change from James to Charles and how far it reflects a change from peace to war (125). The question, in that form, can hardly be answered. The wars of 1625 to 1630 were Charles's and Buck- ingham's wars and they were responsible for the tensions which these conflicts imposed on English society, just as they were responsible for the introduction of Arminianism as the official doctrine of the Church.

1. I. Macalpine and R. Hunter, *George III and the Mad Business* (1969), pp. 201 ff.
2. The fundamental study is C. G. C. Tite, *Impeachment and Parliamentary Judicature in Early Stuart England* (1974).
3. J. Rushworth, ed., *Historical Collections*, I (1682), p. 303.

CHAPTER 33

Court and country : the personal rule of Charles I, 1629–1637

The term 'Personal rule', traditionally applied to the period between the dissolution of Parliament in 1629 and its next summons in 1640, can be misleading in at least two ways. It may seem to imply that there was something inherently improper, even 'unconstitutional', about such unparliamentary rule, but, of course, there was no convention that a sovereign should call Parliament unless he had legislation to lay before it or the need to ask it for money. Queen Elizabeth, as we saw, prided herself on calling Parliament as seldom as possible, and James I had a long period without any effective meeting of Parliament between 1610 and 1621, a virtual 'personal rule' of his own, broken only by the brief 'Addled Parliament' of 1614. Another way in which the term can be confusing is its implication of strong government directed from the centre by a single man. There was, in fact, no such government during these years. After the assassination of Buckingham in 1628 the King had no dominant minister, and in the 1630s different advisers competed for his ear and for the influence over patronage and policy which went with the royal confidence. Throughout the decade Laud, because his Arminian views [G. 6(22)] coincided with those of the King, exercised the principal influence in the Church, and his position received formal recognition with his appointment to Canterbury on the death of Abbot in 1633 (on Laud see (197)). In the late 1630s, although he held none of the high offices of State, Laud was perhaps the King's most influential adviser in secular as well as in religious affairs, but in the early 1630s the most influential minister was Lord Treasurer Weston, who had begun his career as a client of Buckingham. Weston was a secret Catholic and he and his close associate on the Council, Chancellor of the Exchequer Francis Cottington, were strongly pro-Spanish in their attitude to foreign affairs. Laud, who disapproved of the Catholic sympathies of these men and of the Queen, who came to exercise a growing and baneful influence on her husband during these years, found his great ally in Thomas Wentworth, who was created earl of Strafford in 1640 (on Wentworth, see (79)). Wentworth came from an important Yorkshire gentry family and during his early political career he showed himself one of the ablest and most determined opponents of the Crown. His opposition to royal policies led to his dismissal from the prestigious post of *custos rotulorum* of the Yorkshire Commission of the Peace in 1626 and the following year he opposed the forced loan. He was one of the principal protagonists of the Petition of Right in 1628. Throughout his career he had, however, sought office and in 1628, after the end of the parliamentary session of that year, he was raised to the peerage and later appointed President of the Council of the North. In 1632 he was made Lord Deputy of Ireland. These great offices kept him away from court for most of the 1630s. That was unfortunate for the King, for there is no doubt that he was by far the ablest of Charles's ministers during these years, a man of great energy and ruthless determination who, once he had joined the King's camp, whether for reasons of conviction or self-interest must remain uncertain, advocated a policy of 'thorough' [N], in which he, together with Laud, pressed for greater honesty and efficiency in government allied to a tough line with the Crown's critics. Charles, who approved in general terms of Wentworth's aims, was not, however, as consistently strong minded in attempting to enforce them in England as his minister showed himself to be in Ireland, and the latter's advocacy of an administrative 'clean-up' was in any event vitiated by the concern which he showed for his own profits, a concern which made him a very wealthy man during these years.[1]

If Charles's government during the period suffered from the divided counsels of his ministers and advisers, it also suffered from the growing isolation of the Court from the country as a whole. During the 1620s the frequent meetings of Parliament had left Charles in no doubt about the dislike which many of his people in the localities felt about his policies. During the 1630s, when there were no Parliaments, that line of communication between King and subjects was broken, and this meant that Charles was increasingly out of touch with grass-roots opinion among politically conscious people in the shires. That was one aspect of the increasing polarization of 'court' and 'country' attitudes which was a feature of these years and which has been much stressed by historians (37; 58; 60; 106; 125; 155). The idea of court and country differences can be approached at two levels. First of all there is the dislike which many country gentlemen in the early seventeenth century felt for the royal Court itself. Under James they were opposed to its gross corruption, its extravagance and its loose morals; under Charles to its Arminian religion and sophisticated culture, which those outside the charmed circle condemned as 'popery, painting and playacting' (60, *176*). Historians like Professor Zagorin have extended this dichotomy into the political field, arguing that it is fair to make a distinction between a court interest consisting of those members of the political nation who were dependent for their position and livelihood on the government, and a country interent, consisting of those who were not. That, however, is a false dichotomy. The most recent writings on the subject, such as those of Professors Russell, Hirst and Ashton, have rightly emphasized that virtually all members of the gentry class – the backbone of the political nation – had a divided loyalty; to the royal Court to which they owed such status symbols as their appointment as JPs in the localities and to which they looked for future profit in either money or position, and to their own 'countries', the county societies in which they lived and worked and which they could not afford to offend too much if they were to retain their local influence. As Professor Stone so aptly put it, 'the conflict between loyalty to the particularist locality and loyalty to the nation was fought out within the mind of each individual gentleman' (38, *108*). In the 1620s this was true both of those who went to Westminster and of those who stayed at home in their native shires. During the period of the personal rule it obviously applied to these members of the political nation – the great majority – who either occupied or hoped for local office or favour. They had to think all the time of the two elements which were essential for the maintenance or advancement of their position and status: loyalty to their neighbours and loyalty to the Crown. It had never been an easy tightrope to walk, but most gentlemen had managed it without undue difficulty under Elizabeth and James I. They found it increasingly difficult during the early years of Charles I, and in the 1630s, when most of them came to find the two roles impossible, there was a growing breakdown in one of the fundamental assumptions behind royal government; that the Crown and local gentlemen should co-operate to a sufficient extent to ensure the effective administration of the localities. The disastrous results for Charles were seen in the events at the end of the 1630s.

The growing disillusionment of the gentry with Charles I's government coincided with a difficult period for the country's economy. The period between the beginning of the personal rule and the outbreak of civil war was a time of relatively poor harvest conditions. A normal span of fourteen years would have produced five or six good harvests, but there were only two between 1629 and 1642 – those of 1639 and 1641 – with three bad and the rest average (228). During the 1630s food prices rose by about 17 per cent and industrial prices by 6 per cent (224, *10*), and high food prices help to explain the government's urgent instructions to local officials to enforce the Poor Laws effectively. The Privy Council was particularly urgent in its exhortations at the beginning of the decade, when the bad harvest of 1630 coincided with a trade slump in 1629–31. The conclusion of peace in 1630 did bring some benefits to trade as the decade advanced, but even here there was no cause for rejoicing as these years saw a continuing fall in the export of the undressed cloths which had dominated London's and the country's overseas trade at the beginning of the century but had fallen to 35 per cent of London's exports by 1640 (242, *137*). The indifferent harvests, the high food prices and the slumps in the textile industry indicate that these were hard years for the lower orders, but their difficulties have too often been underestimated by historians amidst the emphasis which they have traditionally given to the government's paternalistic social policies during the decade and in light of Clarendon's well-known picture of these years as a period of economic plenty the like of which 'was never enjoyed by any nation' (14, vol. 1, *84*). That judgement is a travesty of the reality just discussed, but Clarendon's memory was doubtless distorted both by the lapse of time – he wrote this passage of his great work during the late 1660s – and by the fact that the 1630s were indeed golden economic years for some members of his own class, gentlemen who were now reaping the benefits of the large rises in rents which had been a feature of the late Elizabethan and early Stuart periods.

There is no evidence, in fact, that the common people ever looked back to the 1630s as a happy period or gave Charles and his ministers much thanks for the concern which they undoubtedly showed for the poorer members of the community. In general, historians have laid too much stress on that concern, with the implication that it was in some way unusual. All English governments of the time were preoccupied with the conditions of their less fortunate subjects for reasons of security – hungry men were liable to take part in riots – as well as for moral considerations. The personal rule opened, as we saw, in the very difficult economic conditions of 1629–31 and the Book of Orders of 1631 (154), which instructed local governors to see to the efficient administration of poor relief, was the kind of measure which could reasonably have been expected from any government. Professor Jordan, in a general survey of JPs responses, concluded that they virtually ignored the instructions, fobbing the Privy Council off with false reports about their activities (205, *128 ff*), but detailed local studies, now available for such counties as Somerset, Sussex and Cheshire, show that the local governors did in fact respond to the needs of the situation, increasing the amounts paid to the poor, providing or replenishing parish stocks of raw materials for setting the poor on work, and seeing that greater numbers of poor children were placed in apprenticeships (154; 156–7). It is possible to go some way to reconciling Jordan's arguments with the findings of the more detailed local studies by pointing out that the growth in public poor relief which undoubtedly did take place in the 1630s was part of a generally rising trend in state provisions for the poor which developed from 1600 onwards and continued during the Interregnum. Comparison of poor relief in Warwickshire during the 1630s and 1650s shows that JPs handled nearly three times as many poor relief cases in the latter decade as in the former, and that at a time when the central government had abandoned the kind of direction from the centre which had characterized the 1630s. During the 1650s the local authorities were left to deal with their own poor as they thought best (253). Clearly, JPs during both the 1630s and the 1650s applied themselves with considerable zeal to the relief of the poor and it looks as if their energies during the 1630s may have been due more to their own appreciation of the problem than to any directions from the centre. The false reports which *were* undoubtedly sent to the Privy Council can then be explained, in part at least, by the resentment of local governors at what they regarded as undue interference by the central authorities in a situation which they regarded themselves as both well equipped and willing to handle effectively. It can be concluded, therefore, that Charles's social policies, as typified by his approach to poor relief, were well intentioned but relied too much on instructions from the centre which merely served to irritate local officials without increasing the effectiveness of the measures.

His financial policies during the 1630s have also undergone reappraisal in recent years with results which seem similarly unfavourable to the government. At first sight the financial achievement during these years looks very impressive. Ordinary revenue, which averaged little more than £600,000 per annum during the early part of the decade, rose to an annual average of about £900,000 during the later 1630s, the greatest part of the increase coming from higher customs revenues which were secured partly by the increased volume of trade during these years of peace and partly by higher valuations of, and new impositions on, the goods traded. This very large increase might have been expected to solve the Crown's financial problems, but it did not. Expenditure continued to rise, especially in the royal household, and much of the revenue was anticipated throughout the decade; that is to say the Crown borrowed money on the security of revenues which were not due in for several years. It had, therefore, less ready cash available for its needs during these years once its creditors had taken their due. It was a vicious circle with revenues constantly being anticipated further and further ahead. In the spring of 1633 over £200,000 of future revenue was mort-gaged and the amount rose steadily in the following years, reaching over £300,000 in 1637 when one minor branch of the revenue was anticipated fourteen years ahead (35; 249). Moreover, the Crown's methods of raising the increased reve-nues which it did secure gave rise to much discontent. The customs duties and impositions, so much higher than ever before, continued to be collected without parliamentary authorization. From 1630 onwards all gentlemen worth at least £40 per annum who had not presented themselves for knighthood at the King's coronation, as traditionally they were supposed to do, were fined large sums. This revival of an archaic custom brought in about £175,000 during the decade. The revenues from wardship were sharply increased – they doubled between the mid-1620s and 1640 – and heavy fines were imposed on landowners who had techni-cally encroached on royal forests. The Statute of Monopolies [E. 4(23)], which had been passed in 1624 and which had confined monopolies to corporations, was circumvented by the technical skill of the lawyers to allow domestic monopolies, such as the notorious soap monopoly, which benefited individuals. By the end of the 1630s such monopolies were bringing about £100,000 per annum to the Exchequer, but their cost to the consumer was perhaps eight times as much. The difference went into the pockets of the monopolists who were doubly unpopular for making their large profits at a time of considerable economic difficulty for the average citizen. The increased revenue which these measures brought in was hardly worth the hostility towards the Crown which they provoked from a wide spectrum of the population, ranging from gentry and merchants to the poorer members of the community. All of the measures were arguably legal, but Charles and his advisers, more and more out of touch with opinion in the country at large, failed to see that the main point was no longer their technical legality but the political cost of imposing them.

So far, we have been discussing additions to the Crown's ordinary revenue, but the most notorious of all the financial expedients of the 1630s was ship money, an extraordinary tax which was imposed from 1634 onwards to increase the strength of the navy. There were good precedents for such a tax, both from the sixteenth century and from James I's reign, but under Charles it soon became clear that he intended it to become permanent, despite the fact that the country was at peace. He extended it to inland as well as coastal counties in 1635 and justified it on grounds of 'national emergency' of which he himself should be the sole judge. John Hampden, a wealthy Buckinghamshire landowner, was one of those who refused to pay, and when his case was heard before all the common law judges in 1637 they decided in favour of the Crown, though only by the narrow majority of seven to five [E. 5(27)]. This meant that the King was given a free hand in deciding what constituted a national emergency and the right to impose what amounted to direct taxation to pay for it. It was a decision with very important constitutional implications as it raised the possibility that kings in future might be able to dispense totally with Parliaments. That possibility was, however, eventually dashed by the taxpayers' strike of 1639–40, when about 80 per cent of the ship money due could not be collected. As late as 1637–38 about 90 per cent of the tax was still being paid, but its levy gave rise to considerable administrative problems and local officials were swamped with complaints about inequitable ratings which added enormously to their already heavy workload and caused them to view the central government with still more disenchanted eyes. It is now apparent that it was these administrative upheavals which the tax caused in county societies rather than its constitutional implications which did the King most damage in the eyes of members of the political nation (155).

The general unpopularity of the King's financial demands during the 1630s was compounded by dislike of the Arminian policies (60) which Laud pursued throughout the decade with the King's full approval and encouragement. It has been argued that, 'if there is one person to whose actions and policies the fall of the Stuart monarchy can be attributed, that person is William Laud' (37, *110*), and there is no doubt that the good intentions of Laud and his fellow Arminian clerics were vitiated by their total failure to comprehend the depth of resentment, on political and economic as well as on more narrowly theological grounds, which their policies aroused among the great majority of influential Englishmen and the damage which they therefore did to both the Church and the monarchy which Laud loved so much and so genuinely wished to improve and exalt. The elevation of Arminian bishops to many of the most important English sees between 1625 and 1629, appointments reinforced by further Arminian promotions during the 1630s, left Laud and his lieutenants in control of much of the administrative machinery of the Church, and their sincere belief in a divine right inherent in their episcopal office made them doubly eager to impose upon the Church the 'beauty of holiness' which was a fundamental aspect of the Laudian programme. They laid great stress on the upkeep of the fabric of churches and reverent behaviour of the congregations within them, while their emphasis on the sacramental rather than the preaching aspects of their office was symbolized by their insistence that altars should be railed off at the eastern end of churches. These ceremonial emphases, when combined with their anti-Calvinist theology, gave rise to understandable if totally false accusations of popery against Laud and critics, who were told that he had refused the offer of a cardinal's hat, could justly reply that the significant fact was not the refusal but that the Pope could have made the offer in the first place.

The theological divisions between the Laudians and the rest of the community were exacerbated by the involvement of the hierarchy in secular affairs. Bishops had always been administrators as well as pastors, but in Charles's reign they were increasingly drawn into secular affairs. Laud himself ranked as one of the most influential members of the Privy Council and in 1636 William Juxon, bishop of London, was appointed Lord Treasurer, the first churchman to hold that great office since the reign of Edward IV. The Court of High Commission, the supreme power in the Church under the Crown, used its censorship of books for political as well as religious purposes. This tendency towards a fusion of the lay and ecclesiastical civil services inevitably suggested a return to pre-Reformation days when clerics had played such a large role in the upper reaches of royal government. Laud's attempts at theological change and his desire to give the clergy a greater role in secular affairs were partly a reflection of his determination to raise the status of ecclesiastics from the comparatively lowly level to which it had fallen in the post-Reformation era. He was also aware of the need, if such improved status was to be achieved, to improve their economic position. His efforts in this field (192), which aroused such violent hostility among the laity, were founded on the principle that church property was inalienable and that Henry VIII and his successors had committed sacrilege by despoiling monasteries, chantries and bishoprics. The Laudians obviously could not attempt to regain the former monastic lands for the Church – though some laymen feared that that was their ultimate objective – but they did attempt to increase the amount of the tithes [N] which the laity paid for the support of the clergy and endeavoured to ensure that laymen who held tithes – the so-called impropriated [N] tithes – paid a higher proportion of these to the clerical vicars who did the actual work of the Church in parishes where tithes were impropriated. It seemed indeed to many members of the laity, both gentry and poorer citizens, that the Laudian clergy were attacking their property rights or their purses, or both.

Such generalizations about the unpopularity of all aspects of Laudianism suggest that it must have encountered bitter resistance at grass-roots level, and a recent study of its impact in Sussex shows that this was indeed the case. (156). During most of the 1630s Sussex, which in ecclesiastical terms was the diocese of Chichester, was governed by Richard Montagu, the notorious author of the *New Gag*, whose Arminian propaganda had caused such a stir in the Parliaments of the 1620s. Montagu, who regarded all predestinarian Calvinists as Puritans, made a sustained effort to impose the ritualistic elements of Laudianism in his diocese, but he encountered fierce resistance from the local gentry and was severely hampered in his efforts to improve the fabric of churches by the very low standards which most of the churchwardens of the diocese found perfectly acceptable. Many ordinary parishioners – if they came to church at all – continued to behave in ways which made a mockery of the Arminian ideal of reverent and attentive congregations. There were cases of churchgoers who played cards and stuck pins in each other during services, as well as instances of the traditional jostling and spitting which were clearly characteristic of both pre- and post-Reformation parish behaviour. The general impression of ecclesiastical life in Sussex during the 1630s is of a determined bishop struggling against a combination of hostility and apathy to enforce even the most elementary aspects of the Laudian programme. The most important result of the policies was the bitter resentment which they provoked among the gentry. As Mr Fletcher concludes, 'Arminianism, probably more than any other single issue . . . hardened many gentry . . . against Charles I, his Court and his regime' (156, *93*).

Charles's genius for making enemies among his influential subjects extended to his relationships with the greater part of the London merchant community (37; 258). Professor Ashton has shown that between 1624 and 1629 there was a crucial realignment of forces within the London business world with those who were primarily interested in foreign trade allying with Parliament against the much smaller number of businessmen who held domestic concessions like monopolies and customs farms from the Crown. These foreign merchants, who had previously faced considerable hostility from the Commons towards the chartered trading companies in which they were incorporated, now discovered that Parliament was prepared, in the Monopolies Act of 1624, to exempt them from the prohibition which was then attempted on domestic monopolies. Also, the Crown showed itself unable or unwilling to protect merchant interests effectively in the wars of the 1620s and its demands for the payment of tonnage and poundage without parliamentary assent after 1625 aroused considerable hostility in the merchant community. This breakdown in the traditional alliance between the Crown and the London trading companies remained, and indeed was intensified during the personal rule with continued merchant resentment over the issue of tonnage and poundage and royal disputes with some of the most important chartered companies, especially a bitter quarrel with the East India Company which continued for much of the decade.

East India Company merchants were infuriated by royal support of or sympathy for interlopers in their trade during the 1630s and their resentment was a minor aspect of the very widespread feeling throughout the country that Charles was making radical attempts to overturn traditional values. His opponents stressed their own conservatism in the face of the King's financial expedients and, above all, of his religious policies. The local gentlemen, who resented more and more strongly the additional burdens heaped upon their shoulders by such measures as the Book of Orders of 1631 and ship money did not, however, have a parliamentary forum in which to express their anxieties and resentments, and it has been argued (125, *426*) that in 1637 Charles's position was actually stronger than it had been in 1627. Professor Russell bases that belief on what he sees as the solvency of the regime in 1637 and the willingness of the local governors to serve it. The argument is unconvincing. Charles's solvency depended on a continuing ability to raise large loans from a City of London most of whose prominent citizens were hostile to important aspects of royal policy and by 1637 the willingness of local governors to continue in their roles of unpaid royal servants in the localities was near to breaking point. There was an increasing realization among the gentry class that it was becoming impossible to preserve their traditional loyalty to each of the two bases of their authority, Court and country: by 1637 country as opposed to court interests were predominant in the minds of most local gentlemen. It only required a major crisis to bring this into the open and that came following the Scottish troubles of 1637 onwards. As Professor Woolrych has pointed out, Charles could not hope to avoid war indefinitely and 'even if he had avoided the self-inflicted wound of the Scottish rebellion the first breath of war from any other quarter would have blown down the whole house of cards'[2]. The crisis came sooner rather than later because Charles's actions in Scotland were even more misguided than his policies in England.

---

1. J. P. Cooper, 'The fortune of Thomas Wentworth, earl of Strafford', *EcHr*, 2nd Ser., **11** (1958–59), 227 ff.
2. A. Woolrych, 'Court, country and city revisited', *History*, **65** (1980), 240.

CHAPTER 34

The Scottish rebellion and the road to civil war, 1637–1642

King James's sureness of touch in Scottish affairs, founded on intimate personal knowledge of his native land, continued relatively unimpaired after 1603 despite the fact that he revisited Scotland only once after his accession to the English throne. Charles I, in contrast, who had been born in Scotland in 1600, left it as a young child. He had practically no first-hand knowledge of his native kingdom – he did not even go there for coronation until 1633 – and this, combined with his general inflexibility, caused him to make the most serious errors in his conduct of Scottish business (49; 159). At the very beginning of his reign in 1625 he revoked all grants of ecclesiastical property made to laymen in Scotland since the Reformation. The King's intentions were much more modest than this sweeping measure seemed to suggest – commissioners were empowered to deal with those who held ecclesiastical property 'unlawfully acquired . . . and yet fitting to be secured unto the present possessors upon reasonable conditions' (49, *297*) – and the revocation had limited practical effects, but the secrecy of its introduction and the sweeping assertions of principle which it contained made virtually all Scottish landowners feel insecure and thus stirred up bitter resentment among the nobility and lairds on whose co-operation the King depended for the successful government of Scotland.

The anger of the lay notables was further increased by other royal attacks on their status and influence. Many members of the nobility were forced to resign hereditary offices, like that of sheriff, which they had previously held, and lay influence on the Scottish Privy Council was steadily eclipsed during the 1630s by the growing attendance of bishops. By the late 1630s Charles was relying for the government of Scotland on a small clique of courtier-peers and ecclesiastics who were increasingly out of touch with opinion in the country. This was especially ominous as Scotland was not exempt from the Arminian reaction which affected England in the 1620s and 1630s. During these years anti-Calvinist theological trends began to make themselves felt north of the border among a small number of clergymen and in the 1630s these men, encouraged by the King, began to introduce ceremonies and practices which were anathema to the overwhelming bulk of Protestant Scots who remained committed to the strong Calvinism of the Knoxian tradition.

By 1636 Charles had managed to offend the great bulk of the nobility, gentry and Presbyterian clergy of Scotland, the most influential men in the nation, and matters came to a head in 1637 when he tried to impose a new Prayer Book on the Scottish people.[1] That was a result of discussions conducted between Charles, Laud and the Scottish bishops during the three previous years and imposed English practices on the Scots. If its contents infuriated the Presbyterian ministers and very many members of the laity, the method of its imposition served to unite virtually the whole Scottish political nation, ecclesiastical and lay, against the Crown. The King did not seek the approval of either a Scottish Parliament or Church Assembly, he simply commanded the use of the new Prayer Book by proclamation. The result was riots and even the Scottish Council felt that the Prayer Book should be withdrawn. The King, totally out of touch with the reality of the situation, refused to give way and the result was the National Covenant of February 1638, a document in defence of traditional Scottish religious and political rights which was sworn to by vast numbers of Scots. Charles's persistence with ill-advised policies had united almost the entire Scottish people against him. His folly was compounded by the fact that he had no effective coercive power in Scotland. If he was to impose his will it would have to be through an English army. By the summer of 1638 he had decided to raise one. It was, perhaps, the most fateful decision of his reign, as it led to the two 'Bishops' Wars' of 1639–40. Charles did raise quite substantial armies, but his need for troops and money from his English subjects revealed the fatal weaknesses of his regime south as well as north of the border.

In England the years 1639–40 saw the effective breakdown of royal control over the administration of the country. During the later 1630s royal demands for the enforcement of the unpopular policies of the personal rule in the localities led to a growing reluctance on the part of gentlemen to become JPs, a situation which led, for example, to a net loss of ten magistrates in Somerset between 1635 and 1640 (154, *303–4*). Ship money, with the strains which its administration imposed on local society, made the gentry throughout the country more and more aware that Charles's policies were disruptive of that peace and order in the localities which they prized above all else. In 1639–40, on top of all this, came demands for troops and money from the shires to fight the Scots. The result was the taxpayers' strike of 1639–40 when, 'local government ground to a halt' (155, *29*). The King was desperate for funds, but the combination of a business slump and his strained relations with London made the city fathers reluctant or unwilling to grant substantial loans (258). Charles did manage to get help from the customs farmers, who were both bitterly unpopular with the bulk of the merchant community and totally dependent upon the Crown for their privileges, but this did not prevent the defeat of his army in the Second Bishops' War and the occupation of northern England by the Scots in the autumn of 1640. The King had to agree to pay them £850 a day and the only way he could secure such sums of money was through the summoning of Parliament.

There had already been a Parliament in April and May of 1640. This Short Parliament was called after the abortive First Bishops' War of 1639 in which there was no actual fighting. Charles then made substantial concessions to the Scots, but only as a means of gaining time in order to crush them more effectively later. The Short Parliament, however, refused to grant him the large sums of money he needed without substantial concessions about grievances and the King lost patience and dismissed it after it had been in session for just over three weeks. He was not able to dispose so easily of the Long Parliament, which met in November 1640, soon after Charles's defeat by the Scots in the Second Bishops'

War, and which was not constitutionally dissolved until 1660. The Commons in the autumn of 1640 contained an impressive majority of men – about 400 out of less than 500 MPs elected – who were committed to a 'country' position (37). The determination of these men to obtain concessions from the King in both the political and the religious spheres can be explained principally by their dislike of Charles's domestic policies from the 1620s onwards, which had alienated the bulk of the London merchants as well as the vast majority of the country gentry. They had also, however, been alienated by his foreign policy, which had seemed to subserve Spanish interests during the 1630s, at a time when Protestantism in Europe was threatened by the resurgent forces of Counter-Reformation Catholicism.[2] Royal permission for Spanish silver to be minted in England for the payment of Spanish troops on the Continent and the fact that Charles allowed a Spanish army to march across southern England in 1639 for re-embarkation to the Netherlands, to mention only two specific examples, gave rise to complaints in England that he was criminally endangering the European Protestant cause and even to fears that he might be planning to crush all domestic opposition to his regime with Catholic foreign aid. Such ideas of a royalist–Catholic plot to crush English liberties constantly bedevilled the debates in the Long Parliament, inflaming all other causes of tension, and it is clear that they must have been of considerable significance in building up the largely united opposition which the King faced in the Commons in 1640.

It is crucial to remember, too, that at the beginning of the Long Parliament a majority of members of the House of Lords sympathized with the Commons' aim of reversing some of the royal policies in Church and State which had prevailed since the beginning of Charles's reign. One of the most important trends in recent historical writing on the early seventeenth century had been to stress the significance of the peerage as well as the gentry in the great parliamentary affairs of the period (58; 125); the House of Lords is now beginning to receive the attention which is undoubtedly its due. Professor Christianson, indeed, has argued that peers may well have taken the lead in inspiring the great reforming measures of the early months of the Long Parliament.[3] One can disagree with him and still accept the vital significance of co-operation between royal critics in the Upper and Lower Houses during 1640 and 1641. That was essential for the mass of constructive legislation which was passed. The nobility and gentry who dominated affairs in the early months of the Long Parliament were moderate reformers who were convinced that Charles's actions during the 1630s had been a threat to their traditional political liberties and to the Protestant religion of the country as it had been established by Queen Elizabeth and maintained by King James. Their arguments were essentially conservative and their aim was to restore the 'balanced constitution' of previous days which, they argued, had been upset by Charles's innovations. Once the King's revolutionary policies of the 1630s had been reversed they hoped for a restoration of the traditional situation in which the political nation could maintain a balance between its loyalties to Court and country while serving both. Meanwhile, it was necessary, they believed, to take an overwhelmingly country line to secure this desirable objective. That attitude of the bulk of peers and MPs in 1640 explains their support for the reforming measures of the first session of the Long Parliament, which lasted until September 1641. The King's lack of substantial support combined with the threat of the Scottish Army in the North ensured that he would comply, however reluctantly, with their demands.

Two basic tasks faced the reforming MPs and noblemen: they had to get rid of their leading opponents among the King's advisers, and they had to pass measures which declared that the policies of the last decade had been illegal and ensured that they could not be repeated (for the events after the meeting of the Long Parliament see (*32, 129 ff*; 106, *198 ff*)). Some of Charles's leading ministers, such as Lord Keeper Finch, who had delivered a very unpopular judgment in the ship money case, and Secretary of State Windebank, accused of favouring Catholic recusants, fled abroad to escape the wrath of Parliament, but the other judges who had supported ship money were attacked (see [E.5(28)]), and some monopolists were expelled from the Commons. The greatest prizes were, of course, Laud and Strafford. Both were impeached in 1640, but the former, now an old and failing man, was allowed to live on in prison until he was finally executed in 1645. Strafford was a different matter. The parliamentarian leaders recognized his great energy and abilities and were determined to be rid of him. 'Stone dead hath no fellow' was their motto, and, as it was impossible to prove judicially that he had been guilty of high treason, he was finally executed in May 1641 by Act of Attainder, a measure to which Charles gave his assent only with the greatest reluctance.

The King always regretted his weakness in agreeing to Strafford's execution, but he was under enormous pressure, and the first session of the Long Parliament saw a succession of measures which significantly limited his future powers. In February 1641 the Triennial Act [E.5(29)] provided that Parliament should henceforth meet at least once every three years and laid down an elaborate procedure for summoning it without the King's participation if he failed to call it himself. In May another Act was passed which prohibited the dissolution or adjournment of the present Parliament without its own consent [E.5(30)]. At the time the motives behind this were largely financial – the Crown's creditors were only prepared to go on lending money if it could be guaranteed that Parliament would continue – but it had enormous political implications which were to become very obvious in the years ahead. Having ensured its own continued existence, both for the present and the future, Parliament proceeded to destroy the financial abuses and prerogative instruments of the personal rule. The Tonnage and Poundage Act of June 1641 (16 Charles I, c. 8) declared that all customs duties levied without parliamentary consent were illegal and proceeded to hammer the point home by granting the customs revenues to the king for a period of two months only. In August ship money was declared illegal (16 Charles I, c. 14), the exaction of compositions for knighthood was prohibited (16 Charles I, c. 20), and the boundaries of the royal forests were firmly defined (16 Charles I, c. 16), thus making impossible in future the King's exploitation of forest laws during the 1630s. These financial statutes were accompanied by others which abolished the prerogative courts. In July the courts of High Commission [G.6(24)] and Star Chamber [E.5(31)] were abolished, and the effective judicial powers of the Privy

Council, the Council in the North and the Council in the Marches of Wales were suppressed (16 Charles I, cc. 10,11). All this amounted to 'a constitutional . . . revolution . . . [in which] the heritage of the Tudor monarchy was taken to pieces' (106, *199*). The Lords and Commons had not only forced the King to accept the illegality of his practices during the personal rule, they had attacked and abolished some of the principal foundations of the English State as it had developed since the Reformation. The abolition of the High Commission was linked to their dislike to Laudian ecclesiastical developments, and in December 1640 the House of Commons condemned the Arminian canons which Convocation had passed in the spring of 1640 and which represented the final triumph of the Laudian regime in the Church on the very eve of its downfall. The Commons declarations, which were approved by the Lords during the following summer, affirmed that Convocation had no power to bind either the clergy or the laity without the consent of Parliament and thus attacked its traditional right to legislate with the royal assent alone (106). Dislike of Laudian innovations did not necessarily mean approval for the radical plans which some MPs had to abolish bishops altogether, and it is notable that the Lords and Commons, who agreed on so many constitutional and political issues during the first session, were much less united in their attitude to religion. Religious differences in Parliament were, indeed, one of the principal factors in the breakdown of the largely united front which it had opposed to the Crown during the early months of its meeting. By November 1641 there were mutually opposed parties in the Commons and it is important to understand how this breakdown of parliamentary unity came about and led on to civil war in 1642.

The fundamental reason was the lack of security which the parliamentary leaders felt and which led them to make more extreme demands upon the Crown. Charles never forgave John Pym and his associates for their role in the execution of Strafford. He genuinely believed that they were prepared to deprive him of the basic attributes of sovereignty and he was quite prepared to consider the use of force against Parliament – he was sympathetic to the army plot against it in the spring of 1641. The opposition leaders, on the other hand, feared not only for the permanence of the peaceful constitutional revolution which they achieved in 1641 but also for their own lives if a royal coup succeeded. In this atmosphere of fear and mutual distrust they conceived the need for further safeguards against the Crown, and from June 1641 they demanded that the appointment of royal ministers should be subject to parliamentary approval. This was a very drastic invasion of the royal prerogative and it was opposed by many moderate peers and MPs who had fully approved of Parliament's stand against the innovations of the personal rule. The uneasiness which these moderate parliamentarians felt was increased by religious developments during 1641 and by the role which popular agitation played in influencing events. During the 1630s an increasing number of Puritan Englishmen, furious at the growing persecution of Calvinists by Arminian bishops and disillusioned by the inability of the remaining Calvinists in the hierarchy to defend those who shared their doctrinal ideas, rejected episcopalianism altogether. They embraced Presbyterianism or even Congregationalism, and one result of this growing Puritan militancy was the petition which London citizens presented to the House of Commons in December 1640 calling for the abolition of episcopacy 'root and branch' [G.6(23)]. The issue was discussed in the House of Commons on numerous occasions between February and August 1641, but no agreement was reached. It is clear that the subject caused considerable disharmony among MPs. Virtually all of them were opposed to the Laudian interpretation of episcopacy, but that was quite a different matter from wanting to abolish bishops altogether. Also, there was a notable growth in the number and influence of extremist religious sects in London at that time. It is easy to understand, therefore, why a growing number of peers and MPs were unhappy about the way in which the religious situation was developing. Their fears were compounded by the fact that London mobs were active in agitations against the bishops. Indeed, Dr Manning has argued (221) that the role of the 'people', the population of London, was decisive in the creation of a royalist party and one does not have to go all the way with him to recognize that popular pressure, which was very important in securing the acceptance by Parliament of the Bill of Attainder against Strafford, was bitterly disliked and resented by many peers and MPs.

The situation when the second session of the Long Parliament began in October 1641 was, therefore, that the country opposition, which had been basically united in securing the great reforming measures of the first session, contained a growing number of men in both Houses of Parliament who were increasingly uneasy about some of the more extreme political demands of the Commons leaders and about both the religious developments and popular pressures which had been evident during the previous months. It was just at this time that Englishmen received news of the Irish rebellion of October 1641 (for Ireland under Charles I, see (51; 163–4)). Strafford spent most of the 1630s in Ireland where he was Lord Deputy between 1633 and 1640. During these years he applied a policy of 'thorough' which not merely alienated all sections of Irish opinion but raised fears in England that he would pursue similarly ruthless policies at home if he got the chance. These fears help to explain the implacable determination with which leaders of the parliamentary opposition pursued him to the death in 1641, but the removal of his strong hand from Ireland was largely responsible for the outbreak of a Catholic rebellion in Ulster which soon spread to the whole island and brought horrifying stories of atrocities against Protestants to the receptive ears of the London Parliament. The rebellion clearly required an English army to suppress it, but it emerged in the nine months following its outbreak that a substantial proportion of the political nation was no longer prepared to trust the King with the control of the nation's armed forces, whether of an army to combat the rebellion itself or of the militia which would have to defend England from a possible Irish attack. They feared that the troops might be used against themselves and from December 1641 onwards Pym and the parliamentary leaders demanded control of the militia. Charles refused point-blank, arguing with considerable conviction that command of the country's armed forces was a basic attribute of kingship. Neither side would give way in this dispute which was the immediate cause of the decisive break between King and parliamentary opposition in 1642 and hence of the actual start of the Civil War. It is important to remember that the issue was given both its urgency and much of the heat which it engendered by the developments in Ireland.

The Irish rebellion, which further inflamed the fears of the parliamentary leaders, could not, however, conceal the swing to Charles's camp which was very evident by November 1641 and could be seen in the reaction of MPs during that month to the Grand Remonstrance, a document summing up the parliamentary leaders' grievances against the King (13). It led to a long and bitter debate in which members almost came to blows with each other and was eventually passed by only 159 votes to 148. The decision which was taken to print it was seen by many of the members who had opposed it as an inflammatory appeal to the people and indicated to the King that, if he followed moderate policies, he might hope to increase still further the support which had come to him during the last few months. Events in London in December 1641 and January 1642, however, significantly weakened his position. The city aldermen who, like most of the political nation, had been moderate parliamentarians in the early months of the Long Parliament, had swung back to the King's side in the autumn of 1641, but this very important accession of strength for Charles was short-lived. In a municipal revolution in December 1641 supporters of the parliamentary leadership seized control of the city government and with it of the trained bands, the London militia (158; 258). It was in this sympathetic city that the five leaders of the Commons opposition – Pym, Hampden, Holles, Strode and Haselrig – took refuge on 4 January 1642 when the King tried to arrest them personally in the House on charges of high treason. It was a grave mistake which made many moderate men who had been inclining to the King's side think again and six days later, recognizing that he had lost control of his capital, Charles left it. It was clear that he would only be able to win the city back by force of arms and, granted the overwhelming importance of London in the life of the kingdom, that fact alone made civil war highly probable from then onwards.

The King's departure from London directed attention to the situation in the country at large (155; 221). There were extensive riots and protests by the lower orders in the localities during the period between the meeting of the Long Parliament in November 1640 and the outbreak of civil war in August 1642. These were a reflection of discontent with high food prices and industrial depression and members of the local gentry were afraid that, at a time of political upheavals, they might lead to a complete breakdown of law and order. In this situation there seems to have been an overwhelming desire among members of the political nation in the localities that their differences with the King should not be allowed to continue. They hoped that their representatives at Westminster would be able to settle these quickly so that a reunited ruling class could face the social threat posed by the local disorders. When it became clear that the differences could not be quickly settled then the gentry in the localities reacted in three major ways. A number turned to royalism; a number continued to support the parliamentary opposition; and a very large number, perhaps the majority, tried to remain neutral. Dr Morrill points out that in 1642 attempts were made to neutralize whole areas of the country, and he has found evidence for attempted neutrality pacts in twenty-two English counties and in many English boroughs as well (155, 36–7). Given this very widespread desire for peace among the ruling classes in the shires the outbreak of war must be explained by the fact that activists on both sides, royalists and parliamentarians, seized the initiative and started a struggle which the majority wished to avoid. The moment of decision for most men came when they were faced with Parliament's Militia Ordinance or the Royal Commission of Array, each of which commanded their military service. The Militia Ordinance [E.5(32)], passed by Parliament in March 1642, was declared by the Lords and Commons at Westminster to have the force of law despite the fact that it lacked the King's signature, and those who obeyed the revolutionary constitutional implications of this document must have been aware that they were accepting a decisive break with constitutional propriety. That many *were* prepared to do so shows the depth of distrust of the King which had built up since the beginning of his reign. By the autumn of 1642, then, King and Parliament were at war. Why had the great changes of 1640–41 occurred and why did they lead on to civil war? Some of the answers to these questions will already be obvious, but it is important to examine the issues within a wider perspective.

---

1. G. Donaldson, *The Making of the Scottish Prayer Book of 1637* (Edinburgh, 1954).
2. C. V. Wedgwood, 'Charles I and the Protestant cause', *Proceedings of the Huguenot Society of London*, **19**, No. 2 (1954), 19 ff.
3. P. Christianson, 'The peers, the people and parliamentary management in the first six months of the Long Parliament', *JMH*, **49** (1979), 575 ff.

CHAPTER 35

The causes of the crises of 1640–1642

Historians have used a wide variety of terms to describe the events of the period 1640–60; the Great Rebellion, the English Civil War, the Puritan Revolution, the English Revolution. Unfortunately, however, these labels have all too often been applied indiscriminately to the period as a whole or to parts of the period without sufficiently careful definition of the precise meaning which the writer is attaching to them. Yet such definitions are necessary if we are to make sense of the great variety of changes which took place between the meeting of the Long Parliament in 1640 and the Restoration of 1660. One has to explain, first of all, the causes of the peaceful 'constitutional revolution' of 1640–41. That, as we have seen (Ch. 34), altered the whole political power structure, with the imposition of hitherto unparalleled restrictions on royal power. It was the result of a situation in which civil war seemed impossible; the King had such limited support in 1640 that he could not have fought one. The changes of 1640–41 were of great significance in the long as well as in the short term – they survived the Restoration – but they were limited in scope. They were essentially political and though there *were* undertones of religious and even possible social revolution during these years, the vast majority of the political nation were still wedded to the traditional structure of monarchy, House of Lords, House of Commons and episcopacy which had ruled the country for centuries. The next task is to explain the causes of the Civil War, to understand why the united country opposition of 1640 disintegrated by 1642 to such an extent that the King had a substantial body of followers prepared to take up arms on his behalf. In the years after 1642 there was a radicalization of political, religious and social attitudes. The Civil War of 1642–46 acted as a solvent of hitherto almost unchallenged assumptions and the result was the events of the period 1646–49, which culminated in the abolition of the monarchy and the House of Lords in the latter year. To put it another way, the revolutionary events of 1646–49 were a result of civil war and bore virtually no relationship to the ambitions of members of the political nation in either 1640 or 1642. Indeed, the events of the later 1640s were highly distasteful to the vast majority of the English gentry. It was a minority within the political nation which secured the abolition of episcopacy in 1646 and an even smaller minority which abolished the monarchy and the House of Lords in 1649.[1]

In discussing the causes of the constitutional revolution of 1640–41 the basic disagreement among historians is the time perspective which should be adopted. Professor Stone argues that in examining the origins of these events it is necessary to go right back to the early sixteenth century, the period of the Henrician Reformation (38). That kind of long-term interpretation is not a new one. It emerged in the seventeenth century itself, when James Harrington, a perceptive contemporary commentator, argued that the primary reason for the upheavals of the 1640s was a change in the balance of social forces within England in the century and a half from about 1500 onwards (66, *23 ff*; 214). In these changes, he pointed out, the Crown, the Church and the aristocracy lost substantial amounts of land to the gentry and the yeomen. The revolutionary changes from 1640 onwards were merely a political recognition of this crucial social change. Harrington's interpretation is, therefore, essentially a social and economic one and in this he is followed to a considerable extent by Stone. The latter, while certainly not ignoring political and religious developments lays great stress on the social background to the crisis of 1640. Professor Russell, on the other hand, suggests that in examining the origins of the events of 1640–41 it is necessary to go back only to about 1625, the beginning of Charles I's reign. (60, *1 ff*) This much shorter-term interpretation also has its roots in the seventeenth century, in the writings of Edward Hyde, earl of Clarendon, who became a leading adviser of Charles I during the 1640s and the chief minister of Charles II after the Restoration. In his *History of the Rebellion*, the most important contemporary account of the events of the 1640s, he stated , 'I shall not . . . lead any man further back in this journey, for the discovery of the entrance into these dark ways than the beginning of this king's reign. For I am not so sharp-sighted as those who have discerned this rebellion contriving from (if not before) the death of Queen Elizabeth.' (14, vol. 1, *3*) Clarendon's explanation of the events of 1640–41 within this comparatively short-term context of the years from 1625 onwards is essentially a political one and in this he is followed to a considerable extent by Russell who plays down or rejects social factors and stresses the importance of politics and, above all, of religion. Other explanatory time-scales are, of course, possible – in a recent book Professor Ashton goes back to 1603 (37) – but it may be helpful to discuss the Stone and Russell approaches a little further.

Both men, of course, just like all other historians who have written on the subject, regard the events of Charles I's reign as crucial in producing the united opposition to the Crown which existed in 1640, although they differ substantially about the relative importance of different factors within the period from 1625 onwards. We have already discussed (Chs. 32–4) the wide variety of grievances which members of the landed and merchant classes had against the Crown in 1640, but it is important to stress once again that the political nation was much more receptive in 1640 than used to be thought to the complaints of the lower orders, who had been suffering widespread economic distress during the 1630s and a considerable number of whom had the right to vote in parliamentary elections. Many of these common people blamed the Crown for their situation and their anger, stimulated by the dislike which they also felt for Charles's fiscal and religious policies, strengthened the hands of Lords and Commons against the King in 1640 as well as raising the threat of popular pressure on Parliament if their interests and wishes were not recognized and considered (122; 221). Professor Russell and others who think like him believe that discussion of these events of 1625–40 is basically sufficient to explain the crisis of 1640. Protagonists of longer-term explanations, however, stress that disputes about the exact point of balance in the constitution can be traced back into the sixteenth century – they can, for example, be seen in such disputes as those over free speech and monopolies in Elizabethan Parliaments (see above, Ch. 5) – and recall that even if there were no serious disputes between the hierarchy and the Puritans in the later sixteenth century over fundamental points of doctrine, there were certainly disagreements over many other matters, such as the roles of ceremonial and preaching in the Church. Above all, however, those who favour a long-term perspective on the events of 1640–41 can draw attention to Professor Hill's interpretation of intellectual developments in the century or so before 1640 and to long-term social and economic trends from the 1530s onwards.

Professor Hill has argued that in the 100 years before 1640 a number of strands of thought sapped men's belief in established institutions (281). In this context he points to developments in science, in the writing of history and in the law, all of which, he believes, provided a new intellectual climate for the men who brought about the constitutional revolution of 1640–41 as well as later developments. These intellectual trends, he claims, stressed that the world and man's lot within it could be improved by human reason and effort and that ideas which applied the test of usefulness to institutions were important as well as those which emphasized tradition. Without such changes in the intellectual climate, he believes, political revolution would have been much more difficult. Hill, therefore, assigns to men like Bacon, Ralegh and Coke, whom he places at the centre of these intellectual developments, the kind of role traditionally assigned to the French *philosophes* in the years before 1789; they undermined respect for the English *ancien régime* of the late sixteenth and early seventeenth centuries and thus helped to bring about its collapse in 1640. We cannot go into the details either of Professor Hill's thesis or of the criticisms which have been made of it,[2] but it is important to stress that early seventeenth century political thought was overwhelmingly conservative. If the men of 1640 were substantially affected by new ideas of progress most of them concealed the fact remarkably well in their speeches. It was only in later years of the Long Parliament that the subversive ideas of the pre-1640 period made a significant impact.

If doubt arises about the significance of long-term intellectual trends in the context of the events of 1640–41, it has also been expressed about the 'rise of the gentry' in the century before 1640. In 1941, in a seminal article, Professor Tawney argued that the rise of the gentry – that amorphous group between the peerage on the one hand and the yeomanry on the other – was the most important factor in social changes which took place in the century before the Civil War (215). Following Harrington he stressed that the gentry as a group acquired a great deal of land, much of it from the Crown and the Church, during this period, and that many gentlemen made large profits by farming that land efficiently at a time when a rapidly rising population put heavy pressure on the food supply. Twenty-four years later, in 1965, Professor Stone dealt with the peerage in a massive work (217) in which he argued that members of the titled nobility lost much of their prestige during the late sixteenth and early seventeenth centuries as the result of a many-sided crisis in their affairs, a crisis which was only partly and not principally due to economic difficulties. He accepted Tawney's broad conclusions about the rise of the gentry, only maintaining that it was made to seem even more dramatic by the simultaneous slump in the prestige of the aristocracy. If Tawney's and Stone's arguments are accepted we can see good social and economic reasons for the decisive role which the gentry in the House of Commons were able to take in the events of 1640–41. These men and the class which they represented had become increasingly wealthy and well educated in the century before 1640. This, Tawney and Stone argue, goes far in explaining why they had the self-confidence to seize so much of the political initiative in 1640–41 and thereafter.

If Tawney and Stone both saw a rising gentry as the decisive factor in social changes in the century before 1640 Professor Trevor-Roper painted a very different picture in his article on 'The gentry, 1540–1640', published in 1953 (216), arguing instead that the decisive social development in that century was the decline in the economic standing of the great mass of 'mere' gentry – those who depended on land for their livelihood and did not have access to the profits of office-holding or trade. Since Tawney and Trevor-Roper wrote their original articles there has been much detailed research on the fortunes of the gentry and the peerage. One of the results of that may be, as Professor Russell puts it, that the evidence for a crisis in the affairs of the peerage 'remains uncertain' but Russell is surely on much more doubtful ground when he argues that it has also shown that while 'there were some rising gentry and some declining gentry . . ., no general picture emerges' (60, 6, 7). It is true, of course, that research has revealed many declining as well as many rising gentry families, a situation which would be true of virtually any period of English history, but the *overall* picture is well summarized by Professor Stone who writes that 'both relatively and absolutely there was an impressive rise of the gentry as a status group in terms of numbers and wealth, whatever fluctuations there may have been in the fortunes of some of the individual families who composed it' (38, *74*). The gentry rose substantially in numbers, from perhaps 5,000 to 15,000 families between 1540 and 1640 at a time when the population of the country only doubled, and by the latter date gentlemen as a group undoubtedly held a larger proportion of the land of the country than had been in their possession a century earlier.

What conclusions, if any, can be drawn about long- and short-term explanations of the crisis of 1640–41? It must be said at once that there is no simple answer. In the last resort, each student has the task of deciding for himself in a field where the experts are profoundly divided in their views. Nevertheless, it may be suggested that while short-term explanations may be preferable in some aspects of the problem, longer-term considerations are more appropriate in others. As far as short-term explanations are concerned, it is becoming more and more obvious as a result of recent research that there was a real break in the political and religious fields about the time of Charles I's accession. Professor Ashton's work on the attitudes of the London merchant class and Professor Russell's on the Parliaments of the 1620s (125; 258) have shown that the period 1624–29 saw a serious worsening of relationships between the Crown and the most important sections of the political nation, and it can also be maintained that the extent and unpopularity of the non-parliamentary taxation which Charles I demanded during the 1630s represented an unprecedented refusal to consider the wishes and susceptibilities of the governing classes. In the religious sphere,

Charles's adoption of Arminianism and his attempt to force it on the Church at grass-roots level during the 1630s was a decisive break with the past. As a result of these unwise and unpopular actions there was a virtual breakdown in local administration when Charles made still further demands on the localities to finance the war with Scotland which he had brought upon himself by equally foolish political and ecclesiastical measures in his northern kingdom. When the Short Parliament and even more the Long Parliament met, the King had to face the anger of an almost uniformly hostile ruling class. It is at this point in the argument that longer-term considerations seem relevant. Just at the time when Charles produced policies in both politics and religion which were highly objectionable to the great mass of the political nation, long-term social and economic developments made it easier for the gentry to resist and in 1640, in alliance with the bulk of the peerage, to reverse these innovations. The gentry were able to do this partly because they were wealthier and more self-confident as a group than they had been a 100 years earlier, although it is more doubtful if they were significantly influenced in 1640–41 by the new intellectual trends which Professor Hill has dissected.

If the causes of the constitutional revolution of 1640–41 can be discussed in widely differing ways, in long-term or short-term contexts, the reasons for the breakdown of the broad country consensus of 1640–41 and the outbreak of civil war in 1642 are much less controversial (see above, Ch. 34). The King's hostility to the changes which were forced upon him in 1641 led to growing fears among the parliamentary leaders that he might mount a coup against them which would lead both to the reversal of the reforms already accomplished and possibly even to the loss of their lives. These fears led in turn to the increasingly radical constitutional demands – for a veto on royal ministerial appointments and control of the militia – which they had made by the beginning of 1642. More moderate parliamentarians at Westminster and in the country at large now felt that the parliamentary leadership was going too far, and they were also increasingly afraid of the possible religious and social revolutions which were implicit in the 'root and branch' movement, the growth of sectarianism and the increasing politicization of the London mob. These anxieties produced the extent of support for the King which was symbolized in the debates about the Grand Remonstrance in November 1641 and, despite Charles's foolish actions in December 1641 and January 1642, which lost him a good deal of support, they were sufficient to win and keep for him enough committed followers to pose a serious challenge to the parliamentary leadership. The immediate cause of the final breakdown of relations between King and Parliament, the dispute over the control of the militia, was given added point by the situation in Ireland created by the Catholic rebellion of October 1641, and the crunch for members of the political nation came during the following summer when they had to decide whether they would obey either Parliament's Militia Ordinance or a Royal Commission of Array. Despite the very considerable strength of neutralist opinion in the localities there were sufficient activists on either side among members of the gentry class to start a civil war.

Why did those who did not manage to stay neutral finally choose either one side or the other? There is no clear answer to this question and the final decision in many cases must have been the result of a mental battle in the minds of men who were torn between instinctive loyalty to the King and a strong dislike of his past policies and distrust of his present intentions. Traditional ties did keep the great majority of the peerage loyal to the Crown, although important noblemen, like the earls of Essex and Manchester, helped to give respectability to the parliamentary cause. There were, indeed, no clear-cut social or economic divisions between the two sides. Members of the greater and lesser, rising and declining gentry, office holders (107), merchants and other townsmen were found on both sides, though in different proportions. The lower orders, both in towns and countryside, probably had little choice but to take the side of their social superiors in the immediate vicinity, but it must be emphasized that there is little evidence in 1642 of enthusiastic popular support for a supposedly paternalistic king. On the other hand, religion clearly played a vital role in determining men's final attitudes (142). Although the constitutional dispute about control of the militia was the cause of the final breakdown in relations between Crown and Parliament, Dr Morrill has argued convincingly that this issue did not loom large in the provinces, where both royalists and parliamentarians assumed that political problems were capable of settlement by negotiation. In most counties the activists among the royalists were strong defenders of episcopacy who saw in the policies of the parliamentary opposition an explicit or implicit challenge to the whole structure of the Church and, by extension, to all social order and hierarchy. The parliamentarians, on the other hand, were those who were determined to introduce a Godly reformation of the Church which, at the most, would leave room for only a very modified form of episcopacy. This general analysis receives specific support in such local studies as that of Dr Cliffe, who has pointed out that exactly 50 per cent of the Yorkshire gentry families which fought for Parliament during the Civil War were solidly Puritan in their sympathies. On the other hand, only 10 per cent of the royalist gentry in Yorkshire were Puritans, and Cliffe concludes that it is difficult to see how a parliamentary party could have evolved at all within the Yorkshire gentry without the dynamic leadership which the Puritans provided (155; 252). It is an analysis which the great nineteenth-century historians like Gardiner would have welcomed. They may have oversimplified the issues, but they were not far wrong after all in pointing to the decisive importance of religion in determining the taking of sides in 1642. By that date religious divisions in England which were, to a considerable extent, a long-term result of the sixteenth-century Reformation, played a vital role in a civil war which was a traumatic shock to the English polity and had repercussions throughout the whole of the British Isles.

These repercussions reflected, to a considerable extent, the fact that Scotland and Ireland played a vital role in the events of 1640–42. It was the Scottish rebellion of 1637 and Charles I's failure to suppress it which made the calling of the Short and Long Parliaments necessary, and it was the Irish rebellion of 1641 which inflamed Protestant Englishmens' horror of Catholicism and suspicion of the King's attitude and, above all, brought to the fore the crucial question of control of the armed forces. 'Without the Irish rebellion, as much as without the Scottish', writes Professor Russell, 'Charles I would have overcome opposition and stayed in power.' (*60, 13*) Not all historians may accept that judgement but it does highlight the vital importance of extra-English events in creating the situations in which the constitutional revolution of 1640–41 took place and in which the Civil War broke out in 1642.

———————

1. For useful comments on some of these points, P. Christianson, 'The causes of the English Revolution: A re-appraisal', *JBS*, **15**, No. 2 (1976), 40 ff; J. H. Hexter, 'Power struggle, Parliament and liberty in early Stuart England', *JMH*, **50** (1978), 1 ff.
2. See e.g. G. E. Aylmer's review in *EHR*, **81** (1966), 783 ff.

PART FIVE

An age of revolution: Civil war and interregnum, 1642–1660

FRAMEWORK OF EVENTS 1642–1660

1642   Attempt by the King to arrest the 'five members' (Jan); the King leaves London (Jan). The Long Parliament continues: Bishops' Exclusion Bill passed (Feb); Militia Ordinance passed by the Lords and Commons (Mar).

Gradual beginning of hostilities between supporters of the Crown and supporters of the parliamentary opposition. The King denied entry to Hull by Sir John Hotham (Apr); the King issues Commissions of Array (June); the navy declares for Parliament (July); the King raises his banner at Nottingham (Aug); Battle of Edgehill (d,[1] Oct); royalist forces advance to Turnham Green (pv, November); Eastern Association established (Dec).

Long Parliament orders the closing of all theatres.

1643   Royalist successes in North and West (Jan); death of John Hampden (June); relief of Gloucester (pv, Sept) First Battle of Newbury (d, Sept); Parliament concludes Solemn League and Covenant with the Scots (Sept); the Scots agree to send an army to help Parliament (Nov); death of John Pym (Dec).

Westminster Assembly set up by the Long Parliament to discuss a religious settlement (June).

New fiscal system introduced by Parliament: 'weekly pay' (assessment) – Feb; capital levies on royalists (Mar); excise (July).

Parliament revives censorship.

1644   Royalist Parliament summoned at Oxford (Jan). Scottish Army crosses the border to assist the Long Parliament (Jan). Battle of Marston Moor (pv, July) – the King's control of the North ended; Battle of Lostwithiel (rv, Aug); Second Battle of Newbury (d, Oct). Committee of Both Kingdoms set up.

New Directory of Worship approved by Westminster Assembly.

Excise extended to food.

Milton's *Areopagitica*, a notable protest against censorship.

1645   Uxbridge negotiations between King and Parliament fail (Jan–Feb). Execution of Laud (Jan). Self-denying Ordinance (April). Creation of New Model Army (Apr): Fairfax Commander-in-Chief. Battle of Naseby (pv, June); Battle of Langport (pv, July). Activities of 'clubmen' widespread in southern England.

New Directory of Worship authorized by Parliament (Jan) and use of the Prayer Book prohibited (Aug); parliamentary ordinance on Presbyterianism (Aug).

Compositions with royalists begin.

1646   Surrender of Charles I to the Scots (May); Oxford surrenders to Parliament (June). End of the First Civil War.

Newcastle Propositions presented by Parliament to the King (July).

Parliament orders a Presbyterian Church system to be set up throughout England (Mar); offices of bishop and archbishop formally abolished (Oct) – bishops' lands to be sold.

Abolition of the Court of Wards by Parliament.

First of 5 successive (1646–50) bad harvests.

Thomas Edwards, *Gangraena*, a famous attack on the growth of extremist religious sects; Edward Hyde, later earl of Clarendon begins his *History*, first published in the early eighteenth century.

1647   Scots hand Charles I over to Parliament (Jan). Parliament orders the army to disband without arrears of pay (May). King seized by the army (June). Direct military action by the army against Parliament in order to secure fair treatment for

303

troops (Aug). *Heads of the Proposals* presented by the army to the King (Aug).

Beginning of the period of major Leveller importance (1647–49): First Leveller Agreement of the People (Oct). 'Agitators', strongly influenced by Leveller ideas, are appointed to represent the army rank and file. Debates in the General Council of the Army at Putney (Oct–Nov). Leveller-inspired mutiny in the army (Nov). The King escapes from the army's custody and flees to the Isle of Wight (Nov). Charles signs an 'Engagement' with the Scots (Dec).

Severe parliamentary ordinance on press censorship.

1648   Vote of 'No addresses' passed by Parliament (Jan). Second Civil War (Apr–Aug) Scottish invasion of England on behalf of the King (July); Battle of Preston (Aug) – defeat of the Scots; end of Second Civil War.

Treaty of Newport (Sept): negotiations between the King and Parliament. Cromwell, in Edinburgh, insists that supporters of the Engagement be excluded from Scottish public life. Second Leveller Agreement of the People (Dec). Pride's Purge of Parliament (Dec).

Peace of Westphalia: end of the Thirty Years War.

1649   The 'Rump' of the Commons assumes supreme power in the nation by resolution (Jan). Trial and execution of Charles I (Jan); Charles II proclaimed king in Edinburgh (Feb); abolition by the Rump of the monarchy and the House of Lords (Mar); England declared a free commonwealth (May). Third Leveller Agreement of the People (May). Leveller mutiny in the army (May).

Cromwell in Ireland (Aug): sieges of Drogheda (Sept) and Wexford (Oct)- both taken by storm by Cromwell.

Winstanley and the Diggers begin to cultivate the waste at Walton-on-Thames in Surrey (Apr).

John Milton, *The Tenure of Kings and Magistrates*, a defence of the execution of Charles I. Parliament orders the sale of Charles's splendid collection of paintings.

1650   Cromwell returns from Ireland to England (May): the conquest of Ireland continues in his absence; Cromwell Lord General – Commander-in-Chief of all the forces of the Commonwealth – in succession to Fairfax (June). Charles II lands in Scotland after swearing to the Covenants (June). Cromwell invades Scotland (July); Battle of Dunbar (Sept): Cromwell defeats the Scots; Edinburgh Castle surrenders to the English (Dec).

Rump Parliament provides that all court proceedings are henceforth to be in English; statutes enjoining compulsory attendance at parish churches repealed by the Rump.

Height of the Ranter mvt: 'Blasphemy Act', directed mainly against the Ranters, passed by the Rump (Aug.). Height and collapse of the Digger mvt.

Parliamentary newspaper *Mercurius Politicus* established.

1651   Charles II crowned King of Scots at Scone (Jan). Cromwell captures Perth (Aug); Stirling Castle surrenders to the English (Aug); Scottish Army crosses the border into England (Aug); Battle of Worcester (Sept): Cromwell defeats a Scottish Army in England; English Army storms Dundee (Sept). Charles II escapes to France (Oct).

Negotiations at The Hague for an alliance between England and the United Provinces break down.

The Fifth Monarchist mvt begins.

Parliament attempts to assert control over those English colonies in America which had remained loyal to the Crown. Navigation Act (Oct) – English attack on the Dutch carrying trade. Rate of interest on loans cut by the Rump from 8 per cent to 6 per cent.

Hobbes's *Leviathan*.

1652   An Act 'for the Settling of Ireland' (Aug) begins the great Cromwellian land confiscations there. Hale Commission on Law Reform set up.

War with the United Provinces (May) – a result of trade disputes and of English claims to sovereignty in the British seas: Battle of the Downs between the English under Blake and the Dutch under Tromp (May) – the Dutch retreat; victory by Blake over the Dutch in the Channel (Sept); Dutch victory over English fleet at Dungeness (Nov).

American colonies recognize parliamentary authority.

Gerrard Winstanley's *Law of Freedom*.

1653   Cromwell expels the Rump (Apr). Barebone's Parliament (July–Dec) includes members from Scotland and Ireland: it votes for the abolition of Chancery, the abolition of lay patronage of clerical livings, and also mounts an assault on tithes. Height of Fifth Monarchist influence. Instrument of Government, a written Constitution for Britain (Dec): Cromwell Lord Protector of England, Scotland and Ireland; MPs from all three countries to sit in Parliament.

Beginning of Glencairn's rising (1653–55) in Scotland.

Battle of Portland (Feb): indecisive naval engagement between the English and the Dutch; Battle of the Texel (July) – the greatest battle of the Anglo-Dutch War: Tromp mortally wounded and Dutch defeated.

I. Walton, *The Compleat Angler*.

1654   The Union of Scotland and England formally proclaimed (Apr). George Monck, Commander-in-Chief in Scotland (April) makes considerable progress during the year in subduing Glencairn's rising. Colonel Gerard's plot to kill Cromwell (May): Gerard arrested and executed. Ordinance for the reform of Chancery (Aug).

First Protectorate Parliament meets (Sept, and continues until Jan 1655): it attempts to restrict religious toleration and attacks the Instrument of Government.

Treaty of Westminster (Apr): peace with the United Provinces and a defensive alliance between the two states. Treaty with Sweden (Apr). Treaty with Portugal (July). Treaty with Denmark (Sept).

Cromwellian State Church created by ordinance: Commission of Triers (March); local Commissions of Ejectors (Aug).

Expedition against the Spanish colonies in the West Indies and mainland America sails (Dec). Capture of Nova Scotia from France.

1655   Cromwell dismisses First Protectorate Parliament (Jan). Penruddock's royalist rising in Wiltshire defeated (Mar). Rebellion in Scotland ended (May). Organization of a new militia (summer); introduction of the major-generals (Oct): they are given wide control over local government generally as well as over military affairs.

War with Spain in the colonies: Cromwell's expedition to the West Indies captures Jamaica (May). Defensive treaty with France (Nov) – exiled Stuarts excluded from France. Blake asserts English seapower in the Mediterranean.

Readmission of the Jews to England.

1656   Second Protectorate Parliament meets (Sept, and continues until June 1657): attempts to restrict religious toleration; Parliament agrees that war with Spain is necessary and promises to support it vigorously; disputes over the major-generals whose unpopularity in the country at large is reflected in Parliament.

Blake fails to intercept Spanish treasure fleet from the New World on its way to Spain (spring); a later Spanish treasure fleet is intercepted in European waters and the ships either captured or destroyed – a huge amount of treasure captured (Sept).

Nayler's entry into Bristol in imitation of Christ's entry into Jerusalem (Oct).

Harrington's *Oceana* published.

1657   Second Protectorate Parliament continues until June: major-generals abolished; *Humble Petition and Advice* (May): Cromwell refuses the Crown but accepts some amendments to the Instrument of Government. Second Inauguration of Cromwell conducted with great ceremony in Westminster Hall (June).

Offensive alliance with France against Spain (Mar): Battle of Santa Cruz – great naval victory by Blake in the Canaries (Apr); death of Blake (Aug); Mardyke captured from Spain (Sept).

First of 5 successive (1657–61) bad harvests; beginnings of trade depression.

New university college at Durham.

1658   Second Session of Second Protectorate Parliament (Jan–Feb): a contentious meeting marked by bitter wrangles between the Commons and the new Upper House. Death of Cromwell (Sept); Richard Cromwell becomes Protector at the age of 33.

French alliance prolonged by a new treaty (Mar); Battle of the Dunes (June): French and English forces defeat a Spanish army; surrender of Dunkirk by Spain (June); Dunkirk handed over to England.

1659   Richard Cromwell's Parliament meets (Jan–Apr); Richard Cromwell resigns (May) – end of the Protectorate. The Rump recalled by the army (May): disputes between the army and the newly recalled Parliament. Booth's rising, a royalist revolt in Cheshire (Aug): defeated by Lambert; Booth sent to the Tower. Rump expelled by the army (Oct) and later recalled for the second time (Dec).

Treaty of the Pyrenees between France and Spain (Nov).

Fears among the propertied classes of a Quaker rising.

1660   General Monck marches south from Scotland with his army; he reaches London (Feb). Monck readmits to the Rump those members of the Long Parliament secluded at the time of Pride's Purge (Feb); the Long Parliament dissolves itself (Mar). Declaration of Breda by Charles II (Apr). A Convention Parliament, elected on the traditional franchise, meets (25 Apr); Charles II proclaimed (8 May) and enters London on 29 May.

Samuel Pepys begins his *Diary*.

---

1. d = drawn or indecisive battle; pv = parliamentarian victory; rv = royalist victory.

CHAPTER 36

The first civil war, 1642–1646

The outbreak of civil war in 1642 bore witness to the final collapse of the Tudor system of government which had been created during the sixteenth century and had shown ever increasing signs of stress during the reign of Charles I. The years 1642–60 saw a struggle to find a new system to replace it. First of all, however, King and Parliament tested their fortunes in a war which lasted from 1642 to 1646 (40; 147 see also O.6).

The armies which fought in the war were small by Continental standards – no single army reached 20,000 in number until the later stages of the war – and only a minority of the population were ever actively engaged in the struggle either as participants or as committed supporters of either side. We have already noted the strength of neutralism in 1642, an attitude associated with the deep desire among many men of all classes to keep the localities where they lived free from military strife. It is important as well to stress that, although there was a rough geographical division between the two sides, with the King controlling the North, Wales and parts of the South-west in 1642–43 and Parliament drawing its strength mainly from the richer and more populous southern and eastern half of England, there were significant pockets of royalist supporters in parliamentarian areas and of adherents to the parliamentary cause in parts of the country under royalist authority. Parliament controlled London throughout the war, a fact of very considerable significance in view of the city's importance as a supplier both of money and of men. Most of the larger towns in the country were also under parliamentary authority as were most of the seaports, even those in pre-dominantly royalist areas. Control of London and the other ports gave the parliamentarians the ability to collect most of the customs revenue which continued to flow into the country and they were able to use the navy – under their authority from the beginning of the war – to ensure that their general control of the coasts was maintained and to move food and men to ports which were threatened by royalist attack. Parliament, therefore, controlled the greater part of the country's wealth and manpower, and the major issue during the war was whether it would be able to bring this superior material strength to bear in an effective assault upon the King. Charles did have some initial assets. Parliament lacked good trained troops in the early stages of the war, whereas the King soon had a dashing cavalry force at his disposal commanded by his nephew, Prince Rupert of the Rhine. If he could have achieved some quick military triumphs he might have won the day, especially in view of the fact that his parliamentary opponents were divided in their political aims from 1642 onwards with 'war' and 'peace' parties and a 'middle group' in Parliament each competing for the support of the large numbers of MPs who did not belong to any grouping (108; 128).

These divisions were compounded by the reluctance of the leading parliamentary generals, the earls of Essex and Manchester, to fight too ruthlessly against their anointed sovereign. Charles, in contrast, should have been able to take advantage of his own unquestioned leadership of the royalist cause to impose a firm and united policy on his supporters. In fact, he listened to too many different voices in his council of war and failed to form and stick to an effective policy, a fact which significantly hindered his negotiations with the parliamentarians who, not without reason, suspected him of double-dealing. His inability to win a decisive victory in 1642 or 1643, when he held the military initiative, gave his opponents the opportunity to begin to organize their superior material assets. In 1643 Parliament began to raise large sums of money by new methods and formed an alliance with the Scots which had important military consequences the following year.

The King was never able to match the revenue which the parliamentarians enjoyed from 1643 onwards as the result of the introduction of an entirely new fiscal system founded on a productive excise [N] a Dutch inspired novelty; on a 'weekly pay' later known as the 'assessment' [N], which was a much more effective direct tax than the subsidy; and on capital levies on royalists in the areas under parliamentary control. Parliament was able in the same year to exploit Scottish desires to see a Presbyterian Church in England to conclude a Solemn League and Covenant [G.6(26)] with the Scots which brought the military aid which played an important part in the notable parliamentary victory at Marston Moor in 1644, a battle which gave Parliament control of the north of England. The following year Parliament refashioned its own forces by the creation of a 'New Model Army', a national force which was under the command of Sir Thomas Fairfax and Oliver Cromwell, men who were prepared to press Parliament's military campaigns much more vigorously than the now largely discredited Essex and Manchester. The King was defeated in the Midlands at Naseby in 1645, and the following year, realizing that further resistance was useless, he surrendered to the Scots. He had been overcome by the superior material strength at Parliament's disposal. His one real chance, a quick military victory, had gone by 1643, and if it would be an exaggeration to say that the entry of the Scots into the war in that year sealed his fate, Parliament's reorganization of both its finances and its military forces between 1643 and 1645 certainly ensured a royalist defeat which looked increasingly unavoidable after 1644.

Parliament had gone to war with the King in 1642 partly at least to resist what most MPs regarded as his attacks on the 'ancient Constitution'. In view of this it is ironic that the parliamentarians showed little concern for traditional forms in the government which they imposed on the areas of England under their control during the war. Their realization that in a revolutionary situation strong measures were needed helped them to maintain the control which was necessary to raise the new taxes which played such a significant part in their ultimate military victory. It seems likely that it was the *King* more than his opponents who endeavoured to hold to the normal processes of administration (155). It is true that the royalists gained the greater reputation for lawlessness, but this was due to the actions of some of the King's senior military commanders – an important example of Charles's inability to control his supporters effectively – and the King's own attitude can be seen in his determination that traditional local courts, above all assizes and quarter sessions, should continue to sit if this was at all possible. Parliament's attitude was very different; comparatively few quarter sessions were held where its influence was dominant, and much of the work previously done by these vital local meetings was now undertaken by the county committees which were the most important administrative innovation of the parliamentarians (59).

It has been said that 'the Civil War was won by committees' (64, *182*), and there is no doubt that Parliament made good use of these bodies as the executive arms of its government at both central and local levels. In the early years of the war a Committee of Safety was established as a supreme war council, but it was a good deal less effective in controlling the localities than its successor, the Committee of Both Kingdoms, created in 1644 as a result of the Scottish alliance of the previous year. The latter showed that it could bring strong pressure to bear in the shires on a wide variety of matters ranging from the punishment of deserters and anti-Scottish rioters to attempts to convince local authorities of the need to allow the use of locally raised troops outside their native counties (37; 109). In the shires, county committees often began in *ad hoc* ways as members of the local gentry met to consider parliamentary instructions. They soon developed into powerful bodies, performing a wide variety of military, financial, administrative and quasi-judicial tasks. They were unpopular both with the local population as institutions responsible for imposing substantial military and fiscal burdens upon them and by the Committee of Both Kingdoms which regarded them as bastions of localism, always reluctant to allow the use of their own resources for the common good of the parliamentary cause. It was in an attempt to overcome such particularism that the parliamentary authorities decided at the end of 1642 to group counties together in regional associations. The new associations, however, did not command the kind of loyalty which men felt for their home shire, and only one, the Eastern Association, where Oliver Cromwell commanded the cavalry, was a real success; its troops formed the nucleus of the New Model Army of 1645 which brought final victory to the parliamentary cause. If the very limited success which the associations had in overcoming the particularism of the shires emphasizes the continuing strength of localism throughout the war, the activities of the 'clubmen', who were very active in the southern regions of England in 1645, reminds us that the neutralism which was so strong in many areas of the country in 1642 was not extinguished and indeed may have been increased by burdens which the royalists and especially the parliamentarians imposed on the country during the war years (155). The 'clubmen' – so called because of the clubs they were supposed to have carried – though they might co-operate with either King or Parliament in particular circumstances did not seek the victory of either. They wanted a national pacification, including the return of traditional methods of government in the localities, and were determined if possible to impose local truces as a means both of protecting their own locality and helping to force the warring sides into a general settlement.

The peace which the clubmen wanted came, at least for a time, with the·defeat of the King in 1646, but that year did not see the return to the traditional forms of government which they also craved; these were only to be restored when Charles II came back from exile in 1660. Meanwhile, during the war years Parliament, urged on by the Scots, had created the legal framework for the establishment of a Presbyterian Church of England (10; 166). In February 1642, several months before the outbreak of armed conflict, the King had reluctantly given his assent to the so-called Bishops' Exclusion Bill [G.6(25)], which prohibited not merely members of the episcopate but all clergymen in holy orders from occupying temporal offices in the State. It was a triumph for the laity over one aspect of Laudianism – that intrusion of clergymen into state positions both at the centre of government and in the localities which had been such a prominent feature of the 1630s – but Parliament soon went far beyond an attack on Laud's innovations when it abolished the episcopal office itself. In January 1643 both Lords and Commons approved a bill which swept away any form of diocesan administration in England and Wales and in October 1646 the offices of archbishop and bishop were formally abolished by parliamentary ordinance [G.6(28)]. It was a break not only with post-Reformation tradition but with the entire historical past of the English Church going back to St Augustine's day, and it went hand in hand with measures for the establishment of Presbyterianism. An ordinance of June 1643 (15, Vol. 1, *180ff*) set up an Assembly at Westminster to make recommendations to Parliament for a church settlement. It consisted of 121 ministers, all appointed by Parliament, with the addition of 10 peers and 20 MPs. Although the majority of the ministers were in favour of Presbyterianism, a vocal minority were not and they had support not merely from the majority of the lay members of the Assembly but from many more MPs in the House of Commons itself. These MPs, both inside and outside the Assembly, feared the establishment in England of the full Presbyterian system as it was known in Scotland, with Presbyterians claiming a divine right to control the Church free from lay interference. They had not rejected the *iure divino* claims of Laudian bishops to replace them with equally exalted Presbyterian ideas and the Solemn League and Covenant [G.6(26)], which they accepted in September 1643, contained a clause which, by providing that the settlement should be 'according to the word of God and the example of the best reformed churches', gave them the latitude, in their ordinances of 1645 and 1646 [G.6(27a,b)], to set up a system which was certainly Presbyterian but was firmly subjected to the control of Parliament. It was an Erastian compromise which disgusted the Scots, but by 1645, with the formation of the New Model Army, Scottish military assistance was no longer as necessary as it had previously been. Meanwhile, in 1644 the Westminster Assembly had produced a new Directory of Worship, 'a sober Calvinist form of service', as Dr Cross has described it (166, *202*), to replace the Prayer Book, and in January 1645 Parliament authorized its use, though the old form of worship was not outlawed until August of the same year (15, vol. 1, *582 ff, 755 ff*).

Legally, then, from 1646 onwards there was provision for the establishment of a Presbyterian Church of England with a hierarchy of courts from parish presbyteries at the bottom to a National Assembly at the top. It remained to be seen whether or not the new organization could establish itself at grass-roots level in the years ahead. Its prospects as a national institution were threatened not merely by the opposition or at best indifference of men who continued to prefer a moderate non-Laudian form of episcopacy but more immediately by the growth of independency during the war years. Independents, who had a good deal of support in Parliament and the army, where their greatest champion was Oliver Cromwell, rejected the idea of a State Church with extensive coercive powers or even, in some cases, of any kind of State Church at all, stressing instead the rights of local congregations in choosing their own ministers and managing their own affairs (166; 167). The breakdown of ecclesiastical discipline during the early 1640s led to the emergence of Independent congregations in many parts of the country; London especially became a centre of independency. These 'gathered churches' had ideas about church membership which distinguished them sharply from both Anglicans and Presbyterians, who believed that the whole population of the parish should be included; membership of the State meant for them membership of the State Church as well. Independents, in contrast, believed that only active Christians should be members of a church; for them 'the people of God', who sincerely tried to follow Christ's teaching, were a leaven in the large lump of the unregenerate. For many independents these differences about church membership and organization were the only major issues which separated them from the Presbyterians.

This was the position of the five prominent Independent or, as they preferred to call themselves, 'Congregationalist' ministers who justified their position in the *Apologetical Narration* of 1644, a plea against any attempt to enforce strict Presbyterianism in England. All these men had fled to the Netherlands during the 1630s to escape Laudian persecution and returned to England during the early 1640s. William Bridge, who may be taken as typical of the conservative Congregationalism which they represented, was a member of the anti-Presbyterian minority among the ministers in the Westminster Assembly and in 1643 and 1644 set up gathered churches in Yarmouth and Norwich from which Congregationalist ideas spread across Norfolk. Presbyterians like Thomas Edwards strongly disapproved of such deviations from national ecclesiastical discipline, but at least men like Bridge differed little from himself in their doctrine or in the form of worship which they adopted in their churches. The same could not be said for the more extreme sectaries whose activities Edwards chronicled with horror in 1646 in his *Gangraena*, the most famous and extensive contemporary account of unorthodox religious practices in England. Edwards listed numerous different varieties of sectaries and enumerated some 270 of their errors. It was a *tour de force* of righteous indignation which, despite its exaggerations, shows the widespread extent of sectarianism in the middle 1640s. He was particularly severe on the rejection of infant baptism by the growing number of Baptists in the country and lurid tales, like that of the troop of parliamentary soldiers in Huntingdonshire who discouraged an infant baptism at Yaxley by baptizing a horse in the church, must have filled conservative gentlemen with fears that the whole moral and social as well as the religious and political order which they had known was crumbling away.

The growth of these extremist religious ideas with their socially subversive implications, was a major reason why gentlemen on both the parliamentary and royalist sides were very anxious to bring the war to a close. Only then would they be able to concentrate on what they increasingly saw as their central task; the preservation of the whole hierarchical structure of society which underpinned their own position and privileges. For them, it was a tragedy that the negotiations between King and Parliament which took place during the war ended in failure. We cannot go into the details of these negotiations here – Charles felt that he could not accept the major further limitations on the royal prerogative and the demands for radical reform of the Church which were presented to him in the winters of 1642–43 and 1644–45 – but by that time he had established a strong claim to be regarded as the defender of the 'ancient constitution' which *Parliament* was now trying to overthrow. In June 1642, even before the war began, he produced a reasoned exposition of the idea of a balanced constitution, in which he stressed that the legitimate powers of the monarchy were necessary to preserve the social order and that Parliament's ambitions to arrogate excessive powers to itself would lead to anarchy (10).

By the end of the war the emergence of radical political as well as religious ideas suggested that the King might be right. The clash between Crown and Parliament, which opened up the whole question of the rightful seat of political power, produced during the Civil War extremist political ideas which made themselves felt during the later 1640s. By 1646 the Leveller party (see Chs. 37, 42) had built up considerable influence in London, and its leaders, like John Lilburne and Richard Overton, were taking up positions which were anti-monarchical, rejected the authority of the Lords and stressed the supreme power of a House of Commons under the strict control of an expanded electorate who were to choose annual Parliaments (282). It was a programme which must have sent shivers down the spines of the propertied classes, who saw economic as the logical corollary of political democracy, but they could take comfort in 1646 from the lack of any general support for such ideas as the abolition of the monarchy. Although there may have been some growth of republican sentiments in Parliament and in the army as the war progressed, the men who propounded them remained a small, uninfluential minority. Charles I could not have been more wrong when, in 1645, he told his uncle Christian IV of Denmark, that Parliament was pursuing a design of 'extirpating the royal blood and monarchy of England' (37, *184*). It was over three years after he wrote these words that a drastically purged House of Commons abolished the kingly office. Republicanism as a major force was a product of the dramatic developments of 1646–49 rather than of the events of the First Civil War. Even so, the fact that it was an issue at all by 1646 was a sign of the distance which men had travelled since 1640.

The Long Parliament had met in that year determined to resist and reverse the revolutionary assaults which they believed that the King and his ministers had made on the traditional constitution and on the Church of England since the beginning of his reign. Continuing distrust of Charles had led many of them to make more extreme demands after they had succeeded in achieving the peaceful constitutional revolution of 1640–41. The resulting breakdown of relations between the King and the majority of MPs led to the Civil War of 1642–46, and we have seen the extent to which the pressure of events during the war years radicalized the policies of Parliament. Men who had complained about arbitrary royal taxation and administrative innovation during the 1630s had actively or passively condoned the imposition of new taxes and a new administrative system which were far more drastic breaks with the past then anything that Charles had dreamed about before 1640. The same men, the great majority of whom had seen themselves in 1640 as defenders of traditional Anglicanism against Laudian extremism, had by 1646 abolished episcopacy altogether. During the early 1640s too, radical political and religious ideas with socially subversive implications began to be openly propounded. The propertied parliamentarians who had defeated the King by 1646 saw before them an open Pandora's box which contained ideas labelled 'political democracy' and 'congregational independence'. By challenging the King they had weakened the hierarchical basis of society; that was not, of course, their intention, and during the years 1646–48 the conservative gentry who dominated Parliament struggled with considerable determination to reach a settlement with the King. Such a settlement had eluded them during the war years, but they were ever more fearful of the threat to their own position in the State if their conflict with the monarchy continued too long.

CHAPTER 37

The quest for settlement: King, Parliament and the army, 1646–1649

The years 1646–49 saw a complex series of struggles about the shape of the final settlement which was to follow the parliamentary victory in the Civil War. The protagonists included the King, Parliament, the army, the Scots, and the 'popular' movement centred on the Levellers. A very broad spectrum of political opinion emerged in the country during these years and the differences among Charles' opponents when added to the manoeuvres of the King himself made any agreed settlement extremely difficult. Charles hoped to snatch political victory from military defeat. He believed that no solution was possible without him and in 1646 he had every reason for his confidence; as we have seen (Ch. 36), despite the anti-monarchical attitude of men like Lilburne and Overton, dedicated republicans were still a tiny minority both inside and outside Parliament at the end of the Civil War. The King's tactics were to play off his opponents against each other in the hope that he would emerge as the ultimate victor in the wake of their squabbles. In July 1646 Parliament presented him with severe terms, the Newcastle Propositions (13), which demanded royal recognition of the new Presbyterian Church of England which had been set up and parliamentary control over the militia for a period of twenty years. Charles was clever enough not to reject these terms outright, offering instead counter-proposals which would have given Presbyterianism a trial run for three years and involved parliamentary control of the armed forces for ten. He knew that there was a good deal of influential opinion, represented by men like Cromwell, which did not want a permanent Presbyterian settlement, and this was confirmed in the Heads of the Proposals which the army presented to him in August 1647 (13). These included suggestions for a wide degree of effective religious toleration and asked for parliamentary control of the militia for only ten years. They were the most statesmanlike suggestion for a settlement which emerged during this confused period, but the King treated them only as a further opportunity to play off the parliamentary majority against the army. Moreover, he was now considering a possible alliance with the Scots and in December 1647 he signed an 'Engagement' (13) with them by which, in return for accepting Presbyterianism in England for three years, he secured their promise of military aid to restore him to effective power. This agreement led to the Scottish invasion of England in 1648 and the Second Civil War, which produced implacable hostility towards the King from many of the leaders and men of the army who, in the last resort, held the reins of effective power. When they realized, in April 1648, that war was inevitable, army officers in a prayer meeting at Windsor resolved that, when it was over, they would bring Charles Stuart, 'that man of blood', to account for the injuries which he had inflicted on England (108, 96). By August the Scots had been defeated and

314

Charles was left to face the wrath of the victorious English Army. At the end of the First Civil War the abolition of the monarchy still seemed virtually unthinkable to most men. At the end of the Second it was a real possibility, though it would need a purge of Parliament by the army in December 1648 before the 'Rump' of members who remained in the Commons agreed to Charles's trial and execution at the beginning of 1649. The King's attempts to play off his opponents against each other had not worked. In making the Scottish alliance he had appealed openly to the power of the sword. When that went against him his only protection was the continuing desire of the majority in Parliament to reach a settlement with him. As the events of December 1648 showed, however, Parliament was impotent against an army which was determined to have its way, and by the end of 1648 the army as a whole was convinced that Charles must go. That was the crucial fact in the events of December 1648 and January 1649 even though Cromwell himself, now the most important figure in the country, only became converted to the need for the King's execution at a very late stage in the proceedings. (The events of 1647–49 are admirably analysed in (108).)

Parliament, which had to be drastically purged at the end of 1648 before the army could secure its assent to the King's trial, was divided during the years 1646–49 between a moderate majority, often called the 'Presbyterians' and a more radical minority, generally called the 'Independents'. (108; 128) These terms. which came gradually into general usage in 1645, have produced even more debate among historians that the complexities surrounding parliamentary politics during the Civil War of 1642–46 itself. Much of the difficulty which historians have experienced in employing the terms lies in the fact that contemporaries used them to cover both political and religious attitudes at a time when not all religious Presbyterians [N] were political moderates nor all religious Independents [N] political extremists. Each term in fact was used to cover men of widely differing political and religious views and they are best understood as polarities against which individual opinions, both political and religious, can be measured. Having said that it is important to remember that throughout 1647 and 1648 the majority of members of the Commons, whether we call them Presbyterians or not, were determined to attempt to reach an agreement with the King broadly similar to their proposals of 1646. The Newcastle Propositions of that year were repeated in only slightly modified forms in the Hampton Proposals of 1647 and the Treaty of Newport of 1648. Even the King's equivocal reply to the latter did not prevent the Commons from voting on 5 December to carry on the negotiations, and further discussions between Crown and Parliament were only prevented by Pride's Purge the next day. The more radical parliamentarians, or Independents if we prefer the term, only rarely had the upper hand in the House, though they were in the ascendant for a brief spell at the beginning of 1648 when Parliament in a Vote of No Addresses broke off all contact with the King following news of his secret agreement with the Scots. The moderates, however, soon regained their majority, and the almost permanent minority position of the radicals in Parliament was one – though not the only – important reason why they generally looked to the army as an ally. The radicals, with their desire for strong measures gainst the King, came into their own again after Pride's Purge, but that drastic action by the army was a symbol of the fact that by the end of 1648 the moderate majority in Parliament was prepared to make peace with the King on almost any terms in order to secure a return to stability. They knew that they had gone too far for the country as a whole – they were well aware that the Second Civil War, in some of its aspects, was a rising of the English provinces against the innovations and impositions of parliamentary rule during the 1640s – and not far enough for influential radical opinion both inside and outside the army. The spectre of military rule, a real possibility from 1647 onwards, haunted their debates, and an agreement with the King, which would enable them to reduce the army to political impotence and allow the ruling class as a whole to concentrate on the restoration of order, seemed ever more essential.

The army was united in the decision to purge Parliament at the end of 1648 and thus prevent what it regarded as a sell-out by selfish parliamentarians to a king who had refused to accept the verdict of God as demonstrated in the First Civil War and had been directly responsible for shedding much innocent blood in the Second. It was, however, divided in other ways during the later 1640s. On the one hand there were the grandees, senior officers like Cromwell, his son-in-law Henry Ireton and the able young Yorkshireman Colonel John Lambert, who were socially conservative and deeply mistrustful of the quasi-democratic attitudes of the emerging Leveller movement which, they feared, might lead to attacks on property rights. On the other hand many of the junior officers and of the rank and file of the army were strongly influenced by Leveller ideas in 1647–49. This clash of views led to the Putney debates in October–November 1647 [E.5(33)] in which Leveller ideas were debated in the General Council of the Army, a body which had been created in the spring of 1647 to represent the rank and file as well as the officers. Cromwell and the conservative officers rejected Leveller pleas during these debates and the result was a minor Leveller-inspired mutiny in the army in November 1647 which was sternly repressed by Cromwell, as was a more serious army revolt in May 1649, when Leveller discontent at the lack of any radical reforms after the King's execution led to mutiny in several regiments.

The army, whatever its internal divisions, has traditionally been regarded as an important political force long before 1647, but Dr Kishlansky has recently argued (148) that it was only in that year that it was effectively politicized. Whatever one makes of his arguments there is no doubt that 1647 was a significant year for the army. The attempt of Parliament, following the defeat of the King in the previous year, to disband part of it and ship the rest off to Ireland without paying the soldiers the arrears which they were due or indemnifying them against lawsuits for acts which they had committed during the war, was crass folly, united all sections of army opinion and led to direct military action against Parliament in August 1647 in an attempt to secure fair treatment for the troops. That was an indication, as Kishlansky has said, that by 1647 'political power had passed from the hands of the men at Westminster to those who held the sword' (148, *273*). It was a reality which Parliament was always reluctant to recognize, but it was demonstrated in stark terms in December 1648 when the army shaped Parliament to its will by the naked use of armed force. Indeed, it may be that it was the grandees' dislike of Leveller influence in the army which, paradoxically, helped to make them take a strong line towards King and Parliament in 1648–49. They were not prepared to meet Leveller demands for a quasi-democratic franchise, and they doubtless hoped that Pride's Purge and the subsequent execution of the King – which, of course, they regarded as necessary for other reasons as well – would help to appease Leveller complaints.

Just like Parliament and the army, the Scots were divided among themselves during the years 1646–49 (49; 160). They had entered the war of 1642–46 largely to promote the establishment of Presbyterianism in England, but in 1647–48 they were split between radical Covenanting leaders and more moderate men who inclined to the King's side. In 1647 the moderates were in the ascendant and under the leadership of James, duke of Hamilton, were prepared to try and restore Charles to power in return for the establishment of Presbyterianism in England for a trial period of only three years. Their moderation was fiercely opposed by the majority of ministers in the General Assembly who still held to the Solemn League and Covenant, and as a result the army of 20,000 or so men which marched into England in July 1648 to the King's aid left behind a deeply divided Scotland. The defeat of the Scots at Preston in August was rapidly followed by the overthrow of moderate influence north of the border, and in October Cromwell, who had marched into Edinburgh, was able to insist that supporters of the 'Engagement' would henceforth be excluded from Scottish public life. The defeat of the Scots led, of course, to more than just internal political changes in Scotland itself. It also eliminated them for a time as a major force in English politics and gave the English Army a much freer hand than it would otherwise have had in imposing its own solution in England at the end of 1648 and the beginning of 1649.

The army, which united to crush the Scots and the royalists during the Second Civil War, was, as we have seen, divided in its attitude to the Leveller movement which came to the fore after 1646. The Levellers will claim more detailed attention in another context (see Ch. 42). Here it is enough to note that they have been well characterized by Mr Thomas as a 'crucial pressure group' which did a good deal to influence the course of events in 1647 and 1648, when they helped to push the army grandees into increasingly radical attitudes towards Parliament and the King (62, 57–8). By 1647 the Levellers had won wide support among the lower middle class in London and in the lower ranks in the army, and between 1647 and 1649 the movement, with its radical political programme, roused the fears and opposition both of the conservative parliamentary leaders and of the army commanders. In 1649 the grandees suppressed it not only as an important force in the army but also as a significant political force in the country as well; just as much as the great majority of members of the Commons they disliked the social implications of Leveller ideas. Cromwell himself never forgot that he was a country gentleman and in the Putney debates in the autumn of 1647 he and Ireton made plain their fears that a wide extension of the franchise would lead to an attack on property rights; if men without property got the vote in large numbers they might demand economic as well as political democracy (16).

The different forces and pressures represented by King, Parliament, army,

Scots and Levellers acted and reacted upon each other to produce the main events of 1646–49, which culminated in the execution of the King and the abolition of the House of Lords. After the Second Civil War of 1648 the determination of the bulk of the army to bring the King to account was matched by the equal determination of the conservative majority in Parliament to continue negotiations with him. This deadlock was broken by the Purge to which Colonel Pride subjected the House of Commons on 6 December 1648. Of the 470 or so members who were entitled to sit in the Commons at the time of the Purge about 270 were permanently removed, either as a direct result of army action or on their own initiative. Of the remainder nearly 100 or more stayed away during the vital weeks between the Purge and the King's execution, only returning to the House in or after February 1649 (128). It is usual to assume that the Purge led almost inevitably to the trial and execution of the King, but it is wrong to oversimplify the course of events in December 1648 and January 1649. Cromwell himself was a late convert to the need for the King's execution. It was only after he had made a final vain attempt in late December to reach a settlement with Charles that he became convinced that his death was absolutely necessary. Having said this, there is no doubt that the events of January 1649 would have been quite impossible without the Purge. The House of Commons as constituted at the beginning of December 1648 would never have consented to the King's execution. The Purge enabled the radical minority which was left to arrange a trial at which Charles conducted himself with great dignity.[1] His impressive arguments did not save him from the executioner's axe on 30 January, convicted as a traitor against the English people [E.5(35)]. That was legal nonsense – treason was only possible against the person of the king – but it made the political point that those who now wielded effective power in the State, the army grandees, had come to the conclusion that no settled peace was possible while Charles lived. They may have been right, but the events of the next eleven years were to be a vain quest for a permanent settlement without a king. The structure of the new polity was worked out in February and March 1649. On 6 February the Commons voted to abolish the House of Lords and the following day they brought the monarchy to an end, resolving that 'the office of a king in this nation . . . is unnecessary, burdensome, and dangerous to the liberty, safety and public interest of the people' (108, *202–3*). These votes were enshrined in formal legislation on 17 March [E.6(36a)] – against the monarchy – and on the 19th [E.6(36b)] – against the Lords. Two months later, on the 19 May, England was declared 'a Commonwealth and Free State . . . governed . . . by the supreme authority of this nation, the representatives of the people in parliament . . . without any king or House of Lords' [E.6(36c)]. By the spring of 1649, therefore, supreme power in England in all its aspects, legislative, executive and judicial, was in the hands of a single chamber; that was a constitutional and political revolution with a vengeance. It had come about not as a result of a great popular swing towards republicanism in the country or even in Parliament, but as a consequence of growing conviction in the army, a conviction shared by only a minority of parliamentarians, that there could be no solution while Charles was alive. The Rump of the Long Parliament who proclaimed themselves the 'representatives of the people' in May 1649 represented in fact neither the population as a whole nor majority opinion within the political nation. They were the effective voice of a revolutionary army which between 1646 and 1649 had established itself as the dominant power in the State.

---

1. C. V. Wedgwood, *The Trial of Charles I* (1964).

CHAPTER 38

Commonwealth and Protectorate, 1649–58: I – Ireland and Scotland subdued: the Cromwellian union of Britain

The execution of the King and the abolition of the House of Lords in 1649 were very radical acts but they placed power in the hands of political revolutionaries, the army grandees and the members of the Rump of the Long Parliament, who were basically social conservatives; they wanted to preserve the existing structure of society within a revised constitutional and ecclesiastical framework. It was men of such attitudes who held power throughout the Interregnum when they were constantly attacked by protagonists of much more radical views – Levellers, Diggers and religious sectaries – whose ideas either implied or else explicitly propounded social revolution. We will deal first of all with the State created by the 'moderate' socially conservative revolutionaries whose greatest representative was Oliver Cromwell. His first task was the conquest of Ireland and Scotland.

After their 1641 revolt against English rule the Irish Catholics soon gained control of most of the country and Charles I greatly damaged his cause in England by his negotiations with them during the 1640s. Most Protestant Irishmen sided with Parliament until the Second Civil War, but in 1648 those in the south of the country declared their support for the King. As a result, at the time of Charles's execution, his Lord-Lieutenant there, the marquis of Ormond, was able to unite these Protestant loyalists with the Catholics in a league against the English Parliament. Soon they were in control of the whole country with the exception of Dublin itself and the ports of Dundalk and Londonderry. The young Charles II, who now formally claimed the succession to his dead father's throne, prepared to set sail for Ireland from his exile in the United Provinces and it was clear that if the Rump did not act quickly Ireland would soon be used as a base for attacks on England. In this situation Cromwell was appointed to the command of an army which was to restore English fortunes in Ireland. He finally landed in Dublin in August 1649 with a well-equipped force of 12,000 men. The story of Cromwell's military exploits in Ireland has often been told and Drogheda and Wexford are still names to conjure with among Catholics in both the north and south of Ireland. Ormond did not have sufficient forces to face Cromwell in the field and was forced to rely on the defence of fortresses while he tried to gather fresh men. One of these strongholds, Drogheda, refused to surrender in September when Cromwell summoned it to do so and the entire garrison which defended it, nearly 3,000 men, was put to the sword. The same thing happened at Wexford during the following month, when civilian inhabitants as well as military men were killed. Cromwell's actions could be justified by the laws of war, but their savagery has never been forgotten. It was not the most promising prelude to the reintroduction of effective English rule in Ireland. After the capture of Wexford other towns soon surrendered and by the end of the year almost all of the eastern and southern coasts of Ireland were in Cromwell's hands. By May 1650 he was able to return to England secure in the knowledge that the tide of English conquest was already rolling inland and that the complete subjugation of the island would not be long delayed; his successors Ireton, Ludlow and Fleetwood brought the whole country once more under English control by 1653.[1]

Cromwell had been recalled to England in the Spring of 1650 because of the situation in Scotland. From 1637 onwards, as we have seen, the Scots had played a vitally important role in the great events which had convulsed the British Isles. Their rejection of Laud's Prayer Book had led to the National Covenant, the Bishops' Wars and the collapse of Charles I's authority in England; the Solemn League and Covenant of 1643 has been followed by their military intervention on Parliament's side in the First Civil War and had pushed the English Parliament into formally establishing a Presbyterian Church of England by 1646; and most recently, their 'Engagement' with the King at the end of 1647 had led to the Second Civil War, which was decisive in convincing the English Army that Charles I must be called to account. The King's execution in January 1649 infuri-ated them and they immediately proclaimed Charles II as King of England as well as Scotland. In 1649–50 they made it plain that they were ready to fight for the restoration of their new monarch in both England and Ireland provided he was prepared to take the Covenant and agree to the establishment of Presbyter-ianism in all three of his kingdoms. In 1650, with his hopes of using Ireland as a royalist base now gone, Charles II had only the Scots to turn to, and in 1650 he reluctantly accepted their terms for his restoration. He landed in Scotland in June and was treated almost as a prisoner by the Presbyterians in power. In the same month Cromwell was appointed Commander-in-Chief of all the forces of the Commonwealth (80). He spoke the truth when he told a friend that he had 'not sought these things' – he had wanted Fairfax to retain the supreme command – but the title was final recognition of his actual position as the most important man in the State and when he added that he had been 'truly . . . called' to his new dignity 'by the Lord' he was bearing witness to one of his most sincerely held beliefs; that the unfolding of events demonstrated God's will. It was that belief which had finally convinced him of the need for the King's execution and it was the same conviction which was to help guide his actions during the rest of his life. Cromwell was convinced that the Scots meant to invade England, but he fore-stalled them in July when he crossed into Scotland at the head of an army of 16,000 men. In September he won a famous victory at Dunbar against a much larger army and a large part of Lowland Scotland was soon under his control. The Scottish Army under its competent commander David Leslie was, however, merely defeated, not destroyed, and the following year Cromwell, believing that the move would hasten the final victory which he confidently expected, encour-aged Charles to lead his Scottish forces into England. Following behind he caught up with the Scots at Worcester where he decisively defeated them in September 1651, exactly a year after the Battle of Dunbar. This English victory at Worcester marked the end of Scottish independence. Cromwell had been careful to leave

General Monck with 6,000 English troops behind when he himself marched south in pursuit of the King, and between August 1651 and August 1652 Monck completed the subjugation of Scotland (49; 80; 159–61).

By 1653, therefore, England had imposed her military authority on both Scotland and Ireland. The English government, dominated by Cromwell, now had to work out policies for the administration of the conquered realms. One constant theme between 1653 and 1660 was legislative union of the three kingdoms. James I's greatest ambition had, it will be recalled, been a 'perfect' union between England and Scotland and the failure of his ideas in this field was his biggest disappointment. Between 1653 and 1660, however, vital steps were taken towards union with the incorporation of Scottish and also of Irish members into the English Parliament. As a result, Parliament for the first time represented, at least nominally, the whole of the British Isles (129). The first Parliament to include members from all three kingdoms was Barebone's Parliament, which met in July 1653. It is sometimes called the 'Nominated' Parliament because most of its 144 members were chosen by the Council of Officers, the body which controlled the army. Six of the members were from Ireland and five from Scotland (130). The first elected Parliament to contain members from England, Scotland and Ireland met in 1654, its membership having been determined by the Instrument of Government of December 1653, the Constitution which formally placed Cromwell at the head of the State with the title of Lord Protector. This provided for 460 members altogether, with 30 each from Ireland and Scotland, and the same parliamentary representation was retained in the Humble Petition and Advice of 1657 (15, vol. 2). The parliamentary union seems to have been generally unpopular in both Ireland and Scotland. In 1659 an Irish spokesman complained that Irishmen could not get their legitimate complaints dealt with by Parliament – 'I pray that they may have some to hear their grievances in their own nation', he affirmed – and a Scottish commentator represented his country as a 'poor bird embodied in the hawk that has eaten it up'. Englishmen, too, were sceptical about the united Parliament and in 1659 there was a determined though unsuccessful attempt to exclude the Irish members (49; 80). At the Restoration the union, which was regarded as automatically invalid because it was the result of legislation which had never received the royal assent, was at once dissolved, and Scotland and Ireland regained their Parliaments. In imposing a parliamentary union on the three countries Cromwell was ahead of his time. He was able to do so not because of any general demand for a united legislature in Scotland or Ireland, but because, during the 1650s these two countries were, in the last resort, conquered provinces under English military rule. Final legislative union had to wait until 1801, when the Irish Parliament was abolished. As Scotland had already been incorporated in a parliamentary union in 1707 that meant that the whole of the British Isles was again under one legislature for the first time since 1660.

The legislative union of the 1650s was a symbol of the English government's determination to impose its effective authority throughout the British Isles. At the beginning of 1653 the Ireland which it was called upon to govern was in a very unhappy state as a result of the 'Twelve Years War' of 1641–52, which had in essence been an attempt by the bulk of the Irish population to throw off English rule. The country in 1652 presented a picture of devastation. The contemporary demographer Sir William Petty estimated that the population fell by well over a third during the war, and observers of the Irish scene in the early 1650s were at one in their descriptions of the havoc which the economic life of the country had suffered as a result of the plague and famine which had accompanied the military struggle. One poet described the conflict in simple but expressive terms as 'the war that finished Ireland' (51, *357*). The depth of the misery in 1653 did, however, leave room for considerable improvements and Dr Cullen has convincingly portrayed the years 1653–60 as a period of relative prosperity for ordinary people who were able to exploit the labour shortage resulting from depopulation to claim both higher wages and lower rents (51, *401*). This betterment in the standard of living of ordinary Irishmen – and it was, of course, an improvement from a *very* low level – must not be allowed to hide the deep distaste which the vast mass of the Irish population felt for Cromwell's policies during the 1650s. These were, in their main outlines, wholly traditional, 'colonisation, conversion, and the impartial administration of justice' (80, *259*; 51, *353 ff*).

Cromwell himself firmly believed in the beneficial effects which the fair administration of justice would bring. 'We have a great opportunity', he affirmed, 'to set up a way of doing justice amongst these poor people, which, for the uprightness and cheapness of it may exceedingly gain upon them' (80, *264*), and the Irish judges whom he appointed were honest and able men. Their virtues could not, however, overcome general Irish hostility founded on the understandable belief that the laws which the judges administered, laws which allowed the forcible confiscation of Irish land and the suppression of Catholic worship, were grossly unjust; the fact that unjust laws were now impartially enforced hardly helped. In religious affairs Cromwell showed a fierce determination to suppress Catholic worship which contrasted with the considerable practical toleration which he showed towards Catholicism in England. The difference can doubtless be explained by the considerable political threat which the Catholic Church in Ireland posed towards his regime, and though he did maintain liberty of conscience in the narrowest form – Catholics were not forced to attend Protestant churches – priests were executed, imprisoned or exiled. In tandem with these repressive measures went attempts to propagate Protestantism through preaching. Independent congregations were founded in many towns and ministers imported from England. The results were disappointing. The number of Protestant Nonconformists in Ireland may have increased as a result of Cromwell's rule, but the vast mass of the population remained loyal to the Catholicism which was now as much a sign of their national political resistance to English domination as the religion of their hearts and minds.

If the attempted conversion of the Irish to Protestantism was a failure, the other main base of Cromwellian policy in Ireland, the confiscation of the property of Irish Catholic landowners and their replacement by English Protestants, was a great success, if such a word can be applied to a social upheaval which still further embittered Irish Catholic attitudes towards England. The demands on Irish land had begun in 1642 when Parliament provided that the money advanced by 'adventurers', many of them wealthy landowners, for the reconquest of

Ireland, should be repaid in land, and in subsequent years it was provided that the pay of the soldiers employed against the Irish should be met in the same way. By the early 1650s the State owed vast sums to these two categories of men and in August 1652 an 'Act for the settling of Ireland' (15, vol. 2, *598 ff*) provided for their reimbursement by confiscating, in whole or in part, the estates of Catholic landowners who had taken part in the rebellion. Their tenants were left behind to work the estates of the new owners but the deprived landlords were transplanted to Connaught in a removal which entailed great suffering. The result of this vast upheaval, which was broadly completed by 1656 and basically confirmed at the Restoration was to place the great bulk of Irish land in the hands of Protestants. In 1641 Catholics still held about 60 per cent of the land of Ireland. As a result of the Cromwellian confiscations they retained just over 20 per cent (51). Cromwell thoroughly approved of the whole process. 'Was it not fit', he enquired, 'to make their estates defray the charges who caused the trouble?' For his fellow Englishmen it was a rhetorical question. They agreed that the Catholic Irish were, as he described them after the massacre at Drogheda, 'barbarous wretches' at an altogether lower level of civilization than themselves (80, *255, 261*).

Cromwell, who was such a typical Englishman of his time in his basic attitudes towards Ireland and the Irish, pursued much less harsh policies in Scotland, which was, after all, a basically Protestant country. There was no equivalent there during the 1650s of the confiscations and proscriptions which marked his rule in Ireland (on Scotland see (49; 80; 161)). There was, of course, one fundamental similarity with the Irish situation; the English Army of Occupation which was stationed at strategic points throughout Scotland. The soldiers were strictly disciplined but their presence was a constant reminder to the Scots that they, like the Irish, were a conquered nation. Scottish resentment flared up in Glencairn's rising of 1653–55, a revolt which posed a serious threat to English control of the country, but it was finally suppressed by Monck, who took over as Commander-in-Chief in Scotland in 1654. From then until 1660 he was by far the most important man in Scotland and established an effective control over both the country itself and the English Army which garrisoned it. During the 1650s Scottish landowners who had supported the royalist cause had their estates confiscated or were heavily fined. This produced financial ruin for some Scottish noble and gentle families, led to serious financial hardship for others and helped to increase support for the Glencairn rising, but there was no equivalent of the sweeping changes in land-ownership which occurred in Ireland at the same time; in the Cromwellian land settlement Scottish delinquents were treated much more like their English than their Irish counterparts. Nor was there any attempt to proscribe Scottish Presbyterianism. It is true that Cromwell's dislike of the coercive powers of the Kirk and of the political influence of the General Assembly led to the forcible dissolution of the latter in 1653 and to the abolition of the jurisdiction of the church courts over non-members, but presbyteries and synods were still allowed to meet. The Scottish Church, deprived of its political power, now had more time to concentrate on preaching the Gospel. Meanwhile the government, faithful to the Cromwellian principle of religious toleration for Protestant dissenters, encouraged and protected the formation of Independent congregations.

The civil administration of Scotland during the 1650s was controlled first of all by a Commission of Eight nominated by the English Parliament in 1651 and from 1655 onwards by a Council of State appointed by the Protector. Each of these bodies was dominated by English military men – a symbol of the effective power of the army in Scotland – but under the Council of State there was a genuine attempt to play down the military aspects of administration and to allow Scots to participate in the government of the country. Efficient and impartial judges were appointed, justices of the peace on the English model were introduced with wide administrative and judicial powers, the hereditary jurisdictions of landlords were abolished, English succeeded Latin as the language of the law. It is generally accepted, indeed, that Cromwellian administration and justice, under the ever vigilant eyes of Monck's soldiers, were both efficient and impartial. The testing time of the regime came in 1658–59, after the death of Cromwell, and it passed with flying colours. In contrast to the deteriorating situation in England, which produced conditions of near anarchy there by the end of 1659, Scotland remained calm and orderly. The Cromwellian regime, therefore, brought effective government to Scotland, but it is clear that many Scots regarded this as very hard won in terms of the heavy taxation and loss of national independence which accompanied it. At the Restoration, when Cromwell's legal reforms were swept away and Scotland regained its Parliament it was plain, however, that his rule there had made little of the fundamental impact which it had had in Ireland. This is ironic because Ireland, where Cromwell's land confiscations produced a social revolution, played no significant part in the Restoration. Scotland, in contrast, where his regime had much less profound effects, played a decisive role in the return of Charles II (see Ch. 44).

---

1. For the events of the 1640s in Ireland and the Cromwellian conquest see the three chapters by P. J. Corish in Moody, Martin and Byrne, eds, *A New History of Ireland*, III, pp. 289–352. There is a good brief account of the conquest and Cromwell's subsequent regime in C. H. Firth, *Oliver Cromwell* (1900), Ch. 13. Firth's book remains the best biography. Among the legion of others R. S. Paul, *The Lord Protector* (1955) is strong on the religious side; A. H. Woolrych, *Oliver Cromwell* (Oxford, 1964) is a brilliant, brief sketch; and C. Hill, *God's Englishman* (1970) present a picture of Cromwell in the general context of the 'English Revolution'.

CHAPTER 39

Commonwealth and Protectorate, 1649–1658:
II – Politics and Administration

The conquest of Ireland and Scotland between 1649 and 1653 and their control by English armies during the 1650s was one aspect of the determination of the English governments of the period to bring stability to the British Isles and thus minimize the chances of a royalist restoration. They also sought that stability in England itself through a variety of constitutional experiments. [1] The Rump, which assumed supreme authority in the early months of 1649 by virtue of the unrealistic claim of its members to be the 'representatives of the people', was very clearly a revolutionary regime; it had abolished the monarchy and the House of Lords. In the circumstances it might have been expected to undertake an extensive programme of reforms. In fact, it did nothing of the kind. The two recent authoritative accounts of its work (108; 128) both stress the very limited nature of legal, social and ecclesiastical reforms which were passed during its period of rule between 1649 and 1653. There were two major reasons for this. First of all, the Rump was faced with very serious difficulties both at home and abroad. There were the royalist threats from England and Scotland which we have already examined and there was also a war with the United Provinces which began in 1652. Moreover, the Rump had to superintend the detailed administration of the country as pre-1640 Parliaments had never had to do. As a result it was overwhelmed with day-to-day business and had little time to plan ambitious reforms. The second reason for its failure, at least as important as the first, was its social conservatism. It may have been a body of political revolutionaries, men who were prepared to execute or acquiesce in the execution of the King, but the 211 or so men who were members at one time or another during its existence were overwhelmingly country gentlemen of the traditional ruling class, most of whom were fundamentally conservative in their social attitudes and therefore hostile to drastic legal, social and ecclesiastical reforms which might challenge the traditional social hierarchy. It is ironic that the one field in which the Rump *did* produce extensive plans for reform led directly to its dissolution. A recent account of its fall has been provided by Dr Worden (128) who has radically revised traditional views about its expulsion. It used to be thought that Cromwell dissolved it because it intended to perpetuate its existence indefinitely, only allowing elections to take place to replace those members who had been purged. Worden, however, puts forward a very different scenario. The Rump had produced proposals for an extensive redistribution of parliamentary seats and for a change in the parliamentary franchise in the counties, and he argues that it intended to dissolve itself *completely* after a new Parliament had been elected on the basis of this revised franchise. Cromwell dissolved it not because it refused to hold elections for all the seats, but rather because it insisted on doing so and he was afraid of the results which such elections would produce. In April 1653, when he expelled the Rump, Cromwell was strongly influenced by Major-General Harrison and the Fifth Monarchy Men, a radical religious sect which he later came to detest. He realized that a new Parliament, elected on the reformed franchise, would almost certainly be very hostile to the ideas of 'godly reformation' advocated by the Fifth Monarchists, ideas which centred on the need to prepare for the Second Coming of Christ. In these circumstances his usual respect for constitutional forms, which had probably prevented him from taking a direct part in Pride's Purge, went by the board and he forcibly dissolved the Rump and decided, with the Council of Officers, to replace it with an assembly of godly men or 'Saints'. During his career, as Professor Underdown has emphasized, he was often pulled in different directions by his 'Puritan idealism' and his 'gentry constitutionalism' (108, *150, 353*). In the spring of 1653, if we are to believe Dr Worden, the former won. Worden's thesis has, however, been challenged by Professor Woolrych who, while emphasizing the complexities and uncertainties of the evidence, has raised serious doubts about the reality of Harrison's influence on Cromwell in the spring of 1653 and favours a modified and highly sophisticated version of the traditional account of the Rump's dissolution (110, *68 ff*).

Whatever the truth about the end of the Rump, Cromwell clearly had high initial hopes of the Parliament of Saints – also known as the Nominated Parliament and most frequently of all as Barebone's Parliament, after one of its members, Praise-God Barebone, a London leather merchant and Baptist lay preacher. These hopes did not last long (61; 130). His original confidence was reflected in his opening speech to the new assembly in July 1653 when he told its members that they were 'called by God to rule with Him and for Him. And you are called to be faithful with the Saints, who have been somewhat instrumental to your call' (18, vol. 3, *61*). The voice of the Saints had, in fact, been the Council of Officers, which nominated almost all of the 144 members, but despite its entirely unrepresentative character the assembly assumed the title of Parliament, with full executive, legislative and judicial powers. Hostile contemporary propagandists like Clarendon argued and textbooks have repeated that most of the members were 'inferior persons, of no quality or name, artificers of the meanest trades, known only by their gifts in praying and preaching' (quoted (61, *69–70*)). In fact, Barebone himself was an unrepresentative figure. At least four-fifths of the members belonged to the gentry class – many admittedly were lesser gentry – and 119 were JPs (110). The Parliament was divided between a moderate majority and an extremist minority which included twelve or thirteen Fifth Monarchists. The extremists were more assiduous in their attendance and were thus able to win crucial votes for radical reforms; for example, they voted for the total abolition of the court of Chancery without working out what was to replace it; they carried a vote to abolish lay patronage of church livings; and they mounted a major assault on tithes and with it on the whole concept of a State Church (110; 199). Cromwell became more and more afraid that their proposals would destroy both the ministry of the Church and established property rights and he accepted with relief in December 1653 when the moderates engineered a coup by which they surrendered their powers back into Cromwell's hands. The Fifth Monarchists never forgave what they regarded as Cromwell's betrayal in accepting the surrender; from then on they were his implacable opponents.

Cromwell's hopes for Barebone's Parliament during its early days certainly marked the high point of his 'Puritan idealism' as applied to constitutional and political affairs. Equally clearly, his disillusionment with the assembly during its later stages showed the limits to that idealism when he became afraid that the work of the Saints might challenge established property rights, the foundation of the whole hierarchical social order. In December 1653 he accepted the Instrument of Government [E.6(37); G.7(30)], the first and only written Constitution which Britain has ever had and under which he ruled as Lord Protector until his death in 1658. The Instrument, like Barebone's before it, was imposed upon the country by the army. Cromwell, who may have been influenced by Harrison in April 1653 now turned to another general, Lambert, who had already drawn up the Instrument. It contained the most ambitious reform of the electoral system before 1832, taking over directly the proposals which had already been made by the Rump. A few growing towns like Manchester, Leeds and Halifax, which lacked representation in the pre-revolutionary House of Commons, were given members for the first time, but overall the number of borough seats was greatly reduced – 'rotten' boroughs like Grampound in Cornwall, Gatton in Surrey and Old Sarum in Wiltshire were disfranchised. The number of county seats was greatly increased and the county franchise was given to the owners of real or personal property to the value of £200 instead of to the traditional 40s. freeholders. It is overwhelmingly probable that this last provision *reduced* the number of those entitled to the vote (122; 128–9) – a sign of the social conservatism both of the Rump which devised the provision and of the Protectorate which accepted it. The Instrument vested executive authority in Cromwell as Lord Protector, but insisted that he acted in all important matters only with the assent of a Council of State whose members he could neither appoint nor dismiss at will. Legislative power was given to a single-chamber Parliament which was to be elected at least once every three years and sit for not less than five months. Cromwell could veto its Acts for only twenty days. A fixed yearly income was provided for the support of the armed forces and civil administration, and a wide degree of religious toleration was guaranteed. No provisions were made for amending the Constitution and Cromwell clearly felt that some at least of its clauses, notably those guaranteeing religious toleration, had a status approaching fundamental law, but the general effect of the Instrument was to establish a system of checks and balances which would, at least in theory, prevent too much power falling into the hands of either the Protector or Parliament. Cromwell has been accused of being a dictator during the Protectorate. In fact, his power was always limited by his need to appease the army and outright dictatorship was also impossible in terms of the provisions of the Instrument. That was substantially amended by the Humble Petition and Advice of 1657 [E.6(39)] which originally offered Cromwell the Crown. He refused the title of king, after prolonged hesitation and almost certainly because of army objections, but the remaining provisions of the Petition were accepted. These included more power for the Protector and Parliament, less for the Council of State – now renamed the Privy Council – and the creation of an Upper House of Parliament, with the members selected by Cromwell. That looked very much like a new House of Lords and it is worth noting that Cromwell had personally argued against the abolition of the old Upper House in February 1649 (108, *202*).

Cromwell, as he himself declared, was not 'wedded and glued to forms of government', which were but 'dross and dung in comparison of Christ'. Nevertheless, as the history of the Protectorate shows, he came more and more to favour a settlement 'with somewhat of monarchical power in it' (81, *95, 107–8*). The general trend in the constitutional experiments of 1649 to 1657 is plain; away from a single-chamber Parliament with absolute powers back towards the old monarchical constitution of government by a single person and two Houses of Parliament which is reflected to such a considerable extent in the Humble Petition. In a purely constitutional sense the Interregnum's logical conclusion was the restoration of the monarchy in 1660, though this is not, of course, to suggest that the return of Charles II was inevitable. Cromwell, who was usually so much in favour of traditional forms of government – his dissolution of the Rump and promotion of Barebone's Parliament in 1653 can be regarded as aberrations which do not invalidate the basic point – realized the need to reduce the importance of the army in politics if his regime was to enjoy widespread support in the country, and during the Protectorate he tried to promote the influence of his civilian at the expense of his military supporters. His agonizing over whether or not to accept the Crown in 1657 was no doubt largely due to his realization that acceptance, as a symbol of a final return to traditional forms, would help to promote stability in the country at large, just as his ultimate refusal reflected his understanding that his power still basically depended on the army.

The Protectorate, when all is said and done, remained a military regime in which Cromwell himself could never take the army for granted. He had always to walk a delicate tightrope between his own desire and that of the majority of the political nation for civilian rule through Parliament and the reality of the army's power. After all, the Rump was dissolved and Barebone's Parliament established by the power of the army, and the Instrument itself was an army constitution. If the return to more traditional forms of government is one major theme of the constitutional history of the Interregnum, the other is surely the tension which always existed between the army and the Parliaments of the 1650s. It can be seen very clearly in the Protectorate Parliaments of 1654 and 1656. The 1654 assembly spent a great deal of time questioning the whole basis of the new constitution which it regarded, not unjustifiably, as merely the reflection of the views of army grandees, and it tried to increase Parliament's control of the army at the Protector's expense. The 1656 Parliament showed implacable hostility to the major-generals, army officers who had been given wide authority in the localities the previous year, and its refusal to pay for their upkeep led to the end of the experiment at the beginning of 1657. These Parliaments, which showed such hostility to the influence of the army in the State, also quarrelled with Cromwell over issues such as religious toleration, which they wanted to restrict. It has been argued that the difficulties between the Protector and his Parliaments were largely a result of Cromwell's inadequate techniques of management,[2] and there is no doubt something to be said for this thesis. Oliver Cromwell was not an expert parliamentary manager like his ancestor Thomas Cromwell during Henry VIII's reign or his contemporary John Pym during the early years of the Long Parliament. But there were more fundamental reasons as well; the franchise provisions of the Instrument, by limiting the electorate to men of fairly considerable property, ensured that the MPs whom these electors chose would be unsympathetic to the degree of religious toleration which was enshrined in the Instrument and which Cromwell was determined to preserve, and Cromwell, however much he desired a civilian basis for his rule, could never go too far with Parliament in attacking an army on which his own power ultimately depended.

In the last resort, just like Cromwell himself, we come back to the army. By Pride's Purge it had made possible the end of the monarchy. In 1657 it prevented the creation of a new Cromwellian kingship. In the years between it set effective limits to the life or authority of successive Parliaments. Its size stood at about 45,000 men in 1649 and it rose to a peak strength of nearly 70,000 in 1652, declining to about 42,000 in 1658. The cost of this large body of men was enormous, about £1.5m. a year in 1649, over £2m. per annum in 1651. Even in 1657 it was still costing about £1.1m. a year (149) and the Humble Petition and Advice stated that £1m. out of the £1.3m. per annum which it allowed for government expenses was to be devoted to the armed forces. Cromwell's uphill task of reconciling the power of this military machine with the constitutional aspirations of a gentry class which wanted civilian rule was one which only he, with his unique influence in both camps, could have attempted with any real chance of success. Even Cromwell, however, could not always square the circle. When he was offered the Crown in 1657 he had to displease either the army or the political nation. His choice, so reluctantly made, showed beyond doubt where ultimate power in the State lay.

The years 1649–58, which saw so many constitutional experiments, also saw important changes as well as a good deal of continuity in English administration. The principal executive institution at the centre of government during these years, both under the Commonwealth and under the Protectorate was the Council of State, renamed the Privy Council in the Humble Petition and Advice in 1657 (on the Council of State see 109, *17 ff*). It is tempting to compare the Councils of the Interregnum with the old Privy Council, but despite obvious similarities there were important differences. The Councils of the Commonwealth did not have the effective advisory powers of the Privy Council and during the Protectorate Councils had theoretical rights of veto over Cromwell's activities which no Privy Council had had over the Crown under the old monarchical system. During the Commonwealth each of the five Councils appointed by the Rump had 41 members, but the normal attendance was much smaller, averaging between 13 and 19 at meetings. Protectorate Councils were much smaller; the Instrument prescribed a size of between 12 and 16, comparable to the Elizabethan Privy Council. All the Councils made extensive use of standing and *ad hoc* committees and, just like those under the monarchy, had staffs of clerks and officials to help them with their work; John Milton, as Latin Secretary under the Commonwealth, was a member of the Council staff. In the localities, despite the upheavals of the 1640s and the unpopular rule of the new county committees during that decade, the 1650s saw the persistence of many of the traditional forms of administration. 'The overwhelming impression afforded by the records of local government is one of continuity', writes Professor Aylmer of the 1650s (109, *305*), and Professor Underdown makes the same point when he reminds us that in 1653, when Cromwell became Protector, 'the old structure of local government had . . . survived all the revolutionary changes of the previous ten years' (62, *170*). Above all, the JPs continued in their essential judicial and administrative work both in and out of quarter sessions. There is no reason to think that they were any less efficient than their Elizabethan or early Stuart predecessors. Indeed, to take just one example, Dr Beier has demonstrated the extent to which the administration of the Poor Laws was more effective in Warwickshire in the 1650s than during any previous period (253).

There were, of course, changes amidst this picture of general continuity. The rule of the major-generals in 1655–56 had no precedent in English history. They were instituted in the wake of Penruddock's rising, a royalist revolt which took place in the South-west early in 1655. Later that year the country was divided into eleven military districts, each under an army officer with soldiers at his back to enforce his authority (61). Their initial task was to supervise security, but they were soon given a wide oversight of local government as a whole. The effectiveness of the major-generals varied depending on the personality of the individual officer and the area of the country where he served – Thomas Kelsey, for example, played an assertive role in Kent, where royalism was strong – but there is no doubt that their rule was disliked by the political nation as a whole, a hostility which Parliament expressed in 1657 when it brought their rule to an end. The major-generals have become notorious to later generations not only as military satraps imposed upon a reluctant civilian population but also for their work in enforcing 'Puritan' manners and morals. Some of their activities in this field, such as their attacks on cruel sports like bear-baiting and cock-fighting, are, however, difficult to condemn, and their work in closing large numbers of alehouses had plenty of precedents in the policies of previous sixteenth and seventeenth century governments which traditionally, and not unjustly, regarded them as potential centres of disorder and subversion. The rule of the major-generals is Cromwell's most obvious innovation in his government of the localities, but there were other important and more deeply significant differences between his rule of the shires and that of his Stuart predecessors. One of these was the tax burden. We have already noted (Ch. 36) the heavy new taxes, the assessment and the excise, which Parliament introduced during the 1640s to help it win the Civil War, and these remained during the 1650s when the taxation of the counties continued at a higher level than at any time under the old monarchy. Cromwell had a very expensive army to support and, despite the large revenue which he enjoyed – at least £1.5m. per annum on average during the 1650s – he was constantly and heavily in debt (109; 250). Also, the social composition of the ruling elite in the shires during the 1640s and 1650s differed significantly from its make-up in the 1630s and earlier decades (62; 255). There was, it is true, no social revolution in the sense of one class replacing another; the local governors in the shires continued to be drawn mainly from the gentry, but it was now from the lesser, 'parochial' gentry rather than from the greater families who had served James I and Charles I. In pre-industrial England, where modern ideas about class conflict are often inappropriate, this shift of effective administrative power from one stratum of the ruling elite to another is of very great significance.

The move away from the traditional dominance of the greater gentry families in English life was not, of course, confined to local government. It can be seen in virtually all the country's institutions, including Parliament and the 'Civil Service'. In his massive study of the latter body during the Interregnum Professor Aylmer has demonstrated (109, *168 ff*) that many more central government officials during the 1650s were of lower social standing than those who served Charles I and that a significant minority came from non-gentry families. He has concluded, too, that there were higher standards of administrative probity among officials during these years than in the pre-1640 period (109, *328*). This was no doubt largely due to the higher salaries which were generally paid and it is tempting to see such developments as a step towards the new conception of public service which finally came to the fore in the nineteenth century when the Civil Service in its modern form was created. Other developments of these years, such as the reduction in absenteeism and in the number of sinecure offices, point in the same direction. On the other hand, patronage was still deeply entrenched and the governments of the 1650s laid greater emphasis on the political reliability of their officials than the early Stuart kings. The Cromwellian Civil Service, despite the important changes of the 1640s and 1650s, was still very far removed in its attitudes from the body which we know today. And like so much else that was innovatory about the 1650s the new developments in the bureaucracy were destined not, by and large, to survive the Restoration. Much of the good work of the Cromwellians in this field was destroyed in the 1660s and had to be built up again on new foundations after 1680, when the Civil Service began the next important phase of its history.

---

1. The fundamental narrative accounts of the period 1649–58 remain S. R. Gardiner, *History of the Commonwealth and Protectorate*, 4 vols (1903) and C. H. Firth, *The Last Years of the Protectorate*, 2 vols (1909).
2. H. R. Trevor-Roper, 'Oliver Cromwell and his Parliaments', *Essays Presented to Sir Lewis Namier*, ed. R. Pares and A. J. P. Taylor (1956), pp. 1 ff.

CHAPTER 40

Commonwealth and Protectorate, 1649–1658:
III – Foreign and colonial affairs

The government of the country was obviously vital to Cromwell in his quest for stability at home. So too was foreign policy, which involved the protection of the British Isles against the intrigues of the exiled Stuarts with foreign courts. Historians would agree about a number of aspects of Cromwell's foreign policy during the years of his dominance.[1] It certainly gave the country an importance in Europe which it had never enjoyed under James I or Charles I. A Venetian diplomat made the point in 1655 when he wrote, with pardonable exaggeration, that 'the Court of England by sheer force has made itself the most dreaded and the most conspicuous in the world' (151, *103*). Rulers from all parts of Europe hastened to make contact with Cromwell's government, a reflection not only of what Professor Hill has called the 'fantastic scope' of his foreign policy, with its positive concern for huge tracts of Europe and America (81, *165–6*), but also of the strength of the armed forces which backed up his designs. The historian of the Royal Navy has drawn a dramatic contrast (144, *302–3*) between the weaknesses of the fleet under Charles I and its strength during the Protectorate when permanent Mediterranean and West Indian squadrons were created as well as a strong home fleet. The 200 ships which were added to the navy during the 1650s made it by far the most powerful in Europe, and Britain's[2] authority was further enhanced by the large standing army, some 40,000–60,000 strong during the Protectorate (149), which made the country a great military force as well as the leading naval power in Europe.

Cromwell's foreign policy, with such formidable military forces behind it, was much more active and aggressive not merely than that of the early Stuarts but also than that of Queen Elizabeth. During her reign, as we saw (Ch. 19), foreign policy was essentially passive, a reaction to threats posed by others. Cromwell's reflected a much more conscious desire to change the diplomatic situation in Britain's favour and we can see a mixture of aims behind his actions. There were religious considerations – he passionately wanted to defend and spread Protestantism; there were economic motives – he wished to expand the country's trade; and, as we have seen, there was security – he wanted to do everything he could to prevent foreign help to the exiled Stuarts which might lead to dangers of a restoration. His concern for aid from abroad for Charles II, which continued throughout the 1650s, was reflected in his treaties with the Dutch in 1654 and with France in 1655, both of which agreed to clauses about the expulsion of royalists from their territóries.

Cromwell's foreign policy, then, was active and aggressive, gave Britain a new importance in Europe, and was founded on a mixture of religious, economic and security considerations. That much would be accepted by virtually all experts in the field. There, however, consensus breaks down and historians disagree profoundly both about the relative importance of religious and economic motivations in foreign policy during the 1650s, and also about the wisdom of the policy as a whole. Mrs Prestwich, among others, has stressed its ideological content, emphasizing that Cromwell was prepared to sacrifice Britain's economic interests to secure the advance of Protestantism, while Professor Hill, in contrast, has argued that his policy was conceived 'in hard practical terms of national and commercial interest (81, *155 ff*; 151)' Cromwell did, of course, indulge in frequent religious rhetoric, as in 1655 when he appealed to fellow Protestant states to join him in assistance to the Vaudois – Protestants who had been massacred in Savoy. The point at issue is not what he said but what he did. Consideration of his policies towards the Dutch and towards Spain throws light not only on this problem but also on the wisdom of his foreign policy as a whole. Contemporaries like Clarendon regarded it as his greatest achievement and this judgement was basically accepted by the nineteenth-century Whig historians. Professor Jones, on the other hand, sees his policy as 'misdirected, unrealistic and unsuccessful' and argues that it 'contributed significantly to the Restoration' (34, *34*).

When Cromwell became Lord Protector at the end of 1653 Britain was at war with the Dutch (152). This conflict, entered into by the Rump in 1652 largely as a result of the pressure of powerful mercantile interests which feared and disliked the Dutch as their main commercial competitors, was heartily disliked by Cromwell who looked upon the Dutch as Protestant brothers first and economic rivals second. He made his attitude plain during the negotiations of 1653–54 which brought the war to an end. By that time he was the dominant influence in the State and he showed that he was prepared to sacrifice British trading interests in the East Indies in return for an Anglo-Dutch alliance against the great Catholic enemy, Spain (151). Even when the Dutch refused to be drawn into such an agreement, he accepted terms in the Treaty of Westminster of April 1654 which were 'extraordinarily mild' (152, *77*) in view of British successes during the war and which were criticized at home for their leniency towards the Dutch. As soon as the treaty was signed, moreover, Cromwell sent an envoy to The Hague for further discussions about an alliance between the two Protestant powers, negotiations which failed, as Secretary of State Thurloe wrote, 'in respect the United Provinces always found it necessary for them to mingle therewith considerations of trade' (151, *106*). Having failed to get his hoped-for anti-Spanish alliance with the Dutch in the spring of 1654, Cromwell did show that trading considerations, while they might take second place in his mind, were still important. In the summer of the same year he signed a treaty with Portugal which gave British merchants full trading rights with the Portuguese colonies in both Asia and America. That was a clear blow against the predominant Dutch trade in the East Indies and an indication to them of the loss which they had suffered as a result of their negative attitude to a political alliance during the negotiations which led up to the Treaty of Westminster.

Further insights into Cromwell's attitude towards the Dutch can be gained by examining his Baltic policy during the 1650s (152; 243). This was founded on two basic considerations. First of all, the Baltic was essential to Britain as a source of naval stores for her expanding fleet, and secondly Cromwell saw King Charles X of Sweden as a Protestant champion, a latter-day Gustavus Adolphus, in a great Protestant confederation against the Habsburgs. Unfortunately for Cromwell's point of view, Charles X was more interested in securing Britain's help against his fellow Protestants the Dutch and the Danes in his struggle with them for Baltic hegemony. Cromwell's plan for a great Protestant alliance was thus doomed from the start because of rivalries among the proposed members, none of whom shared Cromwell's crusading zeal. The Protector himself was determined to defend Britain's essential economic interests in the Baltic and prevent the domination of the area by any one power – that would have been an intolerable threat to Britain's vital naval supplies. His 1654 treaty with Sweden, designed to accomplish this by providing a counterweight to the Dutch partnership with Denmark in the area, did not, however, prevent him continuing to dream of the possibility of a great Protestant alliance. He was always careful to do everything he could to prevent open Anglo-Dutch conflict in the Baltic. It was a policy which Professor Wilson has happily characterized as 'prudent idealism' and which reveals that Cromwell certainly gave far more consideration to religion in his foreign policy than any of the Protestant Baltic powers. The Swedish, Danish and Dutch governments of the day lived in a much more secular world than Cromwell.

As for Catholic Spain, Cromwell certainly regarded her as the great enemy, 'the head of the Papal interest'. He told the admirals in charge of his expedition against the Spanish Indies in December 1654 that God himself had 'a controversy with your enemies; even with that Romish Babylon of which the Spaniard is the great underpropper' (152, 79). Of course, he also hoped for economic gains both in terms of immediate booty and long-term trading advantages from this assult upon the old enemy, but the results were very unsuccessful in terms of his ambitions. He aimed first of all to seize the great Spanish islands of Hispaniola and Cuba in the Caribbean and in the following year to embark on the conquest of mainland Spanish America itself. The expedition, however, failed in its assult upon Hispaniola, and Jamaica, which was captured and which was to be of great long-term importance for Britain as a sugar producer, was of little initial value. Projects for the conquest of the mainland were abandoned, but the war did spread to Europe. This had not been Cromwell's original intention – he had hoped initially that it could be confined to the colonies. That was a vain dream, however, and the powerful mercantile interests which traded with metropolitan Spain were quick to voice their disapproval of a war which cut off their trade. There is little doubt, in fact, that the Spanish War was unpopular with the bulk of the merchant community. Cromwell's ideologically motivated attitude towards Spain had sacrificed British economic interests, and the French alliance of 1657, the capture of Dunkirk the following year and the glorious exploits of the navy could only conceal, not alter, that basic fact. The Spanish War led to the loss of British trade to the Dutch, who benefited from their neutrality, reduced the power of an already declining Spain in Europe, and built up that of an emerging France which was soon to be a most serious political and economic rival of Britain, although Cromwell can hardly be blamed for failing to anticipate the transformation effected by Colbert. It also had serious consequences for Cromwell's relations with the London merchant community. These relations were never, at best, very cordial and the Spanish War, which contributed to the trade depression of the last years of the Protectorate, brought them to a very low point. The City had always refused Cromwell loans in its corporate capacity, and by 1658 he found it increasingly difficult to raise money from individual merchants. He left a large debt and a very difficult financial inheritance for his son and successor Richard Cromwell (151; 250).

Study of Cromwell's relations with Spain and the Dutch makes it difficult to believe, therefore, that he did not sometimes subordinate Britain's economic interests to unrealistic dreams of anti-Catholic crusades against the Habsburgs. This did not, of course, mean that he consistently neglected the country's material interests; his Baltic policy, the 1654 treaty with Portugal and his long-term expectations from the 1654 expedition against the Spanish Empire in the Caribbean are evidence of his commercial concerns. On balance it seems best to conclude that his foreign policy certainly took substantial account of both economic and security considerations but was motivated primarily by his religious outlook. That is hardly surprising in view of the primacy of religion in his thinking as a whole, but it did give an anachronistic appearance to his policies at a time when Catholic powers like France and Spain as well Protestant countries like Sweden and the United Provinces thought primarily in political and economic terms. It made him see Spain as the country's arch-enemy at a time when the major political and economic threats to British interests arguably came from a resurgent France and an economically powerful Netherlands. Indeed, in his very unfavourable view of Cromwell's foreign policy Professor Jones argues that there was no compelling reason for him to ally or go to war with *either* France or Spain (34, *35*). Whatever one's conclusions about that judgement a final verdict on Cromwell's foreign policy will depend on the balance drawn between three factors: the short-term external greatness which it certainly brought to Britain; the longer-term implications which it had for British interests by encouraging the rise of France and the Dutch at the expense of an already declining Spain; and the internal cost to the regime in merchant discontent and financial troubles. On this last point, Professor Jones is by no means the first historian to stress the links between the expensive foreign policy of the 1650s and the popular discontent with high taxation which helped to bring about the Restoration (144, *302*).

Cromwell, who made Britain such a prominent power in Europe, took a great interest in colonial affairs, an interest which went back to a time long before he became the greatest influence in the State (47; 80). He himself may have considered emigrating in his younger days and in 1643 he became officially connected with the colonies when he was appointed to one of the parliamentary commissions for their government. The English colonies founded in James I's reign had expanded greatly under Charles I, especially as a result of the emigration of large numbers of Puritan Englishmen who went to New England to escape from Laud's persecutions. By 1649 there were three groups of colonies: the New England settlements to the north; Virginia and Maryland further south; and small islands, like Barbados, in the Caribbean. The New England colonies, so strongly influenced by Puritanism, were sympathetic to Parliament in its struggle with the King during the 1640s, though by the time the Commonwealth was established in 1649 their political links with the mother country were little more than nominal. The southern settlements and the islands, in contrast, were generally royalist in their attitude, and on the execution of the King Virginia proclaimed Charles II and Barbados rejected the authority of the new republic. In 1651, however, a Commonwealth fleet reduced the rebels to obedience and in that and the previous year Navigation Acts were passed (15, vol. 2) which made England and its colonies an economic unit, closing the colonial trade completely to foreign shipping. These Acts, in their commercial aspects, were essentially designed to boost English trade and shipping at the expense of the Dutch, but they also had a political significance as the first English attempt to legislate for the colonies as a whole. These now appeared in English eyes as part of a single economic and political system centred on London.

By the time the Protectorate was established English authority was accepted, at least nominally, throughout the colonies, and during his rule Cromwell interfered as little as possible with their internal affairs. His most cordial relationships were, not surprisingly, with the New England settlements which, unlike the southern colonies and the islands, were dominated by the Puritan ethos, but the main interest of his regime in the colonial field lies in his zeal for the extension of England's empire overseas. He was 'the first English ruler who systematically employed the power of the government to increase and extend the colonial possessions of England' (80, *383*), and his active policy can be contrasted with that of his early Stuart predecessors who had no similar imperial vision. In 1654, while the Dutch War was still in progress, he dispatched a small fleet to America to capture the Dutch colonies on the borders of New England, and when peace was concluded before an assult could be launched the fleet set off northwards to attack the French settlements in Acadia (Nova Scotia), which were soon captured. The territory remained in English hands until it was returned to Louis XIV eight years after the Restoration. The capture of Jamaica from Spain in 1655 was a small consolation to Cromwell for the failure of the 1654 expedition to seize Hispaniola, but he resolved to make the best of it. The soldiers who conquered the island proved very unsuitable as colonists and died in their hundreds. Cromwell had plans for peopling his new conquest with emigrants from New England, Scotland and Ireland, but these schemes came to nothing and Jamaica was settled with the surplus population of other West Indian islands like Barbados and Nevis. Spain made a number of attempts to reconquer the island but they all failed and England kept it at the Restoration. It became a centre of the seventeenth- and eighteenth-century slave trade and, as such, a vital cog in a British Empire which put the highest valuation on its Caribbean possessions with their wealth in sugar and slaves. Cromwell's expedition against the Spanish Empire in 1654 may have been a failure in his eyes, but its results were of great long-term significance in colonial history. Overall in fact, his colonial attitudes, stressing the value of government intervention to help create an overseas empire which was now regarded as an economic unit, were to have an important and lasting influence in later colonial and imperial theory. Cromwell can certainly be regarded as one of the founders of the British Empire.

---

1. The best detailed studies are S. R. Gardiner, *History of the Commonwealth and Protectorate*, 4 vols (1903), and C. H. Firth, *The Last Years of the Protectorate*, 2 vols (1909). There is no satisfactory recent account. G. M. D. Howat, *Stuart and Cromwellian Foreign Policy* (1974) is an uninspiring sketch, but there are suggestive remarks in J. R. Jones, *Britain and Europe in the Seventeenth Century* (1966), pp. 33 ff.
2. During the Protectorate, as we have seen (in Chapter 38), Scotland and Ireland were united in a parliamentary union with England and it is, therefore, technically correct to refer to Cromwell's foreign policy as 'British' rather than 'English'.

CHAPTER 41

Commonwealth and Protectorate, 1649–1658: IV – Religion

In his administration of Britain and in his conduct of its foreign and colonial policies religion was seldom far from Cromwell's thoughts. For him the secular was undoubtedly of less fundamental concern than the spiritual. His open-mindedness about 'forms of government' was accompanied by very definite ideas about the kind of religious settlement necessary to safeguard the varied views of those active Protestant Christians whom he regarded as the 'people of God'.

By 1646, as we saw (Ch. 36), episcopacy had been abolished and Presbyterianism officially approved. In theory there was nothing to prevent the full-scale development of a Presbyterian Church of England in the following years. If this was to happen, however, a number of practical steps were necessary. Individual parishes had to elect elders who would join ministers in exercising discipline over their congregations; the parish presbyteries so formed had to elect representatives to sit in local *classes* (or synods); and these synods had to choose representatives for provincial and ultimately national assemblies (166). This structure was, however, never fully set up for the country as a whole. That was basically because after 1646 the secular authorities were either unable or unwilling to enforce conformity to Presbyterianism. From the mid-1640s the army was a growing power in politics and its leaders as well as its rank-and-file members were generally hostile to compulsion in religious affairs. In the 1650s, when Cromwell was the chief power in the State, he was an ardent advocate of religious toleration. Between 1646 and 1660, therefore, Presbyterian Church organization could only be set up on a voluntary basis. Many local clergymen, however, refused to share authority with lay elders and in other parishes no elders came forward to work with the minister. Both these difficulties were recorded by London and Manchester *classes* and it is clear that there was no effective Presbyterian organization at parish level in many parts of the country. Despite this lack of general grass-roots support there was some type of organization at synodical level in many English counties during at least part of the period 1646–1660, and in some areas – for example parts of London, Nottinghamshire, Derbyshire and Lancashire – *classes* met throughout the later 1640s and during the whole of the 1650s. Two provincial assemblies were also convened, for London and Lancashire, but no national assembly ever met. Presbyterianism, therefore, never replaced Anglicanism as a truly effective national Church during the 1640s and 1650s. In the 1650s, indeed, the Presbyterian elements in the Church were taken into and became part of the Cromwellian national Church which was set up during that decade.

Cromwell's religion was at the very heart of his being, and he combined acceptance of the dominant Calvinist theology of Elizabethan and early Stuart England with a particular stress on the importance of accepting God's providence as revealed by the unfolding course of events (167). These convinced him that he was an important instrument of God's will, but although he sympathized with the radical sects he never joined one and his religious settlement retained the basic idea of a State Church, though with a wide degree of toleration for Protestant dissenters outside it (166; 198). The Instrument of Government provided for a national Church but set out no details of its structure or beliefs [G.7(30)]. It also gave Cromwell himself, with the consent of the Council, the power 'to make law's and ordinances for the peace and welfare of these nations . . ., which shall be binding and in force until order shall be taken in parliament concerning the same' [E.6(37)], and it was under this provision that he created his State Church in 1654. Its ministers were not required to conform to any specific doctrinal or liturgical position, merely to fundamental Christian principles and a sound Protestantism. In these circumstances the vital issue was the appointment and dismissal of the clergy of the new State Church and this was organized in two ordinances of March and August 1654 (15, vol. 2). That of March set up a Commission of 38 to pass judgement upon the qualifications of those presented to benefices within the Church. It represented a wide spectrum of ecclesiastical opinion, containing Presbyterians, Congregationalists and Baptists. The rights of lay patrons were retained except that they could not appoint men regarded as unfit by the commissioners or 'Triers' as they came to be called. The clergy whom these men appointed held a wide variety of views on both theology and church government, including moderate episcopalians at one end of the spectrum and Baptists at the other. That gives a very good idea of the comprehensiveness of the Cromwellian national Church. The August ordinance set up boards of local commissioners, who came to be known as 'Ejectors', to expel unfit ministers from the Church. The Ejectors were forbidden to carry out doctrinal inquisitions of clergymen whom they examined, but were required to weed out those who were negligent in the performance of their duties or whose conduct was 'scandalous' – a definition which included 'adultery, fornication, drunkenness, common haunting of taverns or ale houses, frequent quarrelling or fighting, frequent playing at cards or dice, profaning of the Sabbath day', a list which gives a good idea of common lay complaints of the time about clerical behaviour. Finally, in September 1654, a third ordinance (15, vol. 2) provided for the union of unduly small, and the division of overlarge, parishes in both towns and the countryside, a long overdue reform of the ecclesiastical structure.

The vast majority of incumbent clergy continued to serve within this broadly tolerant Cromwellian national Church. It has been estimated that during the whole period 1643–1660 only about 2,500 parish ministers out of 9,000 were deprived of their livings and many of these deprivations came in the period before 1653 (166). It is also clear that the Triers and Ejectors did good work. Richard Baxter, who was certainly no friend to the Cromwellian religious settlement, admitted as much when he stated that 'they saved many a congregation from ignorant, ungodly, drunken teachers . . .; many thousands of souls blessed God for the faithful ministers whom they let in'.[1] The Instrument of Government had stated that the clergy should continue to receive tithes until provisions 'less subject to scruple and contention' could be made (15, vol. 2, *821*). No satisfactory scheme was devised, however, and the old system of financing parish ministers, which had been so fiercely attacked in Barebone's Parliament, continued. Cromwell did, however, maintain the policy of the parliamentary governments of the Civil War and Commonwealth periods of increasing the income of local clergymen by augmentations from confiscated episcopal property and from the fines imposed on royalists.

The Cromwellian State Church was clearly a much more tolerant institution than either the Presbyterian or Anglican establishments which preceded it, but clause 37 of the Instrument also provided for considerable religious freedom outside it. Moreover, clause 38, by insisting that no Parliament could make laws contrary to these provisions for religious liberty, enshrined a very wide degree of toleration in the Cromwellian Constitution (15, vol. 2). The two Parliaments of Oliver's Protectorate, composed mainly of gentlemen who were much more conservative than Cromwell himself in their religious views, tried nevertheless to restrict the extent of toleration. They did not easily accept the inviolability of any of the Instrument's provisions; for them no part of a constitution imposed by army officers could properly be regarded as fundamental law. Much of the time of the 1654 Parliament was spent in attempts to draw up a list of 'damnable heresies' which could not be tolerated, but this failed because members could not agree among themselves on the contents of the proposed list (198). The Parliament of 1656 returned to the fray (198). It launched a ferocious attack on the Quaker James Nayler who had re-enacted Christ's entry into Jerusalem in the same year with himself in the role of the Messiah, and in the Humble Petition and Advice of the following year a reluctant Cromwell finally agreed to the exclusion of Unitarians, who rejected the divinity of Christ, and socially disruptive sectaries from official toleration (15, vol. 2).

The wide degree of religious liberty which was recognized in the Instrument of Government and which was so largely an expression of the convictions of Cromwell and other army grandees was also to some extent a recognition of the fact that a great deal of practical religious toleration had developed in the country at large during the 1640s. The breakdown of the jurisdiction of the church courts in the early years of that decade meant that there was no effective means of enforcing attendance at church, and in 1650 the Rump formally recognized the situation when it repealed the Elizabethan statutes about compulsory Sunday attendance at parish churches [G.7(29)]. The Rump seems to have been less than enthusiastic about its own recognition of reality (128, *238–9*) and added a clause requiring everyone to attend *some* form of church service on Sundays, 'to the end that no profane or licentious persons may take occasion by the repealing of the said laws . . . to neglect the performance of religious duties'. That provision could not, of course, be enforced in practice, but the reluctant religious liberalism of the Rumpers should be contrasted with Cromwell's own enthusiastic espousal of the cause of toleration. It was surely his most striking characteristic and one which put him far in advance of the great majority of contemporaries of his own class. Others who did stress the virtues of toleration during the 1640s and 1650s tended to be radicals from the lower orders of society, but many sectaries, too, were much less tolerant than Cromwell. He put the point well in 1655 when he talked of 'a strange itch upon the spirits of men. Nothing will satisfy them unless they can press their finger upon their brethren's consciences to pinch them there.' His own task, in contrast, was to act 'as a constable, to part them and keep them in peace' (quoted (80, *361*)).

The Instrument, as we have seen, excluded from toleration not merely Catholicism but 'prelacy'; that is to say there was to be no licence for committed episcopalians who insisted on using the Book of Common Prayer. In practice both Catholics and Anglicans enjoyed a wide degree of freedom. As we noted (on p. 340), only a minority of clergymen were ejected from their livings during the 1640s and 1650s and the views of many of those who remained must have tended towards a moderate Anglicanism which no doubt satisfied large numbers of their parishioners. There is a good deal of evidence that traditional Anglican services – in theory prohibited since 1645 – were widely conducted, sometimes in full, sometimes with discreet modifications, by ministers of the State Church throughout the 1650s. The secular authorities often condoned these activities and the situation in Sebergham in Cumberland, where it was recorded in the later seventeenth century that 'the common prayer was read in the church . . . in all the late times of trouble and we never had a fanatic in the parish', may have been typical of many parts of England. The 2,500 or so clergymen who were expelled from the national Church during the 1640s and 1650s for overt royalism, unseemly personal conduct or over-enthusiastic loyalty to Anglican traditions presented a more difficult problem for the government than their more moderate brethren who remained within it. These ejected priests were the obvious upholders of the prelacy which was so roundly condemned in the Instrument, but in general the government connived at their private preaching activities and many of them obtained posts as chaplains or tutors in royalist households where they conducted services according to Prayer Book rites. On occasion, as after Penruddock's rising in 1655, the government threatened to curtail their activities, but little was in fact done. Cromwell himself, who did fear the political threat which unrestrained Anglicanism would have posed, was always very reluctant to persecute peaceful episcopalians and even in London itself there was a surprising degree of tolerance of Anglican worship. John Evelyn the diarist attended frequent traditional services in the capital during the Protectorate and in 1659 it was reported that the Prayer Book had been openly used for years in the church of St Peter's, Paul's Wharf (198, *194 ff*).

As for Catholics, they 'probably enjoyed a greater freedom to carry out their own worship in private than they had had under any of the previous monarchs since 1558' (62, *115*). That is a remarkable tribute to Cromwell whose personal abhorrence of Catholic doctrines was even greater than that of Elizabeth or the early Stuart Kings. Contemporaries remarked on the expanding corps of priests attached to foreign embassy chapels where they served the increasing number of English Catholics who heard mass there (198). Cromwell also favoured the readmission to England of the Jews, who had been effectively excluded from the country since the Middle Ages. Public opinion remained hostile and suspicious, but he encouraged an increasing number to settle in the country, where in practice they were allowed freedom of worship (198). The effective resettlement of the Jews in England owed more to Cromwell than to any other man.

The practical freedom allowed to Anglicans, Catholics and Jews had, of course, little or no legal foundation. It was a different matter for radical Protestants who felt unable to remain within the broadly based Cromwellian State Church. They were guaranteed full rights to worship outside it and Cromwell, as we have seen, was determined that his Parliaments should not be allowed to restrict the toleration accorded to members of independent churches and sects. Some of these, such as the Fifth Monarchy Men and Quakers, held extremist views which marked them out as radical revolutionaries. We will be looking at them later. But the Cromwellian period also saw the continuing growth of Congregational and Baptist churches which stood outside the State Establishment but rejected the more extreme views of sectaries like the Fifth Monarchists. Some historians have questioned whether it is legitimate to classify the gathered churches of the Interregnum with labels like 'Baptist' or 'Congregational', arguing that such clear-out denominational names are anachronistic as descriptions of what was essentially a fluid situation. Dr Watts, however, has convincingly rejected such doubts (167, *164 ff*), arguing that 'against the few examples of men and churches which sat at the edge of denominational boundaries must be set the considerable amount of evidence which indicates the early existence of denominational ties and denominational exclusiveness' (167, *166*). A large number of Congregational ministers – perhaps as many as 150 – accepted livings within the State Church while continuing to minister to their own independent churches outside it, but other Congregationalist pastors rejected all connection with the establishment. Congregationalists, of course, accepted the practice of infant baptism which was rejected by the Baptists. The latter were far more reluctant to retain links with the State Church and only nineteen of their ministers seem to have accepted parish livings by 1660. That was at a time when there were probably about 240 Baptist churches in existence throughout the country, divided in almost equal proportions between Particular Baptists who held to the Calvinist doctrine of salvation for the elect alone and General Baptists who preached Arminian ideas about universal grace (167).

The English religious scene during Cromwell's rule presented, therefore, a picture of great diversity. During the 1650s the logic of Protestantism, with its stress on the supremacy of the individual conscience, combined with the extensive official toleration allowed by the State to produce a multiplicity of churches and sects which openly proclaimed the widest range of doctrines. Cromwell, himself the principal protagonist of this degree of official religious liberty, extended it still further in practice by the freedom he allowed to officially proscribed Catholics and Anglicans and even to Jews. However conservative he was in some of his other attitudes, in religion he was undoubtedly a radical, far in advance of the views of most men of his time and class. Contemporary Britain is a pluralistic · society, tolerating all faiths. Such religious liberalism, which we take for granted, was totally alien to the vast majority of our seventeenth-century ancestors, but Oliver Cromwell, though he would have objected to many aspects of the modern religious scene, would have approved of that one. The toleration which he constantly preached and tried so hard to practise is one of the foundations of the modern Britain in which we live.

So far we have been looking at the work of the 'moderate revolutionaries' who challenged the King during the 1640s and seized control of the State during the 1650s. The King was replaced first of all by a republic under a single-chamber Parliament and the Church of England by a Presbyterian State Church which never took firm hold throughout the country. In 1653 the republic gave way to the Cromwellian Protectorate with its loosely organized national Church and wide degree of religious toleration. Scotland and Ireland were united in a parliamentary union with England, and the colonial empire, at least in the theory of the Navigation Act of 1651, became an economic unit, integrated with the home country. At the same time, the power of the army and navy which had been created by the new regimes of the 1640s and 1650s enabled Cromwellian Britain to exercise a vastly increased influence in European affairs. These were very significant developments, but it is important to note the limits of the revolution. An official State Church remained right throughout the period, something which more radical revolutionaries wanted to abolish, and, above all, the social hierarchy was preserved. This retention of the traditional social order was something which virtually all the upper-class contestants, both royalist and parliamentarian, both supporters and opponents of the Protectorate, who dominated politics during the 1640s and 1650s, were agreed upon, irrespective of their very widespread differences on constitutional and ecclesiastical questions. It was their belief in the divine right of the propertied classes to rule which, above all else, divided them from the radical revolutionaries. These radicals, as we shall see, had either explicitly revolutionary social ideas (like the Diggers and the Ranters) or else political and religious ideas with radical social implications (like the Levellers and the Fifth Monarchy Men). Such men came to oppose the Cromwellian Establishment of the 1650s just as much as they had opposed the royal Establishment of the 1640s.

Cromwell himself was, of course, the outstanding figure of the moderate revolution and his gigantic personality and presence dominates the events of the 1650s. The multiplicity of verdicts – Puritan hero, conservative stateman, military dictator, empire-builder – which historians have bestowed upon his career reflect their own interests and prejudices at least as much as the man himself. No final verdict can be expected, but it seems fair to stress three points about him. First of all, he was a great soldier – his genius in this field seems beyond dispute – and it is clear that he would never have become Protector unless he had commanded both the loyalty and confidence of the army. He was, however, as his whole career showed, a soldier who always sought a constitutional basis for military rule; the naked power of the sword was not for him. Secondly, he was a social conservative. It was not a blinkered conservatism – he favoured, as we shall see, reforms in the law and in education – but he was determined to preserve the existing structure of society. He showed this very clearly during the Putney debates in 1647, and his general attitude is well summed up in his famous remark of September 1654, 'a nobleman a gentleman, a yeoman: that is a good interest of the nation and a great one' (18, vol. 3, *435*). This social conservatism helps to explain why, though he did not have fixed views on government, he wanted a monarchical element in the political system; that, he thought, was the best hope for social stability. Thirdly, he was a religious radical. His stress throughout his career on the 'people of God', that élite group among the population with the 'root of the matter' in them, reflects the primacy of religion both in his own life and in his thinking. His profound concern with religion when carried into his foreign policy gave much of it an anachronistic slant, but his advocacy of religious toleration at home put him far ahead of his time and class and added a vital radical element to his fundamentally conservative make-up. The radical revolutionaries of the 1650s came to oppose almost everything that Cromwell stood for. In advocacy of religious toleration, however, he and they were at one. It is obvious, in fact, that Cromwell can never be adequately described in a sentence. His personality, inherently complicated, gained added complexity from the drama of the years in which he lived and the variety of events with which he had to deal.

---

1. J. M. Lloyd Thomas, ed., *The Autobiography of Richard Baxter* (Everyman edn, 1931), p. 71.

CHAPTER 42

The ferment in ideas and society, 1642–60: I

There were, as Professor Hill reminds us in a memorable phrase, 'two revolutions in mid-seventeenth century England' (222, *12*). We have already examined one of them, that of the conservative revolutionaries who triumphed over the royal Establishment in the 1640s and ruled the State during the 1650s. They were challenged during the later 1640s and thoughout the 1650s by the representatives of much more extreme political, social and religious ideas. The existence of these 'radical revolutionaries' helps to remind us that some historians have emphasized elements of class struggle during the conflicts of the period 1640–1660, and also directs attention to the economic background against which the drama of these years took place.

Of the twenty-two harvests between 1640 and 1661 ten were bad, eight good and four average, a worse-than-usual pattern within the context of the early modern period as a whole. The 1640s started well, with four good and two average harvests between 1640 and 1645. Then there was a run of five bad harvests in succession until 1650, followed by six average to good ones between 1651 and 1656; Cromwell launched his Protectorate in excellent harvest conditions. The period closed with five successive bad harvests between 1657 and 1661 [I]. The years 1646–61, therefore, were a bad period, with ten bad harvests out of sixteen rather than the four which might have been expected during a 'normal' run of years (228). During the two bad harvest runs agricultural prices rose sharply, especially between 1646 and 1650 when they rocketed by some 50 per cent. Over the two decades as a whole, however, there was little if any rise in the price of food [K], which seems remarkable in view of the political upheavals, military campaigns and, above all, harvest failures of the period. The basic explanation probably lies in the ending of the population expansion which had been a feature of the sixteenth and early seventeenth centuries. That slowed down during the 1640s and ended during the 1650s, easing the pressure on food supplies. In the field of overseas trade the period 1640–60 as a whole seems to have been one of expansion. Estimates are very difficult in the absence of satisfactory statistics, but Professor Coleman has suggested that there was an increase in the value of foreign trade during the 1640s and 1650s ((44, *133*); see also (250, *49 ff*)). There were, of course, years of considerable difficulty. Historians debate whether the Protectorate as a whole was a period of expanding or declining trade (151; 250), but there was certainly a slump during the years 1657–59 caused by the Spanish War with its closure of important markets for English goods and the accompanying attacks by enemy privateers on English shipping. The economic picture over the period 1640–60 as a whole seems then to be one of trade expansion and stabilization of agricultural prices, but within that generally favourable context there were periods of considerable difficulty, notably the sharp rise in agricultural prices in the later 1640s and the bad harvests of 1657 onwards, coinciding with the trade depression of 1657–59.

It is readily apparent to the historian that these times of economic difficulty, compounded by high taxation, coincided with periods of intense radical agitation in 1647–50 and 1659. Did the economic problems of the later 1640s and later 1650s make men from the poorer sections of the community more sympathetic towards radical ideas? The most obvious answer is that they did, but there is another possibility. It can also be argued that bad economic conditions coming at times of political upheaval associated with military rule make ordinary men wish above all else for the return of civilian government and political stability. That at least would mean that they would have more chance of coping with their economic difficulties in a calm atmosphere. Such an attitude, which would favour conservatism rather than radicalism, a desire to return to the old forms of government rather than to try still more radical experiments, would help to explain the general enthusiasm with which the Restoration was greeted among all sections of the community. It is clear, of course, that each of these attitudes must have prevailed in the minds of some members of the lower orders. Those of them who were inclined to radicalism for other reasons were no doubt confirmed and strengthened by economic difficulties in their determination to secure fundamental changes in society. Others – perhaps the great majority – looked for salvation from a restoration of the stability of the pre-1640 period. The upper classes, of course, were well aware of the potential threat to social order which a run of bad harvests presented. The difficulties of the later 1640s and later 1650s in the economic sphere clearly heightened gentry fears of social anarchy. One reaction to such fears can be seen in their determination to maintain and indeed extend the effective working of the Elizabethan Poor Laws (see above, Ch. 39), partly for paternalistic reasons, largely as a means of dampening down lower-class discontents in the interests of security. Another upper-class reaction, at least as important, was, however, the gentry's resolution to have no truck whatsoever with lower-class radicalism.

Discussion of the economic background to the 1640s and 1650s, with the questions which it raises about the links between economic conditions and radical movements, directs attention to another important issue; the extent to which the events of the period 1640–60 can be seen in terms of class conflict. The Civil War of 1642–46 itself obviously cannot be seen simply in such terms. It began, as we have seen (Ch. 36), as a result of a split within the ruling élite and during it members of different interests within that élite – nobility, gentry, merchants, office-holders – fought, admittedly in different proportions, on both the royalist and parliamentarian sides. The attitude of the 'lower orders' was determined largely by that of their betters in the area where they lived. Marxist historians have argued that the Civil War should be seen as a clash between 'feudal' and 'bourgeois' interests within the ruling élite which resulted in the triumph of the latter and with it the emergence of a dominant capitalism[1]. That, however, seems a very unconvincing picture. Non-Marxists, whatever their other differences, would agree that descriptions of the royalist side as 'feudal' and of the parliamentarian as 'bourgeois' in their economic interests beg so many questions and ignore so many complexities as to be almost worthless (37; 61). Marxist interpretations, in fact, suffer from the necessity of pushing complicated realities into a preconceived pattern. Their stress on men's economic motivations and on the role of the 'lower orders' in the events of the period have certainly helped to enrich our understanding of the middle decades of the seventeenth century, but their use of concepts of 'class' which were developed in analyses of nineteenth-century situations are often very misleading in discussing the seventeenth century when men thought rather in terms of status, based on an almost infinite gradation of ranks within an ordered hierarchy.

The most important social change during the 1640s and 1650s, in fact, was almost certainly a shift of power within the landed gentry – that amorphous group between the aristocracy on the one hand and the yeomanry on the other. As we saw (Ch. 39) the dominance of the gentry continued throughout the period, but the lesser or parochial gentry intruded themselves into prominence in all the institutions of central and local government at the expense of the greater landed families who had traditionally dominated Parliament, Civil Service and localities in the years before 1640. This was a very important shift in social power in the status-obsessed world of the mid-seventeenth century, but the fact remains that the new rulers of the State had far more in common with the men they had supplanted than with the lower orders of society. The new men, like their predecessors, were gentlemen, afraid that too many drastic political changes would lead to social upheaval. They were surely right; the proposals of Levellers, Diggers, Fifth Monarchy Men, Ranters and Quakers, if even a fraction of them had been adopted, would have led, in the longer or shorter term, to a social revolution which would have swept away the dominant role of the landed gentry in English life. The views of the different radical groups were varied and sometimes incompatible with each other but they were united in their opposition to the new regimes which emerged after the overthrow of the monarchy; all of them rejected the gentry-dominated establishments of the Commonwealth and Protectorate. There clearly *were* strong element of 'class conflict', however that is defined, in this overt hostility of the radicals towards the regimes of the 1650s and in the dislike and fear of the Commonwealth and Protectorate governments for these protagonists of a 'second revolution'. We can take the Levellers, Diggers, Fifth Monarchy Men, Quakers and Ranters as representatives of extreme political, social, religious and sexual ideas which would have overturned the world which the conservative revolutionaries of the mid-seventeenth century wished to preserve. Despite the very great differences among them they did have a number of specific ideas in common; all of them wanted the abolition of tithes and of a State Church and drastic reform of the law, all were hostile to accepted class distinctions.

The Levellers (143), led by the charismatic John Liburne, a man who won enormous popularity among the London masses,[2] were the first democratic political movement in modern history. They demanded a wide extension of the franchise, though there is still dispute among historians as to just how wide they wished that extension to be. Some think that they wanted virtually full manhood suffrage, others believe that they advocated more restricted rights with only male heads of households having the vote – the latter being roughly the system which actually existed in Britain between 1885 and 1918 (62). The truth is probably that the Levellers differed among themselves on this point and also that at times they were prepared to modify their views for reasons of political tactics. Professor Hirst's demonstration of the wide extent of the franchise in pre-1640 England (122) has made the practical effect of Leveller ideas in this field seem less dramatic. It must be remembered, however, that the complexities of the pre-1640 franchise puzzled both potential voters and the state authorities who had to organize elections. There was certainly no equivalent in early Stuart England to the Leveller proposals for extending the franchise which were such a feature of the later 1640s. Professor Aylmer is surely right when he says that the whole ethos of the Leveller movement was essentially democratic and that there was no movement to compare with it until late-eighteenth-century developments in England, France and America (143, 9).

The Levellers believed in a written constitution which limited the powers of Parliament, a reflection of their conviction that natural law gave men a number of inalienable rights which no assembly could legitimately withdraw. Each of the draft constitutions which they produced – the Agreements of the People of October 1647, December 1648 and May 1649 – contained fundamentals, such as religious toleration, which no Parliament was to be allowed to abrogate (17). They also believed that Parliaments should be frequent and have fixed terms. In the first Agreement they were to be elected every two years and sit for a period of six months; in the third they were to be elected annually and sit for at least four months. Such provisions reflected Leveller determination to make Parliaments regularly accountable to the enlarged electorate who were to choose them. The Levellers also wanted radical reform of both the Church and the law. The Church was to be completely disestablished and the tithes which supported parish ministers were to be abolished. Each parish was to elect its own minister and support him with voluntary contributions, and there was to be complete freedom of conscience and worship. At a time when the pulpit was by far the most important instrument for influencing public opinion the adoption of Leveller ideas on the Church would have meant that governments would have lost all control over the men who occupied the pulpits, a possibility which no seventeenth-century government could contemplate with equanimity. The law was to be equal for all, court proceedings were to be in English instead of Latin and Norman-French, there was to be no imprisonment for debt and legal penalties were to be made 'equal to offences' – a provision which would have abolished capital punishment for comparatively petty thefts. The importance of these legal demands is obvious when we remember that both contemporaries and later historians have seen the law and the legal system of the seventeenth century as instruments of repression and oppression, important elements in the apparatus by which the ruling gentry maintained their hold over the mass of the population. The Levellers' suggestions, if they had been carried out, would have gone far to ending such control and also to reducing the power and wealth of the lawyers. Such considerations make it plain why nearly all suggestions for really radical legal reforms were defeated in the gentry-dominated Parliaments of the Inter-regnum (on law reform see Ch. 43). Another feature of the Levellers' thinking was the emphasis which they laid on decentralization (221). They envisaged a withering away of the central agencies of government and saw England essentially in terms of a federation of county communities, with each shire governed by elected local officials. It was an appeal to local patriotism and to localism gener-ally, but in a form which would have deprived the gentry of their traditional dominance in the localities.

The strength of the Leveller movement lay in the lower ranks of the army and in the journeymen and craftsmen of London and it was this influence in the armed forces and among the population of the capital which made the Levellers seem a serious threat to the ruling gentry during the difficult economic conditions of 1647–49 when the movement was at its height. The threat was recognized by the army grandees, notably by Cromwell, who, as we have seen, suppressed Leveller-inspired mutinies in the army in 1647 and 1649 (Ch. 37). It was a reflection of his fears of the social implications of Leveller ideas. A movement towards political democracy would lead in due course, he believed, to a frontal challenge to estab-lished property rights and that would be a recipe for anarchy. The Leveller move-ment never recovered from its defeats in 1649. Cromwell was able to suppress it as a serious political force in that year because the Levellers' penetration of the army had not gone too far; the bulk of the soldiers remained loyal to their commanders.

The Levellers' ostensible demands were for political rather than economic democracy. The latter was the avowed objective of the Digger movement and its remarkable leader Gerrard Winstanley, the hero of Professor Hill's book on the radical movements of the period ((222); see also (19)). Very little is known about Winstanley's life – he was probably born in 1609, the son of a Wigan mercer – but between 1649 and 1652 he elaborated his ideas in a series of pamphlets, especially his *Law of Freedom* of 1652, in which he produced the first-ever detailed blueprint for a communist society as well as many other notable ideas. His basic demand was for the total abolition of private property and wage labour; the former, he argued, was the source of all national and international wars and conflicts and its abolition would bring peace among both men and nations. He stressed, however, that abolition would have to be achieved by persuasion rather than coercion. His communist ideas did not come from books. He himself tells us that they came rather as a personal inspiration: as he put it, he saw 'the light . . . rise up within myself' (19, *157*). Among his other ideas were an insistence that all state officials should be elected and that a people's militia should be the only armed force. There was to be complete separation of Church and State, with every congregation electing its own minister and religious toleration for all. Winstanley himself was a pantheist, believing that God pervaded the whole universe and dwelt in every creature. He rejected the possibility of personal immortality and thought that death would make him one with nature. That belief is expressed in the very last lines he wrote, at a time when all his hopes for a communist society had been dashed. They come at the end of the *Law of Freedom*.

O death where art thou? Wilt thou not tidings send?
I fear thee not, thou art my loving friend.
Come take this body and scatter it in the four [elements]
That I may dwell in one, and rest in peace once more. (19, *389*)

Winstanley advocated universal education for both sexes, with due attention to vocational training as well as book learning, but he rejected élitism in all spheres, advocating the abolition of both professional lawyers and a university-educated clergy. He believed in the possibility of human progress and looked to a future in which science would be applied to improve both economic conditions and the quality of human life. In this aspect of his thought he looked both backwards to Francis Bacon and forwards to the modern conservationists.

Winstanley believed that the first step towards a total abolition of private property in England, his ultimate objective, should be communal cultivation of the extensive waste lands in the country. Accordingly, in April 1649 he and a group of followers began to dig the waste in the parish of Walton-on-Thames in Surrey. By the beginning of 1650 other colonies had appeared in Northamptonshire, Kent, Buckinghamshire, Hertfordshire, Middlesex, Bedfordshire, Leicestershire, Gloucestershire and Nottinghamshire, making ten English counties altogether. The public authorities, however, were, as one would expect, hostile and the Digger movement collapsed in the same year. We know the names of ninety-two Diggers altogether. As Hill says, it does not seem, on the face of it, a very important episode in history. The Diggers had clearly no chance whatsoever of establishing themselves on a permanent footing in view of the incomprehension with which they were regarded by the bulk of the population, and above all in face of the implacable hostility of the governing classes. But, of course, numbers and immediate influence are not everything. The Diggers are interesting to us as the first communist movement to produce a detailed description of the society which they hoped to create and also for the very attractive personality of Winstanley which has been so sympathetically and movingly portrayed for us by Professor Hill.

The Diggers and the Levellers were, in their different ways, representatives of one of the two main elements of radicalism in the abortive second revolution which we are now considering. They were concerned principally, though not of course by any means exclusively, with secular matters, as opposed to the Fifth Monarchist and Quaker movements, which were primarily religious sects. In contrast to the secular radicals, who looked in the direction of political and economic democracy and who were at their most prominent in the years 1647–50, the heyday of the Leveller and Digger movements, the religious radicals were at their most influential in 1653, at the time of Barebone's Parliament. As we saw (Ch. 39), Cromwell may have been influenced in his decision to call that Assembly by the Fifth Monarchists, religious revolutionaries who believed that the millennium[3] was at hand and that it was the duty of the elect, the Saints, that is to say themselves, to rule the world in preparation for the Second Coming of Christ (200). The movement was, therefore, essentially anti-democratic. The Fifth Monarchists shared their basic millenarianism with a wide spectrum of religious opinion in mid-seventeenth-century England, but stood out from their fellow believers in two important ways. First of all, they claimed not merely the right but also the duty to take up arms, overthrow existing regimes and establish the millennium by force. Secondly, they produced a detailed description of the political, social and economic structure of their promised land. Their reliance on force led to them being branded by contemporaries as violent revolutionaries hiding behind a façade of godliness, and their political and social ideas do indeed reveal the extent of their radicalism. If their ideas had been put into practice the whole traditional basis of English society would have been overturned. They believed that government should be by a small élite of the godly. Only church members – presumably members of Fifth Monarchist churches – were to have the vote, with each congregation nominating representatives to a kind of Church-Parliament, which was to rule the country until the Second Coming. Fifth Monarchists recognized that the godly might be found in all ranks of society, from the very highest to the very lowest, but the kind of political structure which they envisaged would clearly have swept away the traditional governmental dominance of the gentry; it would, therefore, have been a social as well as a political revolution. This fact was well recognized by contemporaries who accused them of seeking to annihilate the upper ranks of society. They wanted the abolition of the whole existing legal system and with it of professional lawyers. Laymen were to be allowed to plead their own cases in local courts before elected judges and juries. Again, such drastic reforms would clearly have ended the role of the law as an instrument of upper-class dominance of the lower orders. The legal just like the political ideas of the Fifth Monarchists implied social revolution. As far as the Church is concerned the movement rejected lay patronage, tithes, parochial livings, the whole idea of a State Church. On the other hand, it is not completely clear how far the Fifth Monarchists believed in religious toleration.

The movement was essentially an urban phenomenon (except in Wales) and the London area was dominant throughout; it contained at least twenty-nine of the seventy-two Fifth Monarchist groups of which we have record during the second half of the century. During the 1650s, in fact, the strength of the movement lay in the southern half of England and in Wales. Total numbers were small – probably never more than 10,000 – but the Fifth Monarchists made up in dedication and fanaticism for their lack of numerical strength. The leaders were a comparatively small number of clergymen and army officers, of whom General Harrison is the most famous, but the mass of followers were from the lower orders of society, with women outnumbering men. The movement took shape in 1651 and after its moment of glory at the time of Barebone's Parliament in 1653 it was implacably opposed to Cromwell who, the Fifth Monarchists believed, had betrayed both the Saints and his own earlier ideals by his decision to dissolve the Parliament. After the Restoration the Fifth Monarchists were driven underground, but they remained in existence until 1685, when they participated in Monmouth's rebellion.

Today, of course, the Fifth Monarchists are only a memory. It is different with the Quakers, the only significant extremist religious sect of the Interregnum to remain in existence in our own time, though the quietists whom we know today, with their emphasis on good works, are very different from the militants of the 1650s who, just like the Fifth Monarchists, were seen as a threat to established society. The early Quaker story and the lives of its great leaders Fox and Nayler are well known (see e.g. (167; 201–2; 222)), and here it must be enough to emphasize that from obscure beginnings in the later 1640s the movement spread throughout much of England in the 1650s, winning numerous converts among farmers and rural and urban craftsmen. By 1660 there were perhaps 30,000 or 40,000 Quakers (201). The early Quakers were far from being the pacifists of the Restoration period and contemporary fears of a great Quaker rising reached their height in 1659 and were a significant element in the events leading to the return of Charles II. The distinctive Quaker belief was stress on an 'inner light' which brought salvation to those who accepted its guidance. That light was a manifestation of Christ's spirit working within men and Quakers believed that though it might lead to eccentricities in individuals it would also work in them a dramatic moral transformation which would, in due course, transform society itself. Quakers, in other words, put their faith in personal example rather than in politics as the dominant motor in social change. The changes which the Quakers wanted were drastic enough. Their refusal to pay tithes or swear oaths struck at the roots of the ecclesiastical and legal systems and, above all, their contempt for accepted social conventions revealed a rejection of the hierarchical structure of society which helps to explain the extent of gentry fears of the movement by the later 1650s. Quakers who refused to remove their hats in the presence of social superiors and addressed gentlemen in the familiar forms of 'thee'and 'thou' as a rebuke to worldly pride, clearly wanted a totally different social order than the one which prevailed during the 1650s.

The Quakers have always found sympathetic historians but it is only recently that the Ranters have been studied with real understanding (222–3). Ranters held extreme views on most subjects – they have traditionally been regarded as the 'lunatic fringe' of the radical revolution – and two aspects of the movement seem especially noteworthy. First of all, it appealed directly to the urban and rural poor, people at the very bottom of the social heap to whom no other radical movement paid the same attention. Secondly, it preached an extreme version of the permissive society. This was the notorious antinomianism of the Ranters, a conviction that for the true believer traditional moral restraints could be ignored. This can be seen very clearly in the teachings of one of the Ranter leaders, Laurence Clarkson; 'there is no such act' he wrote, 'as drunkenness, adultery, and theft in God. . . . Sin hath its conception only in the imagination. . . . What act soever is done by thee in light and love is light and lovely, though it be that act called adultery. . . . No matter what Scripture, saints or churches say, if that within thee do not condemn thee, though shalt not be condemned.' Or again, 'None can be free from sin till in purity it be acted as no sin, for I judged that pure to me which to a dark understanding was impure: for to the pure all things, yea all acts were pure.' (222, *172–3*) Clarkson was not slow to practise what he preached in his travels around the country when he seduced numerous women. Ranters also held extreme religious and political views. In the religious sphere their most notable belief was that God was present in all living things; like the Digger Winstanley they were pantheists. They believed, therefore, that as God was in them they were themselves in a sense gods. They said this in their writings and it was the expression of this idea together with their rejection of the moral law which was primarily responsible for the Rump Parliament's Blasphemy Act of 1650 (15, vol. 2; 128), which was directed chiefly against the Ranters and denounced anyone who claimed to be God or equal to God together with the idea that there was no such thing as sin 'but as a man or woman judgeth thereof'. The penalty was six months in prison for a first offence and banishment for the second, with death for any condemned person who returned from banishment. The Ranters also preached complete political egalitarianism allied to a kind of primitive communism. Their beliefs in this sphere were reflected in their typical form of address; they called other men 'fellow creature'. The Ranter movement was prominent only for a brief period during the years 1649–51. During 1650 it seems to have attracted a considerable following among the London poor, though there are reports of Ranter activities from almost every part of England. The movement became strong enough in that year, in fact, to alarm the Commonwealth government, which repressed it savagely. Ranter leaders were arrested, imprisoned and forced to recant. By 1651 the movement had been virtually stamped out as a significant force. It is easy to imagine the horror with which Ranters were viewed by all respectable men and women. Their ideas were clearly subversive of the whole structure of society in all its forms – political, religious, hierarchical, sexual. Their views, if ever they had prevailed – and clearly there was not the slightest chance that they could have prevailed – would have produced an anarchical version of the permissive society in its most extreme form; they would have amounted in practice to a dissolution of society.

A Ranter like Laurence Clarkson had little in common with the Leveller John Lilburne, and Levellers and Ranters appealed to very different sections of society, 'respectable' craftsmen and the submerged urban masses respectively, but despite such important differences it is essential to remember that virtually all the leaders and followers of the radical revolutionary movements which we have been examining – Lilburne himself was an exception – came from below the traditional governing classes. Their ideas, which implied or stated social revolution, were a condemnation of the gentry élite which had dominated English society for so long and which they all wanted to replace.

---

1. The classic Marxist view is given by C. Hill, *The English Revolution* (1955 edn).
2. P. Gregg, *Free Born John* (1961).
3. The millennium was a period of godly rule on earth, traditionally of 1,000 years duration. During that period or at the end of it (authorities differed on the point) the Second Coming of Christ would take place.

CHAPTER 43

The ferment in ideas and society, 1642–1660: II

Radical revolutionaries of the 1640s and 1650s, as we have just seen, put forward drastic ideas for legal and educational reforms and advocated the use of science to ameliorate man's lot on earth. Their ideas were, of course, only a part of the vast explosion of discussion of these and other controversial subjects which marked the middle decades of the century and found expression in the work of some of the greatest thinkers and writers of the age.

The period 1640–60 was certainly of the first importance in the history of English political thought. As Professor Zagorin puts it, 'In England no other period of comparable brevity has borne so splendid a harvest', and he goes on to point out that 'most of the leading principles which inspired the eighteenth-century revolutions in Europe and America received their first commanding expression during the years when the Long Parliament defeated the King and Cromwell set up his power.' (282, *1*) We have already emphasized the place of the Levellers' ideas in the history of political democracy, and while some of their views, most notably those on the franchise were not accepted until the nineteenth and twentieth centuries others, such as the calls for annual Parliaments and for the withering away of the State, are still the dreams of extreme left-wing radicals. Winstanley's detailed communist manifesto, with its stress on the links between political liberty and economic equality has also been discussed (Ch. 42), and its significance needs little elaboration in our present-day world with its enormously strong communist movements.

Full recognition of the significance of Winstanley and the Levellers in the history of political thought is a comparatively recent development, but the stature of James Harrington and Thomas Hobbes has long been recognized. Both men were strongly influenced by the 'new philosophy', the scientific movement of the seventeenth century with its emphasis on rational thought founded on math-ematical principles. Harrington, the foremost of the republican theorists of the Interregnum, wanted to erect a commonwealth based on 'scientific' principles. He had, however, a very high conception of the importance of history in the scale of knowledge, believing that an exact science of politics could only be constructed once men had understood the 'historical necessity' which he saw as the root cause of political change and which he believed could be rationally demonstrated to the world. Harrington found his decisive historical factor in the distribution of prop-erty – above all land – and in his greatest work, *Oceana*, published in 1656, he argued that recent disturbances in the English body politic had been caused by a growing imbalance between political power and the ownership of land. The latter had increasingly passed away from the Crown into the hands of others while the King continued to maintain his ancient claims to govern the country. In accordance with Harrington's fundamental doctrine that political authority must, in the long run, inevitably be founded on the ownership of property, the dramatic changes of the 1640s and 1650s were the logical result of the growing imbalance between the King's political pretensions and his material resources. Harrington's solution was the creation of a 'balance' between economic and political power which would ensure that the latter would reflect the realities of the distribution of property. We cannot go into the details of his ingenious solution as set out in *Oceana*, but it was founded on two essentials, an agrarian law strictly limiting the value of the land which any single person could hold, and the idea of rotation of office to prevent the domination of the commonwealth by selfish parties and factions. The result, Harrington believed, would be a state which could exist virtually for ever. He propagated his views with great energy during the later 1650s and, although his ideal republic remained a theory, his doctrine of historical necessity and his penetrating insights into the relationships between economic and political power have strongly influenced much subsequent political thought.

His great contemporary, Thomas Hobbes, produced in 1651 his *Leviathan*, which has been described by Professor Oakeshott as 'the greatest, perhaps the sole masterpiece of political philosophy written in the English language' (20, *viii*). It is certainly a remarkable work, reflecting both Hobbes's opinion of politics as a science and his man-centred rather than God-centred view of the subject; his system was founded not, as was traditional, on a transcendental order dominated by divine and natural law, but on man and his needs. It was, therefore, an important reflection of that secularization of thought which was proceeding apace during the seventeenth century. Hobbes brought into the open the modern doctrine of sovereignty, with the idea that the supreme power in a state – whether the absolute monarch whom Hobbes preferred or some body of men – had complete authority over its subjects, untrammelled by any restrictions of divine or natural law. There is, however, a basic contradiction in Hobbes's thought and historians now lay increasing stress on his views of the rights of individuals, which conflict with his emphasis on the dominance of the absolutist state. The dichotomy arises from the starting-point of his philosophy; the needs of primitive men. Hobbes argued that men gave up certain rights which they had possessed in a state of nature to sovereign authorities in order to prevent anarchy and thus improve their own lives. The sovereign power was absolute, but only as long as it was able to protect its subjects. In the last resort, therefore, individuals had the right to rebel against the sovereign to protect the fundamental advantages which they expected from any governing authority: basic security and, therefore, happiness. Hobbes, traditionally the philosopher *par excellence* of absolutism, can thus give much comfort to liberals who can argue that his stress on the ultimate rights of the individual is the most basic of all his premises.

Political theorists like Hobbes operated, in much of their work, at a high level of abstraction. The realities of the English legal system, in contrast, bore heavily on the mass of the population. We have noted (Ch. 42) that all the radical revolutionaries of the period wanted changes in the law, which they regarded as one of the major instruments by which the ruling élite both oppressed and held in subjection the rest of society. The radicals were certainly the law's most vocal critics, but some members of the ruling élite, while rejecting their more extreme demands, realized the need for law reform. Bacon and Coke had proposed reforms in the early seventeenth century (138) and Cromwell himself was a legal reformer during the Interregnum. The law was criticized both for its workings and for its content (128; 138). Procedure was notoriously slow, and the time taken to hear and settle cases was the subject of frequent and anguished complaints. Chancery which, in its early days, had been renowned for its relative speed and efficiency had by the seventeenth century become a byword for dilatoriness; in a parliamentary debate on the court in 1653 it was asserted that there were 23,000 cases pending before it. It was argued, moreover, that court officials, gaolers and above all the lawyers themselves – those 'verminous caterpillars' of the Commonwealth – exploited the legal system for their own benefit rather than in the interests of their clients. Court officials, who received fees on the basis of the amount of work done, too often organized their business with the primary aim of maximizing their profits; gaolers exploited the helplessness of prisoners, whom they all too often held in appalling conditions, to wring as much money from them as was humanly possible; and complaints – probably exaggerated – about the wealth and greed of the lawyers were legion.

The contents of the law were as open to dissatisfaction as its workings. Punishments often bore little relationship to crimes. During the sixteenth and early seventeenth centuries numerous statutes further increased the severity of already harsh penalties, extending the death sentence to new offences. Cromwell objected to men being hanged for small thefts. 'There are wicked and abominable laws', he told Parliament in 1656, 'that will be in your power to alter. . . . To see men lose their lives for petty matters! This is a thing God will reckon for.' (18, vol. 4, *274*) If the unfairness of punishments was a particular source of complaint in the criminal law, the arcane mysteries of the land law, the most important branch of the civil law, frequently drove litigants to distraction. By the mid-seventeenth century the whole legal system, in both its civil and criminal aspects, clearly needed clarification and simplification. To such general complaints about both the workings and content of the law the radicals added denunciations of its class bias. They understandably believed that laws which had been drawn up and were interpreted by members of the ruling élite subserved their interests rather than those of the mass of the population. Hence the radicals' calls for the abolition of the legal profession or at the very least the ending of its privileges; their demands for a transformation of the structure of the courts, with much more emphasis on the localities at the expense of Westminster; their insistence that all men, irrespective of social status, should receive equal treatment before the law; and their desire for the laws to be simplified and codified in English, in a form which could readily be understood by all.

Such radical dreams, if they had been put into practice, would have transformed not merely the law itself but a host of social assumptions which were built into its structure, and a notable aspect of Interregnum law reform is the limited nature of its achievements in relationship to radical aspirations and demands. The Parliaments of the Protectorate, despite Cromwell's urgings, devoted only a limited amount of time to law reform, but their predecessors, the Rump and Barebone's, each gave the subject a good deal of attention (128; 138–9). The former set up a weighty Commission on Reform in 1652 under the distinguished lawyer Matthew Hale, and the latter resolved both to abolish the court of Chancery and to codify the law, making it 'easy, plain and short'. Neither of Barebone's major proposals was accomplished and it was left to Cromwell to deal with Chancery. He did this in an important ordinance of August 1654 (15, vol. 2), which aimed at reducing the 'trouble, expense and delay' which were notorious in the court. His measure seems to have worked well, simplifying procedure and saving litigants a great deal of expense, but displaced officials and the legal establishment as a whole mounted a powerful campaign against it, and in February 1658 Parliament allowed it to lapse (138). The Rump achievements were more obvious than those of Barebone's. It is true that none of the numerous suggestions of the Hale Commission, which made a wide variety of proposals for procedural and substantive reforms in both the civil and the criminal law, were enacted by the Rump, but it did pass measures to relieve debtors and to deprive MPs and peers of their special legal privileges. Above all, in 1650 it passed an Act insisting that all proceedings in the courts and all law books were henceforth to be in English instead of the traditional Norman-French and Latin. That measure lapsed at the Restoration and was not reintroduced until 1732. Other noteworthy legal reforms of the period 1640–60 were the abolition of the Court of Wards by the Long Parliament in 1646, the transfer of the probate of wills from ecclesiastical courts to the civil authorities, and the introduction of civil marriage ceremonies.[1] Such changes were significant but, of course, they fell far short of radical demands for the total transformation of the legal system and were also a good deal more modest than the changes which Cromwell himself would have liked to see. In April 1657, in a speech to Parliament, he showed his continuing awareness of the need for reform. 'Surely the laws need to be regulated' he told the assembled members, '. . . I confess if any man would ask me, "why, how would you have it done?" I confess I do not know how. But I think verily at the least, the delays in suits, and the excessiveness in fees, and the costliness of suits . . . [require attention] . . . I say certainly that the people are greatly suffering in this respect; they are so.' (18, vol. 4, *483*) It was an appeal which fell on unsympathetic ears. The attitudes of the property-owners and lawyers in the Parliaments of the 1650s explain more than anything else why the legal reforms of the period were so limited (128; 138). The existing legal system, which brought them either substantial profits or high social status or both, suited them very well. They might consider minor amendments but were not prepared to accept major changes in either the criminal or civil law which would put their privileged position in society at risk. Their attitude shows that they accepted the radicals' basic analysis of the English legal system of the mid-seventeenth century as one of the principal institutions by which the ruling gentry and their lawyer allies controlled society in their own interest.

The radicals, who so strongly criticized the English legal establishment, were equally loud in their denunciations of the educational system. The sixteenth and early seventeenth centuries had seen a vast expansion of both higher education and the schools system (see Ch. 24). Contemporary observers like Hobbes saw the universities as nurseries of subversive ideas which helped to bring about the troubles of the 1640s (2, *131*), and later commentators like Professors Curtis and Stone have interpreted the events of that decade partly in terms of the frustrated ambitions of educated men who could not find suitable jobs (213; 219; 263). Radical critics of the higher educational system, however, can have taken small comfort from the fact that the universities may have contributed to the success of the conservative revolution which overthrew the monarchy in 1649. For them the beneficed clergymen who were educated there, just like the lawyers who were trained at the Inns of Court, were a bastion of the established social system, justi-fying and supporting from their pulpits the hierarchical society which was domin-ated by their upper-class patrons. In these circumstances it is not surprising that the Levellers and sectaries like the Fifth Monarchists denounced the university system. The Leveller William Walwyn pointed out that the Apostles were unlearned men and attacked Oxford and Cambridge for persisting in the study of Hebrew, Greek and Latin at a time when the Scriptures were in English. Both episcopalian and Presbyterian clergymen, he argued, 'when they commend learning it is not for learning's sake but for their own; her esteem gets them their livings and preferments and therefore she is to be kept up or their trade will go down' (261, *111*), and John Spittlehouse, a prominent Fifth Monarchist, saw the universities as 'very foundations of atheism and antichristianism'. He believed that classical languages and all learning not to be found in the Bible were useless (200, *188–9*). The Digger leader, Winstanley, was also a bitter critic of Oxford and Cambridge. He wanted them to stop their major traditional task of producing clergymen for the State Church. Such learned ministers, he argued, used their knowledge and authority to prevent worthy laymen from preaching the Gospel. 'The upshot of all your universities and public preachers', he maintained, '. . . is only to hinder Christ from rising.' University scholars were devoted to cheating the poor of 'the freedom of the earth' (19, *47–8*). Winstanley stressed the need for practical studies and his views were shared by the Prussian-born Samuel Hartlib who was a disciple of the great Czech educational reformer Comenius. Hartlib settled in England during the 1620s and was a notable protagonist of reform in a wide variety of fields during the 1640s and 1650s (272). He and his followers argued that the university curriculum should stress scientific subjects at the expense of classical languages and literature. Winstanley and Hartlib had similar criticisms of the schools. These too, they argued, were far too dominated by a curriculum founded on the classics. There was need for much greater emphasis on 'useful' subjects. Winstanley and Hartlib, indeed, preached the virtues of universal education for both sexes (222; 272), and their vision of a vastly expanded schools system which provided practical training for the whole community was a challenge not only to the existing educational establishment but also, by implication, to the whole structure of society which it helped to uphold. Their call for drastic educational reform was, partly at least, an appeal for social revolution.

During the 1640s and 1650s there was a steep fall in private investment in the universities and in the number of students entering them, though it is impossible to be sure whether or not these developments were related to the kind of critical attacks on the higher educational system which we have just been examining. In contrast to an average of over £20,000 gifted by private donors to the universities in each of the first four decades of the seventeenth century, the average in the 1640s and 1650s was less than £6,000 per decade. Similarly, the number of students entering higher education reached a peak during the 1630s, with an average annual intake by the universities and Inns of Court of over 1,200. Numbers fell back sharply during the 1640s and 1650s and, although more lawyers than ever before were called to the bar during the period between the Restoration and the 1688 Revolution, university numbers never recovered to the pre-revolutionary peak during the later Stuart period.[2] New ideas did have an impact on the reduced university population during the revolutionary decades – for example in the medical field (272) – but the more drastic ideas of the radicals came up against Cromwell's determination to defend the traditional role of Oxford and Cambridge as nurseries of the clergy. If there was to be a State Church – and Cromwell, as we have seen, believed that there should be – then it would need ministers with the kind of training which only the universities could give. Cromwell saw very clearly that clergymen educated at Oxford and Cambridge were a powerful bastion of the hierarchical society which he was so determined to defend (80; 261). He kept a close watch on developments in the universities during the 1650s. He became Chancellor of Oxford in 1651 and during the Protectorate appointed fresh Commissions for the visitation of Oxford and Cambridge. He was the driving force behind the creation of a new university college at Durham in 1657 (272). In his attitude to higher education, in fact, just as in his attitude to the legal system, Cromwell emerges as a moderate reformer, rejecting both the extreme views of the radicals and the immobilism of reactionaries. He was anxious for reasonable changes which would not pose a threat to the existing social order.

In contrast to the contraction of the universities and despite the disruption of individual schools, the expansion of the schools system, which had been so notable during the sixteenth and early seventeenth centuries, continued throughout the 1640s and 1650s, with the foundation of new and the improvement of existing schools by private donors (205; 265). Throughout the Commonwealth and Protectorate, moreover, the public authorities systematically devoted part of the revenue from confiscated church lands to the support of schools and schoolmasters. Cromwell's government undertook the task of ejecting unfit schoolteachers and licensing new entrants to the profession (80). Here we can see the beginnings of the modern conception of a state's duty towards education; the provision of funds and the supervision of standards. What was done, of course, fell very far short of the universal education which reformers like Hartlib and Winstanley advocated. That proposal, while wholly admirable as an ideal objective, was quite impracticable in the social and financial conditions of mid-seventeenth-century England.

Hartlib, the radical educational reformer, has recently been seen as a key figure in scientific developments in seventeenth-century England. He appears in this role in a massive study by Dr Charles Webster, who also sees links between

Puritanism and scientific progress in England (272). That latter idea is, of course, an application to English conditions of the thesis that there were important links between the development of European Protestantism, especially in its Calvinist varieties, and the scientific advances of the sixteenth and seventeenth centuries. The argument, in its most general terms, is that Protestantism, by replacing the hierarchical authority of the Catholic Church with a theology which stressed the priesthood of all believers and the supremacy of the individual conscience, promoted a spirit of free inquiry which was an important asset in scientific research. The interpretation as applied to England by scholars like Professor Hill and most recently by Dr Webster sees Puritanism as more conducive to scientific inquiry than the reactionary crypto-Catholic Anglicanism of the Laudian era, and Hill and Webster argue that the new science and Puritanism triumphed together during the 1640s and 1650s, a period which Webster especially sees as being of decisive importance in the overall development of English science during the seventeenth century (272; 281). Both Hill and Webster rightly lay considerable stress on the role of Francis Bacon as a formative influence behind the scientific developments of the mid-seventeenth century; there is no doubt that Bacon's emphasis on the need to build up a body of data, based on empirical knowledge, from which general scientific theories could be established and tested by the process of induction, and his stress on the usefulness of science – his belief that it would give man new powers over nature and thus enable him to build a better life for himself on earth – were extremely influential in that period. On the other hand, the attempts of Hill and Webster to set Bacon's ideas in a Puritan context are not always convincing, and Webster is not helped by his failure to define precisely what he means by the notoriously difficult term 'Puritanism'. In any event, the whole thesis which stresses links between Puritanism and scientific progress ignores or minimizes those anti-scientific trends which were very strong in the Puritan movement; its other-worldliness, anti-intellectualism and biblical fundamentalism, trends which have been stressed by all scholars who have dissected the Puritan movement as a whole (e.g. (183, *339 ff*); see Ch. 18, above).

If doubts exist about the intimate links which some scholars have seen between the development of Puritanism and scientific progress, they also remain about another central point of Webster's thesis, his argument that the work of the scientists of the 1640s and 1650s was central to the whole English scientific revolution, which he believes should be seen in an entirely new perspective with much less weight than usual being given to post-1660 developments and much more to the pre-1660 period. He argues that the political upheavals of the 1640s and 1650s, far from holding back the progress of science, as has often been supposed, actually stimulated its growth. The Puritans and parliamentarians were, he believes, 'the dominant element in the scientific community' (272, *491*) and he maintains that the triumph of the parliamentary cause benefited English science. These arguments are bolstered by statistics which demonstrate the growing number of scientists who entered the profession during the mid-century decades, more than in either the pre-1640 or post-1660 eras (272, *484 ff*). The statistics in themselves, however, tell us nothing about the *quality* of the scientific works which were being produced and many historians of science will take a good deal of convincing that the era of Webster's Puritan projectors should be stressed at the expense of the age which produced the *Principia*, the *Opticks* and other fruits of Newton's genius.

The bulk of Webster's book is taken up by a fascinating analysis of the work of the 'Puritan' intellectuals who are his heroes, the men he sees as dominating the scientific activities of the 1640s and 1650s. They looked to Bacon for their inspiration and concentrated on the advancement of knowledge as a means of improving man's lot on earth. Hartlib is at the very centre of the picture as the co-ordinator and inspirer of much of the work of these men. We cannot go into the details of their schemes. Webster dissects them at length and provides a vast amount of new information about the proposals of the Hartlib circle – suggestions which included a scheme for a decimal currency together with elaborate plans for technical and medical education, including vocational schools as well as London teaching hospitals and even a university of London. These were projects far in advance of their time – they were not realized until the nineteenth or twentieth centuries – and one overwhelming impression which the reader gets about such plans is their total impracticability given the financial restrictions on all seventeenth century governments. Amidst the realities of life in the England of the day the overall programme of the Hartlib circle was clearly Utopian. Moreover, it is doubtful if some of Webster's projectors can properly be called 'scientists' at all, even in terms of the widest possible definition of the word. Many of them seem rather to have been inordinately ambitious social reformers, determined to create a new heaven on English soil through such means as universal education and the provision of vast medical services.

These doubts about some of Webster's major points must not, of course, be allowed to call in question the great importance of his work. He may not convince sceptics that there were intimate links between the rise of Puritanism and scientific progress and his thesis that the mid-century era rather than the age of Newton was the crucial period in the English scientific revolution seems, at best, an interesting hypothesis, but he has revealed the astonishing fertility of the minds of the many intellectuals – whether they were Puritans or not – who flourished during the 1640s and 1650s. Their very ambitious projects for social reform bore comparatively little fruit, but there can be no doubt, after Webster's work, that the revolutionary era was fertile soil not only for the propagation of radical schemes like those of the Levellers, Diggers and religious sectaries, but also for the theories of intellectuals – scientists and other thinkers – who wanted to improve man's lot in this world through the increase and practical application of human knowledge.

The 1640s and 1650s, the age of radical revolutionaries like Winstanley and social engineers like Hartlib, were also of great formative influence in the life and thought of John Milton and John Bunyan, two of the great literary figures of the age (useful surveys of literary developments are (284–6)). It is true that Milton's most famous works, *Paradise Lost, Paradise Regained* and *Samson Agonistes*, were not published until after the Restoration, but during the early 1640s he won notoriety for his writings on divorce in which he argued that marriages could and should be dissolved if the partners were incompatible. That was a shocking idea to most contemporaries, but it reflected the boldness and radicalism of Milton's mind.[3] During this period too, in 1644, a he produced his *Areopagitica*, majestic plea for the freedom of the Press, then under challenge by the Long Parliament. The self-taught tinker Bunyan, so different in background from Milton with his university education, also published his famous work *The Pilgrim's Progress* after the return of Charles II, but it was during the 1640s that he began to study the Bible closely, and any reader of his great book rapidly discovers that it was founded above all else on the Scriptures.

The revolutionary era which, despite continuing attempts by the authorities at censorship, saw the expression of so many radical ideas through the medium of the printing presses, witnessed the end of a great era of English drama with the closure of the theatres in 1642 by order of the Long Parliament. Playhouses had long been under attack by Puritan critics, most notably the ferociously hostile William Prynne, as centres both of moral turpitude and royalist propaganda, and though surreptitious performances continued after the 1642 edict they were discouraged by further parliamentary ordinances of 1647 and 1648 which ordered players to be whipped and members of their audience to be fined. The effective return of the drama had to await the Restoration. Puritans, who were so hostile to stage plays, were also responsible for the burst of iconoclasm which destroyed a great deal of English stained glass, with both cathedrals and parish churches in many parts of the country suffering at the hands of men who regarded their beautiful windows as monuments to superstition and idolatry.[4] It was a sad time for an important part of England's cultural heritage and one which recalls the destructive aspects of the Henrician Reformation when so many monastic treasures were destroyed or dispersed and so many shrines despoiled.

The attacks on the country's wealth of stained glass and the closure of its theatres are evidence of the destructive side of the ferment in ideas which was such a notable feature of the 1640s and 1650s. They must be set against the creative proposals for educational and legal reforms and for scientific advance and social improvement which were designed to ameliorate the lot of the English community as a whole and most notably of its poorer members. Lack of adequate financial resources, quite apart from any other reasons, ensured that most of these projected reforms remained the dreams of radical revolutionaries or visionary intellectuals. The variety of their ideas and the drastic nature of many of their suggestions do, however, bear witness to the extent and depth of the desire for change which existed in the minds of at least some members of the mid-seventeenth-century English community.

---

1. G. B. Nourse, 'Law reform under the Commonwealth and Protectorate', *LQR*, **75** (1959), 512 ff.
2. W. K. Jordan, *Philanthropy in England 1480–1660* (1959), p. 373; L. Stone, 'The educational revolution in England', *P & P*, **28** (July 1964), 51, 54; G. S. Holmes, 'The professions and social change in England, 1680–1730', *PBA*, **65** (1979), 313 ff.
3. For the extent of Milton's radicalism see C. Hill, *Milton and the English Revolution* (1977).
4. C. Woodforde, *English Stained and Painted Glass* (Oxford, 1954), pp. 44 ff.

CHAPTER 44

The road to Restoration, 1658–1660

Oliver Cromwell, who sympathized with some of the ideas of the radical revolutionaries but feared and detested most of them, died in September 1658. Just
over a year and a half later, in May 1660, Charles II was restored, and historians
have rightly seen the rapidity of the Restoration as, in large part, a tribute to
Cromwell's unique ability to keep together during his lifetime warring factions
and interests which soon openly quarrelled after his death. We have to explain
two series of events. First of all, the fall of the protectorship of Cromwell's elder
son Richard in May 1659, and secondly the collapse of the restored Commonwealth and the restoration of the monarchy a year later.[1]

As we have noted (Ch. 39), the whole constitutional history of Oliver Cromwell's Protectorate can be seen as a return to more traditional forms of government. One of the most notable aspects of that trend was the growing importance
during the last years of his life of his civilian supporters, members of old families
like Edward Montague and Charles Howard, whose influence increasingly
balanced that of army grandees like Generals Lambert and Fleetwood. It was that
civilian party which led the successful parliamentary attack on the major-generals
in 1657 and was behind the offer of the Crown to Cromwell in the same year.
Oliver himself valued and encouraged the emergence of these 'new Cromwellians'
as a help in holding the loyalties of the governing class but, ever mindful of his
ultimate dependence on the army, he was careful to keep a balance between them
and the military men (62). His elder son Richard, whom he nominated to succeed
him under the terms of the Humble Petition and Advice, was a mild, well-
meaning man who had none of his father's standing with the army.[2] It was a
serious weakness, especially when he showed a growing tendency to depend on
the new civilian Cromwellians who roused increasing jealousy in army circles.
These difficulties were compounded by a split within the army. The senior officers,
men like Fleetwood, wanted to preserve the Protectorate while re-establishing
their own influence within the regime, but many of their juniors felt no such
loyalty and together with religious sectaries, who disliked Richard's Presbyterian sympathies, looked for a restoration of the Commonwealth. Their
chance came when Richard's Parliament met in 1659. The republican politicians
within it were outnumbered by more conservative members who supported the
Protectorate, but the latter played into their opponents' hands by their anti-
military attitudes which infuriated the grandees as well as the rest of the army.
The senior officers forced Richard to dissolve Parliament in April, but then found
that they had lost control of the situation. They were unable to preserve the
Protectorate in face of the open hostility, not only of the republicans who had
attacked the whole protectoral system in Parliament at the beginning of 1659 but

also of the bulk of the army itself. Early in May the Rump was recalled and later in the same month Richard himself resigned. The Protectorate was at an end. Its fall was due to a combination of discontent within the army and the intrigues of republican politicians on the one hand and lack of adequate leadership and vision from Richard and his natural supporters among the grandees and in Parliament on the other. Those who brought about its downfall spoke for only a tiny minority of the population of the country and they had no viable constitutional settlement to replace it. In this situation the men of property who composed the political nation and who were both a very powerful and an increasingly discontented group awaited developments in the wings.

The year between May 1659 and May 1660 saw the collapse of the restored Commonwealth and the return of the monarchy. It was a period of considerable confusion during which the newly revived Rump was expelled in October 1659 and restored again in December. Among the factors which contributed to the recall of Charles II were the obvious political bankruptcy of both the Rump and the army; the positive enthusiasm of the political nation, in the face of increasing anarchy, for the return of the King; the serious economic and financial situation in the country; the role of General Monck; and, not least, the moderation which Charles II, well advised by Clarendon, showed during these crucial months. Throughout the last year of the Interregnum both the army and the Rump showed little or no sign of the ability to co-operate which was essential if the new regime was to have any chance of survival. They quarrelled about the form of the future constitutional settlement (62), and the parliamentary majority showed little statesmanship in the reckless way in which, after August 1659, they provoked the army, which had restored them to power. The army in turn showed that it had no ability to use constructively the power which it wielded between October and December 1659, the period between the second expulsion and the second restoration of the Rump. It governed through a 'Committee of Safety' which struggled unsuccessfully to halt the increasing drift to anarchy which was very obvious by December, especially in the capital itself.

By the end of 1659, therefore, the Rump and the army had shown very clearly that they were unable, either together or individually, to provide effective government for the country. It was a situation in which massive and increasing pressure built up throughout England for the restoration of the monarchy, and the numerous cries for a 'full and free' Parliament were an ominous indication to both the Rump and the army that their time was running out. In February 1660 General Monck, having marched south from Scotland with his army, readmitted to Parliament those MPs who had been secluded at the time of Pride's Purge in December 1648. The following month the Long Parliament at last dissolved itself and elections were held, on the old pre-1640 franchise, for a Convention Parliament which proclaimed Charles II in May. In the words of Professor Woolrych, 'the Great Rebellion collapsed from within. Monarchy returned to fill a vacuum'. (59, *33*)

The reality of that vacuum was appreciated by the propertied class as a whole, and if the incompetence and unpopularity of the Rump and the army made the Restoration possible it was the positive enthusiasm of the political nation for the return of the King which made it virtually inevitable by the spring of 1660. The history of the Interregnum was largely a search by successive Commonwealth and Protectorate governments for a settlement which would produce a form of constitutional government which would satisfy the great majority of the gentry class, who disliked the events of 1648–49. It was an unsuccessful quest. Most of the gentry remained at best unenthusiastic about and at worst openly hostile to the Commonwealth and Protectorate and their general inclination towards the restoration of the monarchy was immeasurably increased in 1659–60 by the instability of the political situation and above all by the breakdown of public order which led to widespread if exaggerated fears of a coup d'état engineered by increasingly vocal Puritan sects – notably the Quakers (222). The fears of anarchy, so prominent in the minds of the landed class by the end of 1659 were heightened by the country's serious economic and financial situation. We have already noted (Ch. 42) the succession of bad harvests from 1657 onwards and the trade depression of 1657–59, brought on by the Spanish War. The collapse of order in the last months of 1659 intensified the already serious depression and reinforced the determination of the conservative authorities of the city of London to secure the return of civilian and preferably monarchical rule, and it is notable that Monck worked closely with the City Fathers after his arrival in the capital early in 1660. Moreover, the ambitious foreign policy of the Protectorate together with the upkeep of a large army and navy had ensured that there was a substantial public debt, and the solvency of the government was further endangered by a threatened taxpayers strike in the localities in 1659–60. That latter challenge to the authorities was a very ominous one in view of the effect of the similar strike of 1639–40 which heralded the end of the personal rule. The economic and financial just like the political situation in 1660 presented a picture of gloom and confusion and demanded a return to stability which by that time only a restored monarchy seemed likely to provide.

All that was needed by the beginning of 1660 was a catalyst which could control the army and the Rump effectively enough to allow the general enthusiasm for a restoration to find expression in negotiations with Charles II. That catalyst was General Monck who crossed from Scotland to England with his army in December 1659 and reached London at the beginning of February 1660. Monck's exact intentions on his march south are debatable, but his actions after his arrival in the capital at the head of a strictly disciplined army, then the only reliable military force in England, led directly to the Restoration. His key decision was to restore the Rump's secluded members, an action which ensured a monarchist rather than a republican majority in the assembly. His ability to impose his will in England reflected the success of his government in Scotland, which had stayed calm and orderly in 1659 despite the turmoil south of the border ((161); see above, Ch. 38). It is indeed ironic that the success of English government in Scotland during the Interregnum was a major factor in the restoration of the King in 1660. Charles II contributed significantly to his own return by his moderation and good sense. In April 1660 he issued the Declaration of Breda [E.6(40); G.7(31)] in which he announced that he would allow Parliament to settle some of the most important and contentious questions which would require resolution on his homecoming. These included the religious and land settlements and the scope of the pardon which would have to be issued for deeds done during the Civil Wars and the period of the Interregnum. In addition, the army was promised its arrears of pay, a very sensible move in view of the fact that effective power in England at that time, in so far as it existed at all, lay with Monck's soldiers.

What then were the basic reasons for the collapse of the revolutionary regimes and the restoration of the monarchy during the period September 1658–May 1660? The death of Oliver Cromwell was clearly of very great importance. It brought out into the open the rivalries between civilian and military supporters of the Protectorate. The fact that Richard Cromwell was unable either to control or reconcile these rivalries led to his fall and to a situation in which the restored Rump and the army, both increasingly unpopular in the country at large, contested for power amidst growing anarchy, with widespread fears among the propertied classes that extremist religious sects were planning an uprising. The result was an enormous groundswell of opinion, especially among the political nation, for the return of the monarchy. The gentry as a whole had never been reconciled to any of the regimes of the 1650s, and the combination of threatened anarchy in England, Monck's intervention from Scotland and the studied moderation which Charles II displayed in the spring of 1660 enabled the King to return amidst the general acclaim of the propertied classes and to the relief of the country as a whole.

We have discussed the collapse of the Protectorate and of the restored Commonwealth which succeeded it, but the middle decades of the century had seen both the creation of a new state by the moderate revolutionaries who challenged Charles I during the 1640s and the failure of more radical men to replace it by a regime which, whatever its precise nature, would have involved revolutionary social changes which would have been anathema to the men who ruled England during the 1650s. One of the most important reasons for the failure of the radical revolutionaries was surely the social composition of the governing institutions during the period. Parliaments, the Civil Service and local government all continued to be dominated by the gentry, though by a different stratum of the gentry than that which had ruled England in the period before 1640. In the pre-1640 era it was the upper gentry who controlled both central and local government. During the 1640s and 1650s power passed largely into the hands of the lesser or 'parochial' gentry. That was a social change of a very important but also of a limited kind. It was a shift of authority *within* the governing élite, not the calling into power of a new class. In other words, it was very different from the kind of changes sought by radicals like the Levellers, Diggers and Fifth Monarchy Men. The fact that the gentry continued to dominate the government machine during these years went far in ensuring the failure of schemes which would have led to both their social and political eclipse. Moreover, the radical revolutionaries, faced with the hostility of an entrenched governing class, were not sufficiently numerous seriously to challenge the ruling élite. They were a tiny minority among the population at large, a fact which becomes very clear when we assess their strength in the army, in London, in the counties, in the Parliaments of the period and the numbers in radical sectarian congregations (108). They were faced, too, with a lack of political and social awareness among the vast bulk of the population and such awareness would have been necessary for a true social revolution granted the general conservatism of the ruling classes. The mass of the population seem to have been concerned mainly with peace and stability at a time of often difficult economic conditions. There is overwhelming evidence that they disliked, above all else, military rule and the heavy taxation which went with it. This was very unfortunate for the radicals for, of course, elements in the army, which was so generally disliked, were among the leading protagonists of radical revolution. Cromwell himself, throughout most of the 1640s and 1650s, acted as a brake on genuinely radical social change. The one exception to this is perhaps his initial support for Barebone's Parliament in 1653, but that support was soon withdrawn. His fundamental social conservatism was evident in his attitude to the Levellers in 1647 and 1649 and in the whole development of the Protectorate between 1653 and 1658 when he strove to increase civilian authority in the government and reduce the power of the army – a statement which is broadly true despite the regime of the major-generals in 1655–56.

The moderate revolutionaries, those protagonists of political and religious change and social stability of whom Cromwell was the greatest representative, did, in contrast, gain power in the later 1640s and keep it during the 1650s. The reasons for their success have been analysed in previous chapters, but the Cromwellian State, the final fruit of their labours, collapsed after 1658. With its downfall the struggle to find a 'new system' to replace the early Stuart monarchy, which had itself collapsed between 1639 and 1642, came to an end with the restoration of Charles II. The return with the King of the House of Lords and an Established Episcopal Church gave the impression that the wheel of change had really turned full circle. That was, of course, an illusion. The events of 1640–1660 could not be erased from the minds of Englishmen, Irishmen and Scotsmen and, even in nominal terms, the apparatus of government through which Charles II ruled England was different from the administrative system which Charles I had had at his disposal during the period 1625–40; the prerogative courts did not come back with the King in 1660.

---

1. The standard account of the period 1658–60 is G. Davies, *The Restoration of Charles II* (Oxford, 1955), but there are much more succinct and analytical discussions by I. Roots, *The Great Rebellion* (1966), pp. 232 ff; A. H. Woolrych, 'Last quests for a settlement 1657–1660', *The Interregnum*, ed. G. E. Aylmer, pp. 183 ff; and J. R. Jones, *Country and Court: England 1658–1714* (1978), pp. 113 ff.
2. There is no satisfactory biography of the second Protector. R. W. Ramsey's *Richard Cromwell* (1935) is superficial.

Conclusion

The absence of prerogative courts together with a general memory of the political and religious upheavals of the 1640s and 1650s may have made the monarchy of Charles II different from that of his father, but it would be quite wrong to conclude that the constitutional struggle between Crown and Parliament had, by 1660, been firmly decided in favour of the latter. During the reigns of Charles II and James II England could well have followed Continental trends and gone the way of absolute monarchy. That possibility is important in reminding us that the turmoil of the period 1640–60 did, in some senses, actually strengthen the restored monarchy, reinforcing its bargaining power with the propertied classes who were very slow to forget the threat to stability in all spheres of life that the abolition of the kingship had introduced or intensified. The gentry class had managed to prevent the dramatic religious and political changes of the mid-seventeenth century from overturning the whole social hierarchy, but there can be no doubt that they regarded the events of these years as a 'genuine' revolution, a view which would be shared by those historians who do not accept the Marxist thesis that the only 'real' revolutions are social ones. Indeed, in considering trends in the historiography of early modern England a writer is struck by the number of 'revolutions' which he is now invited to accept in the context of the period 1529–1660 as a whole. Recent research has also emphasized the important influence which wars had on England's internal affairs and stressed the need for more investigation of court factions and local politics at the expense of previous over-emphasis on parliamentary history.

Struggles for power and influence at Court and in the shires were continuous, whereas Parliaments were occasional phenomena, depicted by Professor Russell as comparatively unimportant, their significance a mirror of their limited life-spans. They 'should not', he writes, 'be seen as the makers of the major historical events of the 1620s, but as *ad hoc* gatherings of men reacting to events taking place elsewhere. Major political decisions were usually taken at Court, and other major political events tended to take place in the country, well away from the palace of Westminster.' (125, *1*) These are salutary words, especially when we remember the intimate links between country and Court. The tentacles of faction stretched out from the centre into the shires and the concerns of county communities were reflected in Parliament – essentially a collection of gentlemen from the localities. It is a picture which has been splendidly delineated in the work of Dr Hassell Smith on Elizabethan Norfolk (153), and it helps to explain the importance of that private parliamentary legislation which was of such significance both to individual gentlemen and to the towns and counties which they represented. The growing interest of historians in local factions, which can be

369

linked both with the central politics of the Court and with events in Parliament, also reflects that wider concern with 'localism' which is now such an important aspect of historical studies. Professor Everitt may not always command complete assent for his thesis that England was little more than a federation of county communities, but the picture which he and other local historians have drawn for us of the rich political life of individual shires has done much to deepen our understanding of the history of the period.

Parliament, within the comparatively reduced role that is now being assigned to it, is seen more and more as a legislative rather than as a political institution, with the House of Lords now looming larger and the House of Commons much less dominant than it seemed in the works of Neale and Notestein (see especially (116)). These are essentially healthy historiographical developments, though there are signs that some aspects of the reinterpretation of parliamentary history may be going too far; revisionists who quite rightly stress their predecessors' neglect of the legislative achievements of early modern Parliaments seem some-times in danger of denying that political conflicts within them were significant. That is surely to fly in the face of the evidence and it is clearly important to give considerable weight to both the political and the legislative aspects of parliamen-tary activities; failure to emphasize their legislative work makes them seem both more dramatic and more contentious than they really were, while failure to give due weight to political and constitutional arguments can, when carried to extremes, make the events of the 1640s seem incredible.

Early modern English sovereigns usually called Parliaments to vote supply, and most of the limited amount of money which they granted to the Crown between 1529 and 1660 was for the defence of the realm. Details of campaigns and war strategy are part of a now relatively unfashionable branch of historical studies – military history – but the significance of wars for the *internal* evolution of countries is, in contrast, of growing concern to historians. During the 1540s Henry VIII and Edward VI financed their enormously expensive Continental and Scottish campaigns mainly from debasements of the coinage and from sales of monastic and chantry lands, but the ending of debasements in 1551 was a water-shed in financial history. By then most of the monastic and chantry lands had been sold and the Crown's few years of relative affluence were over. Had Henry and Edward kept and exploited their newly acquired lands they could have greatly strengthened the financial and therefore the general political position of the monarchy in the years ahead, but their failure to do so meant that as early as Mary's reign it was becoming apparent that the Crown, even with good financial management, could not afford wars. The French War at the end of Mary's reign was of limited duration, but Elizabeth's Spanish War lasted from 1585 until 1604 and the struggle which Charles I waged against France and Spain at the beginning of his reign occupied the years 1625–30. The Elizabethan War was in a popular cause, but it imposed enormous strains upon English society at grass-roots level and the much less popular Caroline struggle, with its series of naval and military disasters, led to hitherto unprecedented resistance to the Crown's demands and culminated in the crisis of 1628–29 which found such dramatic expression in the parliamentary session of the latter year. It was a warning to Charles I that he should avoid future wars at almost any cost, and when the foolish policies of the personal rule led to armed conflict with Scotland, his calls upon England for men and money ended in the virtual collapse of royal administration in the shires. He had failed to carry the 'local governors' with him in his policies, and he could not rule without them. That failure is the most effective possible commentary on his reign, just as Elizabeth's general success in retaining the loyalty and co-operation of the great majority of the 'political nation' was the most important single element in her overall success.

The collapse of the personal rule and the summoning of the Long Parliament mark the beginning of the 'English Revolution' of 1640–60, the second of the two revolutions which mark the limits of our period. The other is, of course, the Henrician Reformation of the 1530s, and each of them had enormous consequences for both the Church and the Crown. In 1529 the Church in England was part of a great international organization, subject to the overriding authority of the Pope in Rome. It made its own laws, free in theory and to some extent in practice from lay control, and it enjoyed vast wealth in monastic, chantry and episcopal lands and in the artistic treasures of its cathedrals and monasteries. In 1660 it was a national institution, subject to no external authority. Between 1529 and 1660 the Crown alone, the Crown in Parliament, and then Parliament alone, successively exercised control over it, denying it independent legislative powers. Monarchs on the one hand and parliamentary peers and gentry on the other, whatever their other differences about ecclesiastical policy, were united in their determination to establish and maintain lay supremacy over the Church. Their success in doing so was clear well before 1660 and it had momentous consequences for English history. The Erastian tradition of the Church of England, which has continued until the present day, became firmly established in the sixteenth century. Most of the landed wealth of the Church had gone by 1640 and so had many of the artistic treasures which had adorned its great buildings. The further spoliations of land which took place after 1640 were reversed at the Restoration, but it was impossible in 1660 to repair the damage to priceless stained glass which had been one of the consequences of Puritan zeal during the same years. The Church of 1660 was much more modest both in its theoretical claims and in its institutional framework than the Church of 1529, which had seemed like a colossus in the realm, with profound influence in the political and in the economic as well as in the spiritual life of the nation.

It was also during the years between 1529 and 1660 that the Church ceased, even in theory, to be identified with the entire population. In the Middle Ages, despite the Lollard heresies, every English man, woman and child was theoretically a member of the official Church and this theory continued to be applied, though with diminishing reality, until the middle of the seventeenth century. Oliver Cromwell, who explicitly granted toleration to religious bodies outside his loosely organized State Church was a harbinger of toleration who was ahead of his time, but the religious diversity of the 1640s and 1650s could not be confined within the strait-jacket of the episcopal Church of England of the post-1660 era, and Cromwellian ideals were enshrined, at least in part, in the Toleration Act of 1689. Cromwell had posed, in the most direct form, a simple question: could religious toleration be reconciled with political and social stability in the conditions of mid-seventeenth-century England? He himself was not always sure of the answer, and the gentlemen of England, who were sure, were certain that the answer was 'no'. The fact that the issue could arise at all in the 1650s is, however, evidence of the distance which separated the religious situation of the mid-seventeenth century from that of 1529. Our period clearly witnessed a momentous revolution in many aspects of Church life.

The Reformation of the 1530s, which reduced the status of the Church in England, exalted the power of the Crown to hitherto unknown heights. Henry VIII united in his person the traditional secular powers of the English monarchy and much of the Pope's former jurisdictional and doctrinal authority. It was a formidable combination, but royal absolutism in the Church died with its creator. Edward VI came to share power over the Church with Parliament, Mary found, to her disgust, that she could only reverse the Edwardian and Henrician Reformations by parliamentary statutes, and in those circumstances Elizabeth's attempts after 1559 to turn the clock back by denying Parliament a role in ecclesiastical affairs have a sense of anachronism about them. From her time onwards Puritan opposition to the church hierarchy became linked with opposition to the Crown, and although the Calvinist James I was regarded by the vast majority of his Protestant subjects as a 'godly prince', the Arminian ideas of Charles I horrified most Englishmen, who thought that their sovereign was at best quite misguided and at worst a crypto-papist. By the 1630s it was clear that the royal supremacy in the Church, which had been such an asset to the power and prestige of the monarchy in the reign of Henry VIII, had, in the long term, become a serious liability for the Crown. Indeed, historians today are virtually unanimous about the vital links between Charles I's religious policy and the fall of the monarchy during the 1640s.

The period 1529–1660 clearly saw revolutionary changes in the position of both the Church and the Crown, changes which led by the 1650s to the abolition of the monopoly claims of the official Church on all Englishmen and to the disappearance, for a period of eleven years, of the very institution of monarchy. Historians who agree that these constitutional and ecclesiastical revolutions took place would almost certainly disagree about the reality of at least some of the numerous other 'revolutions' of the period. The 'legal revolution' of the early sixteenth century, which has been propagated and dissected with such great learning by Dr Baker, can only be adequately evaluated by other experts in the history of English law; the 'scientific revolution' of the sixteenth and seventeenth centuries – a well-established concept in the European history of period – arguably reached its height in England in the post-Restoration Newtonian era; the term 'educational revolution' seems at best of doubtful value in describing changes which penetrated to such a limited extent down the social scale. The 'price revolution' of the period remains one of its most important phenomena, but the agricultural and industrial 'revolutions' which have been favoured by Dr Kerridge and Professor Nef look increasingly unreal in the light of subsequent comment and research. Professor Elton continues to defend his 'administrative revolution' of the 1530s with his accustomed skill and vigour, but this writer at least finds it an unconvincing aspect of his wholly acceptable stress on the momentous significance of the early Tudor era as a whole.

Whether or not each – or any – of these sixteenth and early seventeenth century 'revolutions' truly merits the name, the very fact that historians have described the changes of the period in such terms is surely significant. Early modern England had a least its fair share of dramatic change in the midst of a fundamental continuity which left the England of 1660, just like the England of 1529, an agricultural society, ruled by a gentry élite, where the primary concern of the great majority of the population was the annual harvest.

One field of English life where historians of the sixteenth and early seventeenth centuries have been reluctant to talk of 'revolution' is trade, though there is general agreement that these years were a vital preparation for the 'commercial revolution' of the later seventeenth century. The period 1529–1660 certainly saw a great expansion of the geographical area of English trade accompanied by a considerable growth in English merchant shipping, but these developments, so significant for the future, do not alter the fact that the country's trade remained, throughout our period, overwhelmingly intra-European or that the continent of Europe continued to be the focus of English foreign policy. England's attitude towards Europe did, however, change significantly during the period. Before the Reformation the country, despite its island situation, was an integral part of Catholic Christendom. From the Elizabethan period onwards it was the principal Protestant power of Europe with a sense of its own uniqueness as God's 'elect nation'. This idea, prolonged by Cromwell's anachronistic desire to see Britain at the head of a Protestant crusade against Spain, was to come under challenge, at least at the very top of society, in the reigns of Charles II and James II, with their admiration for the Catholic and absolutist France of Louis XIV, but it survived the Revolution of 1688. Britain of the eighteenth and nineteenth centuries, with its majestic overseas empire, was built largely on foundations which were Elizabethan and Cromwellian in their stress on both the distinctiveness and superiority of the Protestant inhabitants of Great Britain compared especially with the Catholic but also to some extent even with the Protestant inhabitants of the European continent. The basic sentiment is still with us today in the anti-Common Market strictures of 'Little Englanders'.

The sixteenth and early seventeenth centuries, which saw such stress on the differences between England and other countries also witnessed what was arguably the greatest cultural achievement in the history of the British Isles. This was the age of the first vernacular Bibles, culminating in King James's version of 1611, and it produced the poetry of Milton, the prose of Bacon and the plays of Shakespeare. At a culturally less significant but historically important level it was also the age of the robust splendours of the Henrician and Elizabethan Courts as well as of the much more élitist refinements of Caroline court life. Elizabeth's broadly based Court, with its room for virtually all shades of political and religious opinion, was a symbol of the Queen's concern for the basic unity of England. Charles's much more narrowly based Court, with its Arminian and absolutist ethos, was, in contrast, a reflection of his ignorance of or disdain for the attitudes and interests of the great majority of his subjects. The former was the reflection of a successful ruler, the latter an appropriate setting for a failure.

The culture of Elizabethan England is still with us today in its great literary works – the plays of Shakespeare are clearly a significant aspect of contemporary

British life – but the most important historical phenomenon of the Tudor age was probably the emergence of the English nation state. Indeed, the years between 1529 and 1660 were profoundly important for the identity of each of the four national components of the British Isles. It was in these years that the great majority of Irishmen came to dislike their English rulers not merely as conquerors but also in the sixteenth century as Protestants and in the seventeenth century as expropriators of their land as well; the Irish problem as we know it today was created by the rulers of sixteenth- and seventeenth-century England. If Irishmen's sense of identity became bound up with their Catholicism, Scottish national feeling was intimately associated during the same years with the rejection of the old Church. During the Middle Ages the Scots had fought against English claims of secular overlordship. In 1560 they repudiated external spiritual authority as well when they threw off papal jurisdiction in a religious revolution which was much more radical than its English counterpart. Scotland and England, despite their common Protestant ethos from the later sixteenth century onwards and the union of the Crowns in 1603 did not, however, quickly bury their traditional enmity. James I's proposals for a 'perfect union' of the two countries foundered in the early years of his reign on the mutual distrust and hostility of Scots and English, and the Cromwellian union of the 1650s was imposed by an English army. It may be that before 1660 the benefits of union were becoming apparent to some Scots (49), but there was still a long way to go before the inhabitants of England and Scotland could forge a sense of common identity.

When James I's plans for closer union between England and Scotland were rejected by his unwilling subjects, Wales had been incorporated into English judicial and administrative life for about seventy years. The Welsh people continued to feel a strong sense of their own identity, but the Henrician union of England and Wales, one of the most significant of Thomas Cromwell's reforms, was a very important step on the road to the ultimate unification of Great Britain.

England herself asserted her claim to be a 'nation state', free of all external authority, when she rejected papal jurisdiction during the 1530s. It took many years to work out all the implications of that momentous claim, but it set the country in a basic direction which was not altered until the 'return of Rome' – this time an economic rather than a religious Rome – with Britain's accession to the Common Market in 1973. The new English nation state of the sixteenth century was not yet, however, a Great Power. The Cromwellian regime demonstrated that it was possible to raise the troops and build the ships which were necessary to support such a position, but in the years after the Restoration it looked as if England might become a satellite within the French orbit. The Revolution of 1688 and the events which followed it changed all that; England – united with Scotland after 1707 in a permanent parliamentary union – assumed the mantle of a Great Power. But that is another story.[1]

---

1. Told by Professor G. S. Holmes in the third volume in the series.

COMPENDIUM OF INFORMATION

A. MONARCHS AND HEADS OF STATE, 1529–1660[1]

Henry VIII (born 28 June 1491)	22 Apr 1509–28 Jan 1547
Edward VI (born 12 Oct 1537)	28 Jan 1547–6 July 1553
Mary (born 18 Feb 1516)	6 July 1553[2]–17 Nov 1558
Elizabeth (born 7 Sept 1533)	17 Nov 1558–24 Mar 1603
James I (born 19 June 1566)	24 Mar 1603–27 Mar 1625
Charles I (born 19 Nov 1600)	27 Mar 1625–30 Jan 1649 (executed)
Interregnum 30 Jan 1649–8 May 1660	
Oliver Cromwell (born 25 Apr 1599)	Lord Protector 16 Dec 1653–3 Sept 1658
Richard Cromwell (born 4 Oct 1626)	Lord Protector 3 Sept 1658–24 May 1659 (resigned)
Charles II (born 29 May 1630)	8 May 1660[3] (when he was proclaimed in London)–6 Feb 1685

---

1. *Handbook of British Chronology* (2nd edn, 1961), pp. 39–41.
2. Ignores the 'reign' of Lady Jane Grey, 6–19 July 1553.
3. Charles II dated his regnal years from the execution of Charles I on 30 Jan 1649.

B. THE SUCCESSION TO THE THRONE

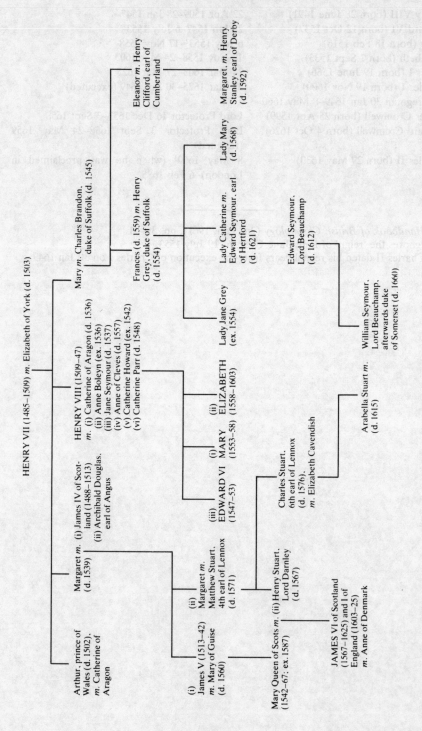

The houses of Tudor, Stuart and Suffolk

The issue of the succession to the throne was one of the most important political consider-ations in England from the 1520s until the accession of James I in the spring of 1603.[1] In 1527 Henry VIII, convinced that he was unlikely to have further children by Catherine of Aragon and worried that his only legitimate heir was a daughter, Mary, set in train the negotiations at Rome for the annulment of his marriage to Catherine which finally led to a complete breach with the Papacy, the establishment of a national Church of England and his marriage, in 1533, to Anne Boleyn, the mother of Princess Elizabeth, born in September of that year. Although the fact that the child was a girl was a bitter disappointment to the King, the infant was placed in line to the throne in the 'First Succession Act' of 1534, in which Parliament declared that she would succeed, failing male issue of the Boleyn marriage.[2] The execution of Anne Boleyn for multiple adultery in 1536 and the subsequent annulment of her marriage to the King by Archbishop Cranmer led to the 'Second Suc-cession Act' of 1536 which bastardized both Mary and Elizabeth and entailed the Crown on the King's as yet unborn heirs by his third wife, Jane Seymour.[3] In 1536, therefore, the succession was even more uncertain than before. The Act recognized this by conferring on Henry the right, failing legitimate heirs by Queen Jane or by subsequent wives, to bequeath the Crown by will – a statutory power never granted to any other English sovereign, either before or since. The birth of Prince Edward in 1537 gave the King an heir who was universally recognized as legitimate, but the death of the Queen soon after the birth and the failure of any of his three subsequent marriages to produce children meant that in 1544 the succession was dependent on the life of a delicate boy of six at a time when the King was planning to lead in person an invasion of France. In these circumstances Parliament passed the 'Third Succession Act' of 1544 which placed Mary and Elizabeth in the suc-cession after Edward and any future children of the King.[4] The Act also permitted Henry to designate the succession by will if both Mary and Elizabeth should die childless. This he did in a document dated December 1546 when he reaffirmed the succession as declared in the 1544 statute and provided that if Mary and Elizabeth died without issue the latter should be succeeded by the heirs of the ladies Frances and Eleanor Brandon, the daughters of his sister Mary, one-time Queen of France, by her second husband, the duke of Suffolk. The Scottish Stuarts, descendants of his elder sister Margaret, who had married James IV of Scotland, were ignored.[5] The will – parts of which may have been altered without Henry's knowledge[6] – did not come into operation until the death of Elizabeth when, of course, it was ignored.

If Henry was unable to control the succession after the lifetime of his younger daughter, the provisions of his will and of the statute on which it was founded did, however, go far in ensuring the succession of Mary, following the attempt by John Dudley, duke of Northumberland, to exclude her from the throne in favour of Lady Jane Grey, the eldest daughter of Frances Brandon. Lady Jane, married to Northumberland's son Lord Guild-ford Dudley, was declared Edward VI's heir in the 'devise' and letters patent[7] which the ardently Protestant young King accepted in 1553 with the prime aim of excluding the Cath-olic Mary from the throne. The overwhelming refusal of the 'political nation' to accept this attempted coup by Northumberland bore witness to the loyalty of the English gentry to the Tudor dynasty and Mary, disappointed in her hope for a child and worried about the religious fate of the nation if the Protestant Elizabeth should succeed her, reluctantly accepted by the end of her reign that there was no way in which she could disinherit her half-sister.

Elizabeth's peaceful accession in 1558 did, however, leave the country once again, as in 1536, without an obvious heir to the throne. The ideal solution, for the Queen to marry and bear a child, remained a possibility until the later 1570s and, during the first twenty or so years of her reign, Elizabeth used her status as a 'virgin queen' to her country's considerable diplomatic advantage. The immediate problem, of course, was what would happen if she died in the early years of her rule. The terrible prospect of civil war was very real in these circumstances. In 1562 the Queen caught smallpox and, at one stage in the illness, seemed on the point of death. The Privy Council, which met to decide who should succeed her, could come to no consensus. Mary Queen of Scots, the heir by hereditary right, was excluded in the councillors' minds both by the terms of Henry VIII's will and by her Catholicism. Lady Catherine Grey, the rightful heir if the will was followed, had some support, but there were voices for the earl of Huntingdon, who had Yorkist royal blood in his veins and had the indubitable advantage from the councillors' point of view of being both male and a committed Protestant. Fortunately for the continuing peace of the realm Elizabeth recovered, but the period from the 1560s to the 1580s saw constant parliamentary attempts both to persuade her to name an heir and to secure the formal exclusion of Mary Queen of Scots from the succession, attempts which Elizabeth always resisted.[8] Following the execution of Mary in 1587 for her part in the Babington Plot against Elizabeth's life, her son, the Protestant James VI of Scotland, became the obvious successor both in terms of hereditary right and religious suitability. Although the Queen never formally recognized him as her heir, thinking Englishmen increasingly regarded his accession as inevitable – 'I do assure myself', wrote Thomas Wilson in his account of England in 1600, 'that the king of Scotland will carry . . . [the succession], as very many Englishmen do know.'[9] In fact Robert Cecil, who carried on a secret correspondence with James during the last two years of the Queen's reign, did much to prepare the way for the Scottish King's peaceful accession in March 1603.[10] Elizabeth had lived long enough for her gamble in refusing to name a successor to pay off, but James's accession was an explicit breach of Henry VIII's will and thus, by implication, of the statute on which it was founded. In 1603 hereditary right to the throne triumphed over the provisions of statute law.

---

1. For good general discussions see M. Levine, *Tudor Dynastic Problems 1460–1571* (1973); J. Hurstfield, 'The succession struggle in late Elizabethan England', *Elizabethan Government and Society* (1961).
2. 25 Henry VIII, c. 22.
3. 28 Henry VIII, c. 7.
4. 35 Henry VIII, c. 1.
5. Levine, *Tudor Dynastic Problems*, p. 163.
6. G. R. Elton, *Reform and Reformation*, pp. 331–2, who points out, however, that the exclusion of the Scots almost certainly represented Henry's personal wishes.
7. For the letters patent, which were the official limitation of the Crown, see Levine, *Tudor Dynastic Problems* pp. 167–9.
8. For these see J. E. Neale, *Elizabeth I and her Parliaments* (1953, 1957).
9. T. Wilson, 'The state of England, Anno Dom 1600', ed. F. J. Fisher, *Camden Misc.*, xvi (1936), p. 5.
10. J. Bruce, ed., *Correspondence of James VI of Scotland with Sir Robert Cecil, Camden Soc. Pub.*, O.S., lxxviii (1861).

C. CHIEF OFFICERS OF STATE, 1529–1660[1]

C.1: Lord Chancellors and Keepers of the Great Seal

A Keeper exercised the same authority as a Chancellor but his office was of less dignity. The office held was Lord Chancellor unless otherwise indicated.

Thomas Wolsey, cardinal archbishop of York	Dec 1515–Oct 1529
Sir Thomas More	Oct 1529–May 1532
Sir Thomas Audley, later Lord Audley	Keeper May 1532; Lord Chancellor Jan 1533–Apr 1544
Sir Thomas Wriothesley, later Lord Wriothesley and earl of Southampton	Keeper April 1544; Lord Chancellor May 1544–Mar 1547
William Paulet, Lord St John, later Marquis of Winchester	Keeper Mar–Oct 1547
Richard Rich, Lord Rich	Oct 1547–Dec 1551
Thomas Goodrich, bishop of Ely	Keeper Dec 1551; Lord Chancellor Jan 1552–Aug 1553
Stephen Gardiner, bishop of Winchester	Aug 1553–Nov 1555
Nicholas Heath, archbishop of York	Jan 1556–Nov 1558
Sir Nicholas Bacon	Lord Keeper Dec 1558–Feb 1579
Sir Thomas Bromley	Apr 1579–Apr 1587
Sir Christopher Hatton	Apr 1587–Nov 1591
Sir John Puckering	Lord Keeper May 1592–Apr 1596
Sir Thomas Egerton, later Lord Ellesmere	Lord Keeper May 1596; Lord Chancellor July 1603–Mar 1617
Sir Francis Bacon, later Viscount St Albans	Lord Keeper Mar 1617; Lord Chancellor Jan 1618–May 1621
John Williams, bishop of Lincoln	Lord Keeper July 1621–Oct 1625
Sir Thomas Coventry, later Lord Coventry	Lord Keeper Nov 1625–Jan 1640
Sir John Finch, later Lord Finch	Lord Keeper Jan 1640–Dec 1640 (fled)
Sir Edward Littleton, later Lord Littleton	Jan 1641–May 1642
Sir Richard Lane	Lord Keeper Aug 1645–Apr 1650
Sir Edward Herbert	Apr 1653–Dec 1657
Sir Edward Hyde, later Lord Hyde and earl of Clarendon	Jan 1658–Aug 1667

Note: Between 1642 and 1660 Parliament and the Protectorate had Great Seals which were in the hands of commissioners.

C.2: Lord Treasurers

Thomas Howard, 2nd duke of Norfolk	Dec 1522–Dec 1546
Edward Seymour, duke of Somerset	Feb 1547–Oct 1549
William Paulet, marquis of Winchester	Feb 1550–Mar 1572
William Cecil, Lord Burghley	July 1572–Aug 1598
Thomas Sackville, Lord Buckhurst	May 1599–Apr 1608
Robert Cecil, earl of Salisbury	May 1608–May 1612

1612–14: Treasury Commissioners

Thomas Howard, earl of Suffolk	July 1614–July 1618

1618–20: Treasury Commissioners

Henry Montague, Viscount Mandeville	Dec 1620–Sept 1621
Lionel Cranfield, earl of Middlesex	Sept 1621–May 1624
James Ley, Lord Ley	Dec 1624–July 1628
Richard Weston, Lord Weston and earl of Portland	July 1628–Mar 1635

1635–36: Treasury Commissioners

William Juxon, bishop of London	Mar 1636–May 1641

1641–43: Treasury Commissioners

Francis Cottington, Lord Cottington	Oct 1643–June 1652

Interregnum

Thomas Wriothesley, earl of Southampton	Sept 1660–May 1667

C.3: Secretaries of State

Date given is that of appointment to office. Secretaries continued in post, unless otherwise noted, until the date of appointment of the indicated successor (in the same column). After 1540 there were usually two secretaries.

July 1529	Stephen Gardiner		
Apr 1534	Thomas Cromwell		
Apr 1540	Sir Thomas Wriothesley	Apr 1540	Sir Ralph Sadler
		Apr 1543	Sir William Paget
Jan 1544	Sir William Petre		
		Apr 1548	Sir Thomas Smith
		Oct 1549	Dr Nicholas Wotton
		Sept 1550	Sir William Cecil
		June 1553	Sir John Cheke (imprisoned July 1553)
		Aug 1553	Sir John Bourn (to March 1558)
Mar 1557	John Boxall		

382

Nov 1558	Sir William Cecil	
July 1572	Sir Thomas Smith (to 1576)	
		Dec 1573 Sir Francis Walsingham (died Apr 1590)
Nov 1577	Thomas Wilson (to 1581)	
Sept 1586	William Davison (to 1587)	

From 1590 to 1596 there was no Principal Secretary.

July 1596	Robert Cecil, later 1st earl of Salisbury	
		May 1600 John Herbert (died 1619)
1612	Robert Carr, Viscount Rochester, later 1st earl of Somerset	
	– conducted the King's correspondence without the title of Secretary of State	
Mar 1614	Sir Ralph Winwood (died October 1617)	
		Jan 1616 Sir Thomas Lake
Jan 1618	Sir Robert Naunton	
		Feb 1619 Sir George Calvert
Jan 1623	Sir Edward Conway, later 1st Viscount Conway	
		Feb 1625 Sir Albertus Morton
		Sept 1625 Sir John Coke
Dec 1628	Dudley Carleton, 1st Viscount Dorchester (died February 1632)	
June 1632	Sir Francis Windebank (fled abroad Dec 1640)	
		Feb 1640 Sir Harry Vane (dismissed Nov 1641)
		Jan 1642 Lucius Carey, Viscount Falkland (killed at Newbury, Sept 1643)
		Sept 1643 George Digby, later 2nd earl of Bristol (resigned 1645, reappointed 1658)

---

1. Principal sources, *Handbook of British Chronology*, pp. 86–7, 103–4, 110–11; *DNB*.

D. PARLIAMENT

D.1: Dates of parliamentary sessions, 1529–1660[1]

Parliament	Dates of sessions	Date of dissolution
Henry VIII		
1529–36	(1) 3 Nov–17 Dec 1529	14 Apr 1536
	(2) 16 Jan–31 Mar 1531	
	(3) 15 Jan–14 May 1532	
	(4) 4 Feb–7 Apr 1533	
	(5) 15 Jan–30 Mar 1534	
	(6) 3 Nov–18 Dec 1534	
	(7) 4 Feb–14 Apr 1536	
1536	8 June–18 July 1536	18 July 1536
1539–40	(1) 28 Apr–28 June 1539	24 July 1540
	(2) 12 Apr–24 July 1540	
1542–44	(1) 16 Jan–1 Apr 1542	29 Mar 1544
	(2) 22 Jan–12 May 1543	
	(3) 14 Jan–29 Mar 1544	
1545–47	(1) 23 Nov–24 Dec 1545	31 Jan 1547
	(2) 14–31 Jan 1547	(dissolved by the King's death)
Edward VI		
1547–52	(1) 4 Nov–24 Dec 1547	15 Apr 1552
	(2) 24 Nov 1548–14 Mar 1549	
	(3) 4 Nov 1549–1 Feb 1550	
	(4) 23 Jan–15 Apr 1552	
1553	1–31 Mar 1553	31 Mar 1553
Mary		
1553	5 Oct–5 Dec 1553	5 Dec 1553
1554	2 Apr–5 May 1554	5 May 1554
1554–55	12 Nov 1554–16 Jan 1555	16 Jan 1555
1555	21 Oct–9 Dec 1555	9 Dec 1555
1558	(1) 20 Jan–7 Mar 1558	17 Nov 1558
	(2) 5–17 Nov 1558	(dissolved by the Queen's death)

Parliament	Dates of sessions	Date of dissolution
Elizabeth		
1559	25 Jan–8 May 1559	8 May 1559
1563–67	(1) 12 Jan–10 Apr 1563 (2) 30 Sept 1566–2 Jan 1567	2 Jan 1567
1571	2 Apr–29 May 1571	29 May 1571
1572–81	(1) 8 May–30 June 1572 (2) 8 Feb–15 Mar 1576 (3) 16 Jan–18 Mar 1581	19 Apr 1583
1584–85	23 Nov 1584–29 Mar 1585	14 Sept 1586
1586–87	29 Oct 1586–23 Mar 1587	23 Mar 1587
1589	4 Feb–29 Mar 1589	29 Mar 1589
1593	19 Feb–10 Apr 1593	10 Apr 1593
1597–98	24 Oct 1597–9 Feb 1598	9 Feb 1598
1601	27 Oct–19 Dec 1601	19 Dec 1601
James I		
1604–10	(1) 19 Mar–7 July 1604 (2) 5 Nov 1605–27 May 1606 (3) 18 Nov 1606–4 July 1607 (4) 9 Feb–23 July 1610 (5) 16 Oct–6 Dec 1610	9 Feb 1611
1614	5 Apr–7 June 1614	7 June 1614
1621	(1) 30 Jan–4 June 1621 (2) 20 Nov–18 Dec 1621	8 Feb 1622
1624	12 Feb–29 May 1624	27 Mar 1625 (dissolved by the King's death)
Charles I		
1625	(1) 18 June–11 July 1625 (2) 1–12 Aug 1625	12 Aug 1625
1626	6 Feb–15 June 1626	15 June 1626
1628–29	(1) 17 Mar–26 June 1628 (2) 20 Jan–10 Mar 1629	10 Mar 1629

Parliament	Dates of sessions	Date of dissolution
1640 (the Short Parliament)	13 Apr–5 May 1640	5 May 1640
1640–1653/60 (the Long Parliament)	30 Nov 1640–20 Apr 1653	20 Apr 1653* (Oliver Cromwell's dissolution of the 'Rump')

* But note that the Long Parliament could only be legally dissolved with its own consent (17 Charles I, c. 7, 1641 – see [E.5(30)] It did not finally dissolve itself until 16 Mar 1660.

The Interregnum

1653 (Barebone's or the Nominated Parliament)	4 July–12 Dec 1653	12 Dec 1653

1654–55	(the Parliaments of the Protectorate)	3 Sept 1654–22 January 1655	22 Jan 1655
1656–58		(1) 17 Sept 1656–26 June 1657	4 Feb 1658
		(2) 20 Jan–4 Feb 1658	
1659		27 Jan–22 Apr 1659	22 Apr 1659

1659–60 (the restored 'Rump' of the Long Parliament)	7 May–13 Oct 1659 26 Dec 1659–16 March 1660 (between 13 Oct and 26 Dec the restored 'Rump' was prevented from sitting by the army)	16 Mar 1660

Charles II

1660 (the Convention Parliament)	(1) 25 Apr–13 Sept 1660	29 Dec 1660
	(2) 6 Nov–29 Dec 1660	

1. *Handbook of British Chronology*, pp. 535–8; S. E. Lehmberg, *The Reformation Parliament* (Cambridge, 1970); S. E. Lehmberg, *The Later Parliaments of Henry VIII* (Cambridge, 1977); J. E. Neale, *The Elizabethan House of Commons* (Peregrine edn., 1963), p. 417.

D.2: The growth of membership of the House of Commons, 1509–1640[1]

	Numbers of members of the House of Commons.			
	Counties	Boroughs	Universities	Total
At the death of Henry VII (1509)	74	222		296
At the death of Henry VIII (1547)	90	251		341
At the death of Edward VI (1553)	90	285		375
At the death of Mary (1558)	90	308		398
At the death of Elizabeth (1603)	90	370		460
At the death of James I (1625)	90	393	4	487
At the meeting of the Long Parliament (1640)	90	413	4	507

1. C. Cook and J. Wroughton, *English Historical Facts 1603–1688* (1980), pp. 83–4.

E. CONSTITUTIONAL LANDMARKS, 1529–1660

E.1: Henry VIII

(1) The Act of Appeals of 1533 (24 Henry VIII, c. 12)
The preamble sets out an important aspect of the theory of the English Reformation; the idea that England was a nation state, subject to no external authority. (On the Act of Appeals see also [G.1(4)].)

> Where by divers sundry old authentic histories and chronicles it is manifestly declared and expressed that this realm of England is an empire, and so hath been accepted in the world, governed by one supreme head and king having the dignity and royal estate of the imperial crown of the same, unto whom a body politic, compact of all sorts and degrees of people divided in terms and by names of spiritualty and temporalty, be bounden and owe to bear next to God a natural and humble obedience; he being also institute and furnished by the goodness and sufferance of Almighty God with plenary, whole and entire power, preeminence, authority, prerogative and jurisdiction to render and yield justice and final determination to all manner of folk resiants or subjects within this realm, in all causes, matters, debates and contentions happening to occur, insurge or begin within the limits thereof, without restraint or provocation to any foreign princes or potentates of the world . . .

(2) The Act of Supremacy of 1534 (26 Henry VIII, c. 1)
This Act, by which Parliament recognized that the King rightfully *was* head of the Church of England, an office which Parliament in no sense conferred, propounded a theory of the royal supremacy which stressed the King's personal headship and relegated Parliament to the vital but essentially subordinate role of enforcing that headship; Henry decided the doctrine of the Church, Parliament enforced his decisions. (On the Act of Supremacy see also [G.1(5)].)

> Albeit the king's majesty justly and rightfully is and oweth to be the supreme head of the Church of England, and so is recognized by the clergy of this realm in their Convocations; yet nevertheless for corroboration and confirmation thereof, and for increase of virtue in Christ's religion within this realm of England, and to repress and extirp all errors, heresies and other enormities and abuses heretofore used in the same, be it enacted by authority of this present parliament that the king our sovereign lord, his heirs and successors, kings of this realm, shall be taken, accepted and reputed the only supreme head in earth of the Church of England, called *Anglicana Ecclesia*, and shall have and enjoy annexed and united to the imperial crown of this realm as well the title and style thereof, as all honours, dignities, preeminences, jurisdictions, privileges, authorities, immunities, profits and commodities, to the said dignity of supreme head of the same Church belonging and appertaining. And that our said sovereign lord, his heirs and successors, kings of this realm, shall have full power and authority from time to time to visit, repress, redress, reform, order, correct, restrain and amend all such errors, heresies, abuses, offences, contempts, and enormities, whatsoever they be, which by any manner spiritual authority or jurisdiction ought or may lawfully be reformed, repressed, ordered, redressed, corrected, restrained or amended . . .

(3) Acts for the union of England and Wales, 1536 and 1543
(27 Henry VIII, c.26; 34 & 35 Henry VIII, c. 26)
From 1534, with the appointment of Rowland Lee, bishop of Coventry and Lichfield, as President of the Council in the Marches of Wales the English government moved towards incorporating the principality of Wales and the Marcher lordships into the English administrative and judicial system. This was done in the two great Acts of 1536 and 1543, which also gaves Wales representation in the English Parliament.

(a) Act of 1536

Albeit the dominion principality and country of Wales justly and righteously is and ever hath been incorporated, annexed, united and subject to and under the Imperial Crown of this realm, as a very member and joint of the same, whereof the king's most royal majesty . . . is very head, king, lord and ruler; yet notwithstanding, because that in the same . . . principality . . . divers rights, wages, laws and customs be far discrepant from the laws and customs of this realm, and also because that the people of the same dominion have and do daily use a speech nothing like nor consonant to the natural mother tongue used within this realm, some rude and ignorant people have made distinction and diversity between the king's subjects of this realm and his subjects of the said dominion and principality of Wales, whereby great discord, variance, debate, division, murmur and sedition hath grown between his said subjects; His Highness therefore, of a singular zeal, love and favour that he beareth towards his subjects of his said dominion of Wales, minding and intending to reduce them to the perfect order, notice and knowledge of his laws of this his realm, and utterly to extirp all and singular the sinister usages and customs differing from the same . . . hath . . . enacted and established that his said country or dominion of Wales shall be, stand and continue for ever from henceforth incorporated united and annexed to and with this his realm of England; and that all and singular person and persons, born or to be born in the said principality . . . of Wales shall have enjoy and inherit all and singular freedoms, liberties, rights, privileges and laws within this his realm, and other the king's dominions, as other the king's subjects naturally born within the same have, enjoy and inherit.

[The Act then proceeded *inter alia* to introduce English at the expense of Welsh land tenure; to insist on the enforcement of English laws at the expense of Welsh customs; to divide the whole of Wales and the Marches into shire ground on the English model; to provide that JPs (introduced to Wales by an earlier Act of the same Parliament, 27 Henry VIII c.5) and other legal officials should hold their courts in English rather than Welsh; to enact that the Welsh shires should be divided into hundreds; and to provide that the Welsh counties and boroughs should be given representation in Parliament.]

(b) Act of 1543

[This very long Act – it runs to sixty-six sections – confirmed, consolidated and elaborated the provisions of the 1536 statute. It provided, to mention only some of the most important clauses: that Wales should be divided into twelve counties, which, in turn were divided into hundreds; that Wales and the Marches should be administered by a President and Council; that judicial sessions, called 'the King's Great

Sessions in Wales' should be held twice a year in each shire; that justices of the peace should exercise their authority in Wales in the same way as in England; and that sheriffs should be appointed yearly in each Welsh county as was the practice in England.]

(4) The Act of Proclamations, 1539 (31 Henry VIII, c. 8)

This statute, once seen as a significant instrument of 'Tudor despotism' is now regarded as an attempt to ensure that royal proclamations, all too frequently ignored, were better obeyed. It did this by setting up a court to enforce them, but that did not work well and the Act was repealed in 1547. The section quoted makes it plain that after 1539 proclamations continued, as before, to be subordinated to both statute and common law. The 'constitutional significance' of the Proclamations Act, in fact, was negligible; its notoriety in the older history books is the result of myths which suggested that it conferred great new powers upon the Crown.

> . . . the king . . . with the advice of his honourable Council . . . or with the advice of the more part of them, may set forth at all times by authority of this act his proclamations, under such penalties and pains and of such sort as to his Highness and his said honourable Council or the more part of them shall see[m] necessary and requisite; and that those same shall be obeyed, observed and kept as though they were made by act of parliament . . .
>
> Provided always that the words meaning and intent of this act be not understood . . . that by virtue of it any of the king's liege people . . . should have any of his or their inheritances, lawful possessions, offices, liberties, privileges, franchises, goods or chattels taken from them . . . nor by virtue of the said act suffer any pains of death, other than shall be hereafter in this act declared, nor that by any proclamation to be made by virtue of this act, any acts, common laws . . . nor yet any lawful or laudable customs of this realm . . . shall be infringed, broken or subverted. . . .
>
> [A later section of the Act, section 4, set up a court to deal with those who offended against proclamations.]

(5) Ferrers' case, 1542
(R. Holinshed, *Chronicles*, III (1808), pp. 825–6)

Members of Parliament and their servants already had, by Henry VIII's reign, the privilege of freedom from arrest in private suits while Parliament was sitting, but until 1542 that privilege had been enforced on the Commons behalf by Chancery. In Ferrers' case the House asserted a right to enforce the privilege on its own behalf, thus establishing a precedent which it upheld thereafter. The King's well-known reaction to the Commons' claims is quoted below.

> The king . . . being advertised of . . . this proceeding, called immediately before him the lord chancellor of England and his judges, with the Speaker of the parliament and other of the gravest persons of the Nether House, to whom he declared his opinion to this effect. First commending their wisdoms in maintaining the privileges of their House (which he would not have to be infringed in any point) he alleged that . . . if the said Ferrers had been no burgess, but only his servant, yet in respect thereof he was to have the privilege as well as any other. 'For I understand', quoth he, 'that you not only for your own persons but also for your necessary servants, even to your cooks and horsekeepers, enjoy the said privilege . . . And further we be informed by our judges that we at no time stand so highly in our estate royal as in the time of parliament, wherein we as head and you as members are

conjoined and knit together into one body politic, so as whatsoever offence or injury (during that time) is offered to the meanest member of the House is to be judged as done against our person and the whole Court of Parliament . . .'

E.2: Edward VI

(6) The Act of Uniformity of 1549 (2 & 3 Edward VI, c. 1)
This Act envisaged a very different interpretation of royal authority in the Church from that suggested in the Act of Supremacy of 1534. The fact that Parliament *authorized* as well as enforced the 1549 Act gave it a positive role in the determination of doctrine which it had not possessed under Henry VIII. The royal supremacy after 1549 was essentially a parliamentary one. (On the Act see also [G.2 (10)].)

[The Act describes the making of the 1549 Prayer Book by Archbishop Cranmer and others. It then continues] that it . . . be ordained and enacted by his Majesty, with the assent of the Lords and Commons in this present parliament assembled, and by the authority of the same . . . that all and singular ministers in any cathedral or parish church, or other place within this realm of England, Wales, Calais and marches of the same, or other the king's dominions, shall from and after the feast of Pentecost next coming be bounden to say and use the matins, evensong, celebration of the Lords' supper commonly called the mass, and administration of each of the sacraments, and all their common and open prayer, in such order and form as is mentioned in the said book and none other or otherwise . . .

E.3: Elizabeth

(7) The Act of Supremacy of 1559 (1 Eliz. c. 1)
The wording of this Act, which asserted that the ecclesiastical powers of the Crown were 'united and annexed' to it 'by authority of . . . parliament' clearly implied that Elizabeth's supremacy over the Church was a parliamentary as opposed to a personal one. It therefore envisaged a type of supremacy similar to that implied in the 1549 Act of Uniformity. In view of the wording of the Act Elizabeth's attempts throughout her reign to deny Parliament a positive role in church affairs seem anachronistic. (On the Act see also [G.4 (14)].)

VIII. . . . such jurisdictions, privileges, superiorities and preeminences spiritual and ecclesiastical, as by any spiritual or ecclesiastical power or authority hath heretofore been or may lawfully be exercised or used for the visitation of the ecclesiastical state and persons, and for reformation, order and correction of the same and of all manner of errors, heresies, schisms, abuses, offences, contempts and enormities, shall for ever by authority of this present parliament be united and annexed to the Imperial crown of this realm . . .
IX. . . . all and every archbishop, bishop, and all and every other ecclesiastical person and other ecclesiastical officer and minister, of what estate, dignity, preeminence or degree soever he or they be or shall be, and all and every temporal judge, justice, mayor, and other lay or temporal officer and minister, and every other person having Your Highness' fee or wages within this realm or any Your Highness's dominions, shall make, take and receive a corporal oath upon the evangelist . . . according to the tenor and effect hereafter following, that is to say: I, *A.B.*, do utterly testify and declare in my conscience that the Queen's Highness is the only supreme

governor of this realm and all other her Highness' dominions and countries, as well in all spiritual or ecclesiastical things or causes as temporal, and that no foreign prince, person, prelate, state or potentate hath or ought to have any jurisdiction, power, superiority, preeminence or authority ecclesiastical or spiritual within this realm . . .

(8) Peter Wentworth's speech of 1576
(S. D'Ewes, *The Journals of all the Parliaments during the Reign of Queen Elizabeth* (1682), pp. 236–9)
Thomas More in 1523 had formally obtained permission for the House of Commons to discuss freely any matters laid before it, but trouble arose during Elizabeth's reign when Paul Wentworth in 1566 and his brother Peter in 1576 and 1587 asserted the liberty of MPs to discuss freely anything they considered necessary for the good of the realm. In 1576 Peter Wentworth was imprisoned by order of the House itself for critical references to the Queen made in the course of the speech quoted here. The Wentworth brothers were clearly ahead of their time in demanding unlimited free speech for MPs, but Sir John Neale was right in the emphasis which he laid on the long-term significance of these claims when he described the 1576 speech as 'the most remarkable . . . hitherto conceived in the parliament of England' (Neale, *Parliaments*, i, pp. 324–5). See also (10) below.

> Mr Speaker, I find written in a little volume these words in effect: sweet is the name of liberty, but the thing itself a value beyond all inestimable treasure. So much the more it behoveth us to take care lest we, contenting ourselves with the sweetness of the name, lose and forego the thing, being of the greatest value that can come unto this noble realm. The inestimable treasure is the use of it in this House.
>
> . . . I conclude that in this House, which is termed a place of free speech, there is nothing so necessary for the preservation of the prince and state as free speech, and without, it is a scorn and mockery to call it a Parliament House, for in truth it is none, but a very school of flattery and dissimulation, and so a fit place to serve the devil and his angels in, and not to glorify God and benefit the common-wealth. . . .
>
> . . . Certain it is, Mr Speaker, that none is without fault, no, not our noble Queen, since . . . her Majesty hath committed great fault, yea, dangerous faults to herself . . .

(9) The Norfolk election case, 1586
(D'Ewes, *Journals*, pp. 398–9)
The court of Chancery traditionally settled disputed parliamentary election results, but in 1586 the Commons asserted its own rights of decision in the celebrated Norfolk election case. The outcome remained uncertain, however, as the Lord Chancellor and judges came independently to the same conclusion as the Commons. The issue was only fully settled in 1604 (see (11) below).

> [11 November 1586] Mr Cromwell, one of the committees for the examination of writs and the returns for the knights of the county of Norfolk . . . maketh report:
> . . . They do find that the first writ and return, both in manner and form was perfect and also duly executed, and the second writ not so; . . . the . . . lord chancellor and the judges had [also] resolved that the said first writ should be returned as that which was in all parts duly and rightly executed, and not the second . . . [It was] thought . . . very prejudicial and injurious to the privilege and liberties of this House to have the said cause decided or dealt in in any sort by any others than only by such as are

members of this House; and that albeit they thought very reverently . . . of the said lord chancellor and judges, and know them to be competent judges in their places, yet in this case they took them not for judges in parliament in this House; and so further required that (if it were so thought good) Mr Farmer and Mr Gresham might take their oaths, and be allowed of and received into this House by force of the said first writ, as so allowed and admitted only by the censure of this House and not as allowed of by the said lord chancellor or judges. Which was agreed unto accordingly by the whole House, and so ordered also to be set down and entered by the clerk.

(10) The Lord Keeper's statement on free speech, 1593
(J. E. Neale, *EHR*, xxxi (1916), 136–7)
In 1593 Lord Keeper Puckering stated the Queen's interpretation of the Commons right of free speech. It was very similar to the one which More had been granted in 1523 and constituted a firm rejection of the ideas of the Wentworths.

. . . For liberty of speech her Majesty commandeth me to tell you that to say yea or no to bills, God forbid that any man should be restrained or afraid to answer according to his best liking, with some short declaration of his reason therein, and therein to have a free voice, which is the very true liberty of the House; not, as some suppose, to speak there of all causes as him listeth, and to frame a form of religion or a state of government as to their idle brains shall seem meetest. She saith no king fit for his state will suffer such absurdities. And though she hopeth no man here longeth so much for his ruin as that he mindeth to make such a peril to his own safety, yet that you may better follow what she wisheth, she makes of her goodness you the partakers of her intent and meaning.

E.4: James I

(11) The Buckinghamshire election case of 1604
(*Journals of the House of Commons*, i, pp. 149, 151–2, 168)
The Commons assertion of a right to decide disputed returns of MPs to Parliament, made in 1586 (see (9) above), was not recognized by the Crown until 1604 when James I formally acknowledged the Lower House as a court of record and a judge of returns. Thereafter the Commons retained control over its own membership.

[22 March 1604] . . . The first motion was made by Sir William Fleetwood, one of the knights returned for the county of Bucks, on the behalf of Sir Francis Goodwin, knight, who upon the first writ of summons directed to the sheriff of Bucks was elected the first knight for that shire; but the return of his election being made, it was refused by the clerk of the Crown *quia utlagatus*: and because Sir John Fortescue, upon a second writ, was elected and entered in that place, his desire was that this return might be examined and Sir Francis Goodwin received as a member of the House. The House gave way to the motion . . .
[23 March 1604] . . . The whole case was at large opened and argued, *pro et contra*, by sundry learned and grave members of the House, and after much dispute the question was agreed upon and made: whether Sir F. Goodwin were lawfully elected and returned one of the knights for Bucks, and ought to be admitted and received as a member of this House? Upon this question it was resolved in the affirmative; that he was lawfully elected and returned and *de jure* ought to be received. Hereupon the clerk of the Crown was commanded to file the first indenture

of return, and order was given that Sir Francis should presently take the oath of supremacy usual and his place in the House . . .

[11 April 1604] . . . The king said . . . that our privileges were not in question . . . He granted it [i.e. the House of Commons] was a court of record and a judge of returns.

(12) The Apology of 1604
(W. Petyt, *Jus Parliamentarium* (1739), as quoted by J. R. Tanner, *Constitutional Documents of the Reign of James I* (Cambridge, 1930), p. 221)

In the course of the discussions about the Buckinghamshire election case James I asserted that the Commons 'derived all matters of privilege from him and by his grant' and members of the Commons hastened to reject this idea in the *Apology and Satisfaction* which some of them drew up. That document was never formally approved by the Commons nor presented to the King, but the section on the rights of the Commons almost certainly reflected the attitude of the vast majority of MPs.

. . . With all humble and due respect to your Majesty our sovereign lord and head . . . we most truly avouch. First, that our privileges and liberties are our right and due inheritance, no less than our very lands and goods. Secondly, that they cannot be withheld from us, denied, or impaired, but with apparent wrong to the whole state of the realm. Thirdly, that our making of request in the entrance of parliament to enjoy our privilege is an act only of manners, and doth weaken our right no more than our suing to the king for our lands by petition . . .

(13) Union with Scotland: James I's speech to Parliament in 1604
(*CJ*, i, p. 143)

At the opening of his first English Parliament in March 1604 James I made the following impressive plea for a close union between England and Scotland.

. . . Hath not God . . . united these two kingdoms both in language, religion, and similitude of manners? Yea, hath he not made us all in one island, compassed with one sea, and of itself by nature so indivisible as almost those that were borderers themselves on the later borders cannot distinguish nor know or discern their own limits? These two countries being separated neither by sea nor great river, mountain, nor other strength of nature, but only by little small brooks or demolished little walls, so as rather they were divided in apprehension than in effect; and now in the end and fullness of time united, the right and title of both in my person, alike lineally descended of both the Crowns, whereby it is now become like a little world within itself, being intrenched and fortified round about with a natural and yet admirable strong pond or ditch, whereby all the former fears of this nation are now quite cut off . . . What God hath conjoined then, let no man separate. I am the husband, and all the whole isle is my lawful wife; I am the head and it is my body; I am the shepherd and it is my flock: I hope therefore no man will be so unreasonable as to think that I, that am a Christian king under the Gospel, should be a polygamist and husband to two wives; that I, being the head, should have a divided and monstrous body; or that being the shepherd to so fair a flock (whose fold hath no wall to hedge it but the four seas) should have my flock parted in two . . .

(14) Union with Scotland: Act for commissioners of union, 1604 (1 & 2 James I, c. 2)
The 1604 session of Parliament passed an Act appointing commissioners to consider,

together with Scottish commissioners, how closer union between England and Scotland could best be achieved.

> Be it therefore enacted . . . [that certain commissioners named in the act] . . . shall by force of this act from and after the end of this present session of parliament have full power, liberty, commission, and authority at any time or times before the next session of this parliament to assemble and meet, and thereupon to treat and consult with certain selected commissioners to be nominated and authorized by authority of parliament of the realm of Scotland, according to the tenor or purport of their authority or commission in that behalf, of and concerning such an union of the said realms of England and Scotland . . . as upon mature deliberation and consideration [the said commissioners] . . . shall in their wisdoms think and deem convenient and necessary for the honour of his Majesty and the weal and common good of both the said realms . . .

(15) Union with Scotland: James on the union, 1607 (James I, *Works* (1616 edn) pp. 10–16)

James wanted the closest possible institutional unity between England and Scotland – it was his favourite parliamentary project – but he was prepared to proceed slowly in the matter. By 1607, however, even modest proposals – for example in matters of trade and common citizenship – had run into considerable difficulties, especially in the English Parliament. James expressed his frustrations in a notable speech to the English Lords and Commons in 1607.

> . . . For myself, I protest unto you all when I first propounded the union I then thought there could have been no more question of it than of your declaration and acknowledgment of my right unto this Crown, and that as two twins they would have grown up together. The error was my mistaking; I knew mine own end but not others' fears. But now, finding many crossings, long disputations, strange questions, and nothing done, I must needs think it proceeds either of mistaking of the errand, or else from some jealousy of me the propounder, that you so add delay unto delay, searching out as it were the very bowels of curiosity, and conclude nothing. . . .
>
> . . . There is a conceit entertained, and a double jealousy possesseth many, wherein I am misjudged. First, that this union will be the crisis to the overthrow of England and setting up of Scotland; England will then be overwhelmed by the swarming of the Scots, who, if the union were effected, would reign and rule all. The second is my profuse liberality to the Scottish men more than the English, and that with this union all things shall be given to them and you turned out of all; to you shall be left the sweat and labour, to them shall be given the fruit and sweet; and that my forbearance is but till this union may be gained . . .
>
> . . . For the manner of the union presently desired, it standeth in three parts. The first, taking away of hostile laws, for since there can be now no wars betwixt you, is it not reason hostile laws should cease? . . . The second is community of commerce . . . For the third point, of naturalization, all you agree that they are no aliens, and yet will not allow them to be natural. . . .

(16) Impositions: Bate's case 1606 (T. B. Howell, ed., *State Trials*, ii (1816), p. 389)

The judgment by the Exchequer barons in Bate's case in 1606 confirmed the Crown's power to regulate English trade by levying, on its own authority, impositions (additional duties on goods entering or leaving the country). In his important judgment Chief Baron Fleming drew the distinction – familiar to lawyers of the period – between the 'ordinary' and 'absolute' powers of the Crown.

> . . . The king's power is double, ordinary and absolute, and they have several laws and ends. That of the ordinary is for the profit of particular subjects, for the execution of civil justice, the determining of *meum*; and this is exercised by equity and justice in ordinary courts, and by the civilians is nominated *jus privatum* and with us common law:.and these laws cannot be changed without parliament . . . The absolute power of the king is not that which is converted or executed to private use, to the benefit of any particular person, but is only that which is applied to the general benefit of the people and is *salus populi*, as the people is the body and the king the head; and this power . . . is most properly named policy and government . . . This absolute law [varieth] according to the wisdom of the king for the common good; and these being general rules and true as they are, all things done within these rules are lawful. The matter in question is material matter of state and ought to be ruled by the rules of policy . . . All customs, be they old or new, are no other but the effects and issues of trades and commerce with foreign nations; but all commerce and affairs with foreigners, all wars and peace, all acceptance and admitting for current, foreign coin, all parties and treaties whatsoever, are made by the absolute power of the king. . . .

(17) Whitelocke on impositions, 1610
(Howell, *State Trials*, ii, pp. 482–3, where the speech is wrongly assigned to Henry Yelverton)

The constitutional implications of the decision in Bate's case were very apparent to many MPs, and in a great debate in the House of Commons in the summer of 1610 James Whitelocke made a notable speech which has seemed to some historians to foreshadow the modern doctrine of parliamentary sovereignty. Note, however, the qualifications which he made in the later part of the excerpt.

> . . . It will be admitted for a rule and ground of state that in every commonwealth and government there be some rights of sovereignty . . .; which sovereign power is *potestas suprema*, a power that can control all other powers and cannot be controlled but by itself. It will not be denied that the power of imposing hath so great a trust in it, by reason of the mischiefs may grow to the commonwealth by the abuses of it, that it hath ever been ranked among those rights of sovereign power. Then is there no further question to be made but to examine where the sovereign power is in this kingdom, for there is the right of imposition. The sovereign power is agreed to be in the king: but in the king is a twofold power – the one in parliament, as he is assisted with the consent of the whole state; the other out of parliament, as he is sole and singular, guided merely by his own will. And if of these two powers in the king one is greater than the other and can direct and control the other, that is *suprema potestas*, the sovereign power, and the other is *subordinata*. It will then be easily proved that the power of the king in parliament is greater than his power out of parliament and doth rule and control it. . . . If a judgment be given in the King's Bench by the king himself, as may be and by the law is intended, a writ of error to reverse this judgment may be sued before the king in parliament. . . . So you see the appeal is from the king out of the parliament to the king in parliament . . ., than which there can be no stronger evidence to prove that his power out of parliament is subordinate to his power in parliament; for in acts of parliament, be they laws,

grounds, or whatsoever else, the act and power is the king's, but with the assent of the Lords and Commons, which maketh it the most sovereign and supreme power above all and controllable by none. Besides this right of imposing there be others in the kingdom of the same nature: as the power to make laws, the power of naturalization, the power of erection of arbitrary government, the power to judge without appeal, the power to legitimate; all which do belong to the king only in parliament. Others there be of the same nature that the king may exercise out of parliament, which right is grown unto him in them . . . by the use and practice of the commonwealth, as denization, coinage, making war; which power the king hath time out of mind practised without the gainsaying and murmuring of his subjects. . . .

(18) The earl of Salisbury's speech of 8 March 1610
(S. R. Gardiner, *Parliamentary Debates in 1610* (Camden Society, 1862), p. 24)
On 8 March 1610 Robert Cecil, earl of Salisbury, in a parliamentary speech, recognized on James I's behalf, the practical limitations on royal power. Note especially the statement that the King had no power to make laws or levy direct taxes without the consent of Parliament.

His Majesty said further that for his kingdom he was beholden to no elective power, neither doth he depend upon any popular applause; and yet he doth acknowledge that, though he did derive his title from the loins of his ancestors, yet the law did set the crown upon his head, and he is a king by the common law of the land. Which as it is most proper and natural for this nation, so it is the most equal and just law in any kingdom in the world. He said further that it was dangerous to submit the power of a king to definition. But withal he did acknowledge that he had no power to make laws of himself, or to exact any subsidies *de jure* without the consent of his three Estates; and therefore he was so far from approving the opinion as he did hate those that believed it; and lastly he said that there was such a marriage and union between the prerogative and the law as they cannot possibly be severed. . . .

(19) James I's speech of 21 March 1610
(James I, *Works*, p. 529)
James's practical good sense, illustrated in the previous excerpt, can be contrasted with the high-flown theoretical pronouncement which he made about the divine right of kings less than a fortnight later. It should be noted that MPs did not object to the concept of divine right as such – they supported the divine right of all duly constituted authority – merely to some of the more extravagant statements which the King made on the basis of it.

The state of monarchy is the supremest thing upon earth; for kings are not only God's lieutenants upon earth, and sit upon God's throne, but even by God himself they are called gods. There be three principal similitudes that illustrate the state of monarchy: one taken out of the word of God, and the two other out of the grounds of policy and philosophy. In the Scriptures kings are called gods, and so their power after a certain relation compared to the divine power. Kings are also compared to fathers of families, for a king is truly *parens patriae*, the politic father of his people. And lastly, kings are compared to the head of this microcosm of the body of man.
Kings are justly called gods for that they exercise a manner or resemblance of divine power upon earth, for if you will consider the attributes to God you shall see how they agree in the person of a king. God hath power to create or destroy, make or unmake, at his pleasure; to give life or send death, to judge all and to be judged

nor accountable to none; to raise low things and to make high things low at his pleasure; and to God are both soul and body due. And the like power have kings: they make and unmake their subjects; they have power of raising, and casting down; of life and of death, judges over all their subjects, and in all causes, and yet accountable to none but God only. They have power to exalt low things, and abase high things, and make of their subjects like men at the chess – a pawn to take a bishop or a knight – and to cry up or down any of their subjects, as they do their money. . . .

(20) Sir Giles Mompesson's case, 1621
(Howell, *State Trials*, ii, pp. 1130–1)

In 1621 the medieval procedure of impeachment, which had not been used since the middle of the fifteenth century, was revived by the Commons in their attack on the monopolist Sir Giles Mompesson. It involved trial before the Lords at the suit of the Commons. It should be noted, however, that impeachment was not during the 1620s an effective weapon for securing ministerial responsibility. It could work effectively only with the co-operation of the Crown and, as Charles I showed in 1626 in the proceedings against Buckingham, this co-operation could be withheld.

[March 26] . . . After a long debate, the Lords agreed upon a judgment. . . . Accordingly a message was sent from the Lords to the Commons that if they and their Speaker, according to the ancient custom of parliaments, come to demand of the Lords that judgment be given against Sir Giles for the heinous offences by him committed, they shall be heard. . . .

The knights, citizens and burgesses of the House of Commons with their Speaker being come up to the Bar, the Speaker repeated the last message which the Lords had sent unto them, and said, 'The Commons by me their Speaker demand judgment against Sir Giles Mompesson as the heinousness of his offences doth require.'

The Lord Chief Justice, as Speaker of the House of Peers, answered: 'Mr Speaker, the Lords Spiritual and Temporal have taken knowledge of the great pains the Commons have been at to inform their Lordships of many complaints brought unto them against Sir Giles Mompesson and others, whereof their Lordships received several instructions from them; and thereupon, proceeding by examination of divers witnesses upon oath, they find Sir Giles and several others guilty of many heinous crimes against the king's majesty and against the commonwealth. Time will not permit their Lordships to deal with all the offenders now; therefore they proceed to give judgment against Sir Giles according to your demand, and hereafter their Lordships will proceed against the other offenders. . . .'

(21) The King's answer of 11 December 1621 to the Commons Petition of 9 December
(J. Rushworth, *Historical Collections*, I (1682), pp. 51–2)

In this passage, in which James refers both to his own letter of 3 December 1621 and to the Commons petition of 9 December in reply to that letter, he affirms the view which he had stated in 1604, in the first parliamentary session of the reign, that the Commons held their privileges by grace rather than by right.

. . . But we cannot omit to shew you how strange we think it that you should make so bad and unjust a commentary upon some words of our former letter, as if we meant to restrain you thereby of your ancient privileges and liberties in parliament. . . .

And although we cannot allow of the style, calling it 'your ancient and undoubted right and inheritance' but could rather have wished that you had said that your privileges were derived from the grace and permission of our ancestors and us (for most of them grow from precedents, which shews rather a toleration than inheritance), yet we are pleased to give you our royal assurance that as long as you contain your selves within the limits of your duty, we will be as careful to maintain and preserve your lawful liberties and privileges as ever any of our predecessors were, nay, as to preserve our own royal prerogative. . . .

(22) *The Commons Protestation of 18 December 1621*
(Rushworth, *Historical Collections*, I, p. 53)

The Commons rejected James's statement that they held their privileges and rights only by his grace in the famous Protestation of 18 December 1621 which so enraged the King that, on the 30 December, he tore it from the Commons Journal with his own hand. It should be noted that the Protestation asserted the *right* of MPs to discuss, on their own initiative, *all* matters affecting both Church and State, an extreme assertion which had little validity either in previously accepted constitutional theory or historical practice.

The Commons now assembled in parliament, being justly occasioned thereunto concerning sundry liberties, franchises, and privileges of parliament, amongst others here mentioned, do make this Protestation following; that the liberties, franchises, privileges and jurisdictions of parliament are the ancient and undoubted birthright and inheritance of the subjects of England; and that the arduous and urgent affairs concerning the king, state and defence of the realm and of the Church of England, and the maintenance and making of laws, and redress of mischiefs and grievances which daily happen within this realm, are proper subjects and matter of counsel and debate in parliament; and that in the handling and proceeding of those businesses every member of the House of Parliament hath, and of right ought to have, freedom of speech to propound, treat, reason, and bring to conclusion the same; and that the Commons in parliament have like liberty and freedom to treat of these matters in such order as in their judgments shall seem fittest; and that every member of the said House hath like freedom from all impeachment, imprisonment, and molestation (other than by censure of the House itself) for or concerning any speaking, reasoning, or declaring of any matter or matters touching the parliament or parliament-business; and that if any of the said members be complained of and questioned for anything done or said in parliament, the same is to be shewed to the king by the advice and assent of all the Commons assembled in parliament, before the king give credence to any private information.

(23) *The Monopolies Act of 1624* (21 & 22 James I, c. 3)

The issue of monopolies caused considerable parliamentary difficulties for the Crown from the 1590s onwards. In 1624 the Monopolies Act, the first important statutory limitation on the royal prerogative during the seventeenth century, restricted the granting of monopolies – except those given to inventors – to companies as opposed to individuals and placed the control of monopolies under the courts of common law. Grievances against monopolies came to the fore again during the 1630s when Charles I's government got round the law by ensuring that individuals were able to benefit by exploiting the monopoly concessions still granted to companies under clause 9 of the 1624 legislation.

I. All monopolies and all commissions, grants, licences, charters, and letters patents heretofore made or granted, or hereafter to be made or granted, to any person or persons, bodies politic or corporate whatsoever, of or for the sole buying, selling, making, working, or using of anything within this realm or the dominion of Wales, or of any other monopolies, or of power, liberty, or faculty to dispense with any others, or to give licence or toleration to do, use, or exercise anything against the tenor or purport of any law or statute, or to give or make any warrant for any such dispensation, licence, or toleration to be had or made, or to agree or compound with any others for any penalty or forfeitures limited by any statute, or of any grant or promise of the benefit, profit, or commodity of any forfeiture, penalty, or sum of money that is or shall be due by any statute before judgment thereupon had, and all proclamations, inhibitions, restraints, warrants of assistance, and all other matters and things whatsoever any way tending to the instituting, erecting, strengthening, furthering, or countenancing of the same or any of them, are altogether contrary to the laws of this realm, and so are and shall be utterly void and of none effect, and in no wise to be put in . . . execution. . . .

[V and VI made exceptions for periods of up to twenty-one years for existing patentees and of up to 14 years for new patentees who were inventors of new processes.] . . .

IX. Provided . . . that this act or anything therein contained shall not in any wise extend or be prejudicial unto the City of London, or to any city, borough, or town corporate within this realm for or concerning any grants, charters or letters patents to them or any of them made or granted, or for or concerning any custom or customs used by or within them or any of them, or unto any corporations, companies, or fellowships of any art, trade, occupation, or mystery, or to any companies or societies of merchants within this realm erected for the maintenance, enlargement, or ordering of any trade of merchandise, but that the same charters, customs, corporations, companies, fellowships, and societies, and their liberties, privileges, power, and immunities, shall be and continue of such force and effect as they were before the making of this act. . . .

(24) The Subsidy Act of 1624 (21 & 22 James I, c. 33)
The appropriation of supplies by Parliament for the war with Spain in the Subsidy Act of 1624 has frequently been regarded as an important invasion of the royal prerogative by the House of Commons. In fact it was the result of conflicts at Court and the proposal came from members of the government.

I. . . . With one consent and voice we have given unto your Majesty [humble advice] to dissolve those treaties [for the marriage with Spain and the restitution of the Palatinate] which your Majesty hath been graciously pleased, to our exceeding joy and comfort, fully to yield unto, and accordingly have made your public declaration for the real and utter dissolution of them, by means whereof your Majesty may haply be engaged in a sudden war. We, in all humbleness most ready and willing to give unto your Majesty and the whole world an ample testimony of our dutiful affections and sincere intentions to assist you therein for the maintenance of that war that may hereupon ensue, and more particularly for the defence of this your realm of England, the securing of your kingdom of Ireland, the assistance of your neighbours the states of the United Provinces and other your Majesty's friends and allies, and for the setting forth of your royal navy, we have resolved to give . . . three whole fifteenths and tenths. . . .

IV. And furthermore, for the great and weighty considerations aforesaid, we the Lords Spiritual and Temporal and the Commons in this present parliament assembled do . . . give and grant to your Highness . . . three entire subsidies. . . .

XXXVI. And be it further enacted . . . that all the sums of money by this present act given and granted to the uses aforesaid shall be paid . . . unto . . . treasurers. . . .

XXXVII. . . . Be it further enacted that the moneys to be received by the said treasurers by virtue of this act shall be issued out and expended for or towards the uses aforesaid to such person and persons and in such manner and form as by the warrant of . . . ten [named] persons [whom] . . . his Majesty hath already nominated and hath made choice of to be of his Council for the War, or any five or more of them . . . under their hands and seals shall be directed and not otherwise. . . .

XLIII. And to the end that as well the said Council of War as the said treasurers may the better observe and perform the trust aforesaid committed unto them, be it further enacted that they shall severally and distinctly take these respective oaths following, that is to say the said treasurers shall take this oath following: you shall swear that you . . . shall not issue any part of those moneys which shall be paid into your hands, or unto the hands of any other by your appointment or consent without the special warrant of those persons which are by his Majesty appointed to be of his Council for the Wars . . . or of five of them at the least . . .; in every such warrant or warrants there shall be expressed that those moneys for which such warrant is given are to be issued for some of those ends mentioned in this present act. And the said Council of War shall take this oath following: you shall swear that you . . . shall make no warrant for any moneys to be issued which are given by this present act but for some of those ends which are expressed in this act, and that all such warrants as shall be made by you shall mention in them that those moneys are to be employed according to the true meaning of this act, and to the best of your means you shall employ the same accordingly. . . .

E.5: Charles I

(25) The five knights' case, 1627
(Howell, *State Trials*, iii (1816), pp. 52–9)
In 1626 Charles I levied a forced loan and imprisoned, among others who refused to pay, five knights who, in 1627, applied for a writ of Habeas Corpus. This was refused on the grounds that they had been imprisoned by 'special command' of the King. This raised the question of the King's right to imprison men without showing specific reasons, but the court of King's Bench upheld his authority. Chief Justice Hyde's judgment is given below.

    . . . The exceptions which have been taken to this return were two; the one for the form, the other for the substance.

        . . . In our case the cause of the detention is sufficiently answered, which is the demand of the writ, and therefore we resolve that the form of this return is good.

    The next thing is the main point in law, whether the substance or matter of the return be good or no: wherein the substance is this – he [the Warden] doth certify that they are detained in prison by the special command of the king; and whether this be good in law or not, that is the question. . . . [After examination of precedents.] Then the precedents are all against you, every one of them, and what shall guide our judgments since there is nothing alleged in this case but precedents? That, if no cause of the commitment be expressed, it is to be presumed to be for matter of state, which we cannot take notice of; you see we find none, no, not one that hath been delivered by bail in the like cases, but by the hand of the king or his direction. . . . We have looked upon that precedent that was mentioned by Mr Attorney – the resolution of all the judges of England in 34 Eliz. . . . The question now is, whether we may deliver this gentleman or not . . . and this resolution of all the judges teacheth us; and what can we do but walk in the steps of our forefathers? . . . If in justice we ought to deliver you, we would do it; but upon these grounds and these records and the precedents and resolutions, we cannot deliver you, but you must be remanded.

(26) *The Petition of Right, 1628* (3 Charles I, c. 1)

By 1628 the King's needs in the wars with Spain and France had led him to exact forced loans, billet soldiers in private houses, proceed by martial law against both soldiers and civilians and resort to imprisonment without cause shown. These proceedings were declared illegal by Parliament in the Petition of Right, which the King accepted. It rapidly became apparent, however, that he regarded it as a statement of existing law, subject to his own interpretation.

The Petition recites complaints about forced loans, arbitrary imprisonment, billeting and proceeding by martial law, and then continues

VIII. They [i.e. the Lords and Commons] do therefore humbly pray your most excellent majesty that no man hereafter be compelled to make or yield any gift, loan, benevolence, tax or such like charge without common consent by act of parliament, and that none be called to make answer or take such oath or to give attendance or be confined or otherwise molested or disquieted concerning the same or for refusal thereof. And that no freeman in any such manner as is before mentioned be imprisoned or detained. And that your majesty would be pleased to remove the said soldiers and mariners, and that your people may not be so burdened in time to come. And that the aforesaid commissions for proceeding by martial law may be revoked and annulled. And that hereafter no commissions of like nature may issue forth to any person or persons whatsoever to be executed as aforesaid, lest by colour of them any of your majesty's subjects be destroyed or put to death contrary to the laws and franchises of the land.

All which they most humbly pray of your most excellent majesty as their rights and liberties according to the laws and statutes of this realm . . .

(27) *Ship money: the judgment of Sir Robert Berkeley*
(Howell, *State Trials*, iii, pp. 1090–9)

John Hampden's refusal to pay ship money led to the celebrated case of 1637–38, held in the Exchequer Chamber before all twelve judges of King's Bench, Common Pleas and Exchequer, a sign of its fundamental importance. Five of the twelve judges found for Hampden – three admittedly on technical grounds – and the fact that the Crown was able to obtain only a narrow majority verdict was regarded by many as a moral victory for Hampden.

The judgment of Sir Robert Berkeley, one of the King's Bench judges, was for the Crown. He made very high claims for royal authority, but was also careful to insist that the King had no general right of arbitrary taxation.

. . . I hope that none doth imagine that it either is, or can be drawn by consequence, to be any part of the question in this case, whether the king may at all times and upon all occasions impose charges upon his subjects in general, without common consent in parliament? If that were made the question, it is questionless that he may not. The people of the kingdom are subjects, not slaves, freemen, not villeins to be taxed *de alto et basso*.

Though the king of England hath a monarchical power, and hath *jura summae majestatis*, and hath an absolute trust settled in his Crown and person for the government of his subjects, yet his government is to be *secundum leges regni*. . . . By those laws the subjects are not tenants at the king's will, of what they have. . . . They have in their goods or property, a peculiar interest, a *meum et tuum*. They have a birthright in the laws of the kingdom. No new laws can be put upon them, none of their laws can be altered or abrogated, without common consent in parliament.

[Berkeley then insisted that ship money was *not* a subsidy. Ships, not money, were to be provided and, although the country was not on the immediate verge of war, there was grave danger on the high seas.]

Now, whether to set the commonwealth free and in safety from this peril of ruin and destruction the king may not of his own royal authority, and without common assent in parliament, impose a change upon his subjects in general to provide such shipping as is necessary in his royal judgment, to join with his majesty's own ships and to attend them for such time as his majesty in his royal wisdom shall think fit . . .? [that is the question.]

There are two [relevant] maxims of the law of England. . . . The first is 'that the king is a person trusted with the state of the commonwealth'. The second of these maxims is; 'that the king cannot do wrong'. Upon these two maxims the *jura summae majestatis* are grounded, with which none but the king himself (not his High Court of Parliament without leave) hath to meddle, as, namely, war and peace, value of coin, parliament at pleasure, power to dispense with penal laws, and divers others; amongst which I range these also, of regal power to command provision (in case of necessity) of means from the subjects, to be adjoined to the king's own means for the defence of the commonwealth, for the preservation of the *salus reipublicae*. Otherwise I do not understand how the king's majesty may be said to have the majestical right and power of a free monarch.

It is agreed that the king is by his regal office bound to defend his people . . . against all disturbers of the general peace amongst them, most chiefly in my judgment against dangerous foreigners. . . .

(28) Clarendon on the judges
(Clarendon, *History of the Rebellion*, W. D. Macray, i (Oxford, 1888), p. 88)
The judges' alleged subservience to royal authority was fiercely attacked by Clarendon, who referred to the ship-money verdict and other cases in the following passage. The judges' verdicts had more weight in law than he allows.

And here the damage and mischief cannot be expressed that the Crown and State sustained by the deserved reproach and infamy that attended the judges, by being made use of in this and the like acts of power; there being no possibility to preserve the dignity, reverence and estimation of the laws themselves but by the integrity and innocency of the judges. And no question, as the exorbitancy of the House of Commons this parliament [i.e. the Long Parliament] hath proceeded principally from their contempt of the laws, and that contempt from the scandal of that judgment, so the concurrence of the House of Peers in that fury can be imputed to no one thing more than to the irreverence and scorn the judges were justly in; who had been always before looked upon there as the oracles of the law. . . .

(29) *The Triennial Act of 1641* (16 Charles I, c. 1)

The Triennial bill, which laid down an elaborate procedure for ensuring that Parliament would meet at least every three years was reluctantly accepted in February 1641 by Charles I, who rightly regarded it as a serious invasion of the traditional prerogatives of the Crown.

II. Be it enacted . . . that in case there be not a parliament summoned by writ under the Great Seal of England and assembled and held before the tenth day of September which shall be in the third year next after the last day of the last meeting and sitting in this present parliament . . ., and so from time to time and in all times hereafter it there shall not be a parliament assembled and held . . . [as aforesaid], then . . . the parliament shall assemble and be held in the usual place at Westminster in such manner and by such means only as is hereafter in this present act declared and enacted and not otherwise, on the second Monday which shall be in the month of November then next ensuing. . . . [Detailed provisions for calling a new parliament without royal co-operation follow.]

(30) *The Act against dissolving the Long Parliament without its own assent* (17 Charles I, c. 7)

This Act, passed in May 1641, meant that the Long Parliament was not legally dissolved until 1660. Like the Triennial Act it was obviously an important restriction on the royal prerogative.

Whereas great sums of money must of necessity be speedily advanced and provided for the relief of his majesty's army and people in the northern parts of this realm, and for preventing the imminent danger it is in, and for supply of other his majesty's present and urgent occasions, which cannot be so timely effected as is requisite without credit for raising the said monies; which credit cannot be obtained until such obstacles be first removed as are occasioned by fears, jealousies and apprehensions of divers his majesty's loyal subjects, that this present parliament may be adjourned, prorogued, or dissolved, before justice shall be duly executed upon delinquents, public grievances redressed, a firm peace between the two nations of England and Scotland concluded, and before sufficient provision be made for the re-payment of the said monies so to be raised; all which the Commons in this present parliament assembled, having duly considered, do therefore most humbly beseech your majesty that it may be declared and enacted.

And be it declared and enacted . . . that this present parliament now assembled shall not be dissolved unless it be by act of parliament to be passed for that purpose; nor shall be at any time or times during the continuance thereof, prorogued or adjourned, unless it be by act of parliament to be likewise passed for that purpose. . . .

(31) The Act abolishing Star Chamber, 1641 (16 Charles I, c. 10)

The court of Star Chamber became increasingly unpopular during the 1630s, when it was an important instrument of the King's 'personal rule'. Its abolition, together with the ending of the jurisdiction of the other prerogative courts in 1641, severely weakened royal authority.

> . . . Forasmuch as all matters examinable or determinable before . . . the court commonly called the Star Chamber may have their proper remedy and redress, and then due punishment and correction by the common law of the land and in the ordinary course of justice elsewhere; and forasmuch as the reasons and motives inducing the erection and continuance of the court do now cease, and the proceedings, censure and decrees of the court have by experience been found to be an intolerable burden to the subjects, and the means to introduce an arbitrary power and government. . . .
>
> For settling whereof and preventing the like in time to come, be it ordained and enacted . . . that the said court commonly called the Star Chamber . . . be from the first day of August in the year of our Lord God 1641 clearly and absolutely dissolved, taken away and determined. . . .

(32) The Militia Ordinance, 1642
(C. H. Firth and R. S. Rait, eds, *Acts and Ordinances of the Interregnum*, i (1911), pp. 1–5)

In this ordinance, passed in March 1642 by the Lords and Commons, the two Houses of Parliament usurped the legislative function. They demanded acceptance of the ordinance in the country despite the fact that the King firmly refused his consent and stressed the illegality of Parliament's proceedings.

> Whereas there hath been of late a most dangerous and desperate design upon the House of Commons, which we have just cause to believe to be an effect of the bloody counsels of Papists and other ill-affected persons, who have already raised a rebellion in the kingdom of Ireland; and by reason of many discoveries we cannot but fear they will proceed not only to stir up the like rebellion and insurrections in this kingdom of England, but also to back them with forces from abroad.
>
> For the safety, therefore, of his majesty's person, the parliament and kingdom in this time of imminent danger:
>
> It is ordained by the Lords and Commons now in parliament assembled, that Henry, earl of Holland shall be Lieutenant of the county of Berks, Oliver, earl of Bolingbroke shall be Lieutenant of the county of Bedford etc. . . .
>
> And severally and respectively have power to assemble and call together all and singular his majesty's subjects within the said several and respective counties and places, as well within liberties as without, that are meet and fit for the wars, and them to train, exercise and put in readiness, and them after their abilities and faculties well and sufficiently from time to time to cause to be arrayed and weaponed, and to take the muster of them in places most fit for that purpose. . . .
>
> And it is further ordained that such persons as shall not obey in any of the premises, shall answer their neglect and contempt to the Lords and Commons in a parliamentary way, and not otherwise nor elsewhere, and that every the powers granted as aforesaid shall continue until it shall be otherwise ordered or declared by both Houses of Parliament and no longer.

(33) The Putney debates, 1647
(A. S. P. Woodhouse, ed., *Puritanism and Liberty* (2nd edn, 1974), pp. 53–8)
These debates in the General Council of the Army were held in October and November 1647. The 'agitators' (representatives of the rank and file of the army) and a few officers, wanted a significant extension of the franchise in line with Leveller demands; the majority of officers, including Cromwell, feared that such a trend towards political democracy might eventually threaten established property rights and thus the whole social fabric.

The following passages in the debate took place on 29 October, with Henry Ireton speaking for the conservative officers and Thomas Rainborough, though himself an officer, for the more radical elements.

Rainborough . . . I really think that the poorest he that is in England hath a life to live, as the greatest he; and therefore truly, sir, I think it's clear that every man that is to live under a government ought first by his own counsel to put himself under that government; and I do think that the poorest man in England is not at all bound in a strict to that government that he hath not had a voice to put himself under. . . .

Ireton . . . I think that no person hath a right to an interest or share in the disposing of the affairs of the kingdom, and in determining or choosing those that shall determine what laws we shall be ruled by here – no person hath a right to this that hath not a permanent fixed interest in this kingdom. . . . We talk of birthright. Truly [by] birthright there is thus much claim. Men may justly have by birthright, by their very being born in England . . ., that we should not refuse to give them air and place and ground, and the freedom of the highway, and other things, to live amongst us. . . . That I think is due to a man by birth. But that by a man's being born here he shall have a share in that power that shall dispose of the lands here, and of all things here, I do not think it a sufficient ground. . . .

Rainborough . . . I do hear nothing at all that can convince me why any man that is born in England ought not to have his voice in election of burgesses. It is said that if a man have not a permanent interest he can have no claim, and we must be no freer than the laws will let us be, and that there is no chronicle will let us be freer than that we enjoy. . . . I do think that the main cause why Almighty God gave men reason, it was that they should make use of that reason, and that they should improve it for that end and purpose that God gave it them. . . . I do not find anything in the law of God that a lord shall choose twenty burgesses, and a gentleman but two, or a poor man shall choose none; I find no such thing in the law of nature, nor in the law of nations. But I do find that all Englishmen must be subject to English laws, and I do verily believe that there is no man but will say that the foundation of all law lies in the people. . . .

Ireton . . . All the main thing that I speak for is because I would have an eye to property. I hope we do not come to contend for victory – but let every man consider with himself that he do not go that way to take away all property. For here is the case of the most fundamental part of the constitution of the kingdom, which if you take away, you take away all by that. Here men of this and this quality are determined to be the electors of men to the parliament, and they are all those who have any permanent interest in the kingdom, and who, taken together, do comprehend the whole interest of the kingdom. . . . Now I wish we may all consider of what right you will challenge that all the people should have right to elections. Is it by the right of nature? If you will hold forth that as your ground, then I think you must deny all property too. . . .

(34) Commons' resolutions, 4 January 1649
(Journals of the House of Commons, vi. p. 111)
After Pride's Purge the Rump of the Commons assumed full legislative powers. From then on they described all measures which passed their own House as 'Acts'.

. . . the Commons of England, in parliament assembled do declare that the people are, under God, the original of all just power:

And do also declare that the Commons of England, in parliament assembled, being chosen by and representing the people, have the supreme power in this nation:

And do also declare that whatsoever is enacted or declared for law by the Commons in parliament assembled hath the force of law; and all the people of this nation are concluded thereby, although the consent and concurrence of king or House of Peers be not had thereunto.

The first 'Act' which the Rump of the Commons passed in terms of these resolutions without the assent of the Lords was that of 6 January 1649, setting up a High Court to try the King (Firth and Rait, *Acts and Ordinances*, i, pp. 1,253 ff).

(35) The sentence of the High Court upon Charles I, January 1649
(J. Rushworth, Historical Collections, IV, ii (1701), p. 1,418)
The sentence of death upon Charles which the High Court pronounced on the 27 January 1649 branded him as a 'traitor'. That, of course, was a legal absurdity in English law as it had been traditionally understood. Treason had been against *the person of the king*.

. . . Charles Stuart, being admitted king of England, and therein trusted with a limited power to govern by and according to the law of the land and not otherwise . . ., yet nevertheless, out of a wicked design to erect and uphold in himself an unlimited and tyrannical power to rule according to his will, and to overthrow the rights and liberties of the people . . ., to the same end hath traitorously and maliciously levied war against the present parliament and people therein represented . . . and . . . hath thereby caused and procured many thousands of the free people of this nation to be slain. . . .

Now, therefore, upon serious and mature deliberation . . . this Court is fully satisfied in their judgments and consciences . . . that he hath been and is the occasioner, author, and continuer of the said unnatural, cruel, and bloody wars, and therein guilty of high treason. . . . For all which treasons and crimes this Court doth adjudge that he, the said Charles Stuart, as a tyrant, traitor, murderer, and public enemy to the good people of this nation, shall be put to death by severing of his head from his body.

E.6: Interregnum

(36) The abolition of the monarchy and the House of Lords; England declared a commonwealth, March–May 1649.
Early in February, following the execution of the King on 30 January 1649, the Commons resolved to abolish both the monarchy and the House of Lords. The necessary legislation was passed in March. Two months later England was formally declared a commonwealth.

(a) *'Act' abolishing the office of king, 17 March 1649*
(Firth and Rait, *Acts and Ordinances*, ii (1911), p. 19)

And whereas it is and hath been found by experience that the office of a king in this nation and Ireland, and to have the power thereof in any single person is unnecessary, burdensome, and dangerous to the liberty, safety and public interest of the people, and that for the most part, use hath been made of the regal power and prerogative to oppress and impoverish and enslave the subject; and that usually and naturally any one person in such power makes it his interest to incroach upon the just freedom and liberty of the people, and to promote the setting up of their own will and power above the laws, that so they might enslave these kingdoms to their own lust; be it therefore enacted and ordained by this present parliament . . . that the office of a king in this nation shall not henceforth reside in or be exercised by any one single person; and that no one person whatsoever shall or may have or hold the office, style, dignity, power, or authority of king of the said kingdoms and dominions, or any of them, or of the prince of Wales. . . .

(b) *'Act' abolishing the House of Lords, 19 March 1649*
(Firth and Rait, *Acts and Ordinances*, ii, p. 24)

The Commons of England assembled in parliament, finding by too long experience that the House of Lords is useless and dangerous to the people of England to be continued, have thought fit to ordain and enact, and be it ordained and enacted by this present parliament and by the authority of the same that from henceforth the House of Lords in parliament shall be and is hereby wholly abolished and taken away. . . .

(c) *'Act' declaring England to be a commonwealth, 19 May 1649*
(Firth and Rait, *Acts and Ordinances*, ii, p. 122)

Be it declared and enacted by this present parliament and by the authority of the same, that the people of England and of all the dominions and territories thereunto belonging, are and shall be, and are hereby constituted, made, established and confirmed to be a Commonwealth and Free State, and shall from henceforth be governed as a Commonwealth and Free State by the supreme authority of this nation, the representatives of the people in parliament, and by such as they shall appoint and constitute as officers and ministers under them for the good of the people, and that without any king or House of Lords.

(37) The Instrument of Government, 1653
(Firth and Rait, *Acts and Ordinances*, ii, pp. 813 ff)
The first and only written Constitution that Britain has ever had was drawn up by a group of officers headed by Major-general Lambert. It was adopted by Cromwell on 16 December 1653. The extracts which follow deal with some of the more important constitutional provisions. (For the religious clauses see [G.7(30)].)

The government of the Commonwealth of England, Scotland and Ireland and the dominions thereunto belonging.

I. That the supreme legislative authority of the Commonwealth of England, Scotland, and Ireland, and the dominions thereunto belonging, shall be and reside in one person, and the people assembled in parliament: the style of which person shall be the Lord Protector of the Commonwealth of England, Scotland, and Ireland.

II. That the exercise of the chief magistracy and the administration of the government over the said countries and dominions, and the people thereof, shall be in the

Lord Protector, assisted with a Council, the number whereof shall not exceed twenty-one, nor be less than thirteen. . . .

VI. That the laws shall not be altered, suspended, abrogated, or repealed, nor any new law made, nor any tax, charge or imposition laid upon the people, but by common consent in parliament, save only as is expressed in the thirtieth article.

VII. That there shall be a parliament summoned to meet at Westminster upon the third day of September 1654, and that successively a parliament shall be summoned once in every third year, to be accounted from the dissolution of the present parliament.

VIII. That neither the parliament to be next summoned, nor any successive parliaments, shall, during the time of five months, to be accounted from the day of their first meeting, be adjourned, prorogued, or dissolved, without their own consent.

IX. That as well the next as all other successive parliaments shall be summoned and elected in manner hereafter expressed; that is to say, the persons to be chosen within England, Wales, the Isles of Jersey, Guernsey, and the town of Berwick-upon-Tweed, to sit and serve in parliament, shall be, and not exceed, the number of four hundred. The persons to be chosen within Scotland, to sit and serve in parliament, shall be, and not exceed the number of thirty; and the persons to be chosen to sit in parliament for Ireland shall be, and not exceed, the number of thirty. . . .

XVIII. That all and every person and persons seised or possessed to his own use of any estate, real or personal, to the value of £200, and not within the aforesaid exceptions [detailed in clauses XIV and XV above] shall be capable to elect members to serve in parliament for counties. . . .

XXIV. That all bills agreed unto by the parliament shall be presented to the Lord Protector for his consent; and in case he shall not give his consent thereto within twenty days after they shall be presented to him, or give satisfaction to the parliament within the time limited, that then, upon declaration of the parliament that the Lord Protector hath not consented nor given satisfaction, such bills shall pass into and become laws, although he shall not give his consent thereunto; provided such bills contain nothing in them contrary to the matters contained in these presents. . . .

XXVII. That a constant yearly revenue shall be raised, settled, and established for maintaining of 10,000 horse and dragoons, and 20,000 foot, in England, Scotland and Ireland, for the defence and security thereof, and also for a convenient number of ships for guarding of the seas; besides £200,000 per annum for defraying the other necessary charges of administration of justice, and other expenses of the government, which revenue shall be raised by the customs, and such other ways and means as shall be agreed upon by the Lord Protector and the Council, and shall not be taken away or diminished, nor the way agreed upon for raising the same altered, but by the consent of the Lord Protector and the parliament. . . .

XXX. That the raising of money for defraying the charge of the present extraordinary forces, both at sea and land, in respect of the present wars, shall be by consent of parliament, and not otherwise: save only that the Lord Protector, with the consent of the major part of the Council for preventing the disorders and dangers which might otherwise fall out both by sea and land, shall have power, until the meeting of the first parliament, to raise money for the purposes aforesaid; and also to make laws and ordinances for the peace and welfare of these nations where it shall be necessary, which shall be binding and in force, until order shall be taken in parliament concerning the same. . . .

XXXII. That the office of Lord Protector over these nations shall be elective and not hereditary. [Future Protectors to be elected by the Council. A quorum of at least thirteen to be present, but the election to be by a simple majority of those present.]. . . .

XXXIII. That Oliver Cromwell, Captain-General of the forces of England, Scotland, and Ireland, shall be, and is hereby declared to be, Lord Protector of the Commonwealth of England, Scotland, and Ireland, and the dominions thereto belonging, for his life. . . .

(38) The Ordinance for the union of England and Scotland, 1654
(Firth and Rait, *Acts and Ordinances*, ii, pp. 871 ff)
The Instrument of Government assumed the administrative and legislative union of the countries of the British Isles, England, Scotland and Ireland, and in April 1654 Cromwell formally promulgated an ordinance for the union of England and Scotland.

His Highness the Lord Protector of the Commonwealth of England, Scotland, and Ireland, etc, taking into consideration how much it might conduce to the glory of God and the peace and welfare of the people of this whole island, that after all those late unhappy wars and differences the people of Scotland should be united with the people of England into one Commonwealth and after and under one government, and finding that in December 1651 the parliament then sitting did send commissioners into Scotland to invite the people of that nation unto such a happy union, who proceeded so far therein that the shires and boroughs of Scotland, by their deputies convened at Dalkeith, and again at Edinburgh, did accept of the said union, and assent thereunto; for the completing and perfecting of which union be it ordained, and it is ordained by his Highness the Lord Protector of the Commonwealth of England, Scotland and Ireland, and the dominions thereto belonging, by and with the advice and consent of his Council, that all the people of Scotland, and of the Isles of Orkney and Shetland, and of all the dominions and territories belonging unto Scotland, are and shall be, and are hereby incorporated into, constituted, established, declared and confirmed one Commonwealth with England; and in every parliament to be held successively for the said Commonwealth, thirty persons shall be called from and serve for Scotland.

(39) The Humble Petition and Advice, 1657
(Firth and Rait, *Acts and Ordinances*, ii, pp. 1,048 ff)
In May 1657 the Instrument of Government was amended by the Humble Petition and Advice. This had originally offered Cromwell the Crown, but he refused it after much agonizing. It should be noted that in the Petition, as passed, the Protector was to nominate his successor, a two-chamber Parliament was restored, and the Council of State was renamed the Privy Council. The tendency was clear; a return to many of the forms of the old monarchical constitution.

. . . 1. That your Highness will be pleased, by and under the name and style of Lord Protector of the Commonwealth of England, Scotland and Ireland, and the dominions and territories thereunto belonging, to hold and exercise the office of chief magistrate of these nations, and to govern according to this Petition and Advice in all things therein contained, and in all other things according to the laws of these nations, and not otherwise. That your Highness will be pleased during your lifetime to appoint and declare the person who shall immediately after your death succeed you in the government of these nations.

2. That your Highness will for the future be pleased to call parliaments consisting of two Houses (in such manner and way as shall be more particularly afterwards agreed and declared in this Petition and Advice) once in three years at furthest, or oftener, as the affairs of the nations shall require. . . .

5. [Those summoned to the Other House] shall be nominated by your Highness and approved by this House, and . . . exceed not seventy in number, nor be under the number of forty. . . .

7. And to the end there may be a constant revenue for support of the government, and for the safety and defence of these nations by sea and land, we declare our willingness to settle forthwith a yearly revenue of £1,300,000, thereof £1,000,000 for the navy and army, and £300,000 for the support of the government, and no part thereof to be raised by a land-tax, and this not to be altered without the consent of the three estates in parliament; and to grant such other temporary supplies according as the Commons assembled in parliament shall from time to time adjudge the necessities of these nations to require; and do pray your Highness that it be enacted and declared that no charge be laid, nor no person be compelled to contribute to any gift, loan, benevolence, tax, tallage, aid or any other like charge, without common consent by act of parliament, which is a freedom the people of these nations ought by the laws to inherit.

8. That none may be added or admitted to the Privy Council of your Highness or successors, but such as are of known piety and undoubted affection to the rights of these nations. . . .

(40) *The Declaration of Breda, 4 April 1660*
(*Journals of the House of Lords*, xi, pp. 7–8)

Charles II's conciliatory Declaration of Breda did much to help him regain the throne. The exerpts below deal with the question of land sales, the payment of arrears to the army, and the issue of a general pardon. (For the religious aspect of the Declaration see [G.7(31)].)

. . . to the end that the fear of punishment may not engage any, conscious to themselves of what is past, to a perseverance in guilt for the future, by opposing the quiet and happiness of their country in the restoration both of king, peers, and people to their just, ancient and fundamental rights, we do, by these presents, declare that we do grant a free and general pardon which we are ready, upon demand, to pass under our Great Seal of England, to all our subjects, of what degree or quality soever, who, within forty days after the publishing hereof, shall lay hold upon this our grace and favour, and shall, by any public act declare their doing so, and that they return to the loyalty and obedience of good subjects; excepting only such persons as shall hereafter be excepted by parliament. . . .

And because in the continued distractions of so many years, and so many and great revolutions, many grants and purchases of estates have been made to and by many officers, soldiers, and others, who are now possessed of the same, and who may be liable to actions at law upon several titles, we are . . . willing that all such differences and all things relating to such grants, sales and purchases, shall be determined in parliament, which can best provide for the just satisfaction of all men who are concerned.

And we do further declare that we will be ready to consent to any act or acts of parliament to the purposes aforesaid, and for the full satisfaction of all arrears due to the officers and soldiers of the army under the command of General Monck; and that they shall be received into our service upon as good pay and conditions as they now enjoy.

411

F. THE CHURCH[1]

F.1: Archbishops of Canterbury 1529–1660

William Warham	Nov 1503–Aug 1532
Thomas Cranmer	Feb 1533–Dec 1555 (deprived)
Reginald Pole	Dec 1555–Nov 1558
Matthew Parker	July 1559–May 1575
Edmund Grindal	Dec 1575–July 1583
John Whitgift	Aug 1583–Feb 1604
Richard Bancroft	Oct 1604–Nov 1610
George Abbot	Mar 1611–Aug 1633
William Laud	Aug 1633–Jan 1645
William Juxon	Sept 1660–June 1663

Dates given in the first column are those of royal nomination, except in the cases of Warham, Cranmer and Pole where they are those of papal provision. Dates in the second column are deaths except where otherwise indicated.

F.2: Archbishops of York 1529–1660

Thomas Wolsey	Sept 1514–Nov 1530
Edward Lee	Oct 1531–Sept 1544
Robert Holgate	Jan 1545–Mar 1554 (deprived)
Nicholas Heath	Feb 1555–July 1559 (deprived)
Thomas Young	Jan 1561 (el.)–June 1568
Edmund Grindal	Apr 1570–Dec 1575 (nominated to Canterbury)
Edwin Sandys	Jan 1577–July 1588
John Piers	Jan 1589–Sept 1594
Matthew Hutton	Feb 1595–Jan 1606
Toby Matthew	July 1606 (el.)–Mar 1628
George Montaigne	June 1628–Nov 1628
Samuel Harsnett	Nov 1628–May 1631
Richard Neile	Feb 1632 (el.)–Oct 1640
John Williams	Dec 1641 (conf.)–Mar 1650
Accepted Frewen	Sept 1660 (el.)–Mar 1664

Dates given in the first column are those of royal nomination (or failing that of election or confirmation), except in the cases of Wolsey and Lee, where they are those of papal provision. Dates in the second column are deaths, except where otherwise indicated.

F.3: Bishops of London 1529–1660

Cuthbert Tunstall	May 1522–Feb 1530
John Stokesley	Mar 1530–Sept 1539
Edmund Bonner	Oct 1539 (el.)–Oct 1549 (deprived)
Nicholas Ridley	Apr 1550–1553 (deprived)
Edmund Bonner	Sept 1553 (restored)–May 1559 (deprived)
Edmund Grindal	June 1559–Apr 1570 (nominated to York)
Edwin Sandys	June 1570–Jan 1577 (nominated to York)
John Aylmer	Mar 1577–June 1594
Richard Fletcher	Dec 1594–June 1596
Richard Bancroft	April 1597 (el.)–Oct 1604 (nominated to Canterbury)
Richard Vaughan	Dec 1604–Mar 1607
Thomas Ravis	Apr 1607–Dec 1609
George Abbot	Dec 1609–Mar 1611 (nominated to Canterbury)
John King	Sept 1611 (consecrated)–Mar 1621
George Montaigne	June 1621–Feb 1628 (nominated to Durham)
William Laud	July 1628–Aug 1633 (nominated to Canterbury)
William Juxon	Oct 1633 (el.)–Sept 1660 (nominated to Canterbury)
Gilbert Sheldon	Oct 1660 (el.)–June 1663 (nominated to Canterbury)

Dates given in the first column are those of royal nomination (or failing that of election or consecration), except in the cases of Tunstall and Stokesley, where they are those of papal provision. Dates in the second column are deaths, except where otherwise indicated.

---

1. *Handbook of British Chronology*, pp. 211–12, 265–6, 240–1.

G. RELIGIOUS LANDMARKS, 1529–1660

G.1: Henry VIII

(1), (2), (3). The three following Acts, taken together, abolished all payments from England to Rome. The first two also ended the executive powers of the Papacy over the English Church. Note how the polite references to the Pope in the 1532 Act have ceased in the 1534 Acts.

(1) *The Act in Conditional Restraint of Annates* (23 Henry VIII, c. 20)

Forasmuch as it is well perceived by long approved experience that great and inestimable sums of money be daily conveyed out of this realm to the impoverishment of the same, and specially such sums of money as the Pope's Holiness, his predecessors, and the court of Rome by long time have heretofore taken of all and singular those spiritual persons which have been named . . . to be archbishops or bishops within this realm of England, under the title of annates, otherwise called first fruits . . .; albeit that our . . . sovereign lord the King and all his natural subjects, as well spiritual as temporal, be as obedient, devout, Catholic and humble children of God and Holy Church as any people be within any realm christened, yet the said exactions of annates or first fruits be . . . intolerable and importable to this realm. . . . It is therefore ordained, established and enacted by authority of this present parliament that the . . . payments of annates or first fruits . . . shall from henceforth utterly cease. . . .

[II. If the Papal Curia should delay or refuse the documents necessary for the consecration of any bishop or archbishop hereafter nominated by the Crown, he is to be consecrated without them.]

III. And to the intent our . . . Holy Father the Pope . . . shall not think that the pains and labours taken and hereafter to be taken about the writing . . . and other businesses sustained . . . for and about the expedition of any bulls hereafter to be obtained or had for any . . . archbishopric or bishopric shall be irremunerated . . . every spiritual person of this realm hereafter to be named . . . to any archbishopric or bishopric of this realm shall . . . pay for the writing and obtaining of his or their said bulls . . . five pounds sterling for and after the rate of the clear and whole yearly value of every hundred pounds sterling . . . of any such archbishopric or bishopric.

IV. And it is also further ordained and enacted by the authority of this present parliament that the King's Highness at any time or times on this side the feast of Easter which shall be in the year of our Lord God 1533, or at any time on this side the beginning of the next parliament, by his letters patent under his great seal . . ., may and shall have full power and liberty to declare . . . whether that the premises or any part, clause or matter thereof shall be observed, obeyed, executed, performed and take place and effect as an act and statute of this present parliament or not. . . .

(2) *The Annates Act of 1534* (25 Henry VIII, c. 20)

[I. Recites 23 Henry VIII, c. 20 and the confirmation of that Act by royal letters patent.]

II. And forasmuch as in the said act it is not plainly and certainly expressed in what manner and fashion archbishops and bishops shall be elected, presented, invested, and consecrated within this realm . . .: be it now therefore enacted by the King our sovereign lord, by the assent of the Lords spiritual and temporal and the Commons in the present parliament assembled, and by authority of the same, that the said act and everything therein contained shall be and stand in strength, virtue and effect: except only that no person nor persons hereafter shall be presented, nominated or commended to the bishop of Rome, otherwise called the Pope, or to the see of Rome, to or for the dignity or office of any archbishop or bishop within this realm . . ., nor shall send nor procure there for any manner of bulls, briefs, palls or other things requisite for an archbishop or bishop, nor shall pay any sums of money for annates, first fruits, or otherwise, for expedition of any such bulls, briefs or palls; but that by the authority of this act such presenting, nominating or commending to the said bishop of Rome or to the see of Rome, and such bulls, briefs, palls, annates, first fruits and every other sums of money heretofore limited, accustomed or used to be paid at the said see of Rome for procuration or expedition of any such bulls, briefs or palls, or other thing concerning the same, shall utterly cease and no longer be used within this realm. . . .

III. And furthermore be it ordained and established by the authority aforesaid that at every avoidance of any archbishopric or bishopric within this realm . . ., the King our sovereign lord, his heirs and successors, may grant unto the prior and convent or the dean and chapter of the cathedral churches or monasteries where the see of such archbishopric or bishopric shall happen to be void, a licence under the great seal . . . to proceed to election of an archbishop or bishop . . ., with a letter missive containing the name of the person which they shall elect and choose; by virtue of which licence the said dean and chapter or prior and convent to whom any such licence and letters missives shall be directed, shall with all speed and celerity in due form elect and choose the said person named in the said letters missives to the dignity and office of the archbishopric or bishopric so being void, and none other. . . .

(3) The Dispensations Act of 1534 (25 Henry VIII, c. 21)

Most humbly beseech your most royal Majesty your obedient and faithful subjects the Commons of this your present parliament assembled . . ., that where your subjects of this your realm . . . by many years past have been and yet be greatly decayed and impoverished by such intolerable exactions of great sums of money as have been claimed and taken and yet continually be claimed to be taken out of this your realm . . . by the bishop of Rome, called the Pope, and the see of Rome . . . [that it be ordained and enacted] by the assent of your Lords spiritual and temporal and the Commons in this your present parliament assembled and by authority of the same, that no person or persons of this your realm . . . shall from henceforth pay any pensions, censes, portions, Peter's pence or any other impositions to the use of the said bishop or of the see of Rome, like as heretofore they have used by the usurpation of the said bishop of Rome and his predecessors and the sufferance of your Highness and your most noble progenitors to do. . . .

[II. Provides that all ecclesiastical faculties and licences hitherto granted by the Pope should be issued by the archbishop of Canterbury.]

(4) The Act of Appeals of 1533 (24 Henry VIII, c. 12)

The preamble has important constitutional implications (see [E.1(1)]). It should be noted that the section of the Act prohibiting appeals to Rome did not specifically forbid such appeals in doctrinal matters.

. . . the King's Highness . . . doth . . . by his royal assent and by the assent of the Lords spiritual and temporal and the Commons in this present parliament assembled, and by authority of the same, enact, establish and ordain that all causes testamentary, causes of matrimony and divorces, rights of tithes, oblations and obventions, (the knowledge whereof by the goodness of princes of this realm and by the laws and customs of the same apperteineth to the spiritual jurisdiction of this realm), already commenced, moved, depending, being, happening, or hereafter coming in contention, debate or question within this realm . . ., whether they concern the King our sovereign lord, his heirs or successors, or any other subjects or resiants within the same of what degree soever they be, shall be from henceforth heard, examined, discussed, clearly finally and definitely adjudged and determined within the King's jurisdiction and authority and not elsewhere, in such courts spiritual and temporal of the same as the natures, conditions and qualities of the causes and matters aforesaid in contention or hereafter happening in contention shall require. . . .

(5) *The Act of Supremacy of 1534* (26 Henry VIII, c. 1)

This Act asserted the King's full power to 'correct' heresy. It therefore rejected any residual papal claims to doctrinal authority which might still have been made after the Act of Appeals. Like that Act, it too had considerable constitutional significance (see [E.1(2)]).

. . . our . . . sovereign lord [the King], his heirs and successors, kings of this realm, shall have full power and authority from time to time to visit, repress, redress, reform, order, correct, restrain and amend all such errors, heresies, abuses, offences, contempts and enormities, whatsoever they be, which by any manner spiritual authority or jurisdiction ought or may lawfully be reformed, repressed, ordered, redressed, corrected, restrained or amended, most to the pleasure of Almighty God, the increase of virtue in Christ's religion, and for the conservation of the peace, unity and tranquillity of this realm. . . .

(6) *The Act against Papal Authority of 1536* (28 Henry VIII, c. 10)

This statute, rejecting papal authority in all its aspects, summed up the revolution of the previous four years.

Forasmuch as notwithstanding the good and wholesome laws, ordinances and statutes heretofore enacted, made and established . . . for the extirpation, abolition and extinguishment out of this realm . . . of the pretended power and usurped authority of the bishop of Rome, by some called the Pope . . ., divers seditious and contentious persons, being imps of the said bishop of Rome and his see, and in heart members of his pretended monarchy, do in corners and elsewhere, as they dare, whisper, inculce, preach and persuade, and from time to time instil into the ears and heads of the poor, simple and unlettered people the advancement and continuance of the said bishop's feigned and pretended authority . . ., be it enacted, ordained and established . . . that if any person or persons dwelling . . . within this realm . . . after the last day of July . . . 1536 shall, by writing, ciphering, printing, preaching or teaching, deed or act, obstinately or maliciously hold or stand with to extol, set forth, maintain or defend the authority, jurisdiction or power of the bishop of Rome or of his see . . . that then every such person or persons . . . shall incur and run into the dangers, penalties, pains and forfeitures ordained and provided by the statute of provision and praemunire made in the sixteenth year of the reign of the noble and valiant prince King Richard II.

(7) The Six Articles Act of 1539 (31 Henry VIII, c. 14)

The Act provided, in sections not quoted here, that those who opposed its first article – which affirmed the doctrine of transubstantiation – were to be burned and that those who opposed the other five were, depending on circumstances, either to forfeit their property and suffer imprisonment at the King's pleasure, or else to be hanged.

> . . . it was and is finally resolved, accorded, and agreed in manner and form following, that is to say: First, that in the most blessed sacrament of the altar, by the strength and efficacy of Christ's mighty word, it being spoken by the priest, is present really, under the form of bread and wine, the natural body and blood of our Saviour Jesus Christ, conceived of the Virgin Mary, and that after the consecration there remaineth no substance of bread or wine, nor any other substance but the substance of Christ, God and man; Secondly, that communion in both kinds is not necessary *ad salutem* by the law of God to all persons, and that it is to be believed and not doubted of but that in the flesh under form of bread is the very blood, and with the blood under form of wine is the very flesh, as well apart as though they were both together; Thirdly, that priests after the order of priesthood received . . . may not marry by the law of God; Fourthly, that vows of chastity or widowhood by man or woman made to God advisedly ought to be observed by the law of God, and that it exempteth them from other liberties of Christian people which without that they might enjoy; Fifthly, that it is meet and necessary that private masses be continued and admitted in this the King's English Church and Congregation as whereby good Christian people ordering themselves accordingly do receive both Godly and goodly consolations and benefits, and it is agreeable also to God's law; Sixthly, that auricular confession is expedient and necessary to be retained and continued, used and frequented, in the Church of God. . . .

G.2: Edward VI

(8) The Act for the Dissolution of the Chantries, 1547 (1 Edward VI, c. 14)

Note the theory of the dissolution: to avoid superstition and improve education and poor relief. In fact, though there was some school funding, most of the money was spent on war.

> The King's most loving subjects the Lords spiritual and temporal and the Commons in this present parliament assembled, considering that a great part of superstition and errors in Christian religion hath been brought into the minds and estimation of men by reason of the ignorance of their very true and perfect salvation through the death of Jesus Christ, and by devising and phantasing vain opinions of purgatory and masses satisfactory to be done for them which be departed, the which doctrine and vain opinion by nothing more is maintained and upholden than by the abuse of . . . chantries and other provisions made for the continuance of the said blindness and ignorance; and further considering and understanding that the alteration, change and amendment of the same, and converting to good and Godly uses, as in erecting of grammar schools to the education of youth in virtue and godliness, the further augmenting of the Universities, and better provision for the poor and needy, cannot in this present parliament be provided and conveniently done, nor cannot nor ought to any other manner person be committed than to the King's Highness, whose Majesty, with and by the advice of his Highness' most prudent Council, can and will

most wisely and beneficially, both for the honour of God and the weal of this his Majesty's realm, order, alter, convert and dispose the same. . . .

[The Act then goes on to convey the chantries to the King.]

(9) The Act allowing priests to marry, 1549 (2 & 3 Edward VI, c. 21)

This statute, which led to the marriage of many priests between 1549 and 1553, was repealed by Mary in the latter year. After Elizabeth's accession clergymen of the Church of England were allowed to marry once again, though the practice was not given renewed parliamentary authority until 1604.

Although it were not only better for the estimation of priests and other ministers in the Church of God to live chaste, sole and separate from the company of women and the bond of marriage . . . and that it were most to be wished that they would willingly and of their selfs endeavour themself to a perpetual chastity and abstinence from the use of women, yet forasmuch as the contrary hath rather been seen . . ., be it therefore enacted . . . that all and every law and laws positive, canons, constitutions and ordinances heretofore made by the authority of man only which doth prohibit or forbid marriage to any ecclesiastical or spiritual person or persons of what estate, condition or degree they be . . . shall be utterly void and of none effect.

(10) The Act of Uniformity of 1549 (2 & 3 Edward VI, c. 1)

The preamble to this Act discusses the making of the 1549 Prayer Book. (For the Act's constitutional significance see [E.2(6)].)

Where of long time there hath been had in this realm of England and Wales divers forms of common prayer commonly called the service of the Church, that is to say, the use of Sarum, of York, of Bangor and of Lincoln; and besides the same, now of late much more divers and sundry forms and fashions have been used in the cathedral and parish churches of England and Wales, as well concerning the matins or morning prayer and the evensong, as also concerning the holy communion commonly called the mass, with divers and sundry rites and ceremonies concerning the same and in the administration of other sacraments of the Church . . .; his Highness . . . to the intent a uniform, quiet and Godly order should be had concerning the premises, hath appointed the archbishop of Canterbury and certain of the most learned and discreet bishops and other learned men of this realm to consider and ponder the premises, and thereupon having as well eye and respect to the most sincere and pure Christian religion taught by the Scripture as to the usages in the primitive Church, should draw and make one convenient and meet order, rite and fashion of common and open prayer and administration of the sacraments, to be had and used in his Majesty's realm in England and in Wales; the which at this time, by the aid of the Holy Ghost, with one uniform agreement is of them concluded, set forth and delivered to his Highness, to his great comfort and quietness of mind, in a book entitled The Book of the Common Prayer and Administration of the Sacraments and other Rites and Ceremonies of the Church after the use of the Church of England.

G.3: Mary

(11) The repeal of the Edwardian religious legislation, 1553 (1 Mary, stat. 2, c. 2)

This Act restored the religious situation to the legal position which had existed at the death of Henry VIII.

Forasmuch as by divers and several acts hereafter mentioned, as well the divine service and good administration of the sacraments as divers other matters of religion which we and our forefathers found in this Church of England to us left by the authority of the Catholic Church, be partly altered and in some part taken from us, and in place thereof new things imagined and set forth by the said acts, such as a few of singularity have of themselves devised, whereof hath ensued amongst us in very short time numbers of divers and strange opinions and diversities of sects, and thereby grown great unquietness and much discord, to the great disturbance of the common wealth of this realm, and in very short time like to grow to extreme peril and utter confusion of the same unless some remedy be in that behalf provided, which thing all true, loving and obedient subjects ought and are bounden to foresee and provide to the uttermost of their power: in consideration whereof be it enacted and established by the Queen's Highness, the Lords spiritual and temporal and the Commons in this present parliament assembled, and by the authority of the same that [all the Edwardian religious acts be repealed].

II. And be it further enacted by the authority aforesaid that all such divine service and administration of sacraments as were most commonly used in the realm of England in the last year of the reign of our late sovereign lord King Henry the Eighth, shall be, from and after the 20th day of December in this present year of our Lord God 1553, used and frequented through the whole realm of England and all other the Queen's Majesty's dominions. . . .

(12) Act restoring papal authority, 1554 (1 & 2 Philip and Mary, c. 8)
This repealed all Henry VIII's anti-papal legislation and restored the Church to the legal position of 1529. After its passage England was once again theoretically a part of Catholic Christendom.

Whereas since the 20th year of King Henry VIII of famous memory, father unto your Majesty our most natural sovereign and gracious lady and queen, much false and erroneous doctrine hath been taught, preached and written partly by divers the natural-born subjects of this realm, and partly being brought in hither from sundry other foreign countries hath been sown and spread abroad within the same; by reason whereof as well the spiritualty as the temporalty of your Highness' realms and dominions have swerved from the obedience of the See Apostolic and declined from the unity of Christ's Church, and so have continued, until such time as your Majesty being first raised up by God and set in the seat royal over us, and then by his divine and gracious providence knit in marriage with the most noble and virtuous prince, the King our sovereign lord your husband, the Pope's holiness and the See Apostolic sent hither unto your Majesties (as unto persons undefiled and by God's goodness preserved from the common infection aforesaid) and to the whole realm, the most reverend father in God the Lord Cardinal Pole, legate *de latere*, to call us home again into the right way from whence we have all this long while wandered and strayed abroad. And we after sundry long and grievous plagues and calamities, seeing by the goodness of God our own errors, have acknowledged the same unto the said most reverend father and by him have been and are, the rather at other contemplation of your Majesties, received and embraced into the unity and bosom of Christ's Church; and upon our humble submission and promise made, for a declaration of our repentance, to repeal and abrogate such acts and statutes as had been made in parliament since the said 20th year of the said King Henry the Eighth against the Supremacy of the See Apostolic, as in our submission exhibited to the said most reverend father in God by your Majesties appeareth. . . .

[II–VIII repeal all statutes, and clauses in statutes, against the Papacy since 1529.]

[XIII–XXVI are chiefly concerned with securing the rights of the holders of the monastic lands.]

(13) The Act renewing the heresy laws, 1554 (1 & 2 Philip and Mary, c. 6)

This Act, which revived the medieval heresy laws which had been repealed in the reigns of Henry VIII and Edward VI, made possible the Marian burnings of 1555–58.

> For the eschewing and avoiding of errors and heresies which of late have risen, grown and much increased within this realm, for that the ordinaries have wanted authority to proceed against those that were infected therewith: be it therefore ordained and enacted by the authority of this present parliament that the statute made in the fifth year of the reign of King Richard the Second concerning the arresting and apprehension of erroneous and heretical preachers, and one other statute made in the second year of the reign of King Henry the Fourth concerning the repressing of heresies and punishment of heretics, and also one other statute made in the second year of the reign of King Henry the Fifth concerning the suppression of heresy and Lollardy, and every article, branch and sentence contained in the same three several acts and every of them, shall from the 20th day of January next coming be revived and be in full force, strength and effect, to all intents, constructions and purposes for ever.

G.4: Elizabeth

(14) The Act of Supremacy, 1559 (1 Eliz., c. 1)

This Act, *inter alia*, authorized the appointment of commissioners to exercise the royal authority over the Church. It was this clause which led to the establishment during the 1560s of the court of High Commission. (For the Act's constitutional significance see [E.3(7)].)

> VIII . . . Such jurisdictions, privileges, superiorities and preeminences spiritual and ecclesiastical, as by any spiritual or ecclesiastical power or authority hath heretofore been or may lawfully be exercised or used for the visitation of the ecclesiastical state and persons, and for reformation, order and correction of the same and of all manner of errors, heresies, schisms, abuses, offences, contempts and enormities, shall for ever by authority of this present parliament be united and annexed to the imperial crown of this realm. And that your Highness, your heirs and successors, kings or queens of this realm, shall have full power and authority, by virtue of this act, by letters patents under the great seal of England to assign, name and authorise, when and as often as your Highness, your heirs or successors, shall think meet and convenient . . . such person or persons, being natural born subjects to your Highness, your heirs or successors, as your Majesty, your heirs or successors, shall think meet, to exercise, use, occupy and execute under your Highness, your heirs and successors, all manner of jurisdictions, privileges and preeminences in any wise touching or concerning any spiritual or ecclesiastical jurisdiction within these your realms . . . and to visit, reform, redress, order, correct and amend all such errors, heresies, schisms, abuses, offences, contempts and enormities whatsoever which by any manner spiritual or ecclesiastical power, authority or jurisdiction can or may lawfully be reformed, ordered, redressed, corrected, restrained, or amended, to the pleasure of Almighty God, the increase of virtue, and the conservation of the peace and unity of this realm. . . .

(15) The Act of Uniformity, 1559 (1 Eliz. c. 2)
This imposed the 1559 Prayer Book on the Church and provided penalties for those
ministers who refused to use it and for those laymen who spoke against it or failed to attend
the services in their parish churches. The provisions against non-attendance stated that

> III. . . . all and every person and persons inhabiting within this realm or any other
> the Queen's Majesty's dominions, shall diligently and faithfully, having no lawful or
> reasonable excuse to be absent, endeavour themselves to resort to their parish
> church or chapel accustomed, or upon reasonable let thereof, to some usual place
> where common prayer and such service of God shall be used in such times of let,
> upon every Sunday and other days ordained and used to be kept as holy days, and
> then and there to abide orderly and soberly during the time of the common prayer,
> preachings or other service of God there to be used and ministered; upon pain of
> punishment by the censures of the Church, and also upon pain that every person so
> offending shall forfeit for every such offence twelve pence, to be levied by the
> churchwardens of the parish where such offence shall be done, to the use of the poor
> of the same parish, of the goods, lands and tenements of such offender by way of
> distress.

(16) The 39 Articles of 1563
(E. Cardwell, *Synodalia*, I (Oxford, 1842), pp. 34 ff)
The thirty-nine Articles of 1563, founded upon the forty-two Edwardian Articles of 1553,
formed a decisively Protestant interpretation of the faith, strongly influenced by Calvinism.
Four of the most significant of the articles are reproduced here.

[No. 10] Of free will,
The condition of man after the fall of Adam is such that he cannot turn and
prepare himself by his own natural strength and good works to faith and calling upon
God. Wherefore, we have no power to do good works, pleasant and acceptable to
God, without the grace of God by Christ preventing us, that we may have a good
will and working in us, when we have that good will.

[No. 11] Of the justification of man.
We are accounted righteous before God only for the merit of our Lord and
Saviour Jesus Christ by faith and not for our own works or deservings. Wherefore,
that we are justified by faith only, it is a most wholesome doctrine, and full of
comfort, as more largely is expressed in the homily of justification.

[No. 12] Of good works.
Albeit that good works, which are the fruits of faith, and follow after justification,
cannot put away our sins, and endure the severity of God's judgment: yet are they
pleasing and acceptable to God in Christ, and do spring out necessarily of a true and
lively faith, insomuch that by them a lively faith may be as evidently known as a tree
discerned by the fruit.

[No. 17] Of predestination and election.
Predestination to life is the everlasting purpose of God whereby (before the foundations of the world were laid) he hath constantly decreed to deliver from the curse
and damnation those whom he hath chosen in Christ out of mankind and to bring
them by Christ to everlasting salvation, as vessels made to honour. Whereupon, such
as have so excellent a benefit of God given unto them be called according to God's
purpose by his spirit working in due season. They through grace obey the calling,

they be justified freely, they be made sons of God by adoption, they be made like the image of his only begotten son Jesus Christ, they walk religiously in good works, and at length, by God's mercy, they attain to everlasting felicity.

As the godly consideration of predestination and our election in Christ is full of sweet, pleasant and unspeakable comfort to godly persons and such as feel in themselves the working of the spirit of Christ, mortifying the works of the flesh and their earthly members and drawing up their mind to high and heavenly things, as well because it doth greatly establish and confirm their faith of eternal salvation, to be enjoyed through Christ, as because it doth fervently kindle their love towards God; so, for curious and carnal persons, lacking the spirit of Christ, to have continually before their eyes the sentence of God's predestination is a most dangerous downfall, whereby the devil doth thrust them either into desperation or into recklessness of most unclean living, no less perilous than desperation.

Furthermore, we must receive God's promises in such wise as they be generally set forth to us in holy scripture, and in our doings that will of God is to be followed which we have expressly declared unto us in the word of God.

(17) The papal bull, Regnans in Excelsis, 1570
(W. Camden, *Elizabeth* (1688 edn), p. 146)

In this bull Pius V excommunicated and deposed Queen Elizabeth. The passages quoted are an interesting reflection both of the powers which the Pope claimed and also of his ignorance of some aspects of the royal claims; note his reference to the Queen as 'Supreme Head' rather than as 'Supreme Governor' of the Church.

He that reigneth on high, to whom is given all power in heaven and in earth, hath committed his One, Holy, Catholic and Apostolic Church, out of which there is no salvation, to one alone upon earth, namely to Peter the chief of the Apostles, and to Peter's successor the Bishop of Rome, to be by him governed with plenary authority. Him alone hath he made prince over all people and all kingdoms, to pluck up, destroy, scatter, consume, plant, and build; that he may preserve his faithful people (knit together with the band of charity) in the unity of the Spirit, and present them spotless and unblameable to their Saviour. . . . But the number of the ungodly hath gotten such power that there is now no place in the whole world left which they have not essayed to corrupt with their most wicked doctrines; and amongst others, Elizabeth, the pretended Queen of England, the servant of wickedness, lendeth thereunto her helping hand, with whom, as in a sanctuary, the most pernicious persons have found a refuge. This very woman, having seized on the kingdom and monstrously usurped the place of Supreme Head of the Church in all England and the chief authority and jurisdiction thereof, hath again reduced the said kingdom into a miserable and ruinous condition. . . . Being therefore supported with his authority whose pleasure it was to place us (though unable for so great a burden) in this supreme throne of justice, we do, out of the fullness of our Apostolic power, declare the aforesaid Elizabeth as being an heretic and a favourer of heretics . . . to have incurred the sentence of excommunication, and to be cut off from the unity of the Body of Christ. And moreover we do declare her to be deprived of her pretended title to the kingdom aforesaid, and of all dominion, dignity, and privilege whatsoever; and also the nobility, subjects, and people of the said kingdom, and all others who have in any sort sworn unto her, to be for ever absolved from any such oath. . . .

(18) Whitgift's articles, 1583
(J. Strype, *The Life and Acts of John Whitgift* (Oxford, 1922), pp. 229–30)
These were the articles with which Whitgift launched his attack on Puritanism at the beginning of his archiepiscopate.

. . . that none be permitted to preach, read, catechize, minister the sacraments, or to execute any other ecclesiastical function, by what authority so ever he be admitted thereunto, unless he first consent and subscribe to these articles following . . .

I. That her Majesty, under God, hath and ought to have the sovereignty and rule over all manner of persons born within her realms and dominions and countries, of what estate ecclesiastical or temporal so ever they be. And that none other foreign power, prelate, state or potentate hath or ought to have any jurisdiction, power, superiority, pre-eminence or authority ecclesiastical or temporal within her Majesty's said realms, dominions and countries.

II. That the Book of Common Prayer, and of ordering bishops, priests and deacons, containeth nothing in it contrary to the Word of God. And that the same may be lawfully used; and that he himself will use the form of the said book prescribed, in public prayer and administration of the sacraments, and none other.

III. That he alloweth the book of Articles of Religion, agreed upon by the archbishops and bishops in both provinces, and the whole clergy in the Convocation holden at London in the year of our Lord 1562, and set forth by her Majesty's authority. And that he believeth all the articles therein contained to be agreeable to the word of God.

(19) Richard Hooker's view of the royal supremacy
(R. Hooker *Of the Laws of Ecclesiastical Polity* (1676 edn), pp. 458–9, 468)
Although Elizabeth accepted that her rule over the Church was founded on the Act of Supremacy, she believed that that Act gave her the right to rule the Church through Convocation and the bishops, free from parliamentary interference. Hooker, the greatest contemporary thinker and writer on the Church, had a very different view; he firmly asserted the right of Parliament to legislate for the Church. He expressed his views in book eight of his *Laws of Ecclesiastical Polity*, completed, in its present form, during 1593. It was the difference between the Queen's ideas and those enshrined in Hooker's work – Elizabeth's parliamentary critics, of course, agreed with Hooker – that led to many of the conflicts between the Queen and members of the House of Commons during her reign.

The parliament is a court not . . . merely temporal. . . . The most natural and religious course in making laws is, that the matter of them be taken from the judgment of the wisest in those things which they are to concern. In matters of God, to set down a form of prayer, a solemn confession of the articles of the Christian faith, and ceremonies meet for the exercise of religion, it were unnatural not to think the pastors and bishops of our souls a great deal more fit than men of secular trades and callings. Howbeit, when all, which the wisdom of all sorts can do, is done for the devising of laws in the church, it is the general consent of all that giveth them the form and vigour of laws, without which they could be no more unto us than the counsel of physicians to the sick. . . . Wherefore, to define and determine even of the church's affairs by way of assent and approbation, as laws are defined in that right of power, which doth give them the force of laws; thus to define of our own church's regiment the parliament of England hath competent authority. . . .

Till it be proved that some special law of Christ hath for ever annexed unto the clergy alone the power to make ecclesiastical laws, we are to hold it a thing most consonant with equity and reason that no ecclesiastical laws be made in a Christian commonwealth without consent as well of the laity as of the clergy, but least of all without consent of the highest power.

G.5: James I

(20) The Millenary Petition, 1603
(T. Fuller, *The Church History of Britain*, iii (3rd edn, 1842), pp. 193–4)
The opening words of the Millenary Petition, so called because it is said to have been approved by over 1,000 ministers, indicate that it represented the views of moderate Puritans rather than Presbyterians or sectaries. Presented to the King on his journey south from Scotland to London in 1603, it led to the summoning of the Hampton Court Conference in the following year.

> . . . Most gracious and dread sovereign, seeing it hath pleased the divine majesty, to the great comfort of all good Christians, to advance your Highness, according to your just title, to the peaceable government of this Church and commonwealth of England; we, the ministers of the Gospel in this land, neither as factious men affecting a popular parity in the Church, nor as schismatics aiming at the dissolution of the state ecclesiastical, but as the faithful servants of Christ and loyal subjects to your Majesty, desiring and longing for the redress of divers abuses of the Church, could do no less, in our obedience to God, service to your Majesty, love to his Church, than acquaint your princely Majesty with our particular griefs. . . . And although divers of us that sue for reformation have formerly, in respect of the times, subscribed to the [Prayer] Book, some upon protestation, some upon exposition given them, some with condition, rather than the Church should have been deprived of their labour and ministry; yet now we, to the number of more than a thousand, of your Majesty's subjects and ministers, all groaning as under a common burden of human rites and ceremonies, do with one joint consent humble ourselves at your Majesty's feet to be eased and relieved in this behalf. . . .

G.6: Charles I

(21) Laud's sermon on the opening of Parliament, 6 February 1626
(W. Laud, *Works*, i (Oxford, 1847), pp. 82–3)
In this sermon Laud asserted one of his most firmly held ideas, that those who wanted to overthrow bishops also planned an attack on the monarchy; they were political as well as religious revolutionaries. He was certainly wrong in 1626, but by the later 1640s there was some truth in the idea.

> I know there are some that think the Church is not yet far enough beside the cushion, that their seats are too easy yet, and too high too. A parity they would have, no bishop, no governor, but a parochial consistory, and that should be lay enough too. Well, first, this parity was never left to the Church by Christ; he left Apostles, and Disciples under them. . . . It was never in use with the Church since Christ; no church ever, anywhere (till this last age) without a bishop. . . .

And one thing more I will be bold to speak, out of a like duty to the Church of England and the House of David. They, whoever they be, that would overthrow *sedes ecclesiae*, the seats of ecclesiastical government, will not spare (if ever they get power) to have a pluck at the Throne of David. And there is not a man that is for parity, all fellows in the Church, but he is not for monarchy in the state. . . .

(22) *Laud's Apologia, 1637*
(W. Laud, *Works*, vi (Oxford, 1857), pp. 42–3)
In this speech in Star Chamber Laud asserted his opinion that bishops held their office by divine right; a true Church was impossible without them. This idea can be contrasted with the views of the great majority of Elizabethan and Jacobean bishops – men like Archbishops Whitgift and Abbot – who held that bishops were the *best* but not the only legitimate form of church government.

Our main crime is . . . [so the critics of the hierarchy say] that we are bishops; were we not so, some of us might be as passable as other men. And a great trouble 'tis to them that we maintain that our calling of bishops is *jure divino*, by divine right: of this I have said enough . . . nor will I repeat [it]. Only this I will say, and abide by it, that the calling of bishops is *jure divino*, by divine right, though not all adjuncts to their calling. . . . And I say further that from the Apostles' times, in all ages, in all places, the Church of Christ was governed by bishops, and lay elders never heard of till Calvin's newfangled device at Geneva.

Now this is made by these men as if it were *contra regem*, against the king, in right or in power. But that's a mere ignorant shift, for our being bishops *jure divino*, by divine right, takes nothing from the king's right or power over us. For though our office be from God and Christ immediately, yet may we not exercise that power, either of order or jurisdiction, but as God hath appointed us, that is, not in his Majesty's or any Christian king's kingdoms, but by and under the power of the king given us so to do. . . .

(23) *The 'Root and Branch' Petition, December 1640*
(J. Rushworth, *Historical Collections*, III, i (1692), p. 93)
This petition sought to sweep away not merely Laudian interpretations of episcopacy but the whole order of bishops. As such it went much too far for moderate members of the House of Commons, witness the deep divisions in the Lower House over this issue during 1641.

To the Right Honourable the Commons House of Parliament.

The humble petition of many of his Majesty's subjects in and about the City of London, and several counties of the kingdom, showeth,

That whereas the government of archbishops and lord bishops . . . have proved prejudicial and very dangerous both to the Church and Commonwealth, they themselves having formerly held that they have their jurisdiction or authority of human authority, till of these later times . . . they have claimed their calling immediately from the Lord Jesus Christ, which is against the laws of this kingdom and derogatory to his Majesty and his state royal. And whereas the said government is found by woeful experience to be a main cause and occasion of many foul evils, pressures and grievances of a very high nature unto his Majesty's subjects in their own consciences, liberties and estates. . . .

We therefore most humbly pray and beseech this honourable assembly, the premises considered, that the said government, with all its dependencies, roots and branches, may be abolished. . . .

(24) The Act abolishing the High Commission, 1641 (16 Charles I, c. 11)
One of the major aims of the Long Parliament was to dismantle the apparatus of prerogative rule and in 1641 it disposed of the court of High Commission, which exercised the
Crown's delegated ecclesiastical authority (see (14) above), on the grounds that it had
oppressed the subject.

> [The preamble recites clause VIII of the Act of Supremacy of 1559 and then
> continues]
> . . . And whereas by colour of some words in the foresaid branch of the said Act
> whereby commissioners are authorised to execute their commission according to the
> tenor and effect of the king's Letters Patent . . ., the said commissioners have to the
> great and insufferable wrong and oppression of the king's subjects used to fine and
> imprison them, and exercise another authority not belonging to [the] ecclesiastical
> jurisdiction restored by that Act, and divers other great mischiefs and inconveniences
> have also ensued to the king's subjects by occasion of the said branch and commissions
> issued thereupon, and the executions thereof; therefore, for the repressing and
> preventing of the foresaid abuses, mischiefs and inconveniences in time to come, be
> it enacted by the king's most excellent Majesty and the Lords and Commons in this
> present parliament assembled . . . that the foresaid branch . . . contained in the said
> Act . . . shall from henceforth be repealed. . . .
> IV. And be it further enacted that from and after the . . . first day of August no
> new court shall be erected, ordained or appointed within this realm of England or
> dominion of Wales which shall or may have the like power, jurisdiction or authority
> as the said High Commission court now hath or pretendeth to have. . . .

(25) The Bishops' Exclusion Act, 1642 (17 Charles I, c. 27)
This misleadingly named Act, which prohibited *all* clergymen from holding secular office,
reflected the dislike of the laity during the 1630s of the growing influence of the clergy in
temporal affairs.

> Whereas bishops and other persons in holy orders ought not to be entangled with
> secular jurisdiction, the office of the ministry being of such great importance that it
> will take up the whole man, and for that it is found by long experience that their
> intermeddling with secular jurisdictions hath occasioned great mischiefs and scandal
> both to Church and state, his Majesty, out of his religious care of the Church, and
> [the] souls of his people, is graciously pleased that it be enacted, and by authority of
> this present parliament be it enacted, that no archbishop or bishop or other person
> that now is or hereafter shall be in holy orders shall at any time after the 15th day of
> February in the year of Our Lord one thousand six hundred and forty-one [i.e. 1642]
> have any seat or place, suffrage or voice, to use or execute any power or authority in
> the parliaments of this realm, nor shall be of the Privy Council of his Majesty, his
> heirs or successors, or justice of the peace . . ., or execute any temporal authority by
> virtue of any commission, but shall be wholly disabled and be incapable to have,
> receive, use or execute any of the said offices, places, powers, authorities and things
> aforesaid.

(26) The Solemn League and Covenant, 1643
(J. Rushworth, *Historical Collections*, III, ii (1692), pp. 478–9)
This reflected both the passionate desire of the Scots to secure a Presbyterian Church
settlement in England and Ireland and the need of the English parliamentarians for Scottish
military support against the King in the Civil War.

We noblemen, barons, knights, gentlemen, citizens, burgesses, ministers of the Gospel, and commons of all sorts in the kingdoms of England, Scotland and Ireland, by the providence of God living under one king, and being of one reformed religion . . . have now at last . . . after mature deliberation, resolved and determined to enter into a mutual and solemn league and covenant. . . .

I. That we shall sincerely, really and constantly, through the grace of God, endeavour in our several places and callings, the preservation of the reformed religion in the Church of Scotland, in doctrine, worship, discipline and government, against our common enemies; the reformation of religion in the kingdoms of England and Ireland in doctrine, worship, discipline and government, according to the Word of God and the example of the best reformed churches; and we shall endeavour to bring the churches of God in the three kingdoms to the nearest conjunction and uniformity in religion, confessing of faith, form of church government, directory for worship, and catechising, that we and our posterity after us may, as brethren, live in faith and love, and the Lord may delight to dwell in the midst of us. . . .

III. We shall with the same sincerity, reality and constancy in our several vocations endeavour with our estates and lives mutually to preserve the rights and privileges of the parliaments, and the liberties of the kingdoms, and to preserve and defend the king's majesty's person and authority, in the preservation and defence of the true religion and liberties of the kingdoms, that the world may bear witness with our consciences of our loyalty, and that we have no thoughts or intentions to diminish his majesty's just power and greatness.

IV. We shall also, with all faithfulness, endeavour the discovery of all such as have been or shall be incendiaries, malignants, or evil instruments, by hindering the reformation of religion, dividing the king from his people, or one of the kingdoms from another, or making any faction or parties amongst the people, contrary to the league and covenant, that they may be brought to public trial and receive condign punishment, as the degree of their offences shall require or deserve, or the supreme judicatories of both kingdoms respectively, or others having power from them for that effect, shall judge convenient. . . .

(27) The erection of a Presbyterian Church in England, 1645–46
In August 1645, in its ordinance 'regulating the election of elders', Parliament set out the form which Presbyterian Church government was to take in England, although it did nothing at that time to put the ordinance into effect. Note how the situation was a fully Erastian one: Parliament had final control of the national assembly and therefore of the Church as a whole. In March 1646, in another ordinance, Parliament ordered that the structure described in August 1645 should be set up, but this was never fully accomplished throughout the country.

(a) An ordinance regulating the election of elders, August 1645
(Firth and Rait, *Acts and Ordinances*, i, pp. 749 ff)
1. That the ruling elders of a parochial and congregational eldership shall be chosen by the several ministers and members of their congregation respectively, being of such as have taken the National Covenant, and are not persons under age, nor servants that have no families. . . .

5. That such shall be chosen for ruling elders as are men of good understanding in matters of religion, sound in faith, prudent, discreet, grave and of unblameable conversation, and willing to undergo the said office.

6. That all parishes and places whatsoever . . . be brought under the government of congregational, classical, provincial and national assemblies; provided that the chapels or places in the houses of the peers of this realm shall continue free for the exercise of divine duties, to be performed according to the Directory. . . .

Concerning the members of the classical and congregational assemblies in the several counties   That in the several counties certain persons, ministers and others, shall be appointed by authority of parliament, who shall consider how their several counties respectively may be most conveniently divided into distinct classical presbyteries, and what ministers and others are fit to be of each classis; and they shall accordingly make such division and nomination of persons for each classical presbytery, which divisions, and persons so named for every division, shall be certified up to the parliament. . . .

And the said several classes respectively, being approved by parliament within their several precincts, shall have power to constitute congregational elderships, where a competent number of persons so qualified for elders as aforesaid, shall be found; and where no persons shall be found fit to be elders as aforesaid, then that congregation shall be immediately under the classical presbytery until that congregation shall be enabled with members fit to be elders as aforesaid.

The congregational assembly shall meet once very week, and oftener if occasions shall serve.

The classical assembly shall meet once every month.

Concerning members of the provincial assembly   The provincial assembly shall be constituted of members sent from every classis within the province. The number of the members sent from each classis shall be so proportioned as that the provincial assembly may be more in number than any classical presbytery within that province, and to that end there shall be at least two ministers and four ruling elders out of every classis. . . .

That the provincial assembly . . . shall meet twice every year. . . .

Concerning the national assembly   That the national assembly shall be constituted of members sent from the several provinces aforesaid. The number of the members from each province to the national assembly shall be two ministers and four ruling elders.

The national assembly is to meet when they shall be summoned by parliament, and to sit and continue as the parliament shall order, and not otherwise.

(b) An ordinance for . . . supplying of defects in former ordinances and directions of Parliament concerning church government, March 1646
(Firth and Rait, *Acts and Ordinances*, i, pp. 833 ff)

That the Lords and Commons assembled in parliament . . . having . . . laid the foundation of a presbyterial government in every congregation with subordination to classical, provincial and national assemblies and of them all to the parliament. . . .

I. Be it ordained that there be forthwith a choice made of elders throughout the kingdom of England and dominion of Wales in the respective parish churches and chapels according to such directions as have already passed both Houses hearing date August . . . one thousand six hundred forty and five . . . and all classes and parochial congregations are respectively hereby authorised and required forthwith effectually to proceed therein accordingly.

(28) An ordinance abolishing archbishops and bishops, 1646
(Firth and Rait, *Acts and Ordinances*, i, pp. 879 ff)

Although effective episcopal jurisdiction in England and Wales ended with the outbreak of civil war the offices of bishop and archbishop were not formally abolished until 1646.

> . . . Be it ordained . . . by the Lords and Commons in parliament assembled and by the authority of the same that the name, title, style and dignity of archbishop of Canterbury, archbishop of York, bishop of Winchester, bishop of Durham and of all other bishops of any bishoprics within the kingdom of England and dominion of Wales be from and after the fifth day of September . . . 1646 wholly abolished and taken away. . . .

G.7: Interregnum

(29) 'Act' repealing the obligation to attend parish churches on Sundays, 1650
(Firth and Rait, *Acts and Ordinances*, ii, pp. 423 ff)
The compulsory attendance at parish churches on Sundays and holy days enjoined by the Elizabethan Act of Uniformity and subsequent statutes of the Queen's reign was seldom rigorously enforced. During the 1640s, however, enforcement of the statutes broke down almost completely. The Rump's Act of September 1650 recognized that *fait accompli*. Its insistence that, after the repeal of the statutes, everyone should take part in *some form* of public or private worship every Sunday was, of course, a pious hope.

> [Repeals all penalties imposed in previous acts of parliament on citizens] for not repairing to their respective parish churches [on Sundays], or for not keeping of holy days or for not hearing common prayer, or for speaking or inveighing against the Book of Common Prayer. . . .
>
> And to the end that no profane or licentious persons may take occasion by the repealing of the said laws (intended only for relief of pious and peaceably-minded people from the rigour of them) to neglect the performance of religious duties, be it further enacted . . . that all and every person and persons within this common-wealth and the territories thereof shall (having no reasonable excuse for their absence) upon every Lord's day, days of public thanksgiving and humiliation, diligently resort to some public place where the service and worship of God is exercised, or shall be present at some other place in the practice of some religious duty, either of prayer, preaching, reading or expounding the Scriptures, or conferring upon the same. . . .

(30) The Instrument of Government, December 1653 – religious clauses
(Firth and Rait, *Acts and Ordinances*, ii, pp. 813 ff)
The religious clauses of the Instrument of Government reflected Cromwell's desire for a broadly based State Church, his determination to secure toleration for Protestant dissenters outside it and his hope that tithes could be replaced by some other form of remuneration for the clergy of the State Church. (For the constitutional clauses of the Instrument, see [E.6(37)].)

> . . . XXXV That the Christian religion, as contained in the Scriptures, be held forth and recommended as the public profession of these nations; and that as soon as may be a provision, less subject to scruple and contention, and more certain than the present, be made for the encouragement and maintenance of able and painful teachers, for instructing the people, and for discovery and confutation of error, heresy and whatever is contrary to sound doctrine. And that until such provision be made the present maintenance shall not be taken away nor impeached.

XXXVI That to the public profession held forth none shall be compelled by penalties or otherwise; but that endeavours be used to win them by sound doctrine and the example of a good conversation.

XXXVII That such as profess faith in God by Jesus Christ (though differing in judgment from the doctrine, worship or discipline publicly held forth) shall not be restrained from, but shall be protected in, the profession of the faith, and exercise of their religion; so as they abuse not this liberty to the civil injury of others, and to the actual disturbance of the public peace on their parts. Provided this liberty be not extended to Popery nor Prelacy, nor to such as, under the profession of Christ, hold forth and practise licentiousness.

XXXVIII That all laws, statutes and ordinances, and clauses in any law, statute or ordinance to the contrary of the aforesaid liberty, shall be esteemed as null and void. . . .

(31) The Declaration of Breda, 4 April 1660
(Journals of the House of Lords, xi, pp. 7–8)*

In the religious clause of the Declaration of Breda Charles II showed his awareness of the diversity of religious opinion in England by that time by his promise of a temporary toleration and by holding out hopes of a permanent provision for religious diversity enshrined in an Act of Parliament. It was a hope which was rapidly dashed by the Anglican zeal of the Cavalier Parliament of 1661–79. (For other clauses of the Declaration see [E.6(40)].)

. . . And because the passion and uncharitableness of the times have produced several opinions in religion, by which men are engaged in parties and animosities against each other, which, when they shall hereafter unite in a freedom of conversation, will be composed and better understood, we do declare a liberty to tender consciences, and that no man shall be disquieted or called in question for differences of opinion in matter of religion which do not disturb the peace of the kingdom; and that we shall be ready to consent to such an act of parliament as, upon mature deliberation, shall be offered to us, for the full granting that indulgence. . . .

H. TUDOR TREASON LEGISLATION

The law of treason was the ultimate legal defence of the Crown and the established order in Tudor and Stuart England. At the beginning of Henry VIII's reign it was founded upon a statute of 1352 which has remained the basis of the treason law until our own day. During the sixteenth century, however, religious and political developments – principally events associated with the Reformation – led to important modifications of the law of treason as it stood at the end of the Middle Ages.[1]

The 1352 Act[2] enunciated three main treasons: imagining the King's death (i.e. planning to kill the King and demonstrating that intention by some overt act); levying war against the king; and adhering to the King's enemies. New statutory treasons were created during the later Middle Ages at times of political upheaval but these were all repealed after the specific dangers which had inspired them had vanished or diminised.

The situation created by the Reformation led to a spate of new statutory treasons – twelve Acts of Henry VIII's reign alone dealt with treason and there were another seventeen under Edward VI, Mary and Elizabeth. The most important Henrician Act, that of 1534[3], provided that those who acted, wrote or spoke against the newly established royal supremacy in the Church were guilty of high treason. The statute did not create the offence of treason by words – judges had construed words as treason in the fifteenth century – but it did give it statutory authority and put a powerful weapon in the hands of Henry VIII and Cromwell in their enforcement of the Reformation during the 1530s. Other Acts of Henry's reign made it treason to attack the royal succession as it stood in the wake of the King's various marriages.[4]

In 1547 Somerset repealed the Henrician treason Acts, but at once reintroduced the offence of high treason for those who acted or wrote against the royal supremacy. Those who spoke against it were to suffer imprisonment at the King's pleasure for the first offence, imprisonment for life for the second, and the penalties of treason for the third.[5] The Act also demanded the testimony of two witnesses in order to secure a conviction for treason, a provision which was repeated in another Edwardian Act, in 1552.[6] There is some doubt about whether this 'two witnesses' clause survived the repeal of the Edwardian treason legislation at the beginning of Mary's reign,[7] but in practice the Crown had rarely relied on a single witness in treason trials, though there had been a notable exception in the case of Thomas More.

Mary's repeal of the Edwardian treason laws in 1553 meant a return to the position of 1352, but the Queen soon found it necessary to extend the protection of treason legislation to her consort, King Philip.[8] In Elizabeth's reign, when nine Acts of Parliament dealt with treason, the main thrust of the legislation was the defence of the Queen and the realm against the gathering forces of the Counter-Reformation. In 1571 a statute[9] repeated the provisions of the 1534 Act, making it a treasonable offence to act, write or speak against the royal supremacy, and another Act of the same Parliament[10] made it high treason to obtain bulls from Rome. In 1581 a statute[11] directed against the Jesuits and seminary priests from abroad who were then entering the country made it treason to attempt to withdraw subjects from their obedience to the Queen in order to persuade them to join the Catholic Church. The continuing success of the work of these priests in the early 1580s inspired a still more drastic Act in 1585[12] which made it treason for all priests ordained either inside or outside the Queen's realms after June 1559 to remain within her dominions for more than forty days after the end of the 1585 parliamentary session. By the end of Elizabeth's reign, therefore, it could be high treason for a man within the Queen's jurisdiction merely to *be* a priest. It was a climax in the clash between the fundamentally different ideologies of the emerging English nation state and the international Catholic Church, a conflict which had been evident since the 1530s.

1. The standard work is J. Bellamy, *The Tudor Law of Treason* (1979).
2. 25 Edward III, stat. 5, c. 3.
3. 26 Henry VIII, c. 13. See G. R. Elton, *Policy and Police*, Ch. 6.
4. 25 Henry VIII, c. 22 (First Succession Act, 1534); 28 Henry VIII, c. 7 (Second Succession Act, 1536); 3 Henry VIII, c. 25 (Act declaring the Cleves marriage void, 1540); 35 Henry VIII, c. 1 (Third Succession Act, 1544).
5. 1 Edward VI, c. 12 (1547).
6. 5 & 6 Edward VI, c. 12 (1552).
7. 1 Mary, stat. 1, c. 1 (1553).
8. 1 & 2 Philip and Mary, c. 10 (1555).
9. 13 Eliz., c. 1 (1571).
10. 13 Eliz., c. 2 (1571).
11. 23 Eliz., c. 1 (1581).
12. 27 Eliz., c. 2 (1585).

I. GOOD AND BAD HARVESTS, 1529–1660

In his important articles[1] on English harvests from the fifteenth to the eighteenth centuries Professor Hoskins classified them under six categories: abundant (when average wheat prices for the harvest year[2] were at least 30 per cent below the norm[3] for that year; good (10–30 per cent below the norm); average (plus or minus 10 per cent of the norm); deficient (10–25 per cent above the norm); bad (25–50 per cent above the norm); dearth (over 50 per cent above the norm).

Good and bad harvests tended to bunch together, with important social and economic implications and potential political consequences. Listed below are all runs of at least three successive harvests between 1527 and 1661 which were (1) deficient or worse, and (2) good or better according to Professor Hoskins's calculations. Dearths are marked * and the percentage price rises above the norm in dearth years are given. It should be noted that only five dearths occurred during the entire period. Four of these came in groups of two: in 1555* (50.3 per cent above the norm) and 1556* (104.5 per cent above the norm); and in 1596* (82.9 per cent above the norm) and 1597* (64 per cent above the norm).

(1) Runs of at least three harvests in a row which were deficient or worse
      1527, 1528, 1529
      1549, 1550, 1551
      1594, 1595, 1596* (82.9%), 1597* (64%)
      1646, 1647, 1648, 1649, 1650
      1657, 1658, 1659, 1660, 1661* (59.1%)

(2) Runs of at least three harvests in a row which were good or better
      1537, 1538, 1539, 1540, 1541, 1542
      1546, 1547, 1548
      1566, 1567, 1568, 1569, 1570, 1571
      1582, 1583, 1584
      1591, 1592, 1593
      1601, 1602, 1603, 1604, 1605, 1606
      1618, 1619, 1620
      1626, 1627, 1628
      1643, 1644, 1645
      1652, 1653, 1654, 1655

The picture presented by Dr Harrison[4], who uses a price based on an average of *three* grain prices – wheat, barley and oats – for each harvest year, is not radically different from that of Hoskins as far as runs of good and bad harvests are concerned.[5]

Harrison's results are as follows.[6]

(1) Runs of at least three harvests in a row which were deficient or worse
      1527, 1528, 1529
      1549, 1550, 1551
      1554, 1555*, 1556*
      1594, 1595, 1596*, 1597 (according to Harrison the 1597 harvest was not
                     a dearth as the average price of the three grains
                     was only 36% above the norm)

(2) Runs of at least three harvests in a row which were good or better

    1536, 1537, 1538, 1539, 1540, 1541, 1542, 1543, 1544
    1546, 1547, 1548
    1569, 1570, 1571
    1591, 1592, 1593
    1602, 1603, 1604, 1605, 1606, 1607
    1618, 1619, 1620

Hoskins' and Harrison's analyses draw attention:

(1) To the generally good harvests of Henry VIII's later years.
(2) To the fact that three of the six harvests of Edward VI's reign were deficient or worse.
(3) To the two dearths (out of a total of only four or five during the entire period) which came in Mary's short reign.
(4) To the generally favourable harvest situation during Elizabeth's reign in the period up to 1594; between 1558 and 1593 there was not a single run of three harvests which were deficient or worse.
(5) To the very bad four years from 1594 to 1597 culminating in the dearth of 1596 and the very bad harvest of 1597.
(6) To the good harvest conditions in the opening years of James I's reign.
(7) To the generally bad harvests from the mid-1640s until after the Restoration.

---

1. W. G. Hoskins, 'Harvest fluctuations and English economic history, 1480–1619', *AgHR*, **12** (1964), 28 ff; 'Harvest fluctuations and English economic history, 1620–1759', *AgHR*, **16** (1968), 15 ff.
2. The harvest year extended from September to September. Thus, the effects of the disastrous harvest in the autumn of 1556 were felt throughout most of 1557.
3. The 'norm' is based on a thirty-one-year 'moving average' of wheat prices in order to allow for the general upward price trend.
4. C. J. Harrison, 'Grain price analysis and harvest qualities, 1465–1634', *AgHR*, **19** (1975), 135–55.
5. Harrison uses the same criteria as Hoskins – prices from 30 per cent below to 50 per cent above a 'norm' based on a thirty-one-year moving average – to define abundant, good, average, deficient and bad harvests and dearths.
6. He only covers the period up to 1634.

J. The Population of England and Wales, 1541–1661

The population of England (estimated to the nearest 1,000) at quinquennial intervals 1541–1661.[1]

1541	2,774,000	(2,968,000)	1606	4,253,000	(4,551,000)
1546	2,854,000	(3,054,000)	1611	4,416,000	(4,725,000)
1551	3,011,000	(3,222,000)	1616	4,510,000	(4,826,000)
1556	3,159,000	(3,380,000)	1621	4,693,000	(5,022,000)
1561	2,985,000	(3,194,000)	1626	4,720,000	(5,050,000)
1566	3,128,000	(3,347,000)	1631	4,893,000	(5,236,000)
1571	3,271,000	(3,500,000)	1636	5,058,000	(5,412,000)
1576	3,413,000	(3,652,000)	1641	5,092,000	(5,448,000)
1581	3,598,000	(3,850,000)	1646	5,177,000	(5,539,000)
1586	3,806,000	(4,072,000)	1651	5,228,000	(5,594,000)
1591	3,899,000	(4,172,000)	1656	5,281,000	(5,651,000)
1596	4,012,000	(4,293,000)	1661	5,141,000	(5,501,000)
1601	4,110,000	(4,398,000)			

The figures in brackets are estimates for the population of England and Wales together. They are obtained by adding a 7% allowance for the population of Wales to each of the English population figures. (Wrigley and Schofield, p. 566, note 20, discuss three different methods of estimating the population of Wales as a % of that of England. These yield figures of 9.2%, 5.9% and 6.6%, with an average of 7.2%.)

1. E. A. Wrigley and R. S. Schofield, *The Population History of England 1541–1871* (1981), p. 528.

K. THE COURSE OF INFLATION, 1400–1700[1]

Indexes of (1) the price of a composite unit of foodstuffs, (2) the price of a sample of industrial products (1451–75 = 100).

	(1)	(2)		(1)	(2)
1401–10	115	107	1551–60	315	186
1411–20	111	107	1561–70	298	218
1421–30	107	108	1571–80	341	223
1431–40	118	106	1581–90	389	230
1441–50	95	101	1591–1600	530	238
1451–60	98	99	1601–10	527	256
1461–70	105	103	1611–20	583	274
1471–80	93	100	1621–30	585	264
1481–90	121	103	1631–40	687	281
1491–1500	100	97	1641–50	723	306
1501–10	106	98	1651–60	687	327
1511–20	116	102	1661–70	702	343
1521–30	159	110	1671–80	675	351
1531–40	161	110	1681–90	631	310
1541–50	217	127	1691–1700	737	331

These are indexes of current prices, that is those which were actually paid or received by consumers and producers. The indexes were originally compiled to try to measure the changing purchasing power of a building worker's money wage and should be used with this knowledge in mind. The figures do, however, probably give a reasonable general view of the upward climb of prices (see Outhwaite, *Inflation in Tudor and Early Stuart England*, pp. 9–10 and p. 10, note 2).

---

1. R. B. Outhwaite, *Inflation in Tudor and Early Stuart England* (1969), p. 10.

L. WAGE RATES, 1450–1650[1]

Estimates of the *purchasing power* of the wages of agricultural labourers and building craftsmen in the south of England (1450–99 = 100).

	Agricultural labourer	Building craftsman
1450–59	105	104
1460–69	100	100
1470–79	104	103
1480–89	86	93
1490–99	104	103
1500–09	97	96
1510–19	89	88
1520–29	80	76
1530–39	80	68
1540–49	71	70
1550–59	59	51
1560–69	66	62
1570–79	69	64
1580–89	57	57
1590–99	49	47
1600–09	50	46
1610–19	44	39
1620–29	50	39
1630–39	47	—
1640–49	50	49

For the method of calculation see Thirsk, *Agrarian History*, IV, pp. 865 ff. The figures given are *decennial* averages. It should be noted that the purchasing power of a building craftsman's wage reached its lowest *annual* level during the whole period between the mid-thirteenth and the mid-twentieth centuries in 1597, when it stood at 29 (see Phelps Brown and Hopkins, in P. Ramsey, ed., *The Price Revolution in Sixteenth Century England* (1971), pp. 38 ff)

---

1. J. Thirsk, ed., *The Agrarian History of England and Wales*, IV, *1550–1640* (Cambridge, 1967), p. 865.

M. CLOTH AND TEXTILE EXPORTS, 1450–1640

Cloths (000s)

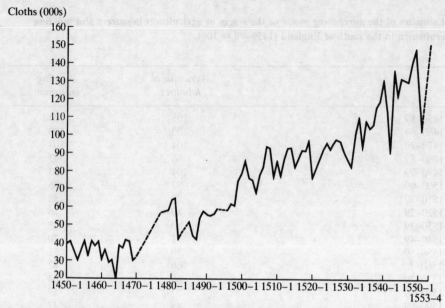

M.1: Cloth exports from England, 1450–1553

Note: A 'cloth' was a national standard cloth to which the various types were reduced for accounting purposes by the contemporary customs' authorities. The years ran from Michaelmas to Michaelmas.

Cloths (000s)

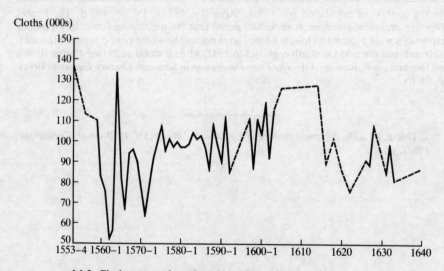

M.2: Cloth exports from London, 1554–1640

Note: After 1606 the years in which the data were recorded changed from Michaelmas–Michaelmas to Christmas–Christmas.

M.3: Total textile exports from England, early seventeenth century[1]

	Estimates of total textile exports, early seventeenth century. (£000)		
	London	Outports	Total
c. 1606/14			
Cloth	880	313	1,193
New draperies	267	80	347
	1,147	393	1,540
c. 1640			
Cloth	580	267	847
New draperies	515	90	605
	1,095	357	1,452

1. D. C. Coleman, *The Economy of England 1450–1750*, p. 64.

N. GLOSSARY

Affinity:	relationship between the relatives of the two partners in a consummated marriage (as opposed to consanguinity, relationship by blood).
Annates:	payments made to the Papacy of the first year's revenue of certain greater benefices, especially bishoprics.
Anticlericalism:	lay dislike of the wealth, power and pretensions of the clergy.
Arminianism:	doctrines generally associated with the Dutch theologian Arminius. They gained an important hold in the English Church in the early seventeenth century. Their main force was to deny or at least to diminish belief in predestination.
Assessment:	a tax introduced by Parliament during the Civil War. Levied first of all weekly and later monthly it was intended to take account of personal property and fees from office as well as income from land. Soon, however, it effectively became a land tax.
Attainder:	an Act of Parliament declaring a man to be a traitor without the requirement of a formal trial.
Bull:	a solemn papal document.
Chantry:	an endowment for saying masses for the souls of the founder and others whom he cared to name.
Commonwealthmen:	supposedly a group of social reformers in Edward VI's reign who stressed the obligations of the upper classes towards the poorer sections of the community. It has recently been demonstrated that no such unified group existed.
Convocation:	a solemn meeting of the clergy of the province of Canterbury or the province of York.
Copyholders:	tenants who held their land on terms set out in a 'copy' of a manorial court roll.
Court of record:	a court which kept written records which had formal legal status.
Curia:	the papal court at Rome.
De iure episcopacy:	the belief that bishops are essential in a true church.
Dissolution (of Parliament; see also prorogation):	the ending of a Parliament.
Enclosure:	the fencing or hedging of land either to improve agricultural productivity or to create sheep runs.
Engrossing:	the amalgamation of two or more farms, leaving at least one farmhouse empty.
Entry fine:	money paid when a new tenant took possession of land.
Erastianism:	the belief that the Church should be controlled by the state authorities.
Excise:	a sales tax on certain commodities – such as beer – introduced by Parliament during the Civil War.
Felony:	a criminal offence which carried the death penalty.
First fruits (see also tenths):	the first year's revenue of all ecclesiastical benefices, paid as taxation to the Crown after the Reformation.
Franchises and liberties:	areas where subjects exercised quasi-independent administrative and judicial authority.

Grand larceny:	the theft of goods worth more than 12d.; conviction carried the death penalty.
Great Cause (or **Matter**):	Henry VIII's attempt to secure the annulment of his marriage to Catherine of Aragon.
Impeachment:	a trial in Parliament in which the Commons acted as the accusers and the Lords as the judges. Originally employed in the Middle Ages it lapsed during the Tudor period but was revived in the 1620s, when Bacon and Cranfield were its most important victims.
Impositions:	duties over and above the normal charges, imposed by the Crown without the consent of Parliament on goods entering or leaving the country.
Impropriated tithes (see also **tithes**):	tithes held by laymen; the clergymen who performed the actual parochial duties were paid limited sums, often pittances.
Independents:	those who, during the later 1640s, stressed either congregational independence in religious affairs or a strong political line against the King, or both.
Indictment:	a formal accusation which began a common law prosecution.
Knight service:	the military service which the Crown's tenants-in-chief theoretically owed to the sovereign. In practice such service was not enforced in the sixteenth and seventeenth centuries though certain legal obligations connected with it continued: the most important of these was wardship.
Leaseholders:	tenants who held their land for a term of years on conditions specified in a contract.
Legate:	a papal representative either sent on a temporary mission or else having more permanent status within a country. His powers varied, but they might be very considerable.
Liberties:	see franchises.
Misdemeanour:	a criminal offence which was less serious than a felony and carried a lesser penalty.
Monopolies:	grants by the Crown of the sole right to make or distribute particular products.
Praemunire:	strictly speaking a writ designed to prevent invasions of royal jurisdictional rights. In a more general sense it was applied to offences (the limits of which were never clearly defined) by the clergy against the King's authority.
Predestination:	the doctrine, characteristic of Calvinist theology, which held that God from the beginning destined some men for eternal salvation and others for eternal damnation. It thus denied the free will of men to work out their own destinies in this world.
Presbyterians:	those who believed in a united national Church governed by a hierarchy of courts. Also used during the later 1640s of political moderates who sought an accommodation with the King.
Prophesyings:	meetings of clergy, often before a lay audience, to expound and discuss Scripture.
Prorogation (of Parliament; see also **dissolution**)	the ending of a session of Parliament while keeping the Parliament itself in being for further sessions.

Puritan:	a man or woman who wanted to 'purify' the Church of England as established by the 1559 settlement. The word, which was often used as a term of abuse, covered a wide spectrum of opinion from moderate episcopalians to Presbyterians and, perhaps, Separatists.
Purveyance:	the right of the Crown to buy supplies for the royal household at less than the market price.
Sacramentarianism:	the belief that there is no real presence of Christ in the consecrated host.
Sanctuary:	the right of criminals to take refuge in a church or other area from which law enforcement officers were excluded; also applied to the place of refuge itself.
Separatists:	those who rejected the idea of a national Church, believing that each congregation should control its own affairs.
Subsidy:	the principal direct tax under the Tudors, imposed either on land or on goods.
Supreme governor:	the title assumed by Queen Elizabeth in 1559; it implied a more strictly lay supremacy over the Church than that of supreme head, borne by her father and brother. The title is still held by the sovereign today.
Tenths (see also **first fruits**):	one-tenth of the annual value of ecclesiastical benefices, paid yearly as taxation to the Crown after the Reformation.
Thorough:	the name sometimes applied to the policies of Laud and Wentworth during the 1630s, with the implication that these policies were efficiently and effectively applied.
Tithes (see also **impropriated tithes**):	the money or produce of the ground, in theory a tenth of their income, which the laity paid for the upkeep of the clergy.
Trained bands:	those members of the militia who, from Elizabeth's reign, received special training for the defence of the realm.
Use:	a legal device designed to keep land out of wardship. The land was handed over to trustees for the use of the effective owner.
Wardship:	the right of the Crown to assume the guardianship of those of its tenants-in-chief (both male and female) who succeeded to their lands as minors. It involved both the administration of the wards' lands and the right to arrange their marriages. These highly profitable privileges were usually sold by the Crown to interested parties.

O. Maps

MacQuillan
MacDonnell
O'Cathain
O'Doherty
Mac Sweeny
O'Neill of Clandeboy
Lordship
of
O'Donnell
Lordship
of O'Neill
Earldom
of
Ulster
Magennis
O'Dowd
O'Hara
O'Connor
Maguire
Mac Mahon
Iveagh
Lordship
of
O'Rourke
Lordship
of
O'Reilly
Burke
of
Mayo
MacDonagh
O'Connor
Don
Trim
O'Malley
O'Farrell
THE
PALE
O'Flaherty
Clan
Rickard
Burke
Lordship
of
O'Kelly
O'Connor
Dublin
Dunne
O'Dempsey
Earl-
dom
of
Kildare
O'Toole
Lordship
of Leix
Lordship
of O'Brien
O'Carroll
O'Kennedy
Lordship
of
O'Byrne
MacMurrough
Mac Mahon
Earldom of Ormond
Fitzmaurice
Earldom of
Desmond
Power
Lordship of
Wexford
Mac Carthy More
Roche
O'Sullivan
Barry
O'Driscoll

| 0 | 60 miles |
| 0 | 80 kms |

Map 1 Ireland *c.* 1530

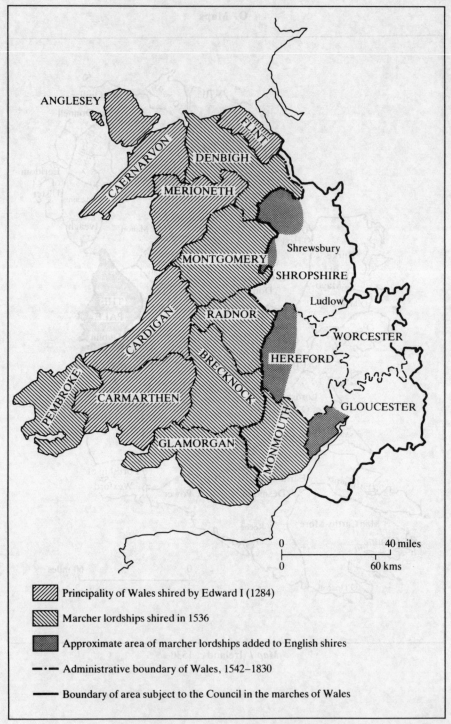

ANGLESEY

FLINT

CAERNARVON

DENBIGH

MERIONETH

MONTGOMERY

Shrewsbury

SHROPSHIRE

Ludlow

RADNOR

CARDIGAN

WORCESTER

BRECKNOCK

HEREFORD

PEMBROKE

CARMARTHEN

GLOUCESTER

GLAMORGAN

MONMOUTH

0   40 miles

0   60 kms

/// Principality of Wales shired by Edward I (1284)

▨ Marcher lordships shired in 1536

■ Approximate area of marcher lordships added to English shires

— · — Administrative boundary of Wales, 1542–1830

——— Boundary of area subject to the Council in the marches of Wales

Map 2 Wales: the union with England, 1536–43

☦ Cathedral city

| | 0 | | 100 miles |
| | 0 | | 150 kms |

Map 3 (a) Dioceses before the Reformation

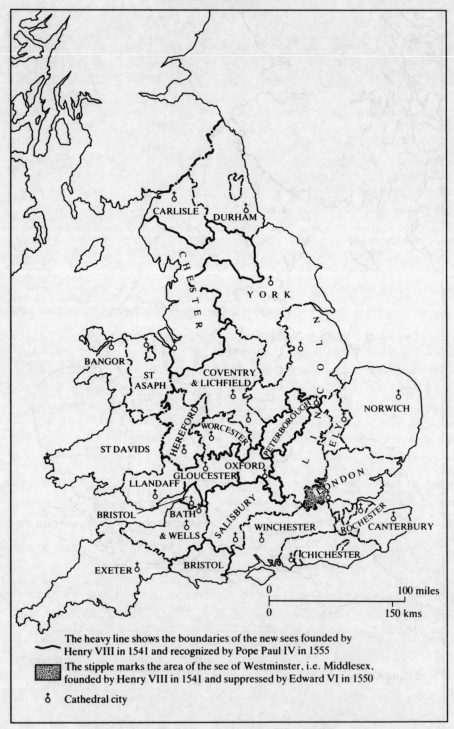

The heavy line shows the boundaries of the new sees founded by
Henry VIII in 1541 and recognized by Pope Paul IV in 1555

The stipple marks the area of the see of Westminster, i.e. Middlesex,
founded by Henry VIII in 1541 and suppressed by Edward VI in 1550

♂ Cathedral city

Map 3 (b) New sees created by Henry VIII

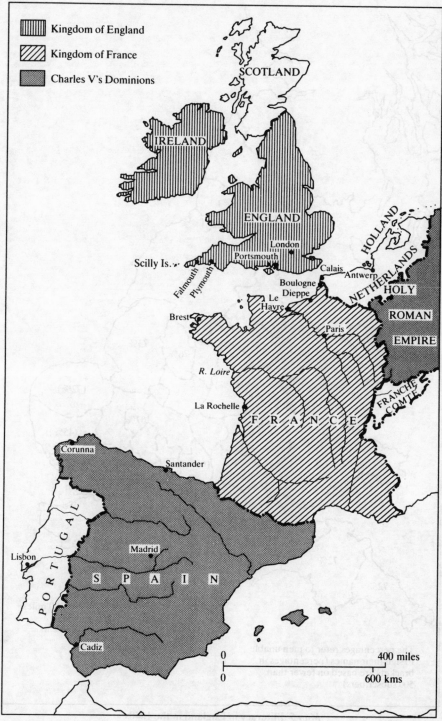

Map 4 Western Europe in 1529

The percentages refer to men unable
to sign their names (percentages in
brackets are based on fewer than
500 subscribers)

Map 5 Illiteracy in England in the 1640s

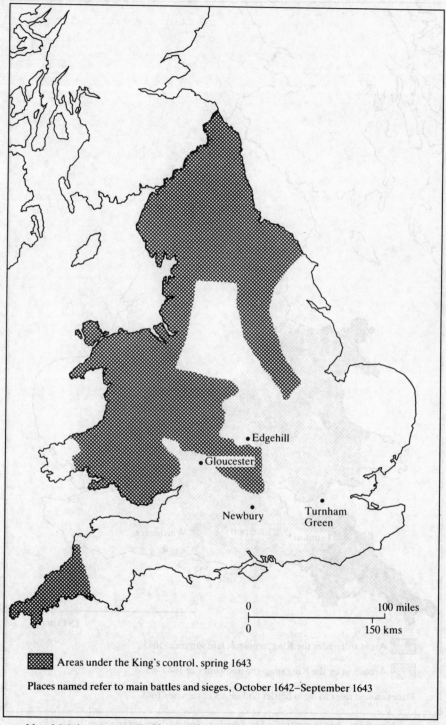

Edgehill

Gloucester

Newbury

Turnham
Green

0   100 miles
0   150 kms

▨ Areas under the King's control, spring 1643

Places named refer to main battles and sieges, October 1642–September 1643

Map 6 (a) Areas controlled by royalists and parliamentarians in the spring of 1643

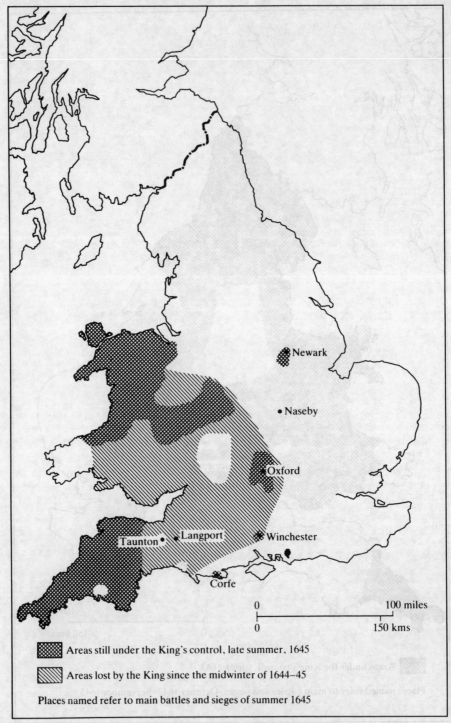

Areas still under the King's control, late summer, 1645

Areas lost by the King since the midwinter of 1644–45

Places named refer to main battles and sieges of summer 1645

Map 6 (b) Areas controlled by royalists and parliamentarians in 1644–45

Newcastle
Carlisle

Scarborough

Marston Moor
(2 July 1644) ×
York

Preston
Leeds
Hull

Adwalton Moor
(30 June 1643) ×
Gainsborough
(27 July 1643)
×
Winceby (11 October 1643) ×

Liverpool

Chester
Lincoln

Rowton Heath ×
(24 September 1645)
× Nantwich
(25 January 1644)
Newark
Nottingham

Hopton Heath ×
(19 March 1643)

Shrewsbury
Leicester

× Naseby (14 June 1645)

Worcester
× Edgehill (23 October 1643)

Powick Bridge ×
(23 September 1643)

Gloucester
Oxford

Lansdown
(5 July 1643)
×

Bristol
Roundway
Down
(13 July 1643)
Reading

Newbury
(20 September 1643
and 27 October 1644)
London

Dover

Langport
(10 July 1645) ×
Sherborne
Cheriton (29 March 1644)

Lyme Regis
Poole
Portsmouth

Stratton
×(16 May 1643)
Exeter

Lostwithiel
(1 September 1644) ×
Braddock Down
×(19 January 1643)
Weymouth

Plymouth
Dartmouth

0   100 miles

0   150 kms

Map 6 (c) Principal battle sites

Land over 1,000 feet

0   60 miles
0   80 kms

Inverness

Aberdeen

Dundee

Perth

Stirling

Leith

Edinburgh

Glasgow   Berwick

Ayr

Map 7 Scotland

Bibliography

The standard bibliographies for the Tudor and Stuart period are C. Read, ed., *Bibliography of British History: Tudor Period, 1485–1603* (2nd edn, Oxford, 1959) and M. F. Keeler, ed., *Bibliography of British History: Stuart Period, 1603–1714* (Oxford, 1970), M. Levine, *Tudor England 1485–1603* (Bibliographical Handbook, Cambridge, 1968) is useful for books and articles published during the late 1950s and early 1960s, while J. S. Morrill, *Seventeenth Century Britain, 1603–1714* (1980), is a splendid annotated guide, covering writings up to the late 1970s. G. R. Elton, *Modern Historians on British History 1485–1945* (1970), has comments on books and articles published between 1945 and 1969. The *Annual Bulletin of Historical Literature*, published each year by the Historical Association enables students to keep up to date with important work.

The following bibliography is organized by categories.

1. Source material
2. Textbooks and general surveys
3. Co-operative works and collected essays
4. Political, constitutional and legal works
5. Religion
6. Social and economic writings
7. Works on education, science, ideas and literature

Note: place of publication is London unless otherwise indicated.

1. SOURCE MATERIAL

1 *Statutes of the realm*, III (1817), IV (1819), V (1819)
2 D. Cressy, *Education in Tudor and Stuart England* (1975)
3 G. R. Elton, ed., *The Tudor Constitution* (Cambridge, 1960) – valuable introductions to the documents. The second edition (1982) appeared too late for use in this volume
4 A. G. Dickens and D. Carr, eds, *The Reformation in England* (1967)
5 J. Hurstfield and A. G. R. Smith, eds, *Elizabethan people* (1972)
6 W. Harrison, *Description of England*, ed. F. J. Furnivall (1877)
7 T. Smith, *De republica anglorum*, ed. L. Alston (Cambridge, 1906)
8 T. Wilson, 'The state of England, anno. dom. 1600', ed. F. J. Fisher, *Camden Miscellany*, **16** (1936)
9 K. Muir, ed., *The Pelican book of English prose*, i, *Elizabethan and Jacobean prose 1550–1620* (1956)
10 J. P. Kenyon, ed., *The Stuart Constitution* (Cambridge, 1966)
11 J. R. Tanner, ed., *Constitutional documents of the reign of James I* (Cambridge, 1930)
12 F. Bacon, *Essays* (Everyman edn, 1906)
13 S. R. Gardiner, ed., *Constitutional documents of the Puritan revolution* (3rd edn, Oxford, 1906)

14 E. Hyde, earl of Clarendon, *The history of the Rebellion*, ed. W. D. Macray, 6 vols. (Oxford, 1888)

15 C. H. Firth and R. S. Rait, *Acts and ordinances of the Interregnum*, 3 vols (1911)

16 A. S. P. Woodhouse, ed., *Puritanism and liberty* (2nd edn, 1974)

17 D. M. Wolfe, ed., *Leveller manifestoes of the Puritan revolution* (New York, 1944)

18 W. C. Abbott, ed., *Writings and speeches of Oliver Cromwell*, 3 vols. (Cambridge, Mass., 1937–47)

19 C. Hill, ed., *Winstanley: The law of Freedom and other writings* (1973)

20 T. Hobbes, *Leviathan*, ed. M. Oakeshott (Oxford, 1946)

2. TEXTBOOKS AND GENERAL SURVEYS

21 J. R. Lander, *Government and community: England 1450–1509* (1980)

22 C. S. L. Davies, *Peace, print and protestantism 1450–1558* (Paladin edn, 1977)

23 G. R. Elton, *England under the Tudors* (2nd edn, 1974)

24 P. Williams, *The Tudor regime* (Oxford, 1979)

25 G. R. Elton, *Reform and Reformation: England 1509–1558* (1977)

26 W. G. Hoskins, *The age of plunder* (1976)

27 A. G. Dickens, *The English Reformation* (1964) – easily the best survey of the subject

28 W. K. Jordan, *Edward VI*, 2 vols. I *The young king* (1968); II *The threshold of power* (1970)

29 D. M. Loades, *The reign of Mary Tudor* (1979)

30 R. B. Wernham, *Before the Armada* (1966) – the only satisfactory general study of Tudor foreign policy

31 G. E. Aylmer, *The struggle for the Constitution 1603–1689* (1963)

32 B. Coward, *The Stuart age* (1980)

33 C. Hill, *The century of revolution 1603–1714* (Edinburgh, 1961)

34 J. R. Jones, *Britain and Europe in the seventeenth century* (1966)

35 J. P. Cooper, 'The fall of the Stuart monarchy', *New Cambridge modern history*, IV (Cambridge, 1970)

36 S. R. Gardiner, *History of England, 1603–42*, 10 vols (1883–84)

37 R. Ashton, *The English Civil War: Conservatism and revolution 1603–49* (1978)

38 L. Stone, *The causes of the English Revolution 1529–1642* (1972)

39 I. Roots, *The Great Rebellion* (1966)

40 S. R. Gardiner, *History of the Great Civil War*, 4 vols (1893)

41 S. R. Gardiner, *History of the Commonwealth and Protectorate*, 4 vols (1903)

42 C. H. Firth, *The last years of the Protectorate*, 2 vols (1909)

43 J. R. Jones, *Country and court: England 1658–1714* (1978)

44 D. C. Coleman, *The economy of England 1450–1750* (1977) – outstanding.

45 L. A. Clarkson, *The pre-industrial economy in England 1500–1750* (1971)

46 P. Ramsey, *Tudor economic problems* (1966)

47 J. A. Williamson, *A short history of British expansion*, I (2nd edn, 1930) – a good brief survey

48 J. Wormald, *Court, kirk and community: Scotland 1470–1625* (1981)

49 G. Donaldson, *Scotland: James V–James VII* (Edinburgh, 1965)

50 C. Smout, *A history of the Scottish people* (1969)

51 T. W. Moody, F. X. Martin, F. J. Byrne, eds, *A new history of Ireland*, III, 1534–1691 (Oxford, 1976)

Bibliography

3. CO-OPERATIVE WORKS AND COLLECTED ESSAYS

52 G. R. Elton, *Studies in Tudor and Stuart government and politics*, 2 vols (Cambridge, 1974)
53 F. Heal and R. O'Day, eds, *Church and society in England, Henry VIII–James I* (1977)
54 J. Loach and R. Tittler, eds, *The mid Tudor polity* (1980)
55 P. Clark, A. G. R. Smith and N. Tyacke, eds, *The English Commonwealth 1547–1640* (Leicester, 1979)
56 S. T. Bindoff, J. Hurstfield and C. H. Williams, eds, *Elizabethan government and society* (1961)
57 A. G. R. Smith, ed., *The reign of James VI and I* (1973)
58 K. Sharpe, ed., *Faction and Parliament: Essays on early Stuart history* (Oxford, 1978)
59 E. W. Ives, ed., *The English revolution 1600–1660* (1968)
60 C. Russell, ed., *The origins of the English Civil War* (1973)
61 R. H. Parry, ed., *The English Civil War and after* (1970)
62 G. E. Aylmer, ed., *The Interregnum* (1972)
63 J. Thirsk, ed., *The agrarian history of England and Wales*, IV, *1500–1640* (Cambridge, 1967) – the fundamental study
64 F. J. Fisher, ed., *Essays in the economic and social history of Tudor and Stuart England* (Cambridge, 1961)
65 P. Clark and P. Slack, eds, *Crisis and order in English towns 1500–1700* (1972)
66 C. Webster, ed., *The intellectual revolution of the seventeenth century* (1974)

4. POLITICAL, CONSTITUTIONAL AND LEGAL WORKS
Biographies

67 A. F. Pollard, *Henry VIII* (1905 edn.)
68 J. J. Scarisbrick, *Henry VIII* (1968)
69 L. B. Smith, *Henry VIII, the mask of royalty* (1971)
70 B. Beckingsale, *Thomas Cromwell, Tudor minister* (1978)
71 A. G. Dickens, *Thomas Cromwell and the English Reformation* (1959)
72 J. E. Neale, *Queen Elizabeth* (Bedford edn, 1938)
73 P. Johnson, *Elizabeth I* (1974)
74 C. Read, *Mr Secretary Walsingham and Queen Elizabeth*, 3 vols (Oxford, 1925)
75 A. G. R. Smith, *Servant of the Cecils* (1977)
76 D. H. Willson, *King James VI and I* (1956)
77 R. Lockyer, *Buckingham* (1981)
78 M. Prestwich, *Cranfield: Politics and profits under the early Stuarts* (Oxford, 1966)
79 C. V. Wedgwood, *Strafford: A revaluation* (1960)
80 C. H. Firth, *Oliver Cromwell* (1900)
81 C. Hill, *God's Englishman: Oliver Cromwell and the English Revolution* (1970)
82 R. S. Paul, *The Lord Protector* (1955)
83 A. H. Woolrych, *Oliver Cromwell* (Oxford, 1964)

Government and administration

84 G. L. Harriss, 'Medieval government and statecraft', *P & P*, no. 25 (July 1963)
85 G. R. Elton, 'Tudor government: The points of contact. III. The Court', *TRHS*, 5th ser., **26** (1976)

86 G. R. Elton, 'Tudor government: The points of contact. II. The Council', *TRHS*, 5th ser., **25** (1975)

87 H. E. Bell, *An introduction to the history and records of the Court of Wards and Liveries* (Cambridge, 1953)

88 E. W. Ives, *Faction in Tudor England* (Historical Association, 1979)

89 B. Bradshaw, *The Irish constitutional revolution of the sixteenth century* (Cambridge, 1979)

90 G. Scott Thomson, *Lords lieutenant in the sixteenth century* (1923)

91 G. R. Elton, *The Tudor revolution in government* (Cambridge, 1953)

92 G. R. Elton, *Policy and police* (Cambridge, 1972)

93 R. W. Heinze, *The proclamations of the Tudor kings* (Cambridge, 1976)

94 J. Hurstfield, 'Was there a Tudor despotism after all?', *TRHS*, 5th ser., **17** (1967)

95 D. E. Hoak, *The King's Council in the reign of Edward VI* (Cambridge, 1976)

96 M. L. Bush, *The government policy of Protector Somerset* (1975)

97 A. F. Pollard, *England under Protector Somerset* (1900)

98 A. G. R. Smith, *The government of Elizabethan England* (1967)

99 W. T. MacCaffrey, *The shaping of the Elizabethan regime* (1969)

100 J. E. Neale, 'The Elizabethan political scene', *Essays in Elizabethan history* (1958)

101 J. Hurstfield, *The Queen's wards* (1958)

102 P. Williams, *The Council in the Marches of Wales under Elizabeth I* (Cardiff, 1958)

103 C. Read, 'Walsingham and Burghley in Queen Elizabeth's Privy Council', *EHR*, **28** (1913)

104 A. G. R. Smith, 'The secretariats of the Cecils, *c.* 1580–1612', *EHR*, **83** (1968)

105 J. G. Pocock, *The ancient Constitution and the feudal law* (Cambridge, 1957)

106 P. Zagorin, *The Court and the country* (1969)

107 G. E. Aylmer, *The King's servants* (2nd edn, 1974)

108 D. Underdown, *Pride's Purge* (Oxford, 1971)

109 G. E. Aylmer, *The State's servants* (1973)

110 A. Woolrych, *Commonwealth to Protectorate* (Oxford, 1982) – the best account of 1653.

Parliament

111 J. S. Roskell, 'Perspectives in English parliamentary history', *Historical studies of the English Parliament*, II, ed. E. B. Fryde and E. Miller (Cambridge, 1970)

112 G. R. Elton, 'Parliament in the sixteenth century: Functions and fortunes', *HJ*, **22** (1979)

113 G. R. Elton, 'Tudor government: The points of contact. I. Parliament', *TRHS*, 5th ser., **24** (1974)

114 S. E. Lehmberg, *The Reformation Parliament 1529–36* (Cambridge, 1970)

115 S. E. Lehmberg, *The later Parliaments of Henry VIII* (Cambridge, 1977)

116 M. A. R. Graves, *The House of Lords in the Parliaments of Edward VI and Mary I* (Cambridge, 1981)

117 J. E. Neale, *Elizabeth I and her Parliaments*, 2 vols (1953, 1957)

118 J. E. Neale, *The Elizabethan House of Commons* (Peregrine edn, 1963)

119 R. W. K. Hinton, 'The decline of parliamentary government under Elizabeth I and the early Stuarts', *CHJ*, **13** (1957)

120 W. Notestein, *The winning of the initiative by the House of Commons* (1924)

121 C. Russell, 'Parliamentary history in perspective, 1604–1629', *History*, **61** (1976)

122 D. M. Hirst, *The representative of the people?* (Cambridge, 1975)

123 W. Notestein, *The House of Commons 1604–10* (New Haven, 1971)
124 T. L. Moir, *The Addled Parliament of 1614* (Oxford, 1958)
125 C. Russell, *Parliaments and English politics 1621–1629* (Oxford, 1979)
126 R. Zaller, *The Parliament of 1621* (Berkeley, 1971)
127 R. E. Ruigh, *The Parliament of 1624* (Cambridge, Mass., 1971)
128 B. Worden, *The Rump Parliament* (Cambridge, 1974)
129 J. Cannon, *Parliamentary reform 1640–1832* (Cambridge, 1973)
130 A. H. Woolrych, 'The calling of Barebone's Parliament', *EHR*, **80** (1965)

Legal

131 J. H. Baker, *An introduction to English legal history* (2nd edn, 1979)
132 J. H. Baker, 'The dark age of English legal history, 1500–1700', *Legal history studies 1972*, ed. D. Jenkins (Cardiff, 1975)
133 J. S. Cockburn, ed., *Crime in England 1550–1800* (1977)
134 J. H. Baker, *Introduction to the reports of Sir John Spelman*, Vol. II (Selden Soc., 1978)
135 J. Bellamy, *The Tudor law of treason* (1979)
136 J. S. Cockburn, *A history of English assizes 1558–1714* (Cambridge, 1972)
137 J. Samaha, *Law and order in perspective: The case of Elizabethan Essex* (New York, 1974)
138 D. Veall, *The popular movement for law reform 1640–1660* (Oxford, 1970)
139 M. Cotterell, 'Interregnum law reform: The Hale Commission of 1652', *EHR*, **83** (1968)

Rebellions

140 A. Fletcher, *Tudor rebellions* (1968)
141 D. M. Loades, *Two Tudor conspiracies* (Cambridge, 1965)
142 A. Fletcher, *The outbreak of the English Civil War* (1981)
143 G. E. Aylmer, *The Levellers in the English Revolution* (1975)

Military and naval

144 M. Oppenheim, *History of the administration of the Royal Navy* (1896)
145 C. G. Cruickshank, *Elizabeth's army* (2nd edn, Oxford, 1966)
146 L. Boynton, *The Elizabethan militia* (1967)
147 A. Woolrych, *The battles of the English Civil War* (1961)
148 M. A. Kishlansky, *The rise of the New Model Army* (Cambridge, 1980)
149 C. H. Firth, *Cromwell's army* (4th edn, 1962)

Foreign policy

150 C. Wilson, *Queen Elizabeth and the revolt of the Netherlands* (1970)
151 M. Prestwich, 'Diplomacy and trade in the Protectorate', *JMH*, **22** (1950)
152 C. Wilson, *Profit and power* (1957)

Local studies

153 A. Hassell Smith, *County and court* (Oxford, 1974)
154 T. G. Barnes, *Somerset 1625–1640* (Oxford, 1961)
155 J. S. Morrill, *The revolt of the provinces* (1976)
156 A. Fletcher, *A county community in peace and war: Sussex 1600–1660* (1975)
157 J. S. Morrill, *Cheshire 1630–1660* (Oxford, 1974)
158 V. Pearl, *London and the outbreak of the Puritan revolution* (Oxford, 1961)

Scotland

159 D. Stevenson, *The Scottish Revolution, 1637–41* (Newton Abbot, 1973)
160 D. Stevenson, *Revolution and counter-revolution in Scotland 1644–1651* (1977)
161 F. D. Dow, *Cromwellian Scotland 1651–1660* (Edinburgh, 1979)

Ireland

162 N. Canny, *The Elizabethan conquest of Ireland. A pattern established, 1565–1576* (1976)
163 H. F. Kearney, *Strafford in Ireland* (Manchester, 1959)
164 T. Ranger, 'Strafford in Ireland: A revaluation', *P & P*, no. 19 (April 1961)

See also:
Government and administration: 3, 10, 11, 13, 23–5, 28, 29, 36, 37, 52, 54–62, 197, 208, 221, 244–6, 250, 258.
Legal: 3, 10, 11, 24, 36, 57.
Foreign policy: 29, 30, 34, 36, 243.
Parliament: 3, 10, 11, 25, 29, 37, 52, 54–8, 60, 62, 179.
Rebellions: 14, 24, 29, 36–9, 59, 60–62.
Military and naval: 40
Local: 251
Scotland: 48–50
Ireland: 51

5. RELIGION

165 R. O'Day, *The English clergy* (Leicester, 1979)
166 C. Cross, *Church and people 1450–1660* (1976)
167 M. R. Watts, *The Dissenters*, I (Oxford, 1978)
168 A. F. Pollard, *Wolsey* (1929)
169 P. Heath, *The English parish clergy on the eve of the Reformation* (1969)
170 J. A. F. Thomson, *The later Lollards 1414–1520* (Oxford, 1965)
171 J. J. Scarisbrick, 'Clerical taxation in England, 1485 to 1547', *JEH*, **11** (1960)
172 D. Knowles, *The religious orders in England*, III (Cambridge, 1959)
173 J. Youings, *The dissolution of the monasteries* (1971)
174 M. Bowker, 'The supremacy and the episcopate: The struggle for control, 1534–40', *HJ*, **18** (1975)

175 C. Haigh, *Reformation and resistance in Tudor Lancashire* (Cambridge, 1975)

176 R. H. Pogson, 'Reginald Pole and the priorities of government in Mary Tudor's Church', *HJ*, **18** (1975)

177 D. M. Loades, *The Oxford martyrs* (1970)

178 C. H. Garrett, *The Marian exiles* (Cambridge, 1938)

179 J. E. Neale, 'The Elizabethan Acts of Supremacy and Uniformity', *EHR*, **65** (1950)

180 V. J. K. Brook, *A life of Archbishop Parker* (Oxford, 1962)

181 P. Collinson, *Archbishop Grindal* (1979)

182 P. Collinson, *The Elizabethan Puritan movement* (1967)

183 M. M. Knappen, *Tudor Puritanism* (Chicago, 1939)

184 P. S. Seaver, *The Puritan lectureships* (Stanford, 1970)

185 A. O. Meyer, *England and the Catholic Church under Queen Elizabeth* (1916)

186 P. McGrath, *Papists and Puritans under Elizabeth I* (1967)

187 W. R. Trimble, *The Catholic laity in England* (Cambridge, Mass., 1964)

188 J. Bossy, 'The character of Elizabethan Catholicism', *P & P*, no. 21 (April 1962)

189 J. Bossy, *The English Catholic community 1570–1850* (1975)

190 C. Haigh, 'From monopoly to minority: Catholicism in early modern England', *TRHS*, 5th ser., **31** (1981)

191 R. B. Manning, *Religion and society in Elizabethan Sussex* (Leicester, 1969)

192 C. Hill, *Economic problems of the Church* (Oxford, 1956)

193 C. Hill, 'Puritans and "the dark corners of the land"', *TRHS*, 5th ser., **13** (1963)

194 M. Curtis, 'The Hampton Court Conference and its aftermath', *History*, **45** (1961)

195 S. B. Babbage, *Puritanism and Richard Bancroft* (1962)

196 C. Hill, *Society and Puritanism in pre-revolutionary England* (1964)

197 H. R. Trevor-Roper, *Archbishop Laud* (2nd edn, 1962)

198 W. K. Jordan, *The development of religious toleration in England*, III (1938)

199 M. James, 'The political importance of the tithes controversy in the English Revolution 1640–60', *History*, new ser., **26** (1941–42)

200 B. S. Capp, *The Fifth Monarchy Men* (1972)

201 W. C. Braithwaite, *The beginnings of Quakerism* (2nd edn, Cambridge, 1955)

202 H. Barbour, *The Quakers in Puritan England* (New Haven, 1964)

See also: 3, 4, 10, 14, 24, 25, 27, 29, 36, 52–7, 60, 62, 68, 99, 106, 108, 114, 117, 125, 128, 155, 156, 205–7, 222, 251, 253, 276, 278.

6. SOCIAL AND ECONOMIC WRITINGS

203 E. A. Wrigley and R. S. Schofield, *The population history of England* (1981)

204 A. B. Appleby, *Famine in Tudor and Stuart England* Liverpool, 1979)

205 W. K. Jordan, *Philanthropy in England 1480–1660* (1959)

206 K. Wrightson, *English society 1580–1680* (1982)

207 G. R. Elton, *Reform and renewal* (Cambridge, 1973)

208 G. R. Elton, 'An early-Tudor Poor Law', *EcHR*, 2nd ser., **6** (1953)

209 W. R. D. Jones, *The mid-Tudor crisis* (1973)

210 C. S. L. Davies, 'Slavery and Protector Somerset: The Vagrancy Act of 1547', *EcHR*, 2nd ser., **19** (1966)

211 M. Campbell, *The English yeoman under Elizabeth and the early Stuarts* (New Haven, 1942)

212 K. R. Andrews, *Elizabethan privateering 1585–1603* (Cambridge, 1964)
213 L. Stone, 'Social mobility in England 1500–1700', *P & P*, no. 33 (April 1966)
214 R. H. Tawney, 'Harrington's interpretation of his age', *PBA*, **27** (1941)
215 R. H. Tawney, 'The rise of the gentry, 1558–1640', *EcHR*, **11** (1941)
216 H. R. Trevor-Roper, 'The gentry 1558–1640', *EcHR Supplement*, no. 1 (1953)
217 L. Stone, *The crisis of the aristocracy 1558–1641* (Oxford, 1965)
218 W. G. Hoskins, 'The rebuilding of rural England, 1570–1640', *P & P*, no. 4 (Nov 1953)
219 M. Curtis, 'The alienated intellectuals of early Stuart England', *P & P*, no. 23 (Nov 1962)
220 R. H. Tawney, *Business and politics under James I* (Cambridge, 1958)
221 B. Manning, *The English people and the English Revolution 1640–49* (1976)
222 C. Hill, *The world turned upside down* (1972)
223 A. L. Morton, *The world of the Ranters* (1970)

The price revolution

224 R. B. Outhwaite, *Inflation in Tudor and early Stuart England* (1969)
225 P. Ramsey, ed., *The price revolution in sixteenth century England* (1971)
226 F. J. Fisher, 'Influenza and inflation in Tudor England', *EcHR*, 2nd ser., **18** (1965)

Agriculture

227 W. G. Hoskins, 'Harvest fluctuations and English economic history, 1480–1619', *AgHR*, **12** (1964)
228 W. G. Hoskins, 'Harvest fluctuations and English economic history, 1620–1759', *AgHR*, **16** (1968)
229 E. Kerridge, *The agricultural revolution* (1967)
230 J. Thirsk, *Tudor enclosures* (Historical Association, 1959)
231 F. J. Fisher, 'The development of the London food market, 1540–1640', *EcHR*, **5** (1934–35)

Industry

232 D. C. Coleman, *Industry in Tudor and Stuart England* (1975)
233 J. U. Nef, *The rise of the British coal industry*, I (1932)
234 J. Thirsk, *Ecomomic policy and projects: The development of a consumer society in early modern England* (Oxford, 1978)
235 D. C. Coleman, 'An innovation and its diffusion: The "New Draperies"', *EcHR*, 2nd ser., **22** (1969)
236 G. Hammersley, 'The charcoal iron industry and its fuel, 1540–1750', *EcHR*, 2nd ser., **26** (1973)

Trade and shipping

237 J. A. Chartres, *Internal trade in England 1500–1700* (1977)
238 R. Davis, *English overseas trade 1500–1700* (1973)

239 R. Davis, *The rise of the English shipping industry* (1962)

240 F. J. Fisher, 'Commercial trends and policy in sixteenth century England', *EcHR*, **10** (1939–40)

241 L. Stone, 'Elizabethan overseas trade', *EcHR*, 2nd ser., **2** (1949)

242 B. Supple, *Commercial crisis and change in England, 1600–1642* (Cambridge, 1959)

243 R. W. K. Hinton, *The Eastland trade and the common weal* (Cambridge, 1959)

Finance and coinage

244 F. C. Dietz, *English government finance 1485–1558* (2nd edn, 1964)

245 F. C. Dietz, *English public finance 1558–1641* (2nd edn, 1964)

246 C. E. Challis, *The Tudor coinage* (Manchester, 1978)

247 J. D. Gould, *The great debasement* (Oxford, 1970)

248 T. S. Willan, *A Tudor Book of Rates* (Manchester, 1962)

249 R. Ashton, *The Crown and the money market* (Oxford, 1960)

250 M. Ashley, *Financial and commercial policy under the Cromwellian Protectorate* (2nd edn, 1962)

Local and urban

251 P. Clark, *English provincial society from the Reformation to the Revolution* (1977)

252 J. T. Cliffe, *The Yorkshire gentry from the Reformation to the Civil War* (1969)

253 A. L. Beier, 'Poor relief in Warwickshire 1630–1660', *P & P*, no. 35 (Dec 1966)

254 A. Everitt, *The local community and the Great Rebellion* (Historical Association, 1969)

255 A. Everitt, *The community of Kent and the Great Rebellion* (Leicester, 1966)

256 P. Corfield, 'Urban development in England and Wales in the sixteenth and seventeenth centuries', D. C. Coleman and A. H. John, eds., *Trade, government and economy in pre-industrial England* (1976)

257 P. Clark and P. Slack, *English towns in transition 1500–1700* (1976)

258 R. Ashton, *The City and the Court 1603–1643* (Cambridge, 1979)

See also: 5–8, 24, 26, 37, 38, 44–6, 63–5, 96–8, 101, 106, 138, 139, 143, 165, 169, 171–3, 188, 191, 192, 196, 199.

7. WORKS ON EDUCATION, SCIENCE, IDEAS AND LITERATURE

259 K. Charlton, *Education in Renaissance England* (1965)

260 J. Simon, *Education and society in Tudor England* (Cambridge, 1966)

261 H. Kearney, *Scholars and gentlemen* (1970)

262 D. Cressy, *Literacy and the social order: Reading and writing in Tudor and Stuart England* (Cambridge, 1980)

263 L. Stone, 'The educational revolution in England, 1560–1640', *P & P*, no. 28 (July 1964)

264 M. Spufford, 'The schooling of the peasantry in Cambridgeshire, 1575–1700', *AgHR*, Supplement (1970)

265 W. A. L. Vincent, *The grammar schools: Their continuing tradition 1660–1714* (1969)

266 M. Curtis, *Oxford and Cambridge in transition* (Oxford, 1959)

267 A. R. Hall, *The scientific revolution* (2nd edn, 1962)

268 A. G. R. Smith, *Science and society in the sixteenth and seventeenth centuries* (1972)

269 H. Kearney, *Science and change 1500–1700* (1971)

270 F. R. Johnson, *Astronomical thought in Renaissance England* (Baltimore, 1937)

271 A. McLean, *Humanism and the rise of science in Tudor England* (1972)

272 C. Webster, *The great instauration: Science, medicine and reform 1626–1660* (1975)

273 A. L. Rowse, *Simon Forman: Sex and society in Shakespeare's Age* (1974)

274 B. Capp, *Astrology and the popular press: English almanacs 1500–1800* (1979)

275 A. O. Lovejoy, *The great chain of being* (Cambridge, Mass., 1936)

276 K. Thomas, *Religion and the decline of magic* (1971)

277 E. M. W. Tillyard, *The Elizabethan world picture* (1943)

278 W. Haller, *Foxe's Book of Martyrs and the elect nation* (1963)

279 A. Macfarlane, *Witchcraft in Tudor and Stuart England* (1970)

280 C. Larner, *Enemies of God: The witch-hunt in Scotland* (1981)

281 C. Hill, *Intellectual origins of the English Revolution* (Oxford, 1965)

282 P. Zagorin, *A History of political thought in the English Revolution* (1954)

283 I. Evans, *A short history of English literature* (Harmondsworth, 1940)

284 G. Sampson, *The concise Cambridge history of English literature* (3rd edn, Cambridge, 1970)

285 D. Bush, *English literature in the earlier seventeenth century* (Oxford, 1945)

286 B. Ford, *From Donne to Marvell* (Harmondsworth, 1956)

287 A. Robertson and D. Stevens, *The Pelican history of music*, 2, *Renaissance and Baroque* (1963)

See also: 2, 9, 14, 16, 17, 19, 20, 105, 138, 139, 143, 198, 200, 202, 205, 207, 214, 219, 222, 223.

Index

Note: subentries in the index are generally arranged in chronological order but where this cannot be established, or the entries are of a more general nature, they are arranged alphabetically before the chronological entries

465